*From Behavioral
Science to Behavior
Modification*

From Behavioral Science to Behavior Modification

Harry I. Kalish

McGraw-Hill Book Company

New York   St. Louis   San Francisco   Auckland
Bogota   Singapore   Johannesburg   London
Madrid   Mexico   Montreal   New Dehli
Panama   São Paulo   Hamburg
Sydney   Tokyo   Paris

Library of Congress Cataloging in Publication Data

Kalish, Harry I
    From behavioral science to behavior modification.

    Bibliography: p.
    Includes index.
    1. Behavior modification.   2. Conditioned response.
3. Psychology, Applied.   I. Title.
BF637.B4K34   153.8'5   80-19796
ISBN 0-07-033245-2

1 2 3 4 5 6 7 8 9 RRD RRD 8 9 8 7 6 5 4 3 2 1

Thomas H. Quinn and Michael Hennelly were the editors of this book.
Mark E. Safran was the designer and Sally Fliess supervised the production. The book was set in Garamond by Haddon Craftsman, Inc.

Printed and bound by R. R. Donnelley and Sons, Inc.

To Millie
Who Kept the Light Lit At The End of the Tunnel

Contents

Preface

The primary objective of this book is to give the reader an appreciation for the relationship between the science of behavior and the application of behavioral principles, and to provide a much-needed historical perspective of the studies and theoretical issues which form the basis of the techniques used in behavior modification.

The book attempts to accomplish this purpose by demonstrating that relatively complex human behavior can be described in terms of principles which apply to both animals and humans and to show how these principles, derived from laboratory investigations with humans and animals, are used to explain the origins of certain behavior disorders and the current methods in behavior modification which are used to alleviate them.

There are at least two ways in which such a book can be organized. The principles may be used to illustrate a particular form of treatment for a specific disorder. In this case the organization would most likely be around behavior syndromes such as depression, anxiety, etc. and a discussion of the behavioral principles underlying the origin or treatment (e.g., operant learning, classical conditioning, or mediated learning) repeated throughout the chapters.

Or, alternatively, as in this volume where the purpose is to emphasize the relationship between science and application, the behavior disorders will be repeated in several appropriate places to illustrate the use of the principles. My preference for this type of organization is based on the belief that unless the origins of the treatment strategies are recognized and enunciated the practice of behavior modification is likely to become immured in techniques.

This book deals with the origin and modification of behavior in terms of three major processes: classical conditioning, operant conditioning, and mediated learning. Each of the three main sections devoted to one of these processes begins with a discussion of the historical background of the learning process, some of the major theoretical issues which have developed, attempts which have been made to resolve them, and the principles which have been abstracted from some of the important laboratory studies.

These principles are subsequently related to a classification scheme to illustrate how they may be used to account for the development of some of the behavior disorders. Each chapter on development is then followed by studies and case material dealing with the application of the specific learning process to the modification of behavior. There are also separate chapters on self-control as choice behavior and biofeedback.

The final chapter is devoted to a discussion of the comparison of behavior modification to other forms of treatment and a review of the ethical and legal issues, in general, which have had an effect on the practice of behavior modification.

Although the chapters were designated to be read in sequence, there is no reason why those dealing with the origin of the behavior disorders (Chapters 3, 7, and 14) could not be eliminated or read cursorily where course time is limited. In the first place, the nature of the explanations for behavioral origins is, of necessity, inclined to be highly speculative. Secondly, there is no necessary relationship between the origin of a specific disorder and the methods which are used to treat it—except in the general sense that both the origin and the treatment may involve learning.

In his trenchant classification of journalists, A. J. Liebling once observed, "There are three kinds of newswriters in our generation, the reporter who writes what he sees, the interpretive reporter who writes what he sees and construes to be its meaning, and the expert who writes what he construes to be the meaning of what he hasn't seen" (1961, p. 225). It is only in this sense that a person who undertakes to write a survey on a subject as vast as behavior modification can be considered an expert.

I am much indebted to Lyn Abramson, Jack Adams, Xenia Coulter, and Arthur Houts who read parts of the book in various stages of development and made invaluable suggestions, and to the Macmillan Publishing Co. for permission to use sections of my chapter Conditioning and Learning in Behavior Modification which appeared in M. H. Marx and M. E. Bunch (Eds.) *Fundamentals and Applications of Learning*, New York Macmillan Publishing Co., 1977. I am especially grateful to my wife Millie whose expert eye saved me from many a stylistic blunder.

H. I. KALISH

chapter one

Behavior Modification: Introduction

In 1969 two psychologists reported the use of punishment training to save the life of a nine-month-old infant with a chronic ruminative disorder. For unknown reasons, rumination is a relatively common occurrence among infants. It consists of voluntary regurgitation of food without nausea or retching, producing death rates as high as 20 percent due to severe malnutrition and lowered resistance to disease in cases of prolonged rumination. In the present case, vomiting persisted for approximately four months, and the infant was literally starving to death (Fig. 1-1) despite several unsuccessful attempts to reverse the behavior by means of antiemetic drugs, physical restraints, and a brief course of psychotherapy for the mother. The psychologists were consulted when the infant weighed less than twelve pounds and behavior modification was considered as a treatment of last resort.

The solution to the problem devised by Lang and Melamed (1969) was a straightforward behavioral one. They made a careful analysis of the entire vomiting response sequence in order to distinguish initial chewing, sucking, and swallowing from the first faint signs of reverse peristalsis in the chain of responses which ultimately leads to vomiting. By monitoring these weak signals through electromyographic recordings of muscle potentials, they isolated the entire sequence of responses involved in vomiting and arrested it without adversely affecting other desirable behaviors such as chewing, sucking, and swallowing. Treatment consisted of a brief, intense electric shock applied to the child's leg at the first sign of regurgitation and repeated at 1-second intervals until vomiting stopped. According to the authors, the first treatment proved successful although five more treatments were subsequently administered. As a result, the child's body weight increased over 20 percent in the two weeks following the first session because of increased nourishment, and he appeared to be both physiologically and psychologically sound in the ensuing 6-month, 1-year, and 2-year follow-up evaluations (Fig. 1-1).

The treatment strategy devised by the psychologists in this case is one of several they could have chosen to deal with the problem. They selected punishment, or aversion, therapy largely because of the child's youth and the apparent danger of starvation. Very little time remained for a consideration of alternatives. They used shock because of its important advantage in the power to disrupt an ongoing response sequence. Other cases of ruminative vomiting, however, have been successfully treated by squirting lemon juice into the child's mouth when signs of rumination appeared (Sajwaj et al., 1974). Another alternative treatment is to withhold attention (see omission training, Chapters 6 and 8) and ignore the child when vomiting occurred (Wright et al., 1978). "Lemon-juice therapy" has even been used to eliminate public masturbation in a severely retarded 7-year-old boy. The parent or the teacher squirted juice into the child's mouth whenever masturbation occurred (Cook et

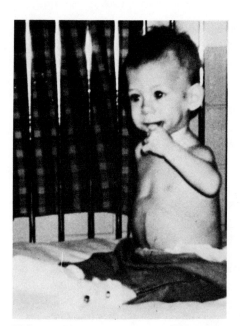 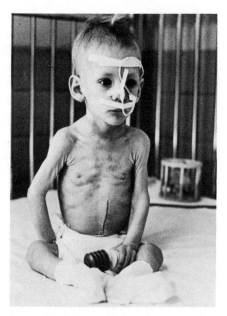

FIG. 1-1 Photographs of the infant with chronic ruminative vomiting before and after treatment. The photograph on the right, taken just prior to treatment, illustrates the child's debilitated condition—weight 12 lbs., lack of body fat, and skin hanging in loose folds. The tape around the face holds a tube for nasogastric feeding. The scar on the abdomen is the result of exploratory surgery. The photograph on the left, taken after treatment and 13 days after the first photograph, indicates a 26% increase in body weight following treatment. (Source: P. J. Lang and B. G. Melamed. Avoidance conditioning therapy of an infant with chronic ruminative vomiting. *Journal of Abnormal Psychology,* 1969, *74,* 1–8. Copyright 1969 by the American Psychological Association and used by permission.)

al., 1978). In none of these cases, however, did the child's life hang in the balance as, indeed, it did when Lang and Melamed decided to use shock.

The important point here is that neither shock, nor punishment in general for that matter, is a uniform procedure for all cases of ruminative vomiting, or, indeed, for any situation where responses are to be eliminated. In fact, its use has generally been restricted to situations where no other methods are feasible, or where other methods are not successful. It would be a mistake, therefore, to regard punishment as a "standardized technique" for eliminating responses in behavior modification.

The inclination to regard the methods of intervention in behavior modification as a collection of standardized techniques is especially misleading. It tends to obscure one of the most important contributions to the understanding of behavior change made by the advent of behavior modification procedures: namely, that for every so-called technique, there is a more fundamental and more general principle of behavior derived from research with animals and/or humans which can be *applied* to the solution of a problem in human functioning. This means, among other things, *that those who intend to use behavior modification to help solve human problems should be aware of these principles and resourceful enough to propose treatment strategies which fit the case after a thorough analysis of the conditions which initiate and maintain the behavior.*

DEFINITIONS

Behavior modification is a general term denoting behavior change resulting from the systematic application of behavioral principles. Behavior modification methods may be applied to any behavior in any setting, but when specifically applied to the alleviation of the behavior disorders, the term *behavior therapy* has generally been used.

Although, as we see subsequently, the growth of behavior modification is intimately associated with the study of learning and conditioning, a definition in terms of behavior principles rather than learning principles leaves room for contributions from any area in the study of behavior. The American Association for the Advancement of Behavior Therapy emphasizes this point by defining behavior therapy as the "primary application of principles derived from research in experimental and social psychology to alleviate human suffering and enhance human functioning. Behavior therapy emphasizes a systematic monitoring and evaluation of the effectiveness of these applications" (AABT, 1974, p. 7).

All behavior modification methods appear to have the following characteristics in common, regardless of the way in which the term is defined:

a. The *methods* are derived from research primarily in the behavioral sciences.

b. The *goal* is the solution of societal problems and alleviation of human suffering through re-education directed toward improving human functioning and measured. by increased skill, independence, and satisfaction.

c. The *practice* typically involves a contractual agreement between both the client and the therapist which specifies the goals and methods of intervention.

d. The *validity* is constantly examined by systematic, critical evaluation of the results of treatment or modification through follow-up studies or experimentation with individuals or groups (Davison & Stuart, 1974).

OBJECTIVES

Most people are in need of therapy either because they cannot do something (behavioral deficiencies) or because they cannot stop doing something (behavioral excesses). The objective of all treatment, regardless of orientation, is to enable them to acquire a sense of control over their own behavior. One generally assumes, therefore, that the goal of all treatment is the alleviation of human suffering, and in this respect the humanitarian objectives of behavior modification are no different from any other form of treatment. Unfortunately, however, this opinion does not seem to be shared by all of those who might make productive use of the procedures in behavior modification, and Box 1-1 shows that frequently the word "behavior" or "behavioristic" itself is enough to create a negative attitude.

Box 1-1
"A Rose by Any Other Name" . . . Just
Doesn't Smell As Sweet

When the term *behavior modification* was used in conjunction with a treatment program at a state training school for delinquent adolescents, the staff appeared openly suspicious and hostile toward the program despite its apparent success and their implicit agreement with the principles and methods being used. A subsequent change of the name to *social learning,* however, eliminated the negative attitude (Reppucci & Saunders, 1974).

A more systematic demonstration of the effect that this term can have on attitudes toward teaching emerged from a study in which the same teaching procedure, called by two different names, produced widely divergent reactions (Woolfolk et al., 1977). Two groups of undergraduates entering a course in educational psychology were shown a videotape describing a teaching procedure. Although the tape was *exactly the same* for both groups, one group saw the tape thinking that they were watching the use of *behavior modification* for the management of children in the classroom. The other group believed they were seeing a demonstration of the development of *humanistic psychology* in education—the integration of affective with cognitive learning. *Actually, the tape shown to both groups depicted a technique in behavior modification called token economy in which the child's academic successes earned points or tokens to be exchanged later for candy and toys.*

When the groups' opinions were sampled on a series of questionnaires, the "humanistic condition" invariably received the more favorable ratings. The teachers in the "humanistic" tape were judged to be more warm, enthusiastic, competent, and effective, and the "humanistic" teaching approach evaluated as more effective and free flowing. A repetition of the same experiment with graduate students in education produced similar results.

Apparently, however, all is not lost. Although the subjects in both groups rated the humanistic condition as more favorable and more desirable, their attitude toward the term "behavior modification" per se was basically not negative, and, in fact, mildly positive. This finding led the authors of the study to conclude that the differences found "did not occur because the response to behavior modification was very negative, but because the response to humanistic education labels was simply more positive" (p. 190).

Barling and Wainstein (1979) have suggested that the results obtained in this study were due to the bias against behavior modification that the students brought with them to the study. The Barling and Wainstein study, a substantial replication of the Woolfolk et al. experiment, determined attitudes for or against behavior modification among a group of individuals in industry before exposing them to videotapes showing organizational behavior modification in use in industrial settings. When the videotape used humanistic terms to describe these methods, those originally opposed to behavior modification rated the methods and leadership characteristics more favorably. *Those in favor of behavior modification rated them negatively.* The situation was reversed for the groups shown the same videotape labeled in behavior modification terms.

Apparently, the bias works both ways, and the solution proposed by many to soften attitudes toward behavior modification by using more "humanistic" terms will simply turn the behavior modifiers off or certainly make them more suspicious. But as the use of learning procedures becomes more widespread, the term "behavior modification" will probably begin to lose its aversive qualities.

Just how did these attitudes develop? One of the answers lies in the extreme position taken by the behaviorists of the twenties and thirties in their break with traditional psychology. Another answer involves the language used to describe the procedures. A third lies in the abuses of behavior modification methods which have recently been publicized.

When Watson broke with the functionalist psychologists and asserted that behavior could be studied objectively, without any reference to mental states, states of consciousness, or to the subjective methods of introspection (looking inward) which were used to study them, he expressed many of the changes in the study of behavior which had already begun to take place. Most psychologists were already convinced, prior to Watson, that chasing will-o-the-wisps such as "consciousness" or "faculties of the mind" were leading to a dead end. They saw that the road to a science of behavior led ultimately to a consideration of the way in which behavior is influenced by the environment. But Watson buttressed his position by a further assumption. He was firm in his conviction that the environment and learning, particularly conditioning, rather than heredity, instincts, or thought processes were the primary agents responsible for the development of behavior.

Objections to this position soon developed, despite its popularity. And it was popular, so popular, in fact, that the renowned "instinct" psychologist William McDougall, who had forecast that it would never happen in America, was forced to change his mind because, as he put it, "[my opinion] was founded upon a too generous estimate of the American public" (Bakan, 1966).

Part of the difficulty with behaviorism, as the movement was called, stemmed from Watson's abrasive, arrogant, and dogmatic manner, which alienated a lot of people. Another problem lay in the extreme position taken by behaviorism itself. Many psychologists, philosophers, and theologians felt that it was a mechanistic, deterministic, and inhumane philosophy which relegated man to the position of an automaton. It disregarded the inner world of contemplation, revery, and feeling, they believed. Willis and Giles (1978), for example, cite several historical documents which bear this out. One in particular, by the philosopher George Santayana, expressed the following viewpoint in an article entitled *Living without thinking:*

> I foresee a behaviorist millenium, countless millions of walking automatons, each armed with his radio . . . all jabbering as they have been trained to jabber, never interfering with one another, always smiling, with their glands all functioning perfectly (which *is* happiness) and all living to a sunny old age . . ." (1922).

Most psychologists today are behaviorists insofar as they subscribe to the idea, expressed by Watson, that psychology is the objective study of behavior which employs the empirical method of experimentation. Many, who study thinking and perception as important behavioral processes, are still behaviorists by virtue of their use of the empirical method and their ultimate concern with the relationship of these inferred processes to overt behavior. No one asserts that people do not have inner lives or private experiences, but as we see in Chapter 13, the usefulness of these experiences for the prediction and control of behavior and the language used to characterize them constitute the major debate among psychologists today.

The "radical behaviorists" (Skinner and his followers), for example, stick close to the relationship between external events and external behavior and see no uses for inferred processes at the present time. Other behaviorists (Hull, Spence, Mowrer, Solomon) talk about mediating processes between the external world and behavior, but they tend to limit their use of these factors and to talk about them in non-mental terms. Cognitive psychologists, on the other hand, emphasize the importance of these internal events in determining behavior and talk about them in terms such as thinking, perception, imagery, attitudes, expectancies, attributions, and so forth.

The bias against behavior modification still persists in some circles today probably because of the language which is used to describe some of the operations. A substantial number of the intervention methods used in behavior modification, for example, derive from studies with animals in classical and operant conditioning. The language used to describe these learning processes—conditioning, shaping, reinforcement, and so on—is also used to characterize the changes in human behavior. All of these terms tend to evoke the feeling that humans are being manipulated as animals are, much against their own will. Of course, a motion picture such as *Clockwork Orange,* which portrays a sadistic post-adolescent being deprived of his right to mutilate and murder through aversive conditioning, does much to reinforce the sinister image of behavior therapy as a mechanistic and dehumanizing method of treatment which forces people to behave against their will and ultimately produces docile members of society. The image has been further strengthened by the tendency to lump behavior modification indiscriminately together with such procedures as drug therapy, electroshock, and psychosurgery.

Fortunately, most of the lurid conceptions of behavior therapy will probably not outlive their publicity value. But some of the bad image is also unwittingly generated by well-meaning, but overzealous, practitioners who misuse the methods of behavior modification in extremely sensitive institutional settings, such as prisons, without consultation or proper regard for the rights of the inmates (Chapter 9). However, abuses of this kind are highly unlikely in the future because professional and governmental committees have been established to oversee the application of behavior modification procedures in prisons, mental health institutions, schools, and community mental health facilities.

PRINCIPLES OF BEHAVIOR IN BEHAVIOR MODIFICATION

For the most part, the methods used in behavior modification are derived from the principles associated with one, or several in combination, of the following behavioral processes: classical conditioning, operant conditioning, and mediated learning.

A principle in psychology, or in any other science for that matter, is an abstract or general expression about a regularly recurring event usually in the form of an "if-then" statement. The principle describing the formation of a conditioned response in Chapter 2, for example, was abstracted from a large number of controlled observations, initially with animals. It states that if a neutral stimulus (a light or tone) is regularly paired with another stimulus (food) which produces a response (salivation), then after a number of such pairings, the neutral stimulus eventually also elicits salivation in the absence of the food. We say "eventually" here because factors such as the number of stimulus pairings, their proximity in space and time, and the amount of food given, for example, affect the length of time it takes to form a conditioned response. These factors are known as variables, and a principle or law in science describes or explains the way in which changes in these variables produce changes in behavior. Chapter 4, for example, contains an account of the way in which the principles of classical conditioning have been applied to deal with chronic constipation, maladaptive sexual behavior, and the elimination of fear-related responses.

Similar principles in operant conditioning describe how a response (bar pressing in a rat for instance) either increases or decreases, depending upon the type, size, or duration of the reinforcer (reward or punishment) that follows the behavior. The principles associated with operant conditioning have had a much wider applicability than those related to classical conditioning, as the studies in Chapters 6 through 11 indicate.

In mediated learning, on the other hand, the situation is not quite as clear. The principles underlying cognitive behavior modification—the name applied to a group of behavior change procedures—are not as explicit as they are in classical and operant conditioning. This is because the methods in cognitive behavior modification all assume that changes in thinking or some internal event must precede changes in overt behavior (Chapters 13 through 15). Because thinking is an unobserved and inferred behavior, we encounter many difficulties in determining precisely how, when, and under what conditions it has been affected.

ASSUMPTIONS

Behavior modification makes two major assumptions, and each has important implications for practice. The first deals with the way in which maladaptive behavior is acquired. The second deals with the relative importance of past and present events in the determination of behavior.

How Maladaptive Behavior Is Acquired

Practitioners of behavior modification assume, for the most part, that behavior problems or behavior disorders are based on learning or learning deficits, i.e., the lack of opportunity to learn appropriate behavior. An example of the former would be the faulty learning which occurs when people become afraid of an object or event that is not instrinsically fear-arousing, as in the phobias, or when they are incapable of inhibiting certain behaviors, as in the obsessive-compulsive disorders. Learning deficits, by contrast, may arise either because the appropriate models are absent or because the behavior has not been properly elicited because of poor management of rewards and punishments.

In Chapters 3, 7, and 14 we explore the possibility that the principles from any one of the three learning models—classical conditioning, operant conditioning, and mediated learning—either singly or in combination, can be used to account for the origin of certain of the behavior disorders. But those discussions also make it clear that the link between learning and the origin of the behavior disorders involves a great deal of speculation based on an extremely small amount of evidence.

Although this assumption is difficult to prove, it has an important corollary that forms the basis for all behavior modification procedures. That is, if certain maladaptive behaviors are learned, then they can also be changed through learning. This corollary, of course, is easier to demonstrate than the assumption from which it originally came. One need only point to the fact that behavioral principles were used to alter the behavior and to predict the changes that did occur. However, this does not necessarily mean that the behavior was acquired through learning, or that the explanation for the change cannot be given in terms other than the principles which were originally employed.

The Role of Past Events in Behavior Modification

Another important assumption in behavior modification is that behavior can be modified by focusing on the existing conditions which initiate and maintain it rather than exploring the influences of the past and the conditions for original learning. This assumption has an important implication. It suggests that the behavior which the therapist observes is, in effect, the target behavior for modification and that the conditions which elicit and maintain the behavior exist in the present and not in the past.

Of course, this assumption opposes the traditional view of therapy, explicitly held by psychoanalytic theory, that past events influence contemporary behavior and must be dealt with before behavior can undergo modification. The idea that the therapist's primary function is to assist clients in discovering the remote undisclosed sources of inappropriate behavior came largely from applying the disease model to the interpretation of the behavioral disorders in the late nineteenth century, as we see in Chapter 3, and it has been reinforced in many ways since (Box 1–2).

BOX 1–2

The Therapist as Detective

In the movie *Spellbound* starring Gregory Peck, Ingrid Bergman, and a cast of appropriately bearded and suitably attired psychiatrist-actors, Mr. Peck appears as a patient who, among other things, is beset by all sorts of difficulties. In a moment either of mischievous prankishness or by accident, he had pushed his younger brother down the stone bannister of their brownstone stoop. The boy was gruesomely impaled on the pointed end of an iron railing surrounding the house, and this memory was the source of Peck's agony. Of course, neither the audience nor Mr. Peck knows of this cause-and-effect relationship until the end of the picture. But Ingrid Bergman, cast as the lovely psychiatrist assigned the awesome responsibility of helping Mr. Peck dredge up the memories surrounding the hideous event in order to free him from its malignant effects, knows that something is bugging Mr. Peck. His behavior, after all, is pretty bizarre.

The movie clearly states two misleading assumptions about therapy and the way it is conducted, and it goes a long way toward strengthening these misconceptions in the public mind. In the first place, it casts the therapist as a detective whose principal purpose is to piece together the clues to *the past event* responsible for the patient's present behavior by poking around in his unconscious to let the repressed material come through. Second, it asserts that *mere knowledge* of the traumatic event is sufficient to change the behavior, discounting the fact, of course, that many a year of bizarre behavior may very well become a strong habit.

What the movie fails to recognize most of all, however, is that the very act of marrying Ingrid Bergman as Mr. Peck does at the end of the picture may, indeed, be all the therapy that anyone needs to solve his problems—especially those created by feelings of inadequacy of one kind or another.

This assumption is constantly being supported by the large number of studies in behavior modification showing that problem behavior can be dealt with successfully by attending to its immediate influences without exploring its origins. Such a practice, however, usually invites the charge that behavior modification deals only with the symptoms of the disorder, much like administering aspirin for the fever produced by typhus. Under the circumstances, the symptoms are bound to reappear when the aspirin wears off. The evidence for reappearance of symptoms or for the occurrence of new behavior in place of the old (symptom substitution) is relatively scarce (Rachman, 1963; Ullmann & Krasner, 1969), although something like symptom substitution could conceivably occur if the conditions which maintain the behavior are not properly evaluated. It is possible, for example, that a child whose tantrum behavior has been eliminated through punishment (a condition which is rarely, if ever, treated in this manner) will begin to set fires. In this case the "real" reason for both the tantrum and fire-setting behavior may be to elicit attention, or love, or concern from adults, and the child will continue to employ and substitute these and other behaviors in order to achieve that goal.

In any event, behavior modification procedures do not thoroughly disregard the past, although emphasis centers on the factors which currently maintain the undesirable behavior. As O'Leary and Wilson (1975) point out, the past is important only insofar as it actively contributes to the person's present problems. It is conceivable, for example, that a woman's attitude toward men in the present might have been colored by a frightening sexual attack in the past, but there is no point in reviewing this experience exhaustively if the current problem is unrelated to the sexual assault (1975, p. 22).

ROOTS

Before we embark on this journey through the principles of conditioning and learning and their applications, a pause in order to get our historical bearings might be a good idea. Every voyage—and especially one into the history of ideas—requires a good map. The shoals and reefs of theoretical dispute fill the trip ahead of us, and even if we do not manage to avoid them, we should at least have the satisfaction of knowing how we got stranded.

Figure 1–2 provides us with such a map. It shows the three main sources from which most, if not all, behavior-change methods are derived. The names on this chart belong to people whose ideas have had a major theoretical or experimental impact on the development of behavior modification. (There are, of course, a great many other individuals whose contribution to the growth of behavior modification have been exceptionally noteworthy, as we see throughout this book.) The ideas at the bottom of the chart and the names associated with them represent the major sources of most of the treatment procedures currently used in behavior modification. (A more detailed history of the origins of behavior modification may be found in *History of Behavior Modification,* by A. E. Kazdin, 1978.)

One striking aspect of the chart in Figure 1–2 merits some brief comment—the overwhelming presence of American psychologists. Most of the names on this list of contributors to learning and learning theory, which has directly or indirectly influenced the development of behavior modification, are those of Americans. The notable exceptions are Pavlov, Bechterev, Freud, and Wolpe (who now resides in the United States although his country of origin was the Union of South Africa).

Although it seems somewhat strange that American psychologists should have so dominated the "learning scene" and "devoted more thought and activity to the construction of learning theory than to any other" behavioral phenomenon (Hall & Lindzey, 1957), the situation is an eminently reasonable one if we assume that scientists, like other human beings, are also influenced by social philosophy.

Despite the myth of the ivory tower, scientists do not operate in a social vacuum, and very often what they choose to investigate (as opposed to how they investigate it which involves the scientific method and is reasonably, although not

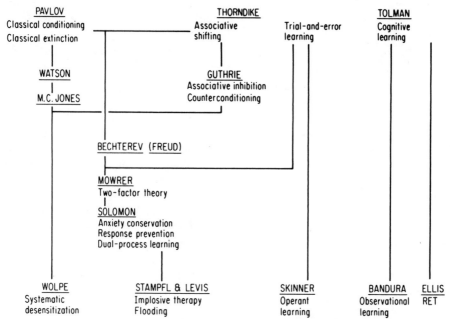

FIG. 1-2 Foundations of behavior modification. In most cases the line drawn between persons represents similar views in the interpretation of behavior rather than direct influence.

entirely, free from human biases) is determined by the social beliefs and the ethos of the society in which they live. This is especially, although not exclusively, true of behavior scientists who deal in human affairs (Kuhn, 1962), and a strong case has been made that the interest of American psychology in learning reflects American–utopian democratic beliefs (Bakan, 1966).

Americans are basically Lockeans. They do not believe in special privilege confirmed by heredity and in authoritarian doctrines. Their very government is an extension of Locke's assertion that the individual is born with a "clean slate" (a tabula rasa) and is ultimately fashioned by the environment. These beliefs are embodied in the doctrines of the Bill of Rights (Bakan, 1966). Emerging from these beliefs is the American melioristic spirit—the conviction that growth, change, progress, and improvement in life can be brought about through human effort. What better way to effect this than to discover the laws of change and adaptation which are the laws of learning and apply them directly to human behavior? Americans not only believed in change, they demanded change and adjustment as a condition for survival. William James's belief in the philosophy of pragmatism and his stress on self-control and habit expressed this melioristic spirit directly, as did Watson's belief that he could train anyone to become any type of specialist—doctor, lawyer, professor—despite his or her inheritance (Chapter 3).

Improvement and change were both regarded as the consummate "good" in the United States, and learning was the way to achieve them. Technology was always of primary interest to Americans. In 1904 Cattell expressed the hope that "the application of systematized knowledge to the control of human nature [would] accomplish results commensurate with the nineteenth century application of physical science to the material world" (Woodworth, 1931). There was, and still is to a very great extent, an abiding faith in the ability of science to take charge of human affairs. Witness Skinner's venture into the planning of utopias (*Walden II,* 1948) and his recent foray into the questions of freedom and dignity (*Beyond Freedom and Dignity,* 1971).

America also has a way of transforming ideas imported from other countries to suit its democratic–environmentalist principles. Bakan has observed that both behaviorism and psychoanalytic theory were equally acceptable to the American scene because both articulated well with the "adjustment of people to a new society" (1966, p. 25). To carry his thinking one step further, both behaviorism (insofar as it emphasized learning and conditioning) and psychoanalysis emphasized behavioral change. In conditioning, Pavlov and Watson showed how the organism could adapt to environmental conditions again and again during its lifetime, making renewal and growth possible. Freud also held out the promise that the personality need not remain fixed despite the "misfortunes" of the past. But neither conditioning nor psychoanalysis was accepted in its original form, and both underwent characteristically American revisions reflecting the social philosophy of progress, growth, and learning.

Pavlov never really divorced the behavioral aspects of conditioning from its neurological events, and he always regarded the conditioning process as a way of bringing a reflex (essentially an involuntary response) under stimulus control—salivation elicited by a light or a tone instead of food.

Pavlov interested himself primarily in the physiology of the nervous system, and he made this point often to distinguish himself from the American psychologists who, he felt, focused primarily on human problems. Watson proved Pavlov's point by completely ignoring the conceptual nervous system which Pavlov had invented to explain conditioning and concentrating mainly on the use of conditioning as a method for solving human problems. Guthrie, as we subsequently see, went one step further. He used the word "response" instead of "reflex" and made the simple occurrence of two events—a stimulus and any response—the basis for learning. Guthrie was also interested in the practical application of conditioning.

In psychoanalysis the shift from biological determinism to cultural determinism was quite consistent with the American belief that culture plays an overwhelming role in shaping behavior. Originally, Freud placed great stress on the id (the instinctual elements in human functioning) and psychosexual development, both of which have their roots in human biology. Gradually, American psychoanalysts began to place more emphasis on the ego (that part of the personality most in touch with the external world), and they played down the significance attached to the instincts considerably. This was not surprising because, as Seely points out in his book, *Americanization of the Unconscious* (1967), *society and social relations are much more amenable to change and improvement than biologically given instincts.* A greater air of optimism unquestionably exists in the American version of psychoanalysis than in Freud's because it is easier to change behavior formed through cultural and environmental influences than to alter biologically based behavior.

AFTERWORD

It should be obvious by now that this book deals almost exclusively with the role of conditioning and learning in behavior modification, and that the emphasis is more on the relationship of the science of behavior to the technology of behavior than on the elements of clinical practice in behavior modification.

Those readers who have more than just a passing acquaintance with the areas of conditioning and learning will see that a relatively elaborate technology of behavior has been stretched over a fragile skeleton of a few fundamental principles abstracted from a very complex subject. But this makes the future prospects of behavior modification even more exciting. If, as we see in the ensuing pages, so much can be accomplished on the basis of a "few fundamental principles," then the scope of behavior modification as a treatment method will surely continue to grow as the scientific base expands.

It would be misleading to suggest that all of the current procedures in behavior modification emerged from the principles of behavior or that they can be explained in terms of them. In fact, one of the points we continue to stress throughout this book is that scientists are chronic skeptics and that scientific explanations are always tentative and subject to challenge. Classical conditioning, operant learning, or mediated learning may generate many of the treatment procedures discussed here, but this does not mean that other explanations may not be reasonable.

Moreover, as we have occasion to observe later, technology frequently has a way of outdistancing science in response to urgent needs, and this is certainly the case in the treatment of behavior problems. The empirical basis of behavior modification, however, requires that all such procedures be tested experimentally, and one of the likely "spin-offs" of such a requirement is the possibility that rigorous study in applied psychology may also contribute to its scientific base.

The growth of behavior modification has brought clinical and experimental psychology much closer together in recent years than they have ever been before, and one of the objectives of this book is to demonstrate the inappropriateness of Rapaport's observation that learning theory, which is the theoretical academic backbone of the majority of clinical psychologists, cannot guide their clinical work, thus making them more reliant on psychoanalytical propositions (1959, p. 144).

chapter two

Classical and Avoidance Conditioning

Not everyone agrees with our conclusion that the elements which make up the practice of behavior modification can be sorted into one of three major classes of learning: classical conditioning, operant conditioning, and mediated learning. In fact, some behavior scientists would suggest a similarity to the tactics of Procrustes, the legendary Greek robber, who stretched his guests or cut off their legs to make them fit his beds. We hope that the facts we choose to ignore and those we choose to expand do not materially affect the body of behavioral science.

Unordered facts are generally confusing, and if imposing order introduces some error, we can only agree with Bacon that truth emerges more readily from error than from confusion. Facts are, after all, only fragments broken off from reality—some broken off by accident, but most, according to some preconceived design. Seldom, if ever, has a fact been discovered, isolated, and described independent of human purposes (English, 1954).

CLASSICAL CONDITIONING—METHODS AND PRINCIPLES

In one of Lope de Vega's plays, *El Capellan de la Virgen (The Chaplain of the Virgin),* written about 1615, the renowned Spanish playwright dramatized the plight of a monk who, as punishment for some infraction, was forced to eat on the floor with the cats.

Saint Ildefonso used to scold me and punish me lots of times. He would sit me on the bare floor and make me eat with the cats of the monastery. These cats were such rascals that they took advantage of my penitence. They drove me mad stealing my choicest morsels. It did no good to chase them away. But I found a way of coping with the beasts in order to enjoy my meals when I was being punished. I put them all in a sack, and on a pitch black night took them out under an arch. First I would cough and then immediately whale the daylights out of the cats. They whined and shrieked like an infernal pipe organ. I would pause for awhile and repeat the operation—*first a cough, and then a thrashing. I finally noticed that even without beating them, the beasts moaned and yelped like the very devil whenever I coughed.* I then let them loose. Thereafter, whenever I had to eat off the floor, I would cast a look around. If an animal approached my food, all I had to do was cough, and how that cat did scat. (Quoted in Bousfield, 1955; italics added.)

Three centuries later, and quite by accident, the great Russian physiologist, Ivan Pavlov, discovered conditioning—the process of learning which Lope de Vega had so accurately depicted in his account of the unfortunate monk.

In conducting his experiments on the physiology of the gastric system in dogs, for which he won the Nobel Prize, Pavlov noted that the animals salivated upon encountering many objects in the laboratory, including the experimenters themselves, just as they salivated to the sight and smell of food. He first reacted with annoyance because these "psychic secretions," as he called them, interfered with his study of the animals' gastric responses to food. Pavlov soon realized, however, that the salivary responses to "extraneous" stimuli were not casual or chance events and that some systematic "connection" existed between his entering the room and the dogs' salivation in the absence of food. In order to study this more precisely, Pavlov isolated the animals from virtually all potentially distracting events and pursued the investigation of conditioning with the same determination and thoroughness he had brought to the study of gastric physiology.

This "connection," Pavlov soon discovered, was specific. In an early experiment, representative of most of the later conditioning studies, a tone, which produced no visible response in a dog and certainly not one of salivation, was sounded for a period of 5 seconds and the animal fed approximately 2.5 seconds after the tone was turned off. This sequence, called a *training trial,* was repeated after varying lapses of time. On the tenth of such trials, food was omitted in order to test for the appearance of a salivary response to the tone alone. These *test trials,* which were interspersed among the training trials, eventually showed that the tone could elicit the salivary response in the absence of food. The number of drops of saliva also increased the more the tone and food were presented together. Lope de Vega had surmised exactly this "connection"—the cats associated the coughing with a beating just as the dogs in Pavlov's experiment associated the tone with food. Then each of these stimuli acquired the ability to produce a response which neither had originally been able to do.

Although it appears from Pavlov's experiments that contiguity—i.e., the closeness in time between the conditioned stimulus (CS) and the unconditioned stimulus (UCS) is the overwhelmingly important relationship in conditioning, another set of conditions must be fulfilled, namely, that the UCS be present whenever the CS is present. All conditioning studies take this relationship for granted because the CS and the UCS are usually contiguous in all conditioning studies. But if this sequence of events was disturbed, and the UCS did not always accompany the CS, then no conditioning was likely to occur because the tone or light (CS) did not always predict the occurrence of food (UCS). So while contiguity is necessary, it is also important that a correlation be established between the CS and the UCS (Rescorla, 1967, 1972).

The diagram below helps to visualize the elements which make up the process of conditioning. Pavlov employed the very terms used in the diagram. The word "conditional" originally conveyed the idea that the ability of a stimulus to elicit a response was "conditional" on its being paired with the reflex. This made a great deal more sense than the term "conditioned" which we now use. But, being creatures of conditioning, we shall lapse into the current usage after this brief excursion into erudition.

The word "reflex," however, is another matter. Two American psychologists, S. Smith and E. R. Guthrie (1921), were primarily responsible for using the word "response" instead of "reflex" for good reasons. As we later see, they intended to broaden the meaning of conditioning to include *any* response the organism is likely to make, not only the involuntary reflex responses that Pavlov observed in his experiments.

Now although the adaptiveness of the organism indeed increases by the rudimentary process of learning we call conditioning, the mere fact that a stimulus can act as a substitute for another in calling out a response does not, in itself, account for the remarkable plasticity of behavior that both animals and humans display. In fact, if the many learned associations acquired through conditioning could not be abandoned because the organism could no longer use them, the advantages of flexibility bestowed by the conditioning process would soon turn into a nightmare of responding in which virtually every event in the environment, however trivial, would exert some control over behavior.

Fortunately, events which have lost their usefulness to the survival and well-being of the organism generally lose their ability to control behavior. Although this generalization apparently admits some exceptions, especially in those instances where humans and animals act in ways that seem to contradict survival (masochism, for example, is not easily reconciled in terms of the individual's well-being), a more precise analysis of the behavior, as we later see, reveals that this is only an apparent inconsistency.

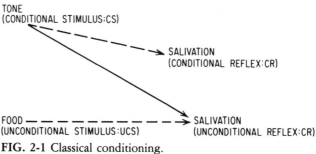

FIG. 2-1 Classical conditioning.

How do animals give up responses that are no longer useful to them? The first simple conditioning experiments answered this and many other questions about the learning process. They also generated a small but significant number of behavioral principles that have formed the foundations of classical conditioning ever since Pavlov first enunciated them. These principles are:

1. Acquisition

2. Extinction

3. Spontaneous recovery

4. Generalization

5. Discrimination

6. Higher-order conditioning

The first principle Pavlov proposed concerned the conditions governing the *acquisition* of the conditioned response. Investigations dealing with how the conditioned response occurs posed numerous questions about the factors influencing the strength of conditioning itself. Does the amount of conditioning depend upon the number of times the CS is presented together with the UCS? How close in time and space must the CS and the UCS be in order to achieve conditioning? Is conditioning influenced by the amount of food given?

Answers to these questions led inevitably to other problems dealing with the durability of the conditioned response and ultimately to the formulation of another principle related to *extinction,* or the way in which conditioned responses disappear. Here Pavlov found that merely presenting the tone (CS) several times in the absence of food (UCS), which he called *reinforcement,* was sufficient to reduce the conditioned response to zero. But he also discovered, much to his amazement, that this was only a temporary state of affairs! If sufficient time elapsed, the response returned in almost full force when the CS was again introduced. This led Pavlov to another principle, one that persuaded him to go beyond the events he could observe in the laboratory.

Pavlov based the third principle, to which he gave the name *spontaneous recovery,* on the observation that conditioned stimuli do not simply disappear upon removal of the unconditioned stimulus or reinforcement. Not only does the conditioned response to the CS return after some lapse of time, but the CR can be revived again and again each time it has apparently been reduced to zero. The amount of the response which returns, however, decreases with each successive rest period until the CR decays completely, and no further presentations of the CS can elicit it. This means that the CR not only diminishes slowly, its disappearance continues to be a temporary state of affairs for some time—a fact one must consider when applying conditioning methods in behavior modification.

Pavlov explained spontaneous recovery in terms of an internal state of the organism called *inhibition.* As a physiologist, he was inclined to think in terms of internal events, and he viewed conditioning in general as the result of two forces in the nervous system—*excitation* and *inhibition.* Excitation builds up when the CR is reinforced by food, and it involves arousal of the cortex and facilitation of learning, remembering, and performing. The negative force, inhibition, on the other hand, accumulates whenever the CR is elicited without reinforcement, and it acts against excitation. Of course, both of these forces are convenient fictions because Pavlov never actually observed them in the organism.

Stimuli never remain exactly the same from moment to moment. Despite these changes in physical characteristics, which may be large or small, conditioning does take place—as though it depended only minimally on the stimulus itself. The fourth principle, *stimulus generalization,* which Pavlov considered an exceedingly important behavioral element in the survival of the organism, takes care of this dilemma. Animals trained to respond to a tone of 700 Hz did not cease to respond even if the tone varied considerably from 700 Hz. Instead, variations in the tone produced variations in the response. When the tone either increased or decreased from the original CS of 700 Hz, the number of drops of saliva showed a corresponding decrease. So animals trained to one stimulus also respond to other similar ones.

It would be terribly uneconomical for the animal to respond to one and only one stimulus, however. Another principle called *discrimination* explains such circumstances. The animal who salivates copiously to 700 Hz soon learns to restrict salivation to this tone if any of the variations from 700 Hz are presented but never reinforced. In other words, by delivering food whenever 700 Hz is present and removing it whenever any other tone is present, extinction occurs for any tone except 700 Hz and responding is confined to that frequency.

The discovery of generalization and discrimination as offshoots of the conditioning process encouraged Pavlov to speculate even more wildly about the internal cortical events which relate to these processes. He firmly believed that conditioning or extinction created a point of excitation or inhibition in the brain which spread in a diminishing wavelike fashion across the sensory cortex. This "irradiation" hypothesis became less acceptable, however, when it was shown that dogs could be conditioned even when the entire cortex had been removed by surgery. In fact, it has been recently demonstrated that a conditioned eye-blink response can be developed in cats with all of the brain except the lower brainstem removed (Norman et al., 1977). This evidence does not support Pavlov's speculations about the importance of the cortex in conditioning.

The last of the five principles important in applying conditioning to behavior modification is *higher-order conditioning.* Figure 2–2 illustrates this process. Here, a stimulus (CS1:tone) which has acquired control over behavior (CR1:salivation) through conditioning with food as reinforcement (UCR1) is now paired with a neutral stimulus (CS2:light).

After a number of such pairings, the light now becomes a CS capable of eliciting salivation (CR2). The third phase of the process shows how the light (CS2) may be used as an unconditioned stimulus (UCS3) in order to condition salivation to yet a third stimulus—tactile stimulation of the skin (CS3). Evidence from several studies suggests that this is about as far as higher-order conditioning can be carried in animals.

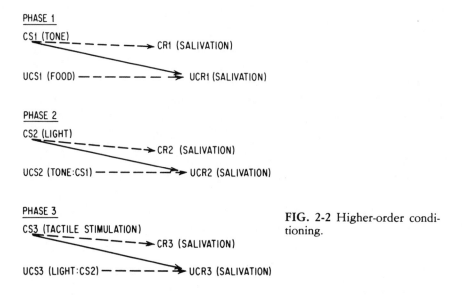

FIG. 2-2 Higher-order conditioning.

For Pavlov the phenomenon of higher-order conditioning took on a special significance. In it he saw the possibility of extending conditioning, as an explanation of learning, from the simple association of sensory events with reflex behavior in animals to language and ideation—the most complex behaviors on the evolutionary scale.

In summary, the study of classical conditioning has generated at least six fundamental phenomena which are important for understanding some of the methods used in behavior modification:

1. *Acquisition:* the formation of conditioned responses and the factors which determine their relative strength.

2. *Extinction:* the elimination of conditioned responses and the factors responsible for their reduction.

3. *Spontaneous recovery:* the reappearance of the conditioned response following extinction.

4. *Generalization:* the elicitation of a conditioned response by a stimulus similar to the conditioned stimulus.

5. *Discrimination:* the formation of a differential conditioned response through the process of reinforcing a response to one stimulus and withholding reinforcement in the presence of another stimulus.

6. *Higher-order conditioning:* the establishment of a conditioned response (salivation) to a conditioned stimulus (light) using a previously conditioned stimulus (tone) as an unconditioned stimulus.

INTEROCEPTIVE CONDITIONING

These examples of classical, or Pavlovian conditioning come from the earliest studies conducted by Pavlov and his associates. Their purposeful simplicity should clarify the relationship between the principles and their experimental origins. But research in classical conditioning has progressed far beyond the original studies, and it has become a complex and varied subject occupying the attention of a large number of researchers for the past three-quarters of a century. In Russia, where the emphasis is still almost entirely on the study of behavior as a conditioning process, interest has extended beyond the simple salivary response that commanded Pavlov's attention to the internal environment of the organism. For some time now, Russian investigators have studied the regulatory mechanisms involved in such physiological responses as heart rhythm, constriction and dilation of the blood vessels, temperature regulation, and digestive-tract action. They found that these responses, so important to the stability of the organism, can serve either as potentially conditionable stimuli to trigger other responses or as responses which themselves can be brought under control through the conditioning process. One of Pavlov's students, K. M. Bykov, first introduced this work to American psychologists in a book called *The Cerebral Cortex and the Internal Organs* (Bykov & Gantt, 1957).

Interoceptive conditioning, as it was subsequently called (Razran, 1961; Adám, 1967), showed that signals from internal organs can acquire control over external responses through conditioning to the same extent that external signals can condition internal events. A typical interoceptive experiment uses water as a CS to stimulate the stomach lining of a dog. The water is introduced and emptied from the stomach through surgical openings made in the stomach walls. At the same time, a UCS, such as electric shock which induces leg flexion or food which elicits salivation, is paired with the stimulation of the stomach mucosa. After a few such pairings, simply wetting the stomach wall produces either leg flexion or salivation as a conditioned response.

Bykov and Gantt describe a more striking example of interoceptive conditioning, both in the laboratory and a natural setting, in a series of studies on the conditioning of thermoregulation (temperature control). In the first of these studies, dogs were repeatedly transferred from their home cages with a temperature of 15° C to an experimental chamber where the temperature was 22° C. At the same time the researchers observed the metabolic changes in the dogs. Measures of metabolism indicate the amount of oxygen consumed and the amount of heat produced as a consequence. When the dogs were transferred to the experimental chamber with the higher temperature, the amount of oxygen production and consequent heat production decreased as it should.

But the experimenters also noticed that one hour before the dogs were to be returned to their home cages with lower temperatures, the amount of oxygen consumption increased. *Evidently, according to Bykov, a conditioned response was created in anticipation of the dogs' return to a lower temperature, and their bodies prepared in advance for this change.* The CS in this instance was temporal—simply the passage of time. With the experimental procedure reversed and the temperature in the experimental chamber reduced relative to the home cage, the exact opposite results were obtained. Transfer back to the home cages after exposure to a lower temperature resulted in a corresponding decrease in oxygen consumption one hour before the expected temperature change to compensate for the anticipated increase in temperature.

After conducting these experiments, the Russians looked for a natural setting with human subjects to support the results found in the laboratory with animals. They found this natural laboratory on a freight train traveling from Leningrad to Lyuban (Box 2–1).

BOX 2–1
The Freight Train Laboratory

Railroad brakemen on the run from Leningrad to Lyuban are constantly exposed to the effects of cold weather because they have to spend their working hours practically unsheltered on a railway car. In conducting tests with these brakemen, Russian investigators found a definite and consistent increase in metabolism during the cold season, *but only on the journey from Leningrad to Lyuban. When the metabolism of the same brakeman was measured on the return trip from Lyuban to Leningrad, it was found to decrease, even though the air temperature remained the same.*

The Russians maintained that the signal for an increase in metabolism was the long, cold run from Leningrad to Lyuban. On the return trip, as the train approached Leningrad and home, the signals were those for entering a warm room, and the man's metabolism decreased accordingly in anticipation of the change in temperature.

The same brakeman, exposed to cold weather while the railroad cars were in town or while tests were being conducted in the laboratory courtyard, did not show any of the behavior observed on the railway car during the regular run. In fact, while he was able to spend many hours on a railway car without suffering from exposure, he could not endure an experiment lasting two hours in the laboratory courtyard. These experiments, repeated with commuters traveling to and from work in automobiles, had similar results (Bykov & Gantt, 1957).

The work in interoceptive conditioning is especially important to behavior modification because it relates directly to some of the procedures used to treat disorders of a physiological nature. Some of the treatment strategies discussed in Chapter 4 are resourceful applications of the fundamental efforts first undertaken by Bykov and his associates.

PAVLOV, GUTHRIE, AND THE IDEA OF COUNTERCONDITIONING

E. R. Guthrie introduced a much broader version of conditioning than Pavlov's. He based it on the notion that any two events can be associated and that one of them need not necessarily be a reflex. The term *conditioned reflex* became *conditioned response,* and, for Guthrie, the most important postulate in learning could be reduced to the principle of contiguity, namely that "stimulus patterns which are active at the time of the response, tend, on being repeated, to elicit that response" (Guthrie, 1938, p. 37). So, in order to associate two events in a way that the occurrence of one will call out the other, the two must simply be contiguous, i.e., occur together in time. Pavlov criticized Guthrie for his emphasis on the one principle of contiguity to explain all of conditioning, but Guthrie replied that Pavlov's version was a highly artificial form of learning and that a more general principle was needed to explain what Pavlov had found in his experiments (Hilgard & Bower, 1966, p. 76).

Another equally important postulate has to do with the way in which responses undergo extinction. According to Guthrie, responses simply do not disappear—they must be replaced by other responses. "The dissociation of a cue from a response is actually the association of that cue with a rival response" (1938, p. 48).

In terms of these two postulates then, habits are acquired when responses occur in the context of a given set of stimuli and are eliminated when they are replaced by new behavior. To break a habit, a new habit (response) must become connected to the old cues. This procedure, called *counterconditioning,* is difficult to accomplish because the old cues will continue to evoke the old response, making it virtually impossible to attach new responses to them.

One of the signals for smoking, for example, is the completion of a meal with all of the attendant cues, the fullness of the stomach, for example. The chief difficulty in dealing with smoking is that the behavior is attached to so many signals —each of which can stimulate smoking before the smoker even becomes aware of it—that substituting other responses is impossible. Guthrie makes this point in a timely excerpt (1935, p. 139).

Drinking or smoking after years of practice are action systems which can be started by thousands of reminders. . . . I once had a caller to whom I was explaining that the apple I had just finished eating was a splendid device for avoiding a smoke. The caller pointed out that I was at the moment smoking. The habit of lighting a cigarette was so attached to the finish of eating that smoking had started automatically.

Many of the techniques suggested by Guthrie in his book *The Psychology of Human Conflict* (1938) for dealing with behaviors such as smoking originated in Pavlov's laboratory. One study, in particular, had exceeding relevance because Erofeeva, one of Pavlov's students, succeeded in converting an intense shock to a dog's skin—a stimulus which normally produces struggling and howling—into a signal for salivation through counterconditioning (Box 2–2).

BOX 2-2
How Masochists Are Made, or Why the
Christians Gladly Went to the Lions

Although Erofeeva had not especially set about to create a masochistic dog, the effect was still the same. What else is one to call an animal who, given a strong electric shock to the skin, turns toward the source of the shock "smacking its lips and producing a profuse secretion of saliva as before eating" (Pavlov, 1927, p. 30)?

Conditioning created this extraordinary behavior, but it was conditioning with a decided difference. Ordinarily, a conditioning experiment starts with a stimulus that does not evoke a response—or at least one that is not likely to interfere with the response to be conditioned. What if the potential CS not only produces a vigorous response itself but also interferes with the potential conditioned response? Can an intense electric shock be turned into a conditioned stimulus for salivation?

Apparently Pavlov and Erofeeva thought so, and they were able to demonstrate that painful stimuli such as shock strong enough to cause a man to withdraw his hand because of intense pain, cauterization, or pricking of the skin deep enough to draw blood can be turned into conditioned stimuli for salivation. This conditioning was so profound that the animals went willingly, if not eagerly, to the laboratory after training. The painful stimulus which would normally arrest both pulse and respiration and create subsequent irregularities in both did not produce the slightest change in pulse and respiration rates after conditioning. The dog just stood there and salivated when shocked, burned, or pricked with a lance.

The secret of the procedure is to arrange the experiment so that conditioning begins with shocks of low intensity which are paired with food. The shock is then gradually increased throughout the course of conditioning until, in full strength, it becomes a conditioned stimulus capable of evoking salivation in the absence of food. Virtually any cue can become a conditioned stimulus if it does not produce a response which interferes with the potential conditioned response. But even if the stimulus does produce such a response, Pavlov and Erofeeva's method shows that gradual "fading in" of the stimulus prevents the interfering response from occurring and makes it possible to associate a different response with it.

Counterconditioning was also successfully demonstrated in young children by M. M. Slutskaya (1928). After pricking the children with a needle until they were fearful of the sight of it, Slutskaya proceeded to feed them each time the needle was applied. In five of the eight children, responses associated with feeding replaced the fearful avoidance responses at the sight of the needle. They opened their mouths and swallowed at each application of the needle.

Why did the dog not continue to howl and struggle while salivating at the same time? Why did the children not continue to be fearful while making anticipatory feeding responses? Although the answer is not readily apparent, it may be that when these stimuli become signals for food their noxious characteristics are altered, and somehow neither the dog nor the children perceived them as threatening and painful any longer. In effect, both the shock and the needle become signals for the food which follows their onset. This close association between painful cues and subsequent pleasurable responses may explain how masochistic behavior is learned and why it is that some individuals actively seek pain.

Pavlov warns us that the results of Erofeeva's experiment can only be obtained in those instances where one reflex is physiologically weaker and biologically less important than another. He based his reasoning on the fact that it was impossible to transfer the defense reaction to shock into a conditioned stimulus for salivation, for example, if the shock was delivered to skin overlying bone without any muscular layer intervening. In this case, apparently, the threat to the dog's survival takes precedence over the desire for food.

Pavlov would probably not have made such sweeping generalizations about the absolute importance of survival if he had seen the implications of Erofeeva's experiment as Sherrington did. On hearing about Erofeeva's study, the great British physiologist was said to have remarked that he could "now understand the joy with which Christian martyrs went to the stake" (Frolov, 1937, p. 95).

Although the procedure used by Erofeeva is customarily used to produce a conditioned response, it contained one notable exception. In order to convert shock successfully into a conditioned stimulus for salivation, the experiment, as Box 2–2 indicates, began with shocks of low intensity which were gradually increased, and the animals received food after each of the shocks. Now, introducing shocks of low intensity initially in the experiment kept the disruptive behavior at a minimum. This made it possible to associate new behavior (salivation) to the old cues (shock). Much to everyone's amazement, the disruptive behavior did not appear even when the shock was gradually increased. The dog merely turned its head toward the source of the shock and salivated.

THE CONDITIONED AVOIDANCE RESPONSE

In the early part of the twentieth century, two men—one in his laboratory in St. Petersburg, Russia, and the other seated at his desk in a consulting room in Vienna —had turned their attention to similar problems in behavior.

At first glance, the Russian physiologist–psychologist Vladimir Bechterev and the Viennese psychiatrist Sigmund Freud appear to have nothing in common. Although Bechterev was also interested in clinical problems, he was intent on interpreting these problems, and indeed all behavior, in terms of conditioning which he had early recognized as an important contribution to the understanding of behavior.

Freud, on the other hand, was convinced that behavior—especially pathological behavior—resulted from the conflict between internal biological forces, and he saw no need for conditioning or learning to explain the origin of the neuroses. Curiously enough, however, Bechterev's work in defense conditioning provided the very touch that Freud's speculations required to make them more credible. Both men were also linked by the idea of "defensiveness" in behavior—an association which O. Hobart Mowrer clearly saw in his seminal paper, *A Stimulus-Response Analysis of Anxiety and Its Role as a Reinforcing Agent,* published in 1939.

Bechterev and Defense Conditioning

Despite their continued and often bitter rivalry (Box 2-3), Pavlov and Bechterev were both interested in studying behavior as an objective, laboratory science. But Pavlov's primary interest lay in the physiology of the nervous system, particularly in the study of the salivary response. As a psychologist and physiologist, Bechterev felt no such constraints on the types of behavior to be investigated.

BOX 2-3
The Pavlov-Bechterev Feud

Scientists are not inherently free from the animosities which affect other people merely by virtue of their association with the high ideals of the scientific method. If anything, the highly competitive race for discovery may make them even more guarded, envious, suspicious, and hostile in their relationships with other scientists—especially those working on similar problems. Most of these animosities tend to remain at the level of "gossip" among the scientists themselves. But occasionally, as in Watson's *The Double Helix,* the feuds become a matter of public record.

It is difficult to say just how the argument between Pavlov and Bechterev began, but given Pavlov's choleric and contentious nature, it is easy to see how it could not have remained at the level of infighting in the scientific journals. One of Bechterev's students had demonstrated that salivary conditioning could not be obtained if a certain point in the brain was cut out. This was not true of similar experiments conducted in Pavlov's laboratory, and the argument went on for a period of two years until Pavlov challenged Bechterev to a "scientific duel," in which Bechterev's claims were to be experimentally and publicly demonstrated.

The salivary centers of two dogs were surgically removed, and on the appointed day Bechterev confirmed his findings by demonstrating that neither of the animals showed a conditioned salivary response when a jar containing some sugar cubes was placed before them. But this was precisely what Pavlov was waiting for —a chance to show how sloppy Bechterev's experimental methods really were. He rose, and taking a jar of weak acid from his pocket, splashed it in one dog's mouth several times. This action immediately produced saliva, and the dog showed a conditioned salivary response to the sight or smell of acid thereafter (adapted from G. A. Miller, *Psychology, the Science of Mental life,* New York: Harper & Row, 1962, p. 184).

Of course, this demonstration did not settle the matter for either contender, and they still continued to take pot-shots at each other whenever possible. Bechterev derided Pavlov's monolithic necessity to explain all behavior by a simplistic

---

extension of the salivary conditioned reflex, disregarding the importance of conditioning involving motor behavior. In *General Principles of Human Reflexology*
(1932), for example, he ridiculed Pavlov for an article which appeared in the
Russian newspaper *Russky Vratch* in 1918. The article asserted that dogs who
secrete saliva freely and cannot spontaneously inhibit this behavior are controlled
by an *"innate freedom reflex"* while dogs who successfully inhibit salivation are
characterized by an *"innate slavery reflex."* Both of these innate reflexes, Pavlov
contended, are also found in man (Bechterev, 1932, pp. 149–150). Bechterev was
attempting to point out Pavlov's absurd tendency to describe complex behavioral
relationships such as slavery and freedom in terms of a relatively simple reflex.

Being dissatisfied with this method [i.e., salivary conditioning] especially because of its
inapplicability to man, I made communication, in the spring of 1907, to the Society of
Physicians of the Hospital of Nervous Diseases, and proved, on the basis of experiments
made by me in collaboration with Dr. Spirtov, the possibility of producing an artificial
association-motor reflex. . . (Bechterev, 1932, p. 197).

With this as an introduction, Bechterev goes on to describe the method he
worked out for producing adaptive changes in motor behavior—finger withdrawal
in man and leg flexion in dogs—a method which has more in common with the
strategy Lope de Vega's unfortunate monk used to safeguard his food from the
hungry cats than it does with Pavlov's salivary conditioning.

Bechterev's experiments involved presentation of a neutral stimulus followed
shortly by a shock to the finger or to the leg in both humans and dogs. The shock
usually resulted in finger withdrawal or leg flexion. Ultimately the neutral stimulus
(now the conditioned stimulus) acquired the capacity to elicit finger withdrawal
or leg flexion in the absence of shock (Bechterev, 1932).

What makes Bechterev's discovery different from Pavlov's? Except for differences in the response—motor in the case of leg flexion and glandular in salivary
conditioning—the two discoveries appear to be remarkably similar on the surface.
In each case, stimulus substitution occurs and a response shifts from one stimulus
to another (Herrnstein, 1969).

The difference comes in the nature of the response. If Bechterev's dog merely
responded to the conditioned stimulus by lifting its leg in the absence of shock,
the situation would compare with the type of conditioning that Pavlov obtained
many times when salivation to a conditioned stimulus occurred in the absence of
food. But often in Bechterev's experiments, conditions were arranged so that the
dog could actually *defend itself against shock by lifting its leg in response to the conditioned
stimulus before shock occurred, thus avoiding the painful stimulus completely.*

Therefore the function that the response serves is different. Salivation occurs
in Pavlovian conditioning as a direct result of the appearance of the conditioned
stimulus, and it is tied inexorably to the stimulus. Whenever the stimulus is presented, the dog has no recourse but to respond. While this is also partly true for
Bechterev's dog, leg flexion has an additional function which distinguishes it from

salivation: *it determines whether or not the unconditioned stimulus (shock) will occur at all.* In other words, given the appropriate conditions, leg flexion or finger withdrawal can act upon the environment in a decisive way to change it. The dog's response in Bechterev's studies and the response of the cats to the monk's cough in Lope de Vega's play both constitute conditioned avoidance responses, each enabling the animal to avoid punishment.

The importance of Bechterev's findings did not entirely escape his attention:

> As a result of reflex movements, a child pricks its hand with a pointed object; consequently, an ordinary *defence* reflex naturally develops [and] the stimulation arising from the prick [becomes] associated with the sight of the pointed object. . . . So, on another occasion, the mere sight of something pointed, although there is no prick, causes a precautionary movement of the hand, which reproduces the previous defence reflex . . . a primary group of association reflexes as necessary for life as are all organic reflexes (Bechterev, 1932, p. 425).

Freud and the Mechanisms of Defense

But what has all this to do with the psychiatrist in his consulting room in Vienna? About the time that Bechterev was advancing his ideas of defense conditioning, Freud was trying to understand the nature of neurotic behavior. He had already proposed a theory, with anxiety as a central concept, to explain how neurotic behavior is developed and maintained. But he was displeased with this formulation, and he set to work on a second.

Influenced by the Law of Conservation of Energy in physics, Freud first advanced the idea that the amount of anxiety exhibited by a patient relates directly to the intensity of the impulse being repressed. He compared the human to a closed energy system in which the energy produced by strong impulses is conserved by being converted into anxiety. Freud based this idea on his clinical observations that patients in analysis who were repressing strong impulses were also generally very anxious.

Soon, however, he abandoned the first theory of anxiety, largely because he could not reconcile it with some of his clinical observations. In conversion hysteria, for example, the patient displays extraordinary symptoms such as hysterical blindness, paralysis of the arms or legs, or peculiar anaesthetic sensations, all of which result from severe psychological disturbances. Yet, despite the repression of strong impulses involved in these disorders, no anxiety is present. In fact, conversion hysteria is especially characterized by the patient's complete indifference to the severity of the symptoms—a state which the French clinicians called "la belle indifference," the beautiful indifference.

In his second formulation of the role of anxiety in neuroses—one which approximates Bechterev's defense conditioning—Freud reversed his original position and made repression a *mechanism of defense* in response to anxiety. Anxiety, according to Freud, is a response to danger. When dangerous impulses create conflict and anxiety in the individual, repression, a form of forgetting, occurs as a first attempt to deal with the anxiety. If repression succeeds, no further avoidance behaviors need develop. But if it does not, the typical defense mechanisms—reaction formation, regression, displacement, and so forth—or neurotic behaviors—phobias, hypochondrias, obsessive-compulsive disorders—develop as a second line of defense. Like Bechterev's dogs, humans produce avoidance behaviors to help protect them from dangerous and threatening impulses. Neurotic behaviors, according to Freud, exist to avoid anxiety, and they are maintained because they succeed in doing so (Freud, 1936).

The Paradox of Avoidance Conditioning

Although one could now understand the relationship between avoidance learning and conditioning, other aspects of avoidance behavior remained puzzling because they just did not seem to fit the facts of conditioning.

In Pavlovian conditioning, for example, the conditioned response (salivation) decreases and ultimately disappears when the conditioned stimulus is presented but the unconditioned stimulus (food) is absent. In avoidance conditioning, this precise relationship no longer seems to hold. As soon as animals learn to avoid punishment by making the appropriate response to a signal—and this happens very rapidly, often after one trial—the unconditioned stimulus (shock or some other aversive event) is no longer present. Despite this, the conditioned stimulus still continues to elicit the avoidance response for remarkably long periods of time—in some instances, for hundreds of trials—before any signs of extinction begin to appear. Animals continue to press levers, jump hurdles, or run in activity wheels in response to a tone or a light despite the fact that punishment no longer occurs. Indeed, the existence of many phobias in humans makes a striking comment on the persistence of avoidance behavior.

Avoidance learning takes place with remarkably few stimulus–response pairings, and it persists for extraordinary lengths of time. What makes it so different from conditioning in general, and can we account for it within the general framework of conditioning?

Enter Two-Factor Theory and the Fear Response

Avoidance learning posed a special problem for those theorists like Hull who proposed that learning occurs through the reinforcement provided by drive reduction (decrease in hunger or escape from punishment). According to this explanation, the avoidance response is first elicited by a noxious UCS (shock), and strengthened when the shock is terminated. But, if the first successful avoidance response eliminates the occurrence of shock, what happens to the drive which is supposed to reinforce and maintain the avoidance response? Why does the avoidance response persist and why do animals and humans continue to give back an extraordinarily large number of responses in exchange for a relatively few painful experiences? This is precisely the problem Mowrer tackled and attempted to clarify in a paper On the dual nature of learning: a reinterpretation of "conditioning" and "problem-solving" (1947).

Mowrer approached the problem of avoidance learning by combining the work of Pavlov, Bechterev, Freud, and Hull with that of Thorndike and Skinner who had investigated yet another form of learning called "instrumental" or "operant" conditioning. In this type of learning (described in detail in Chapter 6) the association is between a response and its consequences. If a response produces rewarding consequences, it is likely to be repeated; if not, it will be abandoned.

Mowrer reasoned that two processes were involved in avoidance conditioning providing two kinds of responses.

The first, *a conditioned emotional response* (CER) results from the pairing of a neutral stimulus with a painful event and is essentially a Pavlovian process. Through *classical conditioning* the neutral stimulus acquires the capacity to elicit fear —the emotional component accompanying the pain—in the same way that a light or tone evokes salivation. It should be recognized, however, that fear is essentially an unobservable response and that an association is *assumed* to be established between the newly conditioned aversive stimulus (CAS) and the unobserved fear response. In general, the greater the number of painful experiences, the greater the fear.

The second response, *the conditioned avoidance response,* is formed when the animal presses a lever or jumps a hurdle to escape. As this response is instrumental in changing the environment by removing the painful event, *instrumental learning or operant conditioning is involved. In effect, learning of fear through classical conditioning is the first process, while learning an avoidance response by operant conditioning is the second.*

The key to the persistence of avoidance behavior in the absence of further shock, Mowrer also proposed, was in the reinforcement of the avoidance behavior by the reduction of fear which followed it. Thus, fear is learned by association with an aversive situation and the avoidance response is acquired and maintained by the reduction in fear which follows avoidance behavior. (It is, of course, a tribute to Freud's genius that he came to the same general conclusions about the role of fear and fear reduction in the development and maintenance of neurotic behavior without so much as touching a white rat).

It is important to note that both Freud and Mowrer make a large number of assumptions about fear and its function in avoidance learning. An experiment conducted by Miller (1948) clearly shows the nature of these assumptions:

Stage I (Pavlovian Conditioning).   A rat placed in a white box is given a brief, intense shock to the feet through an electrified grid. The animal is then permitted to escape the shock by running into an adjacent box through a guillotine door.

Assumption 1—Shock-produced pain is accompanied by fear as an emotional component.

Assumption 2—Fear is the conditionable component of the pain response. A stimulus can acquire the capacity to elicit fear through association with it.

Assumption 3—The white box becomes a conditioned aversive stimulus through association with pain and fear.

Assumption 4—Fear has motivating properties which produce the running response in this experiment.

Stage II (Instrumental Conditioning). The door connecting the two compartments of the experimental box is closed and can only be opened by a wheel made available to the animal. The rat is placed into the white box and shock is no longer presented. In its agitated state the animal at first inadvertently turns the wheel opening the door through which it escapes. On subsequent trials, the time between the placing of the rat in the box and the turning of the wheel (this difference is called the latency of a response) decreases until the animal turns the wheel almost immediately when it is placed into the box. Consequently, wheel turning is learned as an avoidance response.

Assumption 5—The sight of the white box arouses fear.
Assumption 6—Wheel-turning behavior resulting in escape from the white box (aversive stimulus) reduces fear.
Assumption 7—Fear-reduction acts as a reward (or reinforcer) which increases the likelihood that wheel turning will occur when the animal is once again placed in the white box.

It is immediately obvious from the foregoing experiment that fear carries an inordinate share of the responsibility for explaining avoidance learning in two-factor theory. This is, indeed, a heavy burden for a response which is, in essence, not directly observable.

Now the use of the fear concept poses a unique problem in psychology which is discussed in more detail in Chapter 11 on mediated learning. The essence of this problem has to do with the necessity for creating unobserved responses (fear) in order to explain observable behavior. If, for example, we say that someone runs because of the fear of a tiger we can only legitimately claim to be describing (1) the threat or danger which the tiger obviously represents, and (2) the running behavior. To say that the person is afraid under the circumstances is simply to describe what is happening, and, in fact, if we confine ourselves to the observable events— the person runs in order to escape being attacked by the tiger—the term "fear" becomes superfluous.

When fear is used to describe the event it becomes a mediating variable because it occurs first to the sight of the tiger and then motivates running. This is the manner in which two-factor theory uses the term fear.

It seems only fair to say that the view of avoidance learning which espouses the use of fear as a mediating concept is not the only existing view of avoidance learning, although it is the oldest and most prevalent. Another view emerging from operant learning avoids the use of fear, or any other mediating concept for that matter, and attempts to explain avoidance learning solely in terms of observable events.

Problems with the Two-Factor Theory

Essentially, the two-factor theory accomplished what it set out to do. It explained how an avoidance response is acquired and maintained in the absence of shock by proposing a two-process learning sequence: the formation of a conditioned emotional reaction—fear—(CER) through the association of a CS with an aversive event leading to a conditioned avoidance response (CAR), and the strengthening of the CAR through fear-reduction following the completion of the avoidance response.

But this scheme requires that a certain set of relationships exist between fear and the avoidance response; namely that

1. the CER should be acquired before the CAR is learned, i.e., emotional conditioning of fear should precede the avoidance response.

2. fear should decrease after the avoidance response is made.

3. elimination of the avoidance response should occur simultaneously with the extinction of fear or shortly following the elimination of fear.

4. drugs or surgical intervention which affects the fear response should also affect the avoidance response (Rescorla & Solomon, 1967, p. 166).

Tests of these relationships generally involved the use of some physiological response such as heart rate, blood pressure, etc. as an index of fear and the measurement of these responses in relation to the avoidance response itself. Typically, these tests have proved to be inconclusive and, in some cases, contrary to expectations from the theory (Rescorla & Solomon, 1967). In some instances the heart rate (CER) did increase before the avoidance response (CAR) was made, as expected, while, in others, the heart rate increased only after the avoidance response occurred. Often, the avoidance response extinguished long before heart rate—the response on which it was presumably dependent (Black, 1959). Drugs or surgery did not seem to affect the avoidance response once it was firmly established.

These results, as well as the general finding from most avoidance learning studies that the overt signs of fear (agitation, excitability, etc.) rapidly disappeared as the animals responded faster and became more stereotyped in their behavior, were damaging to the two-process speculation and to the assumption that fear was necessary to maintain avoidance.

On the basis of this critical review of the avoidance learning literature Rescorla and Solomon (1967) re-examined the two-process hypothesis in avoidance learning and were persuaded that indices of fear such as heart-rate were, in themselves, conditioned responses, and that these, as well as the avoidance responses, were both still further dependent on a centrally mediated state. They further proposed that a more critical test of the two-process concept involved experiments in which the two learning processes were tested independently.

In one such study conducted by Solomon and Turner (1962), dogs, suspended in a harness, first learned *an instrumental or operant response* to avoid a shock to the paw by turning their heads slightly to move a panel when a light was turned on. The dogs were then completely paralyzed by D-tubercurarine (a curare derivative which immobilizes the skeletal muscles and necessitates artifical respiration to keep the animal alive) and subjected to a *pavlovian discrimination conditioning procedure* during which no motor response could be made. One tone (CS+) was presented with shock (UCS) while a tone of a different frequency (CS−) was presented only when the shock was absent. When the dogs were tested after the drug had worn off, they not only retained the original avoidance response, but, in addition, showed reliable panel pressing to the CS+ and none to the CS−.

Apparently, something was learned during the period when the dogs were exposed to classical conditioning because *the instrumental panel pressing response was now capable of being elicited by the CS+ even though the dogs had never before pressed the panel in the presence of the CS+. In effect, pavlovian conditioning of a CER (CS+ − R fear) during paralysis made it possible for the CS+ to elicit panel pressing by first evoking the fear response which was common to both the CS+ and panel pressing.*

Figure 2-3 is a graphical presentation of the scheme used by Solomon and Turner to test the two-process theory by manipulating each of the factors independently. The relationships shown in Figure 2-3 also suggest several other possibilities for testing the validity of the theory. In principle, it should be possible to increase or decrease the amount of fear and the subsequent avoidance response by varying the number of CS− shock trials or CS no-shock trials while the animal is under the influence of the drug. These results were obtained in two studies.

In the first of these experiments conducted by Black (1958) dogs were immobilized by D-tubercurarine after they had learned to avoid shock by turning their heads following the onset of a CS. During paralysis they were given 55 presentations of the CS without shock. When the drug wore off, and the animals were permitted to make the avoidance response to the CS, they extinguished much more rapidly than control animals which had received an equivalent number of normal extinction trials (presentation of CS and avoidance behavior without drugs) or a group of animals which had received the drug, but no CS presentations during immobilization.

The second experiment (Black, Carlson & Solomon, 1962) showed that fear, and the subsequent avoidance response, could be increased under the same circumstances by pairing the CS with a shock to the foot while the animals were in a drugged state. When this was done the animals showed an increase in avoidance behavior after being released from the drug.

Additional studies by Overmier and Bull (1969) and Overmier and Brackbill (1977) have also confirmed the existence of two, relatively independent, learning processes in avoidance conditioning.

Although the Rescorla-Solomon two-process analysis answered some of the basic questions about the learning components in two-factor theory, it did not shed

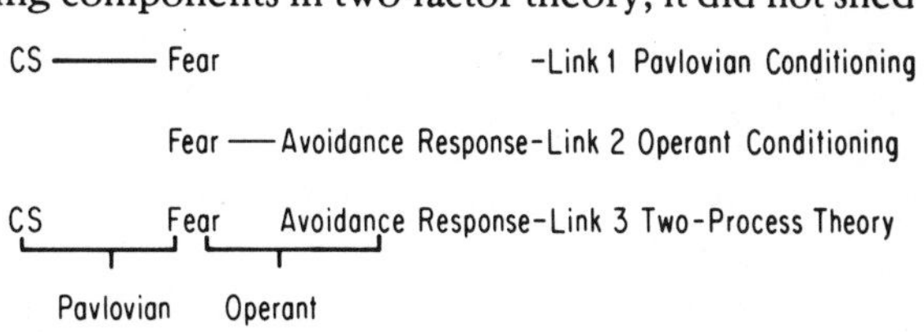

FIG. 2-3 The pavlovian and instrumental links in two-process theory.

any more light on the important relationship between fear and the learning of an avoidance response—particularly on the assumption that fear motivates the avoidance response and that fear-reduction strengthens it. In fact, as we have already indicated, the very persistence of the avoidance response—once it has been established—is inconsistent with the fear-reduction hypothesis because the results of most animal studies show that the overt signs of fear, present during the early stages of conditioning, tend to decrease as avoidance becomes more stereotyped and the animal responds faster.

Clearly, if no fear is present and the organism is no longer being punished, why does the avoidance response persist? Why doesn't it extinguish? Instead, avoidance responses show remarkably high resistance to extinction especially in human behavior where clinicians have observed some well-entrenched phobias (irrational fears) and other fear-related responses continue for the lifetime of an individual without showing any appreciable signs of diminishing. Obviously, this question is of great interest to those who must deal with persistent, irrational avoidance behavior, and Solomon and Wynne set about to attempt to answer it.

The Persistence of Avoidance Through Anxiety-Conservation.   Solomon and Wynne speculated that the very absence of fear during well-established avoidance responses may, in fact, account for the persistence of the avoidance response. In 1954, they ran a study in which dogs were trained to jump a hurdle in response to shock when a light was dimmed. Shock was administered if the dog did not cross the barrier within 10 sec. After this response was well-learned, they unsuccessfully attempted to extinguish it by eliminating the shock. The dogs simply kept jumping faster and faster in response to the dimming light until, at the end of twenty days, they were jumping one or two seconds after the lights were dimmed. This behavior would probably have persisted for very long periods of time without showing any appreciable decrease if the experimenters had not introduced a procedure which hastened extinction and eliminated hurdle-jumping entirely. They merely prevented the dogs from any further jumping by placing a barrier between the two compartments.

This very simple expedient which produced such a dramatic change in the dogs' behavior was based on an elementary but ingenious reformulation of the two-factor theory. Solomon and Wynne reasoned that when the avoidance response is well-learned, jumping takes place even before the CS has an opportunity to elicit fear. If fear never occurs as a response, then it cannot be extinguished because we know from Pavlovian conditioning that extinction takes place only when a response is made and not reinforced. This reformulation introduced a new principle called *anxiety-conservation* which states, in effect, that the avoidance response is maintained for long periods of time because it prevents fear from occurring, and if fear rarely occurs it cannot be extinguished rapidly.

So much for the persistence and durability of the avoidance response. But we know from laboratory studies that it does eventually extinguish. How can the ultimate extinction of the avoidance response be reconciled with the anxiety-conservation hypothesis?

Solomon and Wynne responded to this added perplexity by a careful and detailed analysis of the dogs' behavior from trial to trial. They noticed that "if a dog happened to have an abnormally long latency on a particular trial, he typically acted 'upset' immediately after the (avoidance) response had occurred, and jumped very quickly on the next few trials" (1954, p. 359). According to Solomon and Wynne, it appeared as though the animals were frightening themselves on the long-delay trials. The occurrence of fear on such trials where jumping is delayed serves two purposes. First, it provides an extinction trial for the fear itself, and, secondly, the reduction of fear following avoidance acts to reinforce the jumping response on subsequent trials. In effect then, avoidance behavior should be cyclical —faster on some trials, slower on others—with the overall result that extinction will eventually take place.

Many studies with animals have confirmed the general conclusion reached by Solomon and Wynne that blocking or response prevention in the presence of the aversive stimulus results in more rapid extinction of the avoidance response (Page and Hall, 1953; Page, 1955; Weinberger, 1961; Delude and Carlson, 1964; Schiff, Smith, and Prochaska, 1972; Monti and Smith, 1976) and some also show that the effectiveness of blocking depends, in large measure, on the amount of time the response is blocked and the animal exposed to the aversive CS. In general, the longer response prevention occurs, the faster the avoidance response extinguishes.

Further evidence for the viability of the anxiety-conservation hypothesis was found in an experiment by Levis and Boyd (1979) based on an extension of the anxiety-conservation principle by Stampfl (Levis, 1966). Stampfl suggested that if fear were indeed being conserved by very rapid responding in well-established avoidance behavior, then conservation, and hence resistance to extinction, could be increased by dividing the CS-UCS (shock) interval into several different phases each with a different CS (e.g., tone, light, buzzer) and presenting them serially (tone followed by light followed by buzzer and finally by shock).

According to Stampfl, extinction of the avoidance response would be retarded because response-prevention will produce a reduction of fear to the first stimulus (S1) in the chain and decrease the speed of avoidance as Solomon and Wynne found. But, as S1 and the stimulus which follows (S2) are dissimilar, very little generalization of extinction effects would transfer to S2. Furthermore, as the avoidance response to S1 continues to be delayed, the animal will encounter S2 and "a stimulus change from low-fear to high-fear would take place largely because S2 is more closely associated with shock. In effect, rapid responding and additional fear conservation will again take place in the presence of S1." This procedure, according to Stampfl and Levis, should produce more resistance to extinction than one in which the same stimulus is used in the entire CS-UCS sequence.

An experiment conducted by Levis (1966) verified Stampfl's prediction. In a second, more detailed study, Levis and Boyd (1979) showed that when a tone (S1), white noise (S2), and buzzer (S3) were presented serially and made aversive through association with shock, a group of rats took more than three times longer to extinguish an avoidance response than a comparable group for whom the same stimulus was used in the entire CS-UCS sequence.

An interesting clinical analogue of the Solomon and Wynne study, and one which suggests that prolonged exposure may result in increased fear during the delay period, is provided by Rachman, De Silva, and Roper (1976) in an investigation of the behavior of obsessive-compulsive patients following the prevention of a ritualistic checking response (Box 2-4).

BOX 2-4
Response Prevention and the
Obsessive-Compulsive

Clinicians who work with problem behaviors involving anxiety regard the role of anxiety in the establishment and maintenance of neurotic behavior proposed by Freud as an accurate approximation of what is generally observed in the consulting room. But evidence for this explanation of neurotic behavior has largely been anecdotal, depending upon the invariably subjective and frequently unreliable reports of practitioners. More recently, however, Rachman, De Silva, and Roper (1976) have been conducting a series of controlled laboratory studies with obsessive-compulsive patients at Maudsley Hospital in London which places a great deal of credence in the use of systematically obtained clinical data to support the concept of fear and the way in which it functions to influence overt behavior.

An obsessive-compulsive person characteristically has persistent irrational thoughts and impulses. Sometimes, as in the classical handwashing compulsion, the impulse to engage in handwashing occurs without any obsessive thoughts or any apparent signs of discomfort. Handwashing simply goes on as though it is part of a daily routine—which, of course, it would be if the behavior were not repeated twenty to forty times a day. More often, however, the obsessive thought occurs first—"I must check those packages for a bomb" or "Did I lock somebody in that room?"—and these thoughts create enough discomfort to initiate the "checking response." Most people who are not particularly obsessive-compulsive engage in such behavior as a means of self-assurance, but unlike the obsessive-compulsive, one check generally satisfies them. The obsessive-compulsive ritualizes this activity, and, in severe instances, the necessity to check hundreds of times a day becomes very crippling.

In a series of earlier experiments with obsessive-compulsives, Rachman, Hodgson, and Marks (Rachman et al., 1971; Hodgson et al., 1972; Hodgson & Rachman, 1976) devised a method for dealing with people who were afraid of dirt using a technique called "flooding" (see Chapter 4). This involved exposing them to dirt and preventing them from engaging in ritualistic cleaning behavior. Although the method succeeded, the experimenters thought it advisable to take a closer look at the behavior that occurred when the response was blocked. They chose as subjects eleven adult obsessive-compulsive patients whose condition was moderate to severe and whose main compulsive activity consisted of "checking" rituals. In the first part of the experiment, the subjects were exposed to the provoking stimulus (e.g., a closed door or a paper-wrapped bundle) and then permitted to carry out the checking ritual. In the second part, they were once again exposed to the provoking stimulus, but this time no checking was permitted. In each phase of the experiment, subjects were asked to rate both the urge to carry out the ritual and the discomfort involved before and after exposure to the provoking stimulus and during the blocking period.

Figure 2-4 indicates that the eleven subjects rated themselves highest in discomfort immediately after being exposed to the provoking stimulus and lowest after being permitted to perform the checking ritual. The second part of the figure reveals that after exposure and blocking both the discomfort and the urge to "check" show a sharp increase followed by a gradual decline after three hours. Apparently as the discomfort (fear) from exposure decreases, the urge to check (avoidance response) also declined as in the case of Solomon and Wynne's dogs. If discomfort can be accepted as a measure of fear, then the relationship between the avoidance response and the fear response demonstrated in this study appear to be accurately described by the two-factor theory (Rachman et al., 1976).

A more recent investigation of the handwashing response in obsessive-compulsive patients confirmed Rachman, DeSilva, and Roper's findings. Hornsveld and his associates (Hornsveld et al., 1979) found an increase in "autonomic anxiety/discomfort" for patients with a fear of contamination in anticipation of touching dirt and a decrease after the patients were permitted to engage in handwashing.

Response prevention and exposure to the aversive stimulus is one of several important intervention methods for dealing with behavior involving fear. These methods, known as "systematic desensitization," "implosive therapy," and "flooding," are described in detail in Chapter 5.

Present Status of the Two-Factor Theory.   Unfortunately while the anxiety-conservation hypothesis solves an important problem in the persistence of avoidance responses, it does so only at the expense of another basic assumption in two-factor theory, namely, that fear motivates the organism to respond.

If, as the anxiety conservation-hypothesis suggests, fear is no longer present when the avoidance response is well-learned and the organism is responding almost immediately after the aversive stimulus is presented, what prompts the avoidance response to take place at all? *In other words, what motivates avoidance responding? From all appearances, it seems as though fear is a necessary element in the acquisition and extinction of the avoidance response, but not in maintaining it.*

Several psychologists have attempted to deal with this dilemma, but the results have not proved entirely satisfactory. Seligman and Johnston (1973) suggested, for example, that in well-established avoidance responses the behavior is motivated and maintained by expectancy of shock rather than fear. Levis (1966), on the other hand, reports evidence demonstrating that "short-latency avoidance response (in rats) was elicited by conditioned fear" and not expectancy (p. 118). Obviously, any answer to this issue will depend upon a great deal more research with animals and humans.

At the present time, the two-process theory of avoidance learning with the

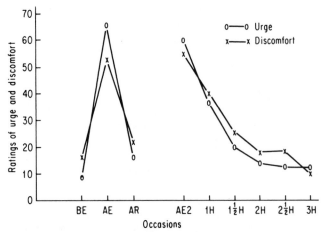

FIG. 2-4 Average (mean) ratings of eleven obsessive-compulsive subjects for urge and discomfort before exposure to the provoking stimulus (BE), after exposure (AE), after the checking ritual (AR), after second exposure (AE2), and half-hour intervals up to three hours (3H). (Source: S. Rachman, P. De Silva and G. Roper. The spontaneous decay of compulsive urges. *Behaviour Research and Therapy,* 1976(b), *14,* 445–453. Copyright 1976 by Pergamon Press and used by permission.)

addition of anxiety conservation is a weaker version of the two-factor theory originally proposed by Mowrer. Although a two-component learning process appears to be a distinct possibility on the basis of the evidence reported by Solomon and his associates, the function of fear as a centrally mediating state in the acquisition and maintenance of avoidance behavior is not yet well established.

As we have already seen, there is ample evidence to suggest that once the avoidance response is learned, fear is no longer necessary to maintain it. The clinical literature has long reported a similar phenomenon called "dysynchrony of fear" in which no visible or covert (physiological) sign of fear occurs as long as the avoidance response can be made. Obviously, any modified version of the two-factor theory will have to account for the persistence of avoidance responding is the absence of fear.

Two-factor theory is a very complex idea which has undergone many revisions since Mowrer first proposed it to explain avoidance learning. Our presentation has been confined to those basic elements in the theory which are useful in explaining how problem behavior may be acquired and helpful in devising treatment procedures for fear-related behavior.

One of the difficulties with two-factor theory is that it is in danger of becoming cumbersome by the addition of new concepts to account for observed phenomena. This kind of expansion often results in a cluttered theory which explains the observations in a tortuous manner. Ptolemy's model of the movement of the sun and planets around the earth suffered such a fate. It began to require all sorts of extraordinary geometric shapes (equants, etc.) to account for the astronomical observations just to maintain the fiction that the circle is the most perfect geometrical form. Ultimately, as we know, it was replaced by a simpler and more elegant view.

The same thing may happen to two-factor theory and, in fact, many have begun to doubt whether two processes are really needed to describe avoidance learning or whether fear is a useful concept. But for the time being the theory provides solace for the clinician, a source for devising new treatment procedures, and an interesting and productive model for generating new experiments. These advantages are not inconsiderable and will probably serve to extend the life of the theory for some time until something better comes along.

In Chapters 3 and 4 we shall explore the use of the principles of conditioning and its extensions—interoceptive conditioning, counterconditioning, and avoidance learning—to explain the way in which some of the behavior disorders are acquired and the methods which are used to treat them.

chapter three

Classical Conditioning, Avoidance Conditioning, and the Behavior Disorders

In this chapter, we attempt to determine how the principles of classical and avoidance conditioning may be used to explain the origin of certain behavior disorders. In many respects this is an impossible task because no one can state with any degree of certainty just what conditions produce behavior disorders or just how they do so. The origin of maladjusted behavior is pretty much a matter of speculation and conjecture for all psychological models—even for those tightly formulated theories of behavior like psychoanalysis. Behavioral explanations are no exception.

It is one thing to *assume* that most behavior disorders result from learning or from the lack of an opportunity to learn as we did in Chapter 1. It is quite another to *prove* it. And that learning can be used successfully to modify certain behaviors does not prove that the behaviors were learned in the first place, even though it tends to make such an assumption seem reasonable.

Proof very clearly requires the equivalent of controlled observation. Anything else is inference. Either the events responsible for the behavior must be witnessed (even under those circumstances the conclusions are subject to all sorts of misinterpretations) or experiments must be performed, taking care to include all those conditions likely to be responsible for the behavior in question.

Because direct experimentation with humans in most instances is neither practical nor desirable—especially where extreme stress and pain are involved—and because peoples' accounts of the events and processes leading to behavior difficulties are notoriously unreliable, psychologists have had to rely on the *analogue* experiment with humans or animals for explanations.

But analogues are only what the word means—things which are similar or comparable to the real thing, not the real things themselves. In the frequently encountered sexual deviation of fetishism, for example, a non-sexual object— shoes, boots, or other items of clothing—acquires the ability to elicit sexual feelings. No one really knows how such behavior originates, but in a cleverly designed analogue study with humans, Rachman (Rachman, 1966; Rachman & Hodgson, 1968) showed that *classical conditioning* could produce fetish-like behavior under the right conditions (Box 3-1).

BOX 3-1
Fetishism and Classical Conditioning

   Black, knee-length women's boots can and often do arouse sexual interest in men because of their sexual connotations. It comes as no particular surprise, then, that women's boots are a common fetishistic object. For some men, the sexual act cannot be consummated unless the woman wears boots. For others, the sight of a woman's boots arouses them to orgasm. Can this behavior be attributed to conditioning? Rachman thought so, and he conducted an experiment to test this supposition.

   It is not an easy matter to find a reliable index of sexual arousal in studies of the sexual response. One could simply ask a person whether he or she finds a situation or photograph sexually stimulating, but the sensitive nature of the subject more likely than not elicits a negative response, even though some stimulation actually occurs. Moreover, some people have relatively high sexual thresholds and cannot give a reliable answer even though they want to cooperate. The obvious solution to this problem is to find a response beyond the person's control which is not subject to these influences. In his study, Rachman chose to measure changes in penis volume resulting from erection by means of an instrument, called a *phalloplethysmograph,* worn around the penis throughout the experiment. (A similar instrument has been devised to measure sexual arousal in females. It is inserted into the vagina and records changes in the vaginal tissues as they become filled with blood during sexual arousal.) These devices have the advantage of detecting very small behavioral changes even though the subject may not be aware of any sexual stimulation.

   With changes in penile volume as the unconditioned response (UCR), Rachman determined that the conditioned stimulus—women's boots—did not elicit any measurable sexual response from his three subjects prior to conditioning. He then paired photographs of the boots with colored slides of attractive nude females (UCS) in the manner illustrated in Fig. 3-1. All three subjects reached the conditioning criterion of five successive penile responses to the boots in approximately 30 pairings. They also *generalized* these responses to other boots of varying shapes and colors. When the slides of the nude females (USC) were eliminated, *extinction* of the penile response occurred in approximately 19 trials, but *spontaneous recovery* followed when the subjects were tested 1 week after extinction.

It is conceivable that certain fetish objects such as boots, hair, and fur are prime candidates for conditioning because they exist in such proximity to the sexual act.

Of course, fetishism in a highly controlled experiment is not fetishism in "real" life, and risks in logic crop up when leaping from the laboratory to real life. Rachman's studies do show that it is possible to produce the *equivalence* of a fetish through classical conditioning. But we may be committing the logical fallacy of *affirming the consequent* by assuming that all fetish behavior is acquired through classical conditioning. In fact, classical conditioning may be only one of several ways in which such behavior is acquired.

Moreover, such studies leave several important questions unanswered. They do not indicate why only certain people acquire the behavior, why surrogate sexual objects come to be preferred over people, or why the fetish produced in the laboratory is so labile and can be extinguished so easily compared to those seen in the clinic.

These questions, and their difficulties of interpretation, are even more complex when animals are used as subjects and one must make the interpretative leap from animal to human behavior.

But the hazards involved in analogue experiments seem relatively small when compared to the benefits of their *judicious* use. Rachman's studies, for example, open up the possibility that fetishism is a learned response rather than the result of arcane forces clashing with one another inside the organism. And the consideration of fetishism as learned behavior makes it possible to use the principles of learning to alter the behavior. Besides, it is no small matter to demonstrate that we can interpret relatively complex human behavior in terms of comparatively simple principles which apply to humans and animals alike.

We need only consider the successes found in the medical and pharmaceutical fields to be convinced of the value of analogue experiments. Pharmacologists never hesitate to try a drug on an animal before it is adopted for human use, and human heart transplants were originally perfected with dogs. Of course, important differences exist between animals and humans, and Ferster (1966) has clearly expressed one of these differences. People who frequently use animals as subjects in physiological experiments or for the purpose of developing new drugs often ask whether psychotic behavior can be produced in animals.

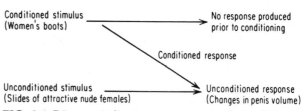

FIG. 3-1 Diagram indicating arrangement of stimuli in the paradigm used to condition women's boots as a fetish object.

The answer to such a question is that animals usually do not have enough behavior to be psychotic. We identify psychosis by noting a discrepancy between the psychotic person's repertoire and the repertoire which is required by his environment. An animal could be psychotic if his repertoire and its controlling environment approached the size and complexity of man's (Ferster, 1966, p. 345).

Obviously, humans and animals differ in many important respects. But where certain types of behavior are concerned—especially that type found in disorganization of function through fear—*humans may be closer to the animals than they are to the gods. Pavlov's discovery of conditioning, and Bechterev's and Freud's elaborations of avoidance learning suggest that, whatever else humans might be and whatever complex forms of additional behavior they might display, they are fundamentally creatures of conditioning and share this form of rudimentary learning in common with all other types of animal life.*

A SOCIAL-LEARNING CLASSIFICATION OF THE BEHAVIOR DISORDERS

The scheme we use throughout this book for discussing the relationship between learning and the behavior disorders is one proposed by Bandura (1968b, pp. 289–299). Essentially, this system classifies behavior disorders in terms of the environmental events (stimuli or reinforcers) which appear to exert control or influence over their occurrences rather than in terms of the behavior clusters upon which classification had been based in the past, e.g., *Diagnostic and Statistical Manual of Mental Disorders II* (1968).

A variation of Bandura's system appears in Table 3-1. It contains the following environmental conditions generally associated with one or another of the "psychological dysfunctions": (1) inappropriate stimulus control of behavior, (2) inappropriate, defective, or impoverished incentive systems, and (3) defective stimulus control of behavior.

Table 3-1 also contains some terms selected from the *Diagnostic and Statistical Manual of Mental Disorders II.* These are included within each of the three broad categories to demonstrate that this type of classification not only encompasses many of the traditional behavior problems, but also orders them in a way which places more emphasis on the factors which appear to control the behavior.

Behaviors as diverse as sexual masochism, alcoholism, drug addiction, antisocial personality, and depression, for example, all have one thing in common—they are under the control of unconventional or impoverished incentives, and thus they fall into the category of defective, inappropriate, or impoverished incentive systems (Table 3-1). People who have these problems either derive their satisfactions from situations that differ from those which satisfy the rest of the population or, as in the case of depression, they do not find sufficient rewards and satisfactions in their daily experiences.

The system, as Bandura has pointed out, is not intended to be exhaustive, and

TABLE 3-1   Social-Learning Classification of the Behavior Disorders

---

A. *Inappropriate stimulus control of behavior*
Stimuli acquire the ability to elicit certain behavior through the process of conditioning. The control is considered inappropriate because these stimuli do not ordinarily evoke the same behavior in others.

1. *Conditioned emotional responses,* such as
psychophysiologic disorders: ulcers, asthma, essential hypertension, etc.

2. *Conditioned avoidance responses*
   a. Shyness, non-assertiveness, etc.
   b. Psychoneurotic disorders: phobias, obsessive-compulsive disorders

3. *Conditioned sexual deviations*

B. *Behavior due to inappropriately administered, addictive, or impoverished reinforcers*
Certain behavior acquired through the inappropriate administration of reward or punishment, or by addictive reinforcers, or by low rates of positive or negative reinforcement.

1. *Behavior deviations under the control of inappropriately administered reinforcement*
   a. Sex typing in children
   b. Self-injurious behavior: masochism
   c. Sexual deviations
   d. Delinquency and dyssocial behavior

2. *Behavior under the control of addictive reinforcers*
   a. Alcoholism
   b. Drug addiction

3. *Behavior under the control of low rates of positive or negative reinforcement,* such as
helplessness and depression

C. *Deficient stimulus control of behavior*
Absence of appropriate behavior due to inadequate or non-existent models, or the presence of inappropriate behavior due to improper models.

1. *Presence of improper models*
   a. Aggression
   b. Dyssocial and delinquent behavior
   c. Sexual deviations

2. *Absence of proper models (deprivation)*
   a. Impaired development
   b. Impaired social functioning

Source: Adapted from A. Bandura, A social learning interpretation of psychological dysfunctions. In P. London and D. Rosenhahn (Eds.). *Foundations of abnormal psychology.* New York: Holt, Rinehart and Winston, Inc., 1968, 293–345. This list is not intended to be exhaustive and contains only a representative sample of some of the behavior disorders assumed to be the result of learning.

some of its classes overlap because people are generally exposed to a variety of social learning experiences which give rise to varying combinations of deviant behavior (1968b, p. 298). *Dyssocial (criminal) behavior,* for example, is not only classified as a *behavior deficit* because in some instances the criminal has had no appropriate models from which to learn the correct values (from society's point of view), but it often also results from *impoverished incentive systems* resulting from the lack of material rewards.

Although the method proposed by Bandura is very largely programmatic and does not significantly add to our understanding of the origins of problem behavior, it does have several advantages over the usual diagnostic system.

In the first place, one traditionally described behavior either in terms of *motives* that *seem* to determine behavior, such as passive-dependent, aggressive, and competitive-exploitive, or in terms of developmental aspects, such as oral, anal, and phallic. Other systems focus on "mental illness" terms such as character disorder, neurosis, and psychosis. These schemes all stress the characteristics of the *person* rather than the relationship between the person and the external environment in which the conditions most likely to produce the behavior are found. This emphasis on the person leads inevitably to speculations about what a person *has* (i.e., the disease entity) rather than on what a person *does* (i.e., the behavior and the conditions which sustain it) (Bandura, 1968b, p. 298).

Secondly, organizing the behavior disorders in terms of the relationship between the person and the eliciting environment makes it possible to alter the behavior by modifying the conditions. Many children who are behavior problems in the classroom, for example, use disruptive tactics to gain attention from the teacher and their peers. Identifying attention-getting as the incentive condition that maintains the behavior enables the teacher to use attention as a reward for non-disruptive behavior by paying attention when the child is non-disruptive.

Lastly, the scheme serves a more immediate purpose. It enables us to explore the interesting possibility that each of the three categories has characteristic, although not exclusive, associations with some specific type of learning: inappropriate stimulus control of behavior with classical and avoidance learning, for example; impoverished incentive systems with operant learning; or defective stimulus control with observational learning.

We cannot, of course, apply this analysis too rigidly. Often behavior disorders are learned in one way and maintained in another. Asthmatic attacks, for instance, may be brought on by a set of stimulus conditions with which they have been associated (classical conditioning), but they can also be maintained by the rewards people get from manipulating the behavior of concerned parents or friends (operant learning).

In this chapter we discuss the way in which classical and avoidance conditioning might conceivably lead to inappropriate stimulus control of behavior.

INAPPROPRIATE STIMULUS CONTROL OF BEHAVIOR

Inappropriate stimulus control of behavior implies the existence of an identifiable stimulus which controls behavior—one of the characteristics which identifies classical conditioning. Consequently, the behavior disorders in this group are those, like phobias, in which an identifiable stimulus has acquired behavioral control.

But what precisely is meant by "inappropriate stimulus control of behavior?" Well, it is appropriate to be somewhat uneasy about thunderstorms, but it is somewhat inappropriate if thunderstorms cause labored breathing, pains in the chest, dizziness, and a feeling of doom, all of which occur as part of an "anxiety reaction." When the resultant behavior is hiding in a closet or under a bed, the stimulus can be said to have acquired inappropriate control of behavior.

To check the door once or twice before going to bed is a normal precaution. To check it twenty-four times and still be uneasy about it is, to say the least, highly unusual. Many people feel apprehensive about having to fly, and the sight of a plane creates uneasiness—especially because devastating accidents do occur. But given the odds that any single such accident will occur, inordinate fear of flying that results in an inability to board an airplane indicates that the airplane, as a stimulus, has acquired inappropriate control over behavior.

Inappropriateness, then, equates with lack of real danger (as opposed to perceived danger which, unfortunately, is always real to the individual who has to deal with it), and inappropriate stimulus control means that a situation has become threatening when, in fact, the danger is minimal or does not exist at all.

Although one can more easily discuss inappropriate stimulus control in terms of fear-related behavior, other kinds of behavior can also be inappropriately controlled. Sexual behavior, for example, can be elicited by stimuli which are not customarily objects of sexual attraction, as in Rachman's fetishism experiment, or part of the sexual encounter may be substituted for the complete sexual act, as in exhibitionism or voyeurism. In principle, any stimulus can gain ascendancy over any response under the proper circumstances.

The Conditioned Emotional Response

Pavlov believed that he had discovered the "rosetta stone" for all behavior in classical conditioning. But he qualified this certainty with the possibility that conditioning, or the ability to be conditioned, depended in part on the specific type of nervous system the individual had inherited. Watson, on the other hand, had no such reservations.

Give me a dozen healthy infants, well-formed, and my own specified world to bring them up in and I'll guarantee to take any one at random and train him to become any type of specialist I might select—doctor, lawyer, artist, merchant-chief and, yes, even beggar-man and thief, regardless of his talents, penchants, tendencies, abilities, vocations, and race of his ancestors (1924, p. 82).

Habits, according to Watson, ranging from the most simple motor movements to emotional responses, are "built into" the organism through conditioning. He also argued that abnormal behavior resulted from a training process that would be revealed by the history of a given maladjustment. To support these arguments, he conducted a study to show that emotional reactions could be elicited by relatively neutral stimuli through conditioning.

The particular experiment conducted with "Little Albert," a 9-month-old boy, is historically important because it challenged the existing notion that most fears arise from a developmental process. By pairing a white rat (CS) which did not originally elicit any fear reaction with a loud noise produced by striking a hammer on a steel bar (UCS), a conditioned fear response was formed to the white rat which generalized to other furry objects. This response persisted for at least one month with only slightly diminishing intensity.

As a result of this study, Watson and Rayner were able to answer three of the four questions they had originally posed: (1) Can a conditioned fear reaction be established? (2) Does the fear generalize to other objects? And (3) will the fear disappear spontaneously with time? A fourth question—can the fear be removed experimentally—was left to speculation because the child was taken from the institution before any attempts could be made to eliminate the fear reaction.

Watson and Rayner's speculations about possible procedures for eliminating the fear reaction were subsequently worked out in a pioneering study by his student, Mary Cover Jones (1924a, b), who anticipated many of the intervention techniques currently being used in behavior modification (Chapter 4).

In principle then, people, objects, events, or ideas are all potential candidates for creating intense emotional experiences, either directly or by association with some aversive event. In reality, however, this has not been so easy to demonstrate, nor have the relatively few laboratory studies uniformly duplicated Watson and Rayner's results.

Shortly after the study with "Little Albert," English (1929) attempted to establish a conditioned emotional response to a painted wooden duck in a 14-month-old girl using Watson and Rayner's methods without any success. And, in another study conducted by Bregman (1934) it was impossible to create a conditioned fear reaction to wooden shapes and colored cloths in 1-year-old babies using a similar procedure.

Because of the artificial nature of the stimuli used as the CS in these studies (painted wooden ducks, for example) it was suggested that perhaps only certain kinds of objects would work as conditioned stimuli and that these may be limited to furry and leather things (Marks, 1977). The "preparedness" hypothesis, recently proposed by Seligman (1971) and tested in the laboratory by Öhmann and his associates (1976), suggests that only objects that may represent a threat to the individual subject are likely to acquire aversive properties through conditioning. Umbrellas, for example, appear less often as phobic stimuli than spiders or rats. (A more detailed discussion of this and related topics appears in this chapter on pp. 63–64.)

Although the total number of laboratory attempts to demonstrate conditioned emotional responses with humans is small, those that have been conducted with both animals and humans using severe, and in most cases "life-threatening," situations show positive results.

Masserman, along with others (Gantt, Liddell), for example, conducted experiments with animals which showed that extreme physiological reactions to stress could be evoked by otherwise neutral stimuli. In these studies a shock or blast of air was delivered to cats which had been trained to lift the lid of a box for food. Ultimately, both the shock and the air blast were discontinued, but the *experimental chamber itself* continued to elicit the responses associated with the noxious stimuli.

Merely placing the cats in the box produced "full pulse, catchy breathing, raised blood pressure, sweating, trembling, hair erection, and other evidence of pervasive physiological tension." They became irrationally fearful and showed extreme startle reactions to minor stimuli such as harmless lights or sounds, closed spaces, air currents, caged mice, and even food itself. "Gastrointestinal disorders, recurrent asthma, persistent salivation or diuresis, sexual impotence, epileptiform seizures or muscular rigidities resembling those in human hysteria or catatonia" were also observed (Masserman, 1943, p. 41). Recent experiments conducted by Wolpe have produced similar results (1952).

Even more dramatic results were obtained by Campbell, Sanderson, and Laverty (1964) in a study designed to show the characteristics of a conditioned emotional response in humans following a single traumatic episode. They used tone as the CS and a drug called Scoline (succinylcholine chlorida dihydrate) as the UCS. Although Scoline produces no pain, it has a terrifying effect because it results in a nearly complete paralysis of the skeletal musculature and interrupts breathing for about 2 minutes.

Just one pairing of the tone and the Scoline was sufficient to produce an intense conditioned heart rate, respiration, galvanic skin response, and muscle potential response which remained substantial even after the delivery of 33 extinction trials with the tone alone. Tests conducted 1 and 3 weeks later indicated that the tone had not lost its effectiveness in producing the conditioned response. In a similar vein, Edwards and Acker (1962) found that World War II veterans retained a galvanic skin response to wartime battle sounds for as long as 15 years after the war. Little doubt remains that if aversive conditions are severe enough, conditioned emotional responses can be obtained.

Psychophysiologic or Psychosomatic Disorders. In a recent discussion of conditioning automatically mediated responses, Kimmel (1974) quotes a statement by Watson (1928) in which he emphasizes the importance of the autonomic nervous system in the ultimate well-being of the individual. "We may earn our bread with the striped (skeletal) muscles," Watson maintained, "but we gain our happiness or lose it with the kind of behavior our unstriped muscles or guts lead us into" (p. 341).

In effect, Watson was saying that the responses of the "unstriped muscles and guts"—heart rate, blood pressure, and so forth—reflect the emotional life of the individual. These responses, in turn, depend upon the activity of the autonomic nervous system which is intimately involved with reactions to stress, tension, and anxiety.

Anxiety and fear (the distinction lies largely in the vagueness of the stimulus producing the emotion: a rattlesnake produces fear; concern about making a good impression at a party is generally regarded as anxiety) are inferred emotions. They equate with physiological reactions (heart rate, sweating, rapid respiration) to an unpleasant or aversive event mediated by the sympathetic branch of the autonomic nervous system. These emotions are usually characterized as subjective feelings of apprehension or dread.

The autonomic nervous system (shown in Figure 3-2) consists of two branches, the sympathetic and parasympathetic systems. Both systems have large responsibilities for controlling the visceral functions of the smooth muscle organs—the heart, intestines, stomach, and so on. In moments of extreme fear, however, sympathetic discharge mobilizes the body for a "fight-or-flight" response, and this reaction produces increased heartbeat, rapid respiration rate, diversion of the blood supply away from the internal organs toward the arms and legs, sweating, and dilation of the pupils of the eyes. At the same time, all vegetative functions related to digestion cease, and the body assumes a "readiness-to-respond" state. Hormonal discharges, such as adrenaline and norepinephrine, also assist in this process by stimulating the release of sugar in the liver, thereby increasing the amount of available energy.

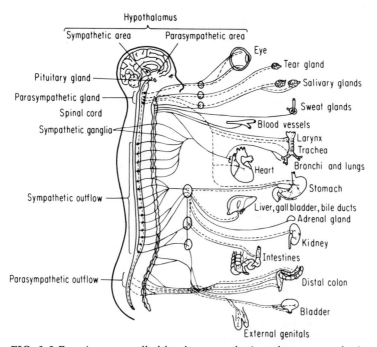

FIG. 3-2 Functions controlled by the sympathetic and parasympathetic nervous systems. (Source: D. Krech, R.S. Crutchfield and N. Livson. *Elements of psychology—a briefer course.* New York: Alfred A. Knopf, 1968. Copyright 1968 Alfred A. Knopf and used by permission.)

TABLE 3-2   Stressful Life Events Arranged in Order of Severity

LIFE EVENT	LIFE-CHANGE VALUE
Death of spouse	100
Divorce	73
Marital separation	65
Jail term	63
Death of close family member	63
Personal injury or illness	53
Marriage	50
Fired from job	47
Marital reconciliation	45
Retirement	45
Change in health of family member	44
Pregnancy	40
Sex difficulties	39
Gain of new family member	39
Business readjustment	39
Change in financial state	38
Death of close friend	37
Change to different line of work	36
Change in number of arguments with spouse	35
Mortgage over $10,000	31
Foreclosure of mortgage or loan	30
Change in responsibilities at work	29
Son or daughter leaving home	29
Trouble with in-laws	29
Outstanding personal achievement	28
Wife begins or stops work	26
Begin or end school	26
Change in living conditions	25
Revision of personal habits	24
Trouble with boss	23
Change in work hours or conditions	20
Change in residence	20
Change in schools	20
Change in recreation	19
Change in church activities	19
Change in social activities	18
Mortgage or loan less than $10,000	17
Change in sleeping habits	16
Change in number of family get-togethers	15
Change in eating habits	15
Vacation	13
Christmas	12
Minor violations of the law	11

SOURCE: T. H. Holmes and R. H. Rahe. The social readjustment rating scale. *Journal of Psychosomatic Research,* 1967, *11,* 213–218. Copyright 1967 Pergamon Press and used by permission.

Of course, this extreme reaction rarely occurs except in moments of real danger to the organism. In less aversive situations, the sympathetic nervous system may innervate only a few of these systems. Lacey (1967, 1970) has called this process *fractionation,* and it may well explain why stress produces different responses involving different organs in the psychophysiologic disorders.

It has been suggested that when an organism finds no adequate solutions to deal with stressful situations, or when it has learned no fear-reducing avoidance response, the prolonged, unrelieved, and uncontrollable exposure to stress can lead to one of several somatic reactions: ulcers, mucous colitis, skin disorders, or essential hypertension, for example.

Some insight is being gained into the nature of the stressful situation which seems to produce the somatic reaction. As we see later, certain studies suggest that animals exposed to unpredictable and/or uncontrollable stress are likely to be afflicted with ulcers or high blood pressure.

Virtually all of the psychophysiological disorders contain a substantial emotional component which is primarily responsible for inducing attacks when they occur. Periods of increased blood pressure, asthmatic wheezing, or severe and painful cramps from mucous colitis have been correlated with stress itself or with events which have been related to stress.

A word about stress.   The stressors that can affect an animal in a laboratory are relatively few compared to those that affect people. Holmes and Rahe (1967) have compiled the life-events and life-change scale listed in Table 3-2 from records of interviews and medical histories. Essentially, they took these stressful events and ranked them from the most stressful—the death of a spouse—to the least stressful —minor violations of the law.

Some interesting relationships emerged from a series of studies using the scale. For example, 50–79% of people with life-change scale values of 200–300 and over during a specific year, indicating a large number of stressful events, became ill the following year. And in a study conducted in Great Britain, 4,500 widowers showed a 40% higher mortality rate than expected in addition to a high rate of illness and depression 6 months after their wives died.

Stress, then, sets the stage for a large number of behavioral changes to take place. Some of these changes express the stress itself directly while others are learned attempts to cope with the tension that stress invariably produces. Can the physiological responses produced by stress be brought under stimulus control in the same manner in which neutral stimuli acquired the capacity to elicit salivation in Pavlov's laboratory? Although the answer must be guarded, evidence suggests that psychophysiologic disorders, like asthma, for example, can be evoked by stimuli with which the symptoms have been associated. Let us examine the evidence for this supposition.

Asthma: an example of a psychophysiological disorder.   Asthma is a psychosomatic disorder in which the air exchange in the lungs, especially expiration, is impaired because of a narrowing of the airways. In a study of 26 patients, 70% of the initial wheezing attacks began with an emotional disturbance (Kleeman, 1967). But while emotional and psychological elements play a pronounced role in the asthmatic response, they by no means predominate. Apparently, over 60% of the cases seem to be due to infective or allergic agents. Evidence indicates, however, that although allergic and infective factors are dominant in children under 5 years of age, psychological variables become increasingly important as the child grows older.

Although ample laboratory evidence suggests that asthmatic-like responses can be induced by previously neutral stimuli which have been associated with the response, and abundant anecdotal evidence suggests that similar results can be obtained with humans, the answer to the question of conditionability is by no means unequivocal.

Clear-cut instances of conditioning in the guinea pig have been reported by Noelp and Noelp-Eschenhagen (1951a, b, c; 1952; cited by Dekker et al., 1957), who exposed guinea pigs to a sound stimulus followed by a protein aerosol or histamine spray to which the animals had been sensitized. Presentation of the sound alone ultimately produced asthmatic-type breathing. Similar results were obtained by Ottenberg et al. (1958), who found that the experimental chamber in which guinea pigs had been sensitized could produce the asthma-like attacks.

Asthmatic attacks in humans have been elicited under unusual circumstances and by extraordinarily strange stimuli according to the clinical literature. For example, one woman who had suffered phasic attacks of asthma since childhood always had these episodes at 3:00 A.M. On one occasion, her husband advanced the clock 1 hour. She awoke at the usual hour and announced that she would soon have an attack. When she was told that it was already 4:00, however, the attack did not occur. Of course, once she discovered the hoax, the attacks continued with their accustomed regularity (Lopez-Ibor, 1956). In another instance, a patient's attacks were traced to his mother-in-law with whom he was in conflict and more specifically to a large picture of her hanging in his bedroom. The attacks could be produced by exposing the picture or eliminated entirely by turning the picture toward the wall (Eysenck, 1965).

A partial list of situations known to produce asthmatic attacks obtained from interviews with patients included the following: (1) radio speeches by highly placed politicians; broadcasts of a children's choir; the national anthem; (2) knitting; the sight of a waterfall or a bicycle race; (3) lifting a sample jewelry case; and (4) goldfish bowl; a bird in a cage; a prison van. These stimuli elicited attacks in six out of twelve instances when patients were exposed to them in the laboratory. *In several cases, the patients had intense emotional experiences while discussing their difficulties or after being exposed to other anxiety-provoking stimuli, but none of these occasions produced an asthmatic response. Only the specific stimulus could trigger the reaction* (Dekker & Groen, 1956). Box 3-2 describes such a case in detail. Such evidence strongly suggests that certain stimuli associated with asthma can gain ascendency over the behavior in a manner reminiscent of conditioning.

BOX 3-2

Asthma in a Goldfish Bowl

At first, Mrs. M. was amused when she was shown a plastic toy goldfish. Eight minutes later her vital capacity had dropped to 29%, and she was in the midst of a severe attack of asthma. She knew it was ridiculous to act this way and even remarked, "Fancy my choking because of that silly toy thing. It isn't even alive!" But Mrs. M. had been having asthma attacks for many years now, and these attacks were triggered by goldfish—and only goldfish.

Dekker and Groen determined this by first showing Mrs. M. a goldfish in a bowl. But before doing so, they permitted her to talk about her problems in general—and especially her son's homosexuality, which troubled her greatly. She showed great emotion and wept when she talked about her son's behavior, *but this anguished display did not produce an asthmatic reaction.* Shortly thereafter, the investigators changed the topic, engaging her in a conversation designed to produce a calming effect. When a goldfish was brought in, she became excited, reproached the physicians for keeping the poor creature in a bowl, where it was suffocating and gasping for breath, and developed a severe attack of asthma within minutes after the introduction of the goldfish.

The interesting thing about Mrs. M.'s asthmatic response is that goldfish were not even involved in her first experience of asthma and must have acquired control of the behavior some time later. The first asthma attack began when her husband, a butcher, made her mop up the blood of a calf which had just been slaughtered. She had a violent emotional reaction to this request, which was immediately followed by an increase in wheezing and shortness of breath (Dekker & Groen, 1965, p. 64).

On the strength of this clinical evidence, Dekker, Pelser, and Groen (1957) devised a study to test the conditioning hypothesis. Patients first inhaled a neutral agent and then the particular substance to which they were allergic and which produced the asthma attacks. Conditioned asthmatic responses to the neutral agent developed in only two subjects although, in one case, just the sight of the inhalator itself elicited a response.

The investigators found this ability to condition no more than two patients particularly disconcerting in view of results with animals and observations in the clinic. But, as the investigators point out, the patients who developed the conditioned attacks were afraid of the allergic investigations, and it may well be that this attitude (fear) was an important factor in facilitating the conditioning process (Dekker et al., 1957, p. 106).

This observation is consistent with the conclusions drawn from their previous study (Dekker & Groen, 1956) that both a specific stimulus and an emotional experience are the necessary prerequisites for an asthmatic attack. Intense emotionality produced by any other than the specific stimulus will not produce the attack.

Removal of the stimulus responsible for the asthmatic attack often results in the termination of the attack. Children whose asthmatic symptoms appeared to be associated with disturbed family relationships, for example, improved significantly when separated from their parents and placed in the homes of substitute parents. Frequency of asthmatic attacks, wheezing, and the amount of medicine required all showed a marked decrease. On the other hand, virtually none of the control children whose asthma was assumed to be induced by allergic or infective agents showed a comparable improvement when they were also removed from the home (Purcell et al., 1969). (It is, of course, entirely possible that the children "learned" to be asthmatic because of the effect this behavior had on the parents. In Chapter 6 we consider the possibility that any deviant response can be learned and maintained because the response manipulates the environment in some way that is advantageous to the individual.)

Emotional responses, whether the direct result of reactions to stress or induced by stimuli which have been associated with stress, also motivate the organism to attempt some solution to reduce the effects of stress. Very frequently, the solution is determined pretty much by the nature of the stress condition itself. Studies with animals and humans have shown, for example, that a predictable and controllable stress situation is less threatening than one which holds neither possibility. The *type* of behavior disorder that develops as a result of stress seems to be a function of the *type* and *amount* of control a situation will permit.

Predictability and Controllability: The Link Between the Psychophysiological and Psychoneurotic Disorders

If, as most behavioral scientists believe, stress is the necessary condition for the development of behavior disorders, then the way in which individuals handle these stress situations—the attempts they make to control them and the extent to which they are actually capable of being controlled—may determine the kind of disorder likely to develop.

Ulcers, for example, usually develop in rats who are given inescapable shock. But Gliner (1972) reduced the frequency of ulcers for a group of rats by permitting them to choose whether a shock would be preceded by a warning signal. Also, rats who were permitted to turn off a shock when they were bar-pressing for food developed fewer stomach lesions than those who were unable to terminate the shock (Moot et al., 1970).

Studies such as those just cited have persuaded some psychologists that the conditions of *uncertainty* and *uncontrollability*, combined with a great amount of *constant effort* and *tension*, seem to produce ulcers and high blood pressure in animals and, perhaps, in humans (Box 3-3).

BOX 3-3
The Executive Monkeys

For some people, promotions and the responsibilities that usually accompany them are as inherently punishing as they are rewarding. At least this is what the "executive monkey" in Brady's extraordinary study found when he was given the responsibility for avoiding shocks to himself and another monkey by pressing a lever 15–20 times a minute to avoid the painful experience. His partner, unfortunately, did not have this doubtful advantage. He had a completely inoperative lever with no effect on the shocks at all, so he continued to receive them on those infrequent occasions when the executive monkey slowed down and shirked his responsibilities. Yet it was the executive who developed ulcers and died after working for 23 days on a 6-hours-on/6-hours-off schedule. His partner, who could not control the shocks, soon gave up interest, stopped pressing the lever, did not develop ulcers, and lived.

The interesting thing about this experiment is that only the "executive" monkeys who were kept on a 6-hour schedule developed duodenal ulcers. When the schedule or the time spent pressing the lever was varied in later experiments, none of the monkeys—executive or not—developed ulcers.

On closer examination of the 6-hours-on/6-hours-off schedule, Brady found that the production of gastric acid (hydrochloric acid in particular) rose sharply at the end of the 6-hour avoidance period and continued to rise for a few hours while the animal was resting. This constant assault on the stomach lining by large amounts of hydrochloric acid without any letup may have been the important factor responsible for the production of ulcers (Brady, 1958).

A subsequent experiment by Weiss (1971) has thrown some additional light on Brady's results. Weiss contends that the important factor in producing ulcers is a condition of uncertainty about the effectiveness of the response in avoiding punishment that keeps the animal constantly at work and in a high state of tension. To test this assumption, he subjected rats to a situation in which they had to turn a wheel in order to escape shock. They were then permitted to delay the onset of shock by turning the wheel a few times before the shock was actually delivered. One group of animals knew precisely how long to turn the wheel to avoid being shocked because they were given a signal which indicated that their efforts were effective in delaying the shock. The other group had no such signal, and as a result, they worked longer and harder to accomplish the same goal. Compared to the first group, the animals without the signal developed considerably more and larger ulcers.

In explaining Brady's results, Weiss points out that Brady virtually guaranteed the development of ulcers in the executive monkeys by selecting them to press the lever *because they were unusually high responders in the initial learning situation.* This doggedness and determination, combined with the uncertainty about how effective their work really was, produced the ulcers that eventually killed them. In fact, Weiss further asserts, this extreme dedication to the job of avoiding punishment resulted in very few shocks for their partners and gave them an ulcer-free existence. The lesson to be learned from all this, of course, is to let the other guy assume the responsibilities!

The Type A and Type B Personalities. People who persist in a struggle for control under stressful conditions like Brady's executive monkey are not uncommon in modern society, and neither is coronary disease. Recent evidence links coronary diseases to a specific personality type (Type A) characterized by competitive achievement striving, a sense of time urgency, and hostility, patterns of behavior which emerge especially under conditions of stress. Type A men have more than twice the rate of heart disease than others, even when traditional risk factors like cigarette smoking, serum cholesterol level, and hypertension are taken into consideration. In fact, greater concentrations of serum cholesterol are found in Type A individuals compared to other less volatile types in subjects as young as 19 years of age (Glass, 1977).

Glass has been conducting laboratory experiments with Type A individuals, and some very interesting, albeit predictable patterns have begun to emerge. When both Type A and Type B (those relatively free of concerns about controlling the environment and, hence, less competitive) individuals are exposed to uncontrollable stress situations consisting of unpleasant noise, Type A people make a greater initial effort to control the noise and persist for greater periods of time than their Type B counterparts. Although the noise was essentially uncontrollable, the Type A individuals even differed in the way they perceived the amount of control that could be exercised. They invariably felt that the situation could be controlled.

It would be highly misleading to conclude from these studies that the main factor responsible for producing psychophysiological disorders is simply the kind of interaction the individual has with the environment under stress conditions. People develop differing kinds of disorders under the same conditions, and some even survive the tension-producing situations relatively unscathed.

Behavioral scientists have only recently begun to appreciate the fact that individuals may react differently to the same stresses because of the differences in their constitutional makeup. It has been demonstrated that some people react to the threat of shock or punishment with elevated heart rates while others show a decrease in heart rate. Some show profuse palmar sweating and increased blood pressure which persists for long periods of time after the stress is removed. Others show much greater flexibility in which the elevated physiological signs return to normal soon after the threats are discontinued. These variations in responding, which Lacey (1967) has referred to as fractionation, indicate the extent to which individual differences in responding laid down in the genes or learned in early developmental history must be taken into account.

Predictability and Controllability: The Effect on Reactions to Stress

Not only do rats develop fewer ulcers when the stressful events are made predictable, as we have already seen (Gliner, 1972), but they also prefer predictable aversive events over unpredictable ones when given the choice. In several studies, for example, rats readily learned to press a lever which produced a warning signal before delivery of the shock rather than accept unsignalled shock, even when the predictable shock was much longer and of greater intensity (Badia & Culbertson, 1972; Badia et al., 1973).

Given the opportunity, humans will also choose predictable over unpredictable shock, and this preference increases as the amount of control over the shock also increases. In an experiment conducted by Averill et al. (1977), 92% of the 65 subjects who acted consistently adopted a vigilant coping strategy (they chose to listen to a warning signal which preceded the shock) when the shock was 100% avoidable. This number decreased as the ability to control shock decreased, but, surprisingly enough, approximately 30% still preferred to listen for the warning signal even though there was no chance they could avoid the shock. And, even more astounding, 5 subjects never chose to listen for the warning signal even when such a strategy would lead to complete avoidance of the shock.

According to Weiss (1977), the executive monkey in Brady's experiment (Box 3-4) had very little going for him which would prevent the formation of ulcers. In the first place, he never knew when the shock was coming. Secondly, the uncertainty of the situation provided very little information about the effectiveness of his efforts to keep the shock at a minimum. And finally, like the Type A personality, he was a very determined and high responder. These factors all combined to keep him in a tense and vigilant state. Both predictability and controllability were markedly reduced.

But control can obviously be an effective way of reducing the effects of stress if it is successful (Miller, 1979). Weiss showed this in his studies with rats, and several studies by Hokanson and his associates illustrate this point.

In a series of earlier studies on the relationship between blood pressure and aggression, Hokanson (1971) showed that when male subjects could "sound off" in a stressful situation where aggression was the appropriate response, the increased blood pressure due to stress lowered considerably. Hokanson speculated that although the aggressive behavior succeeded, it did so essentially as a method for exerting control over the situation. The important factor was the extent to which the subjects believed that the response actually controlled the stressful situation.

To test this assumption, a study was devised in which subjects had to perform a matching task under stressful conditions. They were arbitrarily shocked for poor performance on the average of once every 45 seconds, but they could take 1-minute rest breaks every 20 minutes. One group (control of rest) was permitted to take rest periods whenever they desired. The other group (no control of rest) could not determine their own periods of rest. The conditions of the experiment were so contrived, however, that the number and temporal arrangement of the rest periods were the same for both groups, and both received the same number of shocks. Throughout the entire experiment, the blood pressure for the "no control of rest period" group was uniformly higher than that of the "control" group, demonstrating that control over the stressful conditions—even if only apparent—and not the rest itself was the crucial factor in determining the physiological responses to stress.

More recently, Prindaville and Stein (1978) showed that subjects given unsolvable problems to work out without any information on how they performed were relatively helpless in a subsequent task requiring either avoidance or escape from a highly aversive noise. Subjects provided with solvable problems, and given periodic information on their progress, on the other hand, also performed more successfully in the escape and avoidance situations. The authors suggested that the prediction and control experience for these subjects in the problem-solving task "inoculated" them against the subsequent stress situation and made their behavior more adaptable.

Control over the external conditions producing stress is obviously an effective way of reducing the effects of stress. But often when people find this control impossible for one reason or another, they try to control the fear or anxiety which stress activates by engaging in avoidance behaviors. The avoidance behaviors also reduce the effects of stress, as we shall see, but they do so at the cost of freedom and flexibility of behavior.

Conditioned Avoidance Responses and the Control of Anxiety

Avoidance responses in the behavior disorders, as we saw in Chapter 2, are attempts to control the fear and anxiety which almost always accompany stress. Strangely enough, they succeed even though, as maladaptive responses, they frequently create their own unique problems (inability to drive a car, to ride on a subway, or to enter elevators, or a compulsion to extreme cleanliness or to constantly check doors, for example).

We call this curious state of affairs the *neurotic paradox* because it describes the apparent contradiction involved when the discomfort of anxiety is reduced by behavior which has negative consequences itself. In effect, the avoidance response solves one difficulty only to create others which are also painful.

Psychoneurotic Disorders. The attempt to control the environment or one's own feelings and emotions is a significant factor in the organization of behavior. Although a great many people probably experience some degree of tension and helplessness at one time or another in their lives, most are capable of overcoming these transient feelings of loss of control without any drastic changes in behavior.

Psychoneurotics, by contrast, are always painfully aware of the threat of being overwhelmed by anxiety, and they make extraordinary and self-defeating efforts to control these threats through avoidance behavior. Like the reactions animals show in avoidance-learning studies, psychoneurotic behavior appears to be determined almost exclusively by its success in reducing fear.

Since escape from anxiety is an abiding preoccupation of psychoneurotics, their behavior tends to become extremely overcontrolled, ranging from phobic withdrawal, through compulsive rituals, to rare cases of multiple personality and hysterical blindness or paralysis. In some instances such as the anxiety reaction, control is non-existent, while in others, such as the phobic or compulsive disorders, control is variable and periodic. Table 3-3 illustrates the three major groups into which the psychoneurotic disorders appear to fall in terms of anxiety and control.

Anxiety Neurosis.   Anxiety neurosis, the psychoneurotic disorder of the first group, represents the absence of any kind of behavioral control over anxiety. The behavior is characterized by frightening symptoms—feelings of tenseness and apprehension, palpitations, shortness of breath, sensations of choking, trembling, dizziness, and an intense fear of impending doom that prompted Kierkegaard, the Danish philosopher, to label it the "sickness unto death."

Anxiety neurosis is a widely prevalent disorder, claiming about 4 million victims and constituting about 30–40% of the estimated 10 million who suffer from neurotic disorders. It is an extremely difficult behavior disorder to manage, and it is especially resistive to treatment. The onset most often appears spontaneously, rarely associated with any specific incident or object. For this reason the disorder is frequently called free-floating anxiety, i.e., it is not under the control of any stimulus nor is its intensity diminished by an avoidance response. Frequently, as we see in the discussion of phobic behavior, agoraphobia, the fear of open places, develops out of anxiety neurosis.

Phobia: A Prototype for the Neurotic Disorders.   The behavior disorders of the second group in Table 3-3 are those in which the individual engages in some kind of periodic or repetitive activity in order to maintain control of anxiety. The most uncomplicated and rudimentary of these responses is the simple withdrawal, or avoidance, behavior found in the phobias because it involves the act of withdrawal from the object or event which is considered threatening.

In many ways, the phobic response constitutes the prototype for all of the other neurotic disorders of Groups II and III in Table 3-3. In phobias, the aversive stimulus is clearly apparent, and its relationship to the avoidance behavior is unambiguous. This is not always the case in the other disorders—especially in the conversion hysterias such as paralyses, hysterical blindnesses, multiple personality, and so forth. The clearly defined avoidance response in phobic behavior sheds some light on the "defensive" nature of avoidance and reminds us that the behavior is directed toward one purpose—the management of anxiety.

Although the term *phobia* is generally defined as an irrational fear of an object or event, this definition has usually been reserved for those dramatic instances in which fear and the associated defensive behavior has a pronounced, crippling effect and seriously interferes with daily functioning. But an equally large number of people have fears which also compel them to seek help, even though the associated behavior is not as extreme as that found in the traditional phobias. Shy people, for

TABLE 3-3 Psychoneurotic Disorders and Degree of Anxiety Control

	Degree of Control	Disorder	Description* and Control
I	No control	Anxiety neurosis	Pervasive anxiety bordering on panic. Feeling of uncontrollable dread. Elevated blood pressure and pulse. Breathlessness, palpitations, dizziness.
II	Periodic control	Phobia	Irrational and persistent fear of object or event not inherently dangerous. Becomes increasingly incapacitating as it generalizes to other areas. Control manifested by withdrawal or complete avoidance of phobic object.
		Obsessive-compulsive	Constantly recurring irrational ideas or impulses to perform certain acts. Control usually consists of performing the act or some other act which is counter to the impulse.
		Hypochondriasis	Preoccupation with the body and presumed diseases of various organs. Control consists of attributing discomfort to presumed bodily ailments.
		Depression	Loss of initiative and interest. Saddened mood and sense of loneliness. Control consists of withdrawal from social encounters, reduction in feelings and emotions which are threatening.
III	Complete control	Hysterical disorders Conversion	Physical ailments with no organic basis. Paralyses, tics, tremors, seizures. "Physical symptoms" control the anxiety by making it unnecessary to respond in an appropriate manner, viz., blindness, paralysis, tics, and tremors.
		Dissociation	Amnesias, memory losses, fugue states, and multiple personalities. Control mechanism is complete forgetting of the painful and anxiety-generating experiences, sometimes, as in multiple personalities, by assuming the role of another person.

*Descriptions adapted from *Diagnostic and Statistical Manual of Mental Disorders* [(DSM II), 2d ed.]

example, or those who find it difficult to stand up for their rights, are generally not regarded as phobic although their inability to engage in social relationships or to assert themselves results from fear and is every bit as demoralizing as the inability to drive a car—perhaps even more so because these "quiet" fears that rarely disturb others often bring loneliness and despair.

Statistical counts of phobic disorders indicate an incidence of approximately 77 out of 1,000. But this is probably an underestimation because the less "dramatic" fears like shyness are not included, and it is quite likely that the disorder is more widespread than we realize.

In his analysis of phobias, Marks (1969) has identified several possible situations which may provide the experience necessary for the development of phobic behavior. These include:

1. Actual physical pain
   a. Fear of dogs after a dogbite.
   b. Fear of heights after a fall.
   c. Fear of automobiles after an accident.

2. Psychological trauma involving stress.
   a. Battlefield phobias.
   b. Guilt following forbidden actions.
   c. Interpersonal conflicts.

3. "Calamity syndromes"—disturbances of life situations, e.g., bereavement, menopause, childbirth, divorce, severe illness, failure.

4. Modeling and imitation learning.

Despite its prevalence, the equivalence of clinical phobic behavior has not been produced in the laboratory, and, fortunately, for humanitarian reasons, no real effort has been made to do so. Most of the rationales for conditioning as the basis for the development of clinical phobic behavior have come from laboratory analogues with animals or those clinical situations in which the actual traumatic event and the subsequent avoidance behavior are well documented. However, recent speculations about the formation of agoraphobia by Goldstein and Chambless (1978) may throw some light on the conditioning process involved.

Agoraphobia: fear in search of a control.   Agoraphobia is the irrational fear of being in open or public places. People who are agoraphobic rarely venture out of doors unless accompanied by someone and, in extreme cases, do not leave the house at all. For reasons which are not clearly understood, most agoraphobics are married women.

Unlike the other phobias, agoraphobias harbor a large element of persistent or "free-floating" anxiety which may terminate in debilitating panic attacks. Much speculation has gone on about the origins of the disorder, including one theory proposed by Freud in which he regarded agoraphobia as the "romance of prostitution." Fear of venturing out of the house, he maintained, protected women from their sexual or exhibitionistic impulses (Goldstein & Chambless, 1978).

After comparing data on 32 agoraphobic clients and 36 clients with phobias controlled by other external stimuli, Goldstein and Chambless concluded that agoraphobics can be distinguished from other phobic individuals on the basis of the following characteristics:

1. "Fear of fear" as the most central phobic element.

2. Low levels of self-sufficiency, whether due to anxiety, a lack of skills, or both.

3. A tendency to misapprehend the causal antecedents of uncomfortable feelings. For example, anxiety reliably following interpersonal conflict is interpreted as fear of being on the street alone.

4. Onset of symptoms in a climate of notable conflict. The conflict is generally, but not necessarily, an interpersonal one (1978, p. 51).

Agoraphobics, unlike other phobic individuals, begin as victims of anxiety reactions, with a great deal of "free-floating anxiety. The exact "cause" of the anxiety attacks is not known, but it has been suggested that interpersonal family conflicts—women, for example, who feel trapped by unsatisfactory marriages and heavy responsibilities and cannot flee the marriage—may be one of the responsible factors. In any event, the agoraphobic responds to the slightest sign of anxiety or discomfort, without any awareness of the factor that is actually responsible, with a mounting apprehension.

Eventually, according to Goldstein and Chambless, the slightest sign of fear becomes a CS which produces the CR—a full-blown panic reaction—which the authors interpret in terms of an *interoceptive conditioning process* (internal signals governing external behavior).

Such anxiety attacks generally take place outside the home, while the person is waiting for a bus or shopping in a crowded department store. As a result, anxiety gets associated with the place in which the attack occurred, and these places, then, are likely to become stimuli for the next attack. This development, coupled with the added fear that no help will be available when the unexpected attack occurs, produces an agoraphobic response in which the person cannot leave the house unless accompanied by a family member or friend (Honigfeld & Howard, 1973). Thus, without any awareness on the part of the individual suffering the anxiety attacks, and with much welcome relief, the anxiety reaction is transformed into a phobic response and brought under control through conditioning. Now, as long as department stores or crowded and public places in general can be avoided, the anxiety, which originally had nothing to do with these situations, can be avoided.

The concept of "preparedness" in phobic conditioning. A phobia, according to Seligman (1971), is not just the avoidance of any object which happens to be associated with fear. The fear of crowded places, heights, thunderstorms, animals, insects, blood, and so forth, which are predominant themes in phobic behavior, all have one thing in common: they involve objects which once were dangerous and threatened the survival of the species.

Human phobias, according to Seligman and Hager, "are largely restricted to objects that have threatened survival, potential predators, unfamiliar places, and the dark (1972, p. 465). The phobias involving these objects or situations result from a kind of "prepared" conditioning because the objects already connote danger and are, therefore, more readily conditionable.

Laboratory experiments with humans have, indeed, shown that "prepared" objects, such as snakes and spiders, condition more rapidly and are much more resistant to extinction than circles and triangles, or mushrooms and flowers, which are regarded as "unprepared" objects (Öhman et al., 1976).

This view of phobias proposed by Seligman has interesting implications for phobic behavior in general. According to the preparedness hypothesis, it is reasonable to assume that:

1. The incidence of "prepared" as opposed to "unprepared" phobias, i.e., phobias involving relatively neutral objects, such as plants or colors, should be greater in the clinic populations.

2. The onset of "prepared" phobias should be more sudden, presumably because prepared objects are more easily conditioned.

3. Prepared phobias should be more resistant to treatment, i.e., more difficult to extinguish.

4. Prepared phobias should generalize more easily to other objects or situations.

To test these assumptions, De Silva, Rachman, and Seligman (1977) conducted a survey of 69 phobic and 82 obsessional cases treated with behavior modification techniques at Maudsley Hospital in London for the past 5 years. The case histories of these patients were prepared for evaluation by two raters on each of the questions posed above. Although a greater number of prepared phobias were found in the clinical population, as predicted, their onset was not more sudden than the unprepared phobias, they were not more resistant to treatment, nor did they generalize to other objects or other situations more easily. The authors concluded from these findings that, although the study did not disconfirm the preparedness hypothesis altogether, the concept appeared to have very little clinical utility.

Obsessive-compulsive disorders—phobias with a ritual.

Whenever I walk in a London street,
I'm ever so careful to watch my feet;
    And I keep in the squares,
    And the masses of bears,
Who wait at the corners all ready to eat
The sillies who tread on the lines of the street,
    Go back to their lairs,
    And I say to them, "Bears,
Just look how I'm walking in all of the squares!"
("Lines and Squares," from A. A. Milne, *When We Were Very Young,*
          E. P. Dutton & Co., New York, 1924. By permission.)

In the first stanza of this very insightful poem by A. A. Milne, many of us will recognize the "innocent" games of childhood which consisted of placing oneself in jeopardy and then engaging in behavior which made certain that the danger would never occur as long as the strict rules of the game were precisely followed.

Organizing behavior into routines is probably one of the most conspicuous features of human functioning. Setting alarm clocks, cleaning a house once a week, checking doors before retiring, to mention a few, are some of the socially acceptable ways of reducing discomfort regularly. In fact, society makes a virtue of routine behavior as a way of diminishing the unexpected and maintaining order and stability.

As the degree of discomfort increases, however, both the *frequency* and the *intensity* of the behavior also tends to increase until the simple routine takes on a new urgency and becomes a ritual. In slight cases, the "ceremonial" appears to be only an exaggeration of a justifiable orderliness. The chair must be in a particular place by the bed, the clothes folded and laid on it in a particular order, the bedclothes arranged in a certain manner, and the pillows in a characteristic position. Only then is it permissible to go to bed (Freud, 1959a, p. 26).

When the rituals are confined to an isolated segment of daily life, or when they are expressed through organized religion and public observances at specified times, they are still socially acceptable. Only when the ceremonials begin to seriously interfere with acceptable functioning—as in the obsessive-compulsive disorder—is the behavior likely to be regarded as deviant.

Basically, obsessive-compulsive disorders are phobias. The major difference between the two lies in the nature of the fear-arousing stimulus and the conditioned avoidance response. In phobias, as we have already noted, the aversive stimulus is usually some external situation or object—fear of heights, of flying, or of animals, for example—and the avoidance response is simple withdrawal or escape.

Fear in the obsessive-compulsive disorder, on the other hand, usually becomes aroused by repetitive, intrusive, and unacceptable thoughts frequently related to religion, abhorrent sexual acts, dirt and fear of infection, swearing, or causing someone injury. Since the obsessive-compulsive cannot use the simple phobic mechanism of withdrawal to escape the obsessive ruminations—one cannot escape one's thoughts—avoidance becomes a desperate matter of preventing any of these thoughts from being translated into reality.

The person who constantly fears injuring others will engage in various kinds of "checking" behavior to see that knives or other potentially dangerous instruments are not left "carelessly" lying around or that nobody is standing behind a closed door at the risk of being injured when the door is suddenly opened. Others, who are afraid of being infected by dirt, will take 20 or 30 showers a day, in some extreme cases, to prevent this from happening.

Rachman describes the case of a prosecuting attorney who was troubled by thoughts that he would write, or had already written, a compromising note to a criminal he had prosecuted. To prevent this, he avoided paper, post boxes, or any activity involving writing. He spent a great deal of time recalling in minute detail the events of the day and constantly checked his clothing and drawers for any evidence that he might have written such a note. If he was troubled by the image of a piece of paper containing writing, he would "put matters right" by imagining a blank piece of paper, but this goal might take an hour to attain before it brought any relief (1976, p. 440).

In another case, a woman was disturbed by distressing images of four dead people lying in open coffins in an open grave. When this image occurred, she could not continue with her normal activities until she "put matters right" by imagining these same four people standing and walking about (1976, p. 440). Some rituals, bizarre as they may be, are frequently inadvertantly encouraged by others in order to accommodate the individual with the obsession (Box 3-4).

BOX 3-4
How to Encourage an Obsessive-Compulsive

Dear Abby: I know exactly what Sylvia in Greenwich is going through. She's the wife who's trying to find a chastity belt so she can put her husband's suspicions to rest.

I've been married for 14 years to a wonderful man whose only fault was his unreasonable jealousy. He loved me dearly, and although I've always been a true and faithful wife, he never trusted me out of his sight.

The accusations, denials, and fighting were destroying our marriage, so together we designed something on the order of a chastity belt.

It's a tight fitting rubber panty girdle over which I wear an old-fashioned type corset which laces up the back. My husband laces me into it every morning, tying the lace in a hard knot at the top where I can't reach it, let alone undo it. Over that I wear a snug-fitting wide leather belt which also fastens in the back with a small padlock like those used on suitcases. My husband carries the only key.

Every day he comes home at noon to help me in the bathroom. This may sound like a humiliating solution, and I'm certainly not advocating it for all wives, but it saved our marriage.

—Signed, Happy

Dear Happy: If you're happy in this kind of wedlock, more power to you (Abigal Van Buren, *Newsday,* Nov. 1978. By permission.)

Table 3-4 indicates the variety and duration of ruminations in a group of patients treated with behavior modification (Stern et al., 1973, p. 660).

Problems with the Fear-Conditioning Model

From this discussion, it seems reasonable to suppose that phobic and obsessive-compulsive behavior are conditioned avoidance responses acquired and maintained because they reduce the anxiety created by stress. Although we do not

TABLE 3-4   Nature of Ruminations in a Sample of
Obsessive-Compulsive Patients

AGE	SEX	DURATION OF RUMINATIONS IN YEARS	NATURE OF RUMINATIONS
21	M	6	Teeth are decaying. Particles between teeth.
40	M	8	Fear that harm would befall his children.
29	F	4	Having lumps in breast.
42	M	16	Woman's buttocks. His own eye movements.
21	F	9	Thoughts about strangling people.
55	F	35	Foetuses lying in the street. Killing babies. People being buried alive.
39	F	10	Thoughts of death. Pseudohallucination of "Drop dead."
31	F	16	Harm befalling her children.
24	M	16	Worry about whether he had touched vomit.
43	M	8	Leg veins are varicose.
21	M	9	He will swallow his tongue.

Source: R. Stern, M. Lipsedge, and I. Marks. Obsessive ruminations: A controlled trial of thought-stopping technique. *Behaviour Research and Therapy,* 1973, *11,* 659–662. Copyright 1973 Pergamon Press and used by permission.

discuss them in detail, the behavior disorders listed in Category III of Table 3-3 —the conversion disorders and dissociation—also reduce anxiety due to stress and conflict, but they do it in a more thorough fashion.

Although little disagreement seems to arise about the specific purpose of the avoidance response itself, some legitimate questions have been raised concerning the way in which the basic fear necessary to motivate the avoidance response is acquired. Both Marks (1977) and Rachman (1977, 1978) have questioned the adequacy of the conditioning model on the basis of the following clinical observations:

1. Many phobias in humans do not seem to begin with a clear history of any trauma. While some may be the result of accidents, pain, or threat of injury, others emerge without these aversive states.

2. Preparedness of stimuli seems to play an unusually large role in the type of object or event which acquires the ability to evoke fear. Most of these stimuli do have intrinsic dangerous properties.

3. Major stress situations, such as the holocaust or the air raids in London, do not seem to have produced the number of fears or other behavior disorders commensurate with their severity and the number of people involved.

4. Individual differences in response to stress and in the formation of different avoidance behaviors must be explained. These may involve biochemical and neurological factors as well as family and cultural influences.

Rachman (1977) maintains that although conditioning may well account for the acquisition of fear in certain circumstances—especially in those instances where the stimuli have threatening or dangerous properties (prepared stimuli), fear may also be acquired through vicarious experiences (observational learning) or transmitted through information and instruction. In effect, Rachman suggests that we can learn to be afraid by observing others in fear-arousing situations (see Chapter 14, on observational learning), or by receiving information about frightening events.

Fear and avoidance is a far more complex subject than we have indicated, and we need a great deal more research before anything resembling a reliable relationship between the behavior disorders and conditioning can be established.

Conditioned Sexual Deviations

Sexual behavior, like any other response, is subject to control by stimuli. The ability of any stimulus to control sexual arousal depends, in large measure, on its association with sexual experiences. In most cases, the stimuli are already "prepared," so to speak. They have intrinsic arousal properties because of their association with the opposite sex or because they are usually present during the sexual act itself (articles of clothing, perfumes, cosmetics, and the like). In some cases, however, the objects are somewhat remote from the sexual experience (whips and chains, for example).

Whether or not the stimulus control is inappropriate depends, for the most part, on the sexual object and the sexual act. In heterosexual behavior, the most prevalent form of sexual expression, the object is a member of the opposite sex, and the act itself involves some form of foreplay, intromission, and, generally, consummation through orgasm. The sequence of events in the sexual act may vary widely among individuals without necessarily being regarded as deviant. Generally, however, the behavior is labeled *deviant* when the object is not a sexually mature, living, human member of the opposite sex (homosexuality; bestiality; or relations with animals; pedophilia, or child molestation; necrophilia, or intercourse with a corpse), when some part of the sexual sequence is substituted for the entire act (voyeurism—"peeping tom" behavior—or exhibitionism—sexually provocative disrobing), or when the controlling stimulus is not usually associated with the sexual experience (flagellation—whipping during the sexual sequence or urination).

This definition is not meant to set the standards for sexual behavior. Unfortunately, the term sexual deviation also carries with it the connotations of immorality and illegality. While virtually all forms of sexual expression that did not conform to arbitrary social standards were considered illegal in the not-so-distant past, the mores and, consequently, the laws are rapidly changing to recognize the legitimacy of any kind of sexual expression between consenting adults which does not injure others or violate their rights.

Sexually deviant behavior can be learned in several possible ways. Like conditioned avoidance responses, some sexual deviations and deficiencies are acquired under unpleasant and painful conditions which generate fear. Impotency in men, for example, often results from the fear of being sexually inadequate and failing to live up to some presumed standard of sexual performance. Masters and Johnson (1970) also report cases of men who could not ejaculate during penetration (while inside the vagina) because of certain experiences associated with this act. In one instance, an orthodox Jewish male had been traumatized by one transgression during his premarital years when he made sexual advances to a menstruating woman. Because the Hebraic code of conduct strictly forbids intercourse during menstruation, this sole experience created a fear of vaginal-menstrual contamination and made it impossible for him to have an orgasm intravaginally. Another client came upon his wife in the act of adultery and was unable to ejaculate intravaginally thereafter because "he was faced with the vivid, but castrating mental picture of the lover's seminal fluid escaping his wife's vagina" (p. 134).

If usual heterosexual behavior is punished or forbidden, a deviant sexual response may conceivably become the only acceptable means of expression because it enables the individual to avoid fear by providing an alternative outlet for sexual satisfaction. For similar reasons, the sexual act itself may only be possible if some form of punishment, such as whipping in sexual masochism, precedes it.

But not all sexually deviant behaviors need necessarily develop because of fear. Many are generated under benign and essentially rewarding conditions. The boots in Rachman's fetishism study (Box 3-1, p. 42), for example, acquired their ability to elicit sexual arousal because they became associated with a pleasant experience—the sight of attractive nude females.

The difficulty with laboratory demonstrations of most deviant behavior and the learning model in general is that the "conditioned analogues" produced by experimentation are generally so "short-lived." Rachman's male subjects, for example, extinguished the penile sexual response to boots in about 19 trials. Real-life fetish behavior is not so labile and, in fact, unless treated, may persist for the lifetime of the individual. What, then, is the difference between the fetish-like behavior produced in the laboratory and its counterpart in real life? According to some psychologists, the distinguishing factor is continued reinforcement in the form of orgasm.

As early as 1888, Alfred Binet, of intelligence-testing fame, proposed that sexual deviations are learned as a result of critical, although possibly accidental, experiences. Jaspers (1963) reiterated this belief, but he also pointed out that simple exposure to a casual or chance sexual event could not possibly account for later sexual orientation because it would not explain why a great many people do not become sexual deviants despite the unorthodox nature of their first experience (McGuire et al., 1965, p. 185).

As expected, some form of congenital or constitutional factor was proposed to explain these differences in behavior, but McGuire, Carlisle, and Young found similarities in the case histories of the people they treated for sexual deviations striking enough to suggest an alternative explanation. *It appeared that the early (and often the first) sexual experience was indeed an important element in determining future sexual orientation, largely because it supplied a fantasy which invariably accompanied later masturbation for individuals, some of whom were already convinced that a "normal" heterosexual life was not possible.*

In the conditioning hypothesis proposed by McGuire et al., *"any stimulus which regularly precedes ejaculation by the correct time interval should become more and more sexually exciting,"* and masturbation to a fantasy provides both the stimulus and the optimal setting for this conditioning sequence to take place (1965, p. 186).

But, the authors asked, why should a prospective deviant choose to masturbate to a deviant fantasy rather than to heterosexual thoughts? About three-fourths of the clients they studied supplied this answer. The fantasy used during masturbation, they said, represented "the *first* real sexual experience" they had. Consequently, the stimulus not only had strong stimulus value as a masturbatory fantasy, but it was further strengthened by continued masturbation while other stimuli were weakened because they were not reinforced (Cases 1 and 4 below).

The additional factor which probably served to make the initial sexual encounter more important and to ensure that it would be maintained in fantasy was the belief—verbalized by half of the clients—that a normal sex life was not possible for them (Cases 1 and 4 below). In all instances, this belief predated the sexual deviation and did not arise as a result of the deviant behavior.

McGuire, Carlisle, and Young feel that the hypothesis not only fits consistently with what we know about conditioning in general, it also provides an explanation for the origin of sexual deviations which usually require other explanations. To illustrate this, they present a number of conclusions from the conditioning hypothesis and compare these with some of the case histories obtained from their own patients and other reported cases. The conclusions listed below were drawn from McGuire, Carlisle, and Young (1965, p. 187).

1. No assumptions are made regarding previous sexual interest. Two-thirds of the patients reported heterosexual interest before the sexual deviation emerged. Most deviations began at puberty.

2. Any deviation can be acquired through conditioning.

3. Deviations acquired through conditioning can be "deconditioned." The authors report success in treating their clients with "aversion" therapy. (see Chapter 8.)

4. Guilt, which most of the clients experienced, is not effective in weakening the deviant sexual behavior. The reason is that immediate gratification from masturba-

tion or the practice of the deviant behavior is a much more powerful reinforcer than the punishment which may arise from larger guilt.

5. Any one person may develop more than one deviation. The authors found as many as three apparently unrelated deviations in several patients which were often linked through the original fantasy.

6. "Since females masturbate much less frequently than males (Kinsey, 1953), they should be less likely to develop sexual deviations. Apart from female homosexuality this is certainly true. We have not seen sufficient female homosexuals to account for the difference in that deviation." This particular conclusion is quoted verbatim from McGuire et al. largely because of its potentially controversial nature. Kinsey reported that females enter puberty earlier and begin masturbation much later than males (e.g., 92% of males masturbate at age 20 compared to 33% of females). Also, at age 15, 82% of males masturbate to orgasm compared to 20% of females (Kinsey et al., 1953, p. 149).

(It is interesting to speculate that if there has been any change in these figures since 1949, with an increase in the number of females who masturbate at an early age and who achieve orgasm, the rate of sexual deviations among women should also increase.)

7. The hypothesis also explains why a large number of psychopaths (sociopaths) are also sexually deviant even though they are presumed to be poor learners and not easily conditioned. According to the authors, even the poorest learner can acquire behavior which is practiced so frequently.

The four cases presented below are typical of the 45 clients (21 homosexuals, 7 pedophiliacs, 7 exhibitionists, 5 transvestites, 3 voyeurs, and 2 others) treated by the authors. As they correctly point out, these cases do not constitute proof of the conditioning hypothesis, but they may provide an impetus to further study and a first approximation to a more rigorous conditioning model. (Source: R.J. McGuire, J.M. Carlisle and B.G. Young. Sexual deviations as conditioned behavior: A hypothesis. *Behavior Research and Therapy,* 1965, 2, 185–190. Copyright 1965 Pergamon Press and used by permission.)

Case 1

This 40-year old male had till the age of 20 had normal sexual interests but had been impotent when casual intercourse was attempted. He blamed his impotence on his belief, arising from a strict religious unpringing, that no respectable woman would have sexual relations. While on military service in Asia during the Second World War, he accompanied other servicemen to the brothels where, through fear of venereal disease, and, possibly, fears of impotence, he refused intercourse but allowed the prostitutes to masturbate him. This was his first orgasmic sexual experience with a partner, and the memory of it served as later self-masturbatory fantasies. When he was moved from the town into the jungle, prostitutes were no longer available. He had scruples about having relations with the native married women, and finally resorted to the native children of either sex who would masturbate him, and this remained his only sexual outlet till he was discharged home three years later.

In Britain, his self-masturbatory fantasies continued to be of masturbation by children, and eventually he succumbed and found young boys to masturbate him. He married five years after this but found that he had no interest in sexual intercourse although he was now potent in the heterosexual situation. Self-masturbation continued to his previous fantasies, and intercourse was only possible to these fantasies or to fantasies that his wife was a prostitute. He came to our notice when his wife discovered that for two years the patient had been inducing his son (between the ages of 4 and 6) to masturbate him.

We believe that the above case shows how force of circumstances and self-masturbation to a sexual memory can shape, by simple conditioning, an individual's sexual behavior, so that behavior which was initially substitutive can gain dominance by frequent positive sexual reinforcement.

Cases 2 and 3

We found that the initial incident need not even have been of sexual interest to the individual at the time it occurred. For example, two patients separately reported that they had on one occasion been urinating in a semi-public place when they were surprised by a passing woman. At the time, each had felt embarrassed and left hurriedly. It was only later that the sexual significance of the encounter was appreciated and each of them had then masturbated frequently to the memory of the incident till the thought of self-exposure had acquired, by conditioning, such strong sexual stimulus value that each had in the end taken to public exposure. Neither patient had had the slightest interest in such behavior prior to the incident.

Case 4

An exclusively homosexual patient, aged 25, remembered as his first sexual experience at the age of 11, being taught to masturbate by a male school friend. Very shortly after this he touched a girl's genitals out of sexual curiosity. She complained to her parents who informed the patient's family, with consequent punishment and humiliation for him. From then on he masturbated frequently to fantasies of nude males and had no more heterosexual experiences or interests. This patient also had a large nose which he believed made him ugly. At the age of 22 this was altered by plastic surgery but made no difference to his sexual inclinations.

The Role of the Orgasm in the Formation of Sexual Associations.   According to the hypothesis just discussed, the orgasm is an important source of reinforcement in sexual behavior. Shortly after McGuire et al. formulated their conditioning hypothesis of sexual deviation emphasizing the role of masturbation and orgasm to a sexual fantasy, Davison (1968) and Marquis (1970) used a conditioning procedure involving masturbation for the purpose of "orgasmic reorientation" with individuals who were having sexual difficulties.

Davison's client had sado-masochistic fantasies about women which was disrupting his sexual life. By requiring the client to masturbate to orgasm in the presence of a picture from *Playboy* (CS), Davison succeeded in reorienting his sexual fantasies so that thoughts of punishment were no longer necessary for sexual arousal. Marquis also used "orgasmic reconditioning" successfully for sexual reorientation in 14 cases. In a case similar to Davison's, a 22-year-old woman who had used sado-masochistic masturbation fantasies and regarded herself as a "freak" was capable of carrying through masturbation with normal heterosexual fantasies after conditioning.

Although no studies show unequivocally that stimuli acquire sexual arousal properties through association with orgasm—a condition necessary to support the learning hypothesis—two recent experiments indicate that such a phenomenon is, in principle, possible.

The first of these studies demonstrated that sexual excitement, even to pornographic material, will ultimately decrease if not followed by sexual fulfillment. Male subjects were asked to read pornographic excerpts from Henry Miller's novel *Sextus* to themselves while changes in the diameter of the penis corresponding to erections were recorded. The response to the pornographic material (in contrast to non-pornographic material from the same novel) was an initial increase in tumescence (erection) followed by a decrease when the material was read repeatedly over a period of 2 weeks. But this was not the case for another group of subjects who masturbated to ejaculation immediately following the reading. For them, sexual excitement to the pornographic material continued without any sign of extinction (Schaefer & Colgan, 1977).

A second study conducted by Kantorowitz (1978) showed that penile amplitude increased significantly to stimuli paired with the plateau phase of sexual arousal (immediately prior to ejaculation) and was maintained to these stimuli and to subjective preference measures throughout the course of the experiment. Stimuli paired with the postorgasmic refractory phase, on the other hand, decreased on both the subjective and physical measures.

The actual conditioning process involved in increasing levels of sexual awareness to new stimuli has been worked out in a more precise manner by Keller and Goldstein (1978) with a client who was unable to achieve arousal or orgasm with his wife without the use of a transvestite fantasy. Their procedure focuses more on arousal—hence the name arousal conditioning—than does Marquis's. In treatment the client simply focused on a fantasy of his wife's body (CS) until the image was clear, then switched to the transvestite fantasy (UCS) which produced sexual arousal (UCR). Ultimately, masturbation was possible without the transvestite fantasy, and he was able to have sexual relations with his wife without having to imagine cross-sex dressing.

EPILOGUE

The objectives of this chapter were purposefully limited to a discussion of conditioning and the development of the behavior disorders. We did this in order to stress the role of learning in the development of deviant behavior, but obviously, any attempt to focus exclusively on the learning process must result in the oversimplification of a complex subject leaving a trail of unanswered questions.

Actually, the only thing that can be said about the development of the behavior disorders with any degree of certainty is that sheer number of stress factors is the best way of predicting the onset of such disorders (Langner & Michael, 1963). The more problems a person has, the more likely it is that the attempts to cope with them will become increasingly ineffective.

But even this somewhat trite observation cannot explain why some people break down under stress and develop neuroses while others in similar circumstances do not. Nor does it shed light on why a specific type of neurotic behavior emerges. The factors that have been invoked to answer these questions range from biological and constitutional conditions about which very little is known, through psychological conditions, such as unrealistic ambitions, unacceptable desires, and frustrating decisions, to complex sociological variables, such as social class and extreme deprivation about which only a little more is known.

The position which maintains that most of the behavior disorders are learned cannot overlook these factors. It recognizes that they are important influences in the learning process by determining what is learned and establishing the parameters of learning. Pavlov was probably the first to recognize this when he astutely noticed that all of his dogs did not respond similarly to the same experimental stress conditions.

chapter four

Classical Conditioning and Behavior Change

We might wisely begin this section on applied classical conditioning with a qualification. Many of the studies presented here are isolated instances of successful attempts to change behavior through conditioning. Some are demonstrations rather than well-controlled experiments involving large numbers of subjects, which limits even their clinical usefulness. But these first attempts are especially noteworthy because they illustrate resourceful efforts to use well-known learning principles to change behavior outside of the laboratory.

APPLIED CLASSICAL CONDITIONING: PAVLOV'S SALIVARY RESPONSE "GROWN UP"

The very nature of the classical conditioning procedure dictates the way it is used in behavior modification, and, as a result, its application has been limited to situations in which a *known stimulus* controls behavior and the behavior is *largely involuntary.* So, much of the effort in the application of classical conditioning involves either changing the stimulus that controls the response or substituting a new response for one already under stimulus control.

When changes are made to the stimulus controlling a response, *they involve conditioning a new stimulus to an old response (S1-R1 to S2-R1) or bringing about changes in the characteristics of the stimulus itself to gain improved stimulus control of behavior (S1-R1 to S1a-R1).* Note that in both of these procedures the response itself is not altered, only the stimulus that controls it.

Circumstances which require that the response be replaced usually involve the association of a new response with a stimulus which already elicits other behavior (S1-R1 to S1-R2). We encountered this method of counterconditioning in Chapter 2 when Erofeeva conditioned a dog to salivate to intense shock.

Conditioning a New Stimulus to an Old Response (S1-R1 to S2-R1)

In his book *The Psychology of Conflict* (1935), one of the earliest texts containing practical suggestions for changing behavior derived entirely from learning theory, E. R. Guthrie illustrates the procedure for replacing one stimulus with another by the following anecdote—a device he typically used to make a point. He recounts the exasperation of a mother who could not get her daughter to hang up her clothes upon entering the house no matter how much she pleaded with her. The mother finally resorted to the stratagem of requiring the girl to pick up the garments from the floor, clothe herself completely, return to the street, and re-enter the house, hanging up her clothes properly. In Guthrie's analysis, the clothes were originally hung up in response to the cues of the mother's pleading and the sight of the clothes on the floor (S1-R1). This behavior became disrupted and rearranged *when entering the house became the proper cue* for hanging up the clothes (S2-R1).

Voiding Behavior and the Spinally Injured Patient.   Let us begin with a noble failure. A psychologist by the name of Laurence Ince has devoted a considerable amount of effort to the use of behavior modification techniques in rehabilitation medicine. Most of these efforts have succeeded. People in various stages of paralysis have been trained through operant conditioning (Chapter 8) to use devices designed to strengthen muscles or to use muscles rendered useless by injury (Ince, 1976). In this instance, however, Ince faced a challenging problem which is widely prevalent in patients with severed spinal cords—loss of the ability to control urinary functioning, called a neurogenic bladder. Such patients completely lose urinary control because their brains are severed from the lower portion of their bodies, and normal cortical control over voiding is impossible. To accomplish this bodily function, patients must either be catheterized periodically or have a relatively permanent tube inserted for continuous drainage. In either case, a large amount of residual urine remains in the bladder, and this causes infections that appear to be the leading cause of death in spinally injured patients.

To re-establish bladder control, Ince (1975a) worked out a conditioning technique (Figure 4-1) designed to enable patients with spinal cord injuries to void voluntarily. According to the author, the aim of the research was "to bring the reflex arc of the sacral portion of the spinal cord which controls urinary bladder function under the control of an external stimulus."

He chose two patients, aged 32 and 37, with complete transections of the spinal cord sustained as a result of accidents, as subjects. In order to elicit the

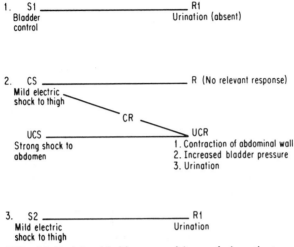

FIG. 4-1 Training bladder control in paralytic patients.

unconditioned response of voiding (UCR), he applied an unconditioned stimulus, an electrical shock (UCS) strong enough to produce contraction of the abdominal muscles, increased bladder pressure, and urination, to the lower abdomen. The conditioned stimulus (CS) was a mild electric shock applied to the inner portion of the thigh, below the region of the spinal lesion, by a small hand-held battery device that the patients could operate. The CS, a mild electric shock to the thigh, did not produce any urination when applied prior to being paired with the UCS (strong shock), indicating that it was, in fact, a neutral stimulus.

At first, the results seemed encouraging. The patients voided almost as much urine in response to the CS alone as they did to the UCS. Although the response to the CS varied, the frequency with which mild electric shock succeeded in stimulating urination indicated that the CS had acquired some control over voiding and that conditioning had taken place. Unfortunately, the patients were discharged from the hospital before the final goal of making them completely independent in bladder function could be achieved.

Ince (1975b) also conditioned another patient who was able to achieve bladder control for about 1 week. After that extinction set in, and the CS failed to resume control, even after additional conditioning trials.

Despite the several failures to obtain conditioning for any reasonable length of time, the study has some interesting and instructive aspects. In the first place, it reaffirms the validity of the "laws" governing conditioning which clearly state that the conditioned stimulus loses its effectiveness and extinction occurs if the unconditioned stimulus is completely removed. Ince, of course, knew this, and he was not entirely surprised that the CS continued to produce urination only a short time after the UCS (the strong shock) was discontinued. This factor is a problem in applying classical conditioning to behavior change in general, and it tends to limit its usefulness as a therapeutic technique. It is resolved in some interesting ways, however, as our discussion of subsequent studies shows.

Secondly, the success of the conditioning procedure used by Ince, short-lived though it was, does demonstrate that it is possible to condition a response at the spinal reflex level involving only a limited part of the spinal cord and not the brain. Such studies tend to confirm the rudimentary nature of classical conditioning as a learning process.

Shifting the Control of Orgasm: Treatment for Women Unable to Have Orgasm During Intercourse.   In Chapter 3 we saw how Davison and Marquis used an "orgasmic reconditioning" procedure to change the content of the fantasy that controlled sexual arousal. Zeiss, Rosen, and Zeiss (1977) used similar methods to train women to be orgasmic during intercourse (Box 4-1). Although their treatment strategy makes no explicit mention of conditioning techniques, using, as it does, fantasies and thoughts about intercourse with the male partner, it appears to fit nicely into a conditioning scheme in which stimulus control of orgasmic behavior shifts from masturbation to intercourse through a series of steps.

BOX 4-1
Training Women to Be Orgasmic During
Intercourse

The wave of sexual liberation and the openness of discussions about sexual functioning have resulted in some very interesting revelations about the sexual behavior of men and women. One of these discoveries is that approximately 20–80% of the women who are treated for "situational orgasmic dysfunctions" remain inorgasmic during intercourse even after treatment—hardly an encouraging result. In view of this, many sex therapists try to convince their clients not to consider themselves sexually deficient if satisfaction can be attained by other means —manual stimulation or oral stimulation, for example—and they encourage women not to overvalue the importance of orgasm during intercourse.

The authors of this study, Zeiss, Rosen, and Zeiss (1977), agree that nothing is basically wrong in seeking stimulation and orgasm by means other than direct sexual intercourse. They also feel, however, that this should not be a standard imposed upon women who seek treatment for sexual dysfunction and whose goal is orgasm during intercourse. With this in mind, they devised a program which successfully achieved this goal through the use of fantasies of insertions, actual vaginal insertion with a dildo (an object used in lieu of a penis for stimulation) and a male partner as stimuli. These stimuli gradually became associated with masturbation and orgasm (Figure 4-2).

In the first phase of the treatment program, the women were asked to produce a fantasy of intercourse and to imagine the penis being inserted by the current sexual partner. If possible, the partner is permitted to be present during masturbation, but only if the woman is comfortable masturbating in his presence.

In phase two, a dildo or some other phallus-like object is used to familiarize the woman with feelings of vaginal containment. The dildo is inserted prior to orgasm which has been stimulated by masturbation and she is asked to produce a fantasy of intercourse with her partner. The male partner again enters the situation so that the woman feels comfortable while reaching an orgasm with her partner present. Eventually, she uses the dildo exclusively for stimulation to produce orgasm.

The final phase of treatment involves actual intercourse with the male inserting his penis just prior to orgasm produced by manual stimulation. As the couple becomes more successful, the male inserts his penis earlier in the sequence during intercourse, and this becomes the sole method for producing orgasm.

In the two cases treated by this method, neither of the women had ever been aroused to orgasm during intercourse. Both women rated sexual satisfaction as slight, and in one case the wife often refused her husband's sexual advances. The desire for sexual engagement changed during treatment, and one of the women reported a change "from thinking of herself as a sexually inhibited cold woman to seeing herself as a sexually creative uninhibited woman" (Zeiss et al., 1977, p. 892). Both women were able to achieve orgasm during intercourse following treatment, and both couples reported that they now accepted sexual initiations with pleasure.

Increasing Heterosexual Arousal in Homosexuals. To reorient homosexuals, Herman, Barlow, and Agras (1974) used a conditioning procedure in which the pleasant sexual sensations (UCR) produced by films with homosexual content (UCS) were paired with slides of nude women (CS). The expectation was that the slides themselves would elicit sexual arousal (CR) and that women would ultimately become objects of sexual attraction.

Changes in the circumference of the penis (erections) measured by a strain gauge were used as indicators of sexual arousal, a measure similar to the one

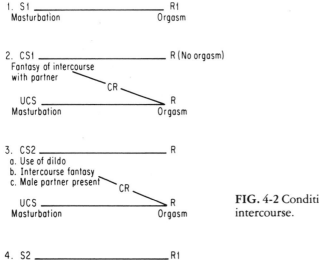

FIG. 4-2 Conditioning orgasm during sexual intercourse.

used in the fetish experiment where sexual arousal was conditioned to the sight of women's boots (Chapter 3, Box 3-1). Additional measures of sexual arousal and orientation were also used. The researchers asked each of the three subjects to record his sexual fantasies and urges in a notebook throughout the day. These included the number of times he became sexually aroused by the sight of a female or had heterosexual fantasies, frequency of masturbation and the content of the associated fantasy, and any occurrence of homosexual or heterosexual encounters outside of the hospital. Each subject also answered a questionnaire, an attitudinal scale called the Sexual Orientation Method (SOM) designed to assess the relative levels of homosexual and heterosexual interests.

For the first subject, the slides of the nude females (CS) and the homosexual film (UCS) were shown alternately in a procedure called *trace conditioning* (Fig. 4-3a). The slides of the nude females were shown for a period of 1 minute and then discontinued, after which the homosexual film was projected for 1 minute. After a series of 16 conditioning trials, the penile response to the CS (female stimuli) increased from a baseline score of 16% to 72% and the response to males decreased to approximately 22%. SOM scores for sexual orientation to females increased to 35 from a preconditioning score of 12, higher than the SOM scores

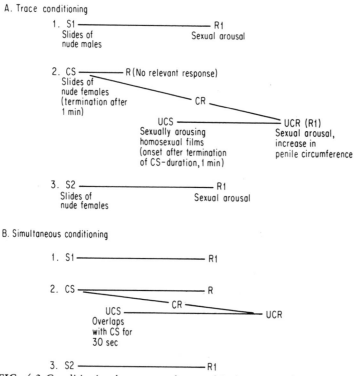

FIG. 4-3 Conditioning heterosexual arousal in homosexuals.

for males. The subject also reported that he now masturbated to female fantasies and had made several attempts to date women.

The same trace-conditioning procedure with Subject 2 did not succeed, and this prompted the experimenters to introduce *simultaneous conditioning* in order to improve the results (Fig. 4-3b). Slides of the nude women and the homosexual film now overlapped for a period of 30 seconds. This procedure increased the likelihood that the slides of the nude women would be present during sexual arousal, in keeping with Guthrie's injunction that the basis for conditioning is the association of the CS with the UCR rather than just the pairing of the CS and the UCS (see p. 23, Chapter 2). Under these conditions, the pictures of the nude women would become associated with the sexual response.

Following the introduction of simultaneous conditioning, the penile response for the second subject rose to 44%, and heterosexual scores on the SOM also increased to 20. The same procedure used with Subject 3 yielded no results.

The subjects' anecdotal responses to the experiments supported the physiological measures. The first subject indicated that he was quite amazed that he responded to the nude females and "was just looking at the slide and automatically began to get an erection" (p. 45). The second subject reported heterosexual fantasies a few days before conditioning took place. He remarked that he was fantasizing having sex with a boy when "all of a sudden a girl popped into the picture" and he continued the fantasy with the girl (p. 45).

One of the difficulties with these studies and with some of the earlier studies in behavior modification is the lack of "follow-up" to determine whether or not the experimental procedures produced any relatively permanent changes in behavior. Although it is important to demonstrate that learning principles can be applied to change deviant behavior, it is equally important to show that these changes are durable—especially because most of the methods employed in these studies will ultimately be used as treatments if they succeed. In fact, some of the journals which publish such studies require a delay of at least 6 months before publication of a study in order to allow for adequate follow-up. We can only assume that, although some immediate dramatic changes in behavior took place for two of the homosexual subjects during the course of the Herman, Barlow, and Agras experiments, their sexual interest in females did not endure. By contrast, some of the conditioning studies discussed later conform more to the research ideals in behavior modification. Not only do they contain relatively larger numbers of subjects, but the follow-up periods range from 6 months in some instances to 6 years in others.

Changing the Characteristics of the Stimulus for Improved Stimulus Control (S1-R1 to S1a-R1)

In many instances the stimulus that controls a particular kind of behavior is absolutely necessary for the organism to function and cannot be replaced by any other. Proprioceptive stimuli from a distended bladder or bowel, for example, elicit urination or evacuation, and much of the organism's well-being depends on the ability to interpret these cues appropriately.

In some cases, the threshold for awareness of these signals is so low that the response takes place even before it is actually necessary (urinary incontinence). In other cases, the threshold may be too high, and the response fails to take place at all (constipation). In still other instances, the stimulus exerts proper control over the response, but the response itself is not made under the correct circumstance or in the correct place (toilet-training in children). The experiments discussed in this section deal with the necessity to change some aspect of the stimulus that controls a particular response without replacing either the stimulus itself or the response it controls.

Restoring the Control of Urination.   The modification of a stimulus to produce improved behavior control is aptly illustrated in the case of a woman treated for urinary incontinence by H. G. Jones (1956). Jones attributed the procedures used in this application to studies of interoceptive conditioning (the use of internal responses as cues, see Chapter 2) conducted by Bykov demonstrating that urinary functioning in human subjects could be controlled by conditioning the bladder to respond to external stimuli (Box 4-2).

BOX 4-2
Conditioning Urination

The urge to urinate usually depends on how full the bladder is. Can this control of urination, which depends basically on internal signals from the bladder, be shifted to another stimulus just as Pavlov's dogs were "taught" to salivate to a tone or a light? The sight or sound of running water does create the urge to urinate in some people, but Bykov wanted to observe this bit of folklore more directly. To do so, he conducted a series of systematic studies with dogs. Actually, Bykov wanted to investigate an even more fundamental question. Can diuresis—the formation and secretion of urine in the kidneys—be increased or decreased through conditioning?

In order to investigate this phenomenon, dogs were surgically prepared so that urine formed in the kidneys could be collected from the ureters themselves, which were externalized for purposes of the experiment. In all of the experiments with these animals, Bykov and his associates found that virtually any stimulus—a tone or a horn, for example—once associated with injections of water into the dog's rectum, could stimulate secretion of fluid by the kidneys. This showed that a process as fundamental as the production of urine by the kidneys could be conditioned (Bykov, 1957).

Can a similar process be accomplished with humans? Because people obviously cannot be surgically prepared, Bykov confined himself to an investigation of bladder conditioning. He introduced warm water through a catheter directly into the bladders of human subjects. At the same time, the changes in pressure created by the volume of water in the bladder were recorded and displayed on a manometer (a pressure measuring device) that the subject could see. The

---

manometer could also be disconnected and manipulated independently by the experimenter without the subject's knowledge.

As the volume of water in the bladder increased, the subjects developed a "connection" between a given manometer reading and the urge to urinate. But, interestingly enough, this urge to urinate could be produced by the experimenter even though the bladder contained very little fluid! He simply disconnected the manometer and artificially increased the reading on the scale to the position at which the subject customarily felt the urge to urinate. The same urge could be evoked by merely calling out the critical number verbally. If, on the other hand, the manometer readings were kept artificially low or at zero, it was possible to fill the bladder with much greater quantities of fluid than that which ordinarily produced urination without even evoking the urge to urinate. This interesting observation led H. G. Jones to devise a method for treating a woman who had to urinate frequently, even though her bladder contained only very small amounts of fluid (Jones, 1956).

Bykov's experiment formed the basis for the method H. G. Jones designed to raise the bladder threshold for urination in order to achieve greater control over voiding (Fig. 4-4).

A 23-year-old woman had given up a stage career as a dancer because of sexual

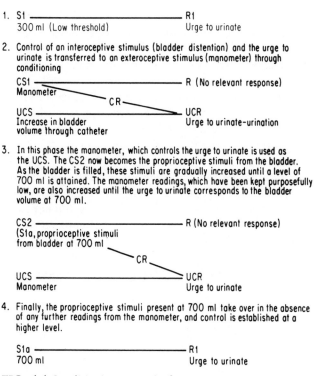

FIG. 4-4 Conditioning control of urination.

and emotional difficulties. She was admitted to the hospital and diagnosed as having an anxiety reaction with hysterical urinary frequency. A course of psychotherapy intended to deal with the problems creating the emotional difficulties lasted for a period of 5 weeks without any appreciable decrease in either the anxiety or the urinary frequency. A physical examination prior to conditioning showed that the patient had the urge to urinate at an abnormally low bladder volume (300 milliliters) and voided approximately every half-hour with abdominal pains.

Conditioning began by introducing varying amounts of saline solution into the patient's bladder and recording bladder pressure on a *manometer,* an instrument similar to the one used to record blood pressure, which the patient could readily observe. The relationship between increases in the volume of saline solution in the bladder and the increased bladder pressure which resulted was explained to her. During the early trials, the manometer reading shown to the patient corresponded to the actual amount of saline solution in the bladder, and she was instructed to relax when a pressure corresponding to 300 milliliters was reached. These conditions brought about some small improvement. But the most dramatic change occurred later in conditioning when the manometer reading was manipulated by Jones so that she did not know the true reading and the volume of saline solution in the bladder continued to increase while the manometer readings were kept artificially low.

This treatment continued for a period of 5 days during which true readings of bladder pressure were alternated with contrived readings. After the fifth day the patient's symptoms disappeared completely, and she was able to retain normal amounts of urine (approximately 700 ml) without difficulty. The ability to exert normal control over urinary functioning resulted in a general improvement in her behavior, and her anxiety reaction was treated by desensitization (a technique discussed later). Follow-up 15 months after discharge from the hospital indicated that she was free of symptoms, had recently married, and was planning to resume her career as a dancer.

Restoring Control of Evacuation.   Modification of stimulus control was also used as a method for treating constipation through conditioning developed by two French physicians, Quarti and Renaud (1962). In the initial phase of treatment, the subjects, two middle-aged women, continued to stimulate bowel movements by taking laxatives, but each bowel movement was accompanied by a slight tingle to the skin generated by a small, battery-powered apparatus worn comfortably around the waist. Gradually, they formed an association between the stimulus from the apparatus and evacuation of the bowels (Figure 4-5).

After 20–30 conditioning trials, electrical stimulation itself took on the properties of the laxative and produced evacuation in the absence of the laxatives. Because the goal of treatment was to transfer control of defecation to a naturally recurring stimulus, the subjects were urged to stimulate evacuation by using the electrical stimulator after breakfast in order to take advantage of the increased activity in the large intestine which follows eating and which often terminates in

1. S1 ————————————————— R1
    Stimuli from   Urge to eliminate (absent)
    large intestine

    This association is virtually non-existent because the stimuli from the
    large intestine have an exceedingly high threshold.

2. Cues from the stimulator are associated with elimination produced
    by the laxative

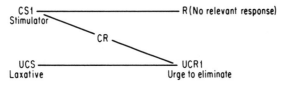

    CS1 ————————————————— R (No relevant response)
    Stimulator

                        CR

    UCS ————————————————— UCR1
    Laxative   Urge to eliminate

3. Natural cues of full stomach associated with elimination induced
    by the stimulator.

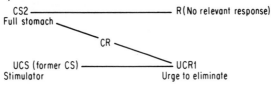

    CS2 ————————————————— R (No relevant response)
    Full stomach

                        CR

    UCS (former CS) ————————————— UCR1
    Stimulator   Urge to eliminate

4. S1a ————————————————— R1
    Fullness of stomach   Urge to eliminate

FIG. 4-5 Restoring control of evacuation through conditioning.

the urge to have a bowel movement. Ultimately, a full stomach and the associated
stimulation of the large intestine became the cues for elimination.

These two studies provide interesting examples of the way in which the
internal cues for a response were modified first by transferring control of the
response to an external stimulus and then by returning control to the appropriate
internal cues. In the study by H. G. Jones, for example, control of the urge to
urinate—essentially an internal process involving stimuli from the bladder—was
taken over by the manometer. By manipulating the manometer readings, the
experimenter kept the patient's urge to urinate purposefully low until the bladder
volume and the associated stimuli from the bladder were both appropriately high
enough for urination to take place. When the manometer was removed, bladder
stimuli once again controlled the urge to urinate.

In the second study by Quarti and Renaud, control of bowel movement was
transferred to the electrical stimulator which enabled evacuation to take place at
the same time that the natural signals from the full stomach were also present. With
removal of the stimulator, control of elimination transferred back to the appropriate internal cues.

Conditioning the Sexual Response to Mature Women.   *Pedophiles* are males who
have a sexual preference for young, pre-pubertal girls. More commonly known as

child molesters, they often have trouble with the law for obvious reasons. In a preliminary investigation, Beech, Watts, and Poole (1971) attempted to redirect the sexual orientation of a pedophile from young, immature girls to sexually mature women through conditioning. The difficulty here was to keep the sexual response to females intact while decreasing the interest in *young* females. They did this through a series of graded, progressive steps in which they gradually changed the characteristics of the original stimulus (young females, S1) controlling the sexual response to those of more mature females (S1a) (Figure 4-6).

Initially, Beech et al. used pictures of young, pre-pubertal girls as the UCS because these consistently produced the the penile response measured by a strain gauge apparatus (similar to the one already described, Herman et al., 1974). Then they paired pictures of slightly more mature females (CS) with those of the younger girls. When the CS (more mature females) acquired the ability to elicit the sexual response, they, in turn, became the UCS and were paired with pictures of sexually mature females which then became the CS for the next phase of conditioning.

After three weeks of conditioning the subject reported an increased sexual arousal for mature females and a declining interest in young females. At first, he was more aroused by simply looking, but a few months after termination of treatment he had satisfactory intercourse with a mature woman. Although still somewhat inhibited, his sexual behavior was more appropriate than before treatment.

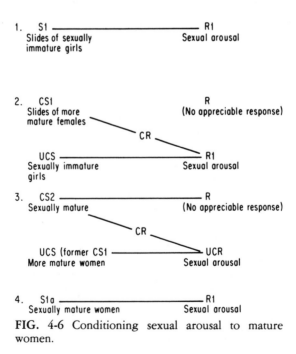

FIG. 4-6 Conditioning sexual arousal to mature women.

Examples of Higher-Order Conditioning.   It may have occurred to the reader that these three studies provide excellent examples of the higher-order conditioning mentioned in Chapter 2 (p. 19). In each of these studies, the CS used in the first phase of conditioning became the UCS in the phase that followed.

For example, in the study by H.G. Jones (see Fig. 4-4), the manometer used as a CS (step 2 in Fig. 4-4) became the UCS in step 3. In the Quarti and Renaud study (see Fig. 4-5), the laxative used as the UCS initially (step 2 in Fig. 4-5) was replaced by the stimulator (CS) which had acquired the ability to control evacuation and became the UCS in step 3. Similarly, in the Beech and Watts study (see Fig. 4-6), the pictures of the young girls originally used as the UCS (step 2 in Fig. 4-6) to elicit the sexual response were replaced by pictures of somewhat more mature girls and used as the CS in step 3.

Virtually all of these studies were first published as case reports or preliminary reports. This means that the authors themselves were uncertain about the long-range effects of the procedures and their ultimate usefulness as clinical tools. Many of the studies in behavior modification will probably remain interesting, one-shot demonstrations of applied learning. Others, however, could conceivably become the bases for standardized treatment techniques. This depends almost entirely on how long the effects of conditioning will endure and on our understanding of the conditions which generate durable changes in behavior. Why do some behavior changes endure while others do not?

The consequences of conditioning are, at best, temporary. This, as we have already noted in Chapter 2, is a good thing because stimuli can therefore lose their control of behavior when they are no longer significant to the organism's survival. This maintains the flexibility so important to learning and re-learning. Remember that Ince learned this important lesson when he failed to maintain urination in the paraplegic and quadriplegic patients with mild shock to the thigh (CS) after the strong shock (UCS) was discontinued.

We can apply this same—admittedly ad hoc—reasoning to the studies with the homosexual and pedophile subjects, and it probably accounts for their negligible successes. In order to maintain a continued interest in their newly formed sexual objects—mature females in both instances—sexual pleasure with mature women has to be experienced soon after conditioning has occurred. If the effort to enjoy sexual experiences with women is frustrated, the homosexual or pedophile will almost assuredly revert to the formerly successful sexual practice. The authors of the study with homosexuals recognize the necessity for these experiences in their closing statement. This suggests the importance of teaching the patient sufficient heterosocial skills to implement his new sexual interests.

Conditioning appeared to be more successful in those instances where the characteristics of the stimulus controlling the behavior were to be modified. In these studies (urinary incontinence and constipation), the conditioning stimuli (manometer and stimulator) came into play as temporary measures, but the control of behavior ultimately returned to the natural signals which lead to elimination.

Counterconditioning: Conditioning a New Response to an Old Stimulus (S1-R1 to S1-R2)

In the conditioning strategies dealt with up to now, behavior has been modified largely through changes in the *stimuli controlling behavior,* but in each instance the response remained the same. In treating the incontinent dancer, for example, H. G. Jones raised the threshold of the stimuli controlling urination so that a larger volume of urine was required before the urge to urinate occurred. However, the urinary response did not change, only the stimuli which controlled it.

In counterconditioning, on the other hand, the situation must be so arranged that a *new response* becomes associated with a stimulus that already elicits another response. This is difficult to accomplish because whenever the stimulus is present it tends to evoke the old response. The new response never really has an opportunity to get attached to the old stimulus.

The subject of counterconditioning raises an interesting problem about response elimination in general which has plagued behavioral scientists for some time and which still continues unresolved. What happens when a response is eliminated? Does it just disappear or must it be replaced by another response? Will the learning of a new response simply eliminate the old response by overshadowing it, so to speak? These are very heady questions despite their apparent simplicity, and no satisfactory explanations for them exist at the present time.

Learning a new habit to an old cue requires some special attention because the old response is always around to interfere with new learning. Guthrie suggests several ways to keep the old response from interfering.

The first of these has already been encountered in the description of Erofeeva's dog who salivated to shock when the shock was gradually introduced in the presence of food. It consists in introducing the "old" stimulus at such weak strengths that it does not evoke the response (or at least only to a small degree) and gradually increasing the stimulus intensity as the new response begins to take hold. Horses, Guthrie suggests, are often broken by this method. First, the bit is introduced into the horse's mouth. Then a light blanket is placed on the back. This is followed by a saddle, and finally, the rider.

The second method is more direct. Here the cues for the undesirable response are presented in full strength while the old response is prevented from occurring. Guthrie recalls that this method worked particularly well on the farm when he was a boy. Dogs who had acquired the habit of killing chickens had the dead chickens tied around their necks. After several days of wearing a "chicken necklace," the dogs no longer bothered the chickens. The following study illustrates how a large number of children were toilet-trained by the simple expedient of preventing one response from occurring and permitting another alternative to take its place.

Training Children Not to Soil in Their Trousers. *Encopresis*—defecating in the clothes—occurs frequently enough among children to represent a problem. While some cases result from difficulties in the muscles controlling evacuation, most result from learning deficits—the child has simply never associated the urge to have a bowel movement with the toilet.

In a large-scale study involving 15 male and 4 female children ranging in age from 4–10 years, Young (1973) used a conditioning process to achieve toilet training. The children were trained by providing them with an opportunity to use the toilet under the same stimulus conditions that usually evoked soiling. As in the study with the constipated women (p. 84), the reflex action that occurs in the intestine following the ingestion of food was used. This action—the *gastro-ileal reflex* —involves a mass movement in the large intestine usually terminating in evacuation. The problem here was to associate the stimuli from the gastro-ileal reflex with evacuation in the toilet.

The relatively simple procedure required only consistency and patience on the part of the parent (Figure 4-7). On rising in the morning, the child was given a warm drink or food, taken to the bathroom 20–30 minutes later, and encouraged to have a bowel movement. The child was praised if a bowel movement occurred and removed from the bathroom if no bowel movement took place after a period of 10 minutes. Most of the children also received a preparation called Senokot the evening before to assist in stimulating the gastro-ileal reflex and to relieve intestinal inertia.

The length of treatment ranged from 2–11 months, with an average of 5 months. In a subsequent follow-up survey varying from 6–72 months following treatment, only 4 of the 19 children had minor recurrences. The remainder were successfully toilet trained.

A Method for Reducing Cold Hypersensitivity. Primary Raynaud's Disease (PRD) is a form of cold hypersensitivity characterized by subjective sensations of coldness and numbness in the toes and fingers, a change in skin color, and sometimes tissue decay (necrosis) due to constriction of the peripheral blood vessels.

Because these symptoms are also occasionally produced by stress, or by stress and cold, and do not have any apparent organic basis, PRD has been regarded as

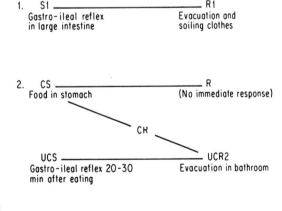

FIG. 4-7 Toilet-training through conditioning.

a psychophysiologic disorder (PRD is also discussed in Chapter 11 on biofeedback).

The normal response to cold exposure is an initial constriction of the peripheral blood vessels followed by periodic vasodilation cycles. Vasoconstriction in response to cold is a physiological measure intended to conserve heat in the central core of the body, while the cycles of vasodilation following continued exposure to cold serves to prevent tissue damage in the extremities from prolonged restricted blood flow.

Because the only difference between the normal response to cold and PRD is the early occurrence of vasoconstriction and the absence of vasodilation cycles in PRD, it is conceivable that the symptoms of PRD might be relieved by restoring the vasodilation cycles following exposure to cold. One of the ways in which this might be accomplished, according to Marshall and Gregory (1974), is through classical conditioning, and more particularly, through counterconditioning.

In the study conducted by Marshall and Gregory, individuals suffering from PRD were selected for conditioning on the basis of abnormally low finger temperature and nerve conduction velocities. They were also screened through physical examinations to rule out the possibility of secondary influencing disease factors.

Baseline measurements of skin temperature and nerve conduction velocities were obtained at room temperatures of 26°C and 0°C in a cold room while the patient was dressed in normal indoor clothing. Following these measurements, counterconditioning was initiated by exposing the patient to 0°C for a period of eight min. and immersing the hands in water heated to 42°C. In effect, the initial response to cold was prolonged vasodilation (S1 cold − R1 vasoconstriction), while the counterconditioned response was vasodilation (UCR) produced by the heated water (UCS) and associated with the cold stimulus (CS). Thereafter, exposure to cold produced initial vasoconstriction followed by vasodilation (S1 cold − R2 vasodilation).

The results of counterconditioning indicated that of the 8 patients treated, skin temperature improved significantly in one case, slightly in five cases, remained relatively stable in one and decreased in one case. Despite these mixed findings, however, "all of the patients treated experienced subjective improvement during cold exposure, i.e., remission of acral skin color changes, disappearance of skin necrosis (if present), and improved comfort without special protection" (Marshall and Gregory, 1974, p. 123). Patients who enjoyed skiing or fishing in cold waters were again able to enjoy these activities.

Conditioned Aversion: A Form of Counterconditioning.   Conditioned aversion as a form of treatment essentially involves a counterconditioning technique. The assumption is that the stimulus for performing a response—a cigarette or a glass of whiskey, for example—acquires its stimulus properties through association with the pleasurable consequences of the response. Associating the stimulus with unpleasant consequences, therefore, should, in principle, eliminate the pleasant associations and replace them with unpleasant ones. Clearly that is counterconditioning. Unfortunately, this potentially ideal procedure for getting rid of bad habits has not worked according to expectations, especially in the addictive behaviors, such as smoking and drinking, where we urgently need some form of treatment and where the aversive methods have been used most frequently.

Rapid smoking: tying the chicken to the smoker's neck. Until the introduction of rapid smoking, most programs designed to break the smoking habit relied on either self-control procedures or the replacement of smoking with an alternative response. In the self-control methods, the smokers usually had to observe a daily cigarette ration until they abandoned the habit through gradual withdrawal. Response-replacement methods instructed the smokers to chew gum or eat candy whenever they felt the urge to smoke, or hypnotic procedures attempted to replace smoking with a feeling of revulsion.

Although some moderate success has been achieved using these methods, the single most effective behavioral technique for breaking the smoking habit appears to be rapid smoking. According to Lichtenstein and Glasgow (1977), who have recently reviewed programs using the procedure, rapid smoking requires the client to smoke at a very fast pace—taking a drag once every 6 seconds—until any further smoking would produce extreme discomfort or nausea. Apparently, under such conditions, all sorts of immediate physiological effects take place that make smoking a noxious event. Instead of the pleasant lift usually associated with normally paced smoking, the smoker experiences the mild toxic conditions that result from increased nicotine concentration. Heart rate and arterial blood pressure increase, and the oxygen-carrying capacity of the blood is reduced due to the inhalation of large quantities of carbon monoxide. All of these changes combine to produce extremely unpleasant feelings, and the aim of the rapid-smoking procedure is to associate these feelings with the urge to smoke or the sight of a cigarette.

Because the technique places some stress on the cardiovascular system, its use requires caution. When Lichtenstein and Glasgow surveyed a large number of academic, clinical, and commercial rapid-smoking programs with an estimated 35,000 clients, however, they found only two reports of non-fatal, minor heart attacks involving persons with previous histories of difficulty. Nevertheless, and with good reason, they strongly recommend a careful screening procedure involving a preliminary history to eliminate clients with a history of heart disease, high blood pressure, diabetes, chronic bronchitis or emphysema, and approval from a physician who is briefed about the possible risks and benefits of the procedure through literature distributed by the therapists.

A smoking cessation study comparing rapid smoking with self-control procedures (Danaher, 1977) demonstrated the use of rapid control methods. Rapid smokers were required to puff a cigarette once every 6 seconds for a period of 8 minutes during a 15-minute session, while a "placebo" smoking group smoked cigarettes at a normal pace, consuming about one cigarette in each 5-minute trial. The groups were further divided into a group of rapid smokers and placebo smokers with whom discussion was conducted to provide insight into their smoking habits and a group given self-control instructions involving control of smoking urges, self-reward, and deep muscle relaxation. The four groups of subjects received a total of six 15-minute sessions in a period of 2 weeks. In a 13-week follow-up survey, the rapid-smoking-plus-discussion group showed greater abstinence than any of the other groups (approximately 36%).

The results of this study are not particularly impressive because only 36% of those who quit smoking remained abstinent 13 weeks after treatment. Moreover, these results are consistent with surveys of the long-term effects of rapid smoking which report that, although a relatively high rate of success is found in a period of 3–6 months following treatment (37–64% abstinence), it declines to a point where only 12.5–45% have stopped smoking completely in the 2- to 6-year follow-up period. Despite the relatively discouraging results, rapid smoking as a form of treatment is still considered superior to other smoking control programs (Lichtenstein & Rodrigues, 1977).

Alcoholism and Conditioned Aversion.   A survey of the vast literature on conditioned aversion treatment of alcoholism (Voegtlin & Lemere, 1942) indicates that the procedures first established by Kantorovich in 1930 are still in use, although not in exactly the same form. The basic idea is to eliminate drinking entirely by pairing the sight, smell, and taste of alcohol (CS) with some aversive event—nausea, retching, illness (UCR)—produced by chemical or electrical means (UCS). Antabuse, which produces violent illness when mixed with alcohol, has been somewhat successful, but its effectiveness depends upon the alcoholic who must take the drug daily. This factor, as well as the serious side effects it produces, has not made it a treatment of choice.

Accounts of the effectiveness of aversion therapy vary considerably. The continuing studies of Voegtlin and Lemere (1950) indicate that of 4,096 cases treated over a 13-year period, 60% abstained from drinking for one year or longer, 51% for 2 years or longer, 38% for 5 years or longer, and 23% for 10 years. The fact that 49% had returned to drinking after a period of 2 years and that 77% were no longer abstinent after a period of 10 years suggests that alcohol is a way of solving problems for these people. This, in turn, suggests that other procedures in addition to aversive counterconditioning must also be used (Wallerstein, 1957; Miller, 1976).

Most studies support the general observation that addictive behaviors such as alcoholism, drug abuse, and even overeating, are especially resistant to change, possibly because the acts are not only pleasurable in themselves, producing euphoria and states of well-being, but also because they are frequently used as a means of reducing anxiety associated with stress. This is probably why most aversive programs produce only modest results. Abstinence occurs early in the treatment because the pain and discomfort associated with drinking, smoking, or overeating is presumably greater than the pain involved from doing without cigarettes, alcohol, or generous amounts of food. Eventually, however, abstinence decreases when direct punishment is discontinued and the programs rely solely on the *anticipation* of discomfort to maintain the inhibition.

Although most studies involving aversive conditioning have assumed that drinking decreases because a conditioned reaction has occurred, none, according to Baker and Cannon (1979), have actually demonstrated the occurrence of a conditioned aversion response. The results have been attributed to factors such as cognitive changes, expiation of guilt, and placebo effects. Their work, however, which involves the use of syrup of ipecac, emetine hydrochloride, and potassium antimony tartrate to initiate and sustain vomiting after drinking alcohol, clearly demonstrates the formation of a conditioned reaction following the conditioning trials. Not only were the patients' subjective attitudes to alcohol as distasteful, unpleasant, and dangerous increased, but physiological measures such as skin conductance and heart rate, both used as CRs, also indicated that alcohol as a CS had been associated with a noxious experience.

It has become increasingly apparent that the origin and treatment of alcoholism are complex subjects and that aversive conditioning oversimplifies the matter. We explore many of the forces that conspire to produce an alcoholic in Chapter 7, and in later chapters we take up some of the treatment methods, such as controlled drinking, which are currently being investigated as alternatives to conditioning.

A Theoretical Dilemma. Up to now, we have followed the processes of behavior change and attributed them to classical conditioning with little difficulty. The operations of Pavlov's experiments were sufficient to describe what took place: the cues used as conditioning stimuli were distinct, and the conditioned responses themselves involuntary—urination, evacuation, and physiological measures of aversion or sexual arousal, for example. In fact, most of the studies were designed with the principles of conditioning in mind, and the basic components of the conditioning procedure—CS, UCS, and CR—were relatively clear and easy to identify. But now we have arrived at one of the theoretical shoals mentioned in Chapter 1, and we must hesitate in order to reestablish our bearings.

Consider the following case. A 22-year-old woman with a temper so uncontrollable that she was actually contemplating suicide referred herself for treatment. Most of her relationships with her husband and son were characterized by violent fits of rage. She screamed at the top of her voice whenever the son misbehaved, smashed household items, and assaulted the child physically. Her husband also became the target of physical and verbal abuse during their frequent arguments. According to her relatives, the client was known for her violent temper which had been a disruptive factor in her associations with other people since childhood (Smith, 1973).

Initially, attempts to deal with this behavior involved a form of desensitization training during which the client was asked to imagine scenes with her husband and son that lead to anger. Although she was instructed to relax whenever the scenes evoked feelings of anger, she could not, and even the most innocuous scene with either her husband or child provoked outbursts of temper. Because straightforward relaxation proved unsuccessful, the therapist decided to employ counterconditioning by explicitly associating each scene with humor.

He began by asking the client to imagine the following humorous scene:

As you're driving to the supermarket, little Pascal the Rascal begins to get restless. Suddenly he drops from his position on the ceiling and trampolines off the rear seat onto the rear view mirror. From this precarious position he amuses himself by flashing obscene hand gestures at the shocked pedestrians. . . (Smith, 1973, p. 577).

Soon the client was able to imagine each of the required scenes without anger and reacted to them with laughter and amusement in the subsequent eight therapy sessions. After three more sessions, her relatives reported a marked improvement in her "temper" and she herself indicated that relationships with her husband and son no longer provoked anger. These positive changes were also confirmed by observations of her interactions with the child in a playroom, especially during those moments when he was obnoxious. Personality scale measurements as well as physiological recordings showed a behavior pattern of decreased impulsiveness, resentment, anger, and tension. The simple expedient of substituting humor as a response to cues which ordinarily provoked anger was sufficient to associate a new response to the old cues.

The case just described cannot easily be interpreted in terms of classical conditioning for a number of reasons.

In the first place, the conditioned stimulus is not as easily identifiable as the cues in the typical classical conditioning study. It consisted of thoughts and images rather than external stimuli such as tones or lights. Although the anger was visible in the case of the woman just discussed, the images or thoughts as cues which provoked the anger were not.

Secondly, the success of the therapist in associating humor with the images of the husband or child depended, to a great extent, on the willingness of the woman to let this occur. She could just as easily have rejected the attempts. In this instance, a volitional element was present in the behavior which was absent in Pavlov's experiments where the dogs were compelled to salivate each time the bell rang, whether they wanted to or not. Apparently, these attempts to change behavior do not fit very neatly into the framework of classical conditioning. But, if not classical conditioning, what kind of learning does take place?

Guthrie, as we saw in Chapter 2, had no doubt that such learning was still an associative process, even though voluntary responses were involved and even though the controlling stimulus was not always easily identified. As long as the two events to be associated were contiguous, the stimulus would eventually come to control the response. Mere association of humor with the images of the husband and son would ultimately replace the woman's anger response.

Guthrie was not terribly concerned with the way in which these responses occurred as long as they were available to be hooked up to the appropriate stimulus. They could be elicited by food as a UCS in Pavlov's experiments or in any other way, as long as they occurred regularly. If the purpose of the experiment had been to condition scratching to a flashing light, for example, then itching powder would serve the same purpose as food. So, for Guthrie, it really makes little difference how the response to be learned is produced, just as long as it occurs in close association with the stimulus.

More often, however, the food, or any other desirable object for that matter, comes as a direct consequence of what the animal or human does. Dogs, for example, may be trained to press a lever whenever a light is turned on in order to receive food. Under these circumstances, the light takes on a different meaning. It signifies, in effect, that if a response is made when the light is turned on, food will probably be obtained. The light, then, simply sets the occasion for the response to take place—it does not act as a conditioned stimulus to force the response. But the response also differs under these conditions. Unless the animal presses the lever, it will not receive any food.

Most animal and human behavior consists of voluntary rather than involuntary responses. When voluntary responses are involved, the consequences of the behavior become a very important issue, as we see in Chapter 6 on operant conditioning. Nevertheless, and with these difficulties fully in mind, we introduce the subject of *behavior rehearsal* as a method for achieving behavior change which appears to be based on the fundamental principle of counterconditioning—the idea that one response is replaced by another under the same stimulus conditions.

Behavior Rehearsal as a Form of Counterconditioning.   "Be sincere, even if you don't mean it!" the slip of paper in the fortune cookie counsels. This bit of paradoxical wisdom suggests that behavior rehearsal—a way of getting rid of old habits by substituting and practicing new ones—is simply a new term for an old way of learning. In fact, Shakespeare, William James, Tolstoy, and I.B. Singer, to mention only a few authors, all subscribed to this method for conquering old, undesirable habits. Hamlet, for example, attempts to persuade his mother, Gertrude, not to continue seeing his uncle Claudius with the following bit of advice:

Assume a virtue, if you have it not, . . .
Refrain tonight
And that shall lend a kind of easiness
To the next abstinence: (the next more easy:
For use almost can change the stamp of nature,
And either master the devil or throw him out
With wonderous potency).

(Hamlet, III, iv.)

In an equally relevant passage, William James also suggests that the way to change behavior and, ultimately, attitudes is to replace one response with another:

The voluntary path to cheerfulness if our spontaneous cheerfulness be lost . . . is to act and speak as if cheerfulness were already there . . . to feel brave act as if we were brave . . . and courage will very likely replace fear . . . to feel kindly toward a person to whom we have been inimical . . . deliberately smile . . . make inquiries . . . and force ourselves to say genial things. *If we act as if from some better feeling, the old bad feeling soon folds its tent like an arab and silently steals away* (W. James, 1899, 1958, p. 133; italics added).

In a remarkably similar vein, the Rabbi in I.B. Singer's short story, *A Piece of Advice,* counsels a man who cannot control his anger and contempt for others to become a flatterer for eight days. Although this advice was odious to him at first, his anger disappeared completely as he practiced his flattery. "And so," Singer concludes, "it is with all things. If you are not happy, act the happy man. Happiness will come later" (Singer, 1963, p. 129).

These counsels fit very nicely into a counterconditioning scheme because all behavior between people consists of reciprocal relationships. If people change their characteristic way of responding toward others, they are also likely to change the behavior of others toward themselves and so alter the stimulus conditions which elicited and maintained the old undesirable behavior.

Behavior rehearsal has also been the basis for two major therapeutic movements. In fixed-role therapy, devised by Kelly (1955), clients are encouraged to abandon their particular system of beliefs in order to achieve increased flexibility by trying out and adopting new roles.

Psychodrama, developed by Moreno (Moreno & Kipper, 1968), attempts to reach a similar goal by requiring the individual to assume and act out roles which represent current difficulties. Apart from helping the client to recognize problem areas, re-enactment promotes a feeling of adequacy and flexibility in social skills and provides a way of attaching new responses to old stimuli.

We leave the further development of behavior rehearsal as a method for changing behavior for Chapter 12 on self-control, where the use of behavior rehearsal in assertiveness training is discussed in more detail.

chapter five

Elimination
of Fear

In his book *Psychiatry in a Troubled World,* W. C. Menninger described some rather puzzling behavior among combat soldiers who were "psychiatric casualties" during World War II. It seems that in the first combat engagements of the American forces in North Africa, soldiers suffering from battle shock, fatigue, and other behavioral difficulties resulting from combat were often transported to a base hospital some 300–500 miles behind the lines. Under these conditions, less than 10% of the men were able to return to duty after treatment. But when immediate, intensive treatment was given within 15–20 miles of the front, generally within the sound and range of gunfire, approximately 60% of the combat exhaustion cases could be returned to duty, and, apparently, the majority of these men readjusted successfully to combat conditions (Ludwig & Ranson, 1947; Menninger, 1948).

Why should distance behind the front lines make a difference in the recovery rate of soldiers suffering from combat exhaustion? To find a possible answer to this question, we shall have to go back in time to Watson and his student Mary Cover Jones, then forward again through a series of events including the pioneer work of Joseph Wolpe, the seminal experiments in "anxiety conservation" of Solomon and Wynne, and the introduction of implosive therapy by Stampfl and Levis.

Watson was among the first to see the implications of conditioning for behavior change, although his student, Mary Cover Jones, ultimately carried out his ideas. In Chapter 3 we described Watson and Rayner's demonstration of how a child could be conditioned to fear white mice by pairing a sudden, loud noise with the mouse as the CS. Although they could not provide evidence that such fears could be eliminated, they did propose a number of methods that they felt sure would be successful in reducing the fear reaction. According to Watson and Rayner (1920, p. 12), extinction of fear could be achieved by:

1. Constantly confronting the subject with those stimuli which called out the fear responses in the hope that habituation would come in corresponding to fatigue.

2. Trying to recondition by showing objects calling out fear responses (visual) and simultaneously stimulating the erogenous zones (tactual). We should try first the lips, then the nipples, and as a final resort the sex organs.

3. Trying to recondition by feeding the subject candy or food just as the animal is shown. This method calls for food control of the subject.

4. Building up constructive activities around the object by imitation and by putting the hand through the motions of manipulation.

The striking thing about these recommendations is that they anticipate, in a somewhat rudimentary form, most of the behavior change methods currently in use. Suggestion 1, for example, approximates flooding or implosive techniques which, as we shall shortly see, involves confronting the subject with the feared object and preventing escape. Both 2 and 3 are essentially counterconditioning techniques which Watson refers to as "reconditioning," and 4 could be construed as imitation learning.

Shortly after these proposals, Mary Cover Jones (1924a) studied the "naturally occurring" fears of hospitalized children and demonstrated that a child's fear of rabbits could be eliminated by gradually introducing the feared stimulus (a rabbit) in the context of pleasurable responses (eating). With the caged rabbit at one end of a room, Peter, the child, was fed at the opposite end. Gradually, the rabbit was brought closer and closer until Peter could ultimately caress and play with the animal, despite his original fear. This study essentially interpreted Watson and Rayner's second and third propositions which stated that "reconditioning" can occur if the aversive or feared stimulus is associated with pleasurable activities or sensations.

Although the technique used by Jones, which she called *direct conditioning,* is generally regarded as the precursor of such methods as "systematic desensitization," she also compared several other methods with direct conditioning in a subsequent study (Jones, 1924b). The *method of distraction,* which replaced the fear response with a substitute activity, and the *method of social imitation,* in which two non-fearful children helped to encourage a positive response from a child who was afraid of dogs, were both found to be effective in reducing fear-related responses. (The methods employed with children in the area of modeling and imitation learning discussed in Chapter 15 appear to be derivatives of the method of social imitation.)

Although neither Watson nor Jones referred directly to a counterconditioning process, the idea was certainly implicit in Watson's term "reconditioning" and in the "direct conditioning" procedures used by Jones. In the study just described, Jones's objective was to replace the responses produced by fear with the pleasurable responses elicited by food—a goal that Wolpe apparently had in mind when he formulated the technique of systematic desensitization.

SYSTEMATIC DESENSITIZATION: A METHOD FOR ELIMINATING FEAR-RELATED RESPONSES

Shortly after its introduction in 1958 with the publication of Wolpe's *Psychotherapy by Reciprocal Inhibition,* systematic desensitization became a standardized technique in behavior modification because it was used so frequently and successfully in the treatment of most behavior disorders in which fear or anxiety played a dominant role. Not only was systematic desensitization the first therapeutic method based on learning principles to receive widespread use in clinical settings, it also opened the door to the clinical use of learning principles in general.

As originally conceived, *systematic desensitization* is a method for reducing fear by confronting the subject with the fear-arousing situation or object and using muscle relaxation as an antagonistic response to inhibit the occurrence of anxiety.

The rationale behind systematic desensitization emerged from Wolpe's view of how neuroses, and phobic behavior in particular, are acquired and how they are relinquished. In a series of experiments he conducted with cats, Wolpe demonstrated that the fear reaction of cats who had received aversive conditioning could be eliminated if the animals were fed while the fear-arousing stimulus was gradually reintroduced into the situation.

Wolpe generalized these findings to human behavior, reasoning that if an individual with a phobia could be made to learn a response which was antagonistic to fear or anxiety, the fear response would ultimately disappear and the alternative response would replace it. In principle, the subject is first taught relaxation as an incompatible alternative response (R2) to replace the responses associated with fear (R1)—clearly a counterconditioning process.

After an initial interview to determine life factors that may be associated with the phobic condition, the treatment procedure is explained to the clients, and they are given instructions in *progressive relaxation*—tensing and relaxing various muscle groups—to provide the alternative, opposing response in desensitization.

A list of fear-arousing objects or situations is then constructed from interviews and arranged in terms of a *hierarchy,* from the least fear-arousing item to the most fear-arousing item—the phobic situation itself. Differing fear situations or gradations of the same situation may make up the list. For example, the list for a person who is afraid of rain and will not venture out if the weather is at all threatening may begin with a series of weather broadcasts predicting rain, gradually shifting to a description of a threatening day with rain imminent, and, finally, to a scene of the client walking in the rain.

During the actual desensitization session, each item on the list is presented in sequence, and the client is instructed to imagine the fear-producing scene. Presentation of the first, mildly stressful, item is followed by instructions to relax in the presence of the imagined scene. When the first item imagined no longer produces reports of anxiety, the second and third more threatening items are presented sequentially until they also no longer elicit fear. If an item continues to arouse anxiety, the client is asked to stop visualizing it and to practice relaxation. This procedure follows from Wolpe's view that *anxiety must be kept at minimal levels* during exposure to the fear-arousing events. Wherever possible, the actual phobic stimulus may be introduced into the desensitization procedure (live animals or hypodermic syringes, for example—a procedure which is known as *in vivo desensitization.*

Wolpe reports that improvement begins to take place at every point in the hierarchy and that reduction of fear to the imagined stimulus is generally followed by a reduction of fear to the real stimulus when the client is actually exposed to it. Since, as Wolpe asserts, most neurotic disturbances consist of intricate systems of phobias, in principle, systematic desensitization can be applied to virtually any situation in which a clearly defined fear stimulus exists.

Systematic desensitization is an extremely rewarding procedure to the therapist who may see phobias of long standing disappear in a relatively short time with very few therapy sessions. But the results can also be very disappointing—especially to the novice—if it is used by itself in an unremitting fashion. Desensitization may help to eliminate fear of social situations, for example, but it may not operate effectively unless deficiencies in social skills are also corrected through training (Chapter 12).

Very often desensitization is ineffective because therapists take the actual phobia itself at face value as the event or object which the client actually fears. In many instances this may actually be the case, and nothing more than a course of desensitization is necessary to eliminate the phobic response. Just as often, however, the client does not fear the situation but the behavior likely to be expressed in the situation. Ben Feather, a psychoanalytically oriented behavior therapist, points out that the ostensible phobic situation is not always the thing which the client actually fears, and illustrates this point in the case of a 37-year-old physiologist who had been in supportive therapy (maintaining adjustment through periodic therapy sessions without actually correcting the behavior disorder) because of recurrent anxiety attacks. It turned out that during the course of therapy the client revealed multiple fears—fear of flying, fear of social situations, fear of sitting in an audience. Feather, as the case history in Box 5-1 reveals, focused on fear of loss of control as the central theme underlying the phobias rather than the environmental conditions reported by the client.

BOX 5-1
Uncovering the "Real" Phobia

Dr. E. had been in supportive therapy for several years before he discovered that he was afraid of flying and was referred to Dr. Feather for desensitization treatment. Although he had been a Navy pilot and enjoyed flying his own plane, he began to avoid flying altogether. This caused him great inconvenience because it prevented him from attending professional meetings and kept him from visiting his mistress who lived at some considerable distance.

But that was not Dr. E.'s only fear. It turned out in subsequent therapy sessions that he was also afraid of sitting in an audience and usually sat in the back row on a folding chair next to the exit. Sitting in the middle or the front of an auditorium so terrified him that he would not attend a lecture or concert if he arrived late. He was also afraid of cocktail parties and social gatherings in general, and conquered his fear of speaking before groups—an absolute necessity in his profession—only by taking large doses of tranquilizers which reduced his anxiety somewhat.

Instead of attempting to desensitize Dr. E. to each of these three phobic situations separately, Feather concentrated on the fantasies associated with the phobias. They revealed that his fear of flying was not related to a fear of dying in an accident but to a fear of losing control, going berserk, and striking out at the passengers if the plane encountered turbulent air or had mechanical difficulties.

His fear of being part of an audience was also associated with loss of control, and while attending a music recital shortly before therapy began, he became so frightened by the thought that he might jump up, wave his arms, and shout obscenities at the people around him that he left in the middle of the concert in a state of acute anxiety. For many years prior to this incident, he had a recurring fantasy of sitting in the second row at Carnegie Hall, disrupting the performance by vomiting all over the man in front of him, and stepping on everyone as he left. At cocktail parties he feared that he might do something stupid, spill a drink, or insult someone. Feather decided to desensitize Dr. E. to the central theme of these phobias—fear of loss of control resulting from anger.

The fear of being part of an audience became the first desensitization target because Dr. E. had several lecture engagements in the near future. First he learned progressive relaxation, then he was asked to imagine sitting in a large audience and doing whatever came to mind. In reporting the scene, he described himself attending a lecture and sitting next to the slide projector while a colleague whom he disliked gave a talk. The noise of the projector annoyed him, and he became angry enough to knock it over on the man sitting next to him, demolishing the projector and disrupting the lecture. On six successive occasions when he repeated the scene, he reported the same violent story. Throughout the session, he could remain relaxed, and he reported very little anxiety.

Dr. E. was instructed to practice relaxation at home and to try sitting in the middle of an audience at a concert before coming for his next therapy session. He succeeded in doing this and was only mildly anxious. The subsequent accounts of his fantasies became less violent. At the end of the session, he was asked to sit in the front row of an audience, which he did successfully and without any anxiety. He reported that he could now sit anywhere he wanted and had resumed flying again. When Dr. E. came in for a follow-up 1 year later, he was free from all phobic behavior and had acquired no other symptoms.

In his summary of the case, Feather suggested that the rapid disappearance of the target phobia and the generalization to other phobias was the result of *applying systematic desensitization, not to the environmental cues themselves, which is customary, but to the imagery of the unacceptable, hostile, and aggressive impulses that Dr. E. feared and that were common to all of his phobias* (Feather, 1970).

In a similar vein, Lazarus (1971) reports the case of a man who came to him for help because he was afraid to cross bridges. After an assessment of the case, Lazarus determined that the fear of bridges was an avoidance response which provided the client with a socially acceptable excuse for staying away from his job. Actually, the man was afraid of an impending promotion and the increased responsibility and scrutiny it would bring. Instead of desensitizing him to bridges, Lazarus focused on his fear of criticism with beneficial results.

How Effective Is Systematic Desensitization

The effectiveness of any therapeutic technique depends on the number of people it helps and the durability of the behavior changes that take place. But effectiveness is not an easy thing to measure given the many uncontrolled factors that are likely to influence the results. Are the clients similar with respect to the disorder being treated? Dissimilarity may bias the results of a study one way or the other. Are the therapists skilled and, if they are conducting several types of therapy in a comparative study, are they biased in favor of one type? Are the outcome reports about the changes in the client's behavior trustworthy and from what sources were they obtained—relatives, friends, the clients themselves? The effectiveness of any new form of treatment—especially where behavior is concerned—is also notoriously influenced by the enthusiasm of its practitioners. This often acts as a placebo, raising the hopes and, in turn, the motivation for treatment of clients who are in a state of despair and ready to believe in anything as a "cure."

Despite these difficulties, systematic desensitization has generated many experiments, demonstrations, and case reports, all of which uniformly confirm that it is a highly effective technique for eliminating fear and fear-related behavior in a relatively short period of time.

The earliest appraisal, of course, appeared in Wolpe's book which originally introduced desensitization as a treatment form (1958). At that time, he listed 88 patients who benefited from desensitization treatment, using a criterion of symptom-free behavior. These cases included inferiority feelings, depression, impotence, claustrophobia, paranoid obsessions, hysterical parasthesias, and others.

Wolpe was careful to point out that the survey made no provision for separating the effects of desensitization as a form of treatment from the effect of simply conducting therapeutic interviews or from the relationships which may have been established in therapy. In a subsequent survey of follow-up studies, Wolpe (1962) found only 4 relapses from among a group of 249 clients.

Wolpe's successful development and application of desensitization encouraged other investigators to replicate his clinical results and many practitioners reported similar successes with single cases. Lazarus (1961), on the other hand, conducted one of the first semi-controlled clinical studies with relatively large groups in which desensitization and interpretative therapy were compared in group therapy. The groups included 11 acrophobics (fear of high places), 15 claustrophobics (fear of enclosed places), 5 impotent men (treated as sexual phobias), and 4 mixed phobic disorders (fear of sharp objects, fear of physical violence, fear of moving vehicles, and fear of dogs). All of the phobias were severe enough to impose limitations on mobility and social-interpersonal relationships.

The patients were assigned at random to three groups matched in terms of sex, age, and nature and severity of the disorder. Desensitization subjects received "group" therapy as a homogeneous unit organized in terms of similarity of phobia. For this group, common stimulus hierarchies—fear of heights, for example—were constructed and presented to the individuals as a group.

A second mixed group of patients was also treated as a unit to determine whether desensitization is effective with heterogeneous phobias. In this group, the clients read the hierarchy items from individual index cards dealing with the phobia specific to them.

The third interpretative group was treated by a form of therapy with re-educative goals devoted to self-exploration and insight into the origins of their phobic disorders. One part of the interpretative group was given relaxation after interpretation to determine the effect of relaxation without desensitization, and all of the clients who failed to recover from their phobic symptoms in the interpretation group had an opportunity to receive desensitization treatment after the study ended.

The criterion of recovery for all clients was the ability to perform the previously feared act 1 month after therapy. Acrophobics, for example, had to climb a fire escape to the third story of a building (about 50 feet), proceed to an 8-story roof garden, and then count the cars below for 2 minutes accompanied by the therapist and an independent observer. The impotent men and members of the mixed phobic group were not tested.

At the conclusion of the study, 13 of the 18 clients receiving desensitization as a form of treatment recovered according to the accepted criterion. None of the clients in the interpretation group recovered, and only 2 of the 8 clients treated by interpretation and relaxation alone were free from phobic symptoms. A subsequent follow-up ranging from 1.5–15 months after recovery indicated that 10 of the 13 clients given group desensitization maintained their recovery. Of the two clients involved in interpretation followed by relaxation alone, 1 relapsed. Eight of the 10 clients in the interpretative group treated by desensitization at the close of the study sustained their behavior changes.

In discussing the possibility of contamination due to experimenter bias because he was the sole therapist, Lazarus indicated that his initial personal preference was for interpretative methods.

Another clinical study conducted by Baker, Cohen, and Saunders (1973) with acrophobics showed that the therapist is not an especially crucial factor in the desensitization process once the client becomes familiar with the elements of the technique. In a self-directed desensitization group, clients who listened to tape-recorded sessions of relaxation training and recorded presentations of fear-evoking scenes made greater behavioral gains, reflected in their own reports of anxiety, than either a therapist-directed group or the waiting-list controls.

The "Theory" Behind Systematic Desensitization

We now come to another of those theoretical shoals which make the journey through the behavioral sciences both exciting and ideologically perilous. *Is systematic desensitization really counterconditioning as Wolpe had conceived it?* If not, what is the learning process? The first part of this question can be answered by examining Wolpe's reasons for the counterconditioning explanation, the second, through an analysis of the elements in desensitization which actually do produce behavior change and a look at implosive and flooding techniques.

Wolpe's ideas for systematic desensitization came from many sources. He believed, along with Guthrie, that the fear-related response must be replaced by another incompatible response before the phobia can be eliminated. But this simple replacement explanation bothered him because it did not adequately account for the disappearance of the old response. Do the phobic responses simply get replaced by other responses—covered up, so to speak? Wolpe suggested that the incompatible alternative response is partly responsible for the disappearance of the phobic response, and this is accomplished through a process called "reciprocal inhibition," a concept he borrowed from the famous British physiologist Sir Charles Sherrington who demonstrated that the contraction of a flexor muscle, which occurs when the arm is bent, automatically produces a "reciprocal" relaxation in the extensor muscle.

At this point, Wolpe took an enormous leap by suggesting that Sherrington's principle could be readily applied to all behavioral situations "in which the elicitation of one response appears to bring about a decrement in the strength of evocation of a simultaneous response" (1958, p. 29). Unfortunately, however, the comparison is not a good one. Bending the arm most certainly brings about a relaxation of the opposing extensor muscle, but this does not decrease the ability to extend the arm again when the occasion arises as Wolpe's statement, "decrement in the strength of evocation," appears to suggest.

In any event, Wolpe went on to say that every time the phobic response is prevented by the alternative response, more and more inhibition builds up and finally takes a more permanent form, called conditioned inhibition. As we know from Pavlov's speculations, inhibition is a force that opposes responding, so the phobic response disappears from the sheer "weight" of conditioned inhibition it has acquired.

Several things are wrong with this explanation. In the first place, no experimental evidence exists to support the concept of conditioned inhibition that Wolpe borrowed from Hull.

Second, responses do not simply disappear because they are not made. In fact, the opposite is the case. Pavlov's definition of the extinction of a conditioned response explicitly requires that a response *be made* in the absence of the unconditioned stimulus in order for extinction to take place—the dog had to keep salivating to the tone and not receive any food. How, then, can a phobic response disappear simply because another response prevents it from being made?

Finally, a counterconditioning explanation of desensitization would require that systematic desensitization and Jones' direct conditioning satisfy two conditions: (1) the elimination of fear; and (2) its replacement by a new response that is under the control of the old, formerly aversive, stimulus. In effect, the child who was afraid of rabbits in Jones's study should show reduction of fear after conditioning as well as some of the signs associated with eating, and Wolpe's patients should relax when confronted by the aversive stimulus.

In reality, it has been very difficult to show that such responses do, in fact, occur. Although evidence suggests that fear-related responses are indeed eliminated by these procedures, nothing comparable to replacement by an alternative response, such as relaxation, occurs.

Searching for the Important Elements. While no one doubted the effectiveness of desensitization as a method for changing behavior, chronic skeptics among the behavioral scientists rejected Wolpe's explanation and began systematically to dismantle (the term proposed by Lang was "sequential dismantling") the desensitization process bit by bit, examining each of its components to determine whether the same results could be achieved with one or several of the presumed important elements missing. In order to accomplish this analogue, studies were employed using animals and college students for the most part.

Because of these studies, the elements of desensitization once thought to be essential have disappeared one by one until, as Yates (1975) pointed out, nothing remained but the well-known Cheshire smile. The only necessary element in the whole desensitization procedure, it turns out, is *exposure to the fear-arousing situation and escape prevention.*

Systematic exposure to a *graded hierarchy* of fear-arousing items was no longer considered important after a number of experimenters demonstrated that it really makes no difference how the items are presented to the subject—in random order or with the fearful event first, by tape recorder or in person—each method was equally effective as long as the person was exposed to the fear-arousing events (Krapfl, 1967).

What about *relaxation* and its role as an antagonistic response? Is it necessary for relaxation to occur during the presentation of the fearful stimuli? Apparently not, but it does serve a useful purpose in that it makes it easier to keep people—especially extremely fearful people—in the presence of the aversive stimuli. As Wilson and Davison (1971) have indicated, the use of relaxation and a graded series of hierarchy items acts to facilitate exposure and helps keep the client from bolting and leaving therapy.

Systematic desensitization, it appears, is not a good candidate for counterconditioning. What is a good explanation? Actually, as we shall see, a simpler explanation in the process of *classical extinction* not only solves the problems created by trying to interpret desensitization in terms of counterconditioning but also brings together two seemingly contradictory processes—desensitization, and flooding and implosive therapy.

ALTERNATIVE EXPLANATIONS FOR SYSTEMATIC DESENSITIZATION

The conclusions drawn from the systematic dismantling of desensitization did indeed erode the certainty with which most psychologists first interpreted desensitization as a counterconditioning process. Because of this, several alternative explanations have been proposed. The one which appears to have most support in terms of clinical and experimental evidence is *classical extinction.*

Extinction: An Alternative to Counterconditioning

The explanation of systematic desensitization as an extinction process developed out of three sources: studies of systematic dismantling, animal studies in avoidance learning, and the use of flooding and implosive therapy.

In the discussion of classical conditioning in Chapter 2, extinction—the elimination of a response—was shown to occur when the conditioned stimulus is presented in the absence of the unconditioned stimulus. When Pavlov withheld the food and continued to present the tone, the salivary response disappeared. But it did not disappear all at once. Trial after trial, the animal continued to salivate even though no food was forthcoming. Eventually, the animal stopped salivating. The important point here is that extinction would not have taken place unless the salivary response *continued to be elicited in the absence of food.* Apparently, responses will not disappear if they are not made. (This fact is central to the anxiety conservation hypothesis which is the theoretical basis for the extinction explanation of desensitization.)

But what is the equivalent of Pavlov's extinction procedure in fear conditioning and avoidance learning? If fear is a classically conditioned response established by pairing a neutral stimulus with some aversive event, then it should be possible to make the conditioned aversive stimulus lose its ability to evoke fear and fear-related behavior when the aversive event is removed. If shock is no longer given to the animal who has learned to turn a wheel to avoid it, the wheel-turning response should lose its significance and eventually disappear. But this does not happen rapidly. Animals extinguish avoidance responses very slowly, and humans suffering from phobias and other behavior disorders related to anxiety almost never recover by themselves. Something must be preventing the fear response—which is assumed to be the basis for the avoidance behavior—from being eliminated.

In the previous discussion of two-factor learning (Chapter 2), we saw that Solomon and Wynne proposed the *anxiety conservation hypothesis* to solve this dilemma. The hypothesis maintains that fear is prevented from occurring because animals make the avoidance response (after it is well learned) before they can be fearful, just as human phobics and obsessive-compulsives engage in avoidance or "setting things to right" before they become anxious. Under the circumstances, if fear is not evoked, it cannot be available to be extinguished.

Solomon and Wynne solved this problem experimentally by keeping the animals exposed to the fear-arousing conditions (a light which had formerly signaled shock) and preventing them from jumping over the barrier to escape the light. When this occurred the animals extinguished the jumping behavior very rapidly. In other words, fear was conserved and not available for extinction while the animals were vigorously engaged in avoidance responding.

Recall from Chapter 2 that additional experiments by Black (1958), Black, Carlson, and Solomon (1962) showed that avoidance responding could be decreased for dogs who were prevented from responding by drug injections and exposed to an aversive CS which had formerly elicited avoidance behavior. Presumably, fear was evoked by the CS during the drugged state and was weakened through lack of reinforcement. By the same token, there was an increase in avoidance responding for other animals when the CS was paired with more shock during the drugged state and fear was, ostensibly, increased.

Apparently, then, fear must be evoked in order to be eliminated. Although these conclusions are drawn from studies of avoidance learning in animals, for the most part, or from inferences about what happens to fear in clinical demonstrations, they were also supported by a precisely controlled experiment with humans involving physiological measurements of the fear reaction. Subjects who benefited from desensitization treatments also showed much higher heart rates during the period when the frightening scenes were presented, reported more fear when their heart rates were high, and exhibited a systematic reduction in heart rate after repeated presentations of the fear-arousing scenes. The subjects who did not improve, on the other hand, showed no such relationship between their verbal reports and the actual physiological responses (Lang et al., 1970).

Schroeder and Rich (1976) obtained similar results. In their experiment, those subjects who showed a higher basal heart rate during the course of desensitization to the fear of snakes also showed greater behavioral and attitudinal improvement than did subjects with lower baseline levels. Although heart rate was high initially during desensitization, it also began to decrease as treatment continued.

Now let us turn our attention to two methods for eliminating fear and fear-related responses through extinction.

Implosive Therapy: Facing the Fear Directly.   About the time that Wolpe published his book on reciprocal inhibition (1958) which introduced the method of desensitization, Thomas Stampfl began a series of clinical studies derived from animal avoidance learning experiments which, 10 years later, culminated in a learning-based technique for treating anxiety-related disorders known as *implosive therapy* (Stampfl & Levis, 1967; Levis & Hare, 1977).

Although, like desensitization, implosive therapy is based on the premise that fear is a learned response and can, therefore, be unlearned, the reduction of fear and the fear-related behavior is achieved by confronting the individual with the frightening event directly and in full strength without either relaxation or a graded hierarchy of fear items which have to be desensitized one by one. In fact, the major objective in implosive therapy is to generate as much fear as possible by requiring the subjects to imagine the most hideous scenes involving either the actual feared event (symptom-contingent cues, fear of heights or enclosed spaces, for example) or some personal-historical conflict experience (hypothesized cues) amplified by the therapist's active verbal contributions. The goal in this type of treatment is to force individuals to face their fears without retreating or hiding behind some defensive behavior which enables them to escape or reduce the anxiety. The following excerpt from an explanation of the procedure often provided to the client prior to the beginning of therapy aptly illustrates this goal.

> If you were learning to ride a horse and you fell off, what would your instructor do? [The usual answer given by the client is to get back on the horse.] Exactly. And, if you didn't, your fear would increase and generalize not only to the surrounding stimuli but may even back up to the entrance of the stable. By forcing yourself to be exposed to what you are afraid of, you can overcome your fears. . . (Levis, 1978, pp. 38–39).

The unique feature of implosive therapy, and one which distinguishes it from flooding, is the assumption that avoidance behavior is multiply determined, involving both internal and external conditioned avoidance cues.

External stimuli are *symptom-contingent cues.* They are the situational or environmental cues, such as the sight of a tall building, driving a car, or being confined to a small space. These are the actual phobic symptoms which Stampfl and Levis assume to have less of an anxiety loading.

Hypothesized sequential cues, on the other hand, are internal and consist of those experiences stored in memory which usually involve "the expression of hostility and aggression directed toward parental figures, retaliation for aggressive acts by the client with cues depicting various degrees of bodily injury, and those related to experiences of rejection, deprivation, abandonment, helplessness, guilt, shame, and sex" (Stampfl & Levis, 1967; Levis, 1978, p. 23–24).

Sometimes hypotheses can be reported by the client. More often, however, they represent inferences made by the therapist from the client's history or from material gathered during the interview. For example, if a claustrophobic client who has a fear of suffocation, helplessness, and dying a slow, agonizing death regards these as a form of punishment for transgressions, the therapists may "introduce logical figures (parents, God, siblings) to apply the punishment" during the course of therapy and also provide descriptions of wrongful acts which explain why the client is being punished (Levis, 1978, p. 29).

Apparently, Stampfl and Levis are not particularly concerned about whether the descriptions are accurate or relevant to the client's case on the grounds that the therapist can ultimately judge this by the client's reaction. The therapist assumes that if they are, a great deal of anxiety will be generated, indicating that the hypothesized cues are the correct ones to pursue. Quite often, however, the rehearsal of scenes in the imagination involving symptom-contingent cues during the early part of therapy results in the reactivation of memories as the case presentations in Box 5-2 illustrate.

BOX 5-2

A Fear of Body Odor

A 30-year-old depressed woman came to therapy because of an extreme fear of crowds. She imagined that she had an offensive body odor that people could detect. As a result, she had no close friends and avoided people at work and in social settings.

After a series of three or four therapy sessions spent gathering data and making the patient feel more at ease, the therapist began with some imagined scenes involving symptom-contingent cues. She was asked to close her eyes and imagine herself in a work situation requiring her to attend a lecture along with a large group of people. The therapist made the scene more vivid by suggesting that she was starting to sweat which made people get up and move to other seats. She knew they were talking about her and about how badly she smelled. Eventually, she was left sitting alone and rejected. The therapist repeated variations of this basic theme over and over again until the client's anxiety began to diminish. Following these sessions the client reported that although she was less concerned about such situations and was able to eat lunch with a group of her colleagues, she still worried that people could detect her body odor in spite of the fact that she maintained good body hygiene.

For the next few sessions the therapist decided to concentrate on the odor itself. The scenes remained essentially the same except that the client was asked to imagine that she could smell her own odor. During one of the scenes, she stated that she could actually smell the odor now and that it was somewhat like the smell of passed gas. At this point, a series of associations occurred which served to introduce material for the hypothesized cues. The client reported that she was not especially worried about the people sitting in front of her as she was about those sitting behind. Suddenly she recalled that at the age of 6, a girlfriend had whispered to her friends, behind her back, "that they shouldn't play with her because she was a bad girl and let the boys touch her." This memory was followed by others involving sexual play and molestation. On several occasions, older boys would take her into the alley and insert their fingers into her vagina. On another occasion, she was molested by an older man who reached under her dress. In the process, the elastic on her panties snapped, which frightened her into imagining that all the people seated behind her knew what was going on and would inform her parents.

The therapist continued to construct scenes in which sweating was substituted for sexual foreplay and in which she suffered the rejection of her parents who discovered her transgressions. In the final scene, she had confessed all her "sins" to God and was condemned to hell. The client visualized herself in the middle of a burning circle, surrounded by people who were pointing at her because they knew all the things she did not want them to know. These scenes were repeated over and over again to decrease the client's guilt and attendant anxiety.

In implosive therapy, each scene is repeated in a relentless and vivid fashion by the therapist until the anxiety produced by the scene is diminished. The client is permitted no escape from the scene precisely because the past escape has been used as a method to prevent fear from occurring and helped to maintain the avoidance response. This principle is dramatically illustrated in the following brief excerpt from a case reported by D. J. Levis (1978).

A 40-year-old man with a multiphobic reaction had been out of work for six months because he could not leave the house for fear of being contaminated by the dog feces in his yard. He showered frequently during the day, was afraid to open his mail believing it would be contaminated, and would not talk to his children when they returned from school until they had changed their clothes. He had even abandoned his car in a parking lot three months earlier because he feared that it was also contaminated.

A number of different versions of the scene reported below had already been presented to the client during the same therapy session, but this one demonstrates the intensity often reached in implosive therapy. The therapist has just asked the client to visualize himself trapped outside the house in the front yard which is filled with all sorts of animals:

> Therapist: Did you get the anus there? Now look at the fecal material starting to come out of that anus. All right. You're right below it. It's slowly coming out. Big stuff, dirty stuff. Those cows are dirty animals. It's coming out and it starts to drop it. You see it falling, falling down, down on your face. Over your face it falls. It almost disfigures your face. It is this dirty, gritty, slimy, yellowish, brownish, shimmering shit. All over your face and you say my God how can this happen? You put your hands up to your face and just push it. This cow feces goes in deeper in the pores of your skin, into your nose, into your mouth. You can feel the chocolaty, dirty, gritty taste of the fecal material. You're swallowing it. You're eating it. It's stuck in your ears, in your hair and it is so dirty, so slimy, you can feel your hair starting to fall off. It has an after-taste to it. It starts to eat away at your skin. See yourself there. You are in that shit. You're covered with it. You're being buried alive in it and there's nothing you can do. Nobody will help you. . . .

> (D. J. Levis. Implementing the technique of implosive therapy. Unpublished manuscript, State University of New York at Binghamton, 1978. Used by permission.)

Flooding.   Like implosive therapy, flooding is also a technique for exposing the person to fear-arousing cues without permitting any escape response to take place. *Unlike implosive therapy, however, no emphasis is placed on the psychodynamic aspects of behavior, no attempt is made to reactivate those memories which are presumed to be responsible for the development of the behavior in the first place, and some feel that the evocation of anxiety during the flooding session is not required for the extinction of avoidance behavior* (Marks, 1978). The evidence, however, as we have seen, tends more and more to support the idea that anxiety must be evoked during exposure in order for implosive therapy or flooding to be effective. The study conducted by Rachman, De Silva, and Roper (Chapter 2, Box 2-4), and the studies by Lang, Melamed, and Hart, and Schroeder and Rich (p. 107), for example, indicate that improvement is generally more effective when it is followed by high physiological responding during the desensitization session. A more recent study comparing flooding with and without drugs (Brevital) also showed that, for some agoraphobics at least, flooding was more effective without anxiety-reducing drugs (Chambless et al., 1979).

In essence, then, *flooding* is both desensitization and implosive therapy reduced to the bare essentials—*prolonged exposure to the fear-arousing cues and response prevention.*

Although much of the procedure in flooding involves the use of the imagination to recreate the fear-arousing conditions, a more frequent practice is to present the actual, real-life conditions which provoke the fear—a method known as *in vivo flooding*. While in vivo flooding may actually be more difficult to administer because it involves escorting the client to an appropriate setting or devising a laboratory-like procedure with real-life stimuli such as cats, dirt, or hypodermic syringes, for example, the advantages are frequently worth the trouble. For one thing, in vivo flooding is the only possible procedure for clients who have trouble imagining the frightening scene. For another, the reduction of fear to the actual feared situation makes it unnecessary to hope that a decrease in fear to the imagined event will also generalize to the actual situation.

In one of the early applications of flooding to several clinical cases, Baum and Poser (1971) describe the use of in vivo procedures with a 41-year-old woman who for 13 years experienced difficulty in handling objects because she believed them to be contaminated with "cancer germs." This obsessive belief began with the birth of her first child but was intensified when her father died of cancer. Among the objects in her home that she feared was raw meat, particularly pork. None of the routine procedures—psychotherapy, antidepressant and tranquilizing drugs, or electroconvulsive shock therapy—brought more than temporary relief, and by the time she was referred for behavior therapy, she was almost totally incapacitated. She washed her hands 20–30 times a day, could not prepare meals, expressed anxiety about her children's welfare, and was almost totally preoccupied with obsessions concerning meat, germs, bird droppings, and so on.

During the flooding procedure, the client was brought into a windowless room and asked to remove the cloth from some pork which lay on a table. She did this very hesitantly and immediately began to sob. The therapist then asked her to make meatballs, which she did with outstretched arms, taking care not to have the meat touch more than just her fingers. This prompted the therapist to pick up a meatball and throw it at her. She caught the meatball and threw it back with the remark, "I know, you hope that one of these will disintegrate and spatter all over me," which, in fact, did occur (p. 251). The client was then brought a dish of dirty water in which to wash her hands. After the flooding sessions, she was urged not to change her clothes for a week. All of these procedures took place while the client was in the hospital.

Eighteen months after the termination of treatment, she was managing her household and, although she reported some preoccupations with her former fears, these did not prevent her from functioning.

In an interesting application of flooding to a urinary problem, Lamontagne and Marks (1973) treated two clients who were unable to urinate outside of their own homes. The onset of the disorder in either case was unrelated to any physical or behavioral problem, although in the case of one client, a woman of 51, urinary inhibition occurred after the removal of an ovarian cyst. The second client, a male 31 years of age, was unable to urinate outside of the home or even at home in the presence of any other person including his wife. He regulated his fluid intake very carefully and rarely participated in social events for fear he might "burst his bladder." Oddly enough, the problem for both clients was confined only to urination and did not seem to affect defecation, sexual activity, or nudity.

Treatment consisted of exposing the clients to the distressing situation without permitting avoidance or escape. Each client was required to remain in a public toilet until urination was completed. Initially, this required 2 hours for the woman and ½ hour for the man. In the early treatment sessions, an appropriate therapist (male or female) remained a certain distance outside the toilet. In later sessions, the distance was decreased. Ultimately, the therapists waited outside the toilet while talking to another person—a situation which the clients found extremely stressful.

After a total of 8 sessions for the male client and 13 for the female, the inhibitory behavior decreased and a subsequent follow-up after 9 months disclosed that they were urinating in public toilets without any signs of distress. Interestingly enough, both still had some residual problems at their places of work—a setting which had not been involved in treatment.

A considerable number of laboratory studies and clinical case reports have documented the effectiveness of flooding, and they indicate that it is an exceedingly valuable addition to the methods for eliminating fear (Watson & Marks, 1971; Emmelkamp, 1974; Emmelkamp & Wessels, 1975; Emmelkamp & Kwee, 1977; Emmelkamp et al., 1978). Several large-scale clinical studies, conducted at the Institute of Psychiatry in London, England, since 1971 by Rachman and his associates with a variety of crippling obsessive-compulsive disorders, have made significant contributions to the understanding of the flooding process in terms of anxiety conservation. One of these studies, already reported in Chapter 2 (Box 2-4), demonstrates the increase and subsequent decrease in discomfort reported by clients during a flooding treatment session when they were prevented from engaging in their ritualistic behavior provoked by obsessive thoughts.

Although flooding and response-prevention procedures have proved useful with obsessive-compulsives, Foa (1979) has recently determined that some patients, namely those who are depressed in addition to their obsessive-compulsive behavior and those who hold strong convictions that their fears are real, do not show the typical decrease in subjective discomfort within a treatment session and from session to session. Instead, the depressed patient continues to have high subjective discomfort both within and between sessions, while the patients with strong convictions show a decrease during the session but return to a high discomfort level at the beginning of the next session.

The use of flooding in agoraphobia also provides an interesting and important comparison between two treatment techniques. As part of their re-analysis of agoraphobia, Goldstein and Chambless (1978) point out that while systematic desensitization has been an effective procedure with phobias in general, it has not worked as well in cases of agoraphobia. Flooding, on the other hand, has been a singularly successful treatment strategy (Emmelkamp et al., 1978). According to the authors, the most important aspect of agoraphobic responses is not the stimulus itself, i.e., fear of public places, but the "fear of fear" (Chapter 3, p. 63). Under the circumstances, arousal of anxiety is a particularly important aspect in the treatment of agoraphobia, and this is best accomplished by exposing the client in vivo to supermarkets and crowded places in general.

Duration of Exposure to the Fearful Stimulus.   All response-prevention procedures place a great deal of emphasis on continued, long durations of exposure to the frightening stimulus in order to ensure intense, emotional experiences which generate a great deal of anxiety. Apparently, this requirement is not a trivial one in view of the studies with animals and humans which show that short-duration exposures to the aversive cues will almost always result in a slower reduction of avoidance and, in some cases, even a paradoxical increase in avoidance responding.

The animal studies which have already been reviewed in the discussion in Chapter 2 dealing with the "anxiety conservation" hypothesis are all in agreement that the greater the duration of exposure to the aversive cues, the faster the extinction of avoidance responses. Short exposure invariably leads to a delay in the elimination of fear-related responses. Moreover, humans who are afraid of snakes exhibited much greater fear if they were exposed for only relatively short periods of time (Stone and Borkovec, 1974). Although optimal exposure time is difficult to determine, long periods of flooding and response prevention are more effective than short periods (Rabavilis et al., 1976; Gauthier and Marshall, 1977).

Flooding—Exposure or Response Prevention?   Several attempts have been made to determine which of the two components of the flooding procedure—exposure or response prevention—is the important factor in eliminating fear and avoidance responses, or whether both are necessary and inseparable. One of the earliest of these reported that, while exposure alone (systematic desensitization) resulted in a reduction of ritualistic behavior for patients with recent onset of the disorder, chronic cases also required the addition of response prevention for effective treatment (Walton and Mather, 1963).

A subsequent study by Mills et al. (1973) found that response prevention alone eliminated ritualistic behavior while exposure alone resulted in no change.

On the basis of these findings, Foa et al. (1980) advanced the hypothesis that "exposure affects anxiety more than does response prevention and that rituals are reduced more by response prevention . . ." (1980, p. 76), and they designed a study to explore the differential effectiveness of flooding and response prevention.

Flooding or response prevention was administered as an initial treatment procedure to two groups of obsessive-compulsive patients with a long history of washing rituals (mean 8.9 years). The four subjects who received exposure first were allowed to wash or clean as they wished following contact with contaminants, but they were further required to recontaminate themselves immediately after washing. Another group of four subjects who received response prevention first were exposed to the contaminants but not allowed to wash themselves, and only one supervised 10-minute shower was allowed every fifth day. Both groups were subsequently treated with exposure and response prevention combined.

The results confirmed the hypothesis. Those patients who received exposure alone initially showed greater reduction in fear (measured by subjective units of discomfort) than those who received response prevention. The response prevention group, on the other hand, showed greater reduction in washing rituals (measured in terms of mean washing time), and both groups continued to improve when a combination of exposure and response prevention was used.

Several explanations have been proposed for these results. Walton and Mather (1963) had previously suggested that ritualistic responses in obsessive-compulsive disorders of long duration acquire "functional autonomy" and are no longer completely dependent on fear to maintain them. While this interpretation does little more than beg the question, it does emphasize the need for some factor to account for dysynchrony in fear-related disorders and the relative absence of fear in well-established avoidance response observed in many experiments and clinical studies (Chapter 2, p. 38).

Foa et al. (1980) interpreted the term functional autonomy to mean that ritualistic behavior becomes associated with many other "second-order" stimuli in the environment in addition to the specific "first-order" stimuli consisting of aversive contaminants. These so-called second-order stimuli also serve to induce fear and provide the necessary reinforcement for the avoidance response. Accordingly, while exposure alone weakens the effect of contaminants, response prevention not only prolongs exposure, but further decreases the fear-arousing and reinforcing properties of the second-order stimuli, allowing other responses to occur. In effect, this view reduces to an explanation involving only exposure since, according to the authors, the main purpose of response prevention is to prolong exposure.

It is entirely conceivable that the answer to the differential effectiveness of exposure and response prevention may be found in two-factor theory and in the procedure used by Foa and her associates rather than in assumptions about second-order stimuli. For example, individuals given exposure first were also allowed to engage in washing rituals some time after being exposed to the contaminants even though they had to recontaminate themselves immediately after washing. Such a sequential arousal of fear during exposure, and reduction of fear after washing could, in principle, act to reinforce the ritual behavior. Something similar to this would probably have happened to Solomon and Wynne's dogs (Chapter 2, p. 34) if they had been prevented from jumping the barrier for a period of time and then permitted to make the avoidance response. While fear would undergo some extinction each time the delay was imposed, jumping would also be reinforced by fear reduction and decrease more slowly. This is precisely what was found for the exposure-alone group in the Foa study, and similar results have been shown in animal experiments. For example, if rats are given the opportunity to make an avoidance response sometime after being restrained, the response occurs with renewed strength (Franchina and Myers, 1976).

The results of the response-prevention group are a bit more difficult to explain, but again the answer may be contained in the procedure. Although the patients in this group were not intentionally exposed to contaminants, some were obviously encountered because, according to the authors, patients "were allowed to avoid contact with any contaminant and were permitted to use gloves or tissue to facilitate avoidance" (1980, p. 72). A relatively small amount of fear would be evoked under this arrangement, due to the use of gloves or tissue, and would, therefore, extinguish more slowly. The washing ritual, on the other hand, would receive no reinforcement and should, in principle, extinguish more rapidly.

Regardless of the explanation used to account for these results there seems to be little doubt that exposure is a necessary but not sufficient condition for effective flooding. If response prevention is not used as well, reinforcement for avoidance will inevitably follow.

A study which relates indirectly to the flooding, response-prevention issue was recently conducted by Greist et al. (1980). This experiment was designed to determine the effects of both avoidance and confrontation (exposure and response prevention) on fear-related behaviors.

The subjects, 23 phobics and 4 obsessive-compulsive ritualizers, were all assigned to both the avoidance and confrontation conditions in sequence. For some of the patients flooding was the first procedure used and confrontation the second; for others the conditions were reversed.

In the avoidance condition, subjects were instructed to keep away from phobic situations on the grounds that this would enable them to conquer their fears. The confrontation condition required the subject to remain in the presence of the fear-arousing stimuli and not yield to the urge to ritualize. All subjects kept diaries of their experiences.

Results were measured by means of five indices:
(1) *Target Problems*—comparisons of pre- and post-test behavior by the subject and an observer who was not aware of the subject's treatment condition, (2) *Fear Questionnaire*, (3) *Obsessive Checklist*, (4) *Depression Scale*, and (5) *Behavioral Avoidance Test* conducted by a "blind" observer. On virtually all of the assessment measures, confrontation led to greater improvement than avoidance, and on one phobic measure avoidance actually led to worsening of behavior.

The results of this study are consistent with the expectations from two-factor theory. Avoidance was less effective than the confrontation condition and, in some instances, actually strengthened the phobic responses. But how can we reconcile the reduction in washing rituals for the exposure-alone condition in the Foa study with the lack of improvement for the avoidance condition in the Greist experiment —especially since both conditions involved avoidance behavior? The answer to this discrepancy appears to be in the procedures used. In the Foa study, it will b' recalled, patients were required to recontaminate themselves after washing, a condition which kept them constantly in the presence of the contaminants. Patients in the Greist study, on the other hand, were permitted to avoid all phobic stimuli (no prolonged exposure).

Another interesting aspect of the Greist experiment was the test for expectancy effects. Although the patients were clearly led to believe that they would benefit from either avoidance or confrontation (confirmed by expectancy measures before and after treatment), only confrontation yielded positive results.

Practical Matters: How to Keep the Anxious Client in Treatment.   Flooding and implosive therapy are effective procedures if the client remains in treatment after the first frightening therapy session. Given the opportunity, some clients will not return to face the second harrowing experience, and many therapists are loathe to use either flooding or implosion for this reason.

Moreover, some studies also show that the effectiveness of response-prevention procedures can be severely limited if the client is too fearful to engage in the necessary behavior or even to visualize the act in imagination. In these cases, many therapists have found that prolonged exposure (in contrast to brief exposure which may actually retard the progress of treatment) to reduced levels of anxiety can be effective. This procedure not only elicits the necessary anxiety, but also enables the clients to experience some initial, small success in conquering their fears. Small doses of drugs have been successfully used for this purpose. Brevital, for example, was used in intravenous injections with one client who could not handle money for fear of being contaminated and had to wash all the money with which she came in contact. The drug enabled her to touch the money without eliminating the anxiety completely (Munjack, 1975). While Brevital succeeded in this case, recent evidence (Chambless et al., 1979) suggests that, at least in some cases, it may actually interfere with treatment because it reduces the amount of fear elicited during the flooding session. Apparently, the precise value of drugs during flooding still remains to be determined.

So, while exposure and response prevention appear to be the important elements in the elimination of fear and fear-related behavior, gradual exposure and encouragement by the therapist are very often necessary additions. This is especially evident in the methods devised by Masters and Johnson (1970) for treating sexual difficulties arising from the fear of sexual performance.

According to Masters and Johnson, the goal of treatment is to alleviate the anxiety of the client so that natural sexual functioning may occur. One of the primary ways of accomplishing this is through a process called *sensate focus* which enables the client who is having sexual difficulties (generally a male suffering from impotency or failure to maintain an erection) to experience pleasure merely by touching and exploring, without the necessity and urgency of having to carry the sexual act through to its completion. In fact, the couple is told specifically not to engage in sexual intercourse for several days during the course of treatment on the grounds that too rapid movement may reinstate the fear of failure which is presumed to be the basis for the sexual malfunction.

Gradually, touching is directed toward the genitals and continues until the male achieves an erection which, according to Masters and Johnson, should occur naturally if sensate focus is successful. This allows the male to experience sexual arousal without the demand for performance. When the male has finally achieved an erection and is able to hold it for an appreciable length of time, a "teasing" game is played in which the female alternates between stimulating the male by stroking the penis or by actual insertion and assuming a relatively non-sexual attitude until the erection is lost. Such a tactic is designed to restore confidence in the male by overcoming the fear of not being able to regain an erection after it has been lost. Eventually, the couple can engage in actual intercourse.

As a technique, sensate focus occurs in the context of other methods used by Masters and Johnson which includes discussions of sexual taboos and inhibitions. But virtually all treatment begins with sensate focus to reduce the fear associated with sexual performance. It is interesting to note that the methods used by Masters and Johnson appear to be consistent with the principles of classical extinction and counterconditioning. By the time that treatment is completed, the sexual cues formerly associated with fear (S1-R1 fear) now evoke the appropriate sexual response (S1-R2).

Desensitization, Flooding, and Battle Shock.   Now what about the puzzling differences in behavior between the two groups of soldiers suffering from combat fatigue and battle shock described at the beginning of this chapter? Does the discussion of desensitization and flooding provide some clue to explain the greater incidence of recovery among the men treated near the front lines compared to those transported far behind the lines? Does the anxiety-conservation hypothesis provide the basis for some reasonable speculations about these differences?

It is conceivable that the soldiers near the enemy lines remained fearful because they were still within the range of gunfire and all of the cues associated with battle, even though they were no longer directly involved in the fighting. Their escape from the battle was only partial. A sufficient amount of fear remained and was available as a response to be eliminated in the presence of the very cues which were responsible for it in the first place.

The soldiers who were transported 300 miles from the battle scene, on the other hand, were no longer exposed to the signs of battle. Their fear must have been reduced considerably, not only because they were no longer confronted with the signs of battle, but also because the distance from the front lines provided them with a powerful avoidance response—the illusion that they had escaped the carnage for good and would no longer be in danger of dying. Fear was no longer present as a response to be extinguished because the battle shock and removal from the front lines effectively reduced it. Under these conditions, attempts to remove the successful avoidance response by treatment would probably be resisted.

AFTERWORD

By this time it should have become obvious that behavior-change techniques derived from classical conditioning and extinction are used mainly when behavior is involuntary and under the control of a well-defined stimulus. It should also be obvious that none of the studies cited in this chapter demonstrates unequivocally that classical conditioning or classical extinction is responsible for the behavior changes that took place. Explanations, models, and theories are tentative. They endure only until they are replaced by a "better" explanation.

In psychology, as in any other science, legitimate results are often obtained for the wrong reasons. Wolpe's desensitization, for example, was conceived as counterconditioning, is presently being nurtured as classical extinction, and will probably undergo several other transformations before it reaches maturity.

Many psychologists involved in the study of behavior modification believe that the elimination of fear—especially in humans—is a far more complicated process than flooding or anxiety conservation can describe. According to them, getting rid of fear involves making decisions about how effective people think they will be in actually engaging in the prohibitive act that evokes fear. We discuss this point of view in Chapter 14. Nevertheless, until they are replaced by better explanations, the principles of classical conditioning and extinction seem to provide the best framework for generating and explaining the methods of behavior change described in this chapter.

chapter six

Operant Conditioning

Operant conditioning, like the lever, was used long before its principles were well understood. Medieval knights, for example, did not depend entirely on valor and their vows of chivalry to help them in their frequent encounters with the enemy. They also employed a mechanical drill instructor known as a *quintain* to perfect their skills with the lance as Figure 6-1 indicates. In its most elaborate form, the quintain was a figure of a swordsman, most probably a Saracen, mounted on a pivot with a flail, sword, or wooden bat in one hand and a shield in the other. The horseman tilting at the quintain had to strike it squarely in the center of the shield to make it fall. If the lance glanced off the shield or if the figure were stuck obliquely, it would pivot and deliver a sharp, painful blow to the horseman's back as he rode by (*The American Behavioral Scientist,* 1961). The quintain is probably one of the first recorded instances of the use of operant conditioning procedures for large-scale training purposes.

An extraordinarily large part of behavior modification methods consists of treatment strategies based on this second type of learning called "instrumental," or "operant," conditioning. The term *operant,* with respect to behavior, indicates that the response acts on or interacts with the environment in some way to change it. The responses of the knight in the illustration above, for example, determined whether or not a blow from the quintain could be avoided. In classical conditioning, by contrast, a dog salivates to the sound of a bell or its metabolism is increased in anticipation of a change in temperature, but neither of these responses changes the environment in any way. If the dog were permitted to press a lever to obtain food, the lever-

FIG. 6-1 Knights practicing tilting with the use of a *quintain*. The figure of the Saracen (lower left-hand corner) had to be struck squarely in the center of the shield; if not, it would pivot and strike the horseman painfully on the back with a flail as he rode by. This engraving appears in Paul Lacroix's *Military and Religious Life in the Middle Ages* (London: Chapman and Hall, 1874) and is a facsimile of a miniature in the 15th-century work *Chroniques de Charlemagne.*

pressing response would be characterized as an operant. Because the responses do not act on the environment, classical conditioning is often referred to as *respondent* learning.

PRINCIPLES AND METHODS

As early as 1898, Thorndike began a series of puzzle box experiments with cats which formed the cornerstone for his system of learning. He placed his hungry cats into a rough wooden crate built of slats. The door to the box was held shut by a catch which the cat could manipulate to gain freedom. When placed in the box, the cat first reacted with a kind of random behavior consisting of exploring and testing, more familiarly known as "curiosity." These trial-and-error movements eventually led to pulling the latch string accidentally and ultimately to escape and food. On repeated occasions, the unsuccessful random behavior began to disappear, and the cats required less time to work the mechanism which led to their freedom and food. Of course, this did not happen all at once, and the cats kept repeating the errors they had previously made until they learned the final escape response. The oscillatory nature of the behavior—useful or functional responses alternating with useless or non-functional responses—convinced Thorndike that most learning was fundamentally a trial-and-error process.

The principles basic to trial-and-error learning, also known as instrumental conditioning, or operant learning, were suggested to Thorndike by these experiments, and his first attempt to account for the learning that took place appeared in his formulation of the Law of Effect (1911). This law essentially elaborates the simple observation that behavior is affected by its consequences. Responses followed by rewards *(positive reinforcers)* are likely to be repeated, while those followed by aversive consequences *(negative reinforcers)* are likely to be altered or abandoned. The presentation of positive reinforcers acts to reinforce behavior. The withdrawal of negative reinforcers also reinforces behavior. Punishment, for example, is effective in suppressing behavior because the punishing stimulus is removed when the behavior stops. (A more detailed discussion of reinforcement is reserved for the section on reward-training procedures.)

In classical conditioning, the association is between the CS (tone) and the UCS (food), and the CR (salivation) is an incidental by-product of this association. In operant conditioning, on the other hand, the association is between the response and the subsequent reinforcement—the response being an integral part of the associative process because it is "instrumental" in obtaining the food. In Thorndike's view, the associations were made and strengthened by rewards and weakened by punishment. Although today we recognize the significance of punishment as a potentially powerful intervention technique, Thorndike prematurely abandoned what he called "the negative law of effect" because evidence from verbal-learning experiments showed that the word "wrong" or slight losses of money for making errors did not disrupt learning.

The introduction of instrumental learning meant that two types of learning were recognized. The first, classical conditioning, was regarded as *stimulus substitution;* that is, a new stimulus, the CS, gained control over behavior. The second, instrumental learning, or operant conditioning, was designated *response substitution* on the grounds that a response is selected from among several and strengthened by reinforcement during the course of learning. The existence of two types of learning is still a much debated issue among learning theorists, some of whom contend that the distinction is skin deep, reflecting differences in training methods only and not in fundamental processes.

Skinner (1935) agreed with Thorndike. He also acknowledged the existence of two types of learning, and like Thorndike, chose to emphasize operant rather than respondent learning as the process which is fundamental to all learning—especially in higher organisms.

In making the distinction between elicited (respondent) and emitted (operant) behavior, Skinner broke with the traditional S-R notion that every response must be tied inexorably to a known stimulus as it is in classical conditioning. For purposes of establishing behavioral principles, all that is necessary is some knowledge of the emitted behavior and the environmental factors which modify it. A knowledge of the stimulus condition is irrelevant for this purpose.

The distinction between emitted and elicited behavior has important implications for the practice of behavior modification. *In classical conditioning, the emphasis is on the stimulus which elicits the behavior. As we have already seen, in Chapters 4 and 5, in order to produce behavior changes in classical conditioning, some aspect of the stimulus-*

response relationship must be changed. In operant conditioning, responses are changed by rearranging the reinforcers (rewards and punishments) on which the behavior is contingent.

The main principle of operant conditioning states that the frequency of any spontaneously occurring response may be increased or decreased if it is followed by an appropriate stimulus. In this case, the stimulus has either rewarding or punishing properties.

Despite their basic differences, both classical and operant conditioning are governed by the same basic phenomena. In operant condtioning, behavior accelerates as the number of reinforced trials are increased (acquisition) and decelerates or extinguishes following non-reinforced trials (extinction). Generalization, discrimination, spontaneous recovery, and higher-order conditioning also occur under the appropriate training conditions.

REINFORCERS AND REINFORCEMENT

The subject of reinforcement is neither obvious nor simple, but its apparent simplicity can easily delude one. It has occupied the center of attention ever since Pavlov first used the term in classical conditioning, and it has been the sine qua non for virtually all learning theories since then.

A *reinforcer* is any stimulus which regularly and reliably elicits a response. Needless to say, reinforcers are exceedingly important elements in learning. Without them learning will not occur, and when they are removed, responses extinguish. But behavioral scientists have not always agreed on the precise function of a reinforcer. Some have felt that they strengthen the association between a cue and a response by reducing bodily needs. Others, like Guthrie, maintained that their function was secondary, their sole purpose being to ensure that the last response in a sequence—the "correct" one—is the response associated with the cues by removing the organism from the situation and preventing other responses from occurring.

Regardless of speculations about how reinforcers function to promote learning, the empirical definition of a reinforcer proposed by Skinner is probably the most defensible. In its simplest form, *a reinforcer is any event which follows a response and increases the probability that the response will be repeated.*

Fortunately, most experiences—eating desirable food, receiving money, making love, or eliciting praise—are pleasurable. These are referred to as *positive reinforcers,* and the process is known as *positive reinforcement.* Sometimes, however, a response may be successful in avoiding or escaping a painful stimulus. This event is also reinforcing because it ensures that the response which removed the noxious stimulus will occur under the same or similar conditions. Removal of an aversive or unpleasant stimulus is called *negative reinforcement.*

Primary and Secondary Reinforcers

Some things, such as food, water, and oxygen, that have intrinsic reinforcement value because they are necessary for the survival of the organism are called *primary*

reinforcers. Many behavioral scientists have proposed that this list of primary reinforcers be expanded to include other behavioral phenomena, such as contact
comfort (cuddling) in young children and social status, which may have no direct
effect on the survival of the organism but which produce behavior disorganization
when they are absent.

Most objects or events shown to be important sources of reinforcement for
humans cannot be classified as primary reinforcers if the definition is restricted to
absolute survival. Yet these sources of reinforcement, known as *conditioned or
secondary reinforcers* because they acquire their value as reinforcers through association with primary reinforcers, are every bit as important as primary reinforcers to
the learning process.

Money, for example, becomes an important source of secondary reinforcement because, although initially valueless as pieces of printed paper, it is associated
with every other important source of human gratification. This process of association is most clearly illustrated in higher-order conditioning (Chapter 2) where a
tone used as a conditioned stimulus in one phase of the experiment is employed
as an unconditioned stimulus, or reinforcer, to elicit the response in the second
phase with yet another conditioned stimulus (Figure 2-2).

Money and social praise are very important examples of secondary, or derived,
sources of reinforcement. This is especially true of money because it is a *generalized
conditioned reinforcer* capable of strengthening virtually any response. But money
also illustrates a significant characteristic of all secondary reinforcers—they lose
their reinforcing value if they are not occasionally paired with primary reinforcers.
The reinforcement value of money, for example, fluctuates during times of inflation or deflation.

One of the fascinating things about reinforcement in general and human
behavior in particular is that primary reinforcers and the survival value upon which
they are based may not always be the dominant incentives for behavior. Often the
distinction between primary and secondary reinforcers in terms of primacy
becomes blurred, and secondary reinforcers become even more powerful incentives. People have been known to commit suicide over unrequited love affairs or
because they have lost their money. In some instances, money, rather than the
things it can buy, becomes an end in itself, and people have been known to starve
to death in the midst of plenty.

Schedules of Reinforcement

People, like pigeons in a laboratory, work because there is a "payoff" for the type
and amount of work performed. But the manner in which a pigeon or a person
is paid off determines, in a very fundamental way, the type of work behavior that
is encouraged. The temporal and spatial arrangements of the response-reward
contingencies governing behavior are known as *schedules of reinforcement.* They
consist of two kinds: *time schedules,* known as *interval schedules,* and *work schedules,*
known as *ratio schedules.* Each of these schedules is further associated with either
a *fixed* or *variable* period.

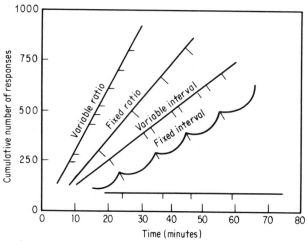

FIG. 6-2 Performance curves produced by the four representative schedules of reinforcement. The steeper the slope of the curve the faster the response. Each pause indicated by a small horizontal line signifies a period of reinforcement. (Source: B.F. Skinner. Teaching machines. *Scientific American,* 1961, 205, 90–102. Copyright 1961 by Scientific American Inc. All rights reserved. Used by permission.)

Each reinforcement schedule generates its own, unique curve of performance. The graph in Figure 6-2 illustrates this phenomenon. The ordinate of the graph reflects the cumulative number of responses—the number of responses for each time period added to the succeeding number for the next time period, and so on. If these units of behavior are measured against elapsed time, the slope of the performance curve varies with the particular schedule employed.

Ratio Schedules. On a ratio schedule, some specified number of responses must be emitted before a reinforcement is received. A person paid according to the amount of work performed and a pigeon required to peck at a key a number of times before receiving a few grains of corn as a reward are both on ratio schedules. Either a fixed or varying amount of work can be required before reinforcement is received.

Fixed-ratio schedules. Fixed-ratio schedules require a specified amount of work to be produced, and they generate very high rates of responding (Figure 6-2), largely because the faster the subject works and the more rapidly the given amount of work is completed, the more often reinforcement will be received. Employers characteristically prefer fixed-ratio schedules because they invariably produce more work for the money. In piece-work, for example, an employee is not paid until a fixed amount of work is completed. The employer can "speed-up" the assembly line, requiring larger amounts of work per unit of reward.

Variable-ratio schedules. These also produce high rates of responding, but unlike fixed-ratio schedules, the reinforcement is received after some variable amount of work which differs each time period is performed. Although the amount of work required generally centers around some average for a long time period, the schedule is much less predictable than that in a fixed-ratio schedule. Las Vegas gamblers playing "one-arm bandits" have been known to generate very high rates of responding (inserting coins and pulling the lever) when they are winning at unpredictable times (variable-ratio schedules), even when their losses are high and the slot machines fixed to pay off at an average rate for any given time period.

Interval Schedules. Unlike ratio schedules, interval schedules pay off after a *given amount of time* has elapsed, regardless of the amount of work performed. Also, unlike ratio schedules, the amount of work performed is not directly under the control of the reinforcer, and, presumably, the only thing rewarded is the passage of time itself. Obviously, workers prefer interval schedules because, as we shall see in fixed-interval schedules, reinforcement does not depend on the amount of work performed, and exploitation is less likely to occur.

Fixed-interval schedules. On fixed-interval schedules, reinforcement occurs after a given amount of time has passed, just like the weekly pay check. Although no work is required during this period, experimenters can generally fool pigeons into believing that some work must be performed, and these schedules do produce relatively high and stable curves of performance (Figure 6-2). But pigeons, like humans, are highly selective about the amount of work performed during these periods, and the "scalloped" performance curve is the result (Figure 6-2).

In such curves, the rate of work is very low immediately after a reward has been received, but it increases very rapidly as the time for another reward draws near. In effect, both the pigeon and the human "loaf along" until just before they are to receive a reward. Then they become very active, emitting a large number of responses in the time remaining. Individuals in factories and offices have been observed to display the same behavior as Friday approaches and it has also been reported that the U.S. Congress maintains a similar fixed-interval work schedule, passing a very few bills during the 3–4 months after a session begins and accelerating bill passage markedly as the time for adjournment draws near (Box 6-1).

BOX 6-1
Congress and the Pigeon

On September 28, 1957, the *Washington Evening Star* published part of an address to the District of Columbia Psychiatric Society by Joseph Brady, Professor of Psychology at Johns Hopkins University, in which he pointed out that the work habits of Congress closely resembled the behavior of pigeons on a fixed-interval schedule of reinforcement.

Fixed-interval schedules of reinforcement are like weekly paychecks. Payment is received merely for the passage of time, regardless of the amount of work performed during that period of time. The important characteristic of such schedules is that they produce the peculiar "scalloped" shaped curves of responding (Figure 6-2). Productivity tends to be low immediately after a reinforcement has been received and remains relatively low, increasing slowly with the passage of time. As the next period for reinforcement approaches, however, a precipitous spurt of activity occurs, reaching a maximum in the period immediately preceding the next reinforcement. The same behavior is repeated with each successive reinforcement.

Weisberg and Waldrop (1972) pursued Brady's trenchant observations of congressional work habits, studying the cumulative number of bills passed during the legislative sessions from January of 1947 to August of 1954 and again from January of 1961 to October of 1968 in detail. In each of these instances, the cumulative number of bills passed was relatively low during the early parts of the congressional sessions in January, February, March, and April, but it rose rather dramatically in the ensuing months as adjournment approached, reaching a peak some time in October when the Congresses adjourned. All Congresses appear to act in a similar fashion (Figs. 6-3 and 6-4).

What reinforcers does Congress respond to? Obviously, public acclaim for hard work or even the sheer joy of passing bills, as an activity in itself, are not potent rewards or else the number of bills passed would show a uniform rate of increase from Congress to Congress, a characteristic of ratio schedules which are sensitive to amount of work performed. Evidence does seem to suggest, however, that one of the major reinforcing elements in the work habits of Congress are the rest periods provided by adjournment (Weisberg & Waldrop, 1972).

Variable-interval schedules.   These produce stable performance curves. Here, the length of time before each reinforcement varies around some average. As in the case of fixed-interval schedules, high rates of responding are not rewarded so performance tends to be somewhat low.

Mixed Schedules of Reinforcement.   Although a number of variations known as mixed, multiple, and chained schedules of reinforcement can be derived from combining basic interval and ratio schedules, these are confined largely to animal studies and have not been used extensively with humans in behavior modification. But other variations, such as *differential reinforcement of high rates of responding* (DRH) and *differential reinforcement of low rates of responding* (DRL), have begun to appear in the methods used to deal with the behavior problems of school children.

Customarily, operant conditioning aims to increase the rate of response to a high level through reinforcement. On some occasions, however, it is desirable to hold responses at a given level—low or high. This can be achieved by using DRH or DRL schedules which impose additional restrictions on the time periods between responses. Thus, for example, reinforcement might be made contingent on waiting a specified period of time after a response is made before another is made. If this interval of time, known as the *inter-response-time* (IRT), is lengthened and

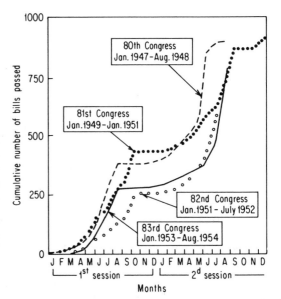

FIG. 6-3 Congress displaying the scalloped curve of fixed-interval responding. The curves depict the cumulative number of bills passed during the legislative sessions from January 1947 to August 1954 (Box 6-1). (Source: P. Weisberg and P. B. Waldrop. Fixed-interval work habits of Congress. *Journal of Applied Behavior Analysis.* 1972, 5, 93–97. Used by permission.)

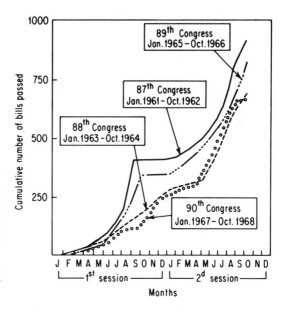

FIG. 6-4 Cumulative number of bills passed during the legislative sessions from January 1961 to October 1968 (Box 6-1). (Source: P. Weisberg and P. B. Waldrop. Fixed-interval work habits of Congress. *Journal of Applied Behavior Analysis,* 1972, 5, 93–97. Used by permission.)

reinforcement given only after long delays between responses, the result is to encourage low rates of responding. If, on the other hand, the interval is shortened, higher rates of responding will occur.

DRL schedules have been especially useful in those cases where a response is to be maintained at a specific level rather than eliminated entirely. In one such study, children in a classroom were reinforced for keeping the number of times they talked out at an acceptable level of 5 or fewer "talk-outs" during a 50-minute period. Using this procedure, the number of outbursts went down from 40 to 5 during the 50-minute period (Dietz & Repp, 1973).

Chains of Behavior.   Chaining is an important concept in operant conditioning because it is the way in which we assume complex behavior is acquired. According to Rachlin (1976), a chain of behavior consists of a series of stimuli and responses in which each stimulus serves as a reinforcer for the response which immediately precedes it and as a cue for the response which immediately follows it. An animal that sees its prey, tracks it, kills it, and eventually eats it, is performing a series of acts, each one of which is related to the other. Accurate tracking is a reinforcer for seeing and a cue for killing which, in turn, becomes a reinforcer for tracking and a cue for eating.

Frequently, we need to know the chains that link behavior in order to bring about behavior change. Punishing the first response in a chain is often more effective than punishing the last response because it disrupts the entire chain. For example, in the chronic ruminative vomiting case described in Chapter 1, shock was delivered when the first faint signs of reverse peristalsis were detected rather than when the vomiting was completed. In Chapter 8, we have occasion to see this technique used in the modification of seizures as well.

RESPONSE-REINFORCEMENT CONTINGENCIES

The connection between behavior and its consequences is known as a *response-reinforcement contingency.* Table 6-1 provides a summary of the operant training procedures and the response-reinforcement contingency specific to each training procedure. The summary in Table 6-1 is relatively simple to interpret. If the consequence of a response is reward (positive reinforcement), the effect is to strengthen or accelerate behavior. A response leading to the removal of a negative or noxious stimulus (negative reinforcement) also strengthens the behavior that is instrumental in avoiding or eliminating the noxious stimulus.

Using Response-Reinforcement Contingencies: Training Procedures

The nucleus of operant-training procedures in which response-reinforcement contingencies are employed can be summarized in three basic steps: 1. The behavior to be changed must be specified in concrete, observable terms. A *functional analysis* is usually conducted to determine how often and under what conditions the undesirable behavior occurs. Target behaviors for change are determined. 2. *Initial baseline measurements* of relevant behavior are recorded for subsequent comparison with later behavior changes. 3. Reinforcers are selected and response-reinforcement contingency schedules are established. The behavior is *"shaped"* by the use

TABLE 6-1 The Four Response-Reinforcement Contingencies and
the Effect on Behavior

Training situation	*Response-reinforcement contingency*	*Effect on behavior*
Reward	If correct response is made, positive reinforcement follows.	Strengthen the correct response.
Omission	If wrong or undesirable response is made, reinforcement is withheld.	Weaken the undesirable or incorrect response.
Punishment	If undesirable response is made, aversive stimulus follows.	Weaken the undesirable response.
Avoidance	If correct response is made, aversive stimulus is avoided.	Strengthen the correct response.

of *successive approximations,* and the reinforcement is applied in a consistent, immediate, and appropriate fashion. Changes in the behavior are recorded for comparison with baseline behavior obtained in 2.

Although these steps are sufficient to produce changes in behavior, some additional steps may be necessary to accomplish certain purposes. In most operant work, it is often desirable, but not always possible for practical reasons, to determine whether the reinforcement is the factor responsible for producing the change in behavior. Customarily, in most experiments using non-operant procedures, this determination is made by conducting a separate study with individuals who receive no reinforcement (a control group).

This procedure has several disadvantages. First, it is often not possible or practical to use a different group of subjects as a control. Secondly, the use of other individuals as controls may introduce new factors into the study—past history, physical condition, and type of behavior, for example—which are not present in the experimental group. A more desirable procedure is to use the subjects as their own "controls" by removing the reinforcement at one point during the experiment and observing the effect of its absence on the behavior. This is known as an ABAB design.

4. After the initial baseline behavior is observed and recorded (A) and behavior change obtained through reinforcement (B), *the reinforcement is simply discontinued for some specified period of time (A).* If the behavior returns to or near baseline during these operations, it could reasonably be concluded that the reinforcer is responsible for the behavior change. Following this determination, the reinforcement is reinstated (B). Figure 6-7 (p. 142) illustrates the use of the ABAB design in a study of operant training with two disruptive children.

5. In the final step, *both the reinforcer and reinforcement setting are changed* to ensure that the behavior acquired in one setting will generalize to others. Reinforcement usually shifts from material to social rewards, and the environment is changed from a laboratory, consulting room, or experimental classroom to a more natural setting. Under these conditions, the reinforcers are more like those found

in the home or at work, and the new behavior has an opportunity to become associated with familiar and prevailing cues.

The Functional Analysis of Behavior: Behavioral Assessment.   The primary purpose of behavioral assessment in behavior modification is to determine the conditions which maintain maladaptive behavior in order to devise strategies for changing the behavior.

The case studies in Boxes 6-2 and 6-3 illustrate and contrast the more traditional methods of psychological evaluation with the behavior assessment techniques currently being used in behavior modification.

BOX 6-2
The Traditional Approach to Assessment

Before the principles of learning were successfully applied to the modification of behavior, and specifically to problem behavior in the classroom, psychologists invariably made the assumption that a child's problems were due (1) to profound emotional disturbances which occurred in the past, (2) to contemporary conflicts within the family between the parents or between the parents and the child, or (3) to some combination of the two. They were also convinced that a detailed analysis of the child's physical, mental, and emotional development, in addition to a precise evaluation of the family relationships, would produce a rationale and a procedure for changing the child's behavior.

Very often, however, the recommendations for treatment, related as they were to unsubstantiated speculations about psychological factors, were themselves vague and generally not appropriate to the child's immediate behavioral problems. If the problems arose in part from some marital conflict, for example, the recommendations for intervention usually focused on the resolution of the conflict as a means of changing the child's behavior without recognizing that many of the factors responsible for maintaining the behavior were, by now, only remotely associated with the marital conflict. Little attention was given to the fact that the child's behavior had to be dealt with directly in order to change it, regardless of whatever other changes were orchestrated in the family itself, and that this required an analysis of the response-reinforcement contingencies in both the home and the classroom.

In many cases, psychologists, faced with the absence of any profound emotional difficulties following assessment on which they might focus as the basis for treatment recommendations, usually avoided the more obvious reasons for the problem behavior. Instead, speculations concerning the number of possible factors responsible for the behavior increased with the psychologist's degree of uncertainty. The following psychological report illustrates the confusion that the traditional assessment usually generated. The idea for the report was inspired by a similar report in a very helpful and informative booklet, *Managing Behavior,* by R. Vance Hall (1971). Although the report is hypothetical, many of the details are taken from an actual case history that appears in Box 6-3 to illustrate and contrast the more recent assessment procedures. Its real counterparts, however, are found in many public school files dealing with the behavior of problem children.

Jim was creating quite a problem at home and in the classroom with his constant scratching. The scratching resulted in large, unsightly sores and scabs covering his entire body, including his scalp, and these often became infected, requiring medical attention.

Jim's mother and father were very patient and understanding. They kept at him constantly, reminding him not to scratch whenever they saw him doing it. One of the several physicians they consulted advised them to keep him in long-sleeved shirts and pants and to keep his hands busy in order to distract him from scratching. To accomplish this, they bought hand grips and balls, and Jim's father even built a seesaw, a swingset, a treehouse, and a go-cart to keep him occupied. But none of these attempts succeeded.

The pediatrician who finally saw Jim found no physical reason for the scratching and recommended that he be seen by the school psychologist. The psychologist who interviewed Jim administered a series of standardized tests to determine his intelligence level, emotional stability, and neurological state. Then he wrote the following report:

Jim is a well-nourished 9-year-old boy of normal intelligence (Wechsler Bellevue Intelligence Scale for Children; IQ = 100) who was referred to the psychological center for severe and frequent scratching verging on self-mutilation. The scratching originated approximately 3 years ago when he had a severe case of poison oak and has persisted since that time without any apparent physical provocation. The sores created by constant scratching often become infected requiring medical attention.

Jim lives with his mother, father, and two siblings. His mother is divorced, but he gets along well with his stepfather who is a kind and generous person. His stepfather is seldom at home, however, due to business commitments. Jim's mother reports that he was a slow developer who did not have many friends and "stuck by her very closely." She is particularly concerned that the boy may have an "emotional problem" because he flinches whenever she or her husband approach him. While it is true that Jim's mother punished him in an attempt to eliminate the scratching, she does not feel that this may have contributed to his insecurities because he also flinches when his father approaches him. She feels confident that the difficulties Jim is having at present are related to his developmental history. Jim gets along reasonably well with his older brother and sister although there seems to be some slight rivalry for the mother's attention and affection. Both siblings have adopted a parental role with regard to Jim's behavior, constantly reminding him not to scratch.

The test results confirm many of the observations made during the interview with the mother. The Bender-Gestalt Test for neurological involvement reveals some slight deficit in motor coordination which may relate to Jim's slow development or to the head injury he sustained from a fall as a child which may have resulted in minimal brain damage. Both the Draw-A-Person and House-Tree-Person Tests show that Jim is a basically insecure and emotionally stunted child who does not relate to other children. The Blum-Blacky Test also shows dependency on the mother, fear of rejection, and competition with the sister and brother for his mother's attention.

These factors strongly suggest that Jim's scratching behavior is multiply determined and the following should be considered as possible causes and suggestions for intervention:

1. Jim's scratching may be the result of insecurities emanating from the divorce and a need to get his mother's attention and affection as reassurance that he will not be abandoned. Counseling should be directed toward helping Jim to gain insight into these feelings.

2. Since Jim's scratching represents an attempt to reassure himself of his father and mother's affection, every effort should be made by the parents to accept the scratching behavior and give him the attention he requires for greater security. The scratching should disappear when Jim feels more secure. Counseling should also be provided for both parents to increase their tolerance for the scratching behavior and to resolve whatever marital difficulties contribute to Jim's insecurities.

3. Both of Jim's siblings should also be seen by the counselor to resolve the problems of competition for the mother's attention.

4. Jim's teacher should continue to be sympathetic about his scratching in class and make whatever allowances are necessary for this behavior until it is eliminated.

5. The slight deficit in motor coordination should be investigated further because of the possibility of minimal brain damage.

It is not difficult to see that the psychologist writing this report is more concerned with the historical factors responsible for Jim's scratching than with the actual behavior itself, and being a psychologist, assumes that the scratching behavior relates to a profound emotional disturbance involving the parents, a genetic-constitutional factor, a physical trauma (the accidental fall and slow development), or the interaction of all three. The assumption is also made that Jim's scratching will continue until these historical factors and Jim's "feelings" about them are explored and clarified. The possibility that Jim's scratching, which began with the poison oak infection, is sustained by the attention he continues to receive from his parents as well as his brother and sister (the manipulative quality of Jim's behavior should not go unrecognized here) has largely been ignored. Box 6-3 presents an actual account of the way this same case was evaluated by a psychologist trained in the use of functional analysis for purposes of behavioral assessment.

BOX 6-3
Behavioral Evaluation Through Functional
Analysis: Another Approach to Assessment

A psychologist trained in the use of functional analysis would proceed to collect approximately the same information regarding Jim's developmental history as the psychologist described in Box 6-3, if only to rule out the possibility that Jim's behavior may be related to physical difficulties. If there were any doubts on this point, further neurological tests would be recommended.

In most instances, however, the problem behavior is usually the result of child-parent interactions and sustained by the very attempts that the parents make to get rid of it. In Jim's case, the psychologist made several important assumptions from the material collected during the interviews:

1. The scratching probably began in response to the poison oak infection.
2. The family was inordinately concerned with Jim's scratching.
3. Scratching was directly related to the amount of attention Jim received from his family and their attempts to deal with it which involved buying items to distract his attention or building the swingset, treehouse, and seesaw. These were important sources of reinforcement which contributed to Jim's scratching and acted to support the behavior.

After two interviews with Jim and his mother, the psychologist arranged to observe the family at home during the evening in order to obtain a sample of Jim's behavioral interaction with his family. The events recorded in Figure 6-5 were observed by the psychologist during the several sessions when the family was visited. The upper half of Figure 6-5 shows the number of times scratching occurred during a 1-hour period. The lower half indicates the number of times some member of the family responded to Jim's scratching by telling him to stop. Figure 6-5 clearly shows that Jim's scratching related directly to the amount of attention he received. When he was preoccupied as in the "play" or "talk" sequences (Fig. 6-5), relatively little scratching occurred. When he was watching television, however, the amount of scratching and the attention he received for it increased dramatically.

Figure 6-6 also demonstrates the relationship between scratching and attention. In this instance, however, the family was instructed, first to behave as usual when Jim scratched and an operant baseline was obtained (Panel A), then to tell him to stop scratching when they saw him (Panel B), and, finally, to ignore the scratching completely (Panel C).

The intervention, or treatment, techniques were based on these observations. The family was instructed in the relationship between behavior and reinforcement and told to ignore the scratching completely. Jim was to be reinforced with attention and affection only when he was not scratching, and he was to be reminded of this during the time that the reinforcement was given. Jim was able to select from among a list of reinforcers consisting of activities he liked whenever an examination of his body revealed a reduction in the amount of sores. Using these methods, the number of sores from scratching was reduced from 20 to 5 in a period of 2 months.

In this particular case, the psychologist found no deficit in the amount of affection Jim received from his parents. It should be noted, however, that even if such a deficit were observed, the intervention techniques would be substantially the same—to increase the amount of attention and affection and to make these contingent on behavior other than scratching. If parental difficulties caused any lack of affection, efforts would also be made to resolve these problems at the same time. (Case report reproduced through the courtesy of Jack MacDowell.)

Behavioral assessments, as we have already indicated, are conducted primarily for the purpose of gathering information for use in devising ways of changing behavior. There are essentially two ways to do this. The first involves *direct observation* of behavior. The case reported in Box 6-3 and the steps involved are examples of this type of behavioral assessment. The central features of direct observation are as follows:

1. *Systematic observation of the problem behavior* (and other behaviors as well) to obtain a response frequency baseline (Fig. 6-6, panel A; Box 6-3). In the case of the child with extreme scratching behavior, this was done by counting the number of scabs produced by scratching and by actually observing scratching in the home. In this instance, the parents were also enlisted and trained as observers.

2. *Systematic observation of the stimulus conditions* following and/or preceding the behavior with special concern for *discriminative cues* (circumstances which seem to produce more scratching) and *consequent reinforcers* (the results of scratching on the surrounding environment). In the present case, the child was observed to scratch more while watching television with his parents and sibs. They, in turn, acted as

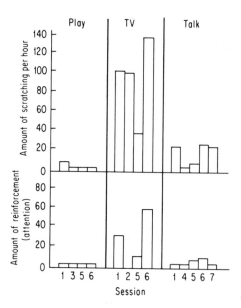

FIG. 6-5 Stimulus control of scratching. Activities during which scratching and the attention received for it occurred. Upper half shows amount of scratching per hour. Lower half shows the amount of attention (reinforcement) during that session. Reinforcement frequency was not recorded during Session 2 (Box 6-3). (Reproduced by courtesy of Jack MacDowell.)

reinforcers by constantly reminding him not to scratch and by being overly solicitous about his sores (Fig. 6-6, panel B, Box 6-3).

3. *Experimental manipulation* of the condition which seems to be functionally related to the problem behavior. In some cases, this might consist of the intervention techniques that will ultimately be used as treatment. In this instance, the parents were told to ignore the scratching, and this resulted in a dramatic decrease in the behavior (Fig. 6-6, panel C, Box 6-3). The child also got rewards both from the therapist and the parents for any visible reduction in the number of sores.

4. In certain instances, although it is not a general rule, the *sources of reinforcement are removed* to see if the behavior returns, as in the ABAB design. When this was done with the child described in Box 6-3, the scratching behavior returned to its pretreatment level.

Although direct observation of behavior is difficult to conduct, involving as it does careful observation under semi-controlled conditions, it is becoming more prevalent, especially in the behavior problems of children where the interaction of the parents and the child cannot be easily verbalized by either and some sample of this interaction must be obtained by observation.

The second method for gathering information to assist in psychological intervention is through interviews. Briefly, four general areas determine the nature of the questions to be asked during the interview. These are:

1. *Definition of the problem behavior.* What is it the person can't do or can't stop doing?

2. *Severity of the problem.* How often does the behavior occur? This is the equivalent of baseline performance, and it is necessary as a point against which to compare any subsequent changes.

FIG. 6-6 Reinforcement control of scratching behavior. The entire session was conducted in the child's home while the family was engaged in normal conversation. The solid lines represent frequency of scratching, the dashed lines the number of instances in which the family asked the child not to scratch. In Panel B, the family was instructed to tell the child to stop scratching when they observed him; in Panel C they were told to ignore the scratching. Note the "extinction burst" in Panel C (see discussion of omission training p. 153). (Reproduced by courtesy of Jack MacDowell.)

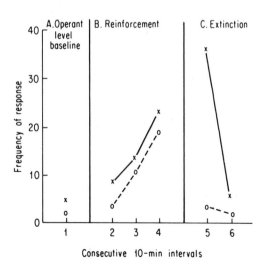

3. *Generality of the problem.* Does it occur everywhere or is it localized to specific situations? Is it pervasive enough to interfere with the person's functioning?

4. *Determinants of the problem behavior.*
     a. What conditions intensify the behavior?
     b. What conditions alleviate the behavior?

In some instances, both interviewing and direct observation procedures are used.

Let us now turn our attention to the use of response-reinforcement contingencies.

Reward Training

There is an old custom in the Jewish tradition that when a child is first introduced to the Torah, the book of laws contained in the Pentateuch, a drop of honey is placed on the page, and the child is required to lick the honey before learning begins. The implications here are obvious, and they suggest that even the ancients were well aware of the importance of rewards in learning.

Reward training is probably one of the most prevalent and successful ways of modifying behavior. However, the methods of rewarding behavior to alter it, and indeed all operant methods, can be deceptively simple and doomed to failure if insufficient attention is given to details such as identifying the type and frequency of the behavior to be changed, analyzing the events which maintain it, and using precision in applying the methods to change it. When, what type, and how much reward should be given are not trivial decisions, and each has genuine consequences for the modification of behavior, as the study in Box 6-4 demonstrates.

BOX 6-4
How Much Reinforcement To Give

On most occasions, the simple rule that the frequency of behavior is increased through positive reinforcement will work. But there are instances in which the amount of reinforcement and the context in which it is given are important factors in determining the outcome of the training procedures.

It never occurred to the psychologists who were conducting a study of children with destructive and disruptive behavior problems that the "density" of reinforcement could conceivably be responsible for the initial failure to change their behavior, but this turned out to be the case. The first observations of the interactions between these children and their mothers showed that the children were receiving constant attention from their mothers for misbehaving, but very little for being good.

As an intervention procedure, the mothers were instructed to pay attention only to the desirable behaviors to be strengthened and to ignore the destructive

---

behavior. Because this method is usually effective in producing behavior change, the researchers were particularly surprised when the destructive behavior escalated and the desirable behavior decreased.

An examination of the behavior of the mothers revealed the reason for these unexpected results. While it was true that desirable behavior was being rewarded and destructive behavior ignored, it was also true that the *total amount of attention the children were receiving dropped almost 25–50% from that which they had formerly been getting merely for being disruptive.* The children simply reverted to a response that had "paid off" more. Obviously, how much reinforcement to give depends, in large measure, on how much had been given to the undesirable response, and a good rule to follow is not to let the level of reinforcement for the new response fall below that of the level of reinforcement for the old response (Herbert et al., 1973).

Parents with newborn children sometimes ignore this rule with their older children, and very frequently the result is a regression to infantile behavior—crawling, bedwetting, temper tantrums, and baby talk—which formerly produced a great deal of attention.

The similarity between the procedures used to train animals in the laboratory and those used in behavior modification is particularly striking in operant learning. In view of this, it would be instructive to examine reward-training procedures by comparing, in a stepwise fashion, the methods used to train a pigeon to peck at a lighted disc with those used to modify the behavior of disruptive children. These procedures are outlined in Table 6-2 and discussed in the ensuing sections.

Training the Pigeon.   Something equivalent to a functional analysis is conducted when the experimenter decides to modify the pigeon's pecking response and proceeds to arrange the situation accordingly.

Steps are taken to confine the animal to a reasonably restricted environment in order to reduce distractibility and limit the range of responses the animal is likely to emit. Grain is selected as a relevant and desirable reward, and training begins by adapting the animal to the noises and strange cues associated with the feeding chamber.

When this is completed, *shaping* is begun using the process of *successive approximations.* This procedure is essentially one in which small units of behavior which approximate the goal response of pecking to the light—turning toward the light, approaching the light and food tray, tentative pecking responses, and so forth—are rewarded.

If the animal is having difficulty learning the response, a *time-out from reinforcement* procedure may be introduced which effectively removes the animal from the locus of reinforcement for some prescribed period. In the case of the pigeon, this may be accomplished by turning off all the lights in the box for 1 minute immediately following a wrong response. Pigeons seem to dislike being in the dark, and

TABLE 6-2 A Comparison of the Operant Procedures Used to Train a Pigeon and a Child

Procedure	Pigeon	Child
1. *Behavior specified; functional analysis*		
a. Assessment of undesirable behavior.	a. Any behavior which interferes with pecking.	a. Temper tantrums, failure to follow parental instructions, impulsiveness, disruptive, uncooperative play.
b. Selection of target behavior.	b. Pecking at disc.	b. Cooperative play behavior (decrease in deviant behavior).
2. *Baseline determinations*		
c. Observing and recording of behavior in the absence of reinforcement.	c. Frequency of disc pecking = 0.	c. Percentage of cooperative behavior = $\dfrac{\textit{cooperative behavior}}{\text{cooperative} + \text{deviant behavior}}$
d. Behavior change setting established.	d. Skinner box.	d. Basement playroom.
3. *Reinforcers and response-reinforcement schedule*		
e. Selection of reinforcer.	e. Grain.	e. Candy, toys, verbal praise = good.
f. Shaping by successive approximations.	f. Small movements toward colored disc rewarded.	f. Cooperative behavior in play. Verbal responses "please" and "thank you" rewarded.
g. Change of schedule from continuous reinforcement (FR1) to variable ratio reinforcement (VR).	g. Bird must peck on the average of 5 times before being rewarded.	g. Every second or fourth response rewarded.

h. Introduction of secondary reinforcers (token reinforcers).	h. Visual or auditory stimulus in place of food.	h. Checks on blackboard to be exchanged for candy or toys.
i. Increase in VR schedule for secondary reinforcers.	i. Increase in average number of pecks required.	i. Increase in number of checks required.
j. Introduction of new stimulus to acquire secondary reinforcing properties.	j. Any stimulus paired with reinforcement.	j. Mother distributes checks and reinforcement (session 30–50, Fig. 6-7).
4. *Test to determine importance of reinforcer*		
k. Reinforcement discontinued.	k. Decrease in number of key pecks.	k. Decrease in cooperative behavior—return to level slightly above baseline (session 20–30, Fig. 6-7).
l. Reinforcement reinstated.	l. Increase in pecking.	l. Increase in cooperative behavior.
5. *Response maintenance procedures introduced to increase generalization*		
m. Change of reinforcer and reinforcement setting.	m. No practical value.	m. Mother continues to reinforce with social reinforcement plus attention by parents for desirable behavior outside the playroom.

SOURCE: O'Leary, K., O'Leary, S.. Becker, W. C., 1967. Their work involved only the training of a child.

they become almost totally inactive. Used correctly, a time-out procedure can markedly increase the rate of learning because it introduces a change in the stimulus conditions when an incorrect response is made by the pigeon, and this assists rapid discrimination.

At first, the animal gets *continuous reinforcement*—every correct response is rewarded—until pecking at the disc is firmly established. A continuous-reinforcement schedule (CRF) is actually a fixed-ratio (FR 1) schedule in which a reinforcer is received for every single appropriate response made. But CRF schedules are not desirable. They produce low rates of responding because the pigeon pauses immediately after each response to get the reinforcer. Also, the response rate is very labile under these schedules, and it will disappear very rapidly if the reinforcer is withheld for any appreciable length of time. To prevent this from happening, some variation of an intermittent schedule of reinforcement is introduced, and rewards are given on an interval or ratio basis.

In the present case, a *variable-ratio schedule* may be introduced in which some multiple of responding is rewarded, say, every fifth, eighth, or tenth response. This has the effect of increasing both the rate of responding and resistance to extinction so that responses are likely to be maintained for longer periods of time when no longer rewarded continuously.

Often, it is desirable to change the nature of the reward by substituting *secondary reinforcers* in place of food, which, as we already know, is a *primary reinforcer.* For the pigeon, any stimulus, such as the noise created by the opening of the food dispenser, may serve as a secondary reinforcer because it has been paired with food. For that matter, any conditioned stimulus or discriminative stimulus is also essentially a secondary reinforcer because it ultimately acts as the food itself in producing a response. Once secondary reinforcers have been introduced, the rate or schedule of reinforcement can be altered for these rewards, but in animals it is often necessary to continue to pair a primary reinforcer with a secondary reinforcer to prevent the secondary reinforcer from losing its value, just as money would if it could no longer purchase food.

In certain situations, it may be desirable to bring the pecking response under *discriminative stimulus control.* This can be accomplished by introducing any stimulus just prior to the beginning of the period during which the pigeon begins pecking at the disc. When this is done, the pigeon will invariably refrain from responding unless the stimulus is present. Under such circumstances, the behavior becomes a *discriminated operant,* as opposed to a *free operant,* and it is under the control of a discriminative stimulus.

A discriminative stimulus bears a certain resemblance to the conditioned stimulus in classical conditioning. Both appear to control behavior, but here the similarity ends. A conditioned stimulus elicits a response in an unremitting fashion. The dog faced with the tone in Pavlov's experiments, for example, can do nothing else but salivate, primarily because the response is a reflex over which the animal has no control. This gives the conditioned stimulus the character of a "goad," something which forces the organism to respond (Skinner, 1969).

The same tone, on the other hand, presented shortly before the pigeon pecks the key to obtain food, takes on a somewhat different meaning. It acts as a cue to the pigeon, indicating that if a response is made while the tone is present, food will probably be forthcoming. The tone, according to Skinner, "sets the occasion upon which the response is likely to occur. . . . It increases the probability of the occurrence of behavior, but does not force it" (1969, p. 175). The pigeon may or may not respond while the tone is present. This is what distinguishes a discriminative stimulus from a conditioned stimulus. Discriminative stimuli do not elicit behavior—they merely increase the probability that the behavior will occur. *A discriminative stimulus that is followed by reward is known as an Sd. One associated with the absence of reward is called an S delta.*

Training the Child. Procedures identical to those used to train the pigeon above were employed by O'Leary, O'Leary, and Becker (1967) to modify the behavior of a 6-year-old boy, Barry, and his 3-year-old brother, Jeff, who frequently engaged in assaultive and destructive behavior. One of the unusual aspects of this study was that the treatment was conducted in the playroom of the children's home because the home environment, including the presence of the parents, was felt to be important in continuing and maintaining the desirable behavior after training.

Although two brothers were involved, Barry, the older 6-year-old, provoked most of the difficulty. He fought with Jeff when they were alone, damaged toys and furniture, threw rocks through a neighbor's window, and roamed away from home. He had been under psychiatric treatment for 2 years, and his psychiatrists described him as "seriously disturbed," an "immature, brain-damaged child with a super-imposed neurosis, although the nature and cause of the brain damage could not be specified" (p. 114).

A functional analysis of Barry's behavior revealed a pattern of temper tantrums, failure to follow instructions, and impulsiveness, all reinforced by the attention both children received from their parents when the behavior occurred. The experimenters then confined both boys to the family playroom to reduce distractibility by limiting the environment and to make it easier to administer the rewards rapidly. A decision was made to reward cooperative play behavior, such as asking for a toy, requesting each other's help, conversation, and playing within 3 feet of each other, and a *baseline of cooperative behavior* was established during the first 10 sessions (Base I, Fig. 6-7).

During the first 2 days of treatment, the slightest sign of cooperative behavior between the brothers was rewarded by the observer who put an M&M candy into the mouth of each child and said "Good." On the third day, the experimenter alternately reinforced every second and fourth cooperative response, and on subsequent days, the boys were instructed that they would receive a reward for saying "please" and "thank you." *A token, or secondary reinforcement system,* was introduced on the fifth day, consisting of checks on the blackboard in addition to M&M candies for desirable behavior. Ultimately, the M&Ms were discontinued and checks made exchangeable for toys, candy, and so forth.

During this period, the amount of cooperative behavior rose from a baseline

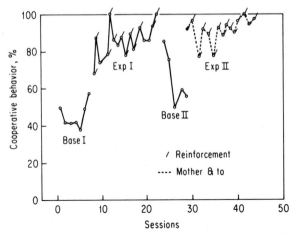

FIG. 6-7 Cumulative response curves for Barry and Jeff. The sessions are divided into four periods. Baseline I (no reinforcement), Exp. I (reinforcement introduced), Baseline II (reinforcement withdrawn), and Exp. II (reinforcement reinstated). During Exp. II the mother distributed the reinforcers and time-out was introduced. The measure plotted on the graph is percentage of cooperative behavior divided by percentage of deviant and cooperative behavior. (Source: K. D. O'Leary, S. O'Leary, and W. C. Becker. Modification of a deviant sibling interaction in the home. *Behaviour Research and Therapy,* 1967, 5, 113–120. Copyright 1967 by Pergamon Press and used by permission).

of 46% to 85% after 25 sessions of 30 minutes each day. A simultaneous decline in deviant behavior also occurred (Exp. I, Fig. 6-7).

During the Base II period (Fig. 6-7), all rewards were discontinued, as in the ABAB design, in order to verify that the reinforcers were responsible for producing the behavior change, and the children were used as their own controls. As a result, cooperative play declined gradually to a value slightly above the original baseline. In the second experimental session (Exp. II, Fig. 6-7), the rewards were reinstated, but the mother was now instructed to run the token reward system in order to ensure that the behavior would endure and have greater generality.

During this period, a *time-out from reinforcement* procedure was also introduced in order to decrease further the amount of yelling and screaming that occasionally occurred. In the time-out procedure, one or the other of the children was confined to the bathroom for a period of 5 minutes when either child became disruptive. The bathroom had been emptied of any objects that would provide amusement. An additional contingency was imposed by requiring a period of 3 minutes of silence before a boy could be released. This ensured that the termination of the time-out would act as *negative reinforcement*—a stimulus that strengthens behavior when it is removed. In this instance, being quiet at the mother's request was the behavior reinforced by release from the bathroom (termination of an undesirable event).

The entire study lasted for a period of 43 sessions during which time the experimenters gradually turned over the reinforcement role to the mother, which she continued during their absence. At the completion of the study, the amount of cooperative behavior increased to 98% with a marked reduction in the frequency of hitting, pushing, kicking, name-calling, and object throwing (Fig. 6-7).

The children's mother continued to reinforce and punish a much wider variety of behavior throughout the normal course of the day. Both parents were advised to give the children a great deal of praise and reward when they were behaving appropriately and to stop spanking Barry. Occasionally, time-out procedures were used to eliminate recurrences of undesirable behavior, but Barry now received consistent rewards for small tasks. His behavior improved considerably as a result of the treatment. Although he occasionally had outbursts of hitting and kicking at school, these incidents decreased markedly. Barry also now asked for things and played well with the neighbors' children.

The similarities in procedure for both the pigeon and the child are apparent, and they emphasize that both the language and the methods of the operant laboratory are readily applicable to the modification of human behavior. The study with the children also demonstrates that some clinical intervention procedures can be conducted with as much rigor as experimental studies employ.

A Further Word on Reinforcement. Those who oppose their use in learning have sometimes called reinforcers bribes. Whether or not a reinforcer is a bribe depends, of course, on the nature of the response being learned. Bribes are usually associated with illicit behavior, which, we can all agree, is hardly the case when a child is being reinforced for learning how to read, for throwing a football, for refraining from self-mutilation, or for any of the countless behaviors that are useful and necessary for daily existence.

But those who advance the argument that operant learning is bribery probably have something else in mind. They are concerned that when a child learns to work for material reinforcers—chocolate-covered candies, money, or toys, for example —he or she will continue to require these kinds of incentives in order to do the things ordinarily expected from everyone.

This criticism has a kind of legitimacy, even though the people who make it lose sight of the fact that their interest in their own jobs depends heavily upon the weekly pay checks they receive. They continue to maintain, nevertheless, that children should do their schoolwork without being bribed because schoolwork must become "intrinsically" rewarding.

It is true that rudimentary material reinforcers, such as candy and toys, cannot continue to serve as learning incentives for long—not because they are not powerful incentives, but because they must ultimately be replaced by other, more natural reinforcers, such as social praise, which are more consistent with rewards found in the "real" world.

Although reinforcers fall into several classes—*material, social,* and *activity*—it takes resourcefulness and planning to avoid using material reinforcers exclusively. The temptation to use candy, money, or toys is great because they are easiest to select, pleasing to most children, and simple to administer. Although they are very important in the initial stages of learning, other, more natural and more durable reinforcers must ultimately be found to replace them.

Some researchers have combined the idea of a "reinforcement menu" (having the child select the reinforcer from a list of desirable things) with some recent findings from animal studies showing that the opportunity to engage in a specific activity is reinforcing. This expands the range of useful natural reinforcers further (Box 6-5). The discussion in Chapter 8 on the use of operant learning in behavior modification deals in more detail with the methods used to replace basic reinforcers with secondary or derived reinforcers.

BOX 6-5
Activity, the Premack Principle and the
Reinforcement Menu

Food and water are not the only things that will stimulate a white rat to learn to press a lever, turn a wheel, or thread its way through a maze. Although these are powerful incentives to performance, David Premack, a psychologist, has discovered that the opportunity to engage in one kind of activity will also act as a reinforcer to encourage the learning of another activity (Premack, 1965). This general rule holds true under certain conditions. The activity to be learned or strengthened (the instrumental response) must be lower in strength than the activity to be used as a reinforcer (the contingent response). The contingent activity must also be performed soon after the instrumental activity, and the animal's ability to perform the contingent activity must be restricted to some degree, i.e., the rat must be deprived of access to the contingent activity in much the same way that an animal is made hungry or thirsty to get it to learn (Timberlake & Allison, 1974). For example, a white rat can be made to increase the frequency of a licking response if licking is followed by wheel turning after the opportunity to turn a wheel has been restricted. In effect, the rat will lick (instrumental response) a larger number of times in order to get to turn the wheel (contingent response). The licking response will be strengthened primarily because it provides access to the wheel-turning activity which, in turn, acts as a reinforcer. This means that behavior itself can be used as a source of reinforcement.

Homme and his associates (Homme et al., 1963) used Premack's expanded notion of reinforcement to modify the behavior of 3-year-old nursery children. The task was to get these children, who loved to scream, push chairs, run around the room, and talk noisily, to sit quietly and attend to the teacher for considerably long periods of time. The teacher had very little control over the children initially, and the children paid very little attention to the teacher's requests to remain seated.

At the outset, Homme et al. decided to make running, screaming, and so on, contingent on the children doing a small amount—a very small amount at first—

of what the experimenters ultimately wanted them to do. Early in the study, the children were requested to sit quietly in chairs and look at the blackboard for very short periods of time—no longer than 3 minutes (the instrumental behavior). This was followed almost immediately by a bell and the command, "Everybody, run and scream now" (the contingent behavior). After a short period, another signal came, and the children had to return to their seats. (Note that the opportunity to engage in the contingent or reinforcing activity was now reduced. The children were not permitted to run and scream freely as before. Instead, the length of time they could engage in noisy periods was decreased.) On some occasions, the bell rang immediately after the children sat down instead of waiting for 3 minutes to elapse. This practice reinforced the children for returning to their seats immediately on command and sitting down quickly. The requirements of the experiment gradually changed, and the children had to sit in the chairs and be attentive for longer periods of time. Ultimately, they received tokens for the desired behavior which they could exchange for free play at the end of the class period. According to the authors, control was established to such an extent that they were able to teach the children in 1 month all the material that was ordinarily taught in first grade (Homme, 1966, p. 34).

Another important aspect of Homme's study is that the contingent behavior, an activity that gave pleasure to the children, would ordinarily not be selected by an adult as a reinforcer. Homme has emphasized this point in another context by using a "reinforcement menu" from which the children selected the activity which served as a reinforcer. Before any attempts were made to involve the child in the procedures for learning, the children constructed a list of desirable activities which served as contingent reinforcers. Such a list prompts a child by introducing a large number of items which may serve as reinforcing events, and it precludes possible errors in selection (Addison & Homme, 1966).

The other operant methods discussed here—omission, punishment, escape, and avoidance training—are almost always used in some combination with reward training because the goal in behavior modification is to facilitate both the elimination of a specific response and its replacement by another. In the case of the two children just described, for example, reward and omission methods were employed. Omission training was introduced in the form of time-out from reinforcement, and the children were occasionally confined to the bathroom to expedite the extinction of disruptive responses such as kicking, screaming, and yelling. Illustrations of the remaining operant methods show that it is difficult, if not impossible, to find pure examples of these techniques which do not at the same time involve instances of reward training.

Aversive Training Procedures

The only alternative to receiving a reward for behavior is (1) to get nothing, (2) to have something of value taken away, or (3) to be subjected to unpleasant or noxious consequences. Since the remaining operant training methods have at least one of these unpleasant options in common, it seems appropriate to include them under the common heading of aversive training procedures. Unlike reward training, removal of a reward or administration of punishment leads to the elimination or suppression of ongoing behavior.

In the discussion of the principles of operant learning earlier in this chapter, we noted that Thorndike was not particularly impressed with the power of punishment as a way to influence learning. But Thorndike's conclusions were drawn from a trivial set of experimental conditions. The threat of losing small amounts of money for not being able to remember words in a verbal learning study, for example, cannot seriously be regarded as a dire consequence of making a mistake, and the results of such an experiment can hardly be used as the basis for sweeping generalizations about the effect of punishment on behavior.

Actually, behavior can be changed rather dramatically through the use of punishment, but whether the behavior is only temporarily suppressed or permanently eliminated depends entirely on the intensity of the punishment, its meaning to the individual being punished, and the resourceful use of the available aversive techniques.

In operant conditioning, aversive training methods are classified into two broad categories: *punishment training* and *omission training.*

Punishment Training.   Punishment training does not really have a great deal going for it as an effective method for changing behavior permanently. In many instances, it acts only to suppress the behavior which invariably surfaces again after the threat of punishment has been removed or when the need to engage in the behavior becomes intense enough.

In the case of undesirable habits, such as smoking, overeating, and addiction, the rewarding consequences of the behavior are immediate and powerful, while the bad effects are too far removed from the act itself to be successful deterrents. The good taste of food or the transient but nevertheless euphoric effects of alcohol and drugs are powerful reinforcers.

Society itself has not yet learned to use punishment effectively. While cost-benefit ratios do seem to play some role in the decision to become a criminal, more often the crime occurs even though the punishment far outweighs any of the advantages to be gained from committing the criminal act. Threats of jail, bodily mutilation, and even death have been only minimally effective in curbing most crimes, and the alarming rate of recidivism among criminals suggests that the rewards of crime (measured by status as well as material reinforcers) are far more powerful incentives, in most cases, than the threats of punishment.

But if punishment is generally such an ineffective way of permanently changing behavior, why is it used so frequently? Well, the specific advantage of punishment is that it invariably stops the annoying behavior immediately, and it acts as a source of reinforcement for the punisher. While this does not take care of the long-term problems of the undesirable behavior, its effectiveness, although temporary, functions as negative reinforcement for the punisher and increases the tendency to use punishment again under the same circumstances. Punishment is also gratifying because it satisfies the desire for justice, equity, and revenge (Luthans & Kreitner, 1975).

Using punishment as the only method for producing changes in behavior has several disadvantages, however, and these have been summarized by Luthans and Kreitner (1975) and Powers and Osborne (1976):

1. *Punishment results in only a temporary suppression of behavior in most instances.* This point has already been made. More permanent changes in behavior can be obtained by punishing undesirable behavior at the same time that some provision is made for rewarding alternative behaviors.

2. *Punishment can often become a discriminative stimulus and a cue for other behavior.* If reinforcement follows punishment, as it did in Erofeeva's experiment in which shock was followed by food, the punishment can become a cue for reward, thereby losing its effectiveness as a deterrent. Children sometimes misbehave just to get punished because punishment brings with it attention and concern.

Punishment may also force the individual to learn to discriminate when and under what conditions the prohibited response may be safely made.

3. *Punishment makes learning difficult.* Punishment elicits associated emotional behavior, such as crying, screaming, and defensiveness, which interferes with the learning of a new response.

4. *Punishment does not in itself lead to the correct response.* It merely points to one of the many incorrect responses.

5. *Punishment also elicits aggression* which, if successful, reduces the effectiveness of the punishment and often represents a threat to the punisher.

6. *Continuous punishment also decreases its effectiveness* by raising the individual's level of tolerance for punishment. Frequently, the intensity of electric shock in animal studies must be raised continuously throughout the experiment in order to maintain effective levels. People also exhibit similar increases in tolerance when their threshold levels are increased—not only for pain, but for other aversive conditions, such as nagging, verbal exhortation, or any other uniquely human attempts to influence behavior.

7. *Punishment may also produce response inflexibility and rigidity* which interferes with further learning. In the studies of "learned helplessness," for example, animals prevented from making escape or avoidance responses early in the punishment sequence do not seem to be able to learn an appropriate avoidance or escape response later in the experiment when it is permitted and can be effective (Seligman, 1975).

In *punishment training,* unpleasant or aversive stimuli are presented, and the behavior options depend upon the objectives of training. If the goal is to suppress a response or eliminate it entirely, then *passive avoidance training* is employed. The response is punished immediately after it is made, but the punishment can be avoided if the behavior is not repeated.

In passive avoidance training, the individual learns *what not to do* by identifying the specific behaviors which produce punishment and by inhibiting these behaviors in order to avoid punishment. This is essentially a passive act, and the result is behavioral restraint.

Active avoidance learning, on the other hand, requires that a response be learned to avoid punishment. Here the individual must learn *what to do* (Solomon, 1964). Active avoidance learning has already been discussed in detail in Chapter 2.

Passive avoidance learning. It may seem paradoxical that after such an involved discussion of the disadvantages of punishment as a method for modifying behavior, we now proceed to demonstrate its usefulness, even in those instances where no other response is being rewarded. But in some circumstances, punishment is the only way to interrupt a sequence of behaviors that would otherwise seriously impede learning or have disastrous consequences. Harless and Lineberry illustrate this point very nicely in an item on the use of punishment taken from their programmed text, *Turning Kids On and Off* (1971).

Suppose that two of your eighth graders, George and William, get into a squabble on the playground. You are nearby. George pulls a knife and approaches William. What do you do?
1. Non-reinforce George's knife-wielding behavior.
2. Stop George from cutting William with threat, punishment, or physical restraint.
3. Reinforce a behavior incompatible with knife wielding.

To heck with the long-term effects of threat and punishment on George. It is the immediate effect on William we are worried about. Number 2 is the only alternative under the circumstances. Sometimes behavior must be suppressed. You can worry about George's long-term attitude later; William can't wait. (From J. H. Harless, and C. S. Lineberry. *Turning Kids On and Off.* Guild V Publications, 1971, p. 50.)

Those who have read Helen Keller's autobiography or who have seen the play or the movie, "The Miracle Worker," in which Anne Bancroft portrayed Anne Sullivan, Helen's devoted and lifelong teacher, will probably never forget the extremely poignant scene in which Miss Sullivan, with great feelings of remorse, decides to use punishment to break the extremely willful behavior of this child who knew no self-discipline (Box 6-6). Anne Sullivan had reached the end of her rope. She felt that she could not teach Helen anything unless she first eliminated the undesirable behavior that Helen's parents had encouraged out of pity for her. *One of the important purposes of punishment, then, is to suppress undesirable behavior in order to permit other, more acceptable, behavior to emerge and be reinforced.*

BOX 6-6
Punishment and Helen Keller

Punishment generally suppresses behavior, but the behavior often surfaces again when the punishing stimuli are removed. For this reason, it is inadvisable to use punishment as the sole technique in behavior modification unless an alternate method cannot be found (as in the case of the child with chronic rumination reported at the beginning of Chapter 1). Occasionally, however, suppression of the old behavior through punishment is necessary so that new behavior can surface to be rewarded.

Anne Sullivan's education of Helen Keller, the remarkable woman who was left totally deaf and blind at 19 months after an illness, illustrates this principle quite dramatically. When Miss Sullivan agreed to undertake Helen Keller's education, she encountered an extremely willful 6-year-old child who tyrannized over her family. According to Anne Sullivan, "Every thwarted desire was the signal for a passionate outburst and as she grew older and stronger these tempests became more violent" (Keller, 1968). It was impossible to coax or compromise with her in order to get her to do essential things for herself. Her parents had encouraged and rewarded this behavior with their indulgence and continued to interfere with Miss Sullivan's attempts to train the child whenever she used force to get Helen to respond properly. In a letter to her friend, Sophia C. Hopkins, Miss Sullivan describes the dramatic confrontation with Helen which marked the beginning of an overwhelming success in teaching her language.

Monday P.M.

I had a battle royal with Helen this morning. Although I try very hard not to force issues, I find it very difficult to avoid them.

Helen's table manners are appalling. She puts her hands in our plates and helps herself, and when the dishes are passed, she grabs them and takes out whatever she wants. This morning I would not let her put her hand in my plate. She persisted, and a contest of wills followed. Naturally the family was much disturbed, and left the room. I locked the dining room door, and proceeded to eat my breakfast, though the food almost choked me. Helen was lying on the floor, kicking and screaming and trying to pull my chair from under me. She kept this up for half an hour, then she got up to see what I was doing. I let her see that I was eating, but did not let her put her hand in the plate. She pinched me, and I slapped her every time she did it. Then she went all around the table to see who was there, and finding no one but me, she seemed bewildered. After a few minutes she came back to her place and began to eat her breakfast with her fingers. I gave her a spoon, which she threw on the floor. I forced her out of the chair and made her pick it up. Finally I succeeded in getting her back in her chair again, and held the spoon in her hand, compelling her to take up the food with it and put it in her mouth. In a few minutes she yielded and finished her breakfast peaceably. Then we had another tussle over folding her napkin. When she had finished, she threw it on the floor and ran toward the door. Finding it locked, she began to kick and scream all over again. It was another hour before I succeeded in getting her napkin folded. Then I let her out in the warm sunshine and went up to my room and threw myself on the bed exhausted. I had a good cry and felt better. I suppose I shall have many such battles with the little woman before she learns the only two essential things I can teach her, obedience and love . . . (Source: H. Keller. *The story of my life.* New York: Dell, 1968. Copyright 1954 Doubleday & Co. and used by permission).

On other occasions, passive avoidance learning is the *only* method for eliminating a response because the behavior is a threat to the individual or to others and must be stopped as soon as possible or because there are no other alternatives to substitute for the undesirable response when it is eliminated. Shock was used in the case of the child with chronic ruminative vomiting described in Chapter 1, for example, because it was imperative to disrupt the vomiting sequence to prevent any further complications from malnutrition. Vomiting was also eliminated without reinforcing another response because the only other alternative to vomiting is not vomiting.

Although the use of punishment without rewarded behavioral alternatives is rare, the literature on passive avoidance learning in behavior modification, described in more detail in Chapter 8, contains several cases. These are largely confined to instances involving involuntary responses, such as vomiting, epileptiform seizures, and tics.

Active avoidance learning.   It may have already occurred to the reader that the subject of avoidance learning appeared as part of the discussion of classical conditioning in Chapter 2. Its reappearance in this chapter, however, will come as no surprise to those who recall that avoidance learning contains the elements of both classical conditioning and operant learning. This is especially appropriate when the concept of fear is invoked to explain avoidance learning, as it is in two-factor theory. The association between fear and the events that induce it are first established as a classically conditioned response. Any subsequent behavior that avoids the impending punishment and reduces fear becomes a discriminated operant response, i.e., behavior which modifies the environment by preventing the occurrence of punishment—one of the criteria used to designate operant learning.

Active avoidance conditioning plays a significant role in the learning of maladaptive behavior, as we saw in Chapter 3. Its usefulness as a procedure for modifying behavior, however, is limited to those instances where the avoidance response itself is a desirable and socially acceptable replacement for the punished behavior. If these conditions are not met, active avoidance learning becomes even more disadvantageous than passive avoidance learning because it forces the individual to engage in behavior that is not rewarding in order to keep from being punished, a situation which is likely to prove even more difficult because of the conflict it produces.

Differences in the success rate for the treatment of alcoholism and sexual perversions support these assertions. The frustrations involved in simply not taking a drink and the failure to maintain abstinence in alcoholics treated with aversion methods provide evidence that simple avoidance without a viable alternative is generally not effective. In some of the more recent attempts to deal with alcoholism, behavior associated with controlled drinking such as sipping drinks, ordering mixed drinks, and limiting the number of drinks has been used as an avoidance response on the grounds that these socially acceptable alternatives may be easier to manage for the alcoholic in the long run than complete abstinence (see Chapter 8).

Active avoidance learning is a more successful strategy in the treatment of sexual disorders, on the other hand, because heterosexual contact with a sexually mature male or female can serve as a potentially powerful and natural alternative for sexual deviation.

Omission Training. Omission training is also designed to prevent a response from occurring. Unlike punishment, however, omission training accomplishes this purpose by *removing a reward* if the response is made. In punishment training, the admonition is, "If you bite your fingernails, you'll get slapped." In omission training, it is, "If you bite your fingernails, you can't go to the movies." Like punishment, omission training is also regarded as an aversive procedure because it results in the loss of a reward. But the major difference between the two is that *punishment involves the presentation of an unpleasant stimulus, while in omission training a pleasant stimulus is withdrawn.*

As an aversive technique, omission training is probably one of the most effective ways of changing behavior—especially if it is used in conjunction with reward for an alternative response. Although omission training cannot be used where immediate and abrupt changes in behavior are necessary, it is preferable to punishment in those instances where behavior change can take place over a period of time. As a method for behavior change, it has almost none of the disadvantages of punishment, which generally interferes with the learning of new behavior; it is not disruptive, nor does it produce the extreme emotional behavior usually associated with punishment.

The appropriate use of omission training depends upon the existence of ongoing response-reward contingencies that can be interrupted by removal of the reward. Of course, this method is implicit in all reward-training situations because no response other than the desirable one is rewarded, and all other responses are reduced in strength through extinction. But omission training goes beyond simple extinction because a *specific* response is singled out for association with removal of reward. Rewards can be removed in three ways: through time-out from reinforcement, ignoring, and response cost.

Time-out from reinforcement. One of the ways to conduct a time-out (TO) procedure is to remove the individual, usually a child, from reinforcement. This method, as we have already seen, was used in the case of Barry and Jeff when each of the children was confined to the bathroom for a prescribed period of time after misbehaving.

The importance of omission training in general and time-out in particular is that it speeds up learning by emphasizing the differences between desirable and undesirable behavior— it enhances discrimination.

Consistency and common sense are the important requirements for the intelligent and effective use of TO. Sending a child to his or her room for some infraction may often mean exchanging one set of rewards for another, especially if the room is filled with toys and a television set.

Teachers often wonder why ordering a child from the classroom to the principal's office for misbehaving does not alter the disruptive behavior. What they often fail to recognize is that being in the classroom is a more rewarding experience for the teacher than it is for the child. Escape from the classroom does not fulfill the requirements for TO. Instead, the student receives negative reinforcement for misbehaving by escaping from an unpleasant and onerous situation, and this is probably further reinforced by the attention the child receives from the teacher and the classmates.

If the TO procedure is to fulfill the requirements of an aversive experience, then obviously some form of deprivation should be involved. An excellent example of the use of both TO and reward training is illustrated in the successful attempts to restore normal breathing in two 8-month-old children who had surgical incisions made in their windpipes to help them breathe during prolonged respiratory illnesses (Box 6-7).

BOX 6-7
Time-out from Reinforcement (TO) and the
Tracheotomized Children

Children who require temporary incisions in the windpipe (tracheotomy) because of illnesses which impair or prevent breathing frequently become addicted to breathing through the tubes (cannulae) inserted in their tracheas, and they often have serious difficulties in restoring normal breathing, even when they are physiologically capable. This type of addiction can apparently have serious consequences in retarding the development of speech, physical and motor performance, and interpersonal and social skills. The likelihood of suffocation seems to increase, the younger the child and the longer the interval between tracheotomy and the first attempt at decannulation.

Wright et al. were asked to solve the problem of decannulation through the use of behavioral methods, and they developed a strategy in which the children were exposed to pleasurable events while breathing normally (reward training) and deprived of these events when breathing through the tube (omission training, TO).

The first step, as in any functional analysis of behavior, was to determine the events thought to be pleasurable for each child. In both instances, social contact with nurses and parents, in addition to play with toys and other objects, were determined to be rewarding. The children were then placed in a deprived environment (no toys, very little social contact) during the time they were breathing through the tubes and in an enriched setting (nurses, parents, and toys present) when the tubes were occluded and the children forced to breathe normally. By increasing the length of occlusion time gradually, the children ultimately could breathe normally for a 36-hour period by the seventh day and were completely decannulated on the twentieth day without any physical difficulties.

At one point in the study, after a period in which the tube had been removed and the hole in the trachea covered by tape, the children actually began crying when the tape was removed for the tube to be reinserted. According to the authors, the children had learned that removal of the tape signaled a return to the deprived and unrewarding environment—the period of time-out from reinforcement (Wright et al., 1969).

Ignoring.　A second way in which omission training can be used to eliminate a response is to ignore the behavior when it occurs. This procedure presupposes, of course, that the behavior is receiving some reinforcement in the form of attention, and this often turns out to be the case.

Withholding of attention was successfully used, for example, in the case of a 20-year-old woman who developed a skin rash which was irritated by constant scratching and which would not respond to treatment by medication and X ray. The rash was a device used by a woman to gain attention from her father who showed a preference for her brother. The psychologist advised members of the family, including the woman's fiancé who accompanied her to the hospital for treatment and helped to apply the ointment, to ignore the ailment and pay attention to her only when she was not complaining about the skin condition. After a period of 3 months following the use of this procedure, the rash disappeared completely, and a 4-year follow-up indicated that she was happily married and gainfully employed (Walton, 1960).

Extinction bursting: an obstacle to ignoring behavior.　Parents, and sometimes psychologists, are frequently discouraged from using the method of withholding attention because of a curiously intimidating phenomenon known as *extinction bursting.*

This interesting behavior was first observed in animals who showed a marked increase in the number—a burst, in fact—and vigor of responses shortly after the reward was discontinued and extinction procedures introduced. Instead of disappearing, the response actually increased in strength for some appreciable time before it began to weaken.

From a simple and superficial viewpoint, it appears as though the animal or human—this behavior does occur in humans as well—is making a forceful attempt to restore the reinforcer, probably because on similar occasions in the past, the use of force and increased responding had been successful.

Whatever the explanation, extinction bursting is often successful in restoring reinforcement. People are generally intimidated by such behavioral outbursts, and the attention demanded is usually given. It is especially difficult to ignore a temper tantrum in a determined child, even though in the long run it is probably the most effective way of dealing with such behavior. One of the distinct disadvantages of yielding to these bursts of behavior, however, is that they are reinforced by the attention they receive, and that compounds the problem even further. Parents are often warned to expect extinction bursting as a consequence of withholding attention.

The behavior is dramatically illustrated in the case of Jim, the child described in Box 6-3, who engaged in self-injurious scratching. Figure 6-6 (panels B and C) clearly demonstrated the direct relationship between the parents' attention and the frequency of scratching. The more the parents called his attention to the scratching, the more he scratched. When extinction was introduced and the parents were instructed to ignore the scratching, however, responding increased in an extraordinary fashion from approximately 20 scratches per 10-minute interval (interval #4, panel B) to approximately 35 scratches per 10-minute interval (interval #5, panel C). But as the parents continued to ignore the behavior, scratching decreased to about 4 in the next 10-minute interval (interval #6, panel C).

Response-cost. Another type of omission training, one encountered frequently in daily living, is response-cost. Very simply, response-cost is having something of material value taken away for some infraction of the rules. Paying a fine for speeding is perhaps the most familiar example. Response-cost can be a very effective training method, but its effectiveness depends very largely on recognizing that it tends to focus on the undesirable behavior early in the training sequence by levying frequent fines during that period. Chapters 9 and 10 provide a more detailed account of the use of response-cost as a behavior modification procedure in the classroom and in industry.

In an attempt to change behavior, parents sometimes try to avoid using punishment by rewarding the non-occurrence of a response. Instead of telling the child, "If you bite your fingernails, you won't be permitted to go to the movies," and establishing a definite contingency, the child often hears, "If you don't bite your fingernails, you will be permitted to go to the movies."

The cardinal rule in operant learning, we have already noted, is that a response must be closely followed by its consequences if the reinforcer is to be effective. When the response is not being made, as in the example just given, at what point should the reinforcer be presented, or, in other words, when should "not responding" (not biting the fingernails) be rewarded? *The moral of all this is that it is far less confusing to the child and much more effective to punish a response for occurring than it is to reward a response for not occurring!*

The purpose of this chapter was to outline the principles involved in operant learning—one of the links in the great chain of behavior between animal and man.

Although the examples illustrate the application of these principles, we concentrated more on elaborating the principles themselves than on demonstrating how they could be applied specifically to solve human problems. The ensuing chapters present a more detailed and systematic discussion of psychology as an applied science. They describe how these principles of behavior are put to work to solve the problems of people in a variety of settings—hospitals, public schools, business, and industry—and they demonstrate even more convincingly than this chapter that the principles discussed here form the basis for a viable and rapidly growing behavior technology.

chapter seven

Operant Conditioning and the Behavior Disorders

Georgie Girl, a Siamese cat, was a masochist. At least this is the way she appeared to the casual observer who would have puzzled about the way in which she placed herself squarely under my wife's feet in order to be stepped on. The first time it happened, it was an accident, but the blood-curdling howl of an abused cat is more than any mortal can bear, and she promptly received food and attention. From that moment on, Georgie saw being stepped on as a neat way of getting food, and she proceeded to make walking about the house a perilous undertaking for all of us. Needless to say, we soon put a stop to this martyrdom by ignoring her completely when she decided to inflict a little self-punishment for the sake of food. This simple account of the way in which a "behavior disorder" was acquired and eliminated suggests that much of what is regarded as aberrant behavior could conceivably be the result of inappropriately reinforced responding.

Georgie Girl was in notable company. President Nixon's dog, King Timahoe, also learned a behavior disorder through inappropriately administered reinforcement. The story has it that Nixon and Kissinger were sitting in the Oval Office at the White House when President Nixon's dog came in and began chewing up the rug. The President commanded the dog to stop several times without any success. Finally, Nixon opened his desk drawer and took out a biscuit that he gave to the dog. "Mr. President," Kissinger declared, "you have taught that dog to chew the rug" (Valariani, 1976).

BEHAVIOR DUE TO INAPPROPRIATELY
ADMINISTERED, UNCONVENTIONAL, OR
IMPOVERISHED REINFORCERS

In speculating about classical conditioning and its relationship to the behavior disorders in Chapter 3, we used several criteria to determine whether some aspect of a given behavior disorder could conceivably be attributed to classical conditioning. In order to be included, the behavior had to be essentially involuntary and under known stimulus control. But, more important, the control exerted by the stimulus had to be inappropriate—fear of public places or the necessity to check packages for bombs, for example. In each of these instances, the person responded to a situation which did not ordinarily elicit a similar response from others.

In operant conditioning, deviant behavior originates and is maintained largely because it is successful in attaining some goal or incentive. The incentive may be an ordinarily acceptable one, such as food, attention, or love, but it is inappropriately administered if the individual has to engage in socially unacceptable behavior in order to get it. In other words, the incentive simply reinforces the wrong behavior.

In certain behaviors, such as alcoholism or drug addiction, the incentive itself is unconventional, and as a result, the behavior it evokes is deviant. In other behavior, the loss of reinforcers, imagined or real, may lead to impoverished incentives and ultimately to depression. This chapter explores the ways in which deviant behavior might originate as a result of such response-reinforcement contingencies.

Behavior Deviations Under Control of
Inappropriately Administered Reinforcement

Psychologists rarely have the opportunity to observe just how bizarre rituals and "senseless" repetitive acts originate in severely disturbed psychotic patients. Haughton and Ayllon (1965) decided to create their own opportunity, and their observations provide us with some insight into one of the ways in which bizarre behavior might arise through inappropriate reinforcement.

A 54-year-old woman, diagnosed as schizophrenic, spent most of her waking moments either lying in bed or walking aimlessly about the ward. Because she also smoked a great deal, the psychologists decided to use cigarettes as a way of reinforcing broom-holding behavior. (This specific behavior was part of a larger program designed to involve patients in rehabilitative tasks.) Each time the broom was placed in her hand, the woman received a cigarette. Within a very short period of time, the behavior became stereotyped, and the woman walked around the ward holding the broom in her hand. The behavior persisted for some period of time after cigarettes were withdrawn and other articles, such as candy or tokens, substituted in their place. Broom holding was finally eliminated completely when all sources of reinforcement were withdrawn.

This simple demonstration by Haughton and Ayllon suggests that very often behavior which appears senseless, i.e., without purpose, to the observer is only so because the "reinforcement" history is unknown. The urge to make sense of strange behavior and to fit it into some logical framework, however, often persuades us to overlook the most obvious explanations.

When psychiatrists on the ward, for example, who were unaware of the conditioning procedure were asked to evaluate the behavior, they suggested that broom holding represented a regression to earlier developmental stages commonly observed among schizophrenic patients. Unfortunately, such speculations about the origins of behavior are unproductive unless they can be tested.

How to Create Sex Differences in Children Through Inappropriate Reinforcement.

According to gender stereotypes, men are strong, independent, and aggressive. Women are weak, passive, and dependent. According to Serbin and O'Leary (1977), *sexual bondage begins in the nursery school* where teachers unwittingly reinforce sex stereotyping by the ways they respond to a child's behavior.

Sex differences in behavior have been accepted as natural for so long that certain rationalizations have grown up around them to explain the differences. Boys mature physically more rapidly than girls and are more active. Boys *need* to rebel against authority whereas girls do not. But recent observations in the classroom strongly suggest that sex typing begins as a learning experience early in the home and continues to be reinforced in the classroom in many interesting and subtle ways that not only magnify the differences between boys and girls but also increase the number of problems boys have with reading and other academic skills.

In a close study of 15 nursery schools, Serbin et al. (1973) found that boys received a great deal of attention when they behaved disruptively by breaking something, hitting another child, or refusing to obey the teacher. They were reprimanded loudly, and a great deal of fuss was usually made about the incident. When a girl was disruptive, on the other hand, she received brief, soft reprimands, which only the child could hear, with very little further fuss. Previous studies by O'Leary et al. (1971) had shown that precisely these patterns of reaction on the part of the teacher strengthened disruptive behavior in boys and eliminated it in girls.

On the whole, boys received a great deal more attention from teachers than did girls. The teachers tended to respond to girls only when they were nearby and not when they were out of arm's reach. Boys, by contrast, received a great deal of attention regardless of where they happened to be. Almost without exception, the teachers would hug and praise the boys when they were nearby and send them off to do things on their own. Girls were praised and helped but not sent off to work on their own (Serbin & O'Leary, 1977, p. 14).

Girls are taught to be dependent while boys are encouraged to be independent, curious, and venturesome. Serbin and O'Leary suggested that the reinforcement of these early sex differences may also account for the differences in academic skills between boys and girls that begin to make their appearance early during the pre-adolescent years. Boys are known to have better analytic problem-solving abilities, spatial reasoning, and mathematical skills. Girls are better at reading and other verbal skills. Although these differences in skills are often regarded as fundamental, teachers do tend to shape such behavior by giving boys step-by-step instructions in how to do things while girls generally have things done for them.

On one occasion when the children were making party baskets, the teacher gave the boys individualized instructions in how to use a staple gun and then permitted the boys to staple the handles of the baskets themselves. When the girls' turn came, the teacher invariably took the basket and stapled the handle for the child. In fact, from their observations, the authors concluded that the only form of teacher attention that the girls received slightly more often than boys was physical assistance when the teacher did something *for* the child (Serbin & O'Leary, 1977, p. 18).

The type and frequency of behavior disorders that children are likely to develop during childhood and when they are adults reflect the sex differences encouraged in the home and shared in the classroom. Passivity and dependence are not apt to be regarded as behavior problems in a child, and because girls learn this kind of behavior, fewer girls are likely to be referred for psychological help. The aggressive behavior of the boys, on the other hand, makes it almost certain that, if aggression continues or intensifies, they will be referred to clinics for problems related to disruptive behavior. In the later years, when women seek psychological consultation, their problems generally relate to disorders associated with dependency, such as depression or anxiety neurosis (free-floating anxiety) (Serbin & O'Leary, 1977, p. 9).

Self-Injurious Behavior.   One of the strangest contradictions in behavior—especially from the viewpoint of survival—is the pain and injury that organisms willingly inflict upon themselves. Rarely observed among animals in their natural state, such behavior occurs often enough among children to be of concern to clinicians because of its life-threatening nature and because of the obstacles it puts in the way of normal social and intellectual development. The most severe types of self-injurious behavior—scratching, biting, or head banging to the point where sutures are required, or punching, face slapping, and pinching severe enough to produce swellings and bruises—are usually associated with autistic, schizophrenic, retarded, and brain-damaged children (4–5% in psychiatric populations). But self-punishment—head banging in particular—also occurs with great frequency among normal children (11–17% at ages 9–18 months and 9% at 2 years of age) (Carr, 1977).

Why do people, especially these young children, inflict pain upon themselves? In a recent survey of studies involving self-injurious behavior, Carr (1977) maintains that the failure of treatment in some cases suggests that self-injurious behavior occurs for a number of reasons, each of which must be considered before a treatment program can be devised.

Because self-punishment violates the commonly accepted principle that organisms generally seek pleasure and avoid pain, behavior scientists have felt a special urge to provide explanations for this very odd and inconsistent behavior. As a result, several hypotheses have been proposed to explain self-injurious behavior.

Some children, it is suggested, need high levels of sensory stimulation because they are somehow deprived of adequate amounts of external stimulation through the usual sensory channels. Others are motivated to injure themselves because of undisclosed defects in the brain and the nervous system. The psychodynamic view regards self-injurious behavior as an attempt on the part of children to establish ego boundaries which differentiate themselves from the world around them or because of guilt.

But the most useful explanations, particularly in terms of research and treatment, emphasize the relationship of self-injurious behavior to inappropriate reinforcement. Children, according to these interpetations, injure themselves in order to gain some advantage not ordinarily available to them otherwise—the *positive reinforcement hypothesis*—or to escape unpleasant experiences that are more painful than the actual physical pain they inflict upon themselves—the *negative reinforcement hypothesis* (Carr, 1977, p. 801).

Pain in the pursuit of pleasure: the positive reinforcement hypothesis. In most experiments with animals, shock produces the expected results. Rats who have been taught to press a lever to obtain food, for example, will stop pressing or slow down considerably if a signal which has been paired with shock is suddenly presented. Under these conditions, shock or punishment has the predicted suppressive effect on behavior. But if the conditions are just right, shock can act to facilitate behavior rather than to suppress it. Erofeeva's experiments demonstrated, for example, that punishment can become a conditioned stimulus for salivation through the simple expedient of pairing graduated amounts of shock with food (Chapter 2, Box 2-2). Of course, Erofeeva used classical conditioning, and the dog could do nothing but respond to the conditioned stimulus. What if animals were given a choice, however? Would they work to restore the shock after it had been withdrawn? From all appearances, it certainly looked as if the subjects in Holz and Azrin's (1961) experiment were eager to continue being punished.

Two hungry pigeons were trained to obtain food by pecking at a disk. When their rates of responding were sufficiently stable, each peck was punished by a shock strong enough to reduce the response rate to 50% of its value before the introduction of punishment. The animals thus received both shock and food during this period. When the shock and the food were subsequently withdrawn, the response rate went down to zero, as might be expected. These procedures provided two baselines—a reinforcement-shock condition and a no-reinforcement/no-shock extinction condition—against which to compare any variations in responding that would result from the subsequent manipulations of shock.

When the animals once again went on a shock-food schedule and the shock was withdrawn, the rate of responding fell below the baseline that had previously been established for this condition. *The animals actually pecked less when the shock was absent even though they received food for responding.* On the other hand, the introduction of shock during the extinction period, when there was little or no responding, produced an increase in pecking that was maintained even after the food was withdrawn. *The animals began to peck when punishment was introduced even though they were receiving only shock and no food. Presumably, punishment had become such an integral part of the stimulus complex leading to food that the animals worked less when it was not there and more when it was.* In the technical language of operant conditioning, punishment had become a *discriminative stimulus* for the animal which increased the probability that food would be obtained when shock was present. Under the right (or wrong) conditions, food was inappropriately administered as a reinforcer for self-inflicted punishment.

Monkeys and children will do the same thing. Rhesus monkeys have been taught to hit themselves on the head to obtain food. Self-injurious children will punish and mutilate themselves more when adults who pay attention to them are around. This does not necessarily mean, of course, that social reinforcement is responsible for creating self-injurious behavior in children, but no doubt exists that attention will maintain it. Lovaas (1965) and others have shown that children will injure themselves more if comforting remarks follow the behavior or if the children may then engage in preferred activities. The opposite is also true: if the child is physically and socially isolated after a period of self-injury (omission training, time-out from reinforcement), the behavior tends to decline rather dramatically.

Self-injurious behavior also responds to different schedules of reinforcement just as any other operant behavior does. When Weiher and Harmann (1975), for example, reinforced only long pauses in which no self-punishment occurred (differential reinforcement of low rates of responding, or DRL—see Chapter 6), they were able to reduce the behavior to negligible levels. These observations, as Carr points out, tend to support the idea that learning is an important element in self-injurious behavior. More specifically, it appears to be a learned operant which, at least in some instances, depends upon social reinforcement for its maintenance. But positive reinforcers are not the only incentives that sustain self-punishment. In certain instances, as we shall presently see, animals and humans, paradoxically, inflict punishment upon themselves in order to escape punishment!

Suffering pain to escape from pain: the negative reinforcement hypothesis.   Consider the following startling experiment. Several groups of rats are trained to escape shock in a starting box by running down a straight alley into a safe goal box. For one group, shock is discontinued to see how long these animals will continue to run after they receive no punishment in the starting box. For the other two groups, shock is also discontinued in the starting box but the grids in the straight alley are electrified, and the animals are shocked if they venture out onto them. For one group, the short-shock group, punishment is present in the last one-third of the alley before they can enter the safe goal box. For the other, the long-shock group, shock is present for the entire length of the runway.

Now none of the animals had any necessity to leave the starting box because it was no longer electrified. *In spite of this, the long-shock and the short-shock groups continued to run faster and for longer periods of time than the no-shock group.* The two groups of animals actually ran into the shock on the alley although there was no need to run at all, and the group that received the longest amount of shock ran faster and longer than the group punished only in the last segment of the runway (Brown et al., 1964).

Despite the rather bizarre and senseless aspects of this behavior, the rats did precisely what the pigeons had done in Holz and Azrin's study. The animals were motivated to run because they feared the starting box even though shock was no longer present. The shock in the alley not only reinforced this fear but also became part of the sequence of events leading to safety. Pain had become a *discriminative stimulus* which signaled escape from shock (negative reinforcement), just as punishment signaled the availability of food for the pigeons. In both instances, punishment was part of a sequence of events which led to reward. In the case of the pigeons, the reward was food. For the rats, it was escape from pain. The animals in the long-shock group ran faster and continued to run longer because the discriminative stimulus (shock) persisted for a longer period of time.

Animals, then, learn any response if it leads to escape from unpleasant conditions—even, paradoxically, a response which leads to pain itself. And so do humans!

Children frequently punish themselves because the act itself inevitably releases them from undesirable demands or other unpleasant circumstances. Therapists working with these children are often compelled to yield to this frightening behavior, enabling the children to escape from the demands and thus reinforcing self-punishment.

Carr, Newsom, and Binkoff (1976) studied self-punishment as a response to demands with a schizophrenic, retarded child named Tim who had been unsuccessfully exposed to virtually every known form of treatment including drugs, restraints (hands tied behind his back), electric shock, extinction, time-out from reinforcement, and reinforcement of incompatible behavior in an effort to curb his self-destructive behavior (Box 7-1).

BOX 7-1
The Lesser of Two Evils?

Most self-injurious behavior results from a desire to draw attention to oneself, and treatment is usually designed so that attention does not depend upon self-punishment. Instead, the child receives attention and affection for other, more desirable behavior, and self-injurious behavior generally disappears because it is ignored. But, as Carr points out, treatment sometimes fails because the reason for self-punishment is misinterpreted as a desire for attention when, in fact, it may be to escape from demands which the child finds onerous or unpleasant.

This was the case with Tim, an 8-year-old boy who was diagnosed as a retarded, schizophrenic child. Apparently, Tim had a choice to make. Should he continue to follow the demands of the adults and teachers that he found particularly unpleasant, or should he engage in behavior so outlandish and startling that the demands would stop? Tim chose what was for him the lesser of the two evils. He punched himself in the face whenever demands were made upon him. The therapists were alerted to Tim's problem when his teachers complained that the self-destructive behavior increased whenever he was put into a classroom situation.

Although the therapists suspected Tim of hitting himself to escape from the classroom situation and from other demands, they decided to observe him in several controlled situations to make certain that this was the case. In the *free time* situation, which was intended to duplicate those periods on the ward when Tim was free to roam about the room or lie down, no demands were made upon him. If he approached an adult to talk, the person would answer him politely and briefly, avoiding a conversation. In the *tact* condition, the adult would call Tim's name, look him in the eye, and deliver a tact regardless of what Tim was doing. (Tacts are what Skinner calls simple declarative sentences, such as "The grass is green" or "The walls are white.") The *mands* situation approximated a structured classroom or therapy session. Here Tim was presented with one of several commands to do something, "Point to the door," for example. (Mands, of course, are orders to be obeyed.)

Figure 7-1 shows how Tim responded to these situations. Self-injurious behavior clearly resulted when demands were placed upon him. Carr reasoned further that if the self-injurious behavior is truly an escape from aversive demands, then it should stop if some stimulus associated with the termination of the demands is presented (a so-called safety signal). This is precisely what happened. When the child was first presented with the signal, "O.K., let's go," a stimulus normally used to terminate the classroom period, he instantly stopped hitting himself. If, on the other hand, he was presented with a neutral stimulus, such as "The sky is blue," which had never been associated with the end of a classroom period, the rate of hitting himself remained high (Carr, 1977, p. 805). This occurred despite the fact that "O.K., let's go" falls into the class of stimuli (mands) that usually elicited self-injurious behavior, and "The sky is blue" is a tact that never evoked self-punishment.

Another interesting fact emerging from this study is that, like all operant responses, self-injurious behavior is sensitive to changes in the specific way in which reinforcement is delivered (the schedule of reinforcement). It was pointed out in Chapter 6 that a "scalloped" curve of responding—low during the first part of a work interval and high toward the end of the interval (Figure 6-2)—usually occurs when reinforcement is given on a fixed-interval schedule, i.e., after a certain amount of time has elapsed (weekly paychecks in contrast to piecework). Tim's self-injurious behavior showed the typical scalloping for the following logical reasons. Each demand session was 10 minutes long, after which the session terminated with the signal, "O.K., let's go." Because these signals provided Tim with an escape from the aversive demands, they were reinforcing (negative reinforcements). After a few such sessions, Tim could expect this to happen every 10 minutes. As a consequence, self-punishment was low during the first part of the 10-minute session and increased markedly during the end of the session in anticipation of the command, "O.K., let's go," which served to terminate the demands.

In the second part of the study, an attempt was made to eliminate self-injurious behavior by a kind of counterconditioning technique which consisted of introducing demands in the context of other, more acceptable and more pleasurable (to Tim) conditions. The original mand condition was modified so that whenever Tim was not being commanded to do something, the adult related to him a simple story concerned with some familiar situation, going swimming, for example. Each of the ten stories was long enough to fill the period between demands and was told in a cheerful and entertaining fashion.

Under these condtions, Tim's self-injurious behavior decreased from approximately 75 hits per minute to 2.0 in the space of 22 experimental sessions. As the experimenters point out, by altering the stimulus properties of a demand situation —i.e., presenting the demands in the context of a cheerful, positive, on-going interaction—it was possible to make demands which Tim obeyed and from which he no longer sought escape through self-punishment (Carr et al., 1976, p. 150).

This study with Tim is especially important because it is a well-controlled clinical investigation which not only isolates the source of the self-injurious behavior (social demands), but also shows, unequivocally, that successful escape from these demands maintained self-punishment. In addition, the experimenters also demonstrated that by counterconditioning—presenting the demands in the context of pleasant and humorous conversation, for example—the escape behavior was eliminated because it was no longer necessary (Carr et al., 1976).

The analysis of the controlling factors in children exhibiting self-injurious behavior was extended by Carr, Newsom, and Binkoff (1980) to children who used aggression as a means of escaping from demand situations. As in the previous studies of self-injury, Carr et al. determined, from a functional analysis of two

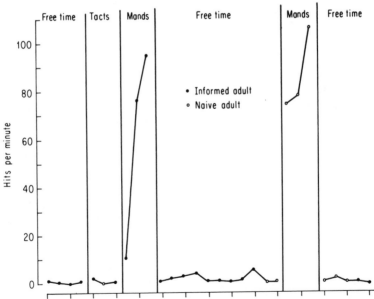

FIG. 7-1 Number of times per minute Tim punched himself during the various experimental conditions. The filled circles are data from an informed observer and the open circles from a naive observer. (Source: E. G. Carr, C. D. Newsom and J. A. Binkoff. Stimulus control of self-destructive behavior in a psychotic child. *Journal of Abnormal Child Psychology.* 1976, *4*, 139–153. Copyright by Plenum Publishing Corp. and used by permission.)

retarded children (9 and 14 years of age), that their aggressive behavior consisting of hitting, scratching, and biting was controlled by demand situations in which the children were given specific instructions (sit in a chair, etc.) and reinforced by their escape from these situations through aggressive behavior. The experimenters showed that aggressive behavior could be eliminated by (1) introducing strongly preferred reinforcers to attenuate the aggressiveness, (2) strengthening alternative nonaggressive responses, or (3) using an escape-extinction procedure. In Chapter 14 we shall also see how aggressive behavior can be learned by observing others who model or exhibit aggression.

When the process is understood and the sources of reinforcement are identified, the paradoxical aspects of self-punishment disappear, and the behavior no longer contradicts what is known, in general, about the way in which learning occurs. The neurotic paradox described in Chapter 3 is only a paradox because we tend to interpret the maladaptive neurotic behavior as self-defeating. However, with the recognition that neurotic responses are maintained because they enable the individual to escape a far greater punishment—fear—the paradoxical elements disappear.

For similar reasons, parents are puzzled when some children act to invite and encourage punishment. Very often, the punishment is followed by an act of contrition on the part of the parents, and they try to make up for the punishment by treating the child with affection. If being punished is the only way they can get attention and affection, then the children, like Holz and Azrin's pigeons, will follow the cues which lead to punishment.

Food as an Inappropriate Reinforcer: The Problem of Obesity.   The average American man and woman is 15–30 pounds overweight according to a study released by the National Center for Health Statistics (1977), and he or she is constantly, but not too successfully, engaged in the process of trying to get rid of the excess fat. (Only about 5–20% lose weight and maintain the weight loss after dieting.)

Obviously, overeating is responsible for these increases in weight, but the causes of obesity, beyond the obvious reason, are not entirely clear. Fat people tend to have fat children, according to Garn at the Center for Human Growth and Development at Ann Arbor, Michigan, and the children of obese parents are generally three times as fat as those of lean parents by the time they reach the age of 17 (Kolata, 1977).

The idea that obesity may, in part, be determined by genetic and constitutional factors is also supported by the fact that severely fat babies tend to become fat adults, and these people have more fat cells than people who become fat as adults. Because the size and number of fat cells remain fairly constant throughout the lifetime of a person, the tendency toward fatness in people who have more fat cells may mean that losing excess fat and maintaining an "ideal weight" presents more of a challenge for them. They may actually have to maintain a statistically normal but biologically abnormal low body weight (Stunkard & Mahoney, 1976).

But before we conclude from all this that fatness is invariably an inherited trait,

Garn hastens to add that the relationship between fat people and their natural children is also equally true for their adopted children and even for their pets! So, while some obesity probably results from organic and biological factors, the larger proportion, by far, seems to be related to eating habits and the environmental factors that control them. In fact, studies in England have shown that most fat babies become lean during their childhood, and fat people whose fatness can be traced to obesity in infancy make up only a small proportion of obese adults (Kolata, 1977, p. 906).

The "causes" of obesity.   Apart from the genetic or constitutional factors, which, as we have just seen, are very difficult to establish, a number of possible determinants of overeating depend upon eating habits begun very early in childhood and continued throughout the lifetime of the individual.

Bruch (1973) sees strong indications that children are programmed to overeat by their parents who unwittingly feed them for the wrong reasons or at the wrong times. Food is often used as a pacifier to quiet the baby's crying or as a reward for good behavior (witness the ever-present chocolate bar). For many fat people, then, overeating is a reflection of a pattern of behavior developed through social learning in the family. Later in life, when problems that create stress and anxiety arise, food becomes an easy and highly satisfying way of reducing the effects of stress.

Eating as a result of emotional arousal.   Excessively overweight animals are rare in nature. Animals generally eat until they are sated, but fat rats have been produced in the laboratory by stimulating the lateral hypothalamus of the brain or by creating conditions of stress.

Lightly pinching a rat's tail generally produces an increase in activity directed toward some object in the rat's immediate environment. If the rat pups are present during the tail pinch, maternal behavior takes place. A mild shock to the tail of a naive male in the presence of a receptive female induces copulatory behavior; in the presence of another male, it induces aggression. But these activities only seem to mask the rat's real intention—to escape the stressful stimulus. If all goal objects are removed, the rat will engage in "nervous grooming" and make an attempt to escape *unless* some highly palatable food or fluid is available. The rats in Rowland and Antelman's study (1976) chose food only when the other options were not available. *Under these conditions, eating took place even when the rat was already full and would normally refrain from eating.*

Will a rat continue to eat until it becomes obese? When the experimenters continued the stress situation in the presence of food, the rats not only overate, they also gained from 39 to 90 grams in the space of 8 days. During the stress phase of the study, the rats ate nothing in their home cages. When the stress was discontinued, however, the animals' weights returned to normal, and they resumed eating in the home cage.

Although no well-controlled human studies relating stress to overeating per se exist, clinical observations and the results of several studies support the supposition that many obese people eat when they are emotionally tense, bored, depressed, or even elated, but rarely in response to actual cues of physiological hunger (Schachter, 1971). It is possible, then, that food, and the general sense of comfort and well-being it produces in appeasing hunger, can, presumably, also act as a *generalized reinforcer* to increase the probability of overeating by diminishing or preventing the unpleasant feelings resulting from stress. (It is interesting to note that just the opposite is also possible. In a condition known as *anorexia nervosa,* food can become a source of *negative reinforcement* which increases the response when it is removed. People—generally adolescent girls—have been known to refuse to eat and literally to starve themselves for fear that eating will somehow alter the image they have of themselves. Many women who want to stay slender in response to social pressure engage in a destructive "cycle of starvation, binge eating, and punishing purges," a condition which has been called *bulimarexia*—the excessive longing for food combined with self-denial and starvation.)

Overeating to reduce stress is also complicated by the "vicious cycle" phenomenon. Negative emotional experiences trigger a little eating which, in turn, leads to concern about the lack of "willpower" and "weak personality" which results in more eating, and so on (Stuart, 1975).

Overeating as a habit and as a response to environmental cues. It would be a mistake, of course, to assert that all obesity is stress- or emotion-related. In affluent societies, obesity also probably results from unrestrained eating habits, compensated for during the vigorous activity of youth but taking their toll when continued unabated into a sedentary old age.

A large number of cues become associated with eating and serve to encourage eating in the absence of actual physiological hunger. For example, people suffering from *hypoglycemia,* a disorder that results in periodic low blood sugar, frequently have to eat small amounts of food at various periods throughout the day. Interestingly enough, when the low blood sugar deficiency was corrected, the patients still continued to eat often between meals.

How many of us begin to "snack" automatically (the very word itself, as well as the phrase "between-meal treats," has become part of the advertising language to induce people to overeat) when we turn on the television set, or open a book or newspaper, or on any number of occasions which are so idiosyncratic that therapists treating obese people often require them to keep a daily log of activities in order to determine under just what conditions eating does occur?

Apparently, the environmental cues which come to control hunger influence the eating habits of obese people more than they do those of non-obese people, who respond more to the internal physiological cues of hunger. The situations that appear to have a marked influence are appointed eating times (obese people generally tend to feel hungry by the clock), palatability of the food, and high visibility and accessibility of food (Schachter, 1971).

A difference in the actual mechanics of eating between obese and non-obese people also exists. Thin women, who have been systematically observed eating in a downtown Los Angeles public cafeteria, are more likely to take smaller mouthfuls at a slower rate, make more extraneous responses (hesitations, toying, putting the utensil down, drinking between bites, wiping the mouth with a napkin), leave food on the plate, stay at the table less long after eating, and appear less tense throughout the whole process (Marston et al., 1977). Similar differences were also found between obese and non-obese children (Marston et al., 1976).

Whether the stimuli which control eating are in the environment or in the process of eating itself, it is necessary to identify them and determine their roles for purposes of treatment. Treatment programs for obesity, as we see in Chapter 12 on self-control, are based on the elimination of cues and responses which encourage overeating. One particular strategy, for example, reduces the process of eating to its absolute minimum and requires the obese client to eat slowly and count the number of "chews" for each mouthful of food. The emphasis on slowness is based on the fact that it takes about 20 minutes for the signals of satiation to reach the brain. Rapid eating is also a unit response in the complex chain that leads to overeating. In order to modify the goal behavior itself (overeating), it becomes necessary to interrupt the unit responses in the chain in order to eliminate or change the behavior.

Sexual Deviations Resulting from Inappropriately Administered Reinforcement.
The question of undesirability or unacceptability of behavior never enters into the diagnosis of a physical illness. The social behavior of a person with pneumonia does not really matter in deciding whether pneumonia does, in fact, exist.

In the behavior disorders, however, departure from societal norms and mores is the principal and, in many instances, the only criterion for making a diagnosis. In the last analysis, then, whether or not a behavior disorder exists depends on the consensus of the particular society in which it occurs. This is especially true of sexual behavior. Cross-cultural studies show that what is considered deviant in one society may be perfectly acceptable in another. On occasion, even the sexual mores within a society undergo change so that what is considered prohibitive at one time is tolerated at another time. Homosexuality, for example, which had long been regarded as deviant in Western culture, and sometimes even pathological, has been "legislated into normality" by the democratic process. A majority vote (58% in favor) of the American Psychiatric Association has recently decided that homosexuality is no longer a behavior disorder.

In Chapter 3, we saw that some sexual deviations may be acquired by conditioning through the association of certain fantasy experiences with masturbation. Clinical observations indicate that deviant sexual behavior may also be learned by children whose parents encourage such behavior and reinforce it with attention and affection. Bandura (1968) cites several cases reported by various authors in which culturally unacceptable sexual behavior was learned through inappropriate encouragement and attention from the parents.

The first of these is the case, described by Litin et al. (1965), of a 5-year-old boy who was encouraged to dress up in his mother's clothes, using cosmetics and jewelry, following an episode in which the mother, in response to the boy's compliment that she looked pretty in her new shoes, offered him her old ones. She continued to encourage this behavior with affection, and the boy was even supplied with feminine apparel by his grandmother and friends who gave him generous quantities of shoes, hats, purses, and other items. The boy finally adopted a completely feminine role and even assumed a girl's name suggested by his mother. When several relatives began to complain about the boy's behavior, his mother instructed him to restrict his "dressing up" to the immediate family.

Inappropriate reinforcement was also evident in the exhibitionism of a 17-year-old boy whose behavior was directly related to the encouragement he received from his mother. She enjoyed disrobing before him, encouraged him to do the same, and complimented him on his "beautiful masculine endowment." A dress fetish was similarly conditioned in a 10-year-old boy by his mother. She responded with feeling and a great show of appreciation whenever he stroked her dress or complimented other women on their attire (Johnson, 1953).

In summarizing these cases and the way in which they illustrate the social learning process, Bandura points out three important influential factors. First is the degree to which the parents themselves served as overt or disguised models for the sexual behavior that they intended to impart to their children. Second, the behavior, once it was elicited, was given extreme positive value through demonstrations of affection—often in the form of physical intimacy. In fact, in some cases this resulted in precocious sexual behavior in the children even before they attained puberty. And finally, the parents maintained the behavior by continuing to reinforce it (Bandura, 1968, p. 315).

Inappropriate Reinforcement and Delinquent Behavior.   The social-learning factors cited by Bandura, which are assumed to be responsible for the development of certain deviant sexual behavior, can also account for the development of delinquent and criminal behavior.

It is a commonly accepted notion that conditions of society, poverty and deprivation in particular, are largely responsible for the development of delinquent and criminal behavior. Although this idea has some credibility—especially because criminal activity does tend to increase somewhat during high periods of unemployment—it does not account for those who do not become criminals despite their impoverished backgrounds or for a substantial segment of society that adopts crime as a life-style although never exposed to deprivation. But all criminals, regardless of their reasons for pursuing a life of crime, are ultimately influenced by a social-learning process involving inappropriately reinforced behavior.

Most adult criminals have a history of criminal transgressions reaching back into their youth when they were first classified as delinquents. But delinquency is not a homogeneous category, and three different types of delinquent have been identified (Quay, 1964).

The first of these is the *sociopath* (psychopath) who is set apart from the rest of the criminal population by the seemingly "congenital," irreversible aspects of his or her behavior. Sociopaths are selfish, callous, irresponsible, and unable to form meaningful human relationships. Although studies show that their actions can be influenced by money rather than threats, this does not mean that their behavior developed through inappropriate reinforcement. In fact, the sociopath's low responsiveness to physical threat and disapproval strongly suggests a breed apart from the ordinary criminal, quite possibly due to inherent constitutional factors.

Unlike the sociopath, the second and third types of delinquent identified by Quay—the *neurotic disturbed* and the *subcultural socialized delinquent*—are influenced by reinforcers other than money and do respond to threats and praise. The neurotic type, characterized by loneliness, worry, and timidity, probably becomes delinquent as a result of the need for attention and affection due to parental and peer rejection. The subcultural socialized delinquent is more prevalent and fits the delinquent stereotype more closely. These people are usually members of a gang with strong allegiances to their friends.

There are several routes to delinquency, each of which can be accounted for by social learning in general and operant learning in particular.

For some delinquents, notably those from the lower class, material and social success is achieved by explicitly rejecting middle-class standards and the "rules of the game." Instead, they adopt their own criteria and become members of a subculture that legitimizes their own values (Cohen, 1955). The reinforcement they receive is two-fold: one, from the material rewards which they can now easily (although with some slight risk) obtain by their own methods; and two, through the acceptance and status that group membership provides.

Other delinquents develop their aggressive, criminal behavior because of a clash of values between the home and society. Dependent behavior is rejected within the family, most notably by a harsh and unrelenting father who demands obedience at home and aggression outside of it. These children are taught that aggression should be met by counteraggression, and any other method for dealing with problems is regarded a sign of weakness and dependency (Bandura & Walters, 1959). This kind of message generally results in a misinterpretation and rejection of attention from others. McDavid and Schroder (1957), for example, demonstrated that delinquent boys were less able to discriminate approval and disapproval for their behavior than a comparable group of non-delinquents. As Bandura (1968) points out, it is difficult to treat people for whom the usual rewards carry a negative message.

Secondary Gains and Inappropriate Reinforcement. Illness in many societies commands a great deal of attention. In most respects, this is fortunate because the individual who is ill obviously requires special consideration. Where the behavior disorders are concerned, however, a solicitous attitude may often serve to perpetuate undesirable behavior, particularly in those instances where individuals can use the illness to manipulate those around them or gain some other advantage.

Often, deviant behavior arising from one set of circumstances is strengthened and maintained by a second set of conditions involving inappropriate reinforcement, hence the term *secondary gains.* The hypochondriac may be afraid of illness because of a sensitization to an actual physical illness, but in all likelihood, that extreme fear of illness will also persist because of its desirable effect on the behavior of others.

Asthma, for example, which may begin as a response to a combination of physiological and psychological factors, such as respiratory infections, allergic reactions, and stress, may persist because the asthmatic child, or adult, finds it a useful way of obtaining affection or of escaping from demands.

The current treatment for asthmatic children recognizes the danger that overprotection may create and recommends that these children receive no special treatment so that the illness will not be used as a device for getting what they want. Davison and Neale (1974) cite the following excerpt from Kluger (1969, p. 361) to illustrate the way in which asthmatic children often attempt to use their illness to avoid demands upon them.

Child: I can't go to school today because my asthma is worse.
Physician: I know, but since it's not contagious, why can't you be in school?
Child (irritated): Because I'm having trouble breathing!
Physician: I can see that, but you'll have trouble breathing whether you go to school or not. Remaining in bed won't help your breathing.
Child (disgustedly): Boy, they don't even let you be sick in this hospital!

The case of Jim, the child who was referred to the clinic because of severe and injurious scratching (Chapter 6, Boxes 6-2 and 6-3), provides an even more striking example of how behavior produced by one causative agent is maintained for other reasons, even though the original reason for the behavior is completely eliminated.

The history of Jennifer, a 17-year-old girl whose coughing became so severe that surgeons considered severing the phrenic nerve to give her some relief, is an especially instructive example of behavior maintained by secondary gains, particularly because the development and course of the disorder is so well documented (Box 7-2).

BOX 7-2
Jennifer

Jennifer's coughing was so severe that surgeons considered an operation to sever the phrenic nerve in order to give her some relief. Although the coughing began when she was about 13 years old and had reached a rate of 48 coughs per minute, and even though she had also become mute sometime before her last physical examination, she showed very little anxiety or concern about her condition. Like most hysterical patients, her "beautiful indifference" prompted her to wonder why everybody was so concerned about her coughing and inability to speak when she herself was not in the least troubled by it.

Jennifer's menses began when she was 10. Menstruation was so frequent and heavy that it caused her embarrassment and anxiety, especially because she believed that she was the only girl in her class who menstruated. She began to develop a sore throat during her periods which, fortunately, also necessitated her absence from school. At the age of 13, she developed a series of colds and was rarely without symptoms of some kind. A complete medical examination, including tests for allergies, was essentially negative. *"Because of her symptoms, Jennifer was excessively absent from school, a condition that worsened to the point of her withdrawing from classes after one one week of her sophomore year. From that time to her graduation, she studied with a home teacher"* (Munford et al., 1976, p. 1010).

Six months later Jennifer was coughing at the rate of 24 coughs per minute. Another medical examination failed to reveal any physical reason for the cough, and she underwent a course of sleep therapy for 1 week with anesthesia administered to a point where no coughing occurred. The cough returned, however, when she woke up. Jennifer left the hospital against medical advice when electroconvulsive therapy was suggested to her, and at this point she also became mute. Jennifer was seen by a psychiatrist in weekly therapy sessions for 2 years during which 12 Amytal interviews were conducted. The cough disappeared while she was under Amytal, but it returned as soon as the Amytal wore off. Four and one-half years after the cough began, she had reached the rate of 48 coughs per minute, and at this point severing of the phrenic nerve was being considered.

By this time, it became obvious that Jennifer's symptoms, which began as learned anxiety-avoidance responses to the onset of menstruation, enabling her to avoid school and other unpleasant interpersonal situations, were now being maintained by the medical and social attention she received. The therapists were somewhat more certain that this analysis was correct after Jennifer refused to cooperate with instructions designed to determine the amount of control she had over the cough and failed to respond to a conditioning procedure in which she was shocked every time she coughed.

To make certain they were on the right track, they decided to observe Jennifer in a variety of settings within the hospital to see what effects these would have on the rate of coughing. The situations ranged from the most isolated—sitting alone occupied by a task—to one in which Jennifer was asked to sit behind a one-way mirror for observational purposes. Figure 7-2 demonstrates quite clearly that Jennifer's coughing was controlled almost entirely by the amount of attention she received.

The course of therapy planned for Jennifer was based on the observations made during this functional analysis of her behavior. The staff in the hospital was instructed to ignore her coughing (omission training) and the rate of coughing declined gradually over a period of approximately 6 months. It was completely eliminated after 2 years (Figure 7-3). It is interesting to note the increase in coughing that took place during the first 5–10 weeks following the removal of attention. This increase in response which takes place after withdrawal of a reinforcer is the extinction bursting described in Chapter 6.

Jennifer's mutism and muscular rigidity were treated by a painstaking shaping procedure that included rewarding her for proper inhalation and exhalation, the production of sounds beginning with plosives, consonants, and vowels, and moving on to words and phrases. Within 6 weeks after discharge from the hospital, she was speaking fluently and appropriately.

Jennifer was hospitalized for a period of approximately 6 months during which she received daily training sessions. She gradually became aware during these sessions that her illness resulted from emotional problems, and she became reconciled to the psychological nature of her problems. She was gradually persuaded to socialize with others and to accept a job as a volunteer teacher's aide to increase the amount of socialization. Twenty months after her discharge from the hospital, Jennifer continued to be symptom free. She majored in biology and earned a 4.0 average for two quarters. She was active in student government, worked as a part-time sales clerk in a department store, and made plans to live away from home and attend a university in another part of the state. A follow-up 41 months after discharge from the hospital indicated that Jennifer continued completely symptom free (Munford et al., 1976).

Behavior under the Control of Addictive Reinforcers

The inappropriateness of reinforcement, as we have already seen, depends pretty much on the behavior for which it is given. If rewards or punishments tend to accelerate and solidify unacceptable behavior, they are, by definition, inappropriate. In other circumstances, these reinforcers might not only be appropriate but also highly desirable as methods for inducing learning.

But some reinforcers can never be appropriate under any circumstances because they always tend to produce undesirable behavior and harmful physical consequences. The two most prevalent addictive reinforcers are alcohol and drugs. However, the new *Diagnostic and Statistical Manual of Mental Disorders* (DSM-III) lists smoking as an addictive mental disorder when restriction of smoking causes distress, or when continued use of tobacco is likely to exacerbate an already existing tobacco-related medical disorder.

Alcoholism.   Where addictive behavior is concerned, yesterday's facts are very likely to be tomorrow's fictions. The belief that some individuals are more susceptible than others to excessive drinking or drug abuse because of their "addictive" or "prealcoholic" tendencies probably emerged from the emphasis that psychoanalytic theory placed on the function which alcohol serves in gratifying the needs of the so-called oral and passive-dependent personalities. These formulations have proved to be of little value to psychologists attempting to understand the origins of alcoholism or to devise uniformly effective methods for treating it.

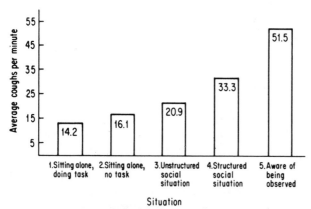

FIG. 7-2 Jennifer's rate of coughing in five situations during the first month of hospitalization. (Source: P. R. Munford, D. Reardon, R. P. Liberman, and L. Allen. Behavioral treatment of hysterical coughing and mutism: A case study. *Journal of Consulting and Clinical Psychology.* 1976, *44,* 1008–1014. Copyright 1976 by the American Psychological Association used by permission.)

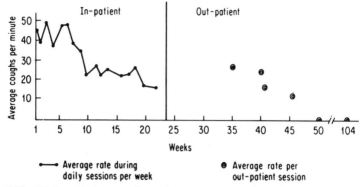

FIG. 7-3 Jennifer's rate of coughing during therapy and follow-up sessions. (Source: P. R. Munford, D. Reardon, R. P. Liberman, and L. Allen. Behavioral treatment of hysterical coughing and mutism: A case study. *Journal of Consulting and Clinical Psychology.* 1976, *44,* 1008–1014. Copyright 1976 by the American Psychological Association and used by permission.)

But even the approaches that rely less on preconceived notions about behavior and more on observation have failed to produce any consistent personality types that might identify alcoholics as distinguished from non-alcoholics. No group of characteristics, physiological, psychological, behavioral, or otherwise, has made it possible to predict the onset of alcoholism with any degree of reliability, nor has it been possible to isolate a consistent physiological or psychological cause for alcohol abuse (Franks, 1970; Verden & Shatterly, 1971).

Another myth which is gradually being dispelled through experimentation is the "craving hypothesis"—the notion that, even when sober, all alcoholics will crave a drink and that one drink will inevitably lead to more and, ultimately, to complete intoxication (Box 7-3).

BOX 7-3
"The Craving Hypothesis"

Most alcoholics do not "crave" alcohol in the sense that they cannot do without it. For that matter, it is not indisputable that once an alcoholic takes a drink, an irresistible compulsion makes the person continue drinking until a severe state of intoxication is reached.

But, in their review of controlled social drinking studies, Lloyd and Salzberg (1975) point out that the "craving" view persisted unquestioned until recently, despite the fact that no well-controlled studies existed to sustain it. In fact, the predominant view, strengthened by support of the World Health Organization, is that alcoholic craving and compulsive drinking is a physiological disorder. One of the strongest reasons for thinking so "is that a case has never been known in which an alcoholic reverted to moderate drinking" (Williams, 1948, p. 53). This notion further encouraged the belief that the only realistic treatment goal for all alcoholics is total abstinence.

In 1964, however, when the prohibitions against giving alcohol to abusers in experimental studies was lifted, some adequate determination could be made of the validity of the craving hypothesis. Since then, all of the studies (some 25) involving deliberate intoxication of alcohol abusers reviewed by Lloyd and Salzberg indicated that physiological or psychological craving for alcohol is not a typical consequence of initial inebriation. In fact, just the opposite was often the case. Many of the subjects stopped drinking even before withdrawal was imposed upon them (1975, p. 819).

One of the first explicit experiments to test the assumption that a single drink inevitably leads to loss of control was conducted by Merry (1960) using Gamma drinkers as subjects. Gamma drinkers are loss-of-control drinkers for whom, according to Jellinek (1960), one drink sets up a chain reaction which is felt as a physical demand for alcohol—once the drinker has started, he or she cannot control the quantity consumed. The results simply did not support the conviction that one drink inevitably leads to more.

Five other studies also supported Merry's conclusions, but, as Lloyd and Salzberg point out, none of these experiments made any attempt to investigate just under what conditions continued drinking will occur.

To study this, Engle and Williams (1972) devised an experiment which would permit the subject to request additional drinks if he developed a strong craving after the first. Forty loss-of-control drinkers received a vitamin mixture with or without a 1-ounce shot of vodka. Some were told that the mixture contained alcohol, others were not. The subjects who were unaware that the vitamin mixture contained vodka showed no increased desire for further alcohol. The subjects who requested additional drinks were those who knew that the mixture contained alcohol. In a similar experiment, Marlatt, Demming, and Reid (1973) also showed that information and expectancy were the sole factors responsible for determining the amount of alcohol consumed by either social drinkers or alcohol abusers. The actual amount of alcohol in the mixtures had no effect upon the amount they drank, and no loss-of-control drinking occurred (Lloyd & Salzberg, 1975, p. 819). Apparently, then, the effects of alcohol on craving appear to be predominantly psychological instead of physiological, at least where initial drinking is concerned.

What implications do these studies have for the treatment of alcoholism? Well, in the first place, the aura of gloom, pessimism, and hopelessness need not necessarily surround the subject of alcoholism as it has in the past. Second, for some alcoholics at least, it may make the often unattainable goal of total abstinence unnecessary. And finally, as we see in the later discussion of treatment strategies for alcoholism in Chapter 8, it opens up the distinct possibility of *controlled* social drinking as a potential treatment goal.

The sequence of physiological, behavioral, and environmental events that lead to alcoholism are probably not vastly different from those involved in the learning of any behavior disorder. If stress is present, alcohol or drugs, like food, will help to reduce the emotional consequences of stress and reinforce the chain of behaviors leading to that "good feeling." In this sense, both alcohol and drugs may operate in the same way as anxiety reduction to reinforce the responses that lead to them. But stress need not be involved in order for alcoholism or drug abuse to develop as long as drugs and alcohol act to reduce inhibitions and generate a sense of euphoria. Both of these appear to be sufficient reasons for learning to occur.

Alcoholism and the "good feeling."   Animals are, at worst, moderate drinkers. They will drink small quantities of alcohol, if it is made available to them, in order to overcome the effects of fear, but they will stop drinking once the stress is over. The cats Masserman and Yum (1946) used in their experiment learned to drink a "milk cocktail" containing 5% alcohol during the time they received shocks while trying to obtain food. Alcohol presumably supplied the "false courage" necessary for them to overcome their fear, but they promptly switched to plain milk when the shock was discontinued. Apparently, the consumption of alcohol for these cats served the same purpose as overeating did for the rats who had their tails pinched—both operated to reduce the effects of stress. Alcohol has a powerful disinhibiting effect on humans as well. People who are shy and timid are often emboldened by drinking, sometimes to the point where they become nasty and aggressive. The type of behavior which emerges after drinking varies for different individuals.

Although alcohol has no intrinsic rewarding properties for animals—they give up drinking as soon as stress is reduced—people will continue to drink in order to experience the euphoric and disinhibiting effects of alcohol. But the mood elevation and general good feeling produced by alcohol are short-term effects which soon give way to depression and dysphoria *unless* something prevents this from happening. The solution to this problem for the alcoholic is the *blackout!*

Blackouts, contrary to the commonly accepted notion, do not involve a loss of consciousness. They are episodes of amnesia brought on by consuming large quantities of alcohol very rapidly ("binge" drinking). The loss of memory for events before the blackout is for the events of any part of a drinking episode and may last from a period of a few hours to several days. During the amnesic period, the person may function reasonably well and even perform complicated tasks. In the "true" blackout state, memory does not return even if the individual resumes drinking (Lloyd & Salzberg, 1975, p. 822).

Apparently, blackouts occur more frequently as a result of drinking than we realize. A Task Force on Alcoholism at the University of Wisconsin in Madison found that more than one quarter of the 2,000 students surveyed suffered blackouts or loss of memory due to drinking and that many students were already beginning to show signs of acute alcoholism (*N. Y. Times,* 1978).

If the blackout does prevent the "letdown" that commonly occurs after the good feeling, and the abuser's last memory is the elevation in mood, the solution for the alcoholic is to produce the amnesic episode as rapidly as possible. *Thus, both the alcohol and the blackout it produces from rapid increases in blood-alcohol concentration become powerful reinforcers for fast drinking, and this is precisely the behavior that distin-*

guishes social drinkers from alcohol abusers! The typical alcohol abuser engages in gulping drinks, consuming straight drinks on an empty stomach, and allowing only a short interval between ordering drinks, all of which is designed to produce rapid increases in blood-alcohol concentration and the ultimate blackout (Lloyd & Salzberg, 1975, p. 822; Sobell et al., 1972).

Alcoholism and social learning. Now that we have a reasonable, although certainly not definitive, explanation of the way in which alcohol abuse might develop through reinforcement, we still face the problem that always confronts us in attempts to trace the origins of behavior. Why do some people become alcoholics and others become social drinkers?

One of the ways to try to account for these differences is in terms of the different experiences that people have. But it should be said at the outset that, while explanations involving different social-learning experiences account for some of the factors responsible for chronic alcoholism, they do not explain why people with similar experiences differ in their response to alcohol.

Apart from stress factors, one of the ways in which alcoholism might conceivably develop is through the social-learning process called modeling. (The topic of modeling is treated fully in Chapter 13. We mention it here to preserve the continuity of discussion.)

Bandura, among others, has pointed out that if alcoholism is attributable to neurotic processes that may involve oral deprivation, self-destructive tendencies, latent homosexuality, indulgent mothering, or feelings of inadequacy, to mention a few, then these processes must be extraordinarily prevalent among the Irish, who surpass all other groups in chronic alcoholism, and curiously absent in the Jews, Moslems, Mormons, and Italians, among whom the rate of alcoholism is exceedingly low (1968, pp. 317–318). But because it is hard to imagine that Jews or Moslems, for example, do not also have their share of the difficulties that might produce deviant behavior, it must be the mores of the group itself—the social learning that goes on within the family—that shape the expression of the deviant behavior.

Among Jews and Italians, drinking is tolerated on social occasions, but excessive drinking and drunkenness is frowned on. This practice of restricting alcohol primarily to mealtimes or to religious ceremonies and other social functions, or of prohibiting it entirely as the Moselms do, brings the use of alcohol under discriminative control and makes it less likely that alcohol will be used as a means to solve problems. On the other hand, where drinking is used as a method for coping with stress and frustrations and where extensive use is made of alcohol, children are likely to imitate their parents and turn to drinking as a solution to their difficulties (Bandura, 1968, p. 318).

This interesting speculation about the relationship between alcohol abuse and family behavior was recently supported by an article in the *New York Times* (1977) which reported that a group of rabbis were concerned about the increasing rate of drinking and drunkenness among Jewish adolescents. Although Jewish family patterns of child rearing have not changed appreciably, the influence of the family on the adolescent has undergone considerable erosion. Opinions of friends and peers have replaced the family's socialization function to a marked extent, and peer drinking is increasing in the high schools. These patterns should be viewed with great concern inasmuch as the next generation of chronic alcoholics is very likely to emerge from the adolescent groups who now find alcohol a relatively cheap, abundant, and readily available way of "being with it." Clearly, the situation calls for preventive measures.

As in the case of obesity, much of the recent focus in the study of alcoholism has been on the drinking habits of alcoholics, and this emphasis has given rise to a form of treatment called controlled social drinking. Actually, as we see in Chapter 8, several strategies have been combined to produce a treatment program for alcoholics that includes some aspects of aversion therapy, operant methods in controlled drinking, and contractual agreements. These programs are now in the process of being tested.

Behavior under the Control of Impoverished Incentives: The Loss or Absence of Reinforcement

When an animal that has been pressing a lever for food or turning a wheel to escape shock suddenly stops doing these things, the experimenter generally checks to see if the animal's efforts are still successful in obtaining the rewards or escaping punishment.

If the food hopper is empty, the experimenter fills it. If something has gone wrong with the apparatus and the animal must expend more energy to get the same amount of food, the mechanism is adjusted to correct the fault. If the behavior of the animal turning the wheel to escape shock produces punishment instead, the conditions of the experiment are rearranged so that shock can be avoided. In each case, the experimenter solves the problem by determining what aspect of the animal's environment is responsible for producing a decline in the expected behavior.

Clinical depression, according to Ferster (1966, 1973), also involves an extreme reduction in the frequency of expected behavior. If a similar functional analysis of behavior could be conducted with depression, it might serve to open some new possibilities for treatment by focusing attention on the environmental events that produce and maintain depressed behavior instead of exclusively on the moods and thoughts of the depressed person, the principal targets for most treatment strategies in the past.

Depression. Everyone knows what it means to be depressed. The behavior is so prevalent that it has been correctly designated as the "common cold" of the behavior disorders, second only to schizophrenia in mental hospital admissions. Approximately 4–24% of the population experiences depression severe enough to warrant attention and hospitalization, but, according to some reports, this estimate is low because it does not include the transient episodes of depression that may last for extended periods and ultimately, like the common cold, disappear with time.

Clinicians have a difficult time defining depression, despite its prevalence. This is because it ranges in severity from the mild mood swings experienced by everyone, to the extreme behaviors of psychotic depression which often require radical treatment measures, such as drugs and electroconvulsive shock therapy. Moreover, depression may also occur in a constellation of other disorders which often introduce their own unique behaviors and serve to complicate the picture. Nevertheless, depression most typically involves a marked reduction in performing behaviors and an increase in dysphoric behaviors.

For the most part, a depressed person usually shows a marked decrease in the ability to work, eat properly, sleep properly, be sexually active, take responsibility for personal appearance, or interact meaningfully with people other than to complain or request help. These are the *performing behaviors,* and it is the failure of these behaviors to occur that creates difficulties for depressed individuals as well as for those around them. At the same time, *dysphoric behaviors*—crying, statements of self-pity, self-blame, and hopelessness, for example—show a marked increase.

Many depressions result from the individual's interaction with the environment and have a known precipitating cause—loss of a loved one, loss of a job, an inability to get promoted, for example. Others appear to have no known external cause and are usually attributed to chemical or physiological changes that occur because of age or for other reasons which are not yet clear.

Depression and the Loss of Reinforcement. Most explanations of the development of depression begin with the assumption that the individual has suffered some loss or deprivation, and all agree that the consequence is a marked reduction in performance and an increase in dysphoria. Beyond this, however, each of these explanations chooses to see the "ultimate" effects of the loss somewhat differently.

Psychoanalysis, for example, places emphasis almost exclusively on the internal events that the theory assumes to be basic to all behavior. Mourning, Freud proposed, is different from melancholia because it involves the loss of a loved object (person, country, or liberty, for example). The period spent in mourning is determined by the time it takes to find a substitute. Melancholia, on the other hand, "displays something else which is lacking in grief—an extraordinary fall in . . . self-esteem, an impoverishment of . . . ego on a grand scale" (1959, p. 155). Although the loss is less tangible than it is in mourning, the individual knows unconsciously that something has been lost and no substitute is possible.

The *cognitive view* of depression, presented in more detail in Chapter 15, emphasizes the way in which individuals perceive these losses and the effect that it has on their thinking. Most depressions, according to Beck (1967), the foremost proponent of this view, develop because of certain attitudes individuals learn as children which predispose them to magnify or distort many negative events into feelings of inadequacy and despair. The cognitive, or mediated, view of depression emphasizes the constant interaction taking place between the individual's internal responses, external behavior, and the environmental events which influence both.

The *operant view* of depression, which was developed by Ferster (1966, 1973), derives very largely from the principles of operant conditioning and focuses entirely on the reduction in the frequency of behavior as a result of environmental events.

How Depressions Are Produced: A View from the Laboratory. The critical and sufficient condition for the development of depression, according to Ferster, is a lowered rate of reinforcement which, in turn, reduces the frequency of behavior, especially that kind of behavior which has been successful in obtaining positive reinforcement from others.

Essentially, the rate of reinforcement can be decreased in two ways. (1) A loss of reinforcement can result from some change in the environment (*loss of positive reinforcement*). Any of the situations already discussed—the loss of a loved one or financial losses, for example—are conditions likely to reduce the frequency of certain behaviors. (2) A loss of reinforcement may also occur if the individual cannot escape punishment or is constantly in the process of trying to avoid punishment *(loss of negative reinforcement)*. Here the consequences may be twofold: (1) certain behaviors, such as withdrawal or isolation, are adopted to reduce anxiety (Table 3-3, Chapter 3); and (2) the acquisition of such behavior means a reduction in the kind of behavior that usually elicits positive reinforcement from others. For example, people become depressed because of continued failure to get along with others. If withdrawal and isolation occur, people are no longer in a position to respond appropriately to elicit social reinforcement from others. In effect, the loss of negative reinforcement (inability to escape from punishment) also reduces the rate of positive reinforcement (friendship, for example).

Depression and low rates of positive reinforcement. Ferster has pointed out that animals will generally decrease the amount of effort they expend or stop working entirely if the quantity of food they work for is decreased for any extended length of time or if a large expenditure of energy is required to produce a significant change in the environment. Some people may also give up and stop trying under the same conditions. In essence, continued deprivation and loss of reinforcement is likely to produce extinction of effort. Paykel et al. (1969), for example, compared the life events of a group of depressed people with those of normal people for the most recent 6-month period and found that the depressed subjects had experienced a larger amount of stress and more situations involving losses and social withdrawal.

Ferster's behavioral view of depression has also been held by others. This is not entirely surprising because, as we have already seen, the concept of loss enters into most explanations of depression.

Lazarus (1968), for example, maintains that depression results from reduced or impoverished reinforcement. The temporary losses in reinforcement and self-esteem which most people experience at one time or another do not generally bring on extended periods of depression. The low period may remain for several days, but normal mood and activity levels are soon reestablished. Some people, on the other hand, seem predisposed to more frequent and more prolonged periods of depression. Lazarus has suggested that when depression is prolonged, it is usually because the individual finds the loss irreconcilable, is unsuccessful at finding alternate sources of reinforcement, and "yearns for the reestablishment of the crucial or pivotal reinforcer."

Lewinsohn's version of the origin of depressed behavior, which has stimulated a great deal of research, is, in effect, an extrapolation and refinement of Ferster's "loss of reinforcement" concept and contains two basic assumptions. The first assumption is essentially a restatement of Ferster's position that "a reduced rate of positive reinforcement is a critical condition for the occurrence of depressed behaviors." The second assumption that "social interactions provide contingencies which strengthen and maintain depressed behaviors" identifies unsatisfactory social interactions as the environmental events presumed to be responsible for the lowered rate of reinforcement (Lewinsohn & Atwood, 1969, p. 166).

In a later version, Lewinsohn (1974) makes it clear that it is not a low rate of reinforcement per se that is responsible for depression but a low rate of *response-contingent reinforcement.* This means that it is not just the absence of pleasures and satisfactions that produces depressed behavior, it is also the *unsuccessful attempts made to obtain the reinforcers.* The conditions that affect the rate of response-contingent reinforcement, either singly or in combination, are (1) the extent to which the individual finds things pleasurable or satisfying (the reinforcing value of events), (2) the number of actual pleasurable events that exist (availability of reinforcers), and (3) the extent to which responses are made to obtain the satisfiers (the degree of skill available to obtain the reinforcers) (Blaney, 1977).

Despite the emphasis they have placed on the relationship between rate of response-contingent reinforcement and depression, Lewinsohn and his associates have not explored the effect each of these three conditions has on producing behavior changes through a reduction in the rate of response-contingent reinforcement. Instead, most of their research has been concerned with correlations between value of the reinforcer, amount of reinforcers available, interpersonal skills, and already existing depression. Actually, as Blaney points out, the theory as it has been tested has more to do with how the depressed person interacts with the environment than it does with the causal antecedents of depression (1977, p. 210).

In the main, Lewinsohn and his associates have found the relationships they proposed between moods of depression and the value, amount, and availability of reinforcers, and interpersonal skills.

First, they have shown that most events do not reinforce depressed people the way they do others. Depressed people tend to find fewer things pleasing and satisfying, and, as a result, they engage less in behaviors which would tend to elicit reinforcement from others (MacPhillamy & Lewinsohn, 1974).

Second, depression is related to the number of available reinforcers. Depressed moods and activities of subjects who were asked to complete a questionnaire at the end of each day were found to relate to the number of pleasant events the subjects experienced during the day. If the number was low, the mood and behavior of the person was also low (Lewinsohn & Libet, 1972; Lewinsohn & Graf, 1973).

Finally, depressed people do show a deficiency in interpersonal skills (Libet & Lewinsohn, 1973) and in the behavior necessary to elicit reinforcement from others. The behavior of the depressed person virtually guarantees rejection. They tend to compliment others less, are inclined to be withdrawn, are less verbal, and when they do talk, their conversations are likely to be devoted to personal problems involving a large number of complaints about ill health. In short, it appears that the depressed person creates the very situation that produces and maintains depression.

Depressions which result from social ineptitude and low activity levels are also likely to last longer than the usual "low" because the behavior of the depressed person continues to reduce the amount of social interaction and further decreases the potential for social reinforcement. People usually avoid depressed persons because their dysphoric mood arouses negative emotions in others (Coyne, 1976) and because their helplessness creates feelings of frustration and futility in their friends who try desperately, but unsuccessfully, to help them.

Although relatively few experiments have been conducted for the specific purpose of determining whether reduction in the rate of reinforcement is a *causal* factor in depression, those that have been undertaken are generally not conclusive. In one study, for example, two groups of subjects who were given a series of tests designed to assess the adequacy of their interpersonal relations and satisfactions in various roles were tested for depression 2 months following the evaluation. Contrary to expectations, the individuals who became depressed did not differ in their personality evaluations from those who did not become depressed. This clearly fails to support the prediction that a depressive episode should be preceded by a drop in social effectiveness (Tanner et al., 1975; Blaney, 1977). In another study on the other hand, subjects who were exposed to false reports of failure in a laboratory task also reported feelings of depression (Wenar & Rehm, 1975).

In Chapter 8, we explore the usefulness of Lewinsohn's formulation for devising effective treatment strategies.

Depression and low rates of negative reinforcement. A second way in which depression can develop, according to Ferster, is through the inability to escape or avoid punishment (a loss of negative reinforcement). Seligman & Maier (1967) found this so when the dogs in their experiment who were exposed to shock developed a helpless and inactive condition that could not be reversed when the conditions were changed and punishment was no longer present. When escape became possible for the animals, they had to be dragged physically away from the shock to the other side of the box before they would respond by themselves. Seligman termed this phenomenon "learned helplessness" and suggested that it was probably the way many reactive depressions develop in humans.

In order to extend the animal analogy to humans, Hiroto (1974; Hiroto & Seligman, 1975) tested human subjects with inescapable noise and found that, like the dogs who had received inescapable shock, these subjects made considerably more errors and took much longer to learn to escape, when it became possible, than other subjects who had been permitted to escape all along.

Further studies with depressed subjects (students receiving high scores on inventories designed to measure depressed behavior) showed that they acted more like non-depressed subjects who had received inescapable noise even though the depressed subjects were never prevented from escaping the noise. They made more errors and took longer to perform the tasks which enabled them to escape the stress (Klein & Seligman, 1976).

Seligman further reasoned that, in humans at least, the sense of helplessness, reduction in activity, and depressed behavior in general were due to a feeling that they could not control the events around them—that they were, in a sense, at the mercy of their environment. This feeling of uncontrollability was not only greater for depressed subjects as a whole, it even extended to situations where it was contradicted by events. Where non-depressed subjects were capable of altering their expectancies of success, depending on the number of successes they had had in the past and whether skill or chance was involved in the task, the depressed subjects could not profit from these experiences and continued to give the same low estimates regardless of the change in the situation (Miller & Seligman, 1975).

On the basis of these and other studies, Seligman has suggested that control, or lack of it, is the major factor in producing helplessness and ultimately depression. Although he acknowledges the influence of low rates of reinforcement, he also feels that reduced reinforcement is simply a subset of lack of control. Having no money, for example, an indication of low rates of reinforcement, means having little control, according to Seligman. And, indeed, many of the rewards that humans hold dear (money, status) are rewarding to the extent that they are useful in controlling the environment (Blaney, 1977, p. 217).

Although loss of control can be construed as the loss of negative reinforcement (inability to escape from stress), Seligman makes further assumptions about the effect of loss of control on the individual which introduce a cognitive element into his explanation and draw him closer to Beck (Chapter 15). Seligman maintains that the depressives' attitudes toward lack of control may have been determined by a continued failure to deal adequately with stress in the past. These experiences served to strengthen the feeling of uncontrollability and eventually led to helplessness and depression.

Seligman's learned helplessness formulation of depression appears in this chapter because, as it was originally conceived, it emphasized the loss of negative reinforcement—clearly an operant explanation. As we see in Chapters 14 and 15, however, recent revisions place more emphasis on the way in which people interpret the loss of reinforcement (attribution), and that brings the model much closer to a mediational explanation.

Afterword

In this chapter, we attempted to account for some of the behavior disorders in terms of operant learning, to show how such complex behaviors as obesity, alcoholism, depression, and delinquency could conceivably result from inappropriately administered, addictive, or impoverished reinforcers.

It might be profitable, however, to review some of the risks and benefits involved in talking about a behavior disorder in terms of one type of learning. In the case of self-injurious behavior, the benefits are somewhat more apparent.

Identifying and removing reinforcement which was given inappropriately (attention, affection, escape from demands) eliminated the undesirable behavior. When these reinforcers were given for other behavior, the child no longer found it necessary to engage in self-mutilation.

But there are obvious risks in dealing with complex behavior in such relatively simple terms. Alcoholism, for example, may begin as a conditioned avoidance response to stress. That "good feeling" becomes associated with the sight, smell, and ingestion of alcohol. The initial mood elevation is short-lived, however, and the alcoholic either has to engage in binge drinking and rapid consumption of alcohol in order to avoid the low which inevitably follows or continue to drink large quantities of alcohol in order to achieve the same results. In either case, alcohol provides a source of reinforcement for rapid and continued drinking because it removes the alcoholic from the dysphoric mood and enables the good feeling to be maintained. Finally, drinking may also be maintained by the specific relationships alcohol abusers have with other people and by their own self-image.

Each of these stages involves a different type of learning: conditioning in the first instance, operant learning in the second, and ultimately, some form of mediated learning. Recognizing this, current treatment methods tend to combine aversive conditioning, modification of drinking habits through controlled drinking, and some form of problem-solving in an effort to cover most of the factors responsible for initiating and maintaining alcohol abuse.

chapter eight

Applied Operant Conditioning

> *Twenty-five hundred years ago it might have been said that man understood himself as well as any other part of his world. Today he is the thing he understands least. . . . We have made immense strides in controlling the physical and biological worlds, but our practices in government, education, and much of economics . . . have not greatly improved. . . . We need to make changes in human behavior and we cannot make them with the help of nothing more than physics or biology. What we need is a technology of behavior.*
>
> *Skinner, 1971, pp. 4–7*

The rudiments of a behavior technology existed from the moment humans first learned to train animals, tried to influence the behavior of others (for better or worse), or sought to understand and control their own behavior. Although the success they achieved in the area of human functioning was modest compared to other areas such as agriculture and industry, clearly people operated according to some vague principles understood only in the most practical terms. These principles did not differ fundamentally from those elaborated in Chapter 6, and, for the most part, they worked.

Medieval knights, as we have seen, learned to handle a lance properly or risked a sore back and possibly a cracked skull. Teachers have been eminently successful at getting children to learn by the lavish, if not indiscriminate, use of gold stars for superior effort. On many occasions, however, the rules did not seem to work. Punishment is often successful in eliminating behavior, but sometimes the behavior returns when the punishment is removed. Society's answer to this problem has been to keep the threat of punishment in front of the individual as a constant deterrent. Teachers awarded gold stars to some students for their efforts and punished others without knowing that punishment (and attention) is like a gold star to the child who is being disruptive.

So, while the tools for behavior technology were in existence even before the advent of the behavioral sciences, they were not always correctly or strategically applied. In this chapter, we show how the relatively simple rules that have been discovered in the study of operant learning have created and refined a technology of behavior and made it useful in alleviating some of the problems of human existence.

REWARD TRAINING: THE USE OF POSITIVE REINFORCERS

We have already discussed the two basic procedures for changing behavior through the use of operant methods—reward and aversive training. This chapter expands the discussion of these principles, illustrates them in detail, and notes their wide applications.

It is important to bear in mind that instances in which either reward or punishment is used exclusively in behavior modification are extremely rare. The objective in most cases is to eliminate already existing behavior and replace it with other behavior. Generally, this is accomplished by rewarding desirable behavior and ignoring (or punishing) undesirable behavior. But in some instances, punishment must be used either initially or exclusively. In view of this, we include examples of operant methods under reward or aversive procedures, depending upon whether reward or punishment is the first procedure to be used.

Restoring Positive Reinforcement in Depression

If the loss of response-contingent reinforcement is the basis for depressed behavior, is it possible to alleviate depression by restoring and increasing the incidence of positive reinforcement? In principle, the answer to this question is yes, even if we subscribe to the idea that lack of control over environmental events is ultimately at the root of all depressed behavior.

One possible way of restoring control is to increase the number of successful attempts to derive pleasure and satisfaction. This can be done in two ways: (1) by increasing the number of potential rewards and making them more available, and (2) by teaching individuals the skills that enable them to make the successful attempts to get the rewards. Most of the efforts to deal with depression have used these procedures.

One of the earliest attempts to alleviate depression through manipulating the amount of reinforcement was made in a clinical case study by Lewinsohn and Atwood (1969). The treatment consisted largely of enriching the client's extremely impoverished social interactions by encouraging her to develop new friendships and engage in rewarding activities outside immediate family concerns. This case study was followed by two others which also achieved positive results by the use of explicit self-reinforcement procedures. (Self-reinforcement and self-control are discussed in more detail in Chapter 12.)

In the first of these cases, Todd (1972) used the Premack differential-probability principle and Homme's notion of coverant control to alleviate a case of severe depression (Box 8-1).

BOX 8-1
Reinforcement in a Pack of Cigarettes

Depressed people find it extremely difficult to say anything good about themselves. One of the goals in the treatment of depression, therefore, is to reconstruct a positive self-image through the manipulation of the proper response-reinforcement contingencies.

In attempting to do this with a 49-year-old severely depressed woman, Todd (1972) made use of Homme's notion (1965) that thoughts, ideas, and ruminations are like overt responses—he calls them *coverants,* that is, covert operants—and that thoughts about one's self can affect the environment like any other operant and can be strengthened or weakened through reinforcement.

Todd also used the Premack *differential-probability principle* (we have already seen how this principle was used to manage the behavior of a group of kindergarten children in Chapter 6, Box 6-5) which states that the probability of behavior which is less likely to occur can be increased if followed by behavior which is more likely to occur. If drinking coffee is high-probability behavior because it occurs frequently throughout the day, in principle it can increase the probability of any behavior which precedes it. For example, the amount of time spent preparing for an exam, which is obviously low-probability behavior, can be increased if drinking coffee is delayed until a certain amount of (gradually increasing) work is completed.

The woman was a 49-year-old physician's wife who was suffering from a depression severe enough to have prompted suicide attempts on three separate occasions. Psychotherapy for a period of 3½ years, including a brief period of hospitalization and a course of antidepressant drugs, had no apparent effect on the depressed behavior. In the initial stages of treatment, a decision was made to concentrate on the elimination of the crippling depression before dealing with other problems consisting of general tension, multiple phobias, psychosomatic disorders, and marital discord.

When the client was asked to describe herself in a series of single words or phrases, her responses were all negative, and she was told that a disparaging self-image was responsible for her depression. After much difficulty and with much prompting from the therapist, she managed to come up with six positive statements about herself. These were printed on a sheet of paper and, in smaller letters, on a card trimmed to fit inside the cellophane wrapper of a cigarette package.

The operation of the Premack principle was explained to the client, and she was instructed to read one or two of the six items each time before smoking and to continue to add positive items to the list. After two weeks, she reported feeling considerably better than she had in the last two years, and she had added 21 positive items to the list. She also indicated that positive thoughts about herself were occurring to her now, even when she was not smoking.

The client was seen for a total of 41 sessions, 6 of which were with her husband. In the three years following therapy, she has not suffered any serious depressions, has become active in volunteer work, is considered an excellent hostess, and has a wide circle of friends. On occasions when she does feel "down," she simply bolsters her spirits by thinking "good things" about herself. Systematic desensitization and behavior rehearsal were also used to deal with the tension and marital discord.

The second of these cases, reported by Jackson (1972), involved a 22-year-old married woman who had been suffering from feelings of worthlessness, depression, and prolonged inactivity for two years. Although she had earned a B.A. degree in sociology and was a thoroughly competent homemaker, her standards for performance were exceedingly high, and she constantly deprecated her own achievements. In fact, she actively *reduced the rate of positive reinforcement from others* by denying compliments when she received them and adding self-deprecating comments of her own. The advice that several therapists had given her to help her gain some insight into the reasons for her depression and become active again was largely ineffective.

In order to restore the confidence and feelings of self-worth that would then enable her to accept the reinforcements available from others, the client was asked to select a routine task in which self-reinforcement was possible. She selected housekeeping, and a 10-day baseline record was kept of the number of times she praised herself, did something she enjoyed, or felt satisfied with her work. A record of depression on a 10-point scale was also kept during the same period. Figure 8-1 indicates that the frquency of self-reinforcement was non-existent during baseline, with a corresponding increase in self-rated depression.

Following the baseline observation, the client was introduced to the idea of self-reinforcement. Because her standards were so high and she had a tendency to set unrealistic goals, she was asked to select several tasks that would guarantee success. When she had achieved the desired goal by completing the task, she was to reward herself with a compliment, a cigarette, or an enjoyable activity. Shortly after receiving these instructions, which the therapist rehearsed with her, the frequency of self-reinforcment began to increase, and self-rated depression went down (Fig. 8-1). The client also began to apply self-reinforcement to other areas of her life, deciding beforehand what her goals were to be and rewarding herself for achieving them. Two months after the completion of therapy, she felt more contentment with her own behavior and had gained a great deal of respect for her own achievements.

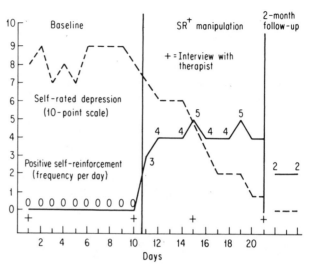

FIG. 8-1 Daily records of depression and frequency of positive self-reinforcement SR$^+$. (Source: B. Jackson. Treatment of depression by self-reinforcement. *Behavior Therapy,* 1972, *3,* 298–307. Copyright 1976 by Academic Press and used by permission.)

The success achieved by using the reinforcement model in individual clinical cases has not been duplicated in large-scale studies. Two studies (Hammen & Glass, 1975; Padfield, 1976) designed to increase rate of reinforcement by requiring groups of women to participate in pleasant activities showed no commensurate decrease in depression.

At first glance, it is difficult to understand why such an eminently plausible method for treating depression worked with individual clients but not with subjects in the large-scale studies, but a closer examination may suggest the reason for the differences. The major difference between the two situations is that the clients in individual therapy did not engage just in pleasant activities, they also administered self-reinforcement in a systematic manner when they completed tasks graded to ensure success. If both loss of response-contingent reinforcement and loss of control are factors necessary in the onset of depression, then increasing rate of reinforcement alone by increasing the number of pleasant activities is not a condition sufficient for alleviating depression. Self-confidence, a positive self-image, and feelings of control can only be restored through successful performance. As we see in Chapter 15, the use of graded tasks guaranteed to produce success and increased availability of reinforcement have become methods for treating depression.

Treating the Hyperactive Child

Estimates show that 5% of all elementary school children in the United States are chronically restless, impulsive, have a short memory span, and routinely "clobber" their classmates at the slightest provocation. Some hyperactive children do show soft neurological signs (soft because their actual presence is uncertain)—immature reflexes and poor motor coordination, for example, which eventually disappear with age (Dubey, 1976). So, while some organic invovement is suspected, we have ample reason to believe that hyperkinesis is also due to inappropriate reinforcement of undesirable behavior.

Approximately 2% of hyperactive children are being treated with drugs (Ritalin and Dexadrine), and, although some children show improvement as a result of medication, gains in treatment are frequently offset by undesirable side-effects such as suppression in height and weight gain, increased heart rate, and elevated blood pressure, all of which disappear when the drugs are eliminated. In some 30–50% of the cases, however, drugs are not effective at all.

The problems created by drug administration have led some psychologists to investigate the possibility that hyperactive behavior could be managed through operant learning. Earlier studies (Patterson et al., 1969) succeeded in reducing hyperactivity in retarded children without medication. More recently, however, behavior modification procedures were shown to be effective with hyperactive children who were otherwise normal in a non-remedial classroom setting.

The first of these studies conducted by O'Leary and his associates (1976) focused on a home-based reward program. Children were rewarded at home for behavior changes in the classroom. As a result, the treatment plan involved both the teacher and the parent. The children selected for the study ranged in age from 8–11 years. They were observed in the classroom by several trained investigators and judged to be severely hyperkinetic in terms of their fidgeting, inability to stay seated, and lack of attention to classroom tasks. All of these children were of average intelligence, and none were receiving stimulant drug therapy, although two had been taking Ritalin prior to the study.

Initially, the program involved conferences with the teachers and parents to select the goals and the target behaviors for change. Although the goals consisted largely of classroom activity—completing work assignments in class, helping other children with their projects, not fighting, and bringing in homework—the rewards for achieving these goals were administered by the parents. The teacher recorded the child's progress on a daily report card that the child brought home and exchanged for reinforcers. The entire program consisted of five components: (1) establishing a child's daily classroom goals; (2) praising the child for efforts made to achieve the goals; (3) evaluating the child's progress toward the goals at the end of the day; (4) transmitting the child's progress to the parents by means of a daily report card; and (5) reward for progress toward the goal by the parents (O'Leary et al., 1976, p. 511).

One of the most critical elements of the program, according to the authors, was the selection and distribution of appropriate rewards. Some of the daily rewards—determined in consultation with the child—consisted of 30 minutes of extra television, a special dessert, spending time with either parent, or money. Weekly rewards, given after a consistently satisfactory record (four out of five good daily reports), included a fishing trip with father, a dinner at a favorite aunt's house, or a family meal at a local restaurant.

When the results of the treatment program were evaluated at the end of 10 weeks, the hyperkinetic children showed a dramatic improvement in behavior compared to the control children who had received the usual attention from the teachers. Problem-behavior ratings for the hyperactive children decreased from an initial score of 5.5, denoting serious or frequent problems, to 3.0—a 25% change. The Teacher Rating Scale, a measure of hyperactivity, also showed similar changes for the hyperactive group, and the overall changes in behavior for the hyperactive children compared well to those achieved with drugs, but without the undesirable side effects.

Although stimulant drugs must be used initially in many instances—particularly in cases where the child is extremely aggressive and unmanageable—the continued use of drugs without some form of behavioral treatment is counterproductive because it does not produce any long-term changes in behavior. According to O'Leary et al., children who have been on medication for a year or more revert to their original hyperactive behavior patterns as soon as the drug is discontinued.

In a second study conducted by S. O'Leary and Pelham (1978), children who were already on stimulant medication had the drugs withdrawn at the same time that a behavior modification program, which included behavior at home as well as in the classroom, was established for them. The children, all boys, selected for the study were 7–10 years of age, and all had been receiving medication for a period of .5–4.5 years. A typical child in the treatment program was 8 years old and in third grade. At home, he fought with his sisters and brothers and paid no attention to their requests. In the classroom, he paid very little attention to the teacher's instructions and failed to complete his schoolwork. He had been receiving Ritalin for a period of 18 months (S. O'Leary & Pelham, 1978, p. 7).

Except for the emphasis placed on individual instructions for the parents, the methods used by S. O'Leary and Pelham were similar to those used by O'Leary. A list of target behaviors in the classroom was developed, and daily reports were sent home to the parents concerning the improvement in these behaviors. In addition, parents were instructed in the use at home of behavior modification procedures, including praise for appropriate behavior, ignoring minor disruptions, and the use of omission training when necessary. Gradually, daily reports were substituted for weekly reports, and weekend activities were used as source of reinforcement. In order to ensure that the children received adequate support and reinforcement, attempts were made to establish goals that they could meet at least 75% of the time.

The entire length of treatment was 4 months, during which time the therapist saw the family and the teacher on an average of once a week initially and once every 2 to 3 weeks later on in the treatment program. The therapists stopped seeing either the teacher or the parents 4 weeks before the final assessment of the child's behavior was made.

The results of this study duplicated those obtained by O'Leary. All measures of hyperkinesis and problem behavior showed a marked decrease, and, with the exception of one child who was being withdrawn from drugs gradually, the medication for all children was discontinued completely. Parents reported less aggressive behavior at home, and, in some cases, the atmosphere in the home "changed radically from that of suspicion, expectation of problems, and hopelessness, to one characterized by shared responsibility, warmth, and an expectation for continued improvement" (S. O'Leary & Pelham, 1978, p. 3; O'Leary, 1980).

The results of these two studies indicate that behavior modification can be an effective alternative to stimulant medication for hyperactive children. Behavioral procedures are preferable, especially when the long-range effects of medication are considered. Continued medication for long periods may simply serve to convince children that the only way they can achieve any control over their own behavior is to take a pill (S. O'Leary & Pelham, 1978, p. 3; O'Leary, 1980).

AVERSIVE METHODS: THE USE OF PUNISHMENT AND OMISSION

Punishment, as we have seen, is a useful method for changing behavior when it is employed in a careful and discriminating manner, with concern for the individuals involved. For punishment to be effective, however, a number of conditions must be satisfied, and these have been outlined by Azrin and Holz in a review of empirical research on punishment (1966, pp. 426–427). Some of these are:

1. Punishment should be as intense as possible and introduced in full strength.

2. Punishment should be administered frequently.

3. Conditions should be arranged so that unplanned escape from punishment is impossible.

4. Reinforcement and punishment should not be associated or else punishment may assume the properties of a conditioned stimulus for the delivery of reinforcement (see Erofeeva's experiment, Chapter 2).

5. *An alternative response should be available which receives the same or greater reinforcement than the punished responses* (italics added).

6. Withdrawal or reduction in positive reinforcement (omission training) may be used in lieu of physical punishment whenever necessary.

Under no circumstances is continuous punishment ever used as a long-term solution—not only because it is morally repugnant but also because it inevitably creates other emotional and behavioral problems that interfere with learning.

Passive Avoidance Training: Learning What Not to Do to Avoid Punishment

All societies maintain stability and order by means of laws. Laws are instances of passive avoidance training, codified examples of the kinds of behavior that individuals should refrain from if they are to avoid punishment.

Whether this type of behavioral control is successful or not is questionable, especially if the goal of society is the elimination of crime. It might conceivably be better, as Azrin & Holz point out in condition #5, to balance injunctions against wrongdoing with rewards for desirable behavior—a combination which is most often employed in behavior modification. But, as we mentioned in Chapter 6, in some instances the use of physical punishment to produce pain and discomfort is necessary in order to interrupt the sequence of ongoing behavior without, at the same time, rewarding any behavioral alternatives. Under these circumstances, for example, vomiting, seizures, and self-injurious behavior will simply disappear when punished, as we shall see.

Chronic Ruminative Vomiting.   The dramatic success that Lang and Melamed (Chapter 1) achieved using punishment to keep a 9-month-old infant from starving to death because of chronic ruminative vomiting was not an isolated instance, and their work led to several other studies which obtained the same results. The first of these was reported by Kohlenberg (1970), who treated a 21-year-old severely retarded woman whose life was endangered because of persistent vomiting.

Vomiting, like most other behavior, occurs at the end of a chain of responses. It begins with stomach contractions and then proceeds up the alimentary canal in the form of a peristaltic wave. Each of the early responses in the sequence serves as a signal for the subsequent response, until vomiting ultimately takes place. Eliminating one of these responses interrupts the sequence of behavior and eliminates vomiting. The responses occurring at the beginning of the chain of behavior are weaker than those at the end because they are more distant from the source of reinforcement so the logical point to introduce punishment in order to break the chain would be somewhere early in the sequence. Lang and Melamed used precisely this strategy when they recorded the first faint signs of vomiting as disturbances in the stomach by means of an electromyographic transducer (a sensitive instrument for recording weak muscle potentials) attached to the child's back. Introducing the shock just at the moment that these signs were detected successfully interrupted the chain and eliminated vomiting.

Kohlenberg accomplished much the same results without the aid of a sensitive detector by making careful observations during the vomiting sequence and looking for external signs related to vomiting. Inasmuch as the woman regurgitated continuously for a period of 1 hour after completing a meal, it was possible to monitor these episodes to determine that abdominal muscle tension invariably preceded each instance of regurgitation. A 1-second shock from a prod delivered to the thigh each time abdominal muscle tension was detected reduced vomiting to zero approximately 48 minutes after the initial shock was administered. The program eliminated vomiting for a period of 10 months enabling the patient to achieve a weight gain of 10.5 lbs. and removing vomiting as a possible hazard to her health. A 1-year follow-up, however, revealed that vomiting had again become a problem and that subsequent treatments would be required.

Several studies have relied less on direct physical punishment such as shock to eliminate vomiting and more on the manipulation of social contingencies. The method used by Wright et al. (1978), for example, involved an omission training procedure similar to that described in Box 6-7 (Chapter 6) with the tracheotomized children. In this instance the child's nurse was simply instructed to leave immediately after the child began vomiting and not to return until after the child was through in order to clean her up. The nurse was also told to be certain there were no objects (toys, etc.) present when she was absent.

After an initial gradual decline in rumination, there was an abrupt drop on the fourth day. When the child was removed from the hospital the parents were instructed to continue the intervention procedures at home. A follow-up approximately 9 and 14 months later showed a continued remission of vomiting.

Bennet and Kennedy (1980) employed verbal reprimand and a DRO schedule [(Differential Reinforcement of Other Behavior) actually, as we shall see, the DRO schedule is a DRL schedule in which low rates of vomiting were systematically reinforced] to decrease habitual vomiting in an 8-year-old severely retarded male. A baseline of vomiting was first established by recording the number of times vomiting occurred in the period one hour after breakfast and one hour after lunch. Observations for 12 sessions indicated that for both of these periods the mean amount of vomiting was 3.5 times.

Following baseline observations the intervention procedure was introduced. Verbal reprimand consisted of saying NO! to the child during vomiting. He was then moved a small distance from the vomitus which was allowed to remain on the floor for 2–3 mins. When the DRO schedule was in effect, the child received a bite of food (after having eaten half his meal) contingent on not vomiting for a set interval of time. The time was gradually increased by 1 min. intervals until a 10 min. DRO was achieved and then further increased by 2 min. intervals. The boy was also hugged and praised for not vomiting during these periods.

After 14 sessions vomiting was reduced to zero and the child was released from the hospital with instruction to the parents to continue the DRO schedule.

As the authors point out, while the use of procedures which do not involve direct physical punishment is preferable, physical punishment is almost inevitable in those instances where habitual vomiting represents a risk to health.

Interrupting the Chain in Seizure Disorders.   Most seizure disorders are associated with epilepsy and occur because of some kind of neurological involvement. They can be identified by a neurological examination including observation of brain waves (electroencephalogram—EEG) and can be successfully controlled by drugs such as Dilantin, Mysolin, Valium, and phenobarbital.

About 5% of all seizure disorders, however, are known as reflex or sensorimotor epilepsy in which seizures can be induced by some known external stimulus. Seizures have been known to be produced by music (in one particular case, country music), certain patterned stimuli such as flashing lights, and sexual fetishes, and many are self-induced.

Wright (1973) reduced the number of "self-induced" seizures by using punishment. The child, a 5-year old retarded boy, was inducing "several hundred" trance-like states each day by waving his fingers back and forth in front of a light source and blinking his eyes at the same time. Electrodes attached to the child's forearm delivered a shock to him each time he raised his arm to stimulate a seizure. As a result, the frequency of seizures was reduced from 175 on the first day to 36 on the fourth day when treatment was discontinued. Seven months later, the mother reported that the child never again attempted to induce seizures by waving his hand before his eyes, although he did stimulate some seizures by blinking his eyes.

In the case just described, the seizures appeared to be a "learned" disorder rather than the result of some brain deficit. Under the circumstance, it would be reasonable to expect that some form of learning or conditioning processes could modify them. But what about those instances where the epileptic behavior suggests some neurological involvement? Could the seizures be controlled by behavioral rather than pharmacological methods in these cases? Zlutnick, Mayville, and Moffat (1975) thought so, and they undertook to eliminate or reduce the frequency of organically related seizures by means of operant-training procedures.

Each of the 5 children selected as subjects in the study was chosen on the basis of three fairly rigorous criteria to decrease the possibility that the epileptic behavior resulted from learning. First, the seizures had to be behaviorally identifiable by two observers, ruling out the possibility of *petit mal* epilepsy, which is difficult to diagnose. Second, the seizures had to occur at least once a day. Finally, a formal diagnosis of epilepsy based upon EEG and/or clinical examination by a neurologist was mandatory. Thirteen children were eliminated from the study because these criteria were not met.

On the assumption that the actual seizure represents the final response in a long chain of pre-seizure behaviors, the authors decided to punish the earliest behavior in the sequence in order to disrupt the chain and eliminate the seizure. In one of the children, a 7-year-old boy who had been diagnosed as autistic and brain damaged and who had had a history of seizures since the age of 2, the sequence of pre-seizure behaviors consisted of (1) a fixed glaze at a flat surface (table top or wall), followed by (2) bodily rigidity, followed by (3) myoclonic spasms (violent shaking), and terminating in (4) a fall to the floor (Zlutnick et al., 1975, p. 320).

Because the fixed stare was the earliest behavior in the series, and inasmuch as it invariably accompanied all seizures, the researchers made a decision to punish this behavior when it occurred by grasping the child at the shoulders, vigorously shaking him and shouting "No!" at the same time.

After 7 weeks, the number of seizures for this particular child dropped from 12 per day during the baseline observation period to 1 or 2 per day, and they were completely eliminated by the tenth week (Fig. 8-2). When the punishment was removed for one day during the tenth week (the researchers were reluctant to remove it for more than one day because of the severity of the seizures) to determine whether it was the effective factor in reducing the seizures, the number of seizures increased to 40 (Fig. 8-2). Punishment was reinstituted, and the seizure behavior dropped to zero. Medication was withdrawn shortly before the end of treatment, and 6 months later the parents reported complete elimination of the staring behavior and only one seizure episode.

The authors emphasize the importance of punishing the pre-seizure behavior in order to eliminate the convulsion itself, pointing out that seizures occurred only

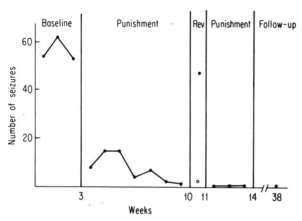

FIG. 8-2 Number of motor seizures for the 7-year-old boy described in the text. Each point represents the sum of all seizures for a given week. Punishment was discontinued between weeks 10 and 11 and reinstated following the eleventh week. Data after the fourteenth week indicate the total number of seizures in the ensuing 6 months following the completion of treatment. (Source: S. Zlutnick, W. J. Mayville, and S. Moffat. In R. Katz and S. Zlutnick (Eds.). *Behavior therapy and health care: Principles and applications.* New York: Pergamon Press, 1975. Copyright 1975 by Pergamon Press and used by permission.)

when the staff members (people in the child's classroom who were trained to administer the treatment) failed to apply the punishment in time, i.e., 15–20 seconds after the onset of staring. Staring also declined as the number of seizures went down. In fact, after 2 weeks of treatment, the child was observed to interrupt his staring in order to see if anyone was approaching.

The same procedure produced similar results for all of the subjects in the study, except in the case of one child with unpredictable pre-seizure behavior. In this instance, the child's mother could only predict approximately 45–50% of his seizures, and the two observers could only agree on 15% of the pre-seizure behavior. Punishment did produce a decrease in seizure frequency from 12 to 7 per day, eliminating those seizures that could be reliably identified by pre-seizure behavior.

The treatment of epilepsy just discussed is a dramatic demonstration of applied behavioral technology. It would be remarkable, indeed, if an organically based disorder such as epilepsy yielded to the relatively simple punishment procedure introduced by Zlutnick and his associates. But, since the study is a relatively isolated one which has not been replicated, any judgment regarding its ultimate effectiveness must be reserved until further research is completed.

Punishment has also been used by Lovaas (1966, 1967) as an adjunctive procedure in the treatment of autistic children, who will often engage in repetitive behavior, trance-like states, or self-injurious behavior in order to avoid demands made upon them. These behaviors must be dealt with before progress can be made in teaching language or any of the other developmental skills necessary to the autistic child. To command the child's attention, Lovaas has resorted to mild electric shock and, in some instances, a sharp slap on the face. Once the undesirable behavior is disrupted, however, the use of punishment decreases as the rewarded alternative behaviors begin to take over.

Punishing Compulsive Verbal Behavior. Punishment does not always involve the application of a painful physical stimulus. On some occasions, the person's own behavior may be the equivalent of a painful stimulus, especially if the behavior is a source of embarrassment or social opprobrium.

This method of exposing people to their own potentially discomfiting behavior was used to reduce the urge on the part of two women to talk uncontrollably about themselves (O'Brien & Raynes, 1973). In one case, a 38-year-old married woman's compulsion took the form of verbal masochistic behavior in which she frequently repeated the desire to gouge out her eyes, burn the hair off her head, jump in front of a car, or jump from the top of a building. She feared harming herself so much that she could not do housework or go into the bathroom when her husband's razor was there. The behavior began about 3 years before O'Brien and Raynes's treatment, and it was probably accelerated by a brief course of psychotherapy in which she was "encouraged" to express these feelings.

In the second case, a 24-year-old married college graduate working as a secretary experienced an uncontrollable desire to talk about her premarital sexual activities and a premarital abortion. Although various environmental stimuli—the make of a car, the number of a house or street—that had been associated with past sexual behavior would evoke thoughts about these events, her husband was the only stimulus which elicited detailed accounts of the premarital experiences. This occurred as frequently as every 15 minutes when they were together, and she would often wake her husband during the night to tell these stories to him. By all accounts, the compulsive desire to confess began when she confided in a girl friend who encouraged her to "tell all" to her husband.

The treatment in both instances required the women to make a tape recording of their compulsive verbal expressions. They also had to listen to these recordings whenever they got the urge to talk about self-injury or sexual experiences, and their husbands monitored these activities to see that they took place.

In the first case, the course of compulsive verbal behavior involving self-injury decreased predictably after the first session in which the patient listened to her own self-destructive verbalizations. While she was required to listen to the tape for only 3 minutes at each compulsive outbreak, she was placed on a schedule (DRL—Differential Reinforcement of Low Rates of Responding—Chapter 6) in which the listening time was increased by 3-minute intervals if the compulsive behavior continued. By the eighth session, the compulsive verbal behavior disappeared completely. The patient found a job and resumed her housecleaning and cooking, tasks which she had not done in over a year.

Although the procedure was basically the same for the second woman with uncontrollable urges to recount her former sexual experiences to her husband, a variation was introduced because of the husband's reluctance to become involved in "playing the silly tapes for her pleasure." A time-out procedure (omission training) was employed in which the husband left the room, increased the volume on the radio, or slept in a separate bedroom whenever the wife felt compelled to talk about her former sexual adventures. This tactic did decrease the amount of time spent in compulsive verbalization by about 50%, but it was not until the patient was convinced to play the tapes to herself that any appreciable reduction took place. By the twelfth session, the "contingent punishment" had reduced the time spent in the compulsive talking to about 10%, and the behavior disappeared completely by the fourteenth session. Follow-up tests indicated that she no longer felt compelled to talk about her former sexual experiences.

Punishment and Exhibitionism.   One way of dealing with a man who derives sexual satisfaction from exposing himself to women is to arrest him on the theory that the shame and embarrassment of a jail sentence will bring about a change in behavior. But the 10 subjects in Maletzky's study (1974) seemed to be impervious to this kind of punishment. Some had been exhibitionists for a very long time (30 years in one case), and even though most were married and had satisfactory sexual adjustments at home, they continued to be arrested time and time again for displaying their genitals to women on the street. Four of the men had even received psychiatric treatment without any benefit. But where one form of punishment failed to produce a change in behavior, another, based on the principles of learning and conditioning, appeared to be effective.

Maletzky used a form of punishment training, known as *covert sensitization,* in which the thoughts and fantasies leading to the undesirable behavior (exposure in this instance) are associated with noxious and aversive events. As it is generally used, the subject is asked to think about or visualize in fantasy the situation which produces sexual excitement and pleasure. The therapist immediately follows this imagined scene with a vivid and repugnant description which includes a detailed account of the subject becoming violently ill, retching and vomiting all over himself. The object of this procedure, of course, is to create a situation in which fantasies of exposure lead to abhorrent thoughts rather than to sexual pleasures and the inevitable deviant sexual action.

Although covert sensitization had been found to be generally effective in the past, Maletzky modified the standard procedure by introducing an extremely malodorous substance, valeric acid, which is reminiscent of decaying human flesh, during the imagination sessions. The subject was initially encouraged to imagine himself in one of several exhibitionist scenes taken from his past. At the point where he was approaching a beautiful blonde woman to expose himself and the sexual pleasure was escalating, the therapist introduced the noxious images and held an uncapped bottle of valeric acid under the subject's nose.

But as you stop the car and start to take (your penis) out that bad smell comes back and that sick feeling in the pit of your stomach. . . . Your stomach turns over and pieces of your supper catch in your throat . . . chunks of vomit gush out of your mouth, dribble down your chin. . . . The smell is making you even sicker . . . the blonde can see you now . . . you quickly clean yourself off and drive away (Maletzky, 1974, p. 37).

The noxious images and the bottle of valeric acid were withdrawn as soon as the subject escaped from the imaginary exposure situation and the fantasy stopped.

After the course of treatment, which consisted of 11–19, 40-minute biweekly sessions, was completed, the subjects received booster sessions at 3-, 6-, and 12-month intervals, and their behavior was monitored during these periods. By the end of the twelfth month, none of the subjects had been apprehended for exposing himself or had any urges or fantasies involving exhibitionistic behavior (Figure 8-3).

To validate the effectiveness of treatment further, "temptation tests" were introduced immediately following treatment and again 1 year later to see whether the subjects would be persuaded to expose themselves in front of a comely model hired for the purpose. The tests took place sometime during the course of the subjects' daily activities—driving to or from work, for example—and the subjects were unaware that tests were taking place. The model waited for a subject's car to approach and then walked toward him in a sexually provocative manner.

All but one of the subjects passed the test immediately following treatment, and none were tempted to expose themselves on the second test conducted 12 months later. (The author raised ethical questions about the use of deception as part of the treatment plan. He felt, however, that it was necessary in order to justify the continued use of the method with other cases. Moreover, the subjects were alerted to expect unusual experimental procedures as part of the treatment.)

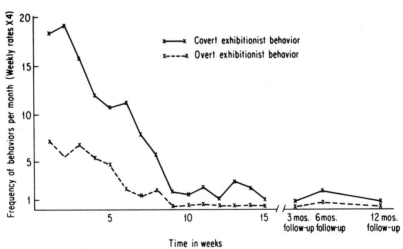

FIG. 8-3 Mean frequencies of covert and overt exhibitionistic behavior during treatment and follow-up. (Source: B. Maletzky. "Assisted" covert sensitization in the treatment of exhibitionism. *Journal of Consulting and Clinical Psychology.* 1974, *42*, 34–40. Copyright 1974 by the American Psychological Association and used by permission.)

The elimination of exhibitionism through the use of punishment illustrates another instance in which the chain of behavior may be broken by interrupting other responses early in the sequence. The act of exposure itself, once it is committed, carries with it a certain amount of reinforcement (the presence of a female, the "surprise" reaction, and the heightened sexual feelings) which may make it more difficult to extinguish. The thoughts and fantasies that precede the actual act, however, like the faint muscle responses in chronic ruminative vomiting and the pre-seizure behaviors in the seizure disorders, are further removed from the source of reinforcement and weaker by comparison. As we already know from previous discussions, punishing these anticipatory behaviors early in the sequence can effectively remove the goal behavior.

Active Avoidance Learning: Learning What to Do to Avoid Punishment

The major difference between active and passive avoidance learning lies in the response itself. Passive avoidance learning, as we have already seen, involves response restraint in order to avoid punishment. Active avoidance specifically requires that a response be made. The objective in passive avoidance is to keep a response from being made—in active avoidance it is to activate responding.

Although active avoidance learning is presumed to be the basis for most of the behavior disorders involving fear and anxiety (neurotic disorders, see Chapter 3), the occasions on which it is used for changing behavior are rare. In the cases which we have already described under passive avoidance learning, the only condition necessary to avoid punishment is to stop doing what elicits the punishment. In active avoidance learning, a *new response* must be learned which prevents the punishment from occurring.

But active avoidance learning as a form of treatment has certain disadvantages. No form of therapy should encourage behavior, the sole purpose of which is to escape punishment. In most instances, this would be like trading off one difficulty for another, much as obsessive-compulsives do when they learn severely crippling rituals such as "checking for nonexistent bombs" in order to avoid or reduce fear. To be effective, the avoidance behavior itself should not merely be an escape from the threat of punishment, it also should be a response which is socially desirable and leads ultimately to positive reinforcement. This is one of the ways it is used in the treatment of alcoholism (see the section on behavior modification and the treatment of alcoholism at the end of this chapter). It has also been used effectively in the treatment of bedwetting.

Learning to Avoid Wetting the Bed. One of the important characteristics of behavior modification that distinguishes it from other methods of treatment in the behavior disorders is the commitment to critical self-examination. Follow-up studies are required to validate the outcome of treatment, and both the theory and method are exposed to constant "public" scrutiny. The treatment of *nocturnal enuresis,* or bed-wetting, is an excellent illustration of the way in which this self-appraisal has operated to change the explanations underlying the methods. Several years ago a discussion of enuresis would have been included in the section on classical conditioning, with many important questions left unanswered. But recent speculations as well as research strongly suggest that the basis for treatment in bed-wetting is probably active avoidance learning.

In his book *Conditioning and Enuresis* (1964) Lovibond estimates that spontaneous recovery from bedwetting for children between the ages of 3 and 4 is approximately 25% for a 12-month period. This rate shows a progressive decline with increasing age until at ages of 11 and 12, the uppermost limits sampled, it is reduced to 16%. No one is very happy about advising a mother to "wait it out," especially because the parent still has to contend with wet beds, offensive odors, a child with a severely depreciated self-image, and strained family relationships. In fact, the literature on child-abuse indicates that, next to crying, bed-wetting is the most commonly stated reason for assaults on children.

No one really knows why some children do not learn to keep dry at night, especially when most have achieved control during the day. Studies of enuretic children indicate that, for the most part, they are no more maladjusted than non-enuretic children. But while enuresis is usually not in itself the result of emotional disorders, it can act as a catalyst for the development of more serious behavioral and emotional difficulties if neglected.

In 1938, Mowrer and Mowrer devised a method for dealing with nocturnal bedwetting based on a model of classical conditioning. The Mowrers considered functional enuresis as a habit deficiency which could be corrected by teaching the child to control urination while asleep. To accomplish this, they designed a basic apparatus consisting of an absorbent pad containing a network of fine wires connected to a buzzer and a 6-volt battery. The wires in the pad represent an open circuit until they are shorted by urine, which is highly conductive. When this occurs, a buzzer or tone sounds until the child wakes up, turns it off, and goes to the bathroom.

The classical-conditioning explanation of these events involves the association of stimuli arising from the bladder (CS) with the response of waking and stopping urination (UCR) which is elicited by the bell and buzzer (UCS) (Fig. 8-4). Presumably, as is the case with all conditioning, the stimuli from the bladder (CS) ultimately acquire an anticipatory function and wake the child even before urination occurs and the signal has sounded—a situation much like that which takes place when a person wakes up before the alarm clock rings in the morning.

But if the children are conditioned to wake up with this method, why is it they

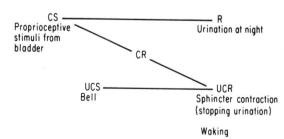

FIG. 8-4 Classical conditioning account of bell and pad training. In avoidance conditioning explanation the CS becomes a signal for sphincter contraction which prevents the child from waking.

eventually learn to sleep through the night without wetting? Furthermore, because conditioned stimuli lose their effectiveness if the unconditioned stimulus is discontinued, why should the child continue to wake up in response to signals from the bladder (CS) if the bell or buzzer (UCS) is no longer present? According to the principles of conditioning, "waking up" should extinguish, and the child should continue to wet the bed. These questions emphasize the dilemma in using classical conditioning to explain enuresis training.

Actually, if the sequence of events is carefully analyzed, it becomes apparent that the child *learns to avoid* urination and that avoidance learning is a more satisfactory explanation of the events. But a wet bed in itself is not uncomfortable enough for the child to stop wetting, especially because most enuretic children continue to sleep soundly through the night, even after urinating in bed. *The ultimate reason may be that sleep interruption, which occurs when the bell rings, is an aversive condition for the children, and they learn to avoid waking up through control of the sphincter muscle which prevents urination.*

Since sphincter contraction is one of the many responses occurring to the sound of the bell and the distended bladder, closing of the sphincter can, in principle, ultimately be conditioned to signals from the bladder. In effect, the distended bladder produces sphincter contraction (an active avoidance response), and the children learn to be dry through the night simply because they do not want their sleep disturbed (Fig. 8-4).

Although no direct experimental evidence exists to support the active avoidance hypothesis just proposed, the results of several studies appear to make such an explanation plausible. In a recent review of behavioral treatment for enuresis, for example, Doleys (1977) points out that the high incidence of failure among children *who do not wake up to the bell* strongly suggests that waking is the crucial factor around which successful treatment appears to revolve.

Azrin, Sneed, and Foxx (1974) have also found evidence that throws some doubt on classical conditioning as an explanation for enuresis training and gives more weight to the avoidance learning hypothesis. Several groups were included in a study designed to compare a "dry-bed" procedure with others, including the traditional classical conditioning approach. Although the dry-bed method proved to be superior in achieving continence at a faster rate, it is a more complicated procedure which involves waking the child several times during the night, having the parents respond to a signal in their room, which is activated when the child wets the bed, and rewarding the child for urinating in the toilet. Because the methods used by Azrin et al. are designed to keep the child awake (hourly awakenings during the night), continence may very well be learned as a way of avoiding being aroused so frequently. *The authors themselves speculate that, in view of the fact that substantial success is also obtained with the traditional "classical conditioning" technique, their results may well be attributed to the child's annoyance at being wakened to wash and change the sheets,* and, in fact, a recent study by Azrin and Thienes (1978) suggests that this may be the case.

Azrin and Thienes report a variation in the "dry bed" method, introduced by Azrin et al., which eliminates the use of the bell and pad to wake the child at night.

According to the authors, the new method is more effective than the bell-and-pad procedure, and it relies almost entirely on "positive reinforcement and positive behavior rather than on the negative aspects of bedwetting" (1978, p. 353).

In Azrin and Thienes's study, children receiving bell-and-pad training alone wet their beds 76% of the nights during the first two weeks of training. The children receiving the new method wet their beds on only 15% of the nights.

The procedure begins with daytime training during which the child is encouraged to increase fluid intake, requested to attempt urination every half-hour, and urged to hold the urine for increasing lengths of time when the need to void arises. Discussions of the disadvantages of bedwetting and promises of rewards for a dry bed are also part of the training.

One hour before bedtime, the child role-plays cleanliness training. The parents pretend that the bed is wet, and the child has to remove the sheets and replace them. Before actually retiring, the child also has to practice getting up and going to the bathroom where an attempt is made to urinate. This process is repeated twenty times! During this time, the child also continues to drink fluids.

After they fall asleep, the children are wakened hourly until 1:00 A.M. and asked whether they need to void. If bedwetting occurs during the night, the children are wakened, reprimanded for wetting, taken to the bathroom, required to change the sheets, and made to practice getting up from bed and going to the bathroom for twenty more trials.

It is fairly obvious that, although the bell and pad are eliminated from this procedure, it still retains the elements of avoidance learning. In fact, if anything, the more effective results reported by Azrin and Thienes are probably due to the increase in the amount of annoyance and "harrassment" associated with wetting the bed rather than the so-called "positive aspects" of the method.

Unfortunately, the study introduces so many changes in procedure simultaneously that it becomes impossible to decide what method or combination of methods actually produces the results. Positive reinforcement appears in the form of rewards for dry periods. Cleanliness practice-training uses role-playing and modeling. Overlearning occurs when the amount of fluid intake is increased before bedtime, and overcorrection and punishment are involved when the child who wets the bed at night is forced to change the sheets and to practice going to the bathroom twenty times.

It may be that each of these components is necessary to produce the results reported in the study, but several aspects of the study suggest that avoidance learning still plays a prominent role in the process.

For example, Azrin and Thienes indicate that, although the new method is more effective than the bell and pad alone, it is not as effective as the dry-bed procedure in a previous study employing a bell and pad (Azrin et al., 1974). And, a more recent study comparing the dry-bed procedure with and without the bell and pad demonstrated that, while all of the children trained with an alarm reached the criterion of 14 consecutive dry nights within 8 weeks of treatment without any relapse during a 2-month follow-up, those trained without an alarm continued wetting the bed almost as frequently as a control group that did not receive any treatment (Nettelbeck & Langeluddecke, 1979). These results suggest that the bell and pad may provide more precise timing sequences that enhance the association of signals from the bladder with the annoyance of being wakened.

Furthermore, the children who used the bell-and-pad method exclusively in the Azrin and Thienes study did not have to change the sheets or put up with the annoying practice of bathroom behavior. These children were awakened by their parents and instructed to go to the bathroom and wash. Then they waited until their parents changed the sheets and reset the alarm.

So, while waking up appears to be the crucial factor in learning to be dry at night, it also seems reasonable to suppose that any condition that further increases the unpleasantness of rising—washing, changing bed linen, and practicing going to the bathroom—will hasten avoidance learning.

In spite of the theoretical difficulties surrounding the interpretation of enuresis training, the results have been uniformly good since the method was first introduced. Reports from over 13 studies indicate that it takes approximately 15–40 sessions with the bell and pad to achieve an initial 100% arrest of bedwetting (defined as a period of 14 consecutive dry nights). Until recently, the relapse rate was found to be quite variable, ranging from 1–48% (median 14%) for a period of 2–36 months follow-up. But Young and Morgan (1972) showed that the relapse rate can be reduced to 10% by introducing a method called "overlearning" which requires the child to maintain bladder control for an additional 14 consecutive dry nights after the first successful dry night while drinking up to 2 pints of liquid in the hour before retiring. These results were obtained in a 4-year follow-up study involving 563 children (see also Morgan, 1978).

A recent large-scale study (Jehu et al., 1977) conducted in a residential training home for children, where nocturnal bedwetting is a widespread problem, reported that 95% of the children treated by "conditioning" were still dry 20 months after the treatment ended. It is interesting to note that two other procedures were employed in this study in addition to the usual bell and pad. *First, the staff was instructed to make certain that the child got up and went to the toilet each time the alarm was triggered. The beds were also remade and the alarm reset on each occasion. Secondly, the overlearning method was introduced, with each child required to drink 1 or 2 pints of water in the hour before retiring for an additional 14 consecutive dry nights after the first success.*

One of the important results of the enuresis training programs that employ behavioral methods is the sense of accomplishment that children derive from being able to master their own difficulties instead of constantly being at the mercy of their environment. While this can be said of all the behavior problems children usually experience, it is especially true of bedwetting because the problem is such a salient one and the child is often subjected to all sorts of peer ridicule (Baker, 1969). The bell-and-pad method makes it particularly easy to conquer this problem because treatment can be administered at home with very little guidance from a professional.

Changing the Sexual Object: Homosexual to Heterosexual Behavior.   At the present time, any discussion involving the subject of homosexuality—especially that dealing with therapy for homosexuals—is bound to generate a great deal of controversy. Some people feel that the majority of homosexuals who request therapy do so only because social pressure prevents them from choosing their own form of sexual expression and not because of any personal deliberate choice for change. Homosexuality, the argument continues, is not a behavior disorder, and the people who seek help for it are responding to the social stigma attached to being homosexual rather than a genuine need to correct maladaptive behavior patterns.

This point of view has recently received considerable support from several sources. The American Psychiatric Association eliminated homosexuality as a behavior disorder from the *Diagnostic and Statistical Manual of Mental Disorders* (*DSM III*), and it has been argued that a therapist should carefully determine whether a homosexual seeking therapy for sexual reorientation is motivated by his own desire for change or the dictates of society. In fact, Davison (1976) has further proposed that the aim of therapy with homosexuals should be to help them improve the quality of their interpersonal relationships rather than to achieve sexual reorientation. Since society ultimately determines the correctness or incorrectness of sexual expression, the merits of such arguments cannot be fully evaluated without exploring the profound ethical questions involving human rights.

Deviant sexual responses were among the first to be treated with aversive methods. The success of such treatment was probably due in large measure to the availability of other, socially acceptable, ways of deriving sexual pleasure that made it possible for people to abandon one method of sexual expression in favor of another. The individual who found sexual satisfaction in bizarre fetish behavior, or by being a peeping Tom, or by exposing himself, could once again derive sexual satisfaction from heterosexual activities, once the deviant response was eliminated.

Most of the early efforts to eliminate sexual deviations by aversive means focused almost completely on the deviant response itself, and no attempt was made to explicitly encourage heterosexual behavior. In 1965, however, a paper was published by Feldman and MacCulloch, describing an "anticipatory avoidance learning" method for the treatment of homosexuality in which heterosexual stimuli played a role. The homosexuals who participated in this treatment program were exposed to a series of nude male slides which were also accompanied by shock. Pressing a button 8 seconds after the slide appeared avoided the shock, removed the slide from the screen and substituted the slide of a female figure. In a subsequent article (MacCulloch, Birtles, Feldman, 1971) summarizing the results of this treatment, the authors concluded that, although the method was uniformly successful in 63 cases, it worked primarily with those people who had a history of prior pleasurable heterosexual experiences (secondary homosexuals) and was largely unsuccessful with those who did not (primary homosexuals). The researchers also suggested that because the suppression of homosexual behavior is much easier and more rapid than the subsequent development of heterosexual behavior, a program for the learning of heterosexual skills be developed.

These suggestions, as well as the anticipatory avoidance method, were incorporated into a well-controlled study by Birk et al. (1971) which punished homosexual imagery and also provided a heterosexual alternative. Pictures of males flashed on the screen before the subject, followed by shock after an interval varying from 2–15 seconds. Failure to respond during this interval elicited a shock. A response terminated the male picture, avoided the shock, and produced the image of a female on the screen.

Group therapy was also provided to reduce heterosexual fears and to stimulate and reward heterosexual responses. A control group received the same treatment, except that the subjects were never shocked—the electric current passed through a light bulb instead. Subjects in the control group also had to respond to the male pictures in order to produce the female figures on the screen, and they were told that "associative conditioning" would occur to facilitate treatment. (The ethical problem of withholding treatment for the control group was dealt with by assuring both groups that these were experimental procedures and by offering them the opportunity to receive whichever conditioning treatment ultimately proved superior.)

The results of the study, including a 2-year follow-up, revealed that homosexual response suppression was produced in 5 of the 8 experimental subjects and in none of the placebo-treated subjects.

Although the studies just discussed involved active avoidance learning in the training procedures, the heterosexual response, once it is learned, is presumably reinforced by the pleasure derived from heterosexual activity rather than the avoidance of sexually deviant behavior. The training techniques involved in the studies considered below illustrate this point. Instead of using heterosexual activity as an escape from punishment, each of the behaviors is treated separately—deviant sexual behavior is punished while appropriate sexual behavior is rewarded. These studies are discussed in the context of a broader issue regarding the necessity for using punishment in the treatment of sexual deviations.

Is punishment necessary in the treatment of sexual deviations?   The use of punishment as a technique to modify behavior—especially that involved in sexual deviations—is accepted by most clinicians only with a great deal of hesitation and misgivings. Although studies employing punishment in the form of covert sensitization to discourage homosexual or exhibitionistic behavior have been successful in many cases, many feel that the emphasis should be placed on strengthening heterosexual urges and skills rather than on eliminating deviant sexual behavior through punishment. Homosexuals who feel the necessity to change sexual orientation, it is further argued, should be assisted through education, positive reinforcement procedures, such as masturbation to orgasm in the presence of an appropriate sexual stimulus (orgasmic reconditioning, see Chapter 4), or the use of systematic desensitization to reduce anxiety associated with heterosexual relationships (Wilson & Davison, 1974).

This argument against the use of punishment in the treatment of sexual deviations implies that a reciprocal relationship exists between heterosexual and deviant sexual behavior, and that heterosexuality is a positive force which rushes in to fill the erotic void produced by the absence of sexual deviations. *But most of the experimental evidence indicates that heterosexual behavior does not automatically emerge when deviant sexual behavior is discouraged, nor, for that matter, does deviant sexual behavior disappear merely because heterosexual urges are encouraged.* Each behavior must be treated independently as the following study shows.

People who have been engaging in sexually deviant practices do not suddenly show heterosexually mature urges when the deviant behavior is eliminated through punishment. The ability to be aroused heterosexually must exist to begin with, according to a recent study on patterns of appropriate and deviant sexual arousal by Brownell, Hayes, and Barlow (1977). If the "correct" sexual expression is not present in some latent form, it must be encouraged by learning.

In this study, all of the subjects were given extensive assessments consisting of interviews, questionnaires, and physiological examinations to determine the strengths and weaknesses in heterosexual arousal, deviant arousal, and social skills with the opposite sex. Two subjects who showed substantial deficits in heterosexual arousal were first treated with orgasmic reconditioning followed by covert sensitization. The remaining 3 subjects received only covert sensitization. In each case, a multiple-baseline experimental design was used in which both deviant and appropriate sexual behavior was monitored throughout the course of treatment by means of self-reports and a penile plethysmograph.

Orgasmic reconditioning for the 2 subjects with inadequate heterosexual strengths consisted of masturbation to heterosexual stimuli. They were first instructed to masturbate to the appropriate deviant stimuli and to substitute the heterosexual just prior to orgasm. When they were able to do this without loss of erection, the heterosexual stimuli were introduced earlier in the sequence until they became the only stimuli present during masturbation.

All 5 of the subjects ultimately received a course of covert sensitization in which the deviant sexual behavior was associated with an image of the realistic consequences of the deviant behavior—being arrested, abandonment by the family, job loss, and so on—or with a less aversive scene—nausea or vomiting, for example—depending upon which of the scenes the subject found most threatening.

The results of this study strongly suggest that strengthening heterosexual urges alone will not reduce the urges toward sexually deviant expression. While orgasmic reconditioning effectively increased heterosexual arousal for the 2 subjects with initially weak heterosexual urges, it did not influence their deviant behavior patterns. Covert sensitization, on the other hand, did reduce the deviant urges, but it did not, at the same time, increase the "correct" sexual urges, even when the subjects were led to expect that it would. Apparently, each form of sexual expression is independent of the other and requires separate attention.

Punishing one form of deviant sexual expression will not affect another type of deviant behavior. Each of the subjects in this study was selected because he exhibited at least two patterns of deviant sexual behavior. In some instances, exhibitionism was combined with sexual arousal to a stepdaughter with sadistic or sadomasochistic urges. Or transvestism was combined with sadomasochism, or hebephilia (sexual urges toward adolescents) with pedophilia (sexual urges toward children). The elimination of one pattern of sexual arousal through covert sensitization did not influence the other. Each pattern of behavior did not decline until it was specifically treated with covert sensitization.

A 6-month follow-up of each subject showed that the deviant urges, measured by erections (penile plethysmograph) and self-report, remained at zero. No relapses were reported, and none of the subjects had been arrested for deviant behavior. The subjects' wives confirmed the reports given by their husbands, and each acknowledged that sexual behavior had become more pleasurable for them.

A subsequent study conducted by Hayes, Brownell, and Barlow (1978) also used self-administered covert sensitization to eliminate exhibitionism and sadism in a 25-year-old married male with a history of deviant sexual practices including homosexual prostitution. Prior to treatment, the subject had been arrested for exhibitionism and attempted rape. Despite the history of deviant sexual behavior, the subject's heterosexual experience and heterosocial skills were strong enough to indicate that suppression of deviant behavior itself would lead to more frequent heterosexual expression. As in the previous study, each of the deviant sexual patterns was eliminated separately through the use of covert sensitization. Exhibitionistic urges disappeared approximately 9 days after treatment was instituted. After 8 weeks, the sadistic fantasies were reduced almost to zero. Both of these behaviors were measured by self-report and the penile plethysmograph.

Apparently, the use of negative and aversive situations is not the only way to reduce sexually deviant behavior. Marshall (1979) has shown, for example, that a form of "satiation therapy," involving prolonged masturbation in the presence of fantasied stimuli, can also be used to eliminate sexual arousal to aberrant stimuli (Box 8-2).

BOX 8-2
Too Much of a Good Thing

We have already seen how masturbation and orgasm can be used as a reinforcer in sexual reorientation in Chapter 3. But, while sexual arousal and orgasm can be powerful sources of reinforcement, prolonged sexual arousal, masturbation, and orgasm can also be "too much of a good thing." Marshall (1979) showed this in the case of two sexual deviates who lost their desire for deviant sexual expression when they were required to engage in prolonged masturbation to the aberrant sexual stimuli in a form of "satiation therapy."

The client in case 1 was a 33-year-old male with a long history of pedophilia involving young girls (4–14 years of age) and a long-standing fetish for women's underwear and shoes. Despite his mutually satisfactory sexual relationship with his wife, he was discovered engaging in sexual acts with a 13-year-old girl and volunteered for treatment after this incident.

Treatment required the client to sit in a darkened room and masturbate while verbalizing aloud the fantasies involving children and fetish objects. He was instructed to masturbate continuously during a 1-hour session, stopping only to wipe himself after an orgasm. Continuous monitoring through a one-way screen and sound system revealed that the instructions were closely followed.

The results of treatment are illustrated in the graphs contained in Fig. 8-5. The uppermost graph indicates how sexual arousal to female children—measured by a penile plethysmograph—declined from the initial baseline measures to the 6-month follow-up period. The initial 6-hour session (ST 1) following baseline dealt with female children 6–8 years old. When the response to these stimuli was reduced below an average amplitude of 10% of full erection, girls of 11–13 years were used as stimuli. The middle graph shows a similar decline for both the shoe and underwear fetish.

After the sexual responses to aberrant stimuli had been substantially reduced, a successful attempt was made to increase the response to adult females through a course of orgasmic reconditioning (OR 1 and 2, Fig. 8-5). In this procedure, the client was instructed to masturbate as in satiation therapy with two important differences: (1) the fantasies were supplied by the therapist (descriptions of enjoyable sexual experiences between the client and an adult female), and (2) he was permitted to stop masturbating after ejaculation to enjoy the postejaculatory feelings. The bottom graph in Fig. 8-5 indicates the increase in sexual arousal toward adult females resulting from orgasmic reconditioning. The client's wife also reported an improvement in the sexual and interpersonal aspects of the marriage and more contact with the family.

Case 2, involving a 36-year-old male with a history of pedophilia, sadistic behavior, and homosexual interests also yielded the same results when treated by satiation therapy. An additional objective in this case, however, was to compare aversion therapy—an unpleasant shock to the leg—with satiation therapy. The aversion procedure was introduced first, but had little effect on sexual arousal for young girls. The satiation therapy which followed resulted in a marked decrease in responsiveness to female children and adult males.

Apparently, satiation therapy works where more direct punishment procedures, such as aversion therapy, may fail. Satiation therapy appears to depend on the way in which sexual stimuli lose their attractiveness after prolonged exposure, but it is also apparent that the special nature of this exposure—prolonged masturbation and the attendant unpleasant qualities—suggests that a very strong punishment component is also present. It is also important to note that, as in the other studies reported, heterosexual responses to adult females did not arise spontaneously as a result of a decrease in deviant sexual arousal. These responses had to be trained separately through orgasmic reconditioning.

The studies just reported suggested that some form of punishment training appears to be necessary in order to extinguish sexually deviant responses. A report by James (1978), however, indicates that, for homosexuals at least, desensitization of anxieties related to social and heterosexual situations under hypnosis, along with erotic arousal training, also under hypnosis, was effective in producing a change of sexual orientation.

Both heterophobic homosexuals (those who had a fear of social situations and

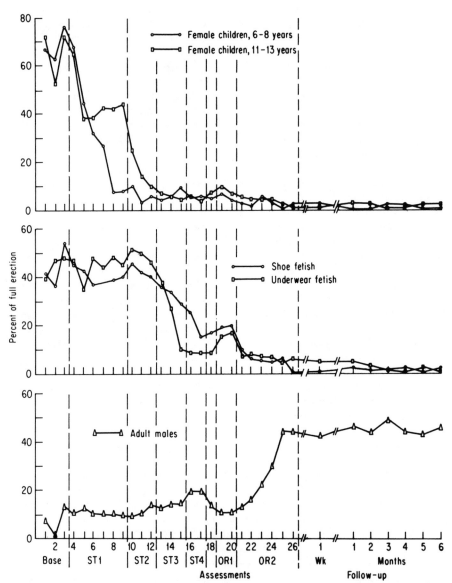

FIG. 8-5 Sexual arousal for Case 1 measured in average amplitude of penile response. Base-Baseline, St1, St2, St3, and St4 are periods during which female children 6–8 years old, female children 11–13 years old, women's underwear, and women's shoes respectively were introduced as fantasied stimuli during prolonged masturbation. OR1 and OR2 are periods of orgasmic reconditioning. (Source: W. L. Marshall. Satiation therapy: A procedure for reducing deviant sexual arousal. *Journal of Applied Behavior Analysis,* 1979, *12,* 377–389. Used by permission.)

heterosexual people) as well as non-heterophobic homosexuals showed greater changes in sexual orientation after desensitization and erotic arousal training than a comparable group of subjects given only aversion training.

The generalization which seems to emerge from all of these studies—whether punishment is used to extinguish the undesirable response or not—is that heterosexual behavior must be elicited and reinforced even though the deviant sexual responses have been successfully eliminated.

Omission Training

Dear Ann (the letter to Ann Landers begins), My husband was a "Food Inspector," too—although not quite as bad as the man in Michigan. There's a chance his wife might cure him if she's willing to try my technique. It worked for me.

Never get into a discussion with your husband about any food he thinks doesn't smell "right" or look "right." The minute he questions something agree with him that it is a little "off." Throw it all out where it can't be retrieved. Then go fix fried eggs.

After that, at the first sign of a wrinkled nose throw everything out immediately and prepare a peanut butter sandwich. If he says he prefers eggs, tell him, "Sorry dear, I need the eggs tomorrow morning for a cake I promised the church bake sale."

Three such incidents and your "Food Inspector" won't be so fussy. He'll eat whatever you put in front of him. Mine does.

(Ann Landers, *Newsday,* Jan. 1978, copyright Field Newspaper Syndicate and used by permission.)

This rudimentary, but highly successful effort to modify a "fussy" husband's behavior describes, in succinct terms, the elements of omission training. In order to train the proper response, to eat the food placed in front of him, the wife who wrote the letter removed it and substituted something less palatable. She was simply practicing a *response-cost* procedure by removing the reinforcer whenever her husband made an inappropriate, unappreciative response.

Omission training, as we have already indicated in Chapter 6, is a more desirable way of changing behavior if aversive methods have to be used. Unlike punishment, omission training has the advantage that it produces no physical pain and reduces to a minimum the side effects that would ordinarily result from punishment.

The proper use of omission training always presupposes that an ongoing reinforcement process which can be stopped exists and that the source of reinforcement can be identified. Obviously, this was not the case in many of the disorders treated with punishment just described. In some instances, such as chronic ruminative vomiting, it was even assumed that the children were regurgitating food in order to attract attention, but regurgitation persisted even though the children were given attention at other times.

Basically, omission training can be used in two ways. Either the source of reinforcement can be removed from the individual *(response-cost)* or the individual can be removed from the source of reinforcement *(time-out from positive reinforcement).*

Response-Cost. The most common and most practical way of using omission training—especially with adults—is response-cost. For the majority of people, the threat of being deprived of something is sufficient to prevent undesirable behavior. For more serious crimes, of course, the individual is frequently removed from the source of reinforcement. To be of maximum value, however, reward training and response-cost should be used in conjunction with each other.

Several Long Island high schools, for example, solved the problem of vandalism in their toilet facilities by using the money which would ordinarily be spent on repairing the ravages of vandalism to fund other desirable projects. The students were informed that certain programs,—handball courts, typewriters, and cameras for the student newspaper and magazine, for instance—would be funded to the extent that vandalism decreased. If vandalism occurred, the amount necessary was allotted for repairs; if not, the student government could use the money for any projects it chose.

The response-cost, reward operation was extremely effective. Money that would ordinarily be allocated for the programs anyway was made contingent on the reduction of vandalism, and the schools actually saved money because the program allowed the maintenance staff to spend more time on normal duties (*Newsday,* 1978). The use of response-cost and reward is also technically known as differential reinforcement of other responses (DRO).

Ignoring a child's undesirable behavior is often a good way to apply response-cost strategies. Most parents, however, find it an extremely harrowing experience, especially because of the increase in the intensity of the unacceptable behavior that is likely to take place initially due to extinction-bursting (Chapter 6).

We have already seen how ignoring behavior reduced the amount of self-injury in a child who created sores and infections by scratching (Chapter 6) and in the case of the child who was hitting himself on the head to stop the demands being placed on him (Chapter 7). In both cases, the behavior was ignored. In other cases, self-injurious behavior was eliminated by creating a reinforcement contingency and withdrawing the reinforcement when the undesirable response occurred.

In one case (Peterson & Peterson, 1968) a 6-year-old boy who was mutilating himself severely was given small amounts of food during a 3–5 second interval in which no self-injurious responses took place. The child then had to walk across a room and sit in a chair whenever he hit himself. If no self-injurious responses occurred during the time it took to get to the chair, his behavior was immediately reinforced with the food and the word "good." After 80 such sessions, the frequency of self-destructive behavior was reduced to almost zero.

Head-banging was similarly eliminated in a 14-year-old, retarded boy who was fed small amounts of applesauce during the periods in which no self-destructive behavior occurred. During the course of training, a DRL schedule (differential reinforcement of low rates of responding) was introduced in which the child was required to refrain from head-banging for successively longer periods of time until the behavior was eliminated completely (Weiher & Harmann, 1975).

The two studies just described illustrate some of the difficulties involved in using omission training as a treatment method. The use of omission training implies the presence of a reinforcement process which can be interrupted, i.e., a reward has to be available so that it can be withdrawn. This was done by giving food as a reinforcer on a non-contingent basis, i.e., regularly, regardless of the behavior, and withdrawing it whenever a self-destructive response occurred. In this way, *the relationship between self-injurious behavior and absence of reward was established.* Where the self-injurious behavior is being maintained by the attention it receives (the scratching child in Chapter 6 and the self-destructive behavior in Chapter 7), a contingency already exists, and the behavior can be eliminated by simply withdrawing the attention.

Response-cost in "real life."   Since 1962, the Cincinnati Bell Telephone Company has unwittingly conducted an interesting experiment with 1 million subjects in the use of response-cost procedures (McSweeny, 1978). Sometime in 1973, a charge was introduced for local directory assisted calls which had been free up to that time. Long-distance directory assisted calls were still provided without charge. For a period of 12 years, from 1962 to 1976, the frequency of calls for local directory assistance had shown a steady increase. When the telephone company received permission to charge for these calls, the number dropped precipitously in 1 month from approximately 52,000 to 16,000 calls per day. Long-distance directory assistance calls, on the other hand, continued to increase.

On a more modest scale, response-cost methods were also used to reduce cash shortages in a family-style restaurant in the Midwest (Marholin II & Gray, 1976). Cash shortages, whether due to carelessness or employee theft, is a particularly serious problem for small business where estimated losses run as high as 6 billion dollars annually. In the past, the methods used to deal with this problem have been very unsatisfactory, either for humanistic reasons or because the results have proved to be disappointing.

Where employee theft is suspected, the answer has usually been to hire private detectives and security personnel or to resort to television cameras and "lie detectors." If the cash shortages are actually due to carelessness, however, the precautions taken to stop theft will be useless.

By spreading the cost of cash shortages among the people who were most likely to be responsible for them, Marholin and Gray were able to reduce financial losses without implying that the losses were due to either theft or carelessness. After a baseline observation for 5 days to determine the actual extent of loss— about 9% of the daily receipts—the 6 cashiers in the restaurant were told that "if any single day's cash shortage equalled or exceeded 1% of the day's sales receipts, the total shortage, divided by the number of cashiers working that day (would be) subtracted from each cashier's salary for that particular day" (Marholin & Gray, 1976, p. 26). On the first day, the shortages went well below the 1% criterion, and this continued for 20 days. On the twenty-first day, when the cost contingency was removed to observe the effects of the response-cost procedure (ABAB design), the percentage of daily shortages increased to about 4.5%, but it decreased below the criterion again after the cost contingency was reestablished.

The authors are careful to point out that the success of this response-cost procedure may not necessarily justify its use for a very important reason. On some days, overages of 1–2% were recorded in the percentage of daily receipts. If employee theft was actually responsible for the shortages, and if the procedure merely shifted the loss from the owner of the restaurant to the customer, the overall problem would still exist.

Time-Out from Reinforcement.   Several years ago a number of parents from Eugene, Oregon, objected strenuously and, it might be added, somewhat justifiably to the use of a time-out procedure with their children in the classroom. It seems the children were forced to spend some period of time confined to a wooden box in the corner of the classroom for misbehaving.

Although time-out has been a highly effective method for modifying behavior when used in conjunction with reinforcement, some people who use it focus mainly on its effect as a punisher rather than on its usefulness in emphasizing the difference between appropriate and inappropriate behavior. The teacher whose time-out procedure created such a furor broke two cardinal rules: the punishment was too severe and the children were not rewarded for subsequent correct behavior. The statement we made about punishment in Chapter 6 bears repetition here: punishment does not in itself lead to the correct response, it merely points to one of the many possible responses, most of which are incorrect.

Time-out from reinforcement has been used effectively in a variety of settings. Box 6-7 (Chapter 6) describes how children with temporary incisions in their windpipes were restored to normal breathing by shifting the child from a socially impoverished setting when the canula was in place to a socially enriched setting when the canula was eliminated. The same general procedure is used in all time-out methods—the child is usually removed to another room when the inappropriate behavior occurs.

Removing a child from the source of reinforcement by confinement to another room is a difficult and often counterproductive way of using time-out. In the first place, most agencies for children are opposed to it because of the adverse publicity that even the most innocuous procedure can generate. Second, people with purely punitive motives can use time-out as a pretext for extended periods of seclusion. Third, some institutions do not have adequate facilities for using isolation. And finally, removing the child from a specific situation may provide an escape from a stressful or demanding situation. Because of these objections, Foxx and Shapiro (1978) devised a "non-exclusionary" time-out procedure—the "time-out ribbon" which does not isolate the child and appears to be equally effective in eliminating disruptive classroom behavior.

Their device, a simple piece of ribbon, was hung around the child's neck during those periods in which the child displayed acceptable behavior. While wearing the ribbon, the children received edible and social reinforcement from the teacher every 2.5 minutes. When the child was disruptive, the ribbon was removed, the child was told the reason for removing the ribbon, and reinforcement was discontinued for a period of 3 minutes.

When this procedure was adopted for a class of 5 retarded children who spent about 50% of their time getting out of their seats, making inappropriate noises, pinching other children, yelling, or injuring themselves, the disruptive behavior went down to a more acceptable level of approximately 10% by the end of 45 days. And, what is more important, the teachers found they were reinforcing the children for appropriate behavior—remaining in their seats and concentrating on work, for example—more often because the ribbons served to remind them of the necessity for rewarding proper behavior.

According to the authors, the time-out ribbon is probably very effective as a time-out procedure for several reasons. First, the density of reinforcement is raised for the children—they were given more reinforcement more often. This also serves to create a more pronounced contrast, making the time-out more aversive when it does occur. Second, the ribbon establishes a clear signal for reinforcement and the absence of reinforcement. Third, the ribbon can be removed almost immediately when the child misbehaves, heightening the discrimination between appropriate and inappropriate behavior. Finally, the child deprived of the ribbon has the opportunity to observe other children receiving reinforcement for correct behavior (Foxx & Shapiro, 1978, p. 134).

BEHAVIOR MODIFICATION AND THE TREATMENT OF ALCOHOLISM

The most recent behavioral approach to the treatment of alcoholism, as we indicated in the last chapter, involves several different learning procedures. Techniques such as aversive and avoidance conditioning, blood-alcohol level discrimination training (BAL), controlled drinking through the use of reward-punishment procedures, alternatives training, behavioral counseling, and alcohol education in various combinations are now part of one or another of the integrated treatment packages that have been devised to deal with alcohol abuse. The treatment of alcoholism has progressed considerably beyond the early, simple use of classical aversion conditioning.

The purpose of aversive conditioning, as we saw in Chapter 4, was to associate the sight, smell, and ingestion of alcohol with unpleasant or aversive conditions in order to achieve a goal of total abstinence. This treatment, it will be recalled from the discussion, was based on the assumption that total abstinence was the only way to deal with alcoholism. But because aversion conditioning, and punishment training in general, tends to suppress behavior rather than to change it, aversive conditioning for long-term treatment of alcohol abuse proved largely ineffective.

Although the use of alcohol to reduce stress is a plausible hypothesis for the way alcoholism is acquired, several psychologists (Cohen et al., 1971; Sobell & Sobell, 1973) have proposed that alcoholism can also be construed as a response maintained by its effect on the environment. It is conceivable, for example, that while an alcoholic may drink to escape the effects of stress, drinking may also be supported by powerful reinforcers such as care, attention, money, or welfare, to mention a few. In fact, it has been shown that these reinforcers are most likely to be dispensed as a result of excessive drinking (Sobell & Sobell, 1973). Several treatment studies have been devised, based on the idea that drinking is an operant response which can be eliminated by removing the sources of reinforcement and providing alternatives.

Alcoholism and Time-Out from Reinforcement

One treatment program for alcoholism, devised by Hunt and Azrin (1973), involved the use of a time-out from positive reinforcement procedure. The program was conducted in a community setting, as opposed to a hospital or institution, with 8 subjects who had been admitted to a state hospital and diagnosed as alcoholics. An additional 8 subjects who did not receive the treatment were used as a control group.

Because time-out from positive reinforcement is essentially a response-cost, omission-training process, reinforcers have to be dispensed prior to treatment before they can be removed for the wrong response. Accordingly, alcoholics in the program were initially provided with vocational counseling and a job, marital counseling, social counseling, radios, television sets, telephones, and transportation, contingent on their abstinence. The patients were informed that any of these could be removed if they resumed drinking. Actually, however, the incidence of time-out from reinforcement was relatively low because drinking rarely occurred after the study was begun. Despite this, the authors maintain that time-out was involved as a procedure because knowledge of the consequences of drinking served as a deterrent.

Figure 8-6 shows that the control group (CTL) spent more than twice as much time drinking, unemployed, away from home, and institutionalized than the community-reinforcement group for a period of 6 months during the course of the study. Moreover, only 1 of the 8 patients in the community-reinforcement group drank as much as his matched control, 4 stopped drinking entirely, and the other 3 drank less than 5% of the time. These differences were obtained despite the fact that the control group received the counseling and instruction that was standard at the hospital and consisted largely of lectures, counseling, and information on the basic operation of Alcoholics Anonymous.

Individualized and Integrated Approaches to the Treatment of Alcoholism

One of the difficulties with research into the treatment of alcoholism is that alcoholics tend to improve on a short-term basis almost regardless of the type of therapy used. The *individualized* (Sobell & Sobell, 1973) and the *integrated* (Vogler et al., 1977) approaches to the treatment of alcoholism were devised in an attempt to improve the long-term effectiveness of therapy by making the goals of treatment more realistic in terms of the alcoholic's own objectives, and by integrating several

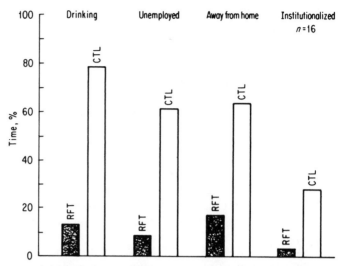

FIG. 8-6 A comparison of the key dependent measures for the reinforcement (RFT) and control (CTL) groups since discharge; mean percentages of time spent drinking, unemployed, away from home and institutionalized. (Source: G. M. Hunt and N. H. Azrin. A community-reinforcement approach to alcoholism. *Behaviour Research and Therapy,* 1973, *11,* 91–104. Copyright 1973 by Pergamon Press and used by permission.)

training procedures to change both the stimulus conditions and the response consequences that serve to maintain drinking.

Both the integrated and individualized programs are based on the idea that heavy, abusive drinking is a discriminated operant response which occurs in selective situations—bars, social occasions, and frequently alone—and which is maintained by the consequences of drinking. The objectives of treatment, therefore, were to identify the stimulus conditions and the inappropriate responses involved in drinking and to train the subject in alternative, socially acceptable responses. Accordingly, then, the following treatment procedures were used in either one or both of the treatment programs.

1. *Punishment Training*

   Samples of drunken behavior were videotaped and played back to the subjects at selected times during treatment. The purpose of this procedure was to provide an aversive state for excessive drinking.

2. *Discrimination Training and Avoidance Conditioning*

   a. *Individualized behavior therapy (IBT)* Subjects who had elected a controlled drinking goal were given a 1-second shock for the following inappropriate drinking behaviors: (1) ordering a straight drink, (2) taking a sip larger than one-sixth (mixed drinks) or one-twelfth (beer) of the drink's total volume, (3) ordering a drink 20 minutes after a previous order, or (4) ordering more than a total of 3 drinks (Sobell & Sobell, 1973, p. 56).

b. *Integrated behavior change (IBC)* Subjects were trained to detect their blood-alcohol levels (BAL) by relating periodic breath samples (taken with a breath analyzer) to bodily sensations and other cues such as concentration of drinks, number of drinks, and consumption time. (This is, in effect, another way of achieving the same discrimination for inappropriate behavior as in the IBT method because BAL is also ultimately related to indiscriminate drinking.)

3. *Behavioral Counseling and Alternatives Training (IBC only)*

To assist subjects in handling situations related to their drinking, daily schedules were analyzed to determine the situations and setting events for excessive drinking and the planning of alternatives. Assertiveness training and contingency contracting were also employed (see Chapter 12, on self-control).

In the IBT program (Sobell & Sobell), the subjects, who were gamma alcoholics (loss-of-control drinkers who cannot stop at one drink), were given a choice of treatment depending on the goal they selected. Those who had requested it, had sufficient support in the environment, and/or had practiced controlled drinking in the past were assigned to the controlled drinking group (CD-E). Those who did not meet these critera were assigned a non-drinking goal (ND-E). The ND-E group did not receive discrimination training for controlled drinking. Instead, they received shock for simply ordering or touching a drink. Two other groups, CD-C and ND-C, were also included as controls.

The results of the study, following a 6-month, 12-month, and 2-year report, showed the experimental groups functioning significantly better than the controls on such measures as abstinence, controlled drinking, and percentage of time drunk. In a 3-year, follow-up, double-blind study (the interviewers had no idea whom they were interviewing), the findings were substantially those of the second-year follow-up report obtained by the Sobells. The CD-E subjects were functioning better than their controls, while the difference between the two non-drinking groups disappeared. The results of the 3-year study (Caddy et al., 1978), covering 49 of the original 70 subjects, are presented in Table 8-1.

Statistical tests indicated that the only reliable differences in Table 8-1 were between the CD-E and CD-C groups on number of days functioning well and on percentage of drunkenness. Apparently, the gains made by the CD-E group were sustained over a period of 3 years after the end of the study while those made by the ND-E group were not. In terms of overall improvement, however, the groups who received IBT functioned better than those in the control group who had received conventional hospital treatment. They were generally superior on such measures as general adjustment, vocational and occupational status, driver's license maintained, and marital status.

Vogler and his associates (1977) went beyond a simple replication of the study conducted by the Sobells in an attempt to determine whether any individual component of the integrated treatment package was more effective than the others.

TABLE 8-1 Percentage of Days Functioning Well, Abstinent, Controlled Drinking, and Drunk for 48 Subjects 3 Years Following Individualized Behavior Therapy (CD-E, ND-E), or Conventional Hospital Treatment (CD-C, ND-C)

	Functioning well	Abstinent	Controlled drinking	Drunk
CD-E (N=14)	*94.9	66	28.7	*5.1
CD-C (N=14)	*74.9	40	34.8	*25.3
ND-E (N=9)	**81.4	76.3	5.1	**18.5
ND-C (N=11)	**66.9	53	14.5	**32.5

*Comparison pairs for which significant differences were found.
**Comparision pairs for which no significant differences were found.

SOURCE: Adapted from G. R. Caddy, H. J. Addington Jr., & D. Perkins. Individualized behavior therapy for alcoholics: A third-year independent double blind follow-up. *Behaviour Research and Therapy*, 1978, *16*, 345–362.

Under the circumstances, one group of alcoholics received punishment training, discrimination and avoidance training, behavioral counseling, and alcohol education; a second group received all but the punishment training; a third, only alcohol education; and a fourth, only the last three conditions. The study was conducted with problem drinkers in the community, as opposed to gamma alcoholics, who were interested in changing their daily patterns and achieving moderation.

The results of the Vogler et al. study indicate that most problem drinkers can learn to reduce their alcohol intake and reduce excessive drinking but that no one set of techniques for producing these changes had any advantage over the other.

This latter finding is especially surprising in view of the significant results among treatment techniques found in the Sobells' study. Vogler has suggested that these differences in the two studies could be attributed to the differences in the alcoholic populations from which the subjects were selected. In the IBC study, the subjects were essentially problem drinkers who functioned well in the community but who were interested in moderating their drinking habits. The subjects in the Sobells' study, on the other hand, were heavy alcohol abusers (gamma drinkers) who had admitted themselves voluntarily to the hospital for alcoholism. The problem drinkers in the IBC program were only drinking 7.5 gallons per year per subject before treatment compared to 14.8 gallons per year for the chronic gamma drinkers. The potential drop in intake, therefore, was twice as great for the chronic drinkers as it was for the problem drinkers. According to Vogler et al., this limited range in potential modification may be the factor responsible for the failure to obtain significant differences in technique among the problem drinkers (1977, p. 277).

The interpretation of alcohol abuse in terms of learning in general, and operant behavior in particular, has introduced some interesting and innovative possibilities for treatment, especially in the form of controlled drinking. The Rand Corporation study (Polich, Armor & Braiker, 1980), for example, recently reported the results of a four-year, half-million-dollar study conducted for the National Institute on Alcohol Abuse and Alcoholism which reaffirmed the findings of a previous study (1976) that some alcoholics can return to controlled drinking. In fact, the study was able to identify a group—men under 40 who had not yet become highly dependent on alcohol—who were less likely to relapse into alcoholism after a return to social drinking than those who abstained. Apparently, controlled drinking is a reasonable goal for some alcoholics while complete abstinence may be the only solution for others. Obviously, further study is needed to determine just who can profit from what form of treatment.

Although the gains made by re-analysis of alcoholism in terms of learning continue to be sustained in large-scale studies (Miller, 1978; De Ricco & Garlington, 1978), the overall picture for long-term treatment effectiveness is still somewhat bleak. Alcoholism still continues to be one of the most pressing behavior problems in many countries.

In this chapter we focused almost entirely on the use of operant principles in clinical settings, often with individual cases. In Chapter 9, these principles are applied on a much broader basis to institutional settings and the community.

chapter nine

Operant Methods in the Classroom

Although the principles of operant conditioning remain the same whether they are applied to individuals or to groups of individuals found in institutions, industry, or the community, the use of operant methods with individuals in such settings has created its own unique problems. Some of these problems, as might be expected, are concerned with the way in which operant principles are applied and related to such important and difficult issues as the maintenance of behavior changes when the setting and conditions for original learning have been shifted (the problem of behavior maintenance and generalization). Others involve the use of the group as a source of reinforcement or punishment.

But the problems which appear to have attracted the most attention, both within and outside the discipline of psychology itself, are those dealing with ethical and legal issues concerning the rights of captive populations—children in a school system, prisoners, or patients in mental hospitals, for example—or the particularly difficult and extremely controversial questions of the goals and purposes of social and human engineering in general. For example, it may come as something of a surprise that some behavior scientists have themselves criticized the use of behavioral techniques to eliminate disruptive behavior in the schoolroom on the grounds that these procedures are inevitably aimed at destroying potentially independent and creative children by transforming them into docile, conforming, and submissive creatures who will not create any difficulties for the establishment (Winett & Winkler, 1972). Others have even gone farther, suggesting that it is patently wrong to "fix" the alcoholic or the criminal as an individual without changing the "societal contingencies that prevail outside of the therapeutic environment and continue to produce alcoholics and criminals" (Holland, 1978, p. 163).

The solutions to most of these problems are neither simple nor immediately obvious. In the final chapter, which is concerned with the ethical and legal implications of behavior modification in general, we make some attempt to explore them in more detail. But, as we see in this chapter, some psychologists have attempted to come to grips with the provocative issues of the goals of social engineering. Graubard, Rosenberg, and Miller, for example (1971), have addressed themselves to the question of "whose behavior gets modified and for what purpose" by demonstrating in an interesting manner that even some aspects of an institution, such as a school system, can be changed to accommodate the behavior of its students rather than the other, more usual way around.

In any event, the ethical and legal issues surrounding the use of operant methods in institutions would not have arisen if the results of such applications were trivial. Obviously, they are not, and the studies cited in the next two chapters demonstrate how behavior modification methods have been employed to deal effectively with some of the more common problems found in social agencies.

BEHAVIOR MODIFICATION IN INSTITUTIONS

An *institution* is an agency which has been created for the purpose of solving a common, pervasive social problem. Behavior modification methods are especially well-adapted to institutional settings for a variety of reasons. The "closed" environment limits the number of distractions that tend to interfere with the behavior being learned. The response-reinforcement contingencies can be monitored continuously and a detailed record kept of the progress. The institution personnel can serve as assistants in the treatment program after a relatively short period of training. For many public institutions—mental hospitals, public schools, schools for the retarded and for delinquent juveniles—the use of behavior modification has meant the difference between wretched, aimless custodial care, completely dependent upon the tenuous good will of an overworked staff, and an active program designed to restore the dignity of the students, inmates, and patients by offering them incentives for improving their lives and the environments in which they live.

But some of these advantages have also turned out to be mixed blessings. Behavior learned under one set of relatively restricted conditions and in one setting, for example, does not automatically transfer to other conditions and other settings. The most significant lesson learned from working with people in institutions is that the transfer of behavior from the institution to a more "natural" setting must be strategically planned to ensure that the new behavior will be maintained.

Behavior Modification in the School Systems

Teaching is not an easy profession, especially when one considers that the teacher faces the behavioral management of 20–30 children for considerable periods during the day before any learning can begin. Of necessity, most teachers have worked out reasonably successful ways to maintain order in the classroom and to motivate children to learn. So, when elementary school teachers enrolled in courses designed to teach the fundamentals of behavior modification for use in the classroom suddenly discover, much to their surprise, that the curriculum is organized primarily around the use of rewards and punishment for classroom management and instruction—the very things they believed themselves to be doing—their initial reaction is one of doubt and rejection. It soon becomes clear to them, however, that a marked difference exists between the instinctive, impulsive, and expedient use of rewards and punishments to deal with momentary behavior and the appropriate and systematic use of these incentives to produce long-term beneficial changes in behavior.

The Use of Teacher Attention as Positive Reinforcement.   For the most part, the formulation of behavior modification techniques for use in the classroom grew out of the observations psychologists made of the procedures used by the teachers themselves, and recent surveys of behavioral methods used in the classroom indicate that teacher attention is one of the most important and the most effective sources of positive reinforcement (Drabman, 1976).

Although most teachers would probably agree that teacher attention is an effective way to influence a child's behavior, very few realize that children may receive the greatest amount of attention in the classroom only when they misbehave or behave inappropriately—a practice surely designed to increase the undesirable behavior. This assumption was first tested in an experiment at the University of Washington Laboratory Preschool by Bijou and Baer (1963) with a 4-year-old child who spent most of her time away from other children and in the company of adults (Box 9-1).

BOX 9-1
Ann Would Rather Be with Adults

"Ann is a strange child," they would say. "She just doesn't like children! She would rather play alone or be with us adults. Isn't that sweet."

Ann was indeed a strange child, but her indifference to other children was not due to anything the psychologists could immediately put their hands on—family background, physical and mental skills, or IQ, all of which seemed perfectly adequate. It was just that the adults paid particular attention to Ann whenever she played alone or decided to join them. And when she did play with the other children, the children hit her, pushed her, or took her toys. No wonder she spent more time away from the children playing by herself or in the company of grown-ups.

After determining that she really spent only about 10% of her play-time with other children, the psychologists decided to ask the teachers to praise Ann when she was with other children and ignore her when she played alone or made an attempt to join the adults. When this happened, the amount of time Ann spent in the company of children rose to 60%. To see whether or not it was adult intervention that really produced the change in behavior, the psychologists asked them to revert to their old behavior with Ann. As expected, the time spent with other children dropped to 20% but returned to its former value when she once again received attention for playing with her peers. Adult attention can, indeed, reinforce all kinds of behavior in children.

Later studies have confirmed Bijou and Baer's findings. In 1970, a survey of public school teachers in Florida reported that 77% of a teacher's interactions with the children were negative, consisting largely of commands and reprimands which actually serve to increase the inappropriate behavior rather than reduce it. The commands "Sit down!" and "Be quiet!" produced more standing behavior and more noise (Madsen et al., 1968, 1970).

Apparently, disapproval for disruptive behavior in the classroom is a universal phenomenon and not confined solely to classrooms in the United States. A group of 10 seventh-grade New Zealand teachers were also found to use disapproval for inappropriate behavior three times more often than approval for appropriate behavior (Thomas et al., 1978).

Teachers may use disapproval so frequently for several reasons. It is conceivable that immediate cessation of disruptive behavior serves to reinforce the teacher's reprimands. It is also possible that teachers feel appropriate behavior is to be expected in the classroom and, therefore, deserves no special recognition or reward.

But while praise for appropriate behavior appears to be more effective than reprimands for inappropriate behavior, it is not always the more desirable or practical way of managing the classroom from a teacher's point of view. Some teachers maintain that praising a child for correct behavior takes considerably more time and that attention directed toward particular children in the class will produce problem behavior in the other children.

In their extensive review of behavior modification in the classroom, O'Leary and O'Leary (1976) put these matters to rest. They report, for example, that in the Madsen et al. (1968) study cited above, the teacher commanded the children to be seated on an average of 27 times in a 20-minute period with about 4 children remaining standing in any 10-second interval during that time. When the children were praised for sitting at the rate of 21 times per 10-minute period, on the other hand, only 1 or 2 children remained standing in a 10-second interval. Praise actually required 25% less effort than reprimands. As for the presumed negative effect on the rest of the class when certain children are selected for attention, the conclusion that the others become disruptive is "not proven." In fact, just the opposite may be the case. According to O'Leary and O'Leary, when a teacher praised one of two second-grade disruptive boys for attending to his work, the second boy's behavior also improved, and the remainder of the class exhibited no behavior problems as a consequence (Broden et al., 1970).

One of the salutary effects of behavior modification methods on the teachers themselves is that they become more aware of the relationship between their behavior and its ultimate effect on the child. But, while most teachers have little difficulty in using praise to reinforce a child's appropriate behavior, some find it extremely difficult to give up reprimands in favor of ignoring undesirable behavior. Two of the 5 teachers involved in a study investigating the use of praise-and-ignore procedures, for example, were absolutely unable to abandon their use of commands and reprimands (Hall et al., 1968). Apparently, as in the case of punishment, the effect of putting an immediate stop to undesirable behavior is more reinforcing than patiently programming long-term changes. Obviously, there are instances in which the behavior of the teacher is as sorely in need of modification as the child's.

Although the systematic use of praising and ignoring is superior to almost any other method at the present time, using those techniques has several potential pitfalls, as Drabman (1976) has pointed out. (1) Simply ignoring undesirable behavior is not effective. Praise must also be given for appropriate behavior (the importance of an alternative response is once again emphasized). (2) Ignoring undesirable behavior may sometimes backfire, especially in those cases where children receive recognition and accolades from their friends and peers for disruptive behavior. This is especially true as the child grows older and peer reinforcement begins to compete with teacher reinforcement. (3) Merely praising (or punishing) a child—especially a young child—is not as effective as describing what it is that the child did to earn the praise (or punishment). (4) Behavior should be monitored continuously in order to observe what changes are taking place.

The use of tokens and back-up reinforcers. While no substitute for teacher attention as a source of reinforcement exists in the classroom, teachers may often find that they need some sort of tangible recognition for achievement to supplement social praise. Where the combination of tangible reinforcers and teacher attention has been used, they have proven to be more effective than attention alone.

Reinforcements—candy, toys, and so forth—are powerful incentives, but they may also create problems unless used judiciously. They should only be used for limited periods of time, the aim being to phase them out completely in favor of other, more "natural" reinforcers. In many studies, for example, candy or toys given as rewards are ultimately replaced by "tokens" which are periodically earned for appropriate behavior and ultimately exchanged for "back-up" reinforcers—candy and toys initially, perhaps, gradually shifting to access to preferred activities.

The virtue of tokens as interim, or secondary, reinforcers is that they teach the child delay of gratification. But perhaps even more important, the token program makes it possible to introduce procedures for ensuring that the desirable behavior

will transfer to situations outside the classroom. (The problem of response maintenance and generalization is discussed in more detail later in this section.)

Token programs are extremely effective in reducing disruptive behavior and
in increasing academic skills according to O'Leary and Drabman (1971), but their
effectiveness depends upon other factors as well. In reviewing the use of token
programs in the classroom, O'Leary and Drabman (1971) concluded that the
success of these programs can vary with the following factors: (1) *the teacher's
effectiveness in using high rates of praise, low rates of disapproval, and soft reprimands to
shape the child's behavior;* (2) *the teacher's attitude toward the program;* (3) *the extent to
which the teacher is familiar with behavior modification procedures;* (4) *the number of
disturbed children in class and the severity of the disturbances;* (5) *the amount of attention
the children receive from their peers for being disruptive;* and (6) *the cooperativeness of the
parents* (O'Leary & O'Leary, 1976).

The Use of Punishment in the Classroom.   Simply ignoring a child's disruptive
behavior may not be an effective way of dealing with it, especially if the behavior
is maintained by attention from classmates. Obviously, the thing to do under the
circumstances is to reduce the amount of attention disruptive children receive from
their peers before attempting to introduce a praise-and-ignore program. Often,
however, the behavior persists despite the absence of peer reinforcement, and
these occasions call for some form of punishment to stop the ongoing behavior.
Spanking, of course, is not a good solution, despite its recent sanction by the U.S.
Supreme Court.

Typically, three types of punishment have been used in the classroom: response-cost, time-out from positive reinforcement, and verbal reprimands. The
first two of these have been discussed in previous chapters, and their use in the
classroom does not differ, in principle, from their use with individuals. However,
certain differences in the implementation of these negative incentives when groups
of children are involved do exist.

Response-cost is an effective behavior-change procedure, but it is rarely used
alone—unless a child is made to lose privileges normally accorded to all children.
Customarily, some agreement is reached with the child or with the entire class in
which they earn tokens or points for appropriate behavior and lose them for
misbehavior. Obviously, the ratio of gains to losses is an important factor in the
success of such programs, but a study by McLaughlin and Malaby (1972) showed
that the losses may, in certain instances, be twenty times as large as the gains
without endangering the success of the procedure. Students in their study earned
5 points for proper study behavior at certain times of the day, for example, but
lost as many as 100 points for fighting and cheating. Despite this rather severe
imbalance, 20 of the 25 class members evaluated the program favorably.

The chief difficulty with response-cost procedures, as O'Leary and O'Leary
(1976) have pointed out, is that they may prompt teachers to look for bad behavior
and thereby increase their use of criticisms, threats, and reprimands. For this
reason, response-cost procedures should not be used alone.

Although time-out has been a common procedure for dealing with problem children, it has rarely been used appropriately or effectively in the school system for reasons already elaborated earlier. Sending a child from the classroom, the traditional way of dealing with disruptive behavior, often removes the child from an unpleasant situation and serves to reinforce the negative behavior. Where time-out has been used effectively, it is combined with reward procedures.

Verbal reprimands are probably used more often than any other form of punishment, but, as we have indicated, their effectiveness is transitory unless they are incorporated in a complete behavior-change program that includes ignoring and praising. When verbal reprimands are used, however, soft reprimands have been found to be more effective than loud reprimands which only serve to increase the disruptive behavior. Two studies cited by O'Leary and O'Leary (1976) showed that misbehavior decreased markedly in a class where the child was called to the desk and reprimanded in a voice which was not audible to the other students.

The Group as the Focus of Reinforcement.   In many studies concerned with the use of behavior modification in the classroom, the individual is the focus of reinforcement and the group is only peripherally involved. But O'Leary and O'Leary (1976) have identified a large number of studies in which the entire class is involved as a group, and they have classified these into three types: Type I, in which the behavior of the individual child is still the main concern, the rewards being shared by the entire class; Type II, where each individual child earns a reward (usually in the form of tokens) with the ultimate "back-up reinforcement" for the group (extra recess, for example) dependent upon the total number of tokens accumulated by the entire class; and Type III, where the rewards are based on the behavior of the class as a whole rather than on each individual child.

It should be immediately obvious that, while there are apparent advantages in using the entire class in any one of these three arrangements, there are also implied hazards. In the Type I situation, for example, where the reward for the entire class is contingent on the behavior of a single child, any failure on the part of the child that prevents the group from receiving a reward will immediately be intensified by the pressure the other children could, conceivably, bring to bear on the child. Of course, such difficulties diminish in the Type II and Type III situations where it is more difficult to identify individual children clearly. Teachers can also avoid such predicaments by guaranteeing that the group will receive a reward by reinforcing a child for minimal changes in behavior.

Children as Behavior Changers.   Psychologists have recently come to appreciate what most parents have known for a very long time—that their children's friends and peers frequently have a greater influence on their child's behavior than do the parents themselves. Most teachers are aware of this, and they have used children as teachers' assistants to help their classmates with academic skills. It seemed reasonable to suppose, therefore, that if children were taught the rudiments of behavior shaping, they could also help teachers to bring about changes in the disruptive behavior of their classmates. Solomon and Wahler (1973) tested this supposition in a well-controlled study which not only confirmed the widely held belief that peers contribute significantly to the deviant behavior of their classmates by the attention they give them, but also that some children can be trained as "therapists" to help produce changes in the behavior of the problem children.

Five children were selected on the basis of their popularity to be "therapists" for 5 disruptive children who frequently violated classroom rules by playing with prohibited objects, combs and nail files, for instance, talking to other children or talking out of turn, and leaving their seats to roam around the room. Each of the 5 "therapists" was seated next to one of the problem children and asked to help improve his or her academic performance by responding positively to the child for appropriate behavior and by ignoring inappropriate behavior. Under these conditions, problem behavior declined markedly, but it increased again when the "therapist" children discontinued their help. When the treatment was introduced again (the customary ABAB research design), the problem behavior continued to decline.

Fig. 9-1 indicates the amount of attention the problem children received from

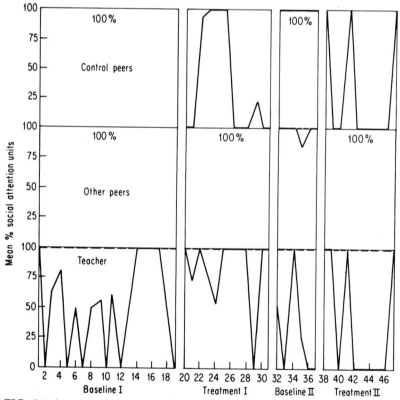

FIG. 9-1 Amount of attention children received for disruptive behavior from their teachers, control peers who acted as "therapists," and other children. (Source: R. W. Solomon and R. G. Wahler. Peer reinforcement control of classroom problem behavior. *Journal of Applied Behavior Analysis*, 1973, *6*, 49–56. Used by permission.)

the teacher and their peers for disruptive behavior during the various phases of the study. This figure is particularly interesting because it illustrates the relationship between problem behaviors and the kinds of attention they elicited from both the teacher and the students. During the baseline period (Fig. 9-1) before the control peers were enlisted and trained as "therapists," they acted like the other-peer children, responding 100% of the time to the problem behavior. Interestingly, the response of the teacher during that period was variable. As the experiment continued, the control peers modified their behavior in accordance with the instructions they received to praise appropriate behavior and ignore disruptive behavior. The other-peer children continued to attend almost 100% of the time to disruptive behavior. Apparently, the control-peer influence was great enough to decrease the disruptive behavior.

"Be Still, Be Quiet, Be Docile!" Who Gets Their Behavior Changed and Toward What End? "Behavior modifiers have used their procedures to serve the goals and values of the existing school system. . . ," say Winett and Winkler. These goals, they further assert, are to "produce a model child who stays glued to his seat and desk all day, continually looks at his teacher or his text/workbook, does not talk or in fact look at other children, does not talk unless asked by the teacher, hopefully does not laugh or sing (at the wrong time)" (Winett & Winkler, 1972, p. 50).

Although somewhat overdrawn, this description of the purposes of behavior modification with children in the school system is consistent with the criteria most studies seem to use for appropriate behavior. Actually, most modification procedures aim at increasing the child's academic skills or reducing the amount of disorder that disruptive children create in the classroom, but there is also no doubt that teachers and supervisory personnel are happier with a quiet, orderly classroom in which each child behaves well and attends to the ongoing lessons.

It is true that, in their eagerness to demonstrate the effectiveness of behavioral methods, psychologists have paid very little attention to the reasons for which the behavior was being changed—a dangerous precedent for scientists in general to follow.

Graubard, Rosenberg, and Miller were among those psychologists who felt strongly that the rules of the dominant culture often suppressed individuality and creativity in children considered deviant. These so-called special-education children were frequently isolated from the classroom, shut up involuntarily in training schools and hospitals, and subjected to loss of prestige and privileges and public ridicule—especially by other children. They were often scapegoated by the normal children who used derogatory terms such as "retards," "rejects from the funny farm," and "tardos" to taunt them (1971, p. 80, 92).

Instead of trying to change the behavior of the special-education children in some way to conform to the expectations of the normal children, Graubard and his colleagues decided to teach the deviant children how to modify the attitudes of the normals by: (1) ignoring negative remarks, walking away from scapegoating sessions, and breaking eye contact with aggressive children; (2) sharing toys and giving candy or compliments to those children who treated them well; (3) initiating activities and reinforcing other children for participating; and (4) helping other children with homework, crafts, and school activities (Graubard et al., 1971, p. 92). Over a period of 7 weeks, positive contacts between the normal and special-education children increased to more than 20 from an initial low of 4.

With the same methods, Graubard and his associates were also able to teach children how to shape the attitudes of their teachers to be more accepting of their special problems (Box 9-2).

BOX 9-2
The Tables Turned

Most of the teachers and administrators of the Visalia School District in California's San Joaquin Valley were generally sympathetic to the use of behavior modification in the classroom. That is why they appointed Graubard, Rosenberg, and Miller to help them with the problem of "reintegrating special-education children into the mainstream of (a) school . . . which was known to be hostile to special-education programs in general and minority group children in particular."

Realizing that it would be fruitless to try to shape the children to meet the unreasonable expectations of these teachers, many of whom scapegoated these children themselves, Graubard and his colleagues decided to make the teachers the targets for behavior modification, and the students the behavior modifiers. The tables were turned completely around!

Seven of the most disruptive children between the ages of 12 and 15 were selected as "behavioral engineers" and told they were going to participate in a scientific experiment to get their teachers to praise them more and punish them less. Because this was to be a "scientific experiment," they were told to observe and record all their interactions with their teachers, a move which no doubt made them more attentive to their own responses and to the effect it had on the teachers.

The children were taught several techniques. They learned to make eye contact with the teachers to hold their attention but to break it when they were being scolded. They were instructed to ask for extra help and extra assignments, to sit up straight as the teachers spoke and nod in agreement, and to use phrases such as "Gee, it makes me feel good and I work so much better when you praise me," or "I like the way you teach that lesson."

One special technique used on the unsuspecting teachers was the "Ah hah" reaction. Even though a student had listened attentively to an assignment and understood it, he was to ask the teacher to explain it once more. Halfway through the second explanation, the student was to exclaim, "Ah hah! Now I understand! I could never get that point before." Very few teachers can resist the massive reward that comes when a student makes a desperate effort to understand and finally gets the point.

Sometimes the childrens' "sweet-talking" backfired, and the experimenters had to use a tape recorder to train the children to be sincere in their responses. Often the children were simply unaware of the effect their original behavior had on the teachers. In an interview, Graubard reports the case of a boy named Willy, an immense child who probably "scared the shit out of the teachers." The problem with Willy was that he didn't know how to smile. "The smile came out more like a leer." The psychologists spent a considerable amount of time teaching Willy how to smile and talk amiably with the teachers (Hilts, 1974, p. 56).

After 7 weeks of "shaping," the average number of positive contacts between the children and the teachers increased from 8 to over 30. The number of negative contacts decreased from 20 to zero. After the seventh week, the children were asked to discontinue reinforcing the teachers in order to see whether the change in the teachers' behavior was due to the things the children were doing, as in the usual ABAB research design. The number of positive contacts did decrease to their former level, but the number of negative contacts remained low. Teachers, according to Graubard et al., are apparently just like other people—they need high levels of reinforcement to maintain their new behaviors.

Another area Graubard and his colleagues tackled was the problem of noise in the classroom. Teachers commonly complained that the classrooms were too noisy. The approach Graubard et al. used was to increase the teachers' tolerance for noise rather than to produce more quiet children.

After initial baseline noise-level readings were recorded by the experimenters, teachers were periodically visited by the special-education supervisor who praised them for their competence and specifically for tolerating the noise levels and permitting the children some freedom of self-expression. The teachers were also requested to permit the use of their classrooms as models, and visitors, including the superintendent of the district, came in to "observe how much freedom of self-expression and behavior a good teacher permits students."

Recordings surreptitiously taken by aides showed a dramatic change from an average of 30 to more than 60 decibels in a period of 5 weeks. The teachers were not only tolerating more noise, they were also creating a less restricted environment for the children (Graubard et al., 1971).

Of course, it should be immediately obvious that changing the behavior of the teachers is not a one-way process. The children themselves had to change their own attitudes in order to modify their teachers' behavior. Most human interactions are like this. If relationships are to undergo a change, the process must be mutual.

Using a technique similar to the one just described in Box 9-2, Stokes, Fowler, and Baer (1978) taught several normal and deviant children to elicit (recruit) praise from their teachers. The children were taught how to increase positive teacher-child interaction on the grounds that these skills might be important to them, especially if they find themselves "bereft" of attention because they do not represent a problem to their teachers. By using phrases such as "Look how much I've done" and "Is this right?" systematically, the children increased the amount of attention and praise they received from their teachers.

The idea that Graubard and his associates developed to train children to modify the behavior of their teachers has also been used in an informal way with children having behavior problems at home. Therapists take the children into their confidence and suggest that they can teach them how to become "psychologists" and "control" the behavior of the parents. Actually, the children are taught how to reinforce their parents for desirable behavior, and this works to the benefit of both. The child's demanding and disruptive behavior decreases, while the parent becomes a more reasonable and consistent person.

Behavior Maintenance and Generalization.   It does little good to change behavior if the behavior does not persevere or if it is confined only to the situation in which it was first acquired. Missionaries to China learned this discouraging lesson many years ago when their "rice-bowl Christians" remained converts only as long as the rice supply lasted. Psychologists who rely exclusively on the use of tangible reinforcers often find themselves in the same dilemma.

It was discovered very early in the application of operant procedures to behavior change that if rewards such as toys, candy, and tokens, used initially for intervention purposes, are removed, the contingent behavior associated with these rewards often disappears. Clearly, psychologists were compelled to devise methods that would ensure the modified behavior would: (1) survive when the program is no longer in effect, i.e., some future time; (2) generalize to other situations from a special class to a regular classroom, for example; and (3) affect behavior which is related to the behavior being changed, reduced swearing in addition to aggressive behavior, for example (O'Leary & O'Leary, 1976).

Response maintenance: how to get behavior to persist.   The central issue in response maintenance is not whether the behavior survives after *all* rewards have been removed—phrased in this manner the question is easily resolved because all behavior must be rewarded in one way or another if it is not to extinguish—but whether the behavior perseveres when the shift is made to other types of reinforcers. As the O'Learys have succinctly put it, because the majority of children learn and behave reasonably well without any specific intervention, the ideal treatment would be one in which problem children would learn to respond to reinforcers available to other children—occasional praise, report cards, personal satisfaction, and the like (1976, p. 501).

Several procedures have been used with varying degrees of success to increase the likelihood that behavior will be maintained. These were summarized in a recent study by Jones and Kazdin (1975) which was designed to create a "maintenance package" by incorporating some of these procedures. In their brief review of other studies, Jones and Kazdin determined that:

1. *Natural reinforcers, such as praise and work satisfaction, had been substituted after tokens or other tangible reinforcers were gradually withdrawn* (reinforcement fading).

2. *Intermittent rather than continuous reinforcement was used to increase the resistance of the response to extinction.*

3. *The natural environment can be programmed. Peers can be used to give and also to receive reinforcements. Parents can also be trained to continue reinforcing specific behavior.*

4. *Other stimuli can be paired with tokens used to maintain behavior.*

5. *Children can be taught to reinforce themselves through personal satisfaction* (1975, p. 154).

The purpose of the Jones and Kazdin study was to demonstrate that behavior can be maintained with a gradual shifting and ultimate withdrawal of all specific reinforcers. In the initial phase of the study, a token reinforcement program was introduced, then later combined with group reinforcement (all the children in class got tokens), peer praise, and delayed back-up reinforcement (intermittent reinforcement). Tokens were subsequently phased out (fading), and the behavior was maintained solely by teacher and peer praise and group reinforcement. Finally, all reinforcement was discontinued.

Four educable mentally retarded children received tokens for being attentive and remaining in their seats during the lessons. The tokens were redeemable for back-up reinforcers such as free time, painting, playing in the sandbox, listening to records, and recess. During the afternoon, all of the children in the class, including the 4 target children, received reinforcers to increase student involvement in the program and make it easier to introduce peer reinforcement. At the end of each school day, all of the students receiving tokens were individually applauded by their peers. An intermittent schedule of reinforcement was introduced by making the back-up reinforcers available in exchange only on alternate days and merely collecting them on other days.

Tokens were phased out during the second part of the study with an announcement from the teacher that the class was so well-behaved that tokens were no longer necessary. All of the class continued to receive rewards (recess, playtime, and so on), however, if the 4 target children continued to be "good." Finally, all forms of reinforcement were discontinued to study the maintenance effects.

The results of the study showed that the reduction in inappropriate motor responses from a baseline mean of approximately 60% to a mean of 10% during the final reinforcement phase was maintained throughout the 12-week follow-up period. The children no longer needed the special reinforcers first introduced to continue the initially obtained changes in behavior.

Generalization of behavior. A dog in an animal laboratory is conditioned to salivate to a tone of 500 Hz. When tones greater or less than 500 are presented, the dog continues to respond, salivating more to tones closer to 500 and less to tones further removed. The psychologist performing this experiment would be extremely surprised if this phenomenon did not occur because all psychologists have come to expect generalization of response as a "naturally" occurring consequence of the conditioning process, and generalization is regarded as a fundamental behavioral principle. Animals will respond similarly to similar stimuli.

A child is having difficulty with his school subjects. He is below grade in most of his academic work, and everybody involved agrees that the problem is due to lack of attentiveness. A behavior modification program succeeds in correcting the child's attention difficulties, but he still cannot read at grade level and continues to be inattentive to his parents' requests at home.

The question is, "Should the psychologists involved in the modification program have expected a change in both the academic program and the child's responsiveness to his parents merely as a consequence of training for improved attention at school?" Until recently, the answer would probably have been "yes" because, as Stokes and Baer (1977) have pointed out, most psychologists would have counted upon the training in attentiveness to transfer to academic skills and to the home situation as part of a "passive process." After all, attention is basic to learning and parents are adults just like the teacher, so there are similarities between the training situation and those to which the behavior should generalize.

But children are also good discriminators, and if rewards are contingent on behaving one way in a set of circumscribed conditions (attentiveness to the teacher), the behavior may not appear in other situations unless specific steps are taken to see that these changes occur. One way of doing this is to "program the generalization process" by employing an explicit technology of generalization (Stokes & Baer, 1977).

Most psychologists have a kind of "train-and-hope" attitude about the transfer of behavior from one situation to another. Although approximately half of the 270 studies reviewed made no explicit attempt to train for generalization, an extraordinarily large percentage achieved it on an after-the-fact basis. If generalized behavior did not occur after the completion of training, measures were usually introduced one after another ("sequential modification") to take care of all the situations in which the new behavior was supposed to occur (Stokes & Baer, 1977, p. 352). For example, a special training session had to be introduced in the morning for a group of adolescent female offenders even though the desired behavior changes were achieved during the afternoon sessions (Meichenbaum et al., 1968). Such strategies not only waste time and effort, they give very little insight into the elements involved in the transfer of behavior. A better procedure would be to anticipate the necessity for generalization and build into the study the conditions that would bring it about. Several methods have been found effective, among them the following (adapted from Stokes & Baer, 1977):

1. *Gradually shift the setting in which the new behavior is to take place and provide more natural reinforcers.* The program devised by O'Leary and his associates (Chapter 7) to deal with hyperactive children illustrates this procedure. Tokens in the form of daily reports for classroom behavior were issued to the children by their teachers, but the actual rewards (fishing trips with father, extra television hours, and so on) were dispensed by both parents at home, thus involving both the parent and the home as the final links in the chain of responses that originated in the classroom.

2. *Associate the response with a number of relevant stimuli.* This can be done in an ad hoc fashion by training the behavior in as many situations as necessary to achieve stimulus control and generalization. For example, even though retarded children were well-trained to greet a specific person, Stokes et al. (1974) found that generalization to the remaining 20 members of the institution took place only after a second person was also involved in the training. This kind of inductive experience was likewise observed in the case of a 30-year-old, retarded woman who was given praise and tokens for correct speech articulation. The response did not appear in the residential cottage until it was specifically trained there. Following these two examples, however, correct articulation generalized to a classroom setting.

Another method is to use stimuli during training which are common to both the training and generalization settings. Although this procedure has rarely been used, some indirect examples indicate its potential usefulness. Stokes and Baer (1976), for example, trained one child with serious learning disabilities to teach another with similar difficulties several word recognition skills. While both children learned the skills, neither performed them in a setting where one or the other was absent. In this case, the absence of a particular stimulus which was present during training presumably caused the disappearance of the response.

3. *Use contingencies that cannot be easily discriminated.* If resistance to extinction can be increased by rewarding a response intermittently (schedules of reinforcement), then, by extension, it might also be possible to increase the likelihood of transfer by varying the setting in which a particular response is rewarded. Under these circumstances, no precise setting is specifically associated with the occurrence or non-occurrence of a reward, and it becomes more difficult for the individual to distinguish in which setting a reward is likely to be given.

4. *Give specific training to generalize.* Instead of training across a number of situations until generalization occurs (method #2), it is conceivable to consider generalization as a response and shape its appearance during training. Teachers often do this when they urge students to form a principle which covers many situations from the one or several examples they are being shown. Goetz and Baer (1973) specifically trained generalization in children engaged in block-building play. The children were reinforced only when a new block form was created and not for any subsequent reappearances of that same form.

Schools of all kinds have turned out to be the most effective proving grounds for behavior modification methods. In institutes for retarded children, for example, some of the most difficult cases requiring constant care and feeding have been taught to feed and dress themselves, freeing the institute personnel for other tasks and making the school a generally happier place. The impact of behavior modification on the regular school systems has even been more impressive. Having recovered from the first blush of success in areas such as the classroom management of disruptive children and the traditional academic problems of reading and arithmetic, psychologists have now begun to apply behavior modification techniques to the more difficult problems in creativity and racial integration. More teachers are now being trained as "behavior modifiers" and are requiring less supervision from other professionals. But classroom problems are rarely ever confined to the classroom. They originate in a matrix of family and societal conditions, and it would be extremely short-sighted to concentrate on the classroom without making an effort to deal with the other areas as well (O'Leary & O'Leary, 1976).

Operant Methods in Institutions

The discussion in Chapter 9 emphasized some of the problems encountered in applying behavior principles to a school system. Perhaps the most important of these problems, apart from the technical difficulties, is that the interests and goals of the institution often conflict with the best interests of the individual and the ultimate objectives of society. In order to function smoothly on a day-to-day basis, for example, most institutions use behavior technology as a method for achieving conformity. Although some conformity is necessary, often what is learned in the institution does not generalize to the outside. Making inmates of a prison "better prisoners" does not by itself improve the chances for rehabilitation once a prisoner is released. The major problem in applying behavior modification to institutional settings, as we shall continue to see in this chapter, lies in devising programs that will facilitate transfer from the institution to society.

BEHAVIOR MODIFICATION IN MENTAL HOSPITALS

The longer people remain in the hospital, the less likely that they will ever have the desire to leave. The back wards of most mental hospitals are filled with patients for whom the sheer length of commitment has destroyed any expectation of recovery and whose desires have virtually been reduced to animal levels (Atthowe, 1976). This chronic hospital population, 50% of which is classified as schizophrenic, occupies two-thirds of the mental hospital beds, and their chances of being discharged from the hospital only 2 years after being admitted is a dismal 6% (Paul, 1969a, 1969b).

But even for those 6 out of 100 patients fortunate enough to be released into the community, only 30 out of 100 will make an average adjustment. The remaining 70 will return to the hospital to create a "revolving-door" phenomenon that spuriously boosts the yearly admission rate and makes it appear as though the incidence of schizophrenia is on the rise in the general population. Actually, however, patients stay in the hospital for shorter periods of time but are readmitted more frequently (Mosher and Feinsilver, 1971).

To a very great extent, tranquilizing drugs are responsible for these conditions. The drugs themselves, of course, have been beneficial in many instances. But the parochial attitude toward treatment in general asserts that drugs alone can accomplish the difficult job of rehabilitation. As Atthowe has pointed out, the major tranquilizers have been extremely helpful in reducing delusions and hallucinations, and they have permitted simple ward adjustments to take place, but drugs can actually be a hindrance where complex skills necessary for a reasonable adjustment to community life outside the hospital have to be learned (1976, p. 247).

Patients are frequently discharged from the hospital into a community which is justifiably hostile because it is burdened with their care without proper assistance or preparation. The patients generally live alone, are unprepared to do anything but take their medication, and roam the streets in a semi-dissociated state.

As recently as July 1978, the community of Long Beach, N.Y., which has been deluged by the release of as many as 2,000 mental patients because existing hotel facilities there can be converted into adult homes, reported that "some of the patients wander aimlessly about, while others panhandle, annoy passersby, and urinate in the streets." The former patients were "dumped here without adequate care or supervision, and they ended up blighting our streets, annoying citizens, and frightening children" (*Newsday,* 1978).

·The patients, as some have characterized the situation, "are merely shifted from back wards to back alleys." Clearly, where the goal is a relatively permanent change to productive behavior, learning and resocialization are indispensable components of any treatment plan.

The Token Economy

Token economies are one correct step in the direction of rehabilitation for mental patients. Designed to rekindle patients' interest in themselves and their environment, they teach them to relate to other people on a non-dependent basis, and they provide patients with the skills necessary to leave the hospital and join the community.

The token economy as a way of changing behavior was first introduced by Ayllon and Azrin (1965) who applied the principles of reinforcement to a chronic hospital population. We have already encountered the use of tokens in the discussion of behavior modification in the classroom. Basically, all token systems involve the use of some medium of exchange (poker chips or coupons, for example) which can be used as a reward for contingent behavior. Token economies in mental hospitals are models of the economic systems that govern the lives of individuals outside of the hospital, and this, of course, facilitates generalization of appropriate behavior from the hospital to the community. They include instances of direct exchange of basic goods (cigarettes, coffee) or privileges (weekend passes, cash allowances) for simple appropriate behavior (smiling, talking to other patients) or for rudimentary services (dusting, making beds, serving meals, running errands). Or, they may involve more complex interactions—banking systems, lotteries, currency (token) manipulation, working with other patients to learn certain skills, or engaging in group discussions on certain topics. Whether simple or complex, token economies in the hospitals appear to be influenced by the same factors that affect the economic systems in real life (Box 10-1).

BOX 10-1.
The Token Economy as a Microcosm of the
"Real World"

Psychologists are beginning to discover that the same "laws" that regulate the economic behavior of most people also affect the behavior of patients in mental hospitals. For example, in the national economy generally, expenditures go as high as 110% of income at the lower end of the income distribution (the availability of credit makes this possible), while at the higher end, expenditure drops off to 90% of income. Patients earning fewer tokens to exchange for cigarettes, coffee, meals, and so on, spent more on these items than did patients with a higher "token income." Moreover, patients who had earned and saved a large number of tokens reduced their earnings by working less and spent more during this time off than they actually earned.

An examination of the relationship between income and type of purchase revealed that patients earning more tokens spent more on luxuries (sweets, drinks, personal items) than the patients with lower token incomes who regularly spent their tokens on necessities (meals). This behavior also duplicates that found in the national economy (Fisher et al., 1978).

What does all this mean? It comes as little surprise that the economic principles at work in the marketplace also operate in token economies because people are common to both situations. What is intriguing, however, is that chronic schizophrenic patients, congenital mental defectives, manic-depressive individuals, and patients with chronic brain syndrome who have been hospitalized for an average of 12 years should continue to function in much the same way that a normal consumer functions, despite long periods of isolation and deterioration. This very fundamental aspect of human functioning is what makes it possible to use tokens as secondary reinforcers, and, ultimately, to use social praise as a source of reinforcement by pairing it with the tokens themselves.

Early token economy programs were tentatively established to test the idea of contingency management with institutionalized patients (Ayllon & Azrin, 1965, 1968). Among these was a program conducted by Atthowe and Krasner (1968) at the Menlo Park Veterans' Administration Hospital with a group of patients who had been hospitalized for an average of 24 years and who did relatively little but sit or sleep in the overstuffed ward chairs. They were so apathetic that they had to be prodded to go to meals or, in some cases, even to the bathroom. At first, the dispensation of tokens to get them to perform the routines usually found in a hospital met with no success. It was not until sitting in a chair itself was made a reward rather than a "routine right" that the patients began to engage in other activities in order to earn the right to sit in a chair. (Recall that in Chapter 6, Box 6-5, Homme et al. used a similar technique—the Premack principle—to get children to sit still. He first made running around the room contingent on sitting still and then deprived the children of the opportunity to run around until they sat still for a certain length of time.)

Unfortunately, although the early pioneering studies served their purpose adequately—they got patients to care for themselves and to learn simple social skills—they were not especially effective as the goals changed from simple modification of ward behavior to the more complex problems involved in release to the community. Although the goal of the Menlo Park VA program was not hospital discharge per se, 24 patients involved in the treatment group were ultimately discharged into the community. Eleven of these patients, however, were rehospitalized within 9 months.

Some psychologists were even alarmed that the newly discovered behavior-change methods were inadvertently being used to enforce hospital policy by creating submissive patients who learned to abide by the traditional institutional values of cleanliness, order, punctuality, deference, and demeanor. Although these behaviors are initially important, their continued emphasis for the purpose of good hospital administration only serves to strengthen the effects of institutionalization (Page et al., 1975; Richards, 1975).

While this criticism is relevant for the early token economy programs, it is not an accurate or appropriate representation of the more recent programs which, by 1969, had already begun to stress gradually developing levels of performance from simple tasks to self-help and self-determination, group living, and a gradual transition from the hospital to carefully supervised community facilities and, finally, to complete autonomy and community involvement (Fairweather, et al. 1969; Atthowe & McDonough, 1969; Atthowe, 1975; Paul & Lentz, 1977).

Comprehensive Treatment Programs

A *comprehensive treatment program* is one in which many sub-goals lead to the final objective of rehabilitation and self-sufficiency. These goals have been emphasized by Paul (1969b):

1. *Resocialization,* including the development of self-maintenance, interpersonal interaction, and communication skills

2. *Instrumental role performance,* including the provision of "salable" vocational skills, and "housekeeping" skills

3. *Reduction or elimination of extreme bizarre behavior,* including appropriate changes in frequency, intensity, or timing of individual acts or mannerisms consensually identified as distressing

4. *Provision of at least one supportive "roommate" in the community,* including either a spouse, relative, parent, or friend (Atthowe, 1976, p. 254)

Following the early pioneering efforts, and encouraged by the significant, although limited, success in reducing the amount of dependence, apathy, and withdrawal in profoundly deteriorated patients, subsequent program-studies were designed specifically with comprehensive treatment goals in mind. The objective of these studies was to achieve stable and enduring changes in behavior leading to rehabilitation and self-sufficiency in the community. The most representative of these was the *Lodge* program (Fairweather et al., 1969), the *Palo Alto* program (Atthowe & McDonough, 1969), and a systematic and carefully controlled comparative study, the *Illinois* program (Paul & Lentz, 1977).

The Lodge Community. Although, strictly speaking, not a token economy program, the *Lodge* community was one of the first to incorporate group-living as a means of social support for the patients when they moved from the hospital into the community. In their book, *Community Life for the Mentally Ill: An Alternative to Institutional Care* (1969), Fairweather and his associates describe these efforts made within the hospital setting to develop a variety of vocational, self-care, and social skills as well as a minimal level of social competence by having patients regulate their own activities and care for themselves. When these goals were achieved, the patients were transferred to the Lodge, a former motel renovated for this purpose. Although the Lodge was initially supervised by a staff member, it was not considered a "half-way house" because supervision was phased out as soon as the patients proved capable of taking care of themselves.

The experiment, which took place over a 3-year period with 75 patients, also included a control group of 75 patients who received the contingency training in the hospital, were eligible for discharge, and also released from the hospital. They did not, however, enter the Lodge program.

After the initial supervisory phase, the patients in the Lodge program managed their own affairs completely and ran a small business. They provided custodial services, painting, hauling, and yardwork for commercial and private customers in the community. In approximately 3 years, the Lodge made a profit of $52,000 which was distributed as income on a weekly basis to members of the Lodge community. The patients also purchased and prepared their own food, and they even maintained themselves on medication with the advice of a physician.

Because the control patients and those participating in the Lodge program were released into the community at the same time, the effectiveness of the Lodge program could be evaluated by comparing the amount of time each group spent in the community and the amount of time each remained in full employment. The Lodge was in operation for a period of 33 months, but the study continued for 40

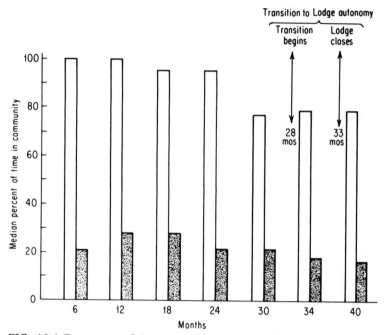

FIG. 10-1 Percentage of time patients in Lodge (white bars) and typical treatment programs (black bars) spent in the community over a 40-month period. (Source: G. W. Fairweather, D. H. Sanders, D. L. Cressler and H. Maynard. *Community life for the mentally ill: An alternative to institutional care.* Chicago: Aldine, 1969. Copyright 1969 by Aldine Publishing Co. and used by permission.)

months in order to provide a 7-month follow-up period. The bar graph in Fig. 10-1 indicates that, on the whole, the Lodge group spent considerably more time in the community than the control group. This difference was maintained even after the Lodge closed: approximately 78% of the Lodge patients remained in the community as opposed to only 18% of the control patients. While virtually *none* of the control patients were employed during the 40-month period after discharge, 40% of the Lodge patients were still involved in full-time employment.

The Palo-Alto Program.   In a comprehensive token economy program, it is not enough to shape the behavior of the patients. The attitudes of the staff must also be modified to accept the program and to administer the rewards on a carefully controlled contingency basis. The token economy program administered by Atthowe and McDonough (1969; Atthowe, 1976) at the Palo Alto Veterans' Administration Hospital began by carefully training the staff and by creating a favorable climate for the study.

The Palo Alto program established three levels of performance for the patients because of differences in patient motivation. Some patients were completely apathetic, others could leave the ward unescorted, and the remaining patients were socially responsive and had made a reasonable adjustment to the hospital. Each of these patients progressed through the three levels, and at each level, more productive and self-sufficient behavior was required and rewarded. Ultimately, the patients transferred to a sheltered workshop on the hospital grounds which provided them with a number of unskilled and semi-skilled jobs and enabled them to earn money in lieu of tokens. Some patients were earning as much as $4.00 an hour in 1971 (Atthowe, 1976, p. 256).

As the patients became more self-sufficient and as they earned more money, they could move from the dormitories to more private quarters which, of course, were more expensive. Ultimately, the patients were formed into groups of 4–6 and assigned to several three-bedroom houses near the hospital which were rented to provide a transition into the community. When they were ready to move into the community, patients moved into rooms rented in a housing complex, and 2 patients were assigned to each apartment. According to Atthowe, moving patients in groups from the hospital was implemented because loneliness appeared to be a major factor in the readmission rate (1976, p. 257).

A follow-up survey 1 year after discharge from the hospital indicated that the readmission rate was less than 12%, compared to the usual 40–50% found for most patients and the larger figure of 60–70% for Veterans' Administration Hospital patients. All of the ex-patients worked a 40-hour week.

The Illinois Project. The Illinois project is a singular example of a large-scale, long-term research venture in the area of treatment programs for chronically hospitalized schizophrenic patients. It involves a complex comparison of three treatment programs conducted in a mental health facility and regional state hospital over a period of 4 years which combines the most effective procedures and long-term goals of the Lodge and Palo Alto programs: token-economy procedures; a step program that enables the patient to progress to more complex behavior; careful and deliberate training of the staff in treatment procedures; and the goal of re-socialization.

Subject population. Because a delay in funding made it impossible to use less deteriorated patients, the subjects selected for the Illinois study were chronically institutionalized patients who had been rejected for a community placement program because they functioned at such low levels of self-care and exhibited excessive bizarre behavior. They were, according to the authors of the project, "the most severely debilitated group ever subjected to a systematic study," and, beyond any doubt, "the most recalcitrant group of people with whom mental hospitals had ever attempted to cope" (Paul & Lentz, 1977 p. 128, 133).

The subjects, half of whom were male and half female, between 18 and 50 years of age, had been hospitalized for an average period of 14 years, and all were receiving chemotherapy at the time the study was begun. Most of the patients had received electroconvulsive shock at one time during their hospitalization, and many had also been subject to insulin shock treatment without any improvement in behavior.

Design of the study. The study was planned primarily to determine the effects of three types of treatment—*milieu, social-learning* (both of these were known as psychosocial programs), and a routine *hospital* program—on overall improvement in hospital behavior, readiness for release into the community, and level of functioning in the community.

The *social-learning* program was explicitly committed to a "non-disease, re-educative model" which regarded the residents as responsible people, emphasized social responsibility, and encouraged the learning of social skills, clarity of communication, i.e., no crazy behavior, and vocational and housekeeping skills. The treatment methods were based largely on operant principles involving a *token economy structure,* using both tokens and systematic social reinforcement for appropriate behavior. Patients were reinforced on an individual basis for acting appropriately and punished through time-out (omission training) and overcorrection (punishment requiring the person to repeat the undesirable behavior ad nauseam). The staff monitored behavior continuously throughout the day and delivered both rewards and punishments for virtually all activities (Paul & Lentz, 1977, pp. 32–33).

The *milieu* program had many features in common with the social-learning program, including the emphasis on a non-disease, re-educative model. In addition, both programs emphasized the goals of re-socialization (learning of social skills and self-maintenance), reduction and elimination of bizarre behavior, and ultimately, release into the community. Furthermore, the operations of the milieu and social-learning programs were described in detail in a manual prepared for the staff participating in the study.

Unlike the social-learning program, the methods involved in milieu therapy were abstracted from a number of previous studies in applied settings rather than established on the basis of "laboratory-derived principles of learning." The crux of the milieu program was the *therapeutic community* in which the patients were permitted to govern themselves within the prescribed rules of the hospital. Residents were reinforced for appropriate behavior in the form of praise, censured for inappropriate behavior, and confined to a room for a prescribed period for intolerable behavior (time-out).

The major focus in the milieu program was on the communication of expectancies (how patients were expected to behave), group pressure, group cohesiveness, and group problem-solving. No token-economy programs were used nor was social reinforcement administered on a systematic basis (Paul & Lentz, 1977, p. 33).

The *hospital* program was concerned largely with traditional custodial procedures involving physical care and drug administration.

In order to control for possible differences in the administration of treatment, both psychosocial programs were carried out by the same staff, which was highly trained for the purpose. The hospital program was administered by the regular hospital staff.

Table 10-1 summarizes the Weekly Program Schedule for the patients in all three programs. It is immediately obvious from the schedule that the residents in the two psychosocial programs spent a great deal more time in classes, meetings, focused activities, and total formal treatment than the hospital group, and considerably less time in drug administration and unstructured activities.

TABLE 10-1

Program content	Hospital comparison	Milieu therapy	Social-learning
Classes, meetings, focused activities	4.9%	58.9%	58.9%
Meals	18.8%	14.7%	14.7%
A.M. and P.M. routines	6.3%	11.6%	11.6%
Unstructured time	63.8%	11.6%	11.6%
Drug administration	6.3%	3.1%	3.1%
Total formal treatment	4.9%	85.2%	85.2%

SOURCE: Paul and Lentz, 1977. By permission.

Program evaluation.   The three programs were very closely monitored during the course of the study, and the ensuing description of the results does not begin to do justice to the voluminous amounts of data collected.

Figure 10-2 shows the behavioral changes in both psychosocial groups for a period of approximately 2 of the 4 years during which the program was in operation. After a week of baseline measures during which appropriate and inappropriate behaviors were sampled prior to treatment, periodic time-sampling of behavior every 3–4 weeks was begun.

The graph in Fig. 10-2 is a condensed version of the sampled time periods contained in the original report for 10-week periods, beginning with baseline behavior. It indicates a decrease in inappropriate behavior for both groups which was also accompanied by a decrease in schizophrenic disorganization and cognitive disorders. Although appropriate behaviors, including self-care, ability to participate in ward activities, and interpersonal skills also increased, the improvement of the social-learning group was clearly superior to the milieu group, and it remained that way throughout the entire 4 years.

In the ensuing 1.5 years following the 2-year period illustrated in Fig. 10-2, the gains made by both groups began to decline. While the social-learning group managed to maintain appropriate behavior appreciably above baseline performance, schizophrenic behavior for both groups increased significantly. Inappropriate behavior for the milieu group decreased below the baseline, with a marked increase in aggressive and assaultive acts.

These reversals in behavior were attributed to several incidents. First, as a result of a statewide directive, the length of the time-out and expulsion periods for assaultive behavior was drastically reduced. Second, an attack on the Department of Health and the local institution by a state representative and the subsequent legislative investigation that resolved the difficulties severely damaged staff and resident morale. And finally, preparation for hospital accreditation required the staff to spend more time in paper work and conferences, leaving less time for direct contact with residents (Paul & Lentz, 1977, pp. 252–255). According to Paul (1979) these events altered the original objectives of the study to such an extent

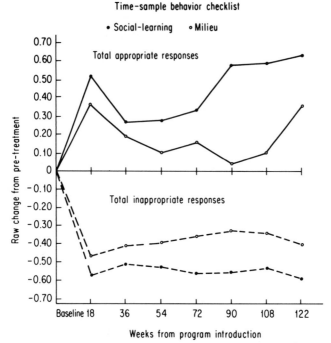

Time-sample behavior checklist

• Social-learning   ○ Milieu

FIG. 10-2 Total appropriate and inappropriate behavior for the
social-learning and milieu groups over the course of 122 weeks
of treatment following baseline measurements. (Source: G.L.
Paul and R.J. Lentz. *Psychosocial treatment of chronic mental patients.*
Cambridge, Mass.: Harvard University Press, 1977. Copyright
1977 by Harvard University Press and used by permission.)

that the data beyond the 122-week period represent the original experimental
design only minimally.

Reduction in the length of time-out, one of the events which had a pronounced disruptive effect on the study, increased the amount of intolerable behavior for both psychosocial groups. But, according to the authors, the considerably greater increase for the milieu residents indicated that the "special
response-cost procedures of the social-learning program still provided some
control of assaultive behavior, even with the ineffectiveness of the short time
period for time-out." It was apparent that "social-learning procedures were
differentially more effective in controlling intolerable behavior than were therapeutic community procedures" used in the milieu group (Paul & Lentz, 1977,
p. 257).

A final statistical analysis of overall functioning in the hospital for the three
groups indicated that the social-learning program was more effective than either
the milieu therapy or the traditional hospital programs (Paul & Lentz, p. 380).

Differences among the groups were also apparent when the residents were
evaluated for release to the community extended-care program. Twenty-seven of

the original 28 residents in the social-learning group were selected, while 19 of the milieu group and 13 of the hospital group were accepted.

Reduction in drug dosage during the last 6 months of treatment also confirmed the superiority of the psychosocial programs over the traditional hospital treatment. By the end of treatment, 100% of the hospital group were receiving either high or low drug dosages as opposed to 11% of the social-learning group and 18% of the milieu group.

Post-release behavior. Although the level of functioning in the extended-care facilities after release from the hospital showed a decline for all groups in the first 6 months of the 18-month follow-up, a slight gain was noted thereafter. Interestingly enough, however, the overall functioning declined more for the psychosocial groups than for the hospital group which actually showed a slight gain.

According to the authors, these changes in post-release behavior occurred for a number of reasons. First, virtually all of the patients, regardless of previous treatment program, were returned to drugs after they were released. Second, although token-economy programs were established in the extended-care facilities for all groups, the extent of the programs represented a decrease in attention for those from the psychosocial programs and an increase in activity and attention for those from the hospital group. Finally, the post-release program, in general, brought only a modest change in treatment for the psychosocial groups and a considerable change for those released from the hospital programs.

Despite these decreases in level of functioning, however, over 90% of the social-learning group remained in the community at the end of the 18-month final follow-up period, and some even stayed for as long as 5 years. Of the milieu group, 70% were still in the community at the final follow-up compared to 50% of the hospital group (Paul & Lentz, 1977, p. 419).

In terms of cost effectiveness, the social-learning program also proved to be superior to the other programs. It was three times less expensive than the traditional hospital program and one-third less expensive than the milieu program.

Considering the reduced state of the residents before treatment, some of whom smeared the walls with excrement, ate their own feces, were assaultive, mute, or incontinent—behavior characteristic of "back ward" patients—one cannot help agreeing with Paul and Lentz that "the social-learning program is clearly the treatment of choice for the severely debilitated, adult, chronically institutionalized patient" (1977, p. 383).

"Flies in the ointment." Comprehensive token-economy programs have increased to the point where most treatment, rehabilitation, correctional, or educational settings use some form of contingency contracting (Atthowe, 1973). The lesson to be learned from most successful programs is that they are indeed comprehensive. Those that have the best records and in which beneficial results endure treat the gradual step-by-step progress in the hospital and the transition from the hospital to the community as larger units of behavior to be rewarded as they approximate the final goal of release. Each step contains more and more of the elements the patient is likely to find in the community, and this facilitates generali-

zation of behavior. The programs devised by Fairweather et al., Atthowe, and Paul and Lentz are excellent examples of the ideal procedure.

But if token-economy programs have proliferated, so have their problems. In 1972, a suit was brought against the State of Alabama to correct some of the outrageous conditions existing in the state institutions for the mentally distrubed. Patients were simply being "stored" in the hospitals without any concern for treatment. Although the suit intended to provide for adequate treatment in the form of a "treatment plan" that included a statement of the patient's problem and specific needs, a description of the treatment procedures including rationale, short-term, and long-term goals, continuous review processes, and criteria for release—aims consistent with those of behavior modification—the effect of the suit went beyond the right to treatment, with some serious consequences for the procedures used in behavior modification.

In *Wyatt v. Stickney,* the court made three major decisions, each of which impacts on the treatment strategies used in behavior modification. In the first place, the decision held that all involuntary patient labor involving hospital maintenance and operation was proscribed unless the patients were paid at the prevailing rate. Second, patients could not be deprived of certain privileges that are legally theirs (because all other patients receive them) for the purpose of using them as goals or incentives. Finally, patients have a right not to be subjected to treatments such as "aversive reinforcement conditioning." Chapter 16 discusses this and other legal decisions as they affect treatment for instirutionalized patients.

BEHAVIOR MODIFICATION IN PRISON SYSTEMS

Using behavior modification procedures for rehabilitation in prisons is, ac-cording to some psychologists, much like "rearranging the deck chairs on the Titanic." Instead of devoting so much time to a system which is ill-conceived for purposes of rehabilitation in the first place, a great deal more effort should focus on "developing alternatives to prisons rather than guidelines for behavioral treat-ment" in prisons (Bandura, 1975; Franks & Wilson, 1975). Although such a sentiment is hardly debatable, the millennium of complete prison reform is still a long way off, and the present system, bad as it is, is what psychologists have to work with. Still, the picture is not so bleak. Several determined psychologists, correction officers, wardens, and prison guards are making an heroic effort to change many aspects of the prison system through behavior modification. To do so, they must also overcome the stigma attached to behavioral methods by some of the early misguided and blatantly punitive programs parading under the banner of behavior modification.

Behavior modification procedures in the prison system are especially open to the charge that they are used primarily to serve the institution's purpose rather than the needs of the inmates. Early prison reform saw to the discontinuation of physical punishment, for example, but several institutions have recently reintroduced it under the guise of aversion therapy. At the prison hospital in Vacaville, California, for instance, an attempt was made to "condition" fear in prisoners who got involved in fighting, stealing, and deviant sexual behavior, and who were unresponsive to group therapy, by administering a curare derivative that induced feelings of suffocation. The prisoners were told to remember these sensations the next time they had the impulse to violate the rules (Kennedy, 1976).

Other "programs" similar to the one at Vacaville came to light following the court suit (*Mackey v. Procunier,* 1973) brought against Vacaville by one of the convicts. Sexual offenders committed to the state prison mental hospital in Atascadero, California, were involuntarily subjected to shocks to their genitalia while watching sexually provocative films, and a program at an Iowa prison used a nausea-inducing drug in an attempt to duplicate the Vacaville program (Kennedy, 1976).

These and several other programs gave rise to a series of prisoner-originated complaints and lawsuits which led to several court rulings on the rights of prisoners and the formulation of guidelines for the use of behavior modification procedures in institutions. One complaint (*Saunders,* ACLU, 1974) and subsequent lawsuit (*Clonce v. Richardson,* 1974) prompted both the Federal Bureau of Prisons and the Law Enforcement Assistance Agency (LEAA) to withdraw support from behavior modification programs in general and from one program (START) in particular.

The START Project: How Not to Conduct a Behavior Modification Program

The purpose of the Special Treatment and Rehabilitative program (START) conducted at the Federal prison in Leavenworth, Kansas, was to rehabilitate hard-core, unmanageable inmates from other prisons who were alleged to have been physically or verbally abusive to the prison guards. According to the description of the project contained in a report to the Subcommittee on Courts, Civil Liberties, and the Administration of Justice of the House of Representatives Judiciary Committee (January 1974), all of the prison inmates "selected" began the project by being intentionally and systematically deprived of their privileges, then moved through eight levels of progressively improved confinement conditions by a system of rewards for good behavior.

At the most severe level—the "orientation level"—the inmate was put in a 6 x 10-foot steel cell with a small window that could be covered to block all light for purposes of punishment. If the inmate adjusted his behavior to the rules of the program willingly, he progressed through various levels of confinement and ultimately returned to the general penitentiary population with the privileges originally taken away restored. A "time-out" procedure was also used to punish prisoners for infractions of the rules. Confined to their rooms for a period of time, they could not earn, lose, or spend points. This confinement continued for as long as the prisoner refused to cooperate and remained disruptive.

Only one of the original 21 prisoners selected for the program completed the entire project. Several were transferred to hospitals because they could not get beyond the initial orientation phase. Seven prisoners staged a 65-day hunger strike, and the project was finally abandoned in 1974 after several lawsuits were brought against it.

The START program elicited protests from the National Prison Project of the ACLU (Saunders, 1974), and in 1974, shortly after the program was voluntarily closed, inmates challenging a number of the aspects of START instituted a lawsuit (*Clonce v. Richardson,* 1974). The inmates alleged that they were forcibly transferred into the START program without charges or a hearing, violating their constitutional rights of due process and equal protection of the law. They further alleged that it was unconstitutional to impose on them an untested, novel, and involuntary behavior modification program which had not been shown to be in accord with the accepted principles of behavior modification.

Three psychologists were appointed by the court to review the START project. Two agreed that, contrary to the allegations brought by the prisoners, the program was a *technically correct* application of behavior modification principles, but the third, H. L. Cohen, *asserted that the objections of the prisoners and the subsequent court trials were inconsistent with the sound practice of behavior modification and would not have occurred if the program were being properly conducted.*

The START program was not a valid behavior modification program, according to Cohen, for the following reasons: (1) inmates were not invited to participate in the program, but, rather, were coerced; (2) no adequate target other than return to the regular prison routine was established for the participants; (3) prisoners were denied any input into the program and threatened with loss of privileges when they did complain; (4) the only back-up reinforcers used were the privileges already taken away from the inmates, and because these had been ineffective in controlling their behavior in the prisons they came from, they were useless as potential incentives for appropriate behavior; and (5) the criterion for success of the program appeared to be a change in the production of brooms (Cohen, 1974).

Cohen's trenchant criticism of the START project directs attention to a violation of one of the most fundamental principles in the practice of behavior modification. If behavior modification is to be regarded as a form of treatment or a method of rehabilitation, voluntary participation on the part of the client is not only mandatory on ethical grounds, it is absolutely necessary to the success of the program. The inmates in the START program did not have this option. Moreover, no long-range goals were established beyond the improvement of conditions of imprisonment, and only the most rudimentary behavior strategy—escape from punishment—was used. In short, the START project was not a well-conceived or properly executed behavior modification program, and its only goal appeared to be the reinforcement of submissive behavior.

Other Prison Projects

The brutalizing methods used at Vacaville and Atascadero and the controversial nature of the START program created an extremely bad image for behavior modification. Opposition to anything even resembling behavior modification became so intense that the Bureau of Prisons was forced to change the name of a new experimental prison, opened in 1976 at Butner, North Carolina, from U.S. Behavioral Research Center, to Federal Center for Correctional Research. Prison activists had threatened to go on a hunger strike to stop the project, penal reform groups lobbied Congress to persuade law groups to cut Federal funds, and hearings were held in both houses on experimentation in general and behavior modification with human subjects in institutions in particular (Trotter, 1976).

Despite this furor, some intrepid souls, most notably McKee, Milan, and their associates of the Rehabilitation Research Foundation (RRF) at the Draper Correctional Center in Elmore, Alabama, are making an effort to apply the principles of behavior modification in a series of well-designed studies emphasizing voluntary participation rather than coercion, contingency contracting, token-economy techniques, and the proper training of correctional officers in behavioral procedures.

The results of these studies are especially interesting because they clearly illustrate the difference that often exists between short-term gains and long-term expectations. They also reinforce the observations made in schools and mental institutions that behavior changes in one setting are often not sustained in another unless specific provisions are made for transfer to occur.

Token Economy in Prisons: Immediate, Short-Term Effects.   Unfortunately, the adverse publicity invited by the Vacaville, Atascadero, and START programs overshadowed the gains being made by the thorough, deliberate, and correct application of behavioral principles at the Experimental Manpower Laboratory for Corrections (EMLC) operated by the Rehabilitation Research Foundation (RRF). Despite the rather pessimistic and somewhat premature conclusions of the Task Force in Corrections of the National Commission on Criminal Justice Standards and Goals that "the use of tokens for behavior reinforcement in a reformatory may not be a suitable application of (the same) approach that works in mental hospitals where secondary gains are not so prominent" (1973, p. 516), Milan and McKee (1974, 1976) conducted a successful experimental "cellblock" token-economy program at RRF.

As early as 1968, Clements and McKee had developed an effective method for encouraging adult offenders to increase their vocational and academic skills through the use of a contingency contracting program which provided money, free time, or privileges as rewards for the successful completion of daily work segments. The inmates agreed (contracted) to finish a specified work assignment after which they were allowed to engage in a desirable activity chosen from a "reinforcement menu" (Chapter 6). The results of these early studies were very encouraging. The percentage of tests passed and work speed increased, and the prisoners became more self-reliant and capable of initiating their own studies.

Following these experiments, which were confined to a circumscribed aspect of prison life (improvement in academic and vocational skills), the RRF group also decided to deal with activities which were important to the operation of the institution—arising at a determined hour, making the bed, cleaning the area in the vicinity of the bed, and maintaining a neat, well-groomed appearance. The decision to deal with these behaviors initially was based on three assumptions: (1) correctional officers would not be inclined to deal with the difficult task of preparing the offenders to return to the community until the basic requirement of institutional management was met; (2) the use of practical problems as target behavior would be an effective way of convincing the administrators of the validity of rehabilitation programs; and (3) the objectives of the study were in the interests of the inmates (Milan & McKee, 1974; 1976, p. 255). A very important part of the RRF program also involved the training of correctional officers as behavioral technicians. For the guards, emphasis was placed on positive reinforcement rather than punishment in dealing with the inmates.

The results of these experiments conducted in a maximum-security correctional institute for adult male felons convicted of grand larceny, child molestation, first- and second-degree manslaughter, and possession and sale of drugs, demonstrated that token-economy programs can be instituted in prison systems, contrary to the negative expectations of the Task Force on Corrections. Unlike the START project, neither of the cellblock token-economy programs began with deprivation of privileges or rights usually accorded prisoners. Instead, prisoners got the opportunity to earn points for canteen items; access to television, pool tables, and lounges; and time off for recreation, study, fishing, and the like. In both the 1974 and 1976 studies, attention to the routine tasks of the institution increased from a moderate 60% level (sometimes less when commands from the guards were used to motivate the inmates) to approximately 90% and above during the course of 420 days.

The experimenters were also somewhat concerned that the availability of reinforcers for these routine institutional tasks would encourage the inmates to spend an inordinate amount of time at maintenance tasks in order to earn more tokens. Actually, however, the prisoners spent less time on these housekeeping activities and more of their earned leisure time on the rehabilitation-oriented remedial education program. The inmates became less regimented and institutionalized as a result of the program.

Token Economy in Prisons: Long-Term Benefits.   The follow-up study, conducted 18 months after the participants in the token-economy program were released from prison, confirmed the observations made with patients in mental hospitals: No long-term benefits can be obtained from token-economy programs that deal exclusively with institutional behavior unless some specific provision is made to sustain the behavior changes in the community. Although the rate of return to prison after release was slower for the "token-economy group," they eventually reached the recidivism level of comparable groups of inmates who had never participated in the token project or who had received a different type of vocational training (Jenkins et al., 1974).

Behavior Modification in Prisons: Quo Vadis?

It is difficult to say exactly where behavior modification programs are going because so much seems to depend on what society is prepared to do for offenders after they are released. No one really has any illusions that the answer to the problems of prison rehabilitation can be solved simply by making the inmates "better prisoners" while they are in prison, but some recommendations have been made to increase the chances of rehabilitation when they are released:

1. Safeguard both the inmate and the reputation of behavioral methods by requiring a systematic review of experimental procedures in prisons (Milan & McKee, 1976). A bill has recently been passed by the Senate protecting the rights of inmates of institutions which would virtually guarantee such systematic reviews (*N.Y. Times,* 1978).

2. Train correction officers in the experimental analysis of behavior so that behavior modification programs will not fail as a result of "well-intentioned," but untrained personnel (Milan, 1976).

3. Allocate enough funds to assist the convict in holding down a job after release from prison (Kennedy, 1976). Continuous employment after release is the best single guarantee that crimes will not be repeated.

4. Instead of releasing offenders into the community immediately after their sentences are served, program useful skills as part of the institutional training and provide a "graduated release," permitting the offender to spend progressively more time away from prison before actual release (Kennedy, 1976).

THE USE OF BEHAVIORAL PRINCIPLES IN INDUSTRY

The goal of any industrial organization is to increase productivity and make money. Obviously, the way to achieve this goal is to keep the cost of production low, and one of the most important factors entering into production cost is labor. In the early days of the Industrial Revolution when jobs were scarce and the newly dispossessed tenant farmers crowded into the cities to swell the labor market, the industrial manager could increase productivity through exploitation by demanding greater output without any commensurate increase in wages. But with the development of trade unionism, industrial management has had to find incentives other than fear and negative reinforcement to motivate the worker and stimulate increases in production. This task is especially difficult now that even money itself is no longer a completely satisfactory contingent reinforcer. Since most employees are paid at fixed intervals (once a week, for example) wages are only minimally related to the actual work the employee must do to earn them.

How to Motivate the Employee

In the opinion of many psychologists, managers and industrial psychologists alike have made two important errors in the attempt to understand organizational behavior in industry and to increase employee motivation. First, they based most of their early efforts on inferences about attitudes, drives, and desires instead of directing them toward external, observable events that could be manipulated and measured directly. When they finally began to consider external events, they committed a second error by choosing too large a unit of behavior for analysis. According to Luthans and Kreitner (1975), the mistake most commonly made in the application of behavioral principles to industry is the failure to use the behavioral event as the lowest common denominator. Behavioral events lead to organizational consequences, but more often, an industrial organization will focus almost entirely on the anticipated outcomes—profitability, effectiveness, reliability, service—without paying much attention to the behavioral events—the specific things that people do in the course of their work—which lead to the outcome.

For example, there is a difference between telling a shopworker to be especially conscious about safety and telling him to clean up any oil spills immediately. Both instructions aim at reducing the number of accidents, but only cleaning up oil spills is a "specific behavioral event." Safety consciousness, unlike cleaning up oil spills, cannot readily be measured in terms of response frequency (Luthans & Kreitner, 1975, p. 65).

When the sequence of behavioral events, performances, and organizational consequences has been determined, the type of reinforcer must be selected. The best way to do this, of course, is to permit the employees a voice in how they should be rewarded for increased productivity and punished for infractions. (With unions doing most, if not all, of the negotiating for wages and working conditions, the choice of reinforcers becomes increasingly difficult. But instead of taking the lead in making recommendations for employee incentives, most industrial organizations have assumed the role of "ogre" whose main function it is to counter the demands made by union negotiators at the bargaining table. In fact, it has been this short-sightedness and lack of "enlightened self-interest" that created the necessity for trade unionism in the first place.)

Typically, employee incentives have been of three types: (1) money, or its equivalent in fringe benefits, stock options, and profit sharing, for instance; (2) status, including promotions, recognition, feedback about performance, and solicitation of advice and suggestions; and (3) job interest, the intrinsic satisfaction an employee receives from doing a specific job.

Money as a Reinforcer. Money still is, and probably always will be, the most important source of reinforcement. It is the primary, and in most cases the only, reason why most people work. But, for a number of reasons, money may be losing its value as an incentive for increased performance.

In the first place, money relates only remotely to the amount of work an individual does. Instead, most pay systems are based on a time-plan (the weekly or bi-weekly pay check is a fixed-interval schedule, as we have already noted in Chapter 6, because reinforcement is given for amount of time rather than the amount of effort expended).

Second, unemployment insurance and welfare, necessary as they are, have diminished the significance of money earned through work (Luthans & Kreitner, 1975, p. 105).

Third, money is given as a bribe in response to threats of strikes and delays.

In the fourth place, wage increases are usually given for promises of increased productivity during labor negotiations, so that the promise rather than the fulfillment is reinforced.

And finally, the employee expects increases regardless of performance—especially during times of inflation.

Given these disadvantages, the obstacles standing in the way of money as a reinforcer are almost insurmountable. One obvious solution is to make money contingent upon production by using some variation of a fixed-ratio schedule (piece work), but these plans are easily abused by employers, and, in the extreme, they become systems for exploitation.

Where experiments have been conducted to test the effectiveness of different pay schedules (schedules of reinforcement), the results have been rather surprising. When rural, Southern tree planters were paid on a continuous reinforcement basis (i.e., for each tree planted) as opposed to a variable-ratio schedule (i.e., where the rate of pay varied from time to time depending upon the amount of work performed) the workers, semi-literate whites and blacks, preferred the continuous reinforcement schedule and worked as well or better under this condition even though they received more money on the variable-ratio schedule (Yukl et al., 1976).

Apparently, the higher earnings from the variable-ratio schedule were not sufficient to compensate for the uncertainty the schedule is bound to have produced. Under continuous reinforcement, they knew precisely how much they would get, while on the variable-ratio schedule, they never knew until a certain amount of work had been performed. Although we can draw no definite conclusions from this study because of the type of workers used as subjects and the kind of work performed, it seems reasonable to speculate that uncertainty of earnings and the requirement of greater effort are two reasons why work on a variable-ratio schedule was rejected as a form of compensation in this instance despite the greater earnings.

Most organizational psychologists agree that money should be made contingent on performance, and various plans have been suggested to accomplish this without resorting to piece work. Cash bonuses for promptness, merit increases for good work, and profit-sharing for increased productivity are among the several ways in which money can be preserved as a reinforcer for increased effort.

Status and Concern as Sources of Reinforcement. The willingness and eagerness with which employees perform a job is determined not only by the money they obtain for doing it, it also depends on the status they receive, the concern shown for their welfare, and the extent to which they feel themselves an integral and vital part of the production process. Many studies have confirmed this since one of the first conducted in the Hawthorne plant of Western Electric showed that the factor most responsible for increased productivity was not the improvement in lighting and other benefits being distributed, but the fact that some concern was being shown for the workers—that they had become the center of attention (Roethlisberger & Dickson, 1939). These conclusions were recently reaffirmed in an interesting program, designed to save money on container utilization, established at the Emery Air Freight Co.

The Emery Air Freight program: How behavior modification pays off. The object of the program at Emery Air Freight was to save as much money as possible through the proper use of air-freight containers. By applying the principles of behavior analysis properly to this problem, Edward J. Feeney succeeded in saving Emery Air Freight $2 million over a 3-year period.

First, a careful analysis was conducted to identify those jobs that had the greatest impact on profit. One of these was the way in which containers were filled for air-freight shipments. The company was bound to lose money if these containers left the loading dock partly filled, and although the warehousemen had been thoroughly trained and encouraged to use empty container space efficiently and actually believed they were doing so, container utilization was found to be about 45% instead of the more profitable 90%.

Instead of providing more training for the dockworkers, Feeny instituted a simple feedback program in which the workers were informed when container utilization fell between 45 and 90%. In addition, the employees were given contingent positive reinforcement by recognizing good work—smiling, nodding encouragement, and offers to buy coffee. According to Feeny, "the emphasis placed on providing feedback to employees about their performance contributed more than any other single factor to the program's success" (Luthans & Kreitner, 1975, p. 67).

Job Interest and Satisfaction as Reinforcers. Although the factors just discussed make a substantial contribution to job interest and satisfaction, the desire to do the job because it is challenging, or a test of skill, or an opportunity to display workmanship also determines the level of performance. Very little is actually known about this form of "intrinsic" motivation largely because it is difficult to characterize. But some psychologists see it predominantly as the ability of individuals to make choices about the type of work they will do, and de Charms (1968) has indicated that people are more likely to prefer self-initiated activities or jobs to those controlled from external sources.

Apparently, the willingness to perform at an optimal level on the job requires a combination of both intrinsic and extrinsic motivation. Half of the wage earners surveyed in a recent Gallup Poll said they could increase their output if they tried, and a study by Hamner and Foster (Franks & Wilson, 1976) suggests that a higher level of performance can be attained by increasing both intrinsic and extrinsic motivation.

BEHAVIOR MODIFICATION IN THE COMMUNITY

In its broadest sense, the extension of behavior modification procedures to problems in the community is somewhat ambitious (and even perhaps a trifle grandiose)

—especially when the proposed goals are to "change the social-environmental determinants of human behavior."

Whose behavior, and what social-environmental determinants are to be changed are important, controversial questions which can only be resolved by the people directly affected. "Behavioral engineers" may make recommendations about the best way to solve a community problem, but these changes cannot be forced on a community that is unprepared to accept them. One would think, for example, that something as innocent as a plan to teach children cooperative, sharing behavior through a series of short films shown on television is beyond controversy. Yet when such an idea was proposed by Robert Liebert, some objections were raised on the grounds that children should learn sharing and cooperativeness as "values" at home and not as "propaganda" through the media!

On a more modest scale, however, behavioral community psychology has made significant contributions in assisting communities to solve problems in mental health, aging, juvenile delinquency, social welfare, and in some of the less compelling, but equally pervasive areas involving litter (Burgess et al., 1971), purchase of soft drinks in returnable bottles (Geller et al., 1973), increase in the use of public transportation (Everett et al., 1974), and a cost-benefit analysis of helicopter patrol in a high crime area (Schnelle et al., 1978).

Like many of the topics we take up here, the research that has been conducted in the areas of community mental health, aging, and juvenile delinquency is far too vast to be treated adequately in a general survey of behavior modification. (A detailed account of research and practice in community psychology may be found in a comprehensive book on the subject, *Behavioral Approaches to Community Psychology*, by Nietzel, Winett, MacDonald, and Davidson, 1977.) Here we present representative studies from several selected areas in order to illustrate the type of work being done.

Aging

As life expectation increases, so do the problems associated with growing old. The disappearance of the extended family, which was devoted both morally and affectionately to the care of the elderly, gave rise to the nursing home as a community obligation. But nursing homes have not proved to be the panacea that was once expected. In fact, nursing homes, for many, have become warehouses of people waiting to die, and the whole area of care for the aged has become "the most troubled, and troublesome, component of [the] entire health care system" (Moss, 1974).

Approximately 77% of the country's nursing homes are run for profit, and many of these have been found physically and medically unsafe. Patients all too frequently fall victim to fires, food poisoning, cruelty, incorrectly administered drugs, virulent infections from poor hygiene, and starvation (Nietzel et al., 1977). But while these problems have been cleared up to some extent following widespread Senate investigations, the problem of simple boredom and depression from neglect and loneliness still persists.

For many of the elderly, institutionalization increases the problems associated with old age—as, in fact it does for many people with emotional and behavior problems. Although continued residence in the community is far preferable to a nursing home, many of the elderly must live in nursing homes for one reason or another. To improve the conditions for the institutionalized aged, McClannahan and Risley (1975) undertook to study the problems of nursing home residents and to redesign their living environments.

One of the most pressing difficulties with the aged, both in the nursing home and in the community, is the problem of apathy. It is difficult to get older persons to participate, even when special facilities are built and special programs are established for them. Studies by McClannahan and Risley have shown that although a lounge area, complete with recreational equipment, was available, the residents of one nursing home spent most of their time by themselves, sitting, lying, or just walking. The amount of participation in activities using the equipment trebled, however, after simple prompting, such as "Would you like to use this?" or "Let me show you." Only a slight increase in stimulation was sufficient to induce the elderly, many of whom were debilitated, to take part in some sort of activity (1975, p. 267), but this stimulation was absolutely necessary.

Participation in programs cannot be taken for granted, even when the elderly have opted to live in the community and are considered capable of taking care of themselves. It has been estimated, for example, that less than 1% of the aged participate in community meal programs sponsored by the Federal government, and that, as a result, many elderly people eat meals that do not provide the minimum daily allowance (Bunck & Iwata, 1978, p. 76).

In a program designed to test various methods for stimulating the interest of the aged in Federally sponsored meal programs, Bunck and Iwata (1978) found that simple prompting through public announcements, although less costly than a reinforcement program, was thoroughly ineffective. When "Give-Away Days" (movies, bingo games, and door prizes) were announced in advance, on the other hand, the meal supplies at the centers were exhausted, and more food had to be ordered. Considering the nominal cost of the "give-away" program ($106 on activity days) the results were very satisfactory.

But such costs would soon become prohibitive if it were necessary to entice the aged with reinforcers on a daily basis. A better procedure, as the authors suggest, would be to advertise the availability of reinforcement on a periodic and unpredictable basis, much like that of a variable-interval schedule. This, they contend, should produce a more consistent attendance (Bunck & Iwata, 1978, p. 84).

The problems of old age are far more complex than these studies suggest. Stimulating and increasing the older person's interests is an important element in preventing depression—a significant feature of growing old. But some of the more important questions, such as those involved in facing the end of life and the imminence of death, are philosophical. Unfortunately, behavior modification cannot readily supply the answers.

Mental Health in the Community

In one important sense, the use of comprehensive token-economy programs with institutionalized patients is a form of community mental health. When these programs are properly conducted, the responsibility for the patients' welfare does not end with release from the hospital. It continues on within the community until the former patients make satisfactory adjustments and are assimilated into society.

Strictly speaking, however, the objectives of the community mental health program, established by an Act of Congress in 1963, were not primarily those of "monitoring" and assisting patients released from mental hospitals. The major intent of the Act was to decentralize mental health services from the standard clinic setting—usually located in a hospital—to convenient and more readily available centers established within the community. Implicit in this movement is the tacit recognition that the difficulties for which most people seek help are problems in living that are only remotely (if, indeed, at all) related to medical problems and that do not require the extensive and costly services of complex hospitals often located some distance from the clients' residence.

A second provision of the Mental Health Centers Act was to make counseling and psychotherapy available to the poor who, for economic and social reasons—the opprobrium attached to "mental" problems or an inability and lack of skill in talking about problems—rarely avail themselves of such services.

The third, and most innovative aspect of the Act was the emphasis on prevention rather than cure. But this feature of the program requires a change in attitude about mental health in general. It suggests a "seeking" rather than a "waiting" mode for the delivery of services in which the personnel of the centers—psychiatrists, psychologists, social workers, and paraprofessionals—engages the public through educational programs (Rappaport & Chinsky, 1974).

The scope of assistance that a community mental health center can render has expanded considerably since Congress passed the enabling Act. Suicide prevention, crisis programs, 24-hour "rap" sessions for younger people, and non-residential drug treatment centers are a few of the services which have been funded through the Act. Behavior modification, and especially the use of operant methods, has made a significant contribution to community mental health in several important areas. Among these are the organization and operation of community mental health centers using behavioral procedures and the community treatment of juvenile delinquents.

Huntsville-Madison: A Behaviorally Oriented Community Mental Health Center.
At the Huntsville-Madison Center, located in Huntsville, Alabama, behavioral principles are not only applied to the treatment plans for the clients, they also constitute the very basis on which the center itself operates. In 1971, the National Institute of Mental Health, United States Public Health Service, provided support for the center to become a "totally behavioral mental health system." From that

point on, all of the interactions with the center's clients, the organization of the center, and the center's relationship to its personnel were conducted according to known behavioral principles.

The behavior of the patient is monitored continuously, and the therapists' records are sampled at random to determine whether the treatment procedures conform to the center's expectations. These evaluations are important for the therapist as well as the patient *because pay increases for the therapists are contingent on their performance.*

One of the outstanding features of the Huntsville-Madison group is its dedication to the use of operant methods in all phases of its operation, including the management of the center itself. Early on, the center developed a contingency contracting system and a token-economy program for the staff. The contract specifies job descriptions, criteria for success, and the rewards for meeting these criteria which are obtained in the form of points exchangeable for salary increments, extra vacation time, or attendance at special training sessions. In effect, the principles of behavior and sound research methodology are the basis for the center's operation.

Does the use of operant procedures make the Huntsville-Madison program a more effective community mental health center? Compared to centers with other orientations, how successful is the Huntsville-Madison program (1) in making services available to the community, (2) in reducing the number of hospital admissions in the area, and (3) in cost-effectiveness? Obviously these are difficult questions to answer, but the commitment of the center to precise record-keeping and continuous self-evaluation has made it possible to answer some of them and to continue gathering information on others.

In 1975, the Huntsville Center completed an evaluation of a 3-year program to train parents of "behaviorally disordered" children in the principles of applied operant learning. The purposes of the study were: (1) to evaluate the effectiveness of some of the operating procedures, i.e., getting parents to do what they were told (process); (2) to compare the results of training parents in child management with no-training (outcome); (3) to compare the effects of professional training level on outcome (master's- vs. doctoral-level instructors); (4) to analyze the relationship between class attendance and socioeconomic level; and (5) to evaluate the cost-effectiveness of the program.

All parents in the training program were required to attend a series of lectures at the center. A response-cost procedure was also established in which each parent was expected to "pay a $30 enrollment fee, $10 of which was refundable if the parents attended classes, arrived on time, completed homework assignments, and produced a positive change in the targeted behavior" (Rinn et al., 1975, p. 379). The problem behaviors of the children included enuresis, temper tantrums, and school attendance. The "no-training group" comprised parents who enrolled too late to be assigned and were asked to wait for the formation of another class.

In terms of process, the operation of the program appeared to be relatively successful. Approximately 79% of the parents completed their homework assignments. Continuous evaluation during the course of the study also showed that the response-cost procedures did affect the parents' behavior positively and led to refinements in the procedure.

At the completion of the study, 92% of the parents reported that the behavior of their children was much improved, as opposed to 0% for the no-training group. This first blush of success did not prevail, however. A follow-up telephone survey conducted in 1973 and 1974 for parents taking the course in 1971, 1972, and 1973 yielded 54% much improved and 30% moderately improved, with an overall improvement level of 84%. Further questioning revealed no serious deterioration in beneficial effects, and only 16% of the 154 parents in the telephone follow-up sample sought further treatment for their children. Moreover, 97% of the parents sampled indicated that they either strongly approved of (64%) or moderately approved of (33%) behavior modification as a child-rearing technique, and 85% reported that they had recommended the course to others.

Another significant finding of the parent training study suggests that paraprofessional and master's-level personnel could be used effectively in training parents. There was no difference in the outcome for parents assigned to a class taught by someone with a master's degree as opposed to a doctorate, even though the parents were aware of the differences in training level.

An analysis of the relationship between socioeconomic level, goal attainment, and meeting attendance was conducted to examine the usefulness of the course for parents of differing economic levels. The low-income group ($5,000 annually) attended fewer meetings (3.1%) and had a lower median goal attainment score (5%) than the middle-income group ($5,000–20,000 annually) who attended 4.9% of the sessions and had a goal attainment score of 93%. These findings led the authors to conclude that because of their verbal deficits, lack of adequate clothing, and diminished experiences of educational success, the lower-income parents may have found the classes aversive (Rinn et al., 1975, p. 385). Future attempts to involve lower income groups in such a program would have to take such factors into consideration.

The training program was also effective in terms of cost benefits. The total cost for all classes, including the individual programming of those who required additional training after the course ("treatment failures") was $26,479. If these same families had been treated as individual outpatients, the cost would have risen to $77,811.

Although this study leaves several important questions unanswered, it does indicate the kind of continuous evaluation procedures each community mental health center must conduct in order to determine the effectiveness of the community center concept in general. Unfortunately, when the personnel of the Huntsville-Madison center attempted to compare the relative effectiveness of this program vis-à-vis other mental health programs, they could not find centers that kept comparable records on "treatment length, goal achievement, persistence of change, and cost per service unit" (Bolin & Kivens, 1974; Nietzel et al., 1977).

Community-Based Programs For Juvenile Offenders. From the time that the courts first recognized the advisability of separating juvenile offenders from mature, seasoned criminals in the administration of justice, a constant struggle has gone on to determine the best way to cope with this rapidly growing social problem.

In 1973, the FBI reported that juvenile crime involving persons under the age of 18 constituted approximately 34% of all documented criminal cases. At least one-third of all male youths between the ages of 14 and 16 in one moderate-sized Midwestern city had at least one police contact, and the rate of juvenile crime appears to be rising faster than the general crime figures (Nietzel et al., 1977). But perhaps even more distressing, the reasonable supposition is that the ever-increasing adult criminal crop is bred and nurtured in the "hothouse" of juvenile crime. Clearly something extraordinary and radical had to be done about the problem of juvenile offenders.

The basis for the behavioral treatment of juvenile offenders stems from the assumption made by many mental health professionals that most juvenile delinquency is the result of inappropriately reinforced behavior. Most juvenile offenders reject middle-class standards and "rules-of-the-game," obtaining their reinforcements through status in group membership and material gain (Chapter 7). It seems reasonable to conclude, then, that if the behavior of the delinquent is to be changed, the contingencies must be rearranged. Reinforcers must now be obtained through other behavior, and the juvenile offender must learn a different set of response consequences. In some instances where the correct responses are not available to be reinforced because they were never learned in the first place, new behavior must be shaped slowly by the method of successive approximations.

One of the primary reasons for the failure of treatment with juvenile offenders, Schwitzgebel and Kolb (1964) reasoned, was that the first link in the chain of responses leading to therapy—the willingness to come and talk to someone—was absent. If the delinquents came to the therapy session at all, it was because the courts forced them to, and, when they finally arrived, the process of simply telling someone about themselves was completely alien to them. One of the first attempts to use behavioral methods with delinquents addressed itself to this problem.

Could a shaping procedure be designed to increase the attendance and cooperation of the delinquent in a therapy-like situation, such as talking into a tape recorder and taking psychological tests (Schwitzgebel & Kolb, 1974, p. 45)? In a series of steps that began by meeting the delinquents in their usual haunts and offering them jobs as experimental subjects to talk into a tape recorder, the interest of the boys slowly increased until they attended the sessions regularly and were no longer erratic in their arrival time. The increased interest slowly led to regular therapy, and a subsequent follow-up of the justice system records for 1-, 2-, and 3-year intervals indicated that the boys who participated in the study had fewer arrests and spent much less time in detention.

The next major advance in the use of behavioral methods with delinquents came when institutions began to use operant methods in the form of contingency-management procedures. Although a great many such studies exist, the most notable, from the viewpoint of large number of youths involved and extensive follow-up observations, were those conducted by Cohen and Filipczak (1971), and Jeness (1974).

The token-economy program developed by Cohen and Filipczak at the National Training School for Boys concentrated on educational achievement. Delinquent youths were encouraged to participate in educating themselves and were rewarded for their efforts. However, despite the significant gains in academic achievement which continued for some period after the boys were released from the institution, a 3-year follow-up disclosed similar rates of recidivism for those delinquents who had been in the program compared to a group who had completed the regular training program.

The study conducted by Jeness under the auspices of the California Youth Authority had similar disappointing results after a period of some promise. Approximately 1,000 youths were involved in a comprehensive study which included many innovations in institutional settings. The boys were assigned to one of two forms of treatment, either experimental behavior modification, or transactional analysis, a method that stresses the importance of interpersonal relationships.

As might be expected, the transactional approach resulted in greater gains in attitudes and self-reports because of its emphasis on self-study, while the behavior modification programs produced greater changes in observed behavior. Both procedures resulted in a drop in illegal behavior and lower recidivism rates for a relatively short time following the completion of the study and the delinquents' release from the institution. Unfortunately, however, these gains were not sustained, and, as in the Cohen and Filipczak study, the recidivism rates returned to their former level after a period of 2 years.

What causes these disappointing results? The promise that followed the behavior changes after the completion of the studies simply did not materialize in the long run, just as the effects of behavior modification procedures with institutionalized adult felons, discussed earlier, also failed to endure. Part of the reason, according to some observers, lies in the very nature of institutionalization itself. The inmates of institutions are very skilled at shaping each other's behaviors. In fact, as one study actually showed, they become better behavior modifiers than the staff itself (Buehler et al., 1966; Fixsen et al., 1976, p. 311). This realization led a group of psychologists to establish a mode of treatment that incorporated family-style homes in the community.

"Achievement Place": The community-based treatment of delinquent youths. The prototype for all "teaching-family models of group home treatment" is the Achievement Place program begun by Ellery and Elaine Phillips in 1967 (Phillips, 1968). With some modification, the many replicas of the Achievement Place concept which now exist use substantially the same token-economy program and reinforcement procedures which were part of the original program (Liberman et al., 1975). In effect, groups of 6–8 youths, generally around 12–16 years of age, who have been in legal trouble are assigned to a house in the community which has been specifically purchased for the purpose. The aim of the program is to teach the youthful offenders the appropriate behaviors necessary to live in the community. Toward this end, their activities are supervised on a 24-hour basis by "teach-

ing parents" who work with the youths in the house and who also interact with parents and teachers to help solve problems.

An entering youth is first familiarized with the token point system by which he either earns or loses his daily privileges. These privileges are basic: use of telephone, tools, and the yard; snacks; television watching; and home time— weekend passes to their natural homes or downtown. Additional privileges to earn are the $1–$3 weekly allowance and a bond savings program (Fixsen et al., 1976, p. 312).

One extremely important aspect of the program is that the youths continue to attend the same schools they went to before they entered the program. Their behavior in school is "monitored" by the teacher, and feedback is provided to both the youth and the Achievement Place "parent" in the form of weekly or, in some cases where necessary, daily report cards. Points are earned or lost depending upon these daily reports. The boys continue to interact with each other at the home after

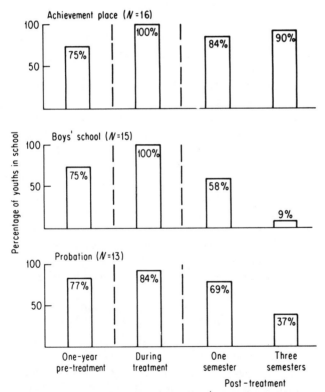

FIG. 10-3 Recidivism rates after treatment for various groups. (Source: D. L. Fixsen, E. L. Phillips, E. A. Phillips and M. M. Wolf. In W. E. Craighead, A. E. Kazdin and M. J. Mahoney (Eds.). *Behavior Modification, principles, issues, and applications.* Boston: Houghton-Mifflin Co., 1976, 310–320. Copyright 1976 by Houghton-Mifflin and Co. and used by permission.)

school, attending daily family conferences, calculating the points they have earned, and engaging in leisure time activities. They are also taught skills such as study and homework behaviors to improve their academic work.

By most of the criteria normally used to evaluate such programs, the "Achievement Place" experiment appears to be a relatively successful venture. Fig. 10-3 shows, for example, that the recidivism rates 12 and 24 months after completion of treatment is considerably less for the youths from the Achievement Place program than for comparable groups of boys from a traditional boys' training school and those placed on probation. In addition, 90% of the Achievement Place youths were still in school 3 semesters after treatment as opposed to 9% for the Boys School graduates and 37% for the boys placed on probation. But one of the most interesting results of Achievement Place shows in the comparative cost of the program. Table 10-2 shows that "the cost per bed of purchasing, renovating, and furnishing Achievement Place was about one-fourth the cost of building an institution," while "the operating costs are less than one-half the operating costs for the Boys School in Kansas" (Fixsen et al., 1976, p. 320).

Although these results are generally impressive, experience with the other long-term failures of the institutional behavioral programs cited earlier suggests that any final judgments about the effectiveness of community-based treatment programs for youthful offenders must be made with caution. It is true that the major difference between the two programs—institutionalization vs. the community—may well be the crucial factor determining the success of one and the failure of the other. But no one really seems to know why Achievement Place may work and why behavior modification programs in institutions apparently do not. Direct comparisons, of course, are not entirely fair, because major differences between the two situations, apart from institutionalization itself, may well account for the results.

Still, if we permit ourselves to speculate about the reasons for the superiority (at least up to now) of the Achievement Place program, it may be that, among other things, the changes which take place in the community-based program occur in the context of cues (peers, environment, status seeking, and so on) that originally controlled the undesirable behavior. Thus cues may lose their ability to elicit

TABLE 10-2   Comparative Costs

	Achievement Place	*Institution*
Capital investment per youth	$6,000	$20,000 to $30,000
Yearly operating cost per youth	$4,100	$ 6,000 to $12,000

SOURCE: D.L. Fixsen, E.L. Phillips, E.A. Phillips, and M.M. Wolf, 1976. By permission.

the inappropriate behavior. For the youthful offender in prison, on the other hand, the cues are carefully preserved because their control is neither extinguished nor associated with other behavior. The difference in the success of the two programs may well be due to the failure to extinguish the influence of the cues which motivate undesirable behavior in the community in addition to the reinforcement the institutionalized delinquent invariably receives from his fellow inmates.

More recently, an Achievement-Place-type program was conducted at the Living and Learning Center in Fort Lauderdale, Florida, in which self-evaluation and external-evaluation token systems were compared. The results of the study showed that the appropriate behavior lasted considerably longer for the self-evaluation group when the tokens were eliminated than it did for the external evaluation group (Wood & Flynn, 1978).

chapter eleven

Biofeedback

Feedback, in general, is a way of maintaining predetermined balance within a system. If a thermostat in a heating system has been set at 68° F, the system works to maintain this temperature more or less constantly through feedback. The thermostat samples the air and "feeds a signal" back, turning the furnace on or off depending upon the need for heat to maintain a constant temperature.

Humans and animals operate in a similar manner to maintain a predetermined balance in the internal environment. In biology, this balance is called homeostasis. Temperature receptors located internally and on the surface of the body, for example, send signals to the central nervous system which, in turn, operates to constrict or dilate the blood vessels, increasing or decreasing the volume of blood to maintain a constant temperature of approximately 98.6° F. In the psychophysiologic disorders when the blood pressure is too high (essential hypertension) or the temperature of the fingers and toes too low (Raynaud's disease), the homeostatic mechanisms for maintaining balance do not operate properly.

In a very important sense, all learning requires feedback in order to be successful, and we have been discussing feedback up to now without actually being explicit about it. Organisms must "know" the consequences of their responding in order to make the continuous adjustments in behavior necessary to maximize the probability of reinforcement. A pigeon, as we have seen, adjusts its pecking behavior to conform to a particular schedule of reinforcement. In effect, *feedback* serves three distinguishable functions in learning: (1) it provides information to the organism about the characteristics and consequences of its responses; (2) it provides information about negative or positive reinforcement; and (3) it makes behavior predictable and potentially controllable (Ruch & Zimbardo, 1971, p. 221).

Biofeedback is essentially another way of modifying behavior through operant conditioning. It might even be more appropriately called interoceptive operant conditioning because, like interoceptive classical conditioning, the response systems are internal rather than external.

The procedure in biofeedback learning is basically the same as it is in other operant strategies. Small units of behavior which approximate the goal response are reinforced until the ultimate goal response is learned. The major difference is that the responses in biofeedback training are internal, essentially unobservable, and produce weak signals. In their original state, they are useless for purposes of biofeedback learning. They must be detected and amplified by sensitive electronic equipment. Typically, heart rate, blood pressure or blood volume, or small muscle potentials are picked up by an appropriate transducer, amplified, and converted to visual or auditory signals that follow the moment-to-moment fluctuations in these responses. (Quartz crystals, for example, are commonly used as pressure transducers because they demonstrate the well-known piezoelectric effect by generating small electric currents when squeezed.)

These auditory or visual signals are generally displayed to subjects who are asked to maintain them at certain levels. The information provided by these signals is frequently sufficient to generate learning, but in many instances, the subjects are further rewarded for their success in raising or lowering the amplitude of a response with money or the opportunity to hear preferred music or see pleasurable slides. The response-reward contingency can also be programmed according to one of the schedules of reinforcement, and some indication exists that the behavior is influenced by the specific schedule used (see Box 11-1, p. 272, for example).

The subject's awareness of the relationship between the response and the auditory or visual signals is, apparently, not a necessary condition for learning to occur. Studies have shown that conditioning can take place when subjects were instructed to increase the clicks they heard in a pair of headphones, even though they did not know that the sound came from muscle potentials in their hands (Hefferline & Perera, 1963). In clinical studies, on the other hand, patients are always specifically instructed to try to vary a response by varying the auditory or visual signals associated with the response.

BIOFEEDBACK: THE CONTROVERSIAL ISSUES

The use of biofeedback to alleviate certain behavior disorders is a relatively recent addition to the learning techniques which form the basis of behavior modification. The persistent belief that autonomically related responses—heart rate, blood pressure, and palmar sweating, or galvanic skin response (GSR)—could not be brought under control by operant conditioning was probably partly responsible for this lag.

We saw in Chapter 2 (Interoceptive Conditioning, p. 21), for example, that responses such as constriction or dilation of the blood vessels or increases and decreases in body temperature could be classically conditioned by an appropriate procedure with relative ease. Can these same responses be brought under operant control simply by reinforcing increases or decreases as they occur during the course of normal fluctuations? Can the same reinforcement procedures used to train a pigeon to peck at a plastic disk or two children to play cooperatively make the heart beat faster or slower or blood pressure increase and decrease by consistently reinforcing (or punishing) these responses as they occur?

Some psychologists did not think so, and in 1928, when Konorski and Miller first began to distinguish between two types of conditioning—classical and operant —they were forced to conclude from the available experimental evidence that autonomic nervous system responses could not be conditioned by operant methods. As late as 1953, even Skinner agreed that changes in the responses produced by the glands and smooth muscles of the organs could not be modified by reinforcement. "We may reinforce a man with food when he 'turns red,' but we cannot in this way condition him to blush voluntarily" (Kimmel, 1974, p. 114). If it could be done, Skinner declared further, children could learn to control their emotions as readily as they do the position of their hands.

The inevitable contradictions were soon to follow, however. In summarizing some of the early evidence for operant conditioning of autonomic responses, Kimmel (1974) points out that positive results began to appear in the reports of experiments in the Soviet Union in which subjects actually learned to turn off a shock when they dilated the blood vessels in the finger, overcoming the natural tendency for shock to cause vasoconstriction. They even learned to avoid shock entirely by dilating the blood vessels to a combination of light and sound which was presented in advance of the shock (p. 326). About the same time, Kimmel (Kimmel & Hill, 1960) began to obtain evidence showing that the increases which are part of the normal fluctuations in the GSR (palmar sweating) could be consistently increased if their occurrence was reinforced with pleasant or unpleasant odors. The next 5 years brought a spate of experiments which removed all doubt that responses associated with autonomic nervous activity could, in fact, be brought under operant control, and in 1967, Kimmel published a very persuasive review of sixteen such studies.

The Controversy Continues

But saying that responses associated with the autonomic nervous system can be operantly conditioned is not the same as saying that the autonomic nervous system itself can be conditioned in this manner.

Psychologists began to observe that changes in responses such as heart rate, for example, were often, if not always, accompanied by simultaneous changes in respiration, and they suggested that maybe, just maybe, the reinforced changes in heart rate were really changes in breathing that were being conditioned and actually producing (or mediating) the observed increases or decreases in heart rate. If this were the case, striate skeletal muscles were being conditioned and not the autonomic nervous system after all.

And, to add more fuel to the fire of dissent, it was also suggested that these so-called autonomic nervous system responses could conceivably be manipulated by the subject's "thinking" about the reactions. In other words, several experiments reported that people who were aware of the relationship between their responses and the subsequent reinforcement did not condition properly, or they were able to increase and decrease their heart rate by merely thinking about it.

Of course, questions like these are rarely resolved experimentally because of the large number of factors that always remain uncontrolled. But it is instructive to sample the kinds of efforts made in an attempt to answer them.

Several experimenters set out to demonstrate that changes in autonomic and central nervous system responses could be operantly conditioned independent of skeletal muscle functioning by using curare to reduce, or completely eliminate, such influences. In one such experiment with animals, Koslovskaya, Vertes, and Miller (1973) demonstrated a change in the level of motor activity of the sciatic nerve (the large nerve that runs down the legs) in a curarized rat by reinforcing either increases or decreases in nerve activity through electrical stimulation of the reward centers of the brain while the rat was kept alive through artificial respiration. They also succeeded in obtaining a decrease in the nerve activity of one leg and an increase in the other by reinforcing the differential responses in both legs when the nerve activity occurred.

Another study, conducted with a volunteer human subject who was partially curarized and capable of only limited movement, demonstrated GSR conditioning in spite of the reduction in respiratory control (Birk, et al., 1966). Finally, several studies have shown that the human salivary response can be either increased or decreased operantly, and it is hard to imagine just how skeletal muscles in the form of tongue-cheek movements can influence this process (Frezza & Holland, 1971).

The second problem, the influence of thought processes on the operant conditioning of autonomic activity, is somewhat more difficult to deal with, if only because thinking can, indeed, influence the response of the autonomic nervous system. Thinking about a frightening event can elevate heart rate, blood pressure, and GSR responses, but this does not rule out the possibility that such processes may also be controlled by events that are independent of thinking. If, however, human subjects can be trained to raise their blood pressures while lowering their heart rates at the same time by reinforcement procedures (Schwartz, 1971), then, as Kimmel points out, those who suggest that some central mediational process, such as thinking, is responsible for these contortions may have some difficult questions to answer (1974, p. 331). Nevertheless, it is virtually impossible to rule out the influence of mediational processes, such as thinking, fear, or small muscle movements for that matter, and whether autonomic activity is directly conditioned or mediated by some other response is not yet clear.

As if this were not sufficient trouble for the biofeedback infant, some have even questioned its legitimacy as an operant offspring. What precisely, they ask, is the reinforcing event in the biofeedback training scheme? In some instances, the subject's response does not really alter the environment in the direct way in which a pigeon's response gets food, or a child's response, candy. Can the information itself be construed as a reinforcer?

It has been suggested that two processes are actually involved. In the first, the subject (or patient) learns to control a response not previously under control by calibrating the feedback signal with the internal response much like a tennis player learns to coordinate posture and stance with the effects of hitting the ball correctly. Once the response is learned, however, it can be brought under further control by reinforcement (Shapiro & Surwit, 1976). But this explanation, unfortunately, cannot handle those instances in which interoceptive learning occurs without any information or any awareness of the contingencies involved.

Interesting as these problems are, and important as they may be for understanding the basic properties of learning, the inability to resolve them has not prevented the procedure itself from being developed for practical application. Therapists have used any combination of factors—conditioning, awareness, instructions, relaxation—in an endeavor to change behavior. The use of biofeedback, as we shall see, has been somewhat limited—it has always promised a great deal more than it could actually deliver—and many problems are associated with sustaining the beneficial effects in real life after they have been obtained in the laboratory. But in certain, selected areas, the effects of biofeedback have been truly fascinating and dramatic.

CLINICAL APPLICATIONS

Clinical applications of biofeedback have generally been of two kinds: training of striate or skeletal muscles to relieve headaches or restore movement and function, and alleviation of disorders associated with the autonomic nervous system.

Training Muscle Movement and Relaxation

Although many of the early studies in biofeedback concentrated on conditioning responses of the autonomic nervous system, one of the first experiments demonstrated that small muscle potentials in the thumb, undetectable by the eye, could be increased through reinforcement (Hefferline et al., 1959; Hefferline & Perera, 1963). Since that time, muscle re-education using operant feedback procedures has proven to be of great value in a number of disorders. In one particularly noteworthy application, a boy of 13 years of age was saved from a radical surgical procedure through the conditioning of the anal sphincter muscle (Box 11-1).

BOX 11-1

Saving a Child from Surgery

A colostomy is a serious surgical procedure involving the creation of a new opening of the large intestine (colon) on the surface of the body through which fecal matter can be eliminated. The operation, which is considered physically and psychologically traumatic, is usually reserved for older people with cancer of the colon or other intestinal obstructions and is rarely performed on a 13-year-old child. But because the boy in this study was a continuous soiler (encopresis) from the age of 6, he had already undergone one type of surgical operation and was recommended for a second. The first operation involved surgical removal of a section of the colon for a suspected congenitally dilated intestine (Hirschsprung's disease) without any effect on the soiling. A colostomy was under consideration at the time of this study on the grounds that continuous soiling was due to inadequate anal sphincter tone and surgery was necessary to bypass the troublesome area.

Continuous soiling is created by one of two conditions. The first is due to withholding stool until it becomes an accumulated mass, forcing the anal sphincter open and allowing a continuous discharge of mucous substance. This type of encopresis has been successfully treated by operant methods involving reinforcement of regular elimination responses and punishment for withholding. In the present case, the encopresis was the result of a dilated sphincter which created a constant fecal discharge. As a last resort, before the operation was to be performed, an attempt was made by Kohlenberg (1973) to modify the child's sphincter tone through operant training.

The boy was placed on a comfortable bed and a small balloon inserted in the rectum to make contact with the anal sphincter. The balloon was connected to a clear plastic tube filled with red tinted water. The height of the water in the tube was controlled by pressure exerted on the balloon from the anal sphincter and served as a visual indication of changes in pressure. The apparatus was arranged so that the child could see the height of the water in the tube (Fig. 11-1).

During phase 1 of the study, the child was told that keeping the water level high—above 22.5 inches—would show that his muscles were working properly and that he would not have to undergo surgery. But this kind of reassurance and visual feedback alone had no beneficial effect on sphincter pressure, and little progress was made. Figure 11-2 shows virtually no change in pressure during this period.

In phase 2, the contingency was changed, and the experimenter looked at the tube every 10 seconds during a 15-minute period. If the height of the water column exceeded 22.5 inches, nickels were dropped into a jar as a reward. No such reinforcement was given, however, if the criterion was not met. Although this schedule resulted in increased sphincter pressure relative to phase 1, the method in phase 2 was not entirely satisfactory for several reasons. Because the schedule used during this phase was essentially fixed-interval reinforcement (reinforcement at the end of a prescribed 10-second period), there was a tendency for the pressure to increase toward the end of the 10-second interval and to decrease shortly after reinforcement producing the familiar "scalloped" curve of perform-ance (Fig. 11-2). Also, the short duration requirements of the study (to reach a pressure goal after 10 seconds) contradicted the long-term requirements of the target behavior—to keep pressure constant over extended periods of time.

The third phase of the study eliminated these difficulties. A timing sequence was introduced which required the child to exert a specific amount of constant pressure for a given length of time in order to obtain the money. Whenever the pressure decreased before the time criterion was met, the timing cycle was broken and starting the timer required increased exertion. In effect, the schedule was changed from fixed interval to fixed ratio, making the reward contingent on the amount of effort expended rather than on the mere passage of time. Figure 11-2 shows that the duration of constant sphincter pressure greatly increased using this method. Measures taken 24 hours after the last training session showed an increase in anal sphincter pressure from 35 to 50 mm Hg.

Surgery was canceled as a result of operant training, and the child was ulti-mately discharged from the hospital. Three days after the last experimental trial, nurses on the ward reported no soiling of the bedclothes. One month after dis-charge, the child's parents reported no soiling for periods of approximately 8 hours in contrast to earlier reports that soiling and odor were present continu-ously. Follow-up after 1 year indicated that neither the hospital nor the referring physician had been contacted by the family for additional treatment (Kohlenberg, 1973).

Biofeedback was also successfully used to train 7 patients who were soiling (fecal incontinence) because they were unable to contract the external sphincter muscles in the rectum for several reasons ranging from surgical intervention to disease. The procedure used was similar to that employed by Kohlenberg (Box 11-1). Recorded responses from balloons inserted in the areas of the internal and external anal sphincter muscles were shown to the patients, and they were encour-aged to increase the amplitude of these responses to approximate normal sphincter pressure. After 4 training sessions consisting of 50 training trials each, the patients learned to increase the amplitude of the external sphincter muscle and to synchro-nize responses so that external sphincter contraction occurred simultaneously with internal sphincter relaxation, a condition necessary for normal fecal retention.

FIG. 11-1 Arrangement of bed, water column indicating pressure, time-lapse camera, and reinforcement jar. (Source: R.J. Kohlenberg. Operant con-ditioning of human anal sphinc-ter pressure. *Journal of Applied Behavior Analysis*, 1970, *3*, 241–245. Used by permission.)

During training, the patients were "weaned" from depending upon the information provided by feedback on several trials when no information was provided. All patients successfully learned to control sphincter function, and follow-up investigations ranging from 3 months to 5 years indicated that the learned sphincter control remained stable (Engel et al., 1974).

Patients suffering from a cerebral stroke which results in a left- or right-sided paralysis (hemiplegia) can often be re-trained to walk after extensive physical therapy requiring a great deal of time and effort. In order to minimize the amount of time and to involve the patient more directly in the process, Johnson and Garton (1973) used a biofeedback technique to increase foot movement by first training very small muscle movements in patients who had suffered cerebrovascular accidents. Fine wire electrodes designed to pick up very small muscle potentials were inserted into the paralyzed leg muscle (tibialis anterior). The patients were then asked to flex or contract the muscles, and the resultant electromyographic responses were shown to them on a screen or heard through a speaker. (If these methods did not work, the electrode was inserted into the opposite leg so that the patients could hear the desired response and then reinserted into the paralyzed muscle.) After some initial training, patients were provided with portable units and told to practice 30 minutes per day. Patients were eliminated from the program when they reached a functional level at which they no longer required a short leg brace for walking. Of the 11 patients who entered the program, only 1 failed to attain the functional level.

One of the most effective uses of biofeedback on a large scale has been for the relief of muscle-tension headaches. These fairly common headaches consist of a dull, "band-like" pain originating in the back of the head which often extends to the forehead region. They are due to sustained contraction of the scalp and neck muscles, and they may last for hours, weeks, and even months. Relaxation of the contracted muscles is the best remedy for these headaches, but very few of the

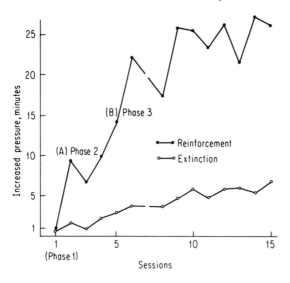

FIG. 11-2 Total time during each session that exerted pressure exceeded the criterion enabling the child to receive a reinforcement during Phase 1, Phase 2, and Phase 3. Note that the nonreinforced pressure response (extinction condition) also increased from 1 to approximately 5 minutes. (Source: R.J. Kohlenberg. Operant conditioning of human anal sphincter pressure. *Journal of Applied Behavior Analysis,* 1970, *3,* 241–245. Used by permission.)

people who suffer from them know how to relax, and, in fact, their behavior in general is characterized by prolonged periods of stress and tension.

Since many disorders, and headaches in particular, are often relieved by suggestion and placebos (medicines or procedures designed to make the patient believe they are therapeutic but which have no known therapeutic effects), studies designed to test the specific effectiveness of feedback for headaches must take these factors into consideration.

An attempt was made to control for placebo effects in a study with 18 people who were frequently afflicted with tension headaches. Each patient was assigned to one of three groups: those who were able to hear the rise and fall of "clicks" in a headphone corresponding to the increase and decrease of tension in the frontalis muscle of the forehead to which the transducers were attached (Group A); those who heard pre-recorded clicks delivered to Group A, but for whom the sound was only randomly associated with the fluctuations in their own muscle tension (Group B); and a third group who received no treatment but were asked to keep a record of the frequency of headaches. The origin of the headaches was explained to Groups A and B, and Group A was further instructed to relax and keep the frequency of clicks as low as possible. Group B was also told to relax, but they were further informed that the purpose of the clicks was to keep out intruding thoughts that would interfere with relaxation. Both groups were also told to practice relaxation at home. Group C was simply told to monitor their headaches.

Only Group A showed a consistent reduction in the frequency of headaches, 3 of the 6 patients maintaining their improvement over a period of 18 months. Although the study is not a complete control for placebo effects, it does demonstrate that biofeedback is superior to relaxation with false feedback and to no treatment at all (Budzynski et al., 1973).

The effectiveness of biofeedback as a uniform treatment procedure for all so-called tension headaches has recently been challenged in a discussion of the theoretical problems of tension headaches (C. Phillips, 1978). According to Phillips, the traditional view of tension headaches, and the notion that all headaches which are non-migraine stem from muscle tension, is untenable. Phillips's research has led her to conclude that three different types of "tension" headaches exist, depending upon the amount of electromyographic (EMG) involvement, each of which may require a different form of treatment (1978, p. 259).

The first is the tension headache with abnormally high EMG levels. In this case, biofeedback works earliest and most effectively in reducing pain. In the second type of headache, EMG abnormalities occur periodically instead of almost continuously. Here biofeedback will be minimally, if at all, effective. Finally, some headaches involve virtually no EMG activity, and these require other behavior modification therapies (behavioral counseling, for example). Once again, the initial assessment of behavior becomes an important factor in devising a treatment strategy.

The use of biofeedback to control muscle groups is expanding at a rapid rate. Dentists, for example, have reported the successful treatment of a painful ailment known as myofascial-pain dysfunction syndrome which is caused by contractions of the masseter muscles in the jaw. By attaching transducers to the masseter muscle and teaching the patient to recognize the difference between tension and relaxation, clinicians were able to achieve significant reductions in pain (Dohrmann & Laskin, 1978). Muscle training with electromyographic procedures has also been employed to help a patient regain use of previously uncontrollable masseter muscles in the jaw and the ability to eat solid food following an operation for cancer of the mouth (Nigl, 1979).

Modifying Autonomic Responses

The success of biofeedback in training and relaxing muscle sets has also been duplicated in the area of autonomic functioning. But, as we shall presently see, certain disorders, such as essential hypertension, create their own unique problems because the decreases in blood pressure obtained in the laboratory or consulting room are rarely ever sustained once the patient leaves the laboratory.

The Use of Feedback in Essential Hypertension.   Essential hypertension—abnormally high blood pressure over long periods of time—is an exceedingly complex disorder that occurs in about 10% of the population 20 years of age or older and in about 40% of those around age 60. Except in the case of kidney disease, the specific causes of hypertension are unknown, although much has been speculated about the responsibility of factors such as congenital susceptibilities, high salt intake, old age, non-specific environmental conditions, and psychological stress (Weiner, 1977).

Because hypertension is widely regarded as a stress-related disorder, much of the early work with autonomic conditioning concentrated on attempts to lower blood pressure through contingency training. And some of the initial results were very promising. Patients suffering from hypertension were taught to lower their blood pressure (both systolic and diastolic) when they received contingent rewards, pleasurable slides or pleasant music, for example, for maintaining pressures at specific predetermined levels that were gradually reduced throughout the experiment. Sometimes the pressure reading was presented to them in the form of a signal with each heartbeat. At other times, the continuation of the music or some other reward indicated that the desirable pressure was being maintained.

For the most part, however, as soon as the patients left the laboratory and returned to their daily routines, their blood pressures returned to their previous elevated levels (Shapiro & Surwit, 1976; Surwit et al., 1978). In some isolated instances, and for unknown reasons, however, a few patients do benefit from treatment and can successfully maintain the gains made in the laboratory. But enduring changes in blood pressure are the exception rather than the rule.

In fact, a very recent study comparing blood-pressure feedback, muscle-potential feedback (EMG), and simple relaxation showed that none were really effective in producing long-term changes in blood pressure, despite significant initial decreases resulting from the blood-pressure method. Extrapolating to a larger population and using life insurance data, these changes in blood pressure through biofeedback would result in a 15% decrease in the mortality rate—a small clinical change compared to the 67% decrease achieved with drugs (Blanchard et al., 1979). These observations have recently been confirmed in a comprehensive survey of the research literature on essential hypertension. "To date, few studies have resulted in blood pressure reductions that are clinically relevant." While substantial reduction can be achieved in the laboratory, no real-life benefits have yet been demonstrated (Seer, 1979, p. 1039).

Why it works when it does. On the basis of recent evidence, we have good reason to believe that relaxation itself may be the most important element in biofeedback training in general, and in essential hypertension in particular. Regardless of whether the patient is told specifically to relax or not during treatment, the situation is highly conducive to the reduction of tension. Typically, patients are placed in a quiet, isolated room with soft lighting and seated in a comfortable chair. They are often told that the purpose of the auditory or visual feedback is to help them relax.

Blanchard and Young (1974) have suggested that biofeedback may actually be an elaborate and highly effective way to teach relaxation. The feedback signal is an added element because it enables the subject to monitor the effectiveness of relaxation training just as it does in muscular training.

A recent review of relaxation procedures in biofeedback, which reports that a combination of feedback and relaxation training is superior to either alone, appears to support this notion (Tarler-Benlolo, 1978). In fact, one of the latest studies comparing cardiovascular feedback, neuromuscular feedback, and meditation (mental and bodily relaxation) in the treatment of borderline hypertension indicated that all were equally effective in producing small changes in blood pressure during the course of training, although blood pressure returned to baseline levels shortly thereafter. The authors of this study also found that the elevated blood-pressure readings obtained during the physical examination were often reduced by as much as 20 mm of Hg systolic and 15 mm of Hg diastolic in the quiet laboratory conditions. Such variability has been noted repeatedly, and it suggests that many of the positive results reported may be due to this kind of habituation and momentary relaxation (Surwit et al., 1978).

Why it often doesn't work. A study of the failures in biofeedback training has provided an interesting array of reasons for its ineffectiveness in many cases. Most of these factors, as Shapiro and Surwit (1976) have pointed out, have to do with circumstances outside of the laboratory that support and reinforce the disorder itself and impede the generalization of any gains made in the laboratory. One of Surwit's patients, for example, expressed a reluctance to "give up" her illness "because it served as an excuse for a poor social life and a dependent relationship with her mother" (Shapiro & Surwit, 1976, p. 102). This patient was particularly candid about her ambivalence toward biofeedback treatment which enabled the therapists to provide social training as an adjunct to biofeedback. Many patients, however, are not even aware of their dependence on these secondary gains.

Another patient's life-style was also an obstacle to the effectiveness of biofeedback training. In the laboratory he would successfully reduce his blood pressure by as much as 20 mm Hg, only to have it increase again when he pursued his favorite weekend pastime—betting on the horses (Schwartz, 1973).

But one of the most important factors responsible for the relative ineffectiveness of biofeedback in essential hypertension is the insidious nature of the disorder. The patient rarely feels any discomfort until it is too late, and, as a consequence, fails to take medication when it is prescribed or to practice the relaxation and/or control procedures learned in the laboratory. Unlike migraine and tension headaches or certain heart irregularities, there are no cues in essential hypertension to warn a patient of an increase in blood pressure. As a result, control outside of the laboratory becomes extremely difficult.

Migraine Headaches and "Handwarming."   Pavlov's discovery of classical conditioning has often been attributed to serendipity—he was engaged in studying gastric function in dogs and found conditioning quite by accident—and many have suggested that "accidental" discoveries occur more often in science than most people think. Whether or not this is actually true for other discoveries, it was substantially the way in which a research project at the Menninger Foundation came upon fairly successful treatment for migraine headaches (Box 11-2).

BOX 11-2
"Serendipity," Migraines, and Handwarming

Sargent and his colleagues at the Menninger Clinic were not specifically studying biofeedback training. They were interested in another phenomenon, called "autogenic training," which is an attempt to bring certain responses under control by concentrating on certain pre-selected phrases. Subjects were taught to control heart rate, experience a sense of warmth in the abdomen and in the extremities, and cool the forehead by repeating to themselves phrases that had been associated with these experiences.

But the experimenters were also aware of the possibilities of combining autogenic and feedback training, and so an experience of one of their research subjects who also happened to be a migraine sufferer did not escape their attention. During a spontaneous recovery from a migraine headache in the laboratory, the subject showed a marked flushing in her hands accompanied by a 10° F increase in temperature within the space of 2 minutes. This prompted two other migraine sufferers who were also research assistants in the laboratory to volunteer for autogenic feedback training in hand-temperature control. One of the volunteers made a complete recovery, and the other showed partial reduction in the frequency of headaches. Primarily on this basis, Sargent began to conduct further studies with people who had migraine headaches. Twelve of the 19 subjects studied showed marked improvement. From this, Sargent concluded that hand-warming was a possible treatment for migraine attacks (Sargent et al., 1973).

But no matter how encouraging Sargent's findings, they did not demonstrate conclusively that hand-warming was the major factor responsible for the reduction in headaches. Too many other things were going on at the same time, and the criteria for successful treatment was poorly defined. Nevertheless, the Menninger group was convinced that hand-warming was the major component in the alleviation of migraine headaches.

In 1975, a case study reported by Turin and Johnson demonstrated that Sargent's speculations were largely correct. A patient instructed to practice hand-warming and able to observe the process through feedback from a thermistor (temperature transducer) attached to the index finger experienced a reduction in the frequency of headaches. The following year, the same investigators published a study, controlled for the possibility of placebo and patient expectancies, extending their preliminary work (Turin and Johnson, 1976).

Seven patients suffering from migraine headaches were trained to achieve hand-warming using temperature biofeedback. Before this, however, they were trained to practice "hand-cooling" on the grounds that, if any specific reduction in headaches occurred from the hand-cooling techniques, the results could be attributed to the patients' expectations that the treatment would be beneficial rather than to the specific method itself. In other words, it would throw a great deal of suspicion on the specific effectiveness of hand-warming.

Interestingly enough, the frequency of headaches remained the same or actually increased for some patients as a result of hand-cooling, even though the patients were led to believe that the treatment would be beneficial. When the same subjects practiced hand-warming, however, the mean number of weekly headaches decreased from a baseline of 2.15 to 1.26 during the final weeks of training. The weekly number of pills consumed also dropped from 4.31 to 1.72, and the number of hours of headache-associated pain decreased from 12.41 to 5.7. On the whole, the results of this study and several others appeared to confirm hand-warming as a therapeutic technique. But why?

Why does handwarming work? The key to the effectiveness of handwarming as a migraine-reducing procedure lies in the physiological characteristics of the migraine headache itself. Again, as in most of the psychophysiologic disorders, stress acting on specific individuals appears to be the culprit. Most migraine attacks, it has been discovered, are responses to increased work pressure, interpersonal problems, difficulties in self-expression, and, in fact, to any problem that the potential migraine sufferer sees as stressful (Bakal, 1975).

In both forms of migraine, classical and common, the actual physiological process is a profound dilation of the peripheral blood vessels in the head. In classical migraine headaches, this may often follow a period of intense constriction of the blood vessels and an aura consisting of the sensation of an array of lights along with impaired vision called prodromal signs. In common migraine, these signs are not usually present. The attack is then followed by nausea, dizziness, vomiting, sensitivity to light, and a painful headache lasting anywhere from a few hours to several days. The important element in this cluster of responses, however, is the abrupt and sudden vasodilation that takes place. The drugs prescribed for the relief of migraine (ergotomine tartrate, epinephrine, or caffeine, for instance) act to constrict the blood vessels.

Figure 11-3 shows what happens to finger temperature as a result of stress and relaxation. The fact that the temperature decreases during stress (threat of electric shock in this case) indicates that the blood vessels are constricting during that period, and the increase in temperature following relaxation suggests that the vascular system in the finger has once again returned to its typically dilated state. On the basis of these observations, Boudewyns (1976) has argued that the hand-warming strategy works because it increases vasodilation. It has also been suggested that the mechanism must be central and not peripheral because *warming the hands with water or some other external device to increase blood volume does not relieve migraines* (Sargent et al., 1973). The actual process must occur somewhere in the autonomic nervous system. Warm hands are an indication that such a process has taken place centrally and that certain changes are also being produced in the cerebral arteries as well.

But why should an increase in peripheral blood volume due to vasodilation in the fingers reduce the frequency of migraine headaches? The specific mechanism proposed to account for this phenomenon appears to be related to the phase of the migraine attack being considered.

Classical migraine headaches, as we have just indicated, are produced by vasospasms consisting of an initial phase of vasoconstriction (prodromal stage) followed by a rapid and painful phase of vasodilation in the intracerebral and extracerebral arteries. It seemed reasonable to suppose, therefore, that any mechanism which acts to constrict the arteries when they are in a state of dilation will terminate the attack. Handwarming, one explanation suggests, accomplishes this

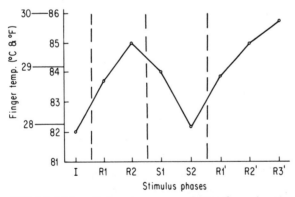

FIG. 11-3 Mean finger temperature during first relaxation phase (R1 and R2), stress phase (S1 and S2), and second relaxation phase (R1, R2 and R3). (Source: P. Boudewyns. Comparison of the effects of stress vs. relaxation on the finger temperature response. *Behavior Therapy,* 1976, 7, 54-67. Copyright Academic Press 1976 and used by permission.)

through a reciprocal action in which vasodilation in the fingers is accompanied by vasoconstriction in the cerebral arteries—a phenomenon which Dalessio and his associates (1979) have termed the "adaptation-relaxation" reflex.

According to results obtained by Dalessio et al. (1979), voluntary warming of the hands through feedback produces a vasomotor reflex (adaptation-relaxation reflex) in which dilation of the peripheral blood vessels in the hand is accompanied by reduced blood flow in the cerebral arteries—a condition necessary to counteract the spasmodic dilation of these blood vessels during a migraine headache. In normal, non-migraine subjects, handwarming by external means produced total vasodilation in both the fingers and the fronterotemporal region of the head measured by pulse volume. When the same subjects were trained to increase their digital pulse volume through feedback, however, the blood vessels in the fingers underwent dilation while those of the temporal and associated regions became constricted. Migraine patients who were successful in reducing the frequency of attacks through feedback and handwarming also showed a similar pattern, but they did not seem to be capable of producing the same degree of vasoconstriction in the cerebral arteries as the normal subjects. Patients who showed no improvement in migraine headaches also showed no vasoconstriction changes in the cerebral arteries even though handwarming increased finger pulse volume.

But contradictory evidence obtained through the use of somewhat more sophisticated devices for measuring blood flow indicates that an alternative hypothesis suggested by Stroebel and Glueck (1976) also merits serious consideration. They proposed that handwarming was effective to the extent that it interrupted the extreme degree of intracerebral vasoconstriction in the first or prodromal phase of the migraine attack and thus prevented extreme vasodilation and the subsequent headache from occurring.

Results obtained by Mathew et al. (1980) appear to support this hypothesis. Thirteen patients suffering from migraine headaches were instructed to either warm or cool their hands and received feedback in the form of a pulsating signal which increased or decreased with changes in finger temperature. At the same time, cerebral blood flow was measured by tracing radioactive xenon gas which the patients had inhaled during baseline and feedback periods. Measurement of the radioisotopes with scintillation counters revealed an increase in cerebral blood flow, and consequently vasodilation, during handwarming.

Although vasodilation during handwarming found by Mathew et al. is inconsistent with the vasoconstriction obtained by Dalessio et al., it is, nevertheless, compatible with the hypothesis advanced by Stroebel and Glueck and suggests that handwarming and subsequent vasodilation "involves the circumventing of the extreme degrees of intracerebral vasoconstriction in the first or pre-headache stage" interrupting the entire headache cycle (1980, p. 26).

Which of these two apparently contradictory hypotheses explains the effectiveness of handwarming in relieving migraine attacks? Although there is no definitive answer to this question at the present time, the following reasons have been proposed to explain why handwarming may act as a prophylactic to prevent headaches from occurring rather than as a palliative to reduce the symptoms after the headache has appeared:

1. Migraine attacks are associated with excessive vasomotor responsiveness and, presumably, increased activity of the sympathetic branch of the autonomic nervous system. The central mechanism which makes it possible to warm the hands volitionally probably also produces a decrease in sympathetic activity preventing vasoconstriction from taking place. There is no reason to assume that this inhibition of sympathetic activity would not generalize and affect the blood vessels in the head as well (Mathew et al., 1980, p. 20).

2. Drugs, which produce constriction of the cephalic blood vessels, bring symptomatic relief only after the headache has occurred; they cannot prevent the headache from occurring (Adams, Feuerstein, and Fowler, 1980, p. 234). On the other hand, handwarming, according to reports by patients, is ineffective once the headache has appeared and only works during the prodromal phase to prevent the headache from occurring. This suggests that handwarming produces vasodilation which acts to prevent vasoconstriction in the initial phase of the attack. As these observations are based on the subjective reports of a few patients, research on the relationship between the effects of handwarming and the phase of the migraine attack in which it is applied seems to be indicated.

The chief difficulty with the Stroebel-Glueck hypothesis is that only 10% of migraineurs have prodromal signs (Adams et al., 1980). If handwarming acts in the vasoconstrictive phase of the attack, as the hypothesis contends, then the prodromal signs would be necessary to inform the patient when handwarming should begin. Yet, individuals who do not exhibit these signs do as well, and in some instances better, in reducing the frequency of migraine attacks through handwarming than those who report prodromal signs (Stout, 1979). Obviously, a great deal more research is needed to resolve these issues.

Primary Raynaud's Disease

Primary Raynaud's Disease (PRD), as we saw in Chapter 4, is a functional disorder of the cardiovascular system consisting of a reduction in blood volume in the hands and feet due to intermittent vasospasms (constrictions of the blood vessels) produced by cold stimulation and/or emotional stress. Although reserpine is frequently prescribed in an attempt to control the disorder, the drug is only moderately effective and often produces distressing side effects in the form of hallucinations or depression.

Chapter 4 also contained an account of a relatively successful attempt to relieve the symptoms of PRD through classical conditioning by pairing exposure to cold (CS) with immersion of the hand in warm water (UCS) to produce vasodilation (CR) when a cold stimulus is encountered (Marshall and Gregory, 1974, Chapter 4, p. 90). Recently, efforts have been made to control PRD by using operant methods and concentrating on reinforced increases in vasodilation alone. In these studies, patients are trained to warm their hands voluntarily and are given feedback (usually in the form of actual temperature readings or tones) when the blood volume in either the hands or feet is increased; successes have been reported in single case studies (Surwit, 1973; Jacobson et al., 1973). Several large-scale studies conducted by Surwit and his associates (Surwit, Pilon and Fenton, 1978; Keefe, Surwit and Pilon, 1980) showed that a combination of relaxation and feedback training is generally effective in reducing the number of vasospastic attacks. The more recent study (1980) compared three treatment procedures (autogenic training, progressive muscle relaxation, and a combination of autogenic training and skin temperature feedback) with a group of twenty-one female patients. The results indicated that all three procedures were equally effective in reducing the number of attacks outside of the laboratory or in the simulated conditions of a laboratory cold room after four weeks of training.

A single case study by Schwartz is particularly instructive because it shows how a patient inadvertently hit on a solution to the problem of transfer of control from the laboratory setting. As part of the treatment for Raynaud's disease the patient was rewarded with an opportunity to see some pleasurable slides each time he successfully increased his blood volume. During one of the sessions a bright, white light flashed on the screen after a projector malfunction. This was immediately associated with sun and warmth, and the patient continued to use these "hot thoughts" as images to successfully control the volume of blood in his feet when they got cold. At the end of 1 year, however, the patient requested further training because he felt he was losing his ability to control the response. The same procedure was unsuccessfully tried with another patient who probably failed to respond because her symptoms were more severe and her motivation for treatment quite low.

BIOFEEDBACK—OTHER POSSIBILITIES

Despite the inconclusive nature of the results with essential hypertension, biofeedback has been useful in the management of such autonomically related disorders as migraine headaches and Raynaud's disease. Investigators are continuing to explore its effectiveness with other disorders, and some recent laboratory studies point to its ultimate utility in the treatment of sexual dysfunction.

Sexual Dysfunction

Although no strategies for the treatment of sexual dysfunction with biofeedback exist at the present time, a recent study by Harris (1978) suggests such a possibility.

Some women are apparently sexually dysfunctional because they are unable to identify the signs of sexual arousal when they occur. While men have little difficulty in labeling their sensations as sexual, women, by contrast, frequently fail to label their sexual feelings accurately because identification is based on interoceptive cues less obvious than an erect penis. Heiman (1975), for example, found that the discrepancy between awareness of sexual arousal and the physiological signs is greater for women who are sexually dysfunctional. This finding was confirmed by Wincze, Hoon, and Hoon (1976) who showed that the vaginal blood-volume measures in a population of women experiencing low sexual arousal was significantly below the same measures in a population of sexually well-adjusted women. Spiess (1977) reports that while most men use the genital response as an index of sexual arousal, women are much less certain about reporting sexual arousal, even when the internal physiological indicators of arousal (increased blood supply in the vaginal walls, lubrication) are all present.

Biofeedback is a method for "putting people in touch with unobservable responses," and it might be possible, therefore, to train women to label their internal sexual signs reliably in order to increase awareness of sexual arousal. The specific purpose of Harris's study, then, was to train women to be aware of sexual arousal earlier in the arousal pattern. Three groups of women subjects were shown erotic films at the same time that a physiological measure of blood volume in the vaginal walls was being recorded by means of an optical plethysmograph (a transducer that measures blood volume by the amount of light reflected from the vaginal walls). These physiological measures as well as self-reports (the subjects pressed a key when they felt they were aroused) were used as indicators of sexual arousal.

After baseline measures to the erotic films were recorded, the subjects were placed in 1 of 3 groups. Those assigned to Group 1 were informed that the sounds heard in their headphones were produced by physiological arousal (contingent feedback). Subjects in the second group were told the same thing, but the sounds they heard were the recorded sounds of Group 1 and not their own (non-contingent feedback). Subjects in Group 3 heard no sounds and were merely told that their arousal was being monitored.

The results of the study indicated that while all of the subjects became sexually aroused merely from watching the film, the level of arousal was higher for those who actually heard the sounds of physiological arousal than for the others. Furthermore, the subjects in Group 1 became aware of sexual arousal at much lower levels of physiological arousal than the subjects in the other two groups. Feedback training for the women in Group 1 resulted in much lower thresholds for sexual arousal (Fig. 11-4). These findings prevailed during the first and second treatment sessions, and even during the experimental session when all the feedback cues were completely eliminated. Women who find it unusually difficult to be sexually aroused, or whose sexual dysfunction appears to be the result of slow levels of arousal, might conceivably benefit from such biofeedback training.

Biofeedback has also been used to correct nearsightedness (myopia) through a combination of feedback and relaxation to the muscles controlling visual acuity, and in some instances 100% acuity changes have been reported (Lanyon and Giddings, 1974). Bruxism (grinding and gnashing of the teeth predominantly at night while asleep) has also been treated with biofeedback and relaxation of the masseter muscles in the jaw (Glaros and Rao, 1977).

BIOFEEDBACK—THE FUTURE

There are many who feel that the behavioral sciences have just barely scratched the surface of biofeedback in its potential usefulness as a research tool and as a clinical method for alleviating a great many of the behavior disorders—especially those associated with autonomic dysfunction.

In some instances, however, it seems almost as though the method is too simplistic given the multitude of factors which can influence behavior. We saw, for example, that secondary gains (social and interpersonal relationships) contribute substantially toward maintaining a disorder once it has been acquired, and it is very difficult to use biofeedback successfully if these rewarding conditions are not also considered. Moreover, a large amount of accumulated evidence indicates that stress does not produce a "characteristic" physiological response in all people. Some, as the Laceys have pointed out (1970), may respond with accelerated heart rate while others may actually display a decreased heart rate to the same threatening stimuli. The picture is even more complicated when we consider the totality of autonomic responding for one individual. Some people over-respond in one

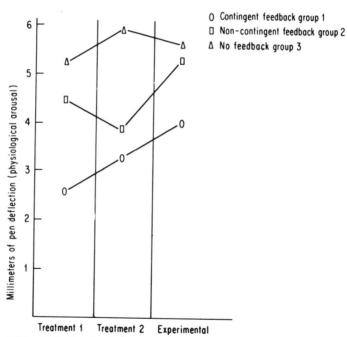

FIG. 11-4 Level of physiological arousal necessary to stimulate awareness of sexual arousal. Note that the physiological level at which sexual arousal is reported by the subject is consistently lower for Group 1 as a result of contingent feedback training. (Source, C. Harris. Unpublished doctoral dissertation, State University of New York at Stony Brook, 1978. Used by permission.)

modality—heart rate or galvanic skin response, let us say—but under-respond in others.

These complicated factors are not likely to make future research in biofeedback any easier. Yet, for those people who cannot take medication because of disastrous side-effects or who have disorders for which no medication exists, biofeedback, even with all its present insufficiencies, appears to be the only alternative. All things considered, however, biofeedback has been remarkably effective in the treatment of certain autonomic disorders such as migraine headaches and Raynaud's disease, and of inestimable value for disorders associated with muscular difficulties.

For the most part, behavioral scientists and practitioners interested in biofeedback have followed Miller's injunction to be bold in what they attempt and cautious in what they claim (Miller, 1973, p. xvii). Often, however, the urgent need for effective treatment methods leads investigators to report results prematurely, creating false expectations, disillusionment, and distrust for those in need of treatment. To avoid the "boom or bust" conditions usually associated with a new type of therapy, and to make certain that the procedures for biofeedback, and indeed for behavior modification in general, have a sound experimental function, Miller (1973) has drawn attention to the following potential problems:

1. Spontaneous changes that lead people to recover only because they are already on the upswing of a cyclical disorder and not because of new procedures used in treatment.

2. Placebo effects in which recovery is due to aroused hope, increased attention, or suggestions made by the investigator. Patients with headaches, for example, frequently respond to attention. As one early physician, Trousseau, advised "treat as many patients as possible with the new drugs while they still have the power to heal" (Shapiro, 1960).

3. Increased enthusiasm on the part of the therapist which often heightens the placebo effect of new therapies. All new techniques should be compared with other therapies.

4. Finally, long-term observations to determine whether the effects of treatment are stable over a substantial period of time.

chapter twelve

Self-Control and Choice Behavior

Choosing a blue suit instead of a brown suit is not generally regarded as an heroic gesture requiring extraordinary resolve and self-control. In fact, the term self-control is never used to describe the behavior involved in selecting clothes, buying automobiles, or in the countless such decisions ordinarily made in the course of a lifetime. The reason for this is rather obvious—both selections are attractive and desirable, and, apart from some conflict, and some small uneasiness about having made the "ideal" choice, choosing one or the other will generally not create feelings of pain or displeasure. In these instances, giving up one goal in favor of another (a blue suit instead of a brown suit) is not usually regarded as an act involving self-control.

The purchase of a blue suit instead of a brown suit is considered a matter of choice. The selection of cottage cheese instead of a chocolate eclair is regarded as self-control. At what point and for what reasons does choice behavior become self-control?

We usually reserve the term *self-control* for those situations in which some form of *self-denial* is involved, where choosing one goal in favor of another is a particularly difficult and distasteful act, and where some delay usually intervenes between the choice and its attainment. A person who goes on a diet, for example, relinquishes the pleasure of eating (certain foods and in large quantities) for the "pain" of abstinence, and the additional pain of waiting a considerable time before some reward in the form of less weight is realized. A student who decides to forgo the pleasure of a movie for the effort involved in studying, or an ascetic who renounces worldly pleasures for a spartan existence and the promise of greater eventual rewards, is said to be exerting a great deal of restraint and self-control. Although all of these situations involve choice behavior, we are strongly inclined to regard them in terms of restraint rather than choice because a more immediate and highly desirable goal is being relinquished and the reasons for the behavior are not readily apparent.

But something else enters along with the use of the term *self-control* which goes beyond the simple notion that pain and displeasure are involved—something which gives the term its surplus meaning. In describing such behavior, we tend to fall back on expressions such as "will-power," "resolve," "ego-strength," or their equivalents, all of which suggest that the choice is governed by forces originating somewhere within the individual and guided by the "inner man" or "executive."

Part of the appeal of explanations containing references to inner forces grows out of the way most people think of motivation in behavior. Motives are generally regarded as the "push from behind" that compels people to act in a specific manner. If certain forces exist that can compel people to do things "against their will," then other forces such as "will-power" or "restraint" are necessary to oppose them. Under the circumstances, the common-sense meaning of self-control— which presumably varies in quantity from person to person—is that of a power which can be mobilized to meet temptation.

SELF-CONTROL: PROBLEMS AND DEFINITIONS

The view of self-control as a restraining force somewhere within the individual is virtually useless for the behavioral sciences because it makes the behavior inaccessible to observation. Several psychologists have even suggested that the term self-control is a fiction because behavior does not take place in a vacuum, and all behavior is ultimately the result of an interaction between the organism and the environment. Bijou (1965) has proposed that that the term *inter-response control* be substituted for self-control on the grounds that the term "self" is almost impossible to define. Inter-response control, on the other hand, refers to the control of one response by another in the same individual—such as removing all distractions to make studying easier or buying certain food when on a diet.

One of the most interesting and fruitful analyses of self-control behavior has recently been conducted by Rachlin (1974) who points out that the need for the concept disappears if the action which we usually call self-control is reduced to choice behavior and analyzed in terms of the variables which influence decision making.

For example, a person who rejects ice cream in favor of cottage cheese (a decision which is almost always interpreted in terms of self-control) is actually making a decision to relinquish a reward *now* (good taste) for a reward *later* (a slim figure). The decision is based on the relative attractiveness of the two goals and the necessity to impose a delay in achieving the more desirable one. To go to a dentist now rather than delay the visit may appear to require enormous amounts of will-power, but in the last analysis, the act really avoids a greater pain later in return for a lesser pain now. Take the temporal issue away (reward or punishment now vs. a greater reward or punishment later) and the issue of self-control disappears along with it (Rachlin, 1974, p. 94). *If the choice were merely between eating ice cream now and losing weight now* (an obviously impossible condition), *delay of gratification would not be involved, and self-control would no longer be an issue.* A person would simply elect to lose the weight (if it could be done immediately) as the more attractive goal.

One of the important advantages of defining self-control in terms of choice behavior and decision making is that the process can be further understood in terms of the factors that appear to influence these behaviors. This, as we see later, is especially significant when it comes to devising methods that enable people to change their own behavior and practice what is usually described as self-control.

Do Animals Show Self-Control?

Until recently, no experimenter would have dared explore the problem of self-control with animals in the laboratory because of its impossibly vague definition. Yet animals do exhibit behavior that can be called self-control, and Rachlin, among others, has shown that such behavior in animals involves choices based upon the attractiveness of the rewards and how long the animal must wait to get them.

One of the ways to study self-control in both animals and humans is through the *delay of reinforcement experiment*. Most self-control behavior, as we have seen, involves a decision to relinquish a small reward for a larger reward later, or to forgo a present reward in order to avoid a future punishment. The inclination to call this behavior self-control in humans and to attribute it to an act of restraint is due to the fact that we rarely think to ask what these individuals might have gained (or lost) if they had not waited. In animal experiments, this tendency to discuss self-control in terms of inhibitory processes is avoided because the delayed rewards or punishments are readily apparent to the experimenter, and it can be demonstrated that animals learn to make choices on the basis of external factors.

Self-Control, Choice Behavior, and the Matching Law

The *matching law* states that the relative rate of responding equals the relative rate of reinforcement.

On the basis of this law, Rachlin and Green (1972) devised an experiment demonstrating that pigeons will select one of two alternative rewards even though the choice required them to wait a longer period of time to get the reward. But this choice, as we shall see, was dictated by the *relative* value of the rewards they received and by the amount of time they had to wait until they got them.

Pigeons were presented with a panel containing two white pecking keys. Pecking at the right white key darkened the pigeon's chamber for a period of 10

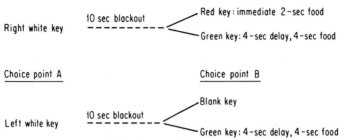

FIG. 12-1 Diagram showing a pigeon's choices in the Rachlin and Green "self-control" study (Source: H. Rachlin and L.S. Green. Commitment, choice and self-control. *Journal of the Experimental Analysis of Behavior,* 1972, *17,* 15–22.)

seconds, after which red and green keys were presented simultaneously. A peck at the red key provided immediate access to 2 seconds of food. A peck at the green key imposed an additional 4-second delay which was then followed by 4-second access to the food.

Pecking at the left white key also darkened the chamber for 10 seconds, but this event was followed by the presentation of the green key only, and a peck at this key produced 4 seconds of delay and then access to food for 4 seconds (Fig. 12-1).

On 65% of the opportunities to select a key, the pigeons chose the white left key which produced a total of 14 seconds' delay for 4 seconds of food rather than on the right key which imposed only a 10-second delay for 2 seconds of food. The pigeons were imposing a control on their own behavior by refraining from pecking the right disk. What was responsible for this self-control? According to Rachlin and Green the contingencies imposed by the matching law and not the pigeon's "willpower." Let us follow their reasoning.

The matching law states that the response choice will be determined by the relative value of the reward. This value can be increased or decreased by a number of factors, one of which is the length of time the pigeon has to wait for the reward. For example, the larger reward is worth almost 1½ times as much as the smaller reward.

$$\frac{\text{Value of larger reward}}{\text{Value of smaller reward}} = \frac{\dfrac{\text{Amount of larger reward}}{\text{Time to larger reward}}}{\dfrac{\text{Amount of smaller reward}}{\text{Time to smaller reward}}}$$

$$\frac{\dfrac{4}{10 + 4}}{\dfrac{2}{10}} = 1.43$$

(SOURCE: Rachlin, 1976, 584–585)

But this was not always the case. On 35% of the occasions when the pigeons chose the right white key and were presented with the red and green keys, they tended to choose the red key which led to an immediate 2 seconds of food rather than the green disk which led to the 4-second delay and then to 4 seconds of food. *Once the pigeon got closer to the goal (choice point B, Fig. 12-1) and had to make a choice at that point, the relative value of the rewards decreased in favor of the smaller reward.* Thus, using the same formula as above it turns out that the smaller reward is "infinitely" more preferable than the larger reward (Rachlin, 1976, pp. 584–585).

$$\frac{\text{Value of the larger reward}}{\text{Value of the smaller reward}} \quad = \quad \frac{\frac{4}{4}}{\frac{2}{0}} = 0$$

(SOURCE: Rachlin, 1976, 584–585)

The Rachlin and Green experiment makes several important points about self-control. It suggests that very often when a concept such as self-control *appears to demand an explanation* in terms of "hidden, controlling factors," the variables influencing the behavior can almost always be found in the external response—that is, in reinforcement contingencies. But, what is perhaps even more significant, the experiment demonstrates that self-control can be interpreted in terms of choice behavior which is further influenced by an interaction between the attractiveness of the rewards and the length of time the organism has to wait to receive them. Apparently, this analysis of self-control in terms of the matching law works equally well for punishment. Deluty (1978) has shown, for example, that rats can be trained to choose a small, immediate punishment in order to avoid a large delayed punishment.

Animals can also learn to delay gratification in the natural setting. A pet raccoon, for example, who was kept chained to a tree learned to ignore the table scraps offered to him in a dish. Instead, the food became a cue for him to climb to the lowest branch, haul the chain up beside him, and patiently await the arrival of the barnyard chickens who were attracted to the food. When the dust had cleared, the raccoon had himself a chicken which he obviously preferred to table scraps.

Self-Control in Humans

Does the reinterpretation of self-control as choice behavior, urged by the Rachlin and Green experiment, define self-control in humans? In most respects it does. Mischel and his colleagues, for example, were able to demonstrate that the reward value of a particular item, as well as the temporal delay in receiving it, were two important factors in determining how well children were able to tolerate delay of gratification (Mischel & Gilligan, 1964; Mischel & Staub, 1965).

But the factors that can influence the making of a choice for humans are considerably more complex than they are for pigeons. Apart from organismic variables—genetic and constitutional differences about which very little is known at present—humans have language and the ability to contemplate future events. Although the general form of the matching law may not change as a function of these characteristics (choices will still be influenced by the relative attractiveness of the goals), predictions about delay of gratification will almost certainly be influenced by them.

For example, the delay of reward values used for pigeons in the Rachlin and Green experiment gave different results when these same values were used in a similar experiment with children. At first, the children behaved just as the pigeons did. At choice point A (Figure 12-1), they invariably selected the longer delay with the greater reward, and at choice point B, the smaller reward with no delay. But their behavior changed as the experiment progressed: they began to select the key associated with the largest reward at either choice point, A or B. Apparently, the pigeons were capable of encompassing events only within a few seconds of the response while the children were able to make choices ranging over longer periods of time (Rachlin, 1976, p. 587).

In another experiment, female college students also behaved like the pigeons. Given a choice between turning an annoying noise off immediately for 90 seconds or waiting an additional 60 seconds and turning it off for 120 seconds, the women showed impulsive behavior by choosing the immediate, smaller reward (90 seconds) rather than the delayed, larger reward (120 seconds). This choice is consistent with predictions from the Rachlin-Green equations. But as soon as a delay was added to both alternatives, the smaller as well as the larger reward, the preferences were reversed, and the choice was predominantly the larger goal. Again, the results equated with the pigeons' choices when delays were imposed on both alternatives (Solnick et al., 1979).

The development of self-control in humans probably begins in infancy when children learn to delay gratification by responding to people and objects that have been associated with attention to their comforts (feeding and toileting, for example). The hungry, crying infant will stop crying as soon as mother appears, but it will probably begin crying again if she is not quick with the bottle. Mother becomes a secondary reinforcer by virtue of her association with food, comfort, and well-being in general.

As the child grows older, language begins to serve as a secondary reinforcing agent. It permits the human to bridge the gap between a present decision and a distant goal. Humans can use language as an interim reinforcer by telling themselves that the goals are imminent. The development of language in humans is probably the most significant element in the development of self-control, largely because it makes self-instruction and self-direction possible, and increases the ability to tolerate long delays of gratification.

Much of the early childhood training in self-regulation is intentionally directed towards increasing tolerance for delays in gratification. Toilet training, for example, is designed to discourage impulsive behavior and to encourage waiting for the appropriate time and place. Toys and other rewards are promised in the future for good behavior now, and some children are even taught to save money for some distant event.

But most of the early lessons in self-control are, of necessity, urgent ones that call for immediate restraint and inhibition. "Don't touch that or you'll burn yourself!" "Don't hit your sister!" The imperative tone of these statements indicates that the behavior must be *stopped, checked,* or *curbed* immediately because the alternatives are obvious and unpalatable. While the element of choice is still present in these situations, the decisions are pretty much preordained.

In any event, these early lessons in restraint serve as the basis for later avoidance behavior mediated by threats of punishment, discomfort, or uneasiness—usually referred to as "conscience." In one sense, the mechanism of conscience and avoidance, which is learned through the early lessons in restraint, is an advantage in the economy of behavior. For most situations, the human organism does not have to stop and decide about the correct or desirable course of action. In another sense, however, these early lessons are a disadvantage because they lead the adult to believe that most of the behavior problems requiring self-control must be dealt with in terms of restraint.

But restraint, as a method of self-control, only seems to work well when the threat of punishment (displeasure or disapproval) is present and imminent. People who decide to go on a diet, for example, are constantly confronted with this dilemma. The reward for eating a chocolate eclair now is considerably greater than the punishment involved in not being able to zip up a dress, or tighten a belt at some future date. Simply "stopping" eating (or smoking, or drinking, or any one of a number of undesirable habits) becomes an increasingly difficult method for controlling behavior as the "props" that support restraint, such as imminent punishment, become more distant and lose their effectiveness. People who initiated their own attempts to stop smoking, for example, were much more successful using such strategies as self-monitoring, self-evaluation, and self-managed rewards to assist them than those who attempted to stop "cold-turkey" (Perri et al., 1977).

Self-Control and Other-Control. We have just concluded that self-control involves choice behavior and that it can be explained on the basis of the variables that affect such behavior. Under the circumstance, it might seem desirable to eliminate the term altogether on the grounds that it is superfluous and carries too much surplus meaning. But in one sense the meaning of the term self-control is unambiguous. When people take steps to control their own affairs, they often arrange to monitor their behavior, to evaluate the effect of the controls they are using, and even to decide under what conditions they are to be rewarded (self-managed or delegated reinforcement). Now this situation is *operationally distinct* from one in which all of these functions are devised and controlled by others, and it provides us with the basis for using the term self-control to distinguish it from control by others. (Whether people are actually managing their own affairs, or whether the very decision to do this is still determined by external factors, is an interesting, but virtually unresolvable question verging on the free will vs. determinism issue.)

Self-control, then, can mean self-directed, self-monitored, and self-evaluated behavior in which the most important problem is delay of gratification. But does this mean that the principles people use to manage their own behavior differ from those that individuals use to manage the behavior of others? According to Skinner, it does not, because

when a man controls himself, chooses a course of action, thinks out a solution to a problem, or strives to increase self-knowledge, he is behaving. He controls himself precisely as he would the behavior of anyone else . . . (Skinner, 1953, p. 228),

and, apparently, with the same mechanisms that are used to control the behavior of others. One uses reinforcement, punishment, and stimulus control to change one's own behavior, and the behavior may include private, unobservable events, such as thinking, as well as public, observable events. Regardless of what type of behavior is involved, however, the process of behavioral control, whether it is self-control or other-control, can only be evaluated in terms of its effect on the environment.

Self-directed behavior, like any other behavior, can be shaped by contingent reinforcement in small, successive steps, and people can be taught to solve their own problems by assessing the alternatives and pursuing a specific course of action.

THE ELEMENTS OF SELF-CONTROL IN BEHAVIOR MODIFICATION

The terms "lack of restraint," "poor self-control," and "low will-power" are often used as though they denoted inherited or constitutional deficiencies in the ability to make decisions and carry them through to completion. The difficulty with these terms is that they are semantic "dead-ends." They bury the reasons for behavior deep in the organism, give very little insight into how these deficiences might be strengthened, and encourage an attitude of resignation. In fact, most people tend to use the term "low will-power" to rationalize failures in self-control.

This attitude toward self-control is probably the result of the many failures typically experienced when attempts are made to solve problems requiring self-control by inhibitory methods that demand that behavior be stopped immediately, checked, or held in restraint without any supports from the environment. What most people do not understand is that failure is most likely if provisions are not made to sustain behavior during the long delays of gratification which are often necessary in most behavior-change situations, and that constant failure reinforces an attitude of defeat, resignation, and withdrawal.

The procedures outlined below have been abstracted from studies and discussions of self-control from a behavioral point of view (Goldiamond, 1965; D'Zurilla & Goldfried, 1971; Thoresen & Mahoney, 1974; Stuart, 1972). They are essentially an expansion of the general principles for changing behavior discussed in Chapter 6). The procedure is first presented in summary form followed by illustrations.

1. Identification of options and selection of goals.

2. Organization and change of environmental conditions to support behavior leading toward the goal and to deal with the factors which may obstruct progress by means of one or all of the following methods:

    a.   Commitments and contracts.

    b.   Systematic changes in the stimulus conditions controlling behavior.

    c.   Establishment of intermediate goals, reinforcers, and punishers. Provisions for self-monitoring.

    d.   Practicing alternative behaviors when necessary through behavior rehearsal.

Identification of Options and Selection of Goals

It should already be fairly obvious by now that self-control is not one behavior but a matrix of behaviors which begins with the decision to pursue a specific goal after weighing all of the alternatives. But while most people know what aspects of their behavior they want to change or what goal they want to achieve and make their decisions on the basis of the relative attractiveness of the goals, some are even incapable of identifying their options or making a selection once the options have been identified. The bewilderment and confusion often observed in these instances can almost always be traced to one of several emotional difficulties—fears associated with being independent, fear of failure, or, even, fear of success.

Ann Landers, whose column contains a representative cross-section of the problems which are often brought to the attention of the helping professions, provides an interesting account of a woman who was incapable of making the most trivial decision—whether to buy a blue dress or a green one, whether to serve shrimp salad or chicken salad to the bridge club—because her mother had never allowed her to make a decision. "It seemed," she reported to Ann Landers, "whenever I attempted to do something on my own (in the past) it turned out badly." Her mother would then invariably say, "See—next time ask *me!*" (Landers, 1978). (This case is an effective reply to those who feel that knowledge of the origin of a response is sufficient to bring about a change in behavior.)

Very often the goal itself is invested with attractive and unattractive aspects that are designed to produce approach-avoidance conflicts. The woman cited above, for example, wanted desperately to achieve a sense of independence, to be able to make decisions without self-doubts, but the fear of failure and disapproval prevented her from making even the first successful attempt. Frequently these conflicts can be resolved by encouragement, assistance in behavior rehearsal, and role-playing, making certain that reinforcements for success are available. In some cases, however, the fears are so overwhelming that some form of therapy, such as desensitization or implosion, is necessary before decision making can begin.

When these difficulties have been resolved and the goals have been selected, measures can be taken to evaluate the factors likely to interfere with progress. This is an exceedingly important step in the procedures for learning self-control because it provides an overview of the conditions that may create difficulties in carrying out the decisions. The methods listed in the next section under Organization and Change of Environmental Conditions are typically used to help minimize the number of distractions and deviations that are likely to interfere with control, but they can also be used as a guide to help identify the potential sources of difficulties in achieving the objectives.

Organization and Change of Environmental Conditions

For many behavioral scientists, the essence of self-control is situational control. It consists, very largely, in manipulating the characteristics of the environment to help support the goal-directed behavior and to prevent exposure to situations which might present problems in "temptation." The following methods and devices have been commonly employed in such instances.

Commitments and Contracts. Human negotiations have taught us that one of the best ways to guarantee performance is by means of a contract spelling out the rights and obligations of both parties entering into the agreement. Contracts are generally successful as guarantors because they have certain behavioral consequences. Pledges that are kept, result in certain rewards; those that are not, entail certain punishments. Contracts are often used in therapy between the client and the therapist. They spell out the forfeits the client must make (usually in the form of money which has been deposited with the psychological center) for not living up to certain conditions agreed on in therapy. Some form of contract has also been used in family therapy to help clarify the relationship between parents and children where confusion exists about their respective roles, and between client and therapist, and husband and wife in marital counseling, and in the treatment of alcoholism and obesity.

People also make contracts or "bargains" with themselves, and, apparently, this has been a very successful device for maintaining self-control, judging from some of the anecdotal accounts which have appeared in the literature from time to time. The well-known American novelist, Irving Wallace, for example, treated novel writing as a form of fixed-ratio behavior by assigning himself a certain number of pages to write each day and by keeping a strict accounting of the number of pages completed in a daily ledger. He also points out that this strategy is not an uncommon one among many authors and quotes from several novelists to support his argument (Box 12-1) (Wallace and Pear, 1977).

BOX 12-1
Trollope on a Fixed-Ratio Schedule

Anthony Trollope, the renowned nineteenth-century British author, was an extremely methodical person and so skilled in writing that he rarely had to wait for the muse to inspire him. He set work goals for himself and wrote when and where he could, even on the London train traveling back and forth to his job as a postal inspector. He describes the details of his work plan in his autobiography (Trollope, 1946).

When I have commenced a new book, I have always prepared a diary, divided into weeks, and carried on for the period which I have allowed myself for the completion of the work. In this I have entered, day by day, the number of pages I have written, so that if at any time I have slipped into idleness for a day or two, the record of that idleness has been there, staring me in the face, and demanding of me increased labour, so that the deficiency might be supplied. According to the circumstances of the time—whether the book I was writing was or was not wanted with speed—I have allotted myself so many pages a week. The average number has been about 40. It has been placed as low as 20, and has risen to 112. And as a page is an ambiguous term, my page has been made to contain 250 words; and as words, if not watched, will have a tendency to straggle, I have had every word counted as I went. . . . There has ever been the record before me, and a week passed with an insufficient number of pages has been a blister to my eye and a month so disgraced would have been a sorrow to my heart.

I have been told that such appliances are beneath the notice of a man of genius. I have never fancied myself to be a man of genius, but had I been so I think I might well have subjected myself to these trammels. Nothing surely is so potent as a law that may not be disobeyed. It has the force of the water drop that hollows the stone. A small daily task, if it be daily, will beat the labours of a spasmodic Hercules. (Trollope, 1946, p. 116–117; quoted by Wallace, 1971.)

Wallace goes on to quote several other authors, including Hemingway, Balzac, Flaubert, Conrad, Huxley, and Maugham who set writing goals for themselves. The most eccentric of all was Victor Hugo who confined himself to his study and had his valet remove every stitch of his clothing on order not to return them until a certain hour when he expected to complete a day's writing (Wallace, 1971).

Systematic Changes in the Stimulus Conditions Controlling Behavior. Some of the greatest obstacles to the implementation of self-control procedures are the actual environmental conditions in which undesirable behavior occurs. Because the behavior is frequently performed in the presence of certain cues, the cues themselves act as conditioned or discriminative stimuli and either elicit the behavior or increase the likelihood that it will take place. Routinely eating in front of a turned-on television set almost guarantees that eating will begin when the set is turned on.

To break up this association and to counteract the influence of such stimulus conditions, behavior therapists typically recommend that clients become aware of the existence of routines in behavior and take steps to interrupt them when they occur (Box 12-2).

BOX 12-2
A Bed Is Not for Worrying!

A client suffering from insomnia regularly went to bed about midnight, but was unable to fall asleep until 3 or 4 A.M. He routinely spent the intervening hours ruminating about the day's events and worrying about relatively trivial problems until, out of exasperation, he turned on the television set and fell asleep while the set was still on. Apparently, the bed and the associated setting (darkness, the particular time of night) all became cues for worrying instead of falling asleep. To correct this, the client was advised to retire at the usual time and attempt to fall asleep. If he was unable to sleep, he was to get up and go to another room until he felt sleepy again. During the first few days following these instructions, the client rose several times during the night, but at the end of 2 weeks he was able to fall asleep without getting up once. Two months after treatment, he reported getting out of bed less than once a week. In this particular case, the client never even saw the therapist. All of the instructions were conveyed to him through the wife, who reported the results to the therapist (Bootzin, 1972).

The stimulus-control hypothesis for the treatment of insomnia has recently been tested in a more rigorous fashion by Zwart and Lisman (1979) who discovered that *both* a contingent condition (get up when unable to fall asleep and return to bed only when sleepy) and a non-contingent condition (subject had to rise a fixed number of times within 20 minutes of retiring whether sleepy or not) were equally effective in reducing insomnia. The authors attempt to resolve this dilemma by suggesting three possible explanations why both conditions should work: (1) both conditions involve contingent disruption of bed and bedtime cues for worrying and tossing and turning in bed because both of these behaviors are likely to occur early in the subject's attempts to fall asleep; (2) both conditions produce contingent punishment—getting out of bed and sitting up can be regarded as aversive; and (3) insomniacs tend to overestimate the time it takes to fall asleep, often considered part of the disturbance. The report of improvement may actually simply reflect a change in the subjects' estimation of the time it takes them to fall asleep.

Students with poor study habits are often advised to create a study area free from the usual stimuli—stereo, food, radio, for instance—thereby controlling behavior incompatible with studying. What is equally important, however, is that they are also instructed to leave the study area if the urge arises to engage in any behavior but studying. Goldiamond (1965) advised a client of his, for example, to leave the desk when she wished to write a letter, read a comic book, or daydream. Although she was only able to spend a total of 10 minutes at the desk during her initial attempts in the first week, her time increased to 3 hours by the end of the semester, something she had been unable to do previously.

The effects of changing the stimulus controlling the behavior is also illustrated in several cases dealing with marital problems reported by Goldiamond (1965). In one instance, the husband could not refrain from screaming at his wife whenever he saw her because of an infidelity she had committed with his best friend 2 years earlier. The remainder of the time he spent sulking and brooding over his abusive behavior. Both the husband and wife wished to preserve the marriage, and Goldiamond used the following strategies to reduce the bickering and screaming. He first suggested that they rearrange the furniture in the house and the use of the rooms. Next, because much of the fighting took place in the bedroom, he suggested that a yellow light be installed which was to be turned on when both felt amorous but was to be kept off otherwise. When the screaming and yelling eventually subsided, the husband increased his sulking behavior. He was then advised to sit on a "sulking stool" in the garage whenever he felt the need to sulk. A record he kept of this behavior showed that sulking decreased from 1.5 hours per day to zero within a period of 3 weeks.

Intermediate Goals, Interim Reinforcers, Self-monitoring, and Self-evaluation. We have already indicated that changing behavior, whether through self-control or through control by others, requires a systematic application of the basic principles of learning. This claim is nowhere more evident than in the necessity for establishing intermediate goals and interim reinforcers in self-regulated behavior, just as small units of behavior are shaped through successive reinforcements in the animal laboratory, and it is especially true when delay of gratification is necessary over a long period of time or when the behavior is excessively resistant to change.

These observations have been confirmed in studies using both animal and human subjects (Mischel & Baker, 1975; Perkins, 1947) and most recently in an experiment dealing with the determinants of self-control in the pigeon (Logue & Mazur, 1979). Using an experimental procedure similar to that of Rachlin & Green (1972), Logue and Mazur showed that the pigeons' choice of a larger, but longer delayed reward as opposed to a smaller, but more immediate reward was, in large measure, influenced by a colored light which was turned on between the time the animal made a choice at point A (Fig. 12-1) and the time the reinforcer was delivered. According to the authors, the colored light, having been paired with food, took on the status of a conditioned or secondary reinforcer which helped to sustain the wait for food. This was later confirmed when removal of the colored light disrupted the birds' self-control behavior.

In many respects, the very crux of self-regulation of behavior consists in the ability to reduce the goal (or the ultimate behavior) itself into its various component parts and constitute each of these as subgoals. Reinforcers can then be established for attaining the intermediate goals, although more frequently success in reaching the goal provides all the necessary interim rewards. The work charts kept by Irving Wallace and Anthony Trollope were, in effect, subgoals defined in terms of the number of pages written, and, although both of these authors emphasized the punitive functions the charts served when the work goals were not met (discomfort, disgrace, and so on) it is easy to imagine the elation each probably felt at reaching or exceeding the projected number of pages.

An attempt to demonstrate the effectivess of subgoals and self-monitoring behavior systematically was made in a study by Rehm and Marston (1968) with male college students who had deficiencies in social skills and were unable to relate adequately to women. These deficiencies were conceived in terms of social anxiety, and each of the study volunteers was required to construct a desensitization-type hierarchy listing the problem behaviors. The ultimate objective, to have the students date girls successfully, was approached systematically by having each student perform the behavior at each level of the hierarchy, evaluate the performance, and reward himself with self-approval for each success.

In order to establish subgoals, each of the subjects was asked to designate a situation on the hierarchy which he would ordinarily avoid because of the discomfort it created. Four such levels were created by designating two points above and two points below the original choice, and each of these levels was used as a goal. One student, for example, designated "taking a seat next to a girl in class" as a first-level item, "Being introduced to a girl while with a group of friends," as a second-level item, "Calling a girl to ask her for a date," as a third-level item, and "Dancing with a girl on a date," as a fourth-level item.

The students reinforced themselves by awarding points for each of the behaviors successfully performed, and they also kept records of their performance which they discussed with the therapist once a week. By following these strategies, the subjects in the self-regulated group made greater changes in their social skills and in their ability to meet women than did a comparable group of students who were given non-directive therapy consisting of reflection and clarification of feelings and low-level interpretations of behavior.

Inefficient and impulsive spending is another of the behaviors (along with overeating and smoking) in which the rewards are immediate and salient and the punishments are delayed. By training students in self-control methods, however, psychologists were able to reduce by more than half the amount of money a group of students were inclined to spend on impulse.

The procedures used to accomplish this consisted in identifying self-defeating habits (excessive use of credit cards, borrowing money from friends, going downtown without a definite purpose), possible alternative responses (watching television, destroying credit cards, not carrying a checkbook), sources of reinforcement (soft drinks, pleasant thoughts or phrases about themselves), and by making long-range goals, such as opening a bank account. Stimulus-control methods were also employed when the subjects refrained from carrying large amounts of money, made shopping lists, and kept cash at home in labeled envelopes for designated purposes.

Twelve weeks after the completion of the study, the self-control subjects who responded to the follow-up questionnaire (50%) were spending considerably less than they had at the beginning of the experiment. The subjects in the placebo condition, on the other hand, who spent time with the therapists discussing the reasons for impulsive spending, tended to show a slight increase in spending. According to the authors, self-monitoring of behavior alone could not have been responsible for the differences between the two groups because both groups recorded the amounts they spent (Paulsen et al., 1977).

The question of self-reinforcement. Several studies in self-control, including the one just cited (Paulsen et al.), maintain that self-monitoring alone, without self-evaluation of progress and self-reinforcement, is not sufficient to produce behavior change (Kanfer & Phillips, 1970; Spates & Kanfer, 1977). But, while intermediate reinforcements appear to be necessary to sustain behavior toward long-term goals, the exact nature and function of these reinforcements is still somewhat ambiguous.

Some psychologists have argued that the term self-reinforcement is a misnomer because all rewards are externally administered and it is impossible for people to reward or punish themselves (Rachlin, 1974; Goldiamond, 1976). Others have asserted that reinforcement is the same in its effects whether self-administered or externally administered, and they have devised studies to show that humans can reward themselves with tangible reinforcers when specific criteria for performance have been met.

Mahoney (1974), for example, demonstrated that overweight people in a weight-control program who were able to reward themselves for losing weight by voluntarily taking envelopes of money provided for the purpose, lost more weight than any of the other groups in the study. Castro and Rachlin (1978), on the other hand, were not entirely convinced that the self-rewards in Mahoney's experiment were equivalent to externally administered rewards, and they devised an experiment that showed that people will still lose weight when they *punish themselves* by paying for each pound lost, or indeed, *even when the amount the subject paid was entirely unrelated to whether they lost or gained weight.* Since all three conditions—reward, punishment, and non-contingent cost—had the same effect on behavior, the money, according to the authors, probably served as a cue to enhance self-awareness and self-monitoring.

It is also conceivable that the loss of weight in itself acts as a source of information about progress, creating pleasure and satisfaction which serve as rewards to sustain the dieting behavior. It could certainly be argued in support of this notion that if people were given a diet which produced a *gain* in weight instead of a loss, they would soon abandon the diet, indicating that the gain in weight acted as a *punisher* to suppress the behavior (dieting) which produced the increase.

Practicing alternative behaviors through behavior rehearsal. Behavior rehearsal, as we saw in Chapter 4, is essentially a counterconditioning process because it requires that new behavior be associated with cues which call out old responses (S1-R1 to S1-R2). Since the self-control process often requires the substitution of one behavior for another, one way to acquire the new behavior and ensure that the old response will not occur is through behavior rehearsal.

The use of behavior rehearsal as a method for modifying behavior was prompted by the observation that often, after therapy, changes in attitude take place without any accompanying changes in overt behavior. Unless people actively participate in the process of changing their own behavior by routinely performing the difficult acts, only minimal verbal and attitudinal changes are likely to occur.

Behavior rehearsal and assertiveness training.   The inability to exercise one's rights—lack of assertiveness—is more often the focus of behavior rehearsal methods than any of the other behavior disorders. Often lack of assertiveness masquerades as depression, homosexuality, obsessive attention to work, or any other behavior designed to cover the behavioral deficits. The method for dealing with unassertive behavior usually involves modeling (Chapter 15) on the part of the therapist in order to demonstrate the client's behavioral deficiencies and rehearsal of the modeled behavior by the client.

The use of these techniques is illustrated in the following case of a 38-year-old engineer who felt depressed, frustrated, and demoralized because he held only junior positions in his work although he had better qualifications. Wolpe and Lazarus (1966) determined that the client's problem was a gross deficiency in assertive behavior and used modeling and behavior rehearsal to train him in the proper attitudes at the office. During one of the sessions, the patient was told to pretend that he was applying for a position and was presenting himself for an interview with a prominent business executive.

At the therapist's deliberately resonant "come in," Mr. P. R. opened the door of the consulting room and hesitantly approached the desk. The therapist interrupted the role-playing procedure to mirror the patient's timid gesture, shuffling gait, downcast eyes, and overall tension. Mr. P. R. was then required to sit at the desk to play the role of the prominent business executive while the therapist reenacted Mr. P. R.'s entry into the room. The patient was asked to criticize the therapist's performance. The therapist then modeled the entry of an assertive individual, asking the patient to note the impact of variations in posture and gait and the all-important absence or presence of eye contact (1966, p. 48).

The correct entrance was repeated several times, and the content of the interview was analyzed, including the patient's speech patterns, hesitant gait, and posture. After each repetition, the therapist modeled the correct behavior, which the patient was required to imitate. After approximately 5 therapy sessions and several months following termination of therapy, the patient reported his promotion to a job more suitable to his ability.

The effectiveness of behavior rehearsal as a method for modifying behavior and as a procedure in teaching self-control has been demonstrated under controlled laboratory conditions (McFall & Marston, 1970) using essentially the same clinical procedures emphasized by Wolpe and Lazarus. Most of the recent research efforts, however, are concerned with the relative contributions that modeling, coaching, and behavior feedback (videotapes and tape recordings) make to the use of behavior rehearsal in assertiveness training. The only clear finding which emerges from these studies is that all three seem to be necessary, depending upon the severity of the behavior. Where the unassertive behavior is less severe (as in the college student population generally used as subjects for these studies), the use of a great deal of modeling and extensive behavior feedback seems to add very little to the effectiveness of behavioral practice (McFall & Twentymen, 1973; Melnick & Stocker, 1977; Turner & Adams, 1977). In actual clinical studies, on the other hand, where unassertiveness verges on withdrawal and depression, extensive modeling, coaching, and feedback appear to be necessary (Marlatt, 1971; Eisler et al., 1973).

Behavior rehearsal is a relatively successful method for obtaining behavior changes very largely because, as Peterson has observed, "more people . . . behave themselves into new ways of thinking than think themselves into new ways of behaving" (1968, p. 41).

OVEREATING, OBESITY, AND SELF-CONTROL

Obesity is one of several problem areas in which self-control methods have been systematically applied with some moderate, but certainly not overwhelming success. Most weight-control programs, including those marketed commercially, such as Weight Watchers Inc., include some variation of the methods that emerged from the early behavioral studies in the control of overeating (Stunkard, 1959; Stuart, 1967).

Although stress and anxiety may play a pronounced role in some instances of obesity ("binge" eating, for example, may be one of the signs) and must be treated with desensitization, most overeating, according to the learning view enunciated by behavioral weight-control programs, is a habit initiated by environmental cues which act as discriminative stimuli and maintained by the eating responses themselves and by the reinforcement involved in the pleasures of eating and the good taste of food. As a result, behavioral treatment of obesity has centered around the following procedures, most of which require self-control in the form of self-monitoring: (1) rearrangement of eating habits by providing reinforcement for other, more appropriate, behavior; (2) decreasing the intrinsic pleasure of food by associating it with noxious consequences; (3) stressing the long-term, negative consequences of overeating (being fat, ill-fitting clothes); (4) eliminating or changing the environmental cues which tempt eating; and (5) restricting the time and place of eating (Wooley et al., 1979, p. 4).

All weight-reduction programs using behavioral methods begin with a stated goal, such as the loss of a specific amount of weight over a given period of time depending upon the physical characteristics of the individual. *Commitments* are then made in the form of *contingency contracts* which usually involve a deposit of money at the beginning of the program and a refund if the provisions of the contract are fulfilled. The contract requires attendance at the treatment sessions and establishes interim goals, such as an intake of no more than 1,000–1,200 calories per day and the loss of 1–2 pounds per week. Money is sometimes provided as an interim reinforcer for weekly losses in weight, but as we have already seen, the money itself probably acts as a source of information or benchmark rather than as a reward unless the amounts are unusually high. In some programs, such as the one devised by Stuart (1967), people are asked to list pleasurable behaviors which can be substituted for those which seem to induce eating. These are used later as problem areas begin to be identified.

Extensive *self-monitoring* in the form of records is also employed. Clients are required to record the amount of food they eat, the way it is prepared, and the circumstances under which it is eaten in order to interrupt the chain of habitual eating and identify some of the situations which act as controlling stimuli to elicit eating (e.g., watching television or reading). Weights are also recorded at specified times during the day.

Time during the treatment sessions is usually spent identifying and discussing the *controlling stimulus conditions* that seem to create temptations to eat. Very often these are group discussions which give the members an opportunity to listen to each other's problems and make suggestions. Stuart, for example, organizes a weight-reduction program around curriculum steps, clearly emphasizing the importance of controlling stimuli. Clients are instructed to remove all food from rooms other than the kitchen on the grounds that much compulsive eating is automatic and people may not be aware that they are eating. They are further instructed to make eating a pure experience and not associate it with any other activity, such as reading, or watching television, to prevent these activities from becoming a conditioned or discriminative stimuli for eating. Finally, they are urged to engage in other activities when the desire to eat arises between meals.

Does it work? Eight of the 10 clients who completed Stuart's program showed a median weight loss of 35 pounds in the subsequent 9-, 32-, and 52-week follow-up periods after treatment. But, according to reviews of behavioral weight-loss programs (Hall and Hall, 1974), this appears to be the exception rather than the rule. Most programs produce dramatic short-term results, but a larger number also show a great deal of backsliding some time after the programs are discontinued.

Kingsley and Wilson (1977) suggested that the variable results usually found in weight-control studies is due to the lack of continued support after the program ends. The experiment they designed to test this possibility showed that, although a group of overweight female subjects given additional "booster" sessions 3, 6, 9, and 12 months after the end of the 8-week program showed greater weight loss than a comparable "social pressure" group who were simply told that weight loss is a matter of proper motivation, backsliding began to take place following the 5-month follow-up period for both groups.

In their extensive review of the theoretical, practical, and social issues in behavior treatments of obesity, Wooley et al. (1979) point out that overweight is a particularly stubborn and refractory behavior disorder and, although learning methods in general have been as good or better than most treatment procedures —especially in the maintenance of weight loss—sustained and permanent weight reduction still remains a difficult and intractable problem for a variety of reasons involving eating and metabolism which are not well understood. These relationships between eating and energy expenditure have undoubtedly acted to thwart most treatment plans and will continue to create serious problems for weight-reduction programs.

For example, Wooley et al. report that

1. Differences in the style of eating between fat and lean people (slow vs. fast, for instance) have probably been exaggerated and are not as important in obesity as once thought.

2. There seems to be little evidence to support the assertion that fat people are less active than lean people. The variability in activity among subjects of normal weight is as great as 400 to 500 calories in resting metabolism, suggesting that activity alone is not a good index in understanding weight gain or loss.

3. Obese patients with the lowest metabolism rate before dieting had the largest drop in metabolic rate during food restriction (i.e., their metabolism slowed down) which may help to explain why weight loss is often very slow to begin with for these people and why they lose very little in overall weight.

4. Adaptive changes in energy expenditure are also very important in studies of obesity. Generally, when food intake is restricted, the body engages in "defensive conservatory responses," such as a decrease in salivation and reduced energy expenditure, to compensate for the loss of food. As a result, the rate of weight loss decreases as food restriction continues. In one study, the amount of weight lost on a fixed diet in successive 4-week intervals was 6.3 pounds, 3.6 pounds, 2.1 pounds, and 1.7 pounds.

In addition, two things happen as the person continues to go on and off diets, First, the metabolic rate falls more rapidly with each successive diet (food is burned less rapidly, leaving more fat), and second, the return to pre-diet metabolism rates takes much longer. In effect, weight is lost more slowly with each diet and regained more rapidly after the diet. Experiments with animals have shown that restriction of food not only predisposes the animal to rapid weight gain after the diet is over, but, what is perhaps even more devastating, the system becomes biased toward excessive storage of fat.

5. There appear to be widespread differences in the utilization of food between fat and lean people. Obese subjects, for example, showed a considerably smaller increase in metabolic rate after ingesting 800 calories of protein (9% after 2 hours) compared to lean subjects (25% after 2 hours). Not only do fat people tend to gain more weight as a result of overfeeding, but they also have a lesser ability to dispose of the excess calories.

These findings, according to Wooley et al., indicate that certain people may become overweight even though they do not eat more than their lean peers, and that specific weight-reduction programs taking individual needs into consideration would tend to offset the depressing effects of treatment failure. Even so, they further maintain, it may be virtually impossible for some people to lose weight and maintain the weight loss (1979, p. 12).

chapter thirteen

Mediated Learning

In discussing the principles of learning and their relationship to the practice of behavior modification in the previous chapters, we concentrated on contributions from classical and operant conditioning, using a relatively simple stimulus-response or response-consequence scheme to describe how organisms behave and how behavior changes occur. We described learning as the result of an automatic conditioning or associative process, and we acted as though nothing much of any consequence in describing behavior goes on within the organism. We kept the explanations accounting for learning purposefully simple in order to reduce the number of assumptions about internal events that are not directly accessible to observation. We made one concession, however, when "fear" was introduced as a construct in two-factor theory in order to help in understanding behavioral events that did not seem to be explainable by reference to external events alone (Chapter 2).

But is this exceedingly sparing view of learning necessarily the best and most viable one for understanding behavior? After all, events do occur between the stimulus and the response or between the response and its consequences. People think, feel, have memories, and respond to mental images, and behavior is, for both animals and humans, a complex, fluid, continuous process instead of the series of discrete and disconnected behavior sequences that the stimulus-response conditioning explanation seems to imply. Many psychologists who regard themselves as associationists disagree with this latter argument. Just because behavior is "represented" in terms of S-R associations does not mean that complex behavior actually consists of such connections. Breaking behavior down into elementary S-R units may misrepresent the way it is actually seen—as a smooth, active, flowing process—just as the solidness of physical matter, as it appears to the senses, is misrepresented by the atomic model. But the final test of either the S-R or atomic model is its ability to represent the facts (Kendler & Kendler, 1962).

What happens between the stimulus and the response? Are there behavioral situations which cannot adequately be described by a simple S-R or response-consequence scheme without using these internal events? Do inferences about intervening events improve the understanding, predictability, and control of behavior? The answers to these questions formed the substance of the debate between the early "behaviorists," who maintained a strict empirical attitude in their study of behavior, and the "cognitivists" who opposed them by introducing such internal events as "thought" and "perception" into the learning process. It was this debate that helped to shape present attitudes toward mediated learning as an additional way of describing the changes that take place in behavior. The term *mediated learning* is the compromise that emerged from this debate. It is a broad term, intended to acknowledge the necessity for making inferences about unobserved events between the stimulus and the response without necessarily specifying the characteristics of these events.

HOW THE ARGUMENT DEVELOPED

The urge to simplify explanations about behavior is in the best, time-honored tradition of psychological theorizing, and most of the pioneers in the behavioral sciences followed the advice of Lloyd Morgan (1894) to avoid explanations of animal behavior in terms of higher mental processes (mentalisms) and to accept the simpler of two alternative explanations for any given phenomenon. So they applied Morgan's rule and refrained from the use of such terms as "thought" and "perception" to explain animal behavior. But somewhere along the way, they also managed to get rid of these higher mental processes as an explanation for human behavior.

Pavlov, Thorndike, and Watson rejected the subjective approach to the study of behavior and resolved to explain all behavior either in terms of conditioning or trial-and-error learning. Watson memorialized this resolution in his famous paper, Psychology as the Behaviorist Views It, which was published in 1913 and is often regarded as the manifesto of the behavioral revolution.

Psychology, Watson announced, was not the study of the mind. It was the study of behavior—overt behavior to be more precise! It involved agreement by observation and experimentation, not by introspection, and its goals were the laws of behavior, not an analysis of the "nature of mind" and the "contents of consciousness." Mind, consciousness, and introspection were expunged from the psychological language! In his zeal to clean house of anything remotely resembling subjectivity, Watson even rejected Thorndike's trial-and-error learning on the grounds that a subjective judgment was involved in determining whether a specific stimulus was a "satisfier" (reward) or an "annoyer" (punishment) to the animal. Pavolvian conditioning, on the other hand, appealed much more to him because he felt it grew out of the more objective tradition in Russian physiology. Watson's position was so persuasive that he set the tone for psychology for many years to come. Psychologists were loath to discuss behavior in any but the most objective terms, and without reference to unobservable, internal processes.

But there were those who did not join the revolution—who did not view learning as a simple matter of stimulus-response or trial and error. The gestaltists, as they were known, disagreed with the early behaviorists that learning was an automatic process involving the gradual strengthening of connections between a stimulus and a response (classical conditioning) or between a response and its consequences (operant conditioning). Their experiments in perception convinced them that learning occurred suddenly, as an insight phenomenon, after the organism had an opportunity to see the problem as a whole and work out the relationships among the elements. This, they said, happened internally, or cognitively (using thought processes), and entirely independent of overt trial-and-error movements.

Animals, they argued, are thoughtful creatures and would not behave as randomly or stupidly as they did in Thorndike's puzzle-box experiments (Chapter 6) if the situation had not been structured to produce stupid and random behavior. The only reason these cats engaged in trial-and-error behavior was that they could not easily see the relationship between the string and the latch that permitted them to escape from the box. This forced the cats to engage in initial random behavior until they accidentally tripped the latch that led to escape and food (Hillix, 1977). What the gestaltists neglected to mention, of course, was that even after the initial success there was no sudden learning—the "aha," or insight experience—and the correct responses continued to build up gradually as the animal proceeded to pull the string faster on each succeeding trial.

But some studies with animals did seem to operate according to the principles proposed by the gestaltists. In some famous experiments conducted by Wolfgang Köhler and described in his book *The Mentality of Apes* (1917, 1925), he uncovered behavior which led him to believe that the animals were capable of insight and intent similar to that found in humans. Köhler's studies required chimpanzees to retrieve bananas placed outside of the cage just beyond their reach or suspended from the ceiling. In most cases, the animals were able to solve the problems by using the materials provided them. They either used a stick, joined two sticks together when a single stick was not long enough, or stacked boxes to reach the otherwise inaccessible bananas.

According to Köhler, the situation provided the animal with an overview of the problem—the stick or box, the banana, the cage—and all the interrelationships of the problem were evident, enabling the animal to "restructure his perceptual field," see the nature of the problem, and behave appropriately without the necessity for random trial-and-error performance. Of course, it was not entirely a matter of the animal sitting and pondering the problem before making the first successful response. On several occasions, some of the chimpanzees threw the stick at the banana or fitted the sticks together purely by accident, but generally the animals appeared to behave as though they viewed the problem as a whole and responded on the basis of a "thought out" solution.

The ability to infer the nature of a problem and recognize its potential solution that Köhler thought the chimpanzee possessed was recently explored further in a study by Premack and Woodruff (1978) with a 14-year-old chimpanzee named Sarah who had been a subject in simplified language experiments from the time she was 1 year old. But instead of having her actually manipulate sticks or rearrange boxes to obtain food as Köhler did with his chimpanzees, Sarah observed videotaped scenes of a human *unsuccessfully attempting* to solve problems in situations similar to those confronting Köhler's chimpanzees.

After observing each of these scenes, Sarah was shown two photographs, one of which depicted the correct method for solving the particular problem. On problems 1, 2, and 3 in the first test, Sarah chose the correct solution right from the onset of testing. In a second test with more complex problems, such as opening a locked door, lighting a gas furnace, attaching a hose to a faucet, or inserting a plug into an electrical socket, Sarah invariably selected the right object for the problem, e.g., a key, a paper torch, a faucet, or an electrical socket.

According to the authors, such problem-solving ability on a representational level (photographs instead of actual performance) lends a great deal of credence to Köhler's supposition that some sort of mediated process is necessary to understand and predict the behavior of these complex animals. Shortly after this experiment was conducted, Woodruff, Premack, and Kennel (1978) showed that Sarah could also solve problems requiring some knowledge of the conservation principle. These problems, which had been devised by Piaget (1976) to demonstrate developmental changes in human cognition, require a child to determine whether two differently shaped containers are filled with identical amounts of liquid—an ability that emerges with increasing chronological age. Sarah not only solved problems requiring the use of conservation as a principle, but, according to the authors, accomplished this on the basis of inferential reasoning.

The work of the gestaltists came as a relief to some psychologists who had challenged the "hard-boiled" view of Watsonian behaviorism. According to Hilgard and Bower, the new behavioral process called "insight learning" heralded a return to a more balanced view of learning—to a consideration of thinking and understanding as an important part of the study of behavior and away from an uncompromising behaviorism in which the organism is "played upon by the pushes and pulls of the environment" (1966, p. 231).

E. C. Tolman, the psychologist who carried the gestalt-cognitive banner into the behaviorist camp, admitted that he sometimes put himself in the place of the rat in order to get ideas for experimentation and to "understand" how the rat went about solving a particular problem. Like many of the other behaviorists, Tolman was an S-R theorist (more precisely, an SR-S theorist as we shall shortly see), but unlike the others he insisted on inserting all sorts of unobservables between the S and the R. He did not do this capriciously, however. Rather, he believed that psychologists were, in fact, talking about unobservables without actually being aware of it.

Take the word "learning" for instance. A rat learns to thread its way through a maze to get food. How do we know that the rat has learned? Why, by its behavior, or, more strictly speaking, by its performance, of course! But, as Tolman pointed out, the rat's performance is a complex affair compounded out of a relatively large number of unidentified and unobserved influences—its physical condition on that particular day, its state of hunger or fear, its previous experience with the maze, and so on. So, although learning does take place, what and how much was learned can only be *inferred* from performance and only accurately measured after the contributions of the other factors have been systematically isolated and identified.

If this can be done with the concept of learning, Tolman argued, there is no reason why other unobservables cannot be inferred from behavior that might help to improve understanding and prediction—providing they conform to certain rules of logic governing the use of such inferences. And this is what Tolman proceeded to do. Humans and animals, he reasoned, learn that making a response in one situation (S1-R1) leads to another situation (S2). (This is the SR-S scheme mentioned above.) A rat traversing a maze and finding food at the other end *learns to expect* food when in the maze again. A person inserting a coin in a vending machine expects that a candy bar or a pack of cigarettes will be delivered. So, what rats and humans actually learn are "expectancies," "means-end-readinesses," or "cognitive maps," which tell them what leads to what. Choices are made on the basis of these expectations, but the expectancies themselves are states of the organism that are not activated until the appropriate motivating conditions prevail. According to Tolman, a rat or a human may "learn" something by merely observing, but this learning may not make its appearance in performance until it is required. Tolman's now classic experiment demonstrated that such latent learning is a distinct possibility (Box 13-1).

BOX 13-1
Learning the Lay of the Land

According to Tolman and Honzik (1930), you really do not have to feed a rat to get him to learn how to run through a maze. Rats will form "cognitive maps" and acquire information about the various parts of the maze simply by exploring the maze without receiving food. To test this assumption, they ran 3 groups of rats in a maze for 10 days. One group found food at the end of the maze every time it completed a run. A second group explored the maze and never received any food. A third also explored the maze for 10 days but only began to receive food in the goal box after the eleventh day. Figure 13-1 shows the results of this experiment. The animals rewarded on every trial demonstrated a considerable reduction in errors for the entire 17 days of the experiment, compared to those who did not receive any reward. But even the unrewarded animals learned something because they also improved slightly. However, the rats who began receiving food on the eleventh day showed a remarkable reduction in the number of errors in just 1 day, equalling the performance of those animals who had been rewarded on every trial for the previous 10 days. Apparently, the rats exploring the maze without food learned many things about the situation that showed up when they were made hungry and rewarded for their performance.

Restle has pointed out that such learning ability is important to animals in the wild state. "The animals need to know the lay of the land in order to locate, trap, and capture their prey," and their ability to learn about the environment cannot simply be related to finding food. They must also be able to gain information and store it without any immediate reinforcement (1975, p. 31).

Enter the Intervening Variable

When Tolman inserted an event (expectancy, cognitive map) between the stimulus and the response, he introduced the intervening variable into the behavioral sciences. Now, basically, an intervening variable is nothing more than a guess as

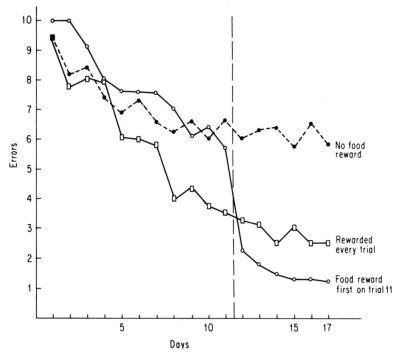

FIG. 13-1 The results of Tolman and Honzik's study. The immediate improvement in performance for the group first rewarded on trial 11 is regarded as evidence for latent learning. (Source: E.C. Tolman and C.H. Honzik. "Insight" in rats. *University of California Publications in Psychology,* 1930, *4,* 215–232. Copyright *University of California Publications in Psychology,* 1930, and used by permission.)

to what factors, other than those under the experimenter's control, are determining the behavior (Spence, 1944). When the guess relates to an actual physiological event, such as the way in which sensory impressions are encoded into nerve impulses and carried to the brain, it is traditionally called a *hypothetical construct.* But when the guess is a convenient fiction, such as a habit, expectancy, or cognitive map, with no immediate counterpart in the physiology of the organism, it is called an *intervening variable* (MacCorquodale & Meehl, 1948). The advantages of such guesses, if they are fruitful, *is that they tend to explain behavior in a way that would otherwise be impossible.*

When behavioral scientists talk about mediating processes in terms of hypothetical constructs, they really ultimately expect to find a corresponding physiological mechanism operating somewhere within the nervous system. For example, some psychologists who study memory feel that the storage of information in the brain occurs as an electrical or electrophysiological phenomenon. Recent evidence suggests that something like this may actually be taking place. When subjects in a short-term memory study were given the task of comparing two numbers flashed in a random order along with two letters, only the first number of the pair to be compared evoked a relatively strong electroencephalogram (EEG) response recorded through electrodes attached to the scalp. The letters, which were considered irrelevant to the task, evoked a considerably lesser response. *But more important, the subjects' accuracy in recalling the number was predictable from the magnitude or strength of the electrical storage component recorded during memorization* (Chapman et al., 1978).

Although many situations in the study of behavior seem to demand the use of some intermediate event to explain a response, most of these are like the terms habit, or expectancy, elements of the particular models used to explain behavior but without any proposed neurophysiological equivalents.

Brown (1961) has identified several instances that are conducive to the use of intervening variables. One of these, for example, is the situation in which a weak stimulus—the creaking of a shutter at night, or the nighttime restlessness of a sick child—evokes an unusually vigorous response. To account for the extremely disproportionate reaction to these stimuli, one would have to assume some readiness or preparedness on the part of the person to respond. This readiness has been variously described as fear, set, or expectancy, all of which suggests that the behavior is being influenced by factors other than those under immediate observation (Brown, 1961, pp. 29–34).

The Search for the Unknown Factors. Intervening variables are neither true nor false. They are either useful or useless, and their utility depends upon: (1) *how well they are defined in terms of experimental procedures; (2) how well they help to organize the existing facts and provide meaningful and unique explanations of the behavior that would otherwise not be possible; and (3) how helpful they are in generating new experiments and new principles in the models of behavior where they are used.* These are stringent criteria, but they are necessary to prevent some serious conceptual errors.

One of the well-known models of personality in which conceptual errors seem to abound is psychoanalytic theory, which employs such intervening variables as ego, id, superego, and libido to describe how behavior originates and how it is influenced by the unobserved interaction of these forces. Like many mediating variables, these terms are convenient fictions invented by Freud to help him organize his observations and speculate about the unobserved conditions which may influence behavior.

While the struggle among these forces proposed by Freud makes a compelling and dramatic description of the way in which behavior may be determined, the terms themselves are really only metaphors which, unfortunately, have been given actual existence (reified). One particularly lurid account of psychosis, for example, has the ego—that part of the personality directly in touch with reality—standing by helplessly as the id—the animal force—shreds the superego—the moral force.

Instead of being given independent meaning, terms such as ego and id are invariably defined in terms of the behavior that they are supposed to have influenced—an operation which leads directly to circular reasoning. For example, two individuals are observed to differ in their responses to continued stress. One functions adequately, the other becomes disorganized and ultimately suffers a breakdown. If, as is often the case, these differences in response to stress are attributed to differences in ego strength, it sounds as though an important statement is being made about influences on behavior that goes beyond what is being observed. Actually, however, the only contribution that the term "ego strength" makes in this instance is to provide a short-hand expression for the actions being observed, and it only repeats in a circular fashion what is already known. "Why did these two individuals respond differently to stress?" "Because of their differences in ego strength!" "What indicates their differences in ego strength?" "Why, their different responses to stress, of course!"

The way out of the tautological trap. One way to avoid circular reasoning in the search for unknown and unobserved factors *is to define them independently of the behavior they are supposed to have influenced.* In one sense, psychoanalytic theory attempts to do this by relating ego strength to the relative contribution that the id, ego, and superego make to behavior, and ultimately, to the way in which these forces developed out of assumed childhood events such as the oral, anal, and oedipal experiences. But because these events are themselves vague and difficult to study systematically, the term "ego strength" depends almost completely on observed differences in reaction to stress for its definition.

Actually, it is fruitless to attempt to define intervening variables in terms of events in the organism's past that are essentially impossible to observe or reproduce. The primary value of an intervening variable is that it demonstrates how behavior is determined by events, other than those currently influencing the behavior, which "set" or "prepare" the organism to respond in a specific manner. This means that we must be able to vary these events in some systematic way to observe their effects on behavior.

One of the ways in which this has been done in the study of motivation, for example, is to assume that drive, or motivation, has an effect upon per-

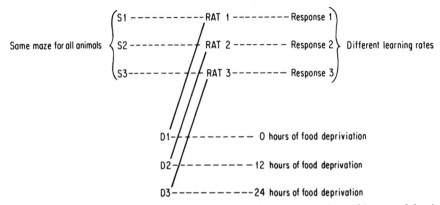

FIG. 13-2 Diagram indicating the relationship between number of hours of food deprivation as antecedent events and maze performance. Food deprivation *prepares* the animal to respond in a specific manner by affecting some mediational process. (Source: J. S. Brown. *The motivation of behavior.* New York: McGraw-Hill, 1961.)

formance and then to study the effects of drive by varying the conditions that produce it. For example, if drive is assumed to be related to the number of hours of food deprivation, this assumption can be tested by observing the behavior of a number of animals in a maze under several deprivation conditions. Under these circumstances, drive, defined in terms of the deprivation histories of the animals, is correlated with the speed of learning in the maze, but it is measured independently of maze learning (Brown, 1961, p. 36). Figure 13-2 illustrates the operations involved in defining drive as an intervening variable. In each case, something done to the animal prepared it to respond in a specific way in the maze-learning situation.

The study by Solomon and Turner (1962) described in Chapter 2 and illustrated in Figure 2-3 shows how fear acts as a mediating variable to relate two separate events the animal has experienced. Dogs who learned to escape shock by pressing a panel were then immobilized by tubercurarine and given several shock trials in the presence of a tone. When they were free to respond again, the tone, which had not elicited a response previously, now evoked panel pressing presumably because it first elicited fear which was common to both the tone and panel pressing and acted as a mediator. In a subsequent study, Black, Carlson, and Solomon (1962) demonstrated that the mediating state could be influenced just as food deprivation influences the hunger drive. Administering more shocks in the presence of the tone while the dog was immobilized *increased* avoidance behavior when the drug wore off. Presentation of the tone without shock during paralysis reduced the fear—presumably through extinction—and *eliminated* the avoidance response.

Wagner and Rescorla (1968) also used memory as an intervening variable to explain classical conditioning and proposed a model which assumes that both the CS and UCS are represented as intervening processes in memory. In studies conducted by Rescorla (1974) the strength of the CR was increased without any additional increases in the number of CS-UCS pairings by simply presenting the UCS alone and increasing its intensity. The results of the experiment were predicted from the model on the grounds that increasing the intensity of the UCS was sufficient to "expand" or "inflate" its representation in memory. Because the CS and CR are both mediated by the memory of the unconditioned stimulus, any increase in the "value" of this memory would also increase the strength of conditioning.

Mediating Events: How to Describe Them

At the beginning of this chapter, we posed a question about the necessity to consider unobserved processes in order to describe and understand behavior. That question is no longer foremost in the minds of many psychologists. The valiant efforts of Tolman and the gestalt psychologists to produce a formalized system of "cognitive learning" did not succeed, true. But the experiments they performed and their attempts to deal with complex behavior were, nevertheless, compelling enough to generate a need for unobserved processes to explain behavior.

Although many psychologists responded to this need, some still stoutly maintain that a description of the environmental events alone is sufficient to explain the occurrence and maintenance of behavior. Operant conditioning, as we saw in Chapter 5, for example, makes no reference to mediating events, and Skinner maintained that even complex behavior could be analyzed in terms of long chains containing elementary conditioning principles and not in terms of "neural, mental, or conceptual events" (1950, p. 194).

Those psychologists who used mediating events to describe behavior, however, were not always in agreement about the form they should take. Hull, for example, avoided the language of mental events and used terms such as drive, habit, excitatory potential, behavioral oscillation, incentive motivation, and so on, combining them in a series of mathematical relationships in order to account for the observed behavior.

Other psychologists, and Tolman in particular, felt that the behavior of animals in a complex learning situation, as well as the "emergent" quality of human thought and language, required different concepts, and, as we have seen, he used terms such as cognitive maps, expectancies, memory, and attention to describe the intervening processes. The difficulty with Tolman's system, as Guthrie once observed, is that instead of predicting behavior it leaves the rat buried in thought!

So, while the argument between the cognitivists and the associationists (Skinner being a notable exception) is no longer about the necessity for mediating events, it still centers around the language to be used to describe them. Quite often, however, either set of intervening variables can explain behavior satisfactorily. The experiments on discrimination-learning in animals and humans by H. H. and T. H. Kendler and L. S. and T. J. Tighe provide an excellent illustration of this point (Box 13-2).

BOX 13-2
The Difference between Rats and College
Students

One of the most ambitious attempts to deal with complex behavior in relatively simple S-R terms is contained in the elegant analysis of discrimination learning conducted by H. H. and T. S. Kendler (1962). Their experiments dealt with the ability of humans and animals to learn to shift from one concept to another. According to the Kendlers, rats and young children do it one way, while older children and adults do it another.

After learning one or another of two concepts (size or color, whichever the experimenter had selected as correct) one of two concept shifts might then be imposed. In the *reversal shift,* the subject, after having been rewarded for responding to the large box, is now rewarded for responding to the small box. Reversal shifts, then, are shifts *within the same dimension*—in this instance a shift from small size to large size. In the *non-reversal* shift, on the other hand, the subject must learn to ignore the size of the box and shift to the color. Non-reversal shifts are shifts *between dimensions*—in this case, from size to color.

Much to the surprise of the experimenters working on this type of discrimination learning, *rats learn non-reversal shifts (from one dimension to another) much faster than they do reversal shifts (from small to large). The opposite is true of college students. They find it much easier to shift from large to small than from size to color.*

The Kendlers analyzed these responses in terms of S-R connections and suggested that the difference between the species was the result of a mediational process in humans (language) that the rats did not have. Animals, they reasoned, respond directly to the stimulus itself (a large box) rather than to the concept of size. If a substantial amount of responding is built up to the large box by continually reinforcing it as the correct choice, this tendency to respond to the large box would first have to be decreased through non-reinforcement before the response could be shifted to small box. But since color (either black or white) has accompanied the correct choice at least 50% of the time (the large and small boxes are both black and white), color, as a dimension, has also accrued a moderate amount of response strength. Under the circumstances, it would be easier for the rats to continue the already moderate tendency to respond to color in the non-reversal shift condition than it would be to change the response to the small box in the complete reversal condition.

Human subjects, on the other hand, especially those with adequate language development, respond on the basis of concepts such as size or color, and discrimination learning builds up mediational responses to these concepts (the concepts themselves are interpreted in terms of internal S-R responses). When a reversal shift from one size to another is required, the mediational response to size already exists, and all the human subject is required to do is to change the overt response from a large object to a small object without the necessity for changing or eliminating the central mediational response to size. But in non-reversal training, both a new mediational response to color and a new overt response to white or black must be acquired. So, the overt and the mediational responses to size first must be decreased before a new response to color can be learned. Under these circumstances, non-reversal training should be more difficult for humans (Kendler & Kendler, 1962).

So far the model accounts for the observed differences between rats and college students, but does it provide any new testable hypotheses? If language development is the crucial factor which distinguishes the behavior of some animals from humans in discrimination learning, the Kendlers reasoned, then there should be a point somewhere between the rat and the adult human where the transfer is made from straightforward stimulus control of behavior to mediational control. They suggested that an obvious place to locate this point would be in the behavior of young children.

The first tests conducted with kindergarten children indicated that they responded *equally well to both reversal and non-reversal shifts as a group.* It appeared as though the children operated in a compromise fashion, with both stimulus and mediational control. But when the fast learners of the discrimination problem were separated from the slow learners, the reason for these findings became apparent. Slow learners behaved like the rats, finding reversal shifts (one size to another) easier. The fast learners performed on the basis of mediational learning, finding non-reversal shifts (size to color) less difficult.

The results of this experiment strongly suggested that language development is a crucial factor in mediating concept shifts. And indeed it was! The percentage of reversal shifts was actually shown to increase with chronological age in a group of children ranging from 10–13 years. Moreover, when children in another experiment were required to verbalize aloud the stimuli to which they were responding, they had less difficulty in executing the reversal shifts from large size to small size.

But is this the end of the story? Can we now assume that shifts in discrimination learning are as the Kendlers have described them? Not as long as there are other psychologists around! L. S. and T. S. Tighe, for example, maintained that the results obtained by the Kendlers could be explained in terms of a "differentiation theory" that used the ideas of perceptual learning, and the Tighes proceeded to demonstrate that the subject's attention to relevant and irrelevant dimensions and the ability to differentiate between them is the important factor in reversal and non-reversal shifts (Tighe & Tighe, 1966).

According to this reasoning, the difficulty of non-reversal shifts in humans could be decreased by making certain that differentiation takes place, and this could be further accomplished by pre-training the subjects in the dimensions to be used during the experimental sessions. Pre-training sessions did not involve choices and rewards. The subjects (children between 67 and 84 months of age) simply made judgments as to whether the pairs of stimuli to be used in the later discrimination experiment were similar or different. The results the Tighes obtained indicated that *reversal-shift* learning during the actual discrimination training was markedly facilitated because of the pre-training trials.

It has been suggested that pre-training was sufficient to develop the sort of mediating process that the Kendlers use in their analysis and that the two "theories" are really not that different from each other. On the other hand, a similar pre-training experience with animals might make it possible to distinguish between the two explanations (D'Amato, 1970, p. 491).

It really doesn't matter that the Kendlers' analysis was the first successful account of the reversal–non-reversal phenomenon in discrimination learning or that their explanation generated new experiments, as long as someone else can explain the results equally well in other terms.

What is the "best" language to describe mediational processes? Unfortunately, there is no easy answer to this question. The Kendlers' description does appear to have a slight edge over the one provided by the Tighes because it accounts for the *difference between animals and humans* in this type of discrimination learning. But it may be that there really is no "best" language and that the S-R description may simply be a more detailed (molecular) way of describing (molar) processes such as thought, perception, memory, or expectancy. In any event, the trend toward using mediating events, and cognitive models in particular, to explain learning is growing.

The Cognitive Model

A cognitive interpretation of behavior is essentially a way of describing how one type of unobserved but inferred behavior—thinking, remembering, feeling—influences or determines another type of observed behavior—overt responding. Figure 13-3 illustrates this concept. A stimulus (S) impinges on an organism and eventually elicits an overt response (B2). The form this response takes, however, is determined (1) by B1—how the individual perceives or interprets (thoughts, feelings, attitudes) the stimulus; (2) by the factors (concurrent and past events) which influence B1 and are retained in memory; and (3) by the feedback from the response consequences.

In some "attributional" studies, for example, the subjects' ability to approach a snake, which they feared, was determined, in part, by their initial memories, perceptions (including attitudes and expectations), and emotions associated with

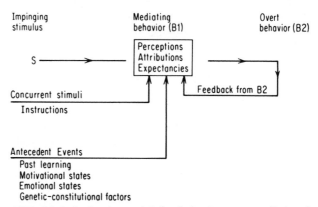

FIG. 13-3 A simple model for behavior as a mediational process.

the snake (S). These mediating events were presumably changed when the subjects listened to *contrived* recordings of their heartbeats (B2) which were slowed down. This apparently led them to believe that they were not as afraid of the snake as they had expected (Valins & Ray, 1967; Carver & Blaney, 1977). Other experiments have also shown that instructions can so alter a subject's response to a specific schedule of reinforcement that the behavior is more consistent with the instructions than it is with the actual schedule (Baron et al., 1969).

Several basic questions emerge from such a mediational model: (1) What is the process that best describes the mediating behavior (B1)? (2) What are the conditions that affect B1? And (3) what is the relationship between B1 and B2—the overt behavior?

Behavior scientists who study cognitive processes attempt to answer these questions through experiments that deal largely with the way information is acquired, stored and retreived. Many have used computer and information-processing models to explain the operation of memory in learning. While much has been discovered about the role of perceiving and remembering in learning (especially as it relates to the process of memorization), no consistent scheme, such as that of classical or operant conditioning with a set of clearly enunciated, easily applied principles, has yet emerged. Consequently, except for Bandura's efforts in observational learning and "self-efficacy" theory, as we shall see, the cognitive method in behavior modification has had to confine itself mainly to the structure rather than the substance of cognitive models.

MEDIATED LEARNING AND BEHAVIOR MODIFICATION

The trend toward using mediated events—cognitive learning in particular—has begun to make itself felt in the area of behavior modification. Those who espouse a "cognitive-learning perspective" are not convinced that classical conditioning and operant learning are sufficient explanations for what goes on when behavior changes. They feel that most behavior modification procedures—especially those used with adult humans—involve changes in thought patterns that are extremely important in affecting overt behavior itself. Influence these thought patterns and you influence the overt behavior. Mahoney (1977), for example, sums up this point of view in four "general assertions" about behavior which, he feels, characterize the "cognitive-learning perspective."

1. Humans respond primarily to their thoughts about the environment rather than to the environment itself. This suggests that virtually all responses are mediated through thought and that such things as *beliefs* and *expectancies* should help to predict behavior better than environmental events alone.

2. Thoughts, like any other response, can be influenced by learning processes such as conditioning.

3. Most human learning is mediated by thought.

4. Thoughts, feelings, and behavior are causally interactive. This means that thoughts and feelings can influence the environment through behavior, and, in turn, be influenced by the environment.

It is clearly apparent, however, that Mahoney's assertions about the importance of cognitive events in behavior modification are little more than articles of faith at the present time.

PROSPECTIVE MEDIATIONAL MODELS FOR BEHAVIOR MODIFICATION

At the present time, two models have influenced the use of mediating variables in behavior modification. The first, *observational learning,* is essentially a reinterpretation of learning through modeling and imitation. The second, *attribution theory,* has had an indirect influence on the development of "cognitive behavior-modification" procedures and has recently been proposed as an explanation for depression and as a source for treatment procedures.

Observational Learning: Learning by Watching

Animals can learn by imitating each other, and humans are capable of learning the most complex behavior by watching other humans perform. One cat sees another pressing a lever to obtain succulent bits of liver. Although the sophisticated cat pressing the lever may have been meticulously trained by the method of successive approximations, which involved rewarding small segments of behavior leading to lever-pressing, the second cat performs the response "full-blown" after merely watching the first.

What an economical way to learn! The animal simply makes the association that lever-pressing leads to food without the painstaking repetitions required in trial-and-error learning. Obviously, learning by observation has important survival and evolutionary value because it enables mature organisms to transmit socially important behavior to the young. Imagine if each new litter of young, naive animals had to acquire adaptive behavior through the energy-consuming and error-filled process of trial-and-error learning. Most populations would not be able to cope with environmental challenges that require rapid changes in behavior for survival. Once the mother ceases to care for the young animal, it must have learned the behavior that will enable it to avoid potential predators, locate food, and find areas for reproductive activities. Obviously, it would be more advantageous to the young if this exceedingly important behavior could be transmitted through a process less cumbersome than de novo trial-and-error learning (Galef, 1975, p. 159).

Children also learn to imitate other children and especially adults who serve as models for most of the behavior learned during the socialization process (this topic is discussed in detail in Chapter 14). We have already seen how Mary Cover Jones—a student of Watson's—made use of observational learning to eliminate a child's fear of dogs (Chapter 4). In this procedure, which she called "the method of social imitation," two children played with a dog while a third child, who was afraid of dogs, watched. Ultimately, the third child was invited to participate. This method helped to rid the child of his fears, but it was not until many years later that Bandura and his colleagues studied observational learning systematically and used the results to formulate treatment methods in behavior modification.

Observational Learning: Experiments and Explanations.   Most attempts to explain imitation in terms of learning have relied very heavily on the immediate or close reinforcement of a copied response in order to explain how the behavior is learned. In their "matched-dependent" model of imitation learning, for example, Miller and Dollard (1941) suggested that this type of learning occurs when a leader indicates the behavior to be followed in order for reinforcement to be obtained.

The operant approach to observational learning proposes a similar Sd-R-Sr+ scheme. One organism watches another respond. The response of the model is the cue (Sd) which the observing organism matches (R) to receive reinforcement (Sr +). Using this scheme, Baer, Peterson, and Sherman (1967) demonstrated that children can be taught a generalized imitation response by first having the model tap on a table, then taking the child's hand and tapping it on the table, and following this sequence by food and praise. Thereafter, the children also learned to imitate other responses which were randomly interspersed among the tapping responses. This experiment suggested that the act of imitating is itself a learned response that can be acquired and generalized on the basis of reinforcement principles alone, without the necessity for invoking mediating variables to explain the behavior.

But the early experiments conducted by Bandura and his associates demonstrated that imitation learning can also occur under those conditions where the modeled response *is not immediately imitated by the observer and where any reinforcement to the observer is delayed.* In several such demonstrations (Bandura et al. 1961, 1963a, 1963b), groups of children viewed aggressive models beat up a stuffed "Bobo" clown, either in real life or on film. When these children were tested some time later under conditions conducive to the expression of aggression, those who watched the aggressive models showed significantly more aggression than those who had watched the subdued, nonaggressive models. When the conditions of observational learning are such that both the response and the reinforcement are delayed, some unobservable process appears to be necessary to explain how the behavior is learned without being performed immediately, how it is retained, and finally, the circumstances under which it is reproduced on a later occasion.

To appreciate this fully, we need only remind ourselves of the distinction Tolman made between *learning* and *performance,* and recall the behavior of the rats in Tolman and Honzik's "latent-learning" experiment (Box 13-1). The animals who ran through the maze when they were not hungry and did not receive any food reward must have learned something during their explorations because, when they were finally given food for their performance, they immediately ran the maze as well as the animals who had learned all along under conditions of hunger and reward. These "latent-learning" animals had learned something about the maze, retained it, and showed an immediate and extraordinary drop in errors when the conditions (hunger) required it. The children in Bandura's experiment showed much the same kind of behaviors (Box 13-3).

BOX 13-3
Learning by Observing

Children, like Tolman's rats, can learn a great deal by simply observing, and what they have learned, or the extent to which they have learned it, may not be apparent until the right conditions occur.

Several groups of nursery children watched a filmed model beat up an adult-sized plastic Bobo doll under one of three conditions. For one group of children, the aggressor was rewarded with a supply of candy, soft drinks, and praise for his hostile behavior. For the second group, the aggressor was berated and spanked (simulated) for his behavior. The third group of children simply viewed the film in which the model received no consequences for his behavior.

In order to measure the spontaneous performance of children in the three groups, each child was left alone in a room filled with toys, including the hapless Bobo doll, and observed behind a one-way screen. Under these conditions, the children who had watched the model being rewarded or receiving no consequences imitated the aggressive behavior of the model to a much greater extent than those who had observed the model being punished. And the boys invariably showed more aggression than the girls (Fig. 13-4).

But the number of imitative responses in Fig. 13-4 tells a different story when the children were offered incentives in the form of decals and fruit juice for imitating the aggressive model in order to test the amount they had learned. Under these conditions, the differences in imitative aggressive behavior which the various groups of children displayed under the no-incentive conditions disappeared completely, indicating that the children had all learned to be "equally" aggressive from observing the model. In fact, the difference in aggressive behavior between boys and girls, which is related to sex-role typing ("girls must not be aggressive"), also disappeared when the girls were offered incentives (Bandura, 1965)!

From this and other experiments, Bandura concluded that:

When a person observes a model's behavior but otherwise performs no overt response, he can acquire the modeled responses while they are occurring only in cognitive, representational forms. Any learning under these conditions occurs purely on the observational, or covert, basis. This mode of acquisition

has accordingly been designated as "no-trial" learning because the observer
does not engage in overt responding trials. . . . According to the author's
formulation, observational learning involves two representational systems—an
imaginal one and a verbal one. After modeling stimuli have been coded into
images or words for memory representation, they function as mediators for
subsequent retrieval and reproduction (1969, p. 133). Astute readers will not
fail to see a resurrection of the gestaltist position in this quotation (see p. 309,
this chapter).

The Elements of Observational Learning.   Now that observational learning—
learning by observing without overt trial-and-error performance—appears to be a
distinct possibility, how does this type of learning differ from what has already been
described in classical and operant conditioning? Actually, the basic requirements
for all three types of learning are the same. In the first place, a stimulus or stimulus

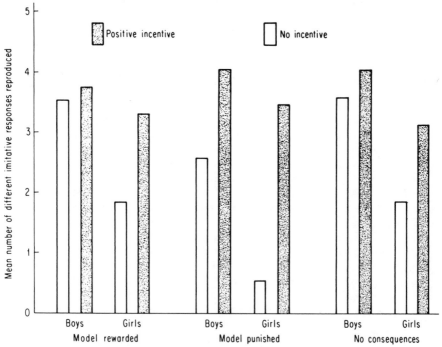

FIG. 13-4 The effect of administering reward, punishment, or neither to the model or
the number of imitative responses produced by observing children. (Source: A. Bandura.
Influence of a model's reinforcement contingencies on the acquisition of imitative responses. *Journal of Personality and Social Psychology,* 1965, *1,* 589–595. Copyright 1965
American Psychological Association and used by permission.)

situation must attract the attention of the organism. Second, the stimulus situation must become part of an associative process because it is important to the organism. And finally, the stimulus situation must be stored in memory for retrieval at some later appropriate time. The essential difference between observational learning and either classical or operant conditioning is that the sequence just described takes place as a series of mediating events because neither the response nor the reinforcement itself is directly observable.

The scheme presented in Fig. 13-5 is really an expanded version of the mediational model described in Fig. 13-3 (p. 319). The difference between the two diagrams is that some of the mediating processes labeled B1 in Fig. 13-3 are further reduced to processes such as attention, retention, and retrieval. In addition, Fig. 13-5 contains a more detailed description of the variables assumed to affect these processes.

The diagram described in Fig. 13-5 is commonly used to characterize the complex mediating processes which are assumed to occur in all learning and in observational learning in particular.

The path labeled A in the diagram indicates the effect a stimulus is presumed to have on the organism if it is merely noticed, but not utilized in behavior. Here the stimulus commands attention by being set apart from other stimuli. Such a stimulus may be retained, and, if retained, can ultimately be recalled on request —"Did you see that lovely dress in the store window as we passed by?"

In order for the stimulus to be utilized in behavior, however, it must follow the course suggested by path B. In this case, an additional attentional process

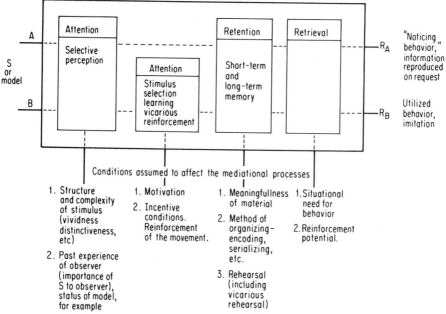

FIG. 13-5 Observational learning as a mediational process.

occurs (stimulus selection), and learning takes place either because the observation itself is reinforced or punished (seeing the model rewarded or punished) or because the actual behavior is reinforced. In observational learning, the behavior is delayed until it is eventually reproduced as imitation.

Certain conditions are assumed to affect learning through these mediating processes, just as increasing the intensity of the unconditioned stimulus was assumed to increase the number of conditioned responses in the Wagner-Rescorla model. These conditions are listed below each of the mediating variables in Figure 13-5.

Although a great deal of research has been conducted in the area of attention, retention, and retrieval, we confine ourselves here mainly to the way in which these inferred behaviors relate to observational learning.

Attention.   Most of the research conducted in this area suggests that attention can be reduced to two more elementary processes—*selective perception* and *stimulus selection*—each of which ultimately leads to different kinds of behavior (D'Amato, 1970).

Selective perception.   Before any learning can take place, the organism must "pay attention" to the characteristics of the situation. Paying attention in this way closely approximates the common-sense meaning of the term. If, for example, we question someone about the color of another person's suit or the events that took place during an automobile ride and no recollection exists, then the person cannot be said to have attended to these events, even though they impinged on the sense organs. In other words, the events simply did not register.

How do certain stimuli become differentiated from others? Well, many things increase selective perception and most of these have to do with the characteristics of the stimulus itself and the specific meaning it may have for the observer (Fig. 13-5). *The structure and complexity of a stimulus, as well as its vividness and distinctiveness, increase the likelihood that it will be noticed.* We tend to notice stimuli that are more unusual—either more intense, larger, or more vivid. *The specific meaning a stimulus has for the observer also enhances its attractiveness.* Liebert and Allen (1969) showed, for example, that models in imitation learning who appear to be experienced or competent are likely to attract more notice and elicit more imitation than others. And, in a study which combined both the distinctiveness of the cue and its apparent meaning to the observer, it was demonstrated that "high-status" jaywalkers—those dressed in freshly pressed suits, shined shoes, ties and shirts—had much greater influence over street-crossing behavior than a comparable model who wore scuffed shoes, soiled and patched trousers, and a wrinkled denim shirt. Under normal circumstances, only 12 out of 1,525 people broke the law and crossed against the light—a scant .007%. When the high status model broke the law, 14% of the people followed him as opposed to only .04% who imitated his disreputable counterpart (Lefkowitz et al., 1955).

Paying attention, however, does not mean that anything has been learned. In selective perception, the stimulus is noticed, retained, and may be described upon request, but it is not learned in the sense that it can be utilized in behavior. This sequence of events is described by path A in Fig. 13-5.

Stimulus selection. For observational learning and imitation to occur, the stimulus, which up to now has merely been "noticed" as a result of selective perception, must now be utilized to bring about some relatively permanent change in behavior. This associative process has been called stimulus selection, and, under these circumstances, the stimulus is not only discriminated from other surrounding and sometimes competing stimuli, it also gains control over behavior.

Motivational factors are important in determining the stimulus-selection process and the extent to which observational learning and imitation will take place, as Fig. 13-5 points out. For example, observers who have a need to imitate a model because they are dependent upon it (see the description of "status envy" in Chapter 14), or who have suffered punishment or deprivation, are also likely to copy the behavior of the models. Black children, for instance, who saw a TV film of an interracial group of children choosing toys to play with, selected the toys chosen by the white children in the film, even though many of the toys they picked were inferior in quality to those that they could have selected (Heckel, 1977). Other studies have shown that young Afro-American children frequently evaluate representations of light-skinned persons more favorably than those of dark-skinned persons (McAdoo, 1970).

Rewards and punishments also play an important role in observational learning, just as they do in operant and classical conditioning. The major difference, however, is that in observational learning, reinforcement is presumed to act *vicariously* rather than directly to increase the likelihood that the observed response will be imitated. Vicarious reward or punishment is assumed to be a mediational process equivalent to the reward or punishment of an overt response, and it occurs when the observer witnesses the consequences of the model's behavior. The children in Bandura's experiment (Box 13-3), for example, saw the model being reinforced or punished for his aggressive behavior, and this affected their own behavior accordingly.

Recent evidence also suggests that the model need not display the critical behavior consistently in order for imitation to occur. Intermittent modeling—a condition in which the model exhibits the crucial behavior only part of the time—is presumably as effective in producing imitation as consistent modeling (Brody et al., 1978). Apparently, observational learning, like other operant behavior, is also affected by the specific schedule of reinforcement.

Vicarious reinforcement serves two purposes in observational learning: (1) it focuses attention on the model's behavior by increasing the interest and importance of the model, and (2) it provides information about the responses necessary to receive reward or avoid punishment (Bandura, 1969).

Liebert and Fernandez (1969) have shown, for example, that rewards to the model can operate to improve observational learning by increasing interest in the modeled behavior. Several groups of first-grade children were exposed to an adult male model who correctly identified states of the United States from colored slides. The material to be learned varied through three levels of complexity—low, moderate, and high—and to each of these levels a second condition was added in which the model was either rewarded or not rewarded for his performance.

Although rewarding the model had a greater effect on the children's ability to reproduce the correct response at all levels of complexity, the influence of vicarious reward became increasingly important as the material become more complex. In other words, vicarious reward facilitated observational learning by enhancing stimulus selection.

Characteristics of a model—age, sex, ethnic status, or social power—can all be made more salient through reinforcement. In all of these instances, models exhibiting these characteristics were copied to a much greater extent when the behavior of the model was reinforced or when the models themselves were construed to be reinforcing.

Retention and retrieval.   While virtually all of the "learning" in observational learning is presumed to take place at the level of stimulus selection, the associations that are formed must be retained until they are translated into overt behavior under the appropriate circumstances. The children in the Bandura, Ross, and Ross (1963a) study retained the impressions they formed while watching the aggressive model being rewarded for usurping all of the toys. The aggressive behavior was not imitated until a later period when the children were given the opportunity to be aggressive. What the children saw on the television screen had to be kept in memory until it was retrieved.

Evidence from research in the area of retention suggests that information can be stored in at least two fundamental ways.

The first, *short-term memory,* is a fragile and labile process and cannot readily account for the retention necessary in observational learning because of its limited storage.

The second, *long-term memory,* is a more permanent storage process in which encoding seems to be a necessary operation. In humans, at least, evidence suggests that the material to be stored is encoded into verbal, or symbolic, information. It is relatively easy to see how verbal encoding and repetition works in the case of a telephone number which must be remembered until it is dialled—the number is simply repeated verbally several times after it has been seen until it is dialled. But laboratory studies also show that encoding can occur as an internal process as well.

In one study (Gerst, 1971; Bandura, 1969) for example, subjects observed a filmed model perform complex motor responses. Various groups were then instructed to do one of the following: code the items into vivid images, create verbal descriptions of the model's actions, label the important responses, or simply watch the film. All three coding operations resulted in greater recall of the model's behavior compared to the recall of the group that simply watched the film.

Very little is actually known about the mechanisms for retrieval of information. It has been shown, however, that information is more easily retrieved when it is stored in some stepwise fashion, the steps following each other in some logical order. Again, as in the learning and retention of information, both motivation and reinforcement are presumed to increase the significance of the material and, ultimately, the ease with which it will be recovered.

Attribution Theory: A Cognitive View of
Behavior Change

People, according to Heider (1958), live in two different causal environments, and they try to make sense out of the multitude of things that happen to them by attributing or assigning a cause to events that is either within themselves or outside of themselves in the environment. The direction of attribution, i.e., whether they see external or internal factors involved, determines, to a marked extent, the quality of their thoughts, feelings, and attitudes, and ultimately, their overt behavior.

The snake-phobic subjects in the attribution studies, it will be recalled, presumably approached the snakes because they were convinced that they were no longer afraid. This new-found fearlessness they attributed to an event within themselves —a decrease in their own (simulated) heart rate when the snake slides were exposed. People in the control group, who were aware of the true nature of the sounds, however, made no such "causal association" about themselves and were still afraid to approach the snake.

Attribution theory was developed by Heider as part of a "psychology of interpersonal relations" to explain how people assign the responsibilities for their own behavior and to understand and predict the behavior of others. Although the principles associated with attribution theory were not precisely formulated, the suggestions made by Heider gave rise to a number of interesting experiments in social psychology and to a theory of personality that assigns an important, if not principal, role to how the individual sees the factors that control behavior—the "locus of control" (Rotter, 1966).

More recently, as we see in Chapter 14 and 15, attribution theory is being used to explain the development of behavior—especially helplessness and depression—and as a means of generating treatment strategies (Abramson et al., 1978). There are even indications that most, if not all of the cognitive methods used in behavior modification are essentially attribution-based procedures, involving, as they do, the person's interpretation of the nature and locus of events that influence behavior.

Afterword

In one sense, the discussion of mediated learning has been somewhat more elaborate than is actually necessary to understand the way in which observational and cognitive learning are used to explain the origins and modification of behavior (Chapters 14 and 15). Although attempts have been made to explain the origins of certain behavior in terms of mediated learning, with the exception of some rudimentary relationships in observational and attribution learning, no explicit principles are used primarily because none are yet available.

The same is also true of the application of mediated learning to behavior modification (see Chapter 15). Here, the use of observational learning, for example, is confined almost solely to the effect of the model on imitation learning without any reference to factors such as attention, memory, and retrieval. And, in cognitive behavior modification, the intervening events—attitudes, beliefs, and expectancies—are used loosely to assert the belief that something goes on within the organism that does help to understand and explain the overt behavior.

Despite this, the somewhat detailed analysis of mediated learning in this chapter serves an important purpose. Given the nature of mediated learning and the necessity for proposing unobservables, there will be a number of attempts to formulate models of behavior based on intervening processes. The use of "self-efficacy" by Bandura in his attempt to pinpoint the important factor in all behavioral intervention procedures, as well as Abramson and Seligman's application of attribution theory to helplessness and depression, are cases in point. Under the circumstances it is important to understand the context in which such attempts should be evaluated. This chapter provides a possible framework for examining the mediational models that we discuss in Chapter 15.

chapter fourteen

Mediated Learning: Behavior Disorders

Some of the black Caribs of British Honduras—escaped Negro slaves who assimilated the culture of the Caribbean natives—and a group of white Boston males have something peculiar in common. Both groups suffer the same symptoms—nausea, vomiting, toothaches, and food cravings—that their wives experience during pregnancy. In fact, the blacks of British Honduras carry this peculiarity even further. Immediately preceding or following the birth of the baby, they practice a custom known as *couvade:* the husband takes to his bed, fasts, goes through purification rituals, and accepts the same attention given his wife (Munroe et al., 1965; Yahraes & Gunders, 1973).

How does this behavior originate, and why is it prevalent in these societies? As it turns out, the black Caribs, the Boston white men, and, indeed, the males from 10 of the other societies studied who also practiced a form of couvade had experiences in common that may explain the behavior. In all of these groups, the mother is the dominant, and, in most cases, the only parent in the household during the child's early formative years. This situation, according to the Whitings (Whiting & Whiting, 1960), results in "status-envy" which produces a close identification with the mother in which her behavior is emulated and copied.

According to John Whiting, a social anthropologist who has spent a considerable amount of time studying the phenomenon, status-envy is one ·of the most important factors governing early childhood learning and subsequent personality development. Simply stated, status-envy means that children in a society come to envy, identify with, and imitate those around them who control such important resources as food, water, love, and freedom from pain. How children respond to others during childhood, and when they mature, is, to a very great extent, a consequence of observing how the important people in their lives—the controllers of these resources—respond, and this means that a child's behavior is largely determined by what is learned through observation. The presence or absence of certain models during childhood, peers as well as parents, often makes for important differences in social behavior later in life as we shall see.

The discussion of the origins of the behavior disorders in Chapter 3 suggested that the behavior which develops as a result of learning could conceivably be related to one of three types of learning situations—classical and avoidance conditioning, operant learning, and mediated or observational learning. Some behavior, it will be recalled, appeared to be more closely associated with inappropriate stimulus control due to classical and avoidance conditioning, while others appeared to be related to inappropriate, defective, or impoverished conditions of reinforcement.

In this chapter, we continue to explore the possibilities listed in Table 3-1, and especially the third likelihood, that some behavior is brought under deficient stimulus control due to the effects of observational learning. In these instances, we assume that control of behavior is deficient, either because no appropriate figure was available to serve as a model for learning (resulting in behavioral deficits) or because an improper model served as a guide to undesirable behavior (producing behavioral excesses).

In discussing the origins of behavior disorders in terms of observational learning, it is extremely important to bear in mind the qualification stressed in Chapter 3. In many instances, behavior is probably learned in one way and maintained in another. Although children learn to imitate the behavior of a significant adult, the responses are not likely to persist unless they have some specific consequences in terms of rewards and punishments.

Sex-role typing in children, for example, probably begins when the parent of the same sex models the appropriate behavior for the child to imitate. Girls are like mothers, boys like fathers. But, as we saw in Chapter 7, these gender stereotypes, which begin with observational learning in the home, continue to be reinforced in the classroom where girls are taught to be dependent and boys are encouraged to be independent, curious, and venturesome. It is extremely important to remember, therefore, that although the classification of behavior disorders in terms of learning emphasizes the importance of one type of learning, behavior more frequently results from the interaction of several types of learning.

OBSERVATIONAL LEARNING: DEFICIENT STIMULUS CONTROL AND IMPROPER MODELS

The successful use of prominent people to promote the sale of products on television and in the news media eloquently expresses the extent to which modeling and imitation continue to be important sources of learning during a person's lifetime.

But even these examples of imitation behavior pale compared to the information recently collected by sociologists which indicates that periodic increases in motor-vehicle accidents and plane crashes may well be disguised instances of suicide, or combined occurrences of murder and suicide prompted by the publicity that such murders and suicides receive on television and in the newspapers.

According to the evidence, fatal crashes of private, business, and corporate executive airplanes increase after murder-suicides are publicized in the news media, and the more publicity given the incidents, the greater the number of plane crashes. Curiously, one study reported that crashes peaked 3 days after such stories appeared in the newspapers, and they were confined primarily to those states in which the news had been publicized (D. P. Phillips, 1978).

Apparently, the people involved in these "accidents" found a solution to their problems in the examples provided by others. The models (murder and suicide) suggested a course of behavior that was appropriate to their mood. Schachter and Singer (1962) found a related effect in an experiment clearly showing that we sometimes allow the behavior of others to define what we are feeling. When people are in an aroused physiological state that they cannot explain, the explanations for their behavior can be influenced by the actions of those around them.

Adrenalin, disguised as "Suproxin"—a fictitious drug—was administered to three groups of students. One group was accurately informed to expect physiological reactions—trembling hands, pounding of the heart, and facial warmth—while the other two groups received no information. Following the injections, the subjects were divided into several groups and either exposed to a student confederate who displayed a happy, euphoric mood or asked to fill out a tedious and insulting questionnaire in the presence of another confederate who complained loudly, tore up the questionnaire, and stalked from the room.

A subsequent evaluation of the mood of the subjects revealed that those who had received accurate information about the effects of the drug were not influenced by the behavior of either of the student confederates. The uninformed groups, on the other hand, showed extreme happiness or anger, depending upon which of the confederates they had observed. In their aroused physiological state, the uninformed subjects, who had no accurate labels for their feelings, were more likely to imitate the behavior of the models.

If relatively mature individuals can be persuaded to purchase products, commit murder and suicide, or misinterpret their own feelings through the influence of models, how much more likely is it that children with considerably less immunity to persuasion can also learn undesirable and antisocial behavior through improper models? Bandura and his colleagues have already demonstrated that children do imitate aggressive acts they have seen, and television provides us with a rare opportunity to observe these laboratory demonstrations recurring in a natural setting.

Aggressive Behavior and Improper Models

A gang doused a small girl with gasoline and set her afire. A boy put crushed glass in the family dinner. Two adolescents murdered an old woman who was their next door neighbor. And a group of boys brutally raped a 9-year-old girl 4 days after a similar scene was portrayed on a television show. Many children have been hurt attempting to imitate Evel Knievel's dare-devil feats, and one 8-year-old boy even talks wistfully about being injured and then being put back together again like the "six-million-dollar man."

These are not rare or isolated instances of aggressive or fantasy behavior in extraordinary children. Each is directly related to a child's exposure to television violence and to the tacit approval of violence that many such programs seem to convey. In the minds of many psychologists, little doubt exists about a relationship between television violence and later aggressive behavior in children. In a study of 100 juvenile offenders commissioned by the American Broadcasting Company, 22 of the teenage violent offenders interviewed indicated that their crimes, 19 of which had gone undetected, were directly inspired by television. An additional 22 had at one time or another thought about committing a crime they had seen on television, and more than half of the youths felt that television had changed their beliefs (Heller & Polsky, 1975).

To demonstrate the effects of television violence on aggressive behavior in a controlled, natural setting, Steuer, Applefield, and Smith (1971) observed a group of 5 pairs of pre-school boys and girls at play before and after they were exposed to Saturday morning children's television programs, largely cartoons. The study showed that the child in each pair of children who had been shown 2 hours worth of Saturday morning programs, in 8-minute segments, exhibited much more physical, interpersonal aggression (kicking, hitting, pushing, choking, holding down, or throwing objects) than the control child who had viewed a selection of neutral programs.

Figure 14-1, which summarizes the results of the experiment, indicates that, in each instance, the child shown the Saturday morning television programs (experimental) exhibited more violent behavior then either of the children showed during the recording of baseline behavior (sessions 1–10). It is interesting to note that not all of the children responded to the television programs with the same intensity. The children exposed to the aggressive programs in pairs 2 and 5, for example, showed considerably less aggression than those in pairs 1, 3, and 4. Obviously, it would be equally important to study the factors responsible for the relative immunity to influence that these 2 children seem to display.

Evidence from more than 50 comprehensive laboratory and field investigations involving upwards of 10,000 children strongly suggests that viewing violence tends to produce aggressive behavior in children. Can this relationship between television violence and aggressive behavior be used in a court of law as a defense against charges of murder? Can television networks be held directly responsible for inciting violence in those cases where adolescents were explicitly copying the violent rape scenes they had witnessed on a television show? Attorneys in Florida

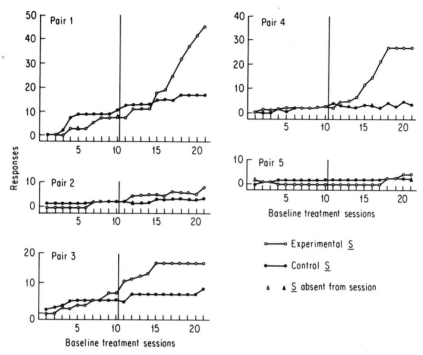

FIG. 14-1 Cumulative number of physical, interpersonal aggressive responses for the five pairs of matched subjects. In each case aggressive behavior increased for the child (experimental) who watched the Saturday morning television programs. (Source: F.B. Steuer, M.M. Applefield, and R. Smith. Televised aggression and interpersonal aggression of preschool children. *Journal of Experimental Child Psychology,* 1971, *11,* 442–447. Copyright 1971 Academic Press and used by permission.)

and California thought so. The former argued that his client was not responsible for the murder he had committed because he was "obsessed with television violence," and the California attorney brought a lawsuit against the National Broadcasting Company for $11 million on behalf of his client who was sexually assaulted in a manner similar to that portrayed in a scene from *Born Innocent* (Box 14-1).

BOX 14-1
"Involuntary Subliminal Television
Intoxication"

"Involuntary subliminal television intoxication," an attorney claimed in defense of his 15-year-old client who, with the aid of a friend, murdered an 83-year-old widow living next door.

The courtroom testimony indicated that from the age of 5 the defendant's devotion to television grew into an obsession. He would sneak out of his bed late at night to watch television, be caught, and sneak out again after being returned to his room. All the games he played were reenactments of television shows, especially *Kojak,* his favorite program, and his customary listlessness disappeared whenever the topic of television arose. "It was the most important thing in his life."

Despite its uniqueness, a plea of "television intoxication" is not inconsistent with Florida law, and a legitimate insanity defense can be based on the prolonged habitual use of an intoxicant. In the pre-trial hearings, the boy's attorney submitted papers indicating that, although in the judgment of several psychiatrists, the defendant would have eventually "developed the murderous tendencies of a sociopath," his madness was hastened by his reliance on television. The boy became an actor in his own television drama, and, according to his attorney, "without the influence of television there would have been no crime." In fact, the boy admitted that he was specifically influenced by a drama he had seen on *Kojak,* and the crime was a reenactment of that program.

The prosecuting attorney, on the other hand, fought the "insanity by virtue of television" defense and successfully argued that the congressional reports on the influence of television violence, research documents, or journals should not be allowed as evidence. He was able to persuade the judge that the defense should be limited solely to television violence as it relates specifically to the defendant and not as an indictment of TV violence in general (*Newsday,* 1977).

During the course of the trial, the attorney for the defense produced two expert witnesses who supported the idea that aggressiveness in children could be traced to television violence. The testimony of one of the witnesses was declared inadmissable, however, because the expert, a psychologist, had declared that instances of crime attributed to television violence were "after-the-fact interpretations" and that no definite statement of causal relationship could be made. From this, the judge concluded that there was no clear evidence that television violence had ever been responsible for the commission of a crime. But the testimony of a second expert was admitted on the grounds that he had personally treated many cases of disturbed and socially deprived children who were affected by what they had seen on television. The expert also declared that the defendant knew right from wrong until he was affected adversely by viewing television violence. On October 6, 1977, the jury delivered a verdict of guilty, and the youth was sentenced to the penitentiary (*Newsday,* 1977).

The suit against NBC brought by the California girl who had been attacked and raped in a manner depicted on one of their television programs was dismissed on the grounds that the plaintiff could not prove that the television network sought to incite the crime by having its viewers imitate the violent sexual attack portrayed in the movie (*N. Y. Times,* Aug., 1978).

At this point, an inconsistency in maintaining, on the one hand, that television is frequently responsible for aggressive behavior in children and noting, on the other hand, that children imitate the behavior of rewarded models more than they do punished models (Bandura, 1965) may be noted. In fact, one of the psychiatrists in the "television intoxication" trial, who was introduced as an expert witness for the prosecution, brought this contradiction to the attention of the court. Because those who engage in violence on television are rarely, if ever, rewarded for their behavior, he argued, it would be difficult to assert that television violence relates to aggressive behavior in children.

Although this argument may sound reasonable, it overlooks an important point, namely, that aggression as a style of behavior is what gets reinforced when a child watches television. Children not only become accustomed to violence and learn to tolerate it, they also learn that violence is the way to settle arguments. Even the so-called proper models, the police, invariably have to engage in violence, often outside the law, in order to restrain criminals. For this they are rewarded. Models on television rarely display sweet reason in attempting to settle differences.

Frequently, parents themselves are models for aggressive and antisocial behavior, and this form of learning is not confined solely to the lower socioeconomic levels where such behavior is often expected and encouraged. Bandura and Walters (1959) reported that delinquents from affluent homes were exposed to parents who constantly practiced antisocial and aggressive behavior while maintaining a smooth and socially correct exterior. Other parents encouraged and rewarded their sons for using aggression to settle arguments with their peers.

When aggression is modeled as a way of solving problems, it often passes from one generation to another as a socially useful pattern. Child-rearing in many Western cultures, for example, is dominated by a form of discipline which emphasizes physical and corporal punishment, and child abuse has recently become recognized as a serious, widespread practice in our culture. According to Steele, who has studied parental abuse of infants and small children, "all the abusing parents who were seen were brought up in much the same manner as that employed in raising their own children." Although they may not have been subjected to severe physical abuse in early life, they felt deeply crushed by disapproval for their failure to behave properly, and all voiced common cliches such as "children have to be taught respect for parents and obedience to authority, etc." (1970, pp. 453, 454). By contrast, the children of the Hutterites, who emphasize pacifism as a way of life, show virtually no aggressive behavior toward each other, despite the harsh conditions and frustrating pressures they are subjected to during their developing years. The culture simply does not model nor reward aggressive behavior (Bandura & Walters, 1959).

Modeling Bizarre Behavior: A Way of Transmitting Behavior Disorders

Clearly, aggression is just one of the many responses that can be influenced through observational learning. Behaviors as strange as psychotic delusions, psychomotor seizures, and a number of phobic conditions have been traced to the opportunity both children and adults have had to observe and imitate these responses. In fact, the term *folie à deux,* meaning literally "the madness of two," was coined in 1877 by Lasègue and Falret to describe the relatively frequent instances where one person imitates the delusions and other psychotic patterns of another person until the behavior becomes indistinguishable from an actual psychotic development. Such relationships have been found between parents and children, husbands and wives, and also between siblings. When the pair is separated and each of the individuals removed to another environment, however, the behavior of the imitator invariably undergoes a change (Box 14-2).

BOX 14-2

"Superguy"

At the age of 5, "Johnnie" was addicted to television cartoons, and he began to worry that the world was going to be taken over by Superguy who could change himself into anyone or anything. He could become a clock or a lamp and send out messages. Superguy could get in anywhere and there was no escaping him. He focused on Johnnie's house because he knew it was the center of the world.

Johnnie's mother had once worked for a crime commission as a secretary, and she had recently begun to imagine that some of the crooks and gangsters, about whom she had typed reports, were going to get even with her. This was especially true of "Mister M" who was still at large because he was very clever and able to assume many disguises which fooled the police. Every person on the street was associated with "Mister M," and the mother was continuously calling the police to report his presence.

Her husband obtained evidence from many sources indicating that she had nothing to fear and that "Mister M" was a figment of her imagination, but Johnnie's mother persisted in her beliefs and the vigilance increased. She referred to him as the "gangster kind," claimed he had magical powers to outwit the police, and used electronic listening equipment. She became suspicious of all items in the house, stopped the clocks as a special precaution, and kept watch by the windows all day long with Johnnie by her side. The doctors were called in, but nothing seemed to help, and the husband became increasingly alarmed at the growing agitation of his wife and son.

Both Johnnie and his mother now had a common persecutor whom they referred to as "super" because of his powers. Neither Johnnie nor his mother would be separated from each other, and both of them ignored the father. After some time, and much against his will, the father had the mother hospitalized. Johnnie became panic-stricken when his mother left, but he soon settled down and forgot all about Superguy when he was given over to the care of his loving grandmother. In the hospital, the mother was diagnosed as paranoid schizophrenic. (From E. J. Anthony, 1970, pp. 575–576.)

Anthony (1968, 1978) has estimated that about 20–30% of childhood morbidity resembles the classical folie à deux pattern brought about through living with one or two schizophrenic parents. Some authors have even gone so far as to suggest that the clue to mental illness lies in these instances of folie à deux (Gralnick, 1942), and that the behavior represents a serious challenge to the biological and hereditary views of schizophrenia.

Others have stressed the immaturity, dependence, suggestibility, passivity, and submissiveness of the imitator as factors that contribute to the origin of folie à deux behavior. In this connection, it is interesting to note that while some individuals succumb to the delusions of their partners, others resist the influence and even shrug off the bizarre behavior with some degree of humor. Anthony (1970), for example, cites the case of a brother and sister living with a mother who believed her food was being poisoned. The sister shared her mother's delusions, while the brother, when asked why he continued to eat at home under the circumstances, replied with a shrug of the shoulders, "Well, I'm not dead yet." In some instances, children have even been known to adopt a double standard of behavior, confining their irrational beliefs to the family circle and abandoning their delusions outside of the home (1970, pp. 576, 594).

Children have also been observed to imitate the behavior of adults in order to achieve specific purposes. A 10-year-old girl, for example, was admitted to the hospital with seizure-like episodes consisting of head-rolling and hair-pulling. A complete physical examination did not reveal any neurological impairment or severe emotional disturbance, but the psychologists discovered that some months prior to the first "seizure" the mother had experienced a headache of such intensity that she "rocked and banged her head" in pain and had to be taken to a hospital. Both the girl and her sister had been competing for the parent's attention, and the mother's experience may have provided a method for the child to receive the attention she saw her mother getting. The case was successfully treated when the parents were advised to ignore the seizures and reward the child with attention for appropriate behavior (Gardner, 1967).

Phobias are frequently transmitted from parent to child through modeling. The child need never have been harmed or have experienced any pain to show terror during thunderstorms or fear when approached by a dog. The fear displayed by the parent (usually the mother) in such instances is sufficient to establish learning. Such "empathic" learning has been demonstrated under controlled conditions in the laboratory by Berger (1962) who showed that subjects observing other people receive a shock following the onset of a light will show an increase in the galvanic skin response (GSR) to the light, even though they themselves had never received a shock.

OBSERVATIONAL LEARNING: DEFICIENT STIMULUS CONTROL AND THE ABSENCE OF PROPER MODELS

It is relatively easy to understand and accept the idea that inappropriate behavior can be transmitted from one person to another by means of modeling and imitation learning. Although it is just as reasonable to assume that the absence of proper models can also produce inappropriate behavior, this relationship is more difficult to demonstrate with humans under controlled conditions similar to those that Bandura and his associates used to study aggression. For obvious reasons, children cannot be intentionally and systematically separated from their mothers or deprived of other human contact for purposes of experimentation, and so much of the information that exists about the effects of such deprivation comes from animal experiments or from situations in which children have been deprived of significant figures because of uncontrollable, or unforeseen, naturally occurring conditions—death, neglect, or child-raising practices specific to various cultures.

Deprivation and Behavioral Impairment

Social isolation, especially during the early, formative years, produces profound and often irreversible changes in behavior. Controlled studies with animals and observations of humans indicate that these changes may appear as *retarded neurological development, reduced defenses to stress, or a deficit in the behavior necessary to function properly within the social group.*

Animals who have been socially deprived during rearing, for example, show a reduction in the receptor surface of neurons in certain areas of the brain as well as changes in the density and size of synaptic connections in the nervous system. A similar transformation in physiological development occurred in fish who were isolated and deprived of the opportunity to see their own species. These animals developed significant structural changes in the optic nerves that did not appear in community-reared fish (Closs & Globus, 1978).

Reactions to stress are also affected when young animals are separated from their mothers at specific times. Rats, for example, who have been separated from their mothers 15 days after birth, develop ulcers when they are exposed to later stress tests, and they also show disturbances in the ability to regulate body temperature, insomnia, and an increase in quiet wakefulness (Ackerman et al., 1978). Liddell (1951) also found that the mother's presence had a pronounced effect on the behavior of young goats during escape conditioning with shock. The kids who were conditioned with shock to the foreleg while the mother was absent all developed complete immobility and one even stopped feeding and died. Those who received the shock while in the presence of the mother did not react in this manner.

Normal, adult social behavior appears to be overwhelmingly dependent on the opportunity to socialize with others during the very early years of psychological and physical development. Animals who are deprived of this opportunity invariably develop extreme behaviors. Either the behavior is out of control, possibly because other animals were not present to influence and moderate the responses, or the appropriate behavior is absent because there was no opportunity to observe and learn from others.

Dogs, for example, who were raised in individual cages with restricted vision from the age of 4 weeks exhibited extremely deviant behavior when they were finally released into a normal environment with other dogs at the age of 19 months. Instead of competing with the other, normally raised dogs for food, the socially deprived animals simply succumbed. None of the deprived animals showed the usual, socially organized curiosity—sniffing, growling, and tentativeness—in the proximity of other unfamiliar dogs. Instead, even after numerous contacts, their behavior continued to be diffuse, disorganized, and characterized by increasing rather than decreasing excitement. The response to humans consisted largely of jerky, withdrawal movements accompanied by increases in agitated behavior (Melzack & Thompson, 1956).

The most extensive research ever carried out on the effects of social isolation and maternal deprivation with animals was begun by Harry Harlow in 1958 (Harlow & Zimmerman, 1958, 1959). Like Pavlov, Harlow was engaged on another project when the discoveries were made. In attempting to maintain a disease-free colony of rhesus monkeys for research purposes, Harlow noted that infant monkeys who had been separated from their mothers at birth:

> ... sit in their cages and stare fixedly into space, circle their cages in a repetitive stereotyped manner and clasp their hands or arms and rock for long periods of time. They often develop compulsive habits, such as pinching precisely the same patch of skin on the chest between the same fingers hundreds of times a day; occasionally, such behavior may become punitive and the animal may chew and tear at its body until it bleeds. Often the approach of a human being becomes the stimulus for self-aggression. This behavior constitutes a complete breakdown and reversal of the normal defensive responses (Harlow & Harlow, 1962, p. 138).

Harlow and his associates continued to observe infant monkeys who had been isolated from their mothers and peers for varying amounts of time after birth. All of these animals exhibited the gross behavior anomalies in their home cage that he had seen and described earlier. They were exceedingly frightened, could not adapt to novel stimuli, often sat clutching themselves rocking back and forth, and had extreme difficulty suppressing or moderating any ongoing behavior.

Several attempts were made to reverse the effects of isolation by providing the infant monkeys with mother-surrogates in the form of a wood frame covered with sponge rubber and terry cloth, or an uncovered wire frame of similar size and shape (Harlow & Zimmerman, 1959). Although each of these sham mothers provided nourishment in the form of milk (a bottle and nipple protruded prominently from the surrogate's chest), the infants clearly preferred the terry-cloth mother. This was true even when the wire mother was the only one of the two who offered milk. The "contact-comfort" provided by the terry-cloth mother did much to alleviate the effects of isolation. The infant monkeys showed less fear and concern when a novel object, such as a toy bear with a drum, was introduced into the cage if the surrogate mother was present so they could rush to her and clutch her. When the surrogate figure was absent on these occasions, however, the infant would often freeze in a crouched position or run screaming from object to object in the cage.

When the isolate-reared monkeys were finally released into the monkey colony after varying amounts of isolation and different deprivation conditions, it was obvious that these experiences had a marked effect on their social behavior as well. Unlike the animals who were raised with mothers, isolate-reared monkeys typically

TABLE 14-1   The Results of Several Years of Studying Monkeys Raised Under Varying Conditions of Social Isolation

EXPERIMENTAL CONDITION	PRESENT AGE	BEHAVIOR				
		None	Low	Almost normal	Probably normal	Normal
RAISED IN ISOLATION						
TOTAL Cage-raised for 2 years	4 years	■ □ ★				
Cage-raised for 6 months	14 months	□ ★	■ □			
Cage-raised for 80 days	10½		■ □ ★			
PARTIAL Cage-raised for 6 months	5 to 8 years		■ ★	□		
Surrogate-raised for 6 months	3 to 5 years		■ ★	□		
RAISED WITH MOTHER						
Normal mother; no play with peers	1 year	★	■			
Motherless mother; play in playpen	14 months		■	□	★	■
Normal mother; play in playpen	2 years					■ □ ★
RAISED WITH PEERS						
Four raised in one cage; play in playroom	1 year				■	★ □
Surrogate-raised; play in playpen	2 years				★	□ ■
Surrogate-raised; play in playroom	21 months					■ □ ★

■ Play
□ Defense
★ Sex

SOURCE: From Social deprivation in monkeys. H. F. & M. K. Harlow. Copyright 1962, *Scientific American, Inc.* and used by permission.

displayed excessive and inappropriately directed aggression, did not engage in play with other monkeys, were incapable of adequate sexual responses, and, what is perhaps most striking, were completely deficient in maternal behavior toward their young (Ruppenthal et al., 1976).

Table 14-1 summarizes the results of several years of study with these monkeys under varying experimental conditions. The table points to some interesting and important implications of social deprivation in animals. In the first place, the monkeys who were isolated for a relatively short period of time—80 days after birth—were less affected by deprivation than those who were isolated for 6 months or 2 years. Apparently, the effect of isolation can be reversed up until the age of 6 months. Beyond this period, the behavior induced by isolation appears to be relatively permanent. Second, although the presence of a surrogate terry-cloth mother had some positive effect on the infant's ability to use normal defenses to withstand stress, the animals were still seriously deficient in play and sex behaviors. Finally, and what is perhaps most astonishing, monkey mothers are absolutely unnecessary to the development of effective social behavior as long as the infant monkeys are permitted to play with each other during the time they are maturing (Box 14-3).

BOX 14-3
A Bad Mother is Better Than None, and
Friends Are Best of All

One of the startling effects of early isolation on the later behavior of female monkeys is that they make terrible mothers when they finally give birth to their own offspring. But even conception is a problem for these females because social isolation has also made them incapable of adequate sexual behavior. Mating simply did not occur, despite the fact that sexually competent, wild-reared males were introduced into the colony. Four of these motherless females were finally inseminated by males, and an additional 16 received artificial insemination.

The socially deprived, motherless mothers were all grossly inadequate with their own infants. Some rejected the baby monkeys and were completely indifferent to any attempts made to remove the infants from the cage. Feral mothers, by contrast, would fight viciously to prevent the removal of their infants. Others became abusive and brutalized their infants, biting off their fingers and toes, stepping and jumping on them, pushing their faces into the grillwork of the cage and, in some cases, attempting to kill them. When this occurred, it became necessary for the staff to intervene in order to save the infant's life. (Arling & Harlow, 1967; Ruppenthal et al., 1976).

Despite the indifference and abuse, the infant monkeys who succeeded in remaining with their motherless mothers made a reasonably good adjustment when they were released into the colony. Their defensive behavior was almost normal, and both play and sexual behavior appeared to be within normal limits, as Table 14-1 indicates. The persistence of some of the infants probably accounts for their subsequent adjustment. As Harlow et al. describe it:

> If denied ventral contact, the infants would seek dorsal contact . . . and worm their way around the mothers' body to the ventral surface. The mothers would persistently scrape the infant off their body, sometimes kicking or crushing its face against the cage floor. In spite of rejection or brutality the infants never gave up. Through this persistence the infants gradually gained some contact with their mothers and in turn, positive behaviors were elicited from the mothers (1966, p. 62).

> What comes as a real surprise is that these infant monkeys who were abused and neglected by their motherless mothers made a better social adjustment than those who were raised in isolation with surrogate mothers. The infants who were raised with terry-cloth mothers showed impaired play and sex behavior and almost normal defense reactions. For those infants reared by a motherless mother, on the other hand, play and sex behaviors were approximately normal (Table 14-1). Apparently then, bad mothers are better than no mothers at all, but what is most extraordinary, as Table 14-1 also shows, mothers seem to be unnecessary as long as the infant monkeys could play with each other.

The studies of deprivation with animals show quite conclusively that those reared in isolation during their early, formative years exhibit deviant social behavior later in life. Whether these behavioral deficits or excesses are due to lack of nurturance and contact-comfort, inadequate reinforcement for appropriate behavior, the absence of proper models, or any combination of these factors is very difficult to say. One can only surmise that the impairment in such social behavior as play, defense, sex, and maternal care of infants which Harlow's monkeys suffered is probably due to the inability of the isolated monkeys to observe these behaviors in other monkeys.

But if it is difficult to draw any definite conclusions about the specific influence of any of these variables in relatively well-controlled experiments with animals, it is even more difficult to study the long-range effects of deprivation in humans. Very little doubt exists that maternal separation in human infants produces learning deficits and retardation in social and emotional behavior, but all of the evidence is based on clinical observation. Studies by Ribble (1943), Spitz (1945), Bowlby (1952), Caldwell (1964), Yarrow (1964) and others indicate that the absence of a mother during the first 6 months of life invariably has serious consequences for the development of the child. Institutionalized children, for example, who have experienced very little human contact, generally become depressed and lethargic. These same investigators have suggested that continued impoverishment eventually leads to a limited capacity to form human relationships.

Yarrow has observed, for example, that when children are separated from their mothers and left in hospitals or institutions, an immediate reaction of crying and protest is usually followed by a period of despair, withdrawal, resignation, and apathy—a situation often misinterpreted by the hospital personnel as evidence that the child has settled down and adapted to the situation. But:

although on the surface the children seem happy and well-adapted to the situation, they act as if mothering or any contact with humans has much significance for them . . . This pattern of "detachment" Robertson and Bowlby consider a precursor of the development of the psychopathic personality or affectionless character (1964, p. 96).

"Masculine Protest" and the Absence of the Father. We have already seen how the concept of status-envy was used to explain feminine identification and the practice of couvade in those males who had been brought up in households where the only adults were women. But, according to the Whitings, if these male-deprived children are subsequently introduced into a predominantly male culture, their early feminine identification inevitably leads them into conflict with the society and difficulty in making later social adjustments. As Beatrice Whiting puts it:

If during the first 2 or 3 years of life a child is constantly with his mother and infrequently sees, and is handled by, his father, he will identify strongly with his mother and not with his father; in short if he is a boy he will have a cross-sex identification. If, later in life, he is involved in a world in which men are perceived to be more prestigeful and powerful than woman, he will be thrown into conflict. He will develop a strong need to reject his underlying female identity. This may lead to an overdetermined attempt to prove his masculinity, manifested by a preoccupation with physical strength and athletic prowess, or attempts to demonstrate daring and valor, or behavior that is violent and aggressive (1965, p. 126).

Evidence from many sources seems to support this hypothesis. The intense couvade males studied by the Munroes, for example, were known as braver men, heavier drinkers, and more frequent cursers than others. In fact, they were considered the prototype of the rugged male.

Support for the masculine protest hypothesis was also found in the high incidence of juvenile delinquincy among lower-class black youths. These youths, according to Rohrer and Edmonson (1960) who analyzed the matriarchal household typical among the Southern black lower classes, came from fatherless households, and they rejected femininity in every form. They saw it in women, effeminate men, laws, morals, religion, schools, and occupational striving. The same relationship was also found in a cross-cultural study of the correlates of crime in 48 societies. Lack of appropriate male models and the opportunity to form an identification with the father was found to be associated with a higher incidence of theft, assault, rape, murder, and other crimes (Bacon et al., 1963).

Further evidence for the relationship between the absent father and aggressive behavior resulting from the masculine protest was found in 2 of the 6 cultures analyzed by Beatrice Whiting (1963). Compared to the other 4 societies studied (Okinawans, Mixtecans, Philippinos, and New Englanders), the Gusi tribe of Kenya, Africa, and the members of the Rajput caste in Uttar Pradesh, India, were discovered to engage in an unusual amount of violence. In both of these tribes, the husband and wife did not work, play, or eat together. They did not even occupy the same bedroom. The children of the other societies, by contrast, had ample and early opportunity to identify with males, and, presumably, as a consequence, the incidence of violent and aggressive behavior was virtually nonexistent.

COGNITIVE FACTORS AND THE BEHAVIOR DISORDERS

Although the incidence of physical and behavioral disorders has been related to the number and intensity (in terms of the amount of social readjustment required) of life-stress changes (see Table 3-2, Chapter 3), not all people break down under similar circumstances. Some survive the most stressful and harrowing experiences like the holocaust, rarely get ill, feel in control, and see change as an opportunity rather than as a threat. Others succumb to considerably fewer and less intense stressful experiences.

For many behavioral scientists, the relationship between the amount and intensity of stress and the incidence of behavior disorders is too simplistic. Several have felt that many cognitive factors, such as the ways in which individuals perceive the stressful situation and their attitudes toward change in general, are important elements in determining their ultimate responses.

This hypothesis was recently supported in a study by Redfield and Stone (1979) who found that responses to a list of life-events, compiled from several life-events schedules, was overwhelmingly determined by how individuals perceived these events in terms of their own situation. Older males, for example, saw events such as pregnancy, childbirth, and marriage as more desirable and meaningful than a group of younger females. Apparently, according to the authors, older individuals are less likely to have their lives disrupted by such incidents, while the younger women perceive pregnancy and childbirth as events involving more drastic personal change.

ATTRIBUTION THEORY: A COGNITIVE FACTOR

Attribution theory further elaborates the idea that the way in which individuals perceive life-changes and stress determines the nature of their responses to these events. It says, in effect, that the person's interpretation of these changes, and more specifically, of the forces that are responsible for them, determines how they deal with these events. The therapy methods used by Beck, Ellis, and Meichenbaum (Chapter 15), for example, are all based on the idea that irrational attributions and self-blame are largely responsible for the difficulties people experience in life.

A more elaborate scheme for understanding helplessness, and depression in particular, within the framework of attribution theory has recently been worked out by Abramson, Seligman, and Teasdale (1977). The authors were compelled to reformulate the original conception of helplessness and depression, based on animal experiments conducted by Seligman and Maier (1967), because of certain inadequacies in the interpretation of similar experiments involving humans.

For example, subjects in an experiment who develop a sense of helplessness when they are told to control an essentially uncontrollable noise may be responding this way for one of two reasons: either they blame themselves for being unable to control the noise, i.e., they tell themselves that other people can control the noise, but that they cannot—or they may believe that the problem is external—that the noise cannot be controlled. Animals, of course, do not make these attributions.

A second inadequacy of basing a helplessness model on animals is that when the subjects in the experiment are told that the noise is uncontrollable, they soon recover from their state of helplessness. Animals require a large number of "assisted" trials over the barrier before they can be induced to overcome their helplessness and jump it on their own.

So, while helplessness (and depression) are states thought to be associated with uncontrollable events, the extent to which these states may be prolonged or transient and the treatment procedures that might be devised to alleviate them depend upon what people believe causes their failure to control. Table 14-2 gives examples of the kinds of attributions a failing student or a rejected woman are likely to make. People might attribute failure to a general or global event or to a specific event. The failure might also be blamed on personal shortcomings and deficits (internal) as opposed to factors in the environment (external). Moreover, the events can be short-term (unstable and capable of change) or longer-lasting (stable and impossible to change).

A woman who has been rejected in a love affair (Table 14-2), for example, may attribute this rejection to one (or more) of these factors, and these attributions will have further implications for how long it takes her to recover from the rejection and for her attitude toward men in the future. In effect, she can:

1. *Make attributions which are global and likely to produce long-term states of helplessness and deficits in performance in new situations with most other men.*

  a. I'm unattractive to men (internal, stable, global).

  b. My conversations sometimes bore men (internal, unstable, global).

  c. Men are overly competitive with intelligent women (external, stable, global).

  d. Men get into rejecting moods (external, unstable, global).

2. *Make attributions which are specific and likely to produce helplessness deficits only with a particular man.*

  a. I'm unattractive to him (internal, stable, specific).

  b. My conversation sometimes bores him (internal, unstable, specific).

  c. He is overly competitive with intelligent women (external, stable, specific).

  d. He was in a rejecting mood (external, unstable, specific).

TABLE 14-2 The Attributional Scheme of Learned Helplessness and Depression

Dimension	Internal		External	
	Stable	Unstable	Stable	Unstable
Global				
Failing student	Lack of intelligence	Exhaustion	ETS gives unfair tests.	Today is Friday the 13th.
	(Laziness)	(Having a cold, which makes me stupid)	(People are usually unlucky on the GRE.)	(ETS gave experimental tests this time which were too hard for everyone.)
Rejected woman	I'm unattractive to men.	My conversation sometimes bores men.	Men are overly competitive with intelligent women.	Men get into rejecting moods.
Specific				
Failing student	Lack of mathematical ability	Fed up with math problems	ETS gives unfair math tests.	The math test was from No. 13.
	(Math always bores me.)	(Having a cold, which ruins my arithmetic)	(People are usually unlucky on math tests.)	(Everyone's copy of the math test was blurred.)
Rejected woman	I'm unattractive to him.	My conversation bores him.	He's overly competitive with women.	He was in a rejecting mood.

SOURCE: L.Y. Abramson, M.E.P. Seligman, and J.D. Teasdale, 1978.

Note: ETS = Educational Testing Service, the maker of Graduate Record Examinations (GRE).

Stable attributions are likely to produce chronic, long-lasting deficits in behavior, while unstable attributions will produce transient deficits. Attributing failure to internal events will also result in loss of self-esteen, while external attributions will not (Abramson et al., 1977, p. 57–58). The woman who blames herself for her failure with men and considers this to be a permanent characteristic is more likely to suffer long-term depressions than the one who blames short-term occurrence events in the environment.

In summary, then, people will generally feel helpless and depressed when the things they want are not likely to occur (loss of positive reinforcement), when they cannot escape aversive situations (loss of negative reinforcement), and when they believe that nothing they can do will change these events (loss of control). The depressions are likely to be related to more events and will last longer if individuals attribute their helplessness to a larger number of situations, to situations which recur, and to characteristics within themselves. The depressions will be more intense to the extent that people are convinced that they cannot control the situation.

According to the authors, using attribution theory as a framework for depression explains why (1) simply expecting an event to be uncontrollable does not necessarily produce depression, (2) lowered self-esteem is often a symptom in depression, (3) depressed people frequently believe they cause their own failures, and (4) depressions are often related to a large number of situations, can be intense, and frequently last for long periods of time (Abramson et al., 1978, pp. 65–67).

The controversy which now surrounds both the original and the reformulated versions of learned helplessness as a model for the origin of depressed behavior has been aired in a special issue of the *Journal of Abnormal Psychology* (1978), and the model has been criticized on the following grounds (Buchwald et al., 1978; Costello, 1978; Depue & Monroe, 1978):

1. The experimental subject on which virtually all of the learned helplessness model is based is the college student. There is little evidence to suggest that depression in college students is the same as depression in a clinical population.

2. Depressed behavior, as it appears in a clinical population, is an extremely heterogenous collection of behaviors ranging from exceedingly intractable psychotic depressions to those which are related to environmental stress, and including anxiety and hostility as part of the symptom picture. Depression resulting from learned helplessness appears to be a "mild subclass" of a more extensive disorder (Seligman, 1978).

3. The reformulation of the learned helplessness model, as Abramson, Seligman, and Teasdale themselves note, is a post hoc attempt to correct the deficiencies of the original model.The new version of the model introduces attribution as a cognitive event. While this addition may improve the explanatory power of the model, it also makes it more difficult to disprove because it now becomes necessary to specify the unobserved cognitive events (the kinds of attributions a person makes when faced with uncontrollable events) that determine helplessness and depressed behavior (Huesmann, 1978).

Because the model is so new there have not been many tests of its validity. The most recent study was designed to test the ability of the model to distinguish the attributional styles of depressed people from others. The responses of depressed college students were compared to non-depressed students in twelve hypothetical situations (i.e., "You have been looking for a job unsuccessfully for some time"). The depressed students invariably blamed their lack of success on personal shortcomings (internal), and long-term events (global) which were impossible to change (stable). Successes, on the other hand, were attributed to factors outside themselves (external) which were capable of being changed (unstable) (Seligman et al., 1979).

In Chapter 13, we saw how difficult it is to infer what goes on inside a person's head and what special care must be taken to avoid circular definitions. This problem is even further compounded by the fact that people are neither aware of nor can they accurately report the influences on their own behavior. After reviewing the data in attribution experiments, Nisbett and Wilson were forced to conclude, "It is frightening to believe that one has no more certain knowledge of the workings of one's own mind than would an outsider with intimate knowledge of one's history and the stimuli present at the time the cognitive event occurred" (1977, p. 257).

Despite these criticisms, the virtues of laboratory-based models of the behavior disorders should not be overlooked. Clinical observations of behavior generally tend to be so overinclusive that it is often difficult to see the forest for the trees. Laboratory models, on the other hand, reduce the number of influences on behavior to a manageable few and define them so that they are capable of being tested. The danger, of course, is that this process may lead to oversimplification as it apparently has in the case of the operant- and learned-helplessness explanations of depression. But it is also interesting to note that the treatment strategies these models have produced—a criterion for determining how valid they may be—were used to alleviate severe clinical depressions, as the cases in Chapter 8 demonstrated. In Chapter 15, we also see how mediational models of the behavior disorders have been used to formulate ideas for treatment.

chapter fifteen

Mediated Learning: Behavior Modification

One of the important differences between the methods of behavior modification derived from classical and operant conditioning described in Chapters 4 and 8 and those related to mediated learning which we discuss in this chapter is the relative emphasis that each places on the role of internal, or mediating, processes in determining behavior. The word *relative* is important here because, although both positions acknowledge the existence of private events not readily accessible to the observer, cognitive behavior therapists attach much more significance to them in their attempts to understand and change behavior.

The previous discussions of conditioning applied to behavior change assumed that responses such as thinking or imagining are involved in, or affected by, the conditioning process. So subjects or clients were required to imagine fearful scenes as part of the *desensitization* procedure, or thoughts about sexual aberrations were punished in *covert sensitization*. Moreover, as in the case of self-control and problem-solving, the choice of alternative goals could conceivably be made on the basis of thinking about them before the actual external, environmental changes were introduced to facilitate self-control.

But many behavior therapists who practice desensitization and other forms of behavioral intervention generally regard thoughts, beliefs, and perceptions as stimulus or response elements in the conditioning process rather than as distinct behaviors requiring special consideration (Wolpe, 1978). Others, who tend to view behavior in terms of operant learning, are inclined to relegate thinking to a secondary role in behavior analysis. They are much more concerned with how behavior is controlled by the environment than how the individual interprets or thinks about the environment.

Proponents of cognitive behavior modification, on the other hand, place a great deal more emphasis on cognitive processes as an essential link in the chain of events that ultimately leads to overt behavior. Thinking both precedes action and is affected by the consequences of the action. For some (Ellis, Beck), it is not enough to try to modify behavior by rearranging the environmental conditions that control it; an attempt must first be made to change the mediational (cognitive) processes through understanding and insight into the attitudes and beliefs assumed to be at the roots of the behavior. For others (Bandura, Mahoney), this process is more of a reciprocal relationship in which a change in overt behavior produces a change in the cognitive processes. The overt behavior is then maintained by both the cognitive processes and the effect it has on the environment (Bandura, 1977).

In this chapter, we survey the attempts that have been made to use mediational processes as the basis for behavior change.

OBSERVATIONAL LEARNING AND BEHAVIOR MODIFICATION

It was almost inevitable that so important a process for acquiring behavior as observational learning would ultimately find its way into the existing clinical methods for changing behavior. As we have already seen, however, the modeling procedures used extensively in behavior modification at the present time can be traced to an early attempt to eliminate children's fears of animals by using other fearless children as models. Following a suggestion by Watson and Rayner (Chapter 4) that fear might be eliminated through imitation learning, Mary Cover Jones (1924b) used a method she called "social imitation" to treat two children (22 and 30 months old) who were afraid of rabbits simply by permitting them to observe other children playing with rabbits.

Modeling, role playing, and imitation learning with adults found its way into clinical use in one form or another through Kelly's fixed-role therapy, Moreno's psychodrama, and Wolpe and Lazarus's use of modeling in behavior rehearsal. But the impetus for using modeling as a clinical tool came from the series of systematic studies on modeling and aggression conducted by Bandura and his associates (see Chapter 13).

Despite Bandura's assertion that "most external influences affect behavior through intermediary processes" (1977b, p. 10), research in observational learning and the clinical modeling strategy that developed out of it have been concerned almost exclusively with the factors which influence imitation learning *directly* and not with the *underlying processes*—attention, retention, and retrieval—which are assumed to act as mediators to behavior. In effect, very little effort has been made to indicate just how the mediational processes relate to the conditions which are assumed to affect them (Figure 13-5, Chapter 13) and how, in turn, these changes in mediation act to produce changes in behavior.

Studies in the clinical applications of observational learning have not been deduced from any theory or scheme of observational learning. Instead, they have been largely concerned with the optimal characteristics of the model—with the way in which imitation learning, for example, is influenced by (1) *live rather than filmed models*, (2) *multiple models and modeling situations rather than a single model*, (3) *participation on the part of the observer rather than simple observation, and (4) models who master the problem situation (mastery models) in contrast to those who cope (coping models) and solve the problem gradually.*

Reduction of Avoidance Behavior through Modeling

Sometime after Wolpe, and Stampfl and Levis had introduced desensitization and implosive therapy as clinical techniques for reducing phobic behavior, it occurred to Bandura that avoidance behavior might also be eliminated by having the apprehensive person watch others in the presence of the fear-arousing stimulus or while performing the dreaded response. The decision to use modeling as a possible clinical tool was suggested to him by Masserman's (1943) somewhat limited success in getting cats who had been made fearful of food to lose their inhibitions after observing other non-fearful cats approaching and eating the food, and by Jones's (1924b) use of imitation learning to reduce children's fear of rabbits.

The initial experiment conducted by Bandura, Grusec, and Menlove (1967) was specifically designed to test the supposition that modeling is an effective technique for reducing avoidance behavior in children who were extremely fearful of dogs. Because it is also conceivable that modeling would not be maximally effective unless the fearful stimulus was associated with pleasant feelings to counteract the anxiety, one condition of the experiment required that modeling take place in a party setting. The results of this study are presented in Figure 15-1. Children in the groups who either saw a boy interact with a dog in a fearless manner on a number of occasions during a party (model + positive context) or observed the model without the party (model + neutral context) were substantially less fearful in a subsequent test that required them to play with the dog or remain in a room with it for some period of time than were the other children who had no exposure to the model but saw the dog at a party (dog + positive context) or simply attended a party (positive context).

One interesting aspect of this study, apart from the relatively large reductions in avoidance behavior that were obtained through modeling, is the lack of difference in a fear reduction between those children who saw the modeling in the context of the party (model + positive context) and those who simply observed the model (model + neutral context) (Figure 15-1). These findings strongly suggest that counterconditioning is not an adequate explanation for those techniques in which individuals are exposed to fear-arousing stimuli to eliminate avoidance behavior, e.g., Jones's (1924 a,b) "direct conditioning" with Peter and the exposure techniques described in Chapter 4. As a learning process, counterconditioning requires that fear be replaced by some other incompatible response, in this

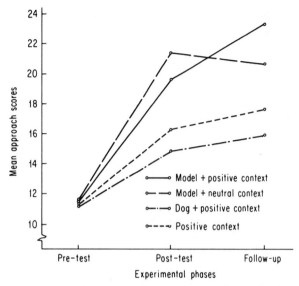

FIG. 15-1 Mean number of approach responses to the dog by dog-phobic children following one of four treatment conditions. (Source: A. Bandura, J.E. Grusec, and F.E. Menlove. Vicarious extinction of avoidance behavior. *Journal of Personality and Social Psychology*, 1967, 5, 16–23. Copyright 1967 American Psychological Association and used by permission.)

case the positive feelings generated by the party. Since the children's fears in the model + neutral group were extinguished without the benefit of a party and the pleasant sensations associated with it, very little in the way of counterconditioning could have occurred.

Live Models, Filmed Models, Multiple Models.   The success of live modeling as a technique for reducing or eliminating avoidance behavior suggested the further possibility that symbolic or filmed models could be used instead in order to make the treatment more practical and less cumbersome to administer. With this in mind, Bandura and Menlove (1968) set out to test the effectiveness of symbolic models in extinguishing avoidance behavior, and to investigate the additional proposition that extinction of the avoidance response would be facilitated by using many models in a variety of situations. In general, the use of filmed rather than live models was effective in extinguishing avoidance behavior of children who were extremely afraid of dogs. But the children who saw a single filmed model did not succeed in approaching the dog in the final test as well as the children who saw a live model in the study described previously. However, this loss of effectiveness in the use of filmed rather than live models was compensated for by the use of many models in a variety of situations. The children who were exposed to the multiple-model condition showed a continued improvement in their behavior and did as well as the children who had viewed the live model.

Modeling and Participation (Behavior Rehearsal). In a further attempt to identify the factors that might help to develop modeling as a useful therapeutic method, Bandura, Blanchard, and Ritter (1969) compared live modeling and active participation on the part of the observer with symbolic modeling and desensitization. The subjects in this experiment were adolescents and adults with severe snake phobias that seriously interfered with their activities and restricted their functioning. Prior to treatment, the extent of the snake phobia was determined for each subject, and each was assigned to one of four groups matched on the basis of the severity of the disorder.

Group I, *live modeling and guided participation,* observed the therapist handle a large king snake. They were encouraged and aided in touching and handling the snake through a series of graduated approaches paced according to the subject's ability to perform each of the tasks.

Group II, *symbolic modeling,* saw a film of children, adults, and adolescents engaging in progressively more fear-provoking activities with a snake. They were also able to regulate their progress by controlling the rate of presentation of the film through a remote device that started, stopped, or reversed the projector. These subjects were also instructed in relaxation.

Group III, *desensitization,* received the standard form of treatment devised by Wolpe in which the subjects were urged to confront a graded series of increasingly fear-provoking scenes with snakes in their imagination. All three groups spent an equal amount of time with the snakes, either live or in symbolic form.

Group IV, *control,* participated in the behavioral and attitudinal tests of snake avoidance but received no treatment.

As Fig. 15-2 indicates, all three of the treatment groups showed a marked decrease in snake-avoidance according to a behavioral test using two snakes of

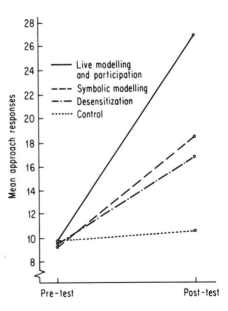

FIG. 15-2 Mean number of approach responses to the snake performed by subjects who received one of four treatment conditions. (Source: A. Bandura, E.B. Blanchard, and B.J. Ritter. The relative efficacy of desensitization and modeling therapeutic approaches for inducing behavioral, affective and attitudinal changes. *Journal of Personality and Social Psychology,* 1969, *13,* 173–199. Copyright 1969 American Psychological Association and used by permission.)

strikingly different colors. In the test, the subjects had to remove a snake from the cage, hold it with bare hands 5 inches from the face, and tolerate the snakes in their laps with their arms hung passively by their sides. These behavioral changes were also accompanied by changes in anxiety and in the attitudes toward snakes.

Follow-up 1 month after the experiment was terminated showed that the subjects, including the controls who were subsequently given treatment, were able to participate in activities such as camping, hiking, and gardening that they had formerly avoided because of the fear of snakes. Some of the subjects even served as model therapists for their acquaintances who were afraid of snakes. Certain fringe benefits were also obtained as a result of treatment. Most of the subjects reported increased confidence in their ability to cope with other fear-provoking events in their lives because of their increased confidence from overcoming the snake phobia (Bandura, 1968b, p. 210).

The superiority in performance of the live-modeling-and-participation group over the other two groups suggests that actually performing the feared act has many advantages over just observing others do it or thinking about doing it, the usual desensitization techniques. It also demonstrates that changes in attitudes are more likely to occur if the person first makes a successful attempt to perform the feared act. We have already seen how a great deal of emphasis is placed on *behavior rehearsal* and *role-playing* (Chapter 12) as a method of acquiring new skills. The behavior of the live-modeling-and-participation group indicates further that a combination of *modeling* and *behavior rehearsal* is a more effective technique for changing behavior than either of these methods used alone. (This issue reappears later in the chapter when the question of cognitive vs. behavioral change is discussed in the section on cognition and behavior modification.)

Mastery Modeling vs. Coping Modeling. Modeling strategies similar to those pioneered by Bandura and his associates have also been used to reduce fear associated with taking examinations and anxiety related to impending medical and surgical procedures.

The prevalence of test anxiety as incapacitating behavior has given rise to a variety of interesting modeling techniques designed to alleviate the fear of taking tests. Virtually all of these methods are based on the assumption that, although fear of failure is ultimately responsible for the poor performance, the behavior that actually interferes with test-taking is the thought of inadequacy and self-depreciation which occurs during the examination itself (Wine, 1971). As a consequence, the models used in these treatment packages generally talk to themselves while taking a test.

Some adopt a *mastery-model role* in which the thoughts expressed are mainly about the most adaptive methods for taking the test ("This question is difficult and needs more time. I'll answer the easy ones first").

Other models display a *coping technique,* first verbalizing the anxiety-arousing thoughts ("If I do badly on this test I'll never get a B in the course. I really need a B for my major"); second, making an adaptive response ("This isn't the time to worry about that, I'll read the next question carefully"); and finally, thinking positively about the performance ("It's working, I'm in control now").

Cooley (1976) has developed a series of modeling videotapes for reducing test-taking anxiety that uses a coping model and statements similar to those described above.

Modeling films have also been used to reduce fear associated with medical procedures. In one study, some of the children, ranging in age from 4–12, who were awaiting elective surgery such as hernia operations and tonsillectomies saw a film entitled "Ethan Has an Operation" showing a 7-year-old boy being prepared for a hernia operation. The children were able to follow the model through scenes showing blood tests being conducted, the operating room, and eventually the recovery room. In each of these scenes, the model displayed coping behavior by expressing his fears and apprehensions, conquering and overcoming them as the crucial moment approached, and completing each event successfully. Another group of children similarly awaiting surgery saw a film about a boy on a nature trip.

On the measures used to determine anxiety prior to surgery and during the 3- to 4-week postoperative recovery period, children who saw the modeling film reported less fear, showed less concern about hospitalization in general, and had fewer physiological signs of fear than did the comparable group of children who had watched the nature film. Moreover, the children who had not watched the surgical modeling film had considerably more problems at home after hospitalization (Melamed & Siegel, 1975). Similar modeling films have also been devised to reduce children's fear of dentists (Adelson et al., 1972; Shaw & Thoresen, 1974).

Building Up Behavioral Deficits: Learning Social Skills through Modeling

The primary purpose of the modeling procedures just described was to reduce avoidance behavior through exposure to a fearless model. Many avoidance behaviors, however, develop not because of the intrinsically threatening properties of the stimulus itself—for example, the danger a dog may convey—but because the necessary skills are simply not available to deal with a specific situation. The fear of social interaction, for instance, arises primarily out of the inability to say the right things or to behave in a manner that encourages others to respond in an amiable fashion. The origin of such behavior can probably be traced to childhood in which children who are not initially gregarious or outgoing remain social isolates largely because social interaction has not been encouraged, practiced, and rewarded. O'Connor (1969) has shown, however, that the use of symbolic modeling with socially withdrawn children can arrest the process by providing appropriate social skills to reduce social fears (Box 15-1).

BOX 15-1
Bringing Children Out With Modeling

The 13 isolate children O'Connor (1969) selected for his experiment were so withdrawn that they averaged less than 2 social interactions with other children in the 80 minutes during which they had been observed. In contrast to the non-isolate children who had more than 9 social interactions during the same period, the isolate children did not engage in any of the usual overtures toward other children that would ordinarily elicit recognition and attention. In fact, most of these socially withdrawn children frequently retreated into corners, closets, and lockers, behavior which had led their teachers to select them as isolates and to confirm the impressions formed by the experimenter-observers.

The modeling film shown to 6 of the 13 socially withdrawn children lasted only 23 minutes, but its effects were dramatic. The film presented a sequence of 11 scenes showing nursery school children in various stages of social interaction with each other and the rewards they got for their efforts. At first a child is shown observing the interaction of other children. The other children talk to the child model, offer him play materials, smile, and generally respond in a positive manner designed to get him to reciprocate. In the final scene, built up to gradually, a group of children gleefully toss play equipment around the room. During these scenes, a woman's soothing voice is heard describing the actions of the model and the responses of other children. The 7 isolate children who were used as controls saw a 20-minute film of cavorting porpoises. (This group was included to determine whether watching a film or attending nursery school in itself had any effect on isolate behavior.)

When the two groups of children were observed following their different experiences, the average number of social interactions for those children who had seen the modeling film increased from 2 to 11, exceeding the baseline of social interactions obtained earlier from a group of children who were not socially withdrawn (Figure 15-3). For some of the children, the number of social interactions actually rose from 2 to 25. The number of social interactions for the children who had seen the control film remained much the same as it had been.

The most extraordinary thing about this experiment, according to O'Connor, is that the changes in behavior were achieved in such a relatively short period of time—considerably less time than an individualized operant-shaping procedure would have taken. In addition, the changes were also obtained without the protracted intimate therapeutic relationship that has always been considered a necessary element in psychotherapy.

In an interesting extension of the experiment described in Box 15-1, which was designed to compare the effectiveness of modeling vs. shaping in modifying social withdrawal behavior, O'Connor (1972) clearly demonstrated that shaping by itself was not sufficient to produce stable behavior changes. The children who

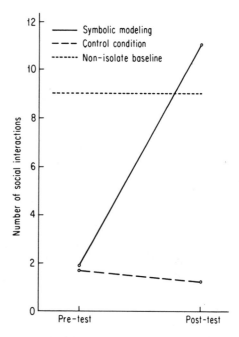

FIG. 15-3 Mean number of social interactions by children before and after exposure to each of the treatment conditions. The dotted line represents interactions of 26 non-isolate children observed during the pretest phase of the study. (Source: R.D. O'Connor. Modification of social withdrawal through symbolic modeling. *Journal of Applied Behavior Analysis*, 1969, *2*, 15–22. Used by permission.)

viewed the modeling film in this study made the same dramatic gains in social responsiveness as the comparable children described in Box 15-1. Those children who received consistent praise and attention (shaping) for all instances of social interaction also showed some increase in social responsiveness, but these gains were highly unstable and did not last beyond the 6-week follow-up period. A combination of shaping and modeling, however, showed durable changes in behavior similar to modeling alone.

The relatively poor performance of the children whose behavior was shaped by operant methods alone raises some substantial questions about contingency management that are not easily resolved—especially because these methods have proved to be uniformly successful in other situations (Chapters 7, 8, 9). One possible explanation for the failure to obtain durable results with the children who received shaping only is that the film provided the children who saw it with a variety of behaviors from which they could choose in social situations. At the same time, they were being "vicariously" reinforced for observing the children in the film engaging in successful interactions. The "shaped" children, on the other hand, had to learn all of these behaviors de novo, so to speak, without the "catalogue" benefit provided by the film. It is conceivable that while modeling is a much more rapid method for teaching new responses, reinforced practice for the shaped group, extended over a longer period, might have provided the same advantages. In any event, if the differences between the two methods continue to recur in similar studies, experiments will have to be devised to tease out the responsible factors.

O'Connor's relatively elaborate method for dealing with social withdrawal was subsequently reduced by Keller and Carlson (1974) to the use of social reinforcement as the most important element in developing and maintaining social interactions. Pre-school children saw four short videotapes of other children praising and approving the behavior of their peers. The amount of social reinforcement and, in turn, social interaction displayed by the children who saw the film increased significantly immediately following the film viewing, and they still maintained this 3 weeks after the initial assessment.

Modeling has also been used to improve social behavior in chronic, hospitalized, schizophrenic and mentally retarded psychiatric patients (Jaffe & Carlson, 1976). The modeling treatment, which was compared to both instructions and attention, involved exposure to videotaped demonstrations of appropriate social behaviors. The models in the videotape showed how to initiate activities, such as having coffee and cigarettes or playing a game of ring-toss with another person, or how to respond to social overtures. After viewing the film, each subject in the modeling group was required to engage in behavior rehearsal by repeating the role of initiator or respondent. The patients in the instruction group merely followed instructions but were not shown the videotape. Those in the attention group simply interacted with the attendant according to a prearranged script without videotape or instructions to imitate. On an overall index of change in social behavior, both the modeling and instruction groups showed significant improvement in appropriate social skills while the attention group remained at their previous level of social adjustment.

The relative success of modeling in treatment has recently been confirmed in a comprehensive review of the use of videotape and film modeling as therapeutic devices (Thelen et al., 1979). After enumerating the large variety of situations in which modeling has been used effectively and discussing its potentially promising future, the authors also point out the urgent need for studies that involve more clinical and disturbed populations, that systematically vary the treatment components, that use several measures to assess behavior change, and that consider the pervasive question of generalization and maintenance of treatment effects.

COGNITION IN BEHAVIOR MODIFICATION

"Psychotherapy," according to Meehl, "is the art of applying a science which does not yet exist" (1960). This observation is nowhere more evident than in the attempts being made to explain behavior change in terms of cognitive learning. Here, unlike applied classical and operant conditioning, the technology seems to have outdistanced the science and given rise to a collection of relatively effective methods for changing behavior which have very little by way of explicit general principles to support them.

But this is no indictment of cognitive behavior modification. Technology frequently precedes systematic explanation. We used the lever, for example, long before we understood its mathematical and physical principles, and the methods for changing behavior that work will undoubtedly continue to be used, even though the explanations for their effectiveness often involve inferences about unobserved events (thoughts, attributions, and so on) which are not carefully defined according to the criteria discussed in Chapter 13 on mediated learning.

Our task in this section, then, is to determine the extent to which the use of mediational processes, such as cognitions, improves the understanding and predictability of behavior. In practical terms, we have the extremely difficult (if not almost impossible) job of deciding whether a primary preoccupation with thoughts, beliefs, attitudes, attributions, and expectations in therapy facilitates behavior change beyond that which could be expected by concentrating solely on the relationship between external, observable behavior and the environment.

Cognitive Restructuring

The term *cognitive restructuring,* which is often used to designate what goes on in cognitive behavior therapy, derives from the cognitive and gestalt theorists' belief that learning is an internal process that involves a restructuring of the perceptual field and a reorganization of thoughts about the relationship of events in the environment (Chapter 13). In cognitive restructuring as a form of intervention, ultimate changes in overt behavior are achieved *primarily* by influencing the thoughts, perceptions, and attributions about external events rather than in changing overt behavior directly by varying some aspect of the environment.

Cognitive restructuring is actually a generic term which includes all those forms of treatment involving cognitive factors. While it is certainly true that the more traditional forms of psychotherapy, such as psychoanalysis, can be called cognitive by these standards, our concern is principally with those treatment strategies in which learning is assumed to play a dominant role and in which the rationale has either been established on the basis of known psychological principles and/or supported by research.

Rational-Emotive Therapy (RET). According to Ellis (1977), its originator, RET emerged out of a desire to establish a more "rational" and behaviorally grounded form of treatment following a disenchantment with psychoanalysis (1977, p. 4). Much of Ellis' earlier work (1949, 1957) clearly suggests that RET began as part of a practical effort to change behavior rapidly by dealing with irrational beliefs in the present, and that its relationship to learning principles in general, and cognitive learning in particular, was established somewhat later (Goldfried & Davison, 1976).

In recent years, RET has grown into a formidable alternative to other psychotherapies, especially for those therapists who prefer a more direct and less protracted behavioral approach. The technique is explicit and free from any elaborate and tortuous conceptions of personality development. It has also influenced some of the other cognitive restructuring therapies, such as Meichenbaum's self-instruction training and Beck's cognitive therapy for depression which attempt to produce behavior change by modifying self-statements and negative thought processes.

The basic ideas behind RET, which Ellis refers to as the ABCDEs, are essentially straightforward and conform in large measure to the simple scheme presented in Figure 13-3 (Chapter 13, p. 319). A, which is equivalent to a stimulus or activating event, is commonly regarded by most people as being responsible for C, the behavioral consequence. For example, A may represent being fired from a good job, and C, the emotional depression and lack of ambition which follows. Most of us are inclined to believe that C is caused by A, but according to Ellis:

> . . . this conclusion does not follow, and represents . . . a *non sequitur.* For what really happened included A (the job loss) and C, the consequence of the loss . . . (no longer getting what we wanted); and even at that C didn't *automatically* follow from A but from B, your Belief about A. What Belief? Well, the fairly obvious Belief, "I liked the job I had; and because I liked it I did not *want* to lose it; and because I did not want to lose it, I consider its loss bad, unfortunate, or disadvantageous." (A. Ellis. In A. Ellis and R. Grieger [Eds.], *Handbook of Rational-Emotive Therapy.* New York: Springer Publishing Co., 1977, p. 6. Used by permission.)

Ellis contends that people get into behavioral difficulties, not because of the things that occur to them but because of the way they view these occurrences (their attributions).

It follows logically from such a view of the development of behavior problems that the most expedient way to change behavior would be to assault the irrational *beliefs* (B1) which are basically responsible for the emotional distress and the inappropriate behavior rather than the onset behavior or the events themselves.

The DEs of the ABCDEs in rational-emotive therapy are the treatment strategies and effects which follow from analyzing the irrational beliefs and dealing with them directly. The beliefs are "defined, discriminated, debated, and disputed" until they are discarded and a new way of thinking—a new cognitive effect (E)—is achieved (Ellis, 1977). The core of RET is assumed to be the debating and disputing in therapy which changes the attributions and expectancies and ultimately the overt behavior itself (Box 15-2).

BOX 15-2
RET—The "Pull-Up-Your-Socks Therapy"

One of the fascinating features of RET is the extent to which the therapist assumes a disarmingly candid and, in some instances, forthrightly belligerent role about the client's tendency to disregard reality or to overlook the irrational aspects of behavior. Ellis frequently brings clients up short, telling them that it is necessary in life to distinguish between a catastrophe and a mere pain-in-the-ass, or that life, whether they like it or not, is generally spelled HASSLE and one rarely gets gain without pain. "Tough!" says Ellis (1977, p. 267).

The most prominent aspect of RET, however, is the way in which the therapist constantly rehearses the ABCDEs of RET with the client as this excerpt from one of Ellis's cases with an unassertive woman illustrates.

Susan had been assuming a submissive role with her friend, Josephine, who always managed to maneuver the most desirable males away from her on blind dates. According to Ellis, although Susan had benefited to some extent from the *activity homework assignments, assertion training (behavior rehearsal)*, and *operant conditioning* by forcing herself to be as determined as Josephine, the real breakthrough in her behavior came after the following session in which Susan "saw what the ABCs of her unassertiveness were all about" (Ellis, 1977, pp. 163–174). The ensuing dialogue took place after Josephine went back on her word not to entice a male who had shown interest in Susan.

Susan: No. My mind's blank.

Therapist: Well, unblank it! What would virtually any woman tell herself if her friend agreed not to go off with a male who was interested in her and then actually did so?

Susan: That . . . that's a dirty deed!

Therapist: Yes, but that's a rational Belief again. For it probably *is*, empirically speaking, a dirty deed. Now, what's the irrational Belief?

Susan: (Looks puzzled. Silence.)

Therapist: And that dirty deed is—? What?

Susan: Awful!

Therapist: Right! "It's *awful* that Josephine did that to me again! How *could* she do it? She *shouldn't* have done that dirty deed."

Susan: Right! She *shouldn't* have done it.

Therapist: Why the hell *shouldn't* she?

Susan: Well, I wouldn't do it to her, for one thing.

Therapist: And *therefore* she shouldn't do it to me? Does that really follow?

Susan: No. I see what you mean. No matter how I would behave, she has a perfect right to behave as she does.
. . .

Therapist: And how about your irrational Belief, "She shouldn't have done that dirty deed!" Well?

Susan: Well, of course, that's nonsense. I can't command that she not do what she does.
. . .

Therapist: Right. Now let's review. Spell out the A-B-Cs that you are making up about Josephine; and how you could Dispute, at D, your irrational Beliefs, at B.

Susan: All right. At A, she Agrees not to be too pushy about walking off with all the attractive men we meet together, especially when one seems to be interested in me. And she then actually does me in and maneuvers the better of the two guys to take her, instead of me, home. At C I feel angry at her, but do nothing to stop her.

Therapist: Right. Because at B—what?

Susan: At B, I'm first telling myself, rationally, that she's doing a dirty deed to me, and I don't like it. Then I'm telling myself irrationally, that she *shouldn't* be doing that bitchy deed and is *a* bitch for doing it.

Therapist: Correct. Now, what can you do, at D, to Dispute your irrational Belief?

Susan: Ask myself, *"Why* shouldn't she be doing that deed?" and "How does it make her *a* total bitch for doing it?"

Therapist: Exactly. And your answer, or the new philosophic Effect, at E?

Susan: That people behave the way they behave, including Josephine. That *it would be nice* if she didn't behave that way, but that's no reason why she shouldn't. And that she isn't a *bitch,* but merely a fucked up human who often acts bitchily.

. . .

Susan: Let me start with C, the way it tells you to do on your Homework report. At C, I act unassertively and feel anxious. At A, Josephine is, as usual, trying to get her way and make off with the more attractive guy. Because at B, I am first telling myself, rationally, "I don't like her behavior, and I'd better stop her before she gets away with it!" But at B I'm also telling myself, irrationally, and much more strongly, "If I stop her she won't like me— and that would be terrible! I *must* have Josephine's approval, even if I keep losing the guys I want because I let her go after them first." And my irrational idea, at B, is the real thing that makes me act so unassertively and weakly at C.

Therapist: Exactly, and what could D and E be?

Susan: Uh, let me see. D—"Why would it be terrible if Josephine doesn't like me?" And, "Where is the evidence that I *must* have her approval?" E—"It's not terrible if Josephine doesn't like me, only inconvenient. And it even has its conveniences! And there is no reason why I *must* have her approval, though it would be nice if I did have it."

Therapist: Right. And what behavioral Effect do you think you'd get, at E again, if you kept Disputing your irrational Beliefs persistently and strongly?

Susan: I think I'd begin to speak up, to assert myself in going off with the good guy, and probably much more often get what I really wanted.

Therapist: I think so, too. Why not try it and see? Force yourself to see the bullshit you are telling yourself, at B, and to Dispute it vigorously at D. Also: *Let's give you the actual homework assignments of (1) speaking to Josephine again about this general problem that you have with her, and (2) definitely speaking up and challenging her the very next time she attempts to walk off with a male in whom you are interested.*

Susan: I'll definitely work on that.

(From A. Ellis, in V. Franks and V. Burtle (Eds.), *Women in Therapy.* New York: Brunner/Mazel, 1974. Copyright 1974 Brunner/Mazel. Used by permission. Italics added.)

The feeling that most people have that they *must* do something is a self-indulgent response that Ellis has labeled "musturbation."

Is it effective—and why? If the voluminous research literature which has accumulated around RET is any measure of its effectiveness, then it must be judged a useful method for dealing with behavior problems (Mahoney, 1974; DiGiuseppe & Miller, 1977; Ellis, 1977) according to a recent survey. Most outcome studies involving RET exclusively, in combination with other forms of behavioral methods, or in comparison with other therapies suggest that "(1) rational-emotive therapy is more effective than client-centered therapy with introverted persons; (2) it is more effective than systematic desensitization in the reduction of general or pervasive anxiety; (3) a combination of cognitive therapy and behavior therapy appears to be the most efficacious treatment for depression; (4) the relative effectiveness of rational-emotive therapy versus assertive training is inconclusive due to limited and confounded research" (DiGiuseppe & Miller, 1977, p. 89).

But *whether* RET works and *why* it works are two basically different questions. Ellis maintains that RET works primarily because it deals with irrational thoughts rather than directly with inappropriate overt behavior. Yet, a significant component in the RET treatment package, as we have already seen from the case report in Box 15-2, is the use of *activity homework assignments* (especially when Ellis assigns Susan the task of speaking to Josephine about the general problem again, and challenging Josephine the next time she attempts to lure a male away from her), *assertiveness training,* and *operant conditioning, all* of which deal directly with overt behavior and do not require a cognitive explanation for their effectiveness.

In a note on Emmelkamp's et al. study (see below) demonstrating the superiority of exposure to cognitive restructuring as a form of treatment for agoraphobics, Ellis (1979) indicates that assignments are almost invariably incorporated into RET, especially in the case of agoraphobia. Under these circumstances, it is impossible to sort out which of the elements in RET are critical without experiments specifically designed to study the components in isolation.

While such studies attempting to determine the relative contributions of cognitive restructuring and behavioral assignments have been rare and generally inconclusive, a recent experiment by Emmelkamp, Kuipers, and Eggerat (1978) argues convincingly against the idea that cognitive restructuring is explicitly necessary to bring about behavioral change in a clinical population.

The subjects in the Emmelkamp et al. study were severe agoraphobics who were unable to venture into public places. Most had been this way for a period of 7 years. One group was administered a treatment package consisting of re-labeling (a method designed to help clients understand the nature of their responses to phobic situations), a variation of RET consisting of an examination and discussion of irrational beliefs specific to agoraphobia, and a form of self-instructional training which enabled the clients to become conscious of negative self-statements during anxious periods and replace them by productive self-statements. A second group was treated solely with prolonged exposure in vivo involving trips to supermarkets and restaurants, for example, in a group accompanied by the therapists.

The results of this study are illustrated in Figure 15-4. Prolonged exposure proved to be clearly superior to cognitive restructuring not only in terms of the actual amount of time spent in feared situations but also on all of the questionnaires used to assess phobic anxiety, mood, and self-expression. In general, the cognitive-reduction group showed very little behavior change.

A more recent study was conducted by Emmelkamp and his associates (1980) to determine the relative contribution of cognitive modification procedures in a treatment strategy involving both self-instructional training and exposure in vivo. Obsessive-compulsive patients were trained to become conscious of their negative self-statements and to replace them with positive self-statements prior to in vivo exposure to the feared stimulus. According to Emmelkamp et al., the addition of self-instructional training did nothing to enhance the effectiveness of in vivo exposure.

There are two possible reasons for the failure of cognitive restructuring with agoraphobics in Emmelkamp's study, and the successes reported by DiGiuseppe and Miller (1977) in their review of RET outcome studies. In the first place, the

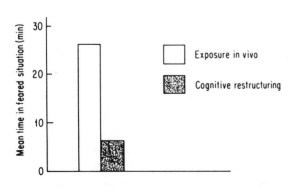

FIG. 15-4 Mean change scores (time spent in feared situations for agoraphobic subjects following exposure in vivo or cognitive restructuring. (Source: P.M.G. Emmelkamp, A.C.M. Kuipers and J.B. Eggerat. Cognitive modification versus prolonged exposure *in vivo:* A comparison with agoraphobics as subjects. *Behaviour Research and Therapy,* 1978, *16,* 33–41. Copyright 1978 Pergamon Press and used by permission.)

subjects used in the RET outcome studies were, for the most part, college students with varying degrees of test-taking, public speaking, or interpersonal anxiety. Compared to agoraphobics, college students exhibit relatively low levels of anxiety that may yield more readily to cognitive methods. Previous studies by Emmelkamp (1979) confirm this observation. When volunteer students were used as subjects, cognitive behavior modification was found to be quite effective. "The difference in outcome between clinical studies and analogue studies" (using college students), according to Emmelkamp (1980), "clearly demonstrates the necessity of testing therapeutic procedures with clinical patients" (1980, p. 65).

Second, and what is perhaps more important, the agoraphobic subjects who received cognitive restructuring only were never exposed to fear-arousing situations, i.e., they were never required to ride on trolleys or go to the supermarket, for instance. In the studies cited by DiGiuseppe and Miller, on the other hand, both cognitive restructuring and overt behavioral procedures were confounded because the subjects were invariably required to face the thing they feared and to practice some form of behavior rehearsal.

The Use of Cognitive Restructuring in Depression. Beck's use of cognitive therapy in the depressive disorders is consistent with the reasoning behind cognitive restructuring in general and, as we shall shortly see, is part of the treatment strategies implied by the recent reformulation of the learned helplessness model.

The major difference between the operant (Ferster, Lewinsohn) and cognitive (Beck, Seligman, et al.) views of depression lies in the relative emphasis each places on the importance of environmental and cognitive events in the formation of depressed behavior. While both views probably agree that the pervasive loss of positive or negative reinforcement is the precipitating event in depression, the cognitive view further assumes that the depressed behavior is ultimately determined by the individual's *interpretation* of the loss.

The difference is important in determining just exactly where treatment is to begin. For Lewinsohn, as we saw in Chapter 8, treatment begins and ends with the rewarded learning of the correct skills necessary to generate social reinforcement from others. Beck, on the other hand, begins with an analysis of the irrational, negative self-attitudes which characterize the depressed condition, and then he proceeds toward the use of behavioral situations designed to change the negative attitudes.

According to Beck, the "primary triad" in depression consists of three major cognitive patterns that force individuals to view themselves, the world, and the future in a negative way. In the first of these, people interpret their interactions with the environment in terms of defeat, deprivation, and disparagement. In the second, they attribute all of the unpleasant experiences they encounter to their own inadequacy and deficiency and make logical errors in interpreting reality. For example, depression-prone people tend to overgeneralize their negative experiences by concluding that they are characteristically stupid or inept on the basis of a few incidents. Finally, they tend to look at the future as a life of unremitting hardship, frustration, and deprivation. This triad leads inevitably to depressed moods, paralysis of will, avoidance wishes, suicidal thoughts, and increased dependency (1967, pp. 255–256).

Because the primary problem in depression, according to Beck, is the misinterpretation and distortion of experience, the goal of therapy is to identify the thoughts and images associated with negative experiences that lead automatically to a depressed state. Once this is done, the therapist enters into a dialogue with the client not unlike that which Ellis employs in rational-emotive therapy and for the same reasons—to challenge the irrational beliefs and self-debasement that form the basis of the depression. Beck views this as the equivalent of formulating and testing hypotheses.

A 38-year-old manufacturer, for example, who had made a series of injudicious decisions which led to financial loss, invariably blamed himself for most of the negative events that touched him one way or another. On one occasion, he took the responsibility for a stock loss his friend had suffered on the grounds that he had, albeit reluctantly, given his friend advice to buy the stock. The advice consisted of a casual "sounds okay" at a party. During therapy, he was disabused of his responsibility in the loss when the therapist pointed out to him all of the other factors that were probably more important in his friend's decision to buy the stock. Actual investigation revealed that the friend had already decided to buy before he had asked the client (Shaw & Beck, 1977, p. 318–319).

As in RET, cognitive behavior therapy for depression employs role playing, behavior rehearsal, and homework assignments, in general, to supplement the cognitive exploration. In the case cited above, for example, the client was assigned a series of simple, but inevitably rewarding tasks to counter the belief that he was totally inadequate. He was asked to wash and dry his own clothes, and despite his negative predictions about the outcome, he was successful. On another occasion, "reverse role playing" was used when the client was asked to assume the role of an acquaintance who had made a mistake adding up the bill at a restaurant. When the client had played himself in this incident, he envisioned others at the table thinking of him as a "basket case" for making the errors. When the role was reversed, however, he was sympathetic to the person who had made the error which helped to "defuse" his own continual self-criticism.

Most of the outcome studies show that a combination of cognitive and behavior therapy for depressed people is superior to no treatment at all, and this establishes the fact that the technique appears to work (Shaw & Beck, 1977). In addition, one ongoing study at the University of Pennsylvania shows clearly that cognitive therapy is much more effective than therapy with an antidepressant drug (imipramine hydrochloride). Seventy-eight percent of the patients in the cognitive therapy group showed marked improvement or complete remission of symptoms, as opposed to 22% of the patients treated with pharmacotherapy. Moreover, the dropout rate was significantly higher with drug treatment (8 patients) than with cognitive therapy (1 patient) (Rush et al., 1977).

It is important to note that, as in RET, some form of direct behavioral intervention, such as contingency management (reward training), prolonged exposure, or behavior rehearsal, is used as an adjunct to the cognitive procedures. Although the combination of the two seems to be an effective method for treating depressions (Shaw & Beck, 1977), the relative weight contributed by each still remains to be determined.

Attribution Theory: Implications for the Treatment of Depression. In revising the learned helplessness model to include attribution as a cognitive element in depression, Abramson, Seligman, and Teasdale have drawn much closer to the treatment methods already proposed and used by Ellis and Beck.

According to the reformulated hypothesis, depression generally occurs when (a) the expectation of rewarding experiences is low or the expectation of aversive or punishing experiences is high, (b) the actual rate of positive experiences is low and the rate of negative experiences high, (c) the events producing positive or negative experiences are regarded as uncontrollable, and (d) individuals attribute the uncontrollability to some general, unchangeable characteristic of themselves (the equivalence of Beck's "overgeneralization") (1978, pp. 69–70).

Because the factors responsible for producing depression (or many of the problem behaviors for that matter) are fairly consistent with those suggested by Ellis and Beck, the treatment strategies are also likely to be the same as those they used. Table 15-1 indicates that this is generally the case. As with Ellis and Beck, the treatment procedures are designed to change expectations and attributions, either directly, by focusing on the illogical and negative thoughts (e.g., B, a, 2 in Table 15-1, "You are not the most unattractive person in the world—consider the counterevidence," and D, a and b in Table 15-1), or by bringing about changes in the environment that will produce changes in the expectations and attributions (A, B, and C in Table 15-1). Most of the proposals for treatment generated by the revised helplessness model still must be tested experimentally.

Modifying What People Say to Themselves: Stress Inoculation. Cognitive processes have been conceptualized in many ways by different therapists, according to Meichenbaum. They have been viewed as (1) behavior similar to overt behavior and following the same laws of learning, (2) part of a response chain, (3) instances of irrational thinking styles (Beck), (4) instances of irrational belief systems (Ellis), (5) instances of problem-solving ability, and (6) instances of defense mechanisms. But, Meichenbaum further asserts, no matter how therapists look at cognitions or what aspect of behavior they choose to emphasize during therapy, the "final common pathway to behavior change is through the alteration in the internal dialogues"—the changes in the things people say to themselves (1976, pp. 224–243).

The difference between abnormal and normal behavior, Meichenbaum argues, is not so much in the quantity or quality of the irrational beliefs or styles that people have, but in the way in which people cope with these beliefs. In fact, the things they say to themselves about their beliefs may ultimately determine their success or failure in managing their problems. This formulation led to a form of treatment which, while employing some of the more standard techniques, such as desensitization and modeling, placed a great deal of emphasis on self-statements and self-instruction as coping skills and, ultimately, gave rise to a procedure known

TABLE 15-1   Implications for Treatment from the Attribution Theory of Learned Helplessness

A. Change the estimated probability of the relevant event's occurrence: Reduce estimated likelihood for aversive outcomes and increase estimated likelihood for desired outcomes.

   a. Environmental manipulation by social agencies to remove aversive outcomes or provide desired outcomes, for example, rehousing, job placement, financial assistance, provision of nursery care for children.

   b. Provision of better medical care to relieve pain, correct handicaps, for example, prescription of analgesics, provision of artificial limbs and other prostheses.

B. Make the highly preferred outcomes less preferred.

   a. Reduce the aversiveness of highly aversive outcomes.

      1. Provide more realistic goals and norms, for example, failing to be top of your class is not the end of the world—you can still be a competent teacher and lead a satisfying life.

      2. Attentional training and/or reinterpretation to modify the significance of outcomes perceived as aversive, for example, you are not the most unattractive person in the world. "Consider the counterevidence" (Beck, Ellis).

      3. Assist acceptance and resignation.

   b. Reduce the desirability of highly desired outcomes.

      1. Assist the attainment of alternative available desired outcomes, for example, encourage the disappointed lover to find another boy or girl friend.

      2. Assist reevaluation of unattainable goals.

      3. Assist renunciation and relinquishment of unattainable goals.

C. Change the expectation from uncontrollability to controllability.

   a. When responses are not yet within the person's repertoire but can be, train the necessary skills, for example, social skills, child management skills, skills of resolving marital differences, problem-solving skills, and depression-management skills.

   b. When responses are within the person's repertoire, modify the distorted expectation that the responses will fail.

      1. Prompt performance of relevant, successful responses, for example, graded task assignment (Burgess, 1968).

      2. Generalized changes in response-outcome expectation resulting from successful performance of other responses, for example, prompt general increase in activity; teach more appropriate goal-setting and self-reinforcement; help to find employment.

      3. Change attributions for failure from inadequate ability to inadequate effort causing more successful responding.

      4. Imaginal and miniaturized rehearsal of successful response-outcome sequences: Assertive training, decision-making training, and role playing.

D. Change unrealistic attributions for failure toward external, unstable, specific; change unrealistic attributions for success toward internal, stable, global.

   a. For failure

      1. External: for example, "The system minimized the opportunities of women. It is not that you are incompetent."

2. Unstable: for example, "The system is changing. Opportunities that you can snatch are opening at a great rate."
3. Specific: for example, "Marketing jobs are still relatively closed to women, but publishing jobs are not" (correct overgeneralization).
  b. For success
1. Internal: for example, "He loves you because you are nurturant not because he is insecure."
2. Stable: for example, "Your nurturance is an enduring trait."
3. Global: for example, "Your nurturance pervades much of what you do and is appreciated by everyone around you."

SOURCE: Abramson, Seligman & Teasdale, 1978.

as *stress inoculation.* The purpose of stress inoculation is to prepare individuals for any future stress situation by teaching them appropriate self-statements and behaviors as coping mechanisms.

Self-statements as self-instruction were initially used in a program to teach impulsive children how to exercise control over non-verbal behavior. Some improvement in performance on the Porteus maze and the WISC was obtained by having the children slow down through a cognitive self-guidance technique in which they watched a model perform a task while verbally instructing himself in the details of the task (Meichenbaum & Goodman, 1969). It soon became apparent, however, that although cognitive modeling was a necessary condition for increasing self-control, it was also important that the impulsive child "try out" the instructions. Cognitive modeling produced slower performance, but cognitive modeling *and* self-instructional behavior rehearsal were required for both slower and more accurate performance (Meichenbaum & Goodman, 1971). It is also interesting to note that while kindergarten children benefited from overt self-instruction, forcing first-grade children to talk to themselves aloud interfered with their performance on a motor task.

The value of self-instruction as a method for reducing anxiety was also demonstrated with the obligatory snake-phobia, speech-anxiety, and test-anxiety groups. In reviewing these studies, Meichenbaum and Cameron (1977) generally support the conclusions drawn from the other cognitive restructuring experiments (Ellis, Beck), that the addition of cognitive methods to the behavioral techniques appears to improve the efficacy of either alone. They also cite a study by Wine (1971) which strongly suggests that simply making test-anxious subjects aware of the self-statements that arouse anxiety can actually be a deteriorative process *unless awareness is accompanied by self-instructions and practice of behavior incompatible with the anxiety-inducing cues.*

Stress inoculation was originally conceived by Meichenbaum and Cameron (1972; Meichenbaum, 1977) as an extension of the self-instructional, coping-skills method specifically designed to prepare people to cope with future stress situations while learning how to deal with current problems.

In the first, or *educational phase,* of treatment, emphasis is placed on "conceptualizing" the problem. The clients concentrate on the thoughts and physiological responses that occur during the fear-arousing situation. In the study reported by Meichenbaum and Cameron (1972), for example, clients who were severely incapacitated by rat and snake phobias were made aware of their increased heart rate, sweaty palms, and bodily tensions, as well as their thoughts and self-statements ("I can't do this. What if the snake gets out. I'll lose control") during the first of six interviews.

The second, or *rehearsal phase* was directed toward learning a set of coping skills consisting of (a) physical relaxation for the purpose of controlling the physiological arousal, and (b) modified self-statements ("Don't worry, worry won't help anything," or "Relax; you're in control. Take a slow deep breath") (Meichenbaum, 1977).

The final, or *application phase* of training consists of exposure to a variety of stressors in the laboratory or consulting room (unpredictable electric shock, cold pressors, failure, and embarrassment have been used in these instances) in order to give the client an opportunity to practice and experiment with the coping skills learned in the previous phase of training. In this situation, the therapist also models several ways in which the coping skills could be used with a stressor.

According to Meichenbaum and Cameron (Meichenbaum, 1977), the stress-inoculation training for the rat- and snake-phobic subjects proved to be more effective in reducing fear of both rats and snakes than desensitization. Moreover, subjects who were given stress-inoculation training for rats only were later able to generalize the coping skills to overcome their fear of snakes as well. For the desensitized subjects, however, only minimal generalization of fear reduction from rats to snakes or vice versa was evident.

Stress-inoculation procedures were also applied to a group of 34 volunteer subjects (18 male, 16 female), ranging in age from 17 to 42, who had serious difficulty controlling their anger (Novaco, 1975; Meichenbaum, 1977). Many were involved in assaults against other people, others had hurled a brick through a window, kicked in a glass door when refused service, or decorated a wall with blood from injuries incurred by intentionally smashing a fist against a wall. Treatment was based on the assumption that anger is generated and maintained by self-statements made in moments of provocation.

Accordingly, the subjects were first made aware of the emotions and thoughts during the educational phase of treatment (anger, perception of threat to self-worth, acts of antagonism to regain control of the situation) and taught cognitive and behavioral alternatives in those situations where loss of control was imminent during the rehearsal phase. They applied the new coping skills in simulated instances where they imagined various provocative situations. As in most other studies where comparisons are made between different treatment methods, a combination of self-instruction and relaxation was reported to be superior to either method alone on physiological and subjective measures of anger obtained in the laboratory. A daily diary of "anger experiences" kept by the subjects also confirmed the laboratory findings.

Stress-inoculation appears to be gaining popularity as a treatment method that combines both cognitive and behavioral techniques. Meichenbaum (1977) cites its use as an experimental procedure for control of pain and in the anger-management training of law enforcement officers. In his candid appraisal of stress inoculation in particular, and self-instructional methods, in general, Meichenbaum suggests that "the efficacy of stress inoculation is encouraging but not proven. The data on full usefulness of the procedure have yet to be obtained" (1977, p. 181).

Cognitive restructuring: an appraisal. At the beginning of this section on cognition and behavior modification, we undertook to determine whether the use of cognitive factors makes a difference in the understanding and control of behavior for purposes of behavior change. Let us now review the available evidence to see whether or not such a determination is possible.

1. *Are there important differences among the cognitive restructuring methods?* Because the aim of all cognitive behavior modification is to change overt behavior by way of changes in faulty attitudes, thoughts, and beliefs, the methods for doing this are bound to be fairly uniform. The differences which do exist among cognitive intervention methods seem to reflect nuances of style rather than crucial differences in theory that might have an important bearing on the effectiveness of treatment.

Ellis, Beck, and the newly reformulated learned helplessness model stress the assumptions, premises, and attributions held by individuals which give rise to problem behavior. Beck and Meichenbaum, on the other hand, seem much less concerned than Ellis with the reasons behind the irrational thinking and more involved in stimulating an awareness of the link between faulty thinking (negative self-statements) and the emotional states they produce. Meichenbaum places more emphasis on the use of problem-solving and coping skills (1977, pp. 197–198). And finally, the revised attribution model of depression seems to incorporate all the procedures used by the others. The lack of research on the relative effectiveness of the different cognitive restructuring methods per se, however, suggests that the advocates of each of the methods may, in fact, regard these differences as trivial.

Whatever minor differences in method exist among the cognitive restructuring procedures, the one thing they all seem to have in common is a widespread use of "adjunctive behavior-therapy" techniques. Desensitization, behavior rehearsal, and response-contingency strategies are extensively employed either as "homework assignments" (Ellis), "graded-task assignments" (Beck), "rational reevaluation during fear-arousal" (Goldfried), "problem-solving" and "coping-skills rehearsal" (Meichenbaum), and "manipulation of environmental events" (Abramson, Seligman, and Teasdale).

The use of these methods indicates an explicit recognition that exposure and practice are necessary parts of behavior change—that making a successful effort to do something that was formerly regarded as impossible is intrinsically rewarding and helps to consolidate the "new way" of thinking.

The use of "behavioral techniques" in cognitive therapy serves a dual purpose, according to Shaw and Beck. The first is "to produce change in the patient's passivity, avoidance, and lack of gratification." The second is "to stimulate empirical evaluation of depressed peoples' belief of inadequacy and incompetence—to reinforce activity and effort" (1977, p. 314).

2. Is it effective and why? Most of the evidence from single case presentations and group studies indicates that cognitive behavior modification is an effective method for changing behavior and alleviating many of the difficult problems in living (Ellis, 1977; DiGiuseppe & Miller, 1977; Goldfried, 1978; Shaw & Beck, 1977; Meichenbaum, 1977). Unfortunately, as we have already seen in the discussion of RET, the presence of behavioral techniques in virtually all of the clinical studies using cognitive restructuring methods makes it impossible to evaluate the importance of the cognitive component alone.

Where comparisons between cognitive methods and desensitization have been attempted (mostly with college students suffering from test-anxiety, speech-anxiety, or fear of rats, spiders, or snakes) the results are inconclusive, sometimes favoring one form of treatment, sometimes another (Ledwidge, 1978).

In those rare instances in which one of the treatment groups receives only cognitive restructuring, i.e., without desensitization, prolonged exposure to the fear-arousing conditions, or behavior rehearsal, the results were strikingly in favor of the group receiving either the behavior procedures alone or in some combination with a cognitive technique (D'Zurilla et al., 1973; Mahoney, 1974; Emmelkamp et al., 1978; Linehan et al., 1979; Emmelkamp, et al., 1980). In fact, in most studies where cognitive restructuring was used without some sort of behavior intervention, the result was weak and inconsistent behavior change.

Apparently, prolonged exposure to the fear-arousing situation (without permitting escape or avoidance to occur) and/or behavior rehearsal are still the necessary elements in any of the procedures for changing behavior. But, since the addition of a cognitive component (rational arguments, exhortation, identification of erroneous and negative self-statements) seems to facilitate the use of behavioral methods, some combination of cognitive-behavioral procedures may have greater practical advantages. However, recent evidence from Emmelkamp et al. (1980), described previously (p. 366), suggests that the advantages of using cognitive and behavioral methods in combination are still to be determined. The effectiveness of exposure in vivo alone, it will be recalled, did not improve with the addition of self-instructional statements for a group of agoraphobic patients.

"Where shall we begin?" Meichenbaum asks. "Should we focus on cognitive structures *or* try to alter inner speech *or* teach new behaviors and manipulate environmental consequences?" (1977, p. 226–227). Some psychologists believe that attitude changes are more easily achieved through changes in overt behavior than the other way around (Bem, 1972; Bandura, 1977). And, in their study of cognitive modification vs. prolonged exposure with agoraphobic clients, Emmelkamp et al. observed a number of clients who reported spontaneously that their thoughts had undergone more of a change during prolonged exposure in vivo than through a procedure which focused directly on such change (1978, p. 40). The primary advantage of dealing with thoughts and feelings first, however, is that it may prepare the individual to engage in the feared behavior in much the same way that relaxation and reassurance in desensitization and implosive therapy help to keep the client exposed to the feared conditions. But it is equally conceivable that if the therapist deals exclusively with cognitive factors without making any attempt to encourage action (a highly unlikely event given the current behavioral therapy methods), the client, like Tolman's rat, is in danger of staying "buried in thought."

At this point, it should be fairly obvious that given the confounded nature of most cognitive restructuring studies (cognitive methods mixed with behavioral techniques) it is no simple matter to determine just how cognitive intervention methods influence behavior change, and, in fact, whether or not they actually do. Bandura's theory of behavioral change in therapy, as we shall see, involves a more rigorous attempt to explain the relationship between cognitive and overt changes in behavior by showing how each of the therapeutic methods operates through a central mediating process called self-efficacy.

Self-Efficacy: A Theory for Behavior Change in Therapy

Bandura's self-efficacy theory is an ambitious project. In one fell swoop, it attempts to reconcile and explain all of the therapeutic approaches we have discussed by subsuming them under one construct, or intervening variable, called *self-efficacy.* The theory is basically an attempt to explain how behavior changes take place in therapy using the principal assumption that most of the therapeutic methods accomplish their purpose by "creating and strengthening expectations of personal efficacy" (1977a, p. 193).

Each of the procedures—desensitization, implosive therapy, response-reinforcement contingencies, biofeedback, or cognitive restructuring—is therapeutic to the extent that each leads individuals to believe that a specific course of action will lead to success *(outcome expectancies)* and that they are capable of taking the specific course of action which will ensure that success *(self-efficacy).* Bandura draws the distinction between outcome expectancies and self-efficacy on the grounds that people may *know* what to expect *if* a particular action is taken, but they may not have the *conviction that they are capable* of engaging in the behavior necessary to produce the outcome. Therapy, in essence, gives them the required assurance. Self-efficacy, like the revised learned helplessness model, is essentially an attribution theory because behavior change depends on whether or not people can expect their behavior to have an effect on the environment.

The diagram in Figure 15-5 is adapted from Bandura's theory and presented in the familiar mediational model form that we discussed in Chapter 13 (Figure 13-3). Essentially, the diagram shows how the self-efficacy concept mediates between the stimulus event and the subsequent response and represents the factors assumed to affect this intervening state.

An individual confronted with a fear-arousing event (S), for example, will be unable to cope with the situation (B2) unless both the outcome expectations and the feelings of personal effectiveness (B1) have been changed to make such behavior possible. The expectation that an individual will be effective in dealing with a particular situation will vary in *magnitude, generality,* and *strength,* depending upon the difficulty of the situation to be mastered, the extent to which success in one situation can be transferred to other equally disturbing situations, and previous

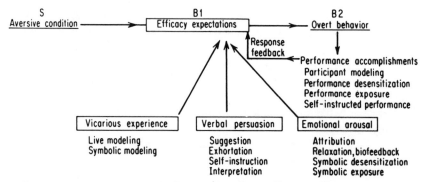

FIG. 15-5 Principal sources of efficacy information affecting efficacy expectations. The resultant overt behavior at B2 is the combined effect of S (aversive situation) and the influence of each of the different sources of treatment on the mediating processes B1. (Adapted from A. Bandura. Self-efficacy: Toward a unifying theory of behavioral change. *Psychological Review*, 1977a, *84*, 191–215.)

successes and failures. Each of these conditions will also vary with the amount of information a person receives about potential effectiveness (efficacy information). The various forms of therapy provide this information in differing ways (Figure 15-5).

Sources of Efficacy Expectations.   The sources of efficacy information provided by the different therapeutic approaches are not all equally effective, according to Bandura. Some, such as performance accomplishments, provide examples of personal mastery and extinguish fear at the same time (1977a, p. 195). It is Bandura's firm conviction that *performance accomplishment* obtained through *behavior rehearsal* is superior to all other methods for changing expectations of personal effectiveness. While *vicarious experiences* (modeling) can increase efficacy information by providing examples of other people overcoming their fears, actual exposure to and participation in the feared event gives people an opportunity to practice the coping skills they have observed during modeling and to experience the benefits of success. The fact that both prolonged exposure to the real fear-arousing situation and participant modeling are more effective ways to reduce fear and avoidance behavior than either symbolic modeling (watching people on film) or symbolic exposure (desensitization and implosive therapy) provides evidence for Bandura's assertion about actual performance.

   Emotional arousal by itself, through symbolic desensitization, symbolic exposure, or modeling, which depends upon the unreinforced elicitation and extinction of anxiety for its explanation (dual-process theory, desensitization, implosive therapy, see Chapters 2 and 4), is effective, according to Bandura, only insofar as it raises efficacy expectations when the heightened physiological state of anxiety is subsequently reduced. In other words, extinction of anxiety does not take place merely as a result of prolonged unreinforced exposure to the aversive stimulus as the classical extinction explanation proposes. Instead, performance accomplishment reduces fear and provides information about success which then acts to raise the level of efficacy expectations.

The least effective way to raise efficacy expectations, according to Bandura, is through *verbal persuasion,* in effect, cognitive restructuring without the behavioral components (exposure and behavior rehearsal). Here Bandura is at odds with Beck, Ellis, and Meichenbaum. *If the clinical applications of the cognitive approach are more effective, Bandura contends following the accumulated evidence, the result is probably due to the use of corrective homework assignments that affect performance accomplishment and increase efficacy expectations. Cognitive changes, he further asserts, follow behavioral changes* (1977b, p. 190).

Exhortation, self-instruction, suggestion, or rational arguments alone are generally not successful in strengthening efficacy expectations, and the experimental evidence strongly indicates that "placebo" conditions designed to raise expectations of improvement produce very little by way of change in overt behavior, especially where high states of anxiety are involved (Lick & Bootzin, 1975). In fact, it has been demonstrated that subjects who are extremely fearful will recover solely on the basis of the treatment regardless of what they have been told to expect (Borkovec, 1973, 1974).

Evidence for the Theory.   In the first of a series of experiments devised to test derivations from the theory, Bandura and his associates (1977a) explored the relationship between self-efficacy and two sources of efficacy expectations (participant modeling and simple observation) as well as the effect of different efficacy expectations on overt avoidance behavior. The subjects in the study were adult snake phobics whose phobia seriously interfered with their normal functioning. The participant-modeling group was assisted by various means in getting closer to and ultimately handling a live boa constrictor. The modeling group, by contrast, simply watched several models handle the snake. A control group received no treatment.

The strength and generality of efficacy expectations were measured at several points during the study—prior to treatment, following treatment, and after the behavioral approach tests. The subjects were asked to designate the snake-approach tasks they thought they were capable of performing from a list of 18 such tasks, and they also rated their expectations for performing these tasks on a 100-point probability scale. An index of efficacy generality was also obtained by having the subjects indicate the extent to which they expected to be able to cope with snakes of several varieties and not just the constrictor used in the study (dissimilar threats).

As predicted, participant modeling produced greater increases than modeling alone in self-efficacy expectations, generality of self-efficacy (ability to handle other snakes as well), and in the actual ability to approach and handle the snakes (Figure 15-6). Moreover, the ratings of self-efficacy (the number of approach tasks the subjects thought they could perform) and the expectations that they might perform these tasks showed a very high correlation. In essence, the probability that a specific approach task would be performed distinctly related to how effective people thought they would be in performing the task.

Self-efficacy also predicts the differences that subjects given the same treatment are likely to show in their ability to approach and handle the snake. For example,

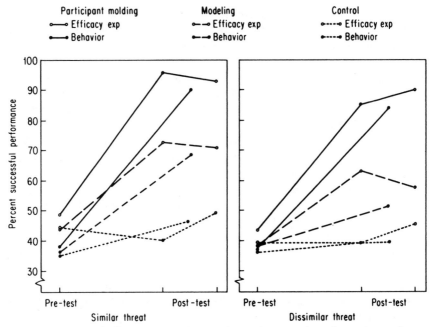

FIG. 15-6 Level of efficacy expectations and actual approach to the snake used as a model (similar) or other snakes (dissimilar) by subjects before and after participant modeling, modeling, or control treatment. (Source: A. Bandura. Self-efficacy: Toward a unifying theory of behavioral change. *Psychological Review,* 1977a, *84,* 191–215. Copyright 1977 American Psychological Association and used by permission.)

although all of the subjects in the participant modeling group were able to handle the snake during treatment, not all of them were able to repeat this performance during the post-test following treatment. This difference among subjects was predictable in terms of their self-efficacy scores. Subjects with relatively low self-efficacy scores were generally unable to perform the approach tasks, while those with higher scores succeeded. *In other words, the identification of a hitherto undisclosed factor (self-efficacy) made it possible to understand why differences in performance occurred under the same stimulus (treatment) conditions.*

Failures are also bound to occur in desensitization, and Bandura and Adams (Bandura, 1977) explored the possibility that these failures to respond to treatment also resulted from differing expectations. Again, as in the study just described, the differing reactions to desensitization treatment related to different self-efficacy expectations.

Self-efficacy Theory: Is It a Useful Explanation of Behavior Change in Therapy?

For several reasons, the use of self-efficacy as a construct to explain the behavior changes which take place in therapy represents an improvement over the explanations that were proposed in cognitive restructuring. Unlike irrational thoughts or self-statements, self-efficacy is unambiguously defined in terms of a subject's response to a rating scale, and factors affecting the strength of self-efficacy are identified (in this case, the operations involved in the various therapeutic approaches) (Figure 15-5). Moreover, predictions are made about the way in which variations in self-efficacy relate to variations in the overt response itself. These factors are important because they make it easier to evaluate the usefulness of self-efficacy as an explanatory concept in terms of the criteria discussed in Chapter 13.

The utility of a mediating variable, it will be recalled, depends upon (1) how well it is defined in terms of experimental procedures, (2) how well it helps to organize and explain existing phenomena, and (3) how helpful it is in generating new hypotheses and new experiments (its heuristic value). On the surface, at least, the concept of self-efficacy seems to satisfy these conditions. A closer examination, however, suggests that this may not be the case.

First, while self-efficacy is presumably defined independently of the performance it is supposed to predict (actual approach and contact with the snake) in order to avoid circularity, there is, in fact, some question as to whether this independence has actually been achieved. One might claim, for example, that the distinction between asking people to designate just how far they are likely to go in approaching and handling a snake on a questionnaire (for purposes of estimating or inferring the strength of self-efficacy) and asking them to show this by performing the act (an overt measure of approach behavior) is, in effect, a trivial one.

For example, let us consider the following statement. "B is unable to approach and handle the snake because his self-efficacy expectation is low." Now the question which inevitably follows, "How do we know that his self-efficacy expectation is low?" can be answered with the usual tautological reply, "Because he is unable to approach the snake!" Have we salvaged the situation by saying instead, "He was asked whether he thought he could approach the snake, and he replied he didn't think he could"? Probably not, because the second statement is simply another way of saying that B cannot approach the snake, and self-efficacy defined in this manner adds little to the understanding of B's avoidance behavior. In this instance, the prediction of snake-approach behavior from self-efficacy (based on a verbal statement of ability to approach the snake) is too close to the criterion variable (actual approach to the snake) for logical comfort.

Another difficulty in defining self-efficacy in terms of verbal behavior lies in the fact that sometimes individuals acknowledge that they are capable of performing a specific act without being able to do so on the actual occasion. Under these circumstances, self-efficacy would be seriously inadequate as a predictor of behavior (because it should invariably predict the ability to perform), and other factors (fear evoked by the actual attempt to handle the snake, for example) would be necessary to explain the difference between thinking about handling the snake and actually doing it.

With regard to the second and third criteria for evaluating mediating variables, Bandura uses the concept of self-efficacy to explain the differences in effectiveness among the various therapeutic approaches and to predict the superiority of the participant-modeling group over the group who merely observed the model. But because the empirical relationships between performance and several of the therapeutic techniques (which presumably determine efficacy information and efficacy strength) had already been determined, at least in part, by other experiments (Bandura et al., 1969; Emmelkamp et al., 1978) it is difficult to see the added advantage of introducing a mediating variable such as self-efficacy to make the same predictions.

In a critique of the concept, Borkovec (1978) argues that self-efficacy is a less parsimonious explanation of how therapy acts to reduce fear than those already proposed on the basis of traditional learning principles, namely extinction as a consequence of prolonged exposure and the learning of incompatible responses. He also suggests that self-efficacy may reflect the cognitive changes that take place *after* the behavior has undergone change and not cause the behavior change, as Bandura proposes.

In the face of all of the evidence, intuitive as well as empirical, it would be pointless to reject the idea that thoughts, feelings, emotions, perceptions, and so on play a critical role in determining human behavior. Advocates of cognitive factors are probably all correct in assuming that factors equivalent to irrational thoughts, self-statements, attributions, or self-efficacy expectations operate in some manner to maintain maladaptive behavior. Undoubtedly, some behavioral scientists will continue to use such concepts to express the idea that private events are in themselves behavior and that they are important aspects of human, and in some cases even animal, functioning. Clinicians, in particular, will continue to discourse with their clients on the basis of a language that refers to thoughts and attitudes, especially because these behaviors are important elements in classical and operant conditioning methods but also because research thus far indicates that some combination of cognitive and behavioral methods is probably more effective than either alone. As Ledwidge has pointed out, however, it is still important to make a distinction between the clinical utility of cognitive methods in general and their conceptual adequacy (1978, p. 371).

Mediating variables help in the discovery, description, and prediction of behavior, and, according to Skinner, "No entity or process which has any useful explanatory force is to be rejected (merely) on the grounds that it is subjective or mental" (1963, p. 958). The danger in using mediating variables in an indiscriminate fashion, however, is that they can be insidiously persuasive in encouraging the belief that an explanation has been found where, in fact, only redundancies actually exist.

chapter sixteen

Comparisons, Caveats, and Conclusions

More attention has probably been focused on the use of applied learning to change behavior in the relatively short period of 10 to 15 years than on any other method of psychological intervention in the last 50 years. Although the reactions to behavior modification have varied from almost unqualified acceptance to undiscriminating rejection, the publicity itself has had a genuinely salutary effect on the field of psychotherapy as a whole for reasons that are not especially difficult to understand.

Behavior modification, as we have already seen, has its roots in the experimental tradition, and this means that its methods are more likely to be exposed to public scrutiny and close professional examination than any of the other less empirical therapies. Such exposure inevitably invites comparisons and criticisms, both of which are vitally necessary to avoid intellectual, scientific, and technological stagnation. Fortunately, by drawing attention to itself, behavior modification has also drawn attention to other behavior-change methods as well, with the result that a healthy skepticism for all therapeutic methods has begun to replace unquestioning acceptance.

For the most part, the issues that accompanied the use of applied learning to change behavior emerged in two major areas: (1) comparisons with other forms of treatment, and (2) some of the ethical and legal problems (discussed briefly in Chapter 10) that arose, in part, from the large-scale use of behavior modification in institutional settings.

COMPARISONS

It may seem somewhat strange at this point to raise questions about the general effectiveness of psychotherapy as a method for changing behavior, especially after so much time and effort has already been devoted in this book demonstrating that at least one variation of it—behavior modification—seems to work. But in 1952 and again in 1965, Eysenck seriously questioned the effectiveness of traditional psychotherapy methods on the basis of a review of several controlled-outcome studies which purported to show that 75% of individuals with problems of one kind or another got well regardless of whether or not they received therapy.

Eysenck's provocative appraisal of the effectiveness of psychotherapy was probably responsible, in part, for the prevailing attitude (offered as testimony before the Colorado State Legislature) that the only thing psychotherapy has been able to prove from research on treatment outcome is that a "third of the people get better, a third of the people stay the same, and a third of the people get worse," regardless of the type of treatment they receive (Smith & Glass, 1977).

Such a challenge to the established and accepted methods for treatment of psychological problems inspired several subsequent surveys of outcome studies. One of the most recent and comprehensive of such surveys, conducted by Smith and Glass (1977), reported a difference in "effect size"—a method devised by the authors for measuring improvement following treatment—of approximately two-thirds of a standard deviation for 25,000 experimental and control subjects (those who did and did not receive therapy) participating in 400 studies. Smith and Glass interpreted these results to mean that the average individual receiving treatment was "better off" than 75% of the controls who did not.

Another way of looking at these findings, however, reveals that the *average* (50th percentile) experimental subject showed only a 22% improvement following treatment compared to the average control subject. And, even this difference may be somewhat inflated, considering the poorly controlled studies that inevitably get into such outcome surveys. The results are, nevertheless, somewhat reassuring, even if they did not completely restore to psychotherapy its former unblemished reputation.

One interesting finding of the Smith and Glass survey is that many people are capable of solving their own problems without the benefit of treatment. Because of this, Frank has maintained that many psychological problems are cyclical in nature, and that the main benefit of psychotherapy may be to speed up the improvement that would have occurred eventually in any case. But, as he has further suggested, even if treatment did no more than accelerate the natural recovery processes, shortening the duration of the client's distress and disability would seem a sufficient justification (1979, p. 311).

Is behavior modification, or applied learning, a more effective form of treatment than any other kind of therapy? Outcome research on the effectiveness of therapy is, in itself, a difficult and generally flawed evaluation procedure. Even the most conscientious outcome studies conducted within a specific discipline (i.e., behavior modification, psychoanalysis, Rogerian, etc.) must deal with differences in client populations, diagnostic descriptions, and the unreliability of measures used to characterize improvement. Consider the additional problems created when an attempt is made to compare different kinds of treatment on the basis of a survey where (1) no attempt is made to distinguish among studies in terms of scientific rigor, (2) as much weight is attached to a client's subjective report of the effect of therapy as to more objective measures, (3) type and severity of disorder is not equated, and (4) the definition of therapy orientation is vague. Despite these problems, Smith and Glass (1977) undertook to relate improvement following therapy to the type of treatment employed.

Table 16-1 indicates the ten types of therapy identified in the survey and the extent of improvement associated with each type. The most effective therapeutic procedure appears to be systematic desensitization with an effect size of .91 indicating that the average person receiving this type of treatment would be better off than 82% of the untreated control subjects. Rational-emotive therapy and behavior modification (identified by the authors as a "Skinnerian Procedure") rank second and third in order of effectiveness.

An interesting corollary to these findings is that problems related to fear, anxiety, and self-esteem—disorders generally treated with behavioral methods—seem to show much greater improvement than those associated with "adjustment and school/work achievement."

TABLE 16-1 The Effectiveness (Effect Size) of Ten Types of Therapy Included in the Smith and Glass Survey

Type of therapy	Average effect size	Number of effect sizes	Standard error of mean effect size	*Mdn* treated person's percentile status in control group
Psychodynamic	.59	96	.05	72
Adlerian	.71	16	.19	76
Eclectic	.48	70	.07	68
Transactional analysis	.58	25	.19	72
Rational-emotive	.77	35	.13	78
Gestalt	.26	8	.09	60
Client-centered	.63	94	.08	74
Systematic desensitization	.91	223	.05	82
Implosion	.64	45	.09	74
Behavior modification	.76	132	.06	78

SOURCE: M. Smith and G. Glass. Meta-analysis of psychotherapy outcome studies. *American Psychologist,* 1977, *32,* 752–760. Copyright 1977 by the American Psychological Association. Used by permission.

When the ten types of therapy are further classified into two major groups, *behavioral* (implosion, systematic desensitization, behavior modification) on the one hand, and *non-behavioral* (Adlerian, Rogerian, rational-emotive, eclectic, transactional analysis) on the other, according to the judgments of a group of clinical psychologists, a small difference in effectiveness in favor of the behavioral group appears. This difference disappears, however, when we compare only those studies in which important elements such as experience of the therapist, nature of the client's problems, duration of therapy, type of outcome measure, and duration of follow-up are equivalent. Nevertheless, as the authors themselves indicate, the differences between individual treatment procedures such as gestalt (.26 of a standard deviation) and systematic desensitization (.91 of a standard deviation) are still substantial (see Table 16-1).

An earlier study by Sloane and his associates (1975) comparing analytically oriented therapy with behavior therapy confirms the results of the Smith and Glass survey. Not only was behavior therapy found to be as effective as psychotherapy with a wide range of moderately severe neurotic and personality disorders drawn from the general patient population, in some instances it was even more effective than psychotherapy with more severely disturbed clients. And, according to Franks and Wilson (1976), the results would probably have been more impressive if a wider range of disorders with children and of sexual difficulties had been included in the study instead of just the problems of well-educated, young, predominantly white, and not too severely disturbed clients.

Although recovery remains the single most important criterion for judging the adequacy of any form of treatment, there are still a number of other factors that must inevitably be used to determine just how useful a procedure is likely to be, especially where two types of therapy have been shown to have equally effective outcomes. Most people would agree that—all other things being equal—the most desirable form of treatment is one which:

a. Is continually developing and improving because its principles are well-defined and constantly being tested experimentally.

b. Can be communicated to others and applied with relative ease.

c. Is widely applicable to largest number of behavior disorders.

d. Can be applied to the largest segment of the population with respect to age as well as socioeconomic status.

e. Does not require inordinate amounts of time and money.

Behavior modification, as it has been defined and described in the preceding chapters, appears to satisfy most, if not all, of these requirements.

CAVEATS

If the dramatic growth in the use of behavior modification and the work cited in these chapters and elsewhere in the literature are regarded as measures of effectiveness, then the application of learning and conditioning to behavior change has, indeed, been at least moderately effective. But this success has brought with it problems and responsibilities that advocates of applied behavior methods must accept as behavioral scientists, practitioners, and members of the human community.

These responsibilities are not unique to behavior modification inasmuch as they arise in every instance where science is applied to solve problems in human affairs, but they are as important for the behavioral scientist as they were for the physicist when principles of nuclear fission were being converted to a nuclear technology.

As scientists and practitioners, psychologists have the responsibility for observing rigor and caution in the investigation and application of the new technology emerging from applied learning, and as members of society, they also have the obligation to consider carefully the ethical and legal implications of the treatment goals they are proposing. As a group, behavior modifiers have been responsive to the ethical and legal problems of treatment, even though, as we shall see, very few of these issues are directly associated with the practice of behavior modification.

The Ethical Issues

Ethical problems involve a conflict of values—the ideals or principles people customarily use to guide their actions. In therapy, these issues are generally associated with the actions that therapists take to safeguard the welfare of their clients. Although ethical problems within most professions are usually resolved by establishing a set of guidelines or standards through the mutual consent and consultation of the members of the profession (see Box 16-1, for example), some of these standards may eventually be enacted into regulation or law.

One such standard governing the use of humans in experimentation, for example, began as a set of loosely structured guidelines concerning the physical and psychological safety of people used in experiments and ultimately became a Department of Health, Education, and Welfare policy. Moreover, in 1974, the National Research Act (PL 93-348) provided for the establishment of a National Commission for the Protection of Human Subjects of Biomedical and Behavioral Research to investigate a number of issues dealing with the use of humans as subjects in experimentation. In addition, the Commission was also asked to determine the need for extending the Department of Health, Education, and Welfare regulations to health services (Brown et al., 1975).

Informed Consent. One of the most formidable of all the ethical issues in activities involving human subjects—whether research or treatment—is that of informed consent. The violation of this principle persuaded the Federal government to establish regulations requiring that written consent be obtained from all subjects in experiments involving humans after they were briefed about the potential risks and benefits involved. Although the regulation requires written consent from all individuals, its primary intent was to safeguard the rights of captive populations in institutions such as schools, prisons, hospitals, and domiciliary homes. In fact, it was the injection of cancer cells into the bodies of the aged in nursing homes that first focused attention on the abuses of human experimentation as a whole.

Although the question of informed consent in individual treatment is just as crucial, the problem is somewhat more difficult to resolve. Where individuals voluntarily seek help for their problems, informed consent merely becomes a matter of having accurate information about the means and goals of treatment, including its risks, potential benefits, length of time, and cost on which to base a decision about treatment. Under these circumstances, the therapist and the client can agree on a contract that specifies the rights and responsibilities of each. But what precisely does informed consent mean for children in a school system, inmates of a school for the retarded, mental patients, and prisoners who are unable or incapable of making their own decisions about treatment or rehabilitation? In effect, who is the client in these instances, the individual or the institution (Brown et al., 1975, p. 20)?

This is the question that led several psychologists to conclude that while the institution was indeed the client in many cases, the best interests of the individual are not always achieved by serving the interests of the institution. As we have already seen in Chapters 9 and 10, what is good for the prison, in terms of maintaining institutional integrity, is not always good for the prisoner, and what is good for the school system is not always in the best interests of the child. The behavioral consultant may have a special contribution to make here in suggesting alternative goals that might enhance the effects of treatment. Graubard and his associates did it by having children subtly modify the behavior of their teachers (Chapter 9); Fairweather and his colleagues focused less on the needs of the mental hospital for tractable, easy-to-manage patients and more on activities that increase the probability of an adjustment into the community; and Clements, Milan, and McKee are attempting to do the same thing for prisoners (Chapter 10).

In 1976, the Committee for the Consideration of Ethical Issues, established by the Association for Advancement of Behavior Therapy, proposed a set of Ethical Practice Guidelines in the form of suggestions or reminders to the therapist that certain questions of ethical importance should be carefully considered prior to treatment. These guidelines were subsequently adopted by the Association in 1977 as Ethical Issues for Human Services (Box 16-1),

---

BOX 16-1
Ethical Issues for Human Services

A. Have the goals of treatment been adequately considered?

1. To ensure that the goals are explicit, are they written?
2. Has the client's understanding of the goals been assured by having the client restate them orally or in writing?
3. Have the therapist and client agreed on the goals of therapy?
4. Will serving the client's interests be contrary to the interests of other persons?

5. Will serving the client's immediate interests be contrary to the client's long-term interest?

B. Has the choice of treatment methods been adequately considered?

1. Does the published literature show the procedure to be the best one available for that problem?
2. If no literature exists regarding the treatment method, is the method consistent with generally accepted practice?
3. Has the client been told of alternative procedures that might be preferred by the client on the basis of significant differences in discomfort, treatment time, cost, or degree of demonstrated effectiveness?
4. If a treatment procedure is publicly, legally, or professionally controversial, has formal professional consultation been obtained, has the reaction of the affected segment of the public been adequately considered, and have the alternative treatment methods been more closely reexamined and reconsidered?

C. Is the client's participation voluntary?

1. Have possible sources of coercion on the client's participation been considered?
2. If treatment is legally mandated, has the available range of treatments and therapists been offered?
3. Can the client withdraw from treatment without a penalty or financial loss that exceeds actual clinical costs?

D. When another person or an agency is empowered to arrange for therapy, have the interests of the subordinated client been sufficiently considered?

1. Has the subordinated client been informed of the treatment objectives and participated in the choice of treatment procedures?
2. Where the subordinated client's competence to decide is limited, have the client as well as the guardian participated in the treatment discussions to the extent that the client's abilities permit?
3. If the interests of the subordinated person and the superordinate persons or agency conflict, have attempts been made to reduce the conflict by dealing with both interests?

E. Has the adequacy of treatment been evaluated?

1. Have quantitative measures of the problem and its progress been obtained?
2. Have the measures of the problem and its progress been made available to the client during treatment?

F. Has the confidentiality of the treatment relationship been protected?

1. Has the client been told who has access to the records?
2. Are records available only to authorized persons?

G. Does the therapist refer the clients to other therapists when necessary?

1. If treatment is unsuccessful, is the client referred to other therapists?
2. Has the client been told that if dissatisfied with the treatment, referral will be made?

H. Is the therapist qualified to provide treatment?

1. Has the therapist had training or experience in treating problems like the client's?
2. If deficits exist in the therapist's qualifications, has the client been informed?
3. If the therapist is not adequately qualified, is the client referred to other therapists, or has supervision by a qualified therapist been provided? Is the client informed of the supervisory relation?
4. If the treatment is administered by mediators, have the mediators been adequately supervised by a qualified therapist?

and this document forms the basis for their Professional Consultation and Peer Review Services. It is interesting to note that item D in the Ethical Issues addresses itself directly to the interests of children and institutionalized individuals, and that question D-3 deals specifically with the potential conflict of interests that may exist between the institution and the "subordinate person."

The Legal Issues

The resolution of ethical conflicts does not involve judicial procedures. Legal issues, on the other hand, arise out of the violation of statutory or Constitutional laws and are decided through formal litigation (Friedman, 1969). The legal issues, which have had some impact on psychotherapy in general, grew out of lawsuits brought by prisoners, mental patients, or their representatives in three main areas: the right to treatment, the right to refuse treatment, and the right to informed consent (Houts, 1979). (The question of informed consent, already considered in a previous discussion, is part of the right-to-refuse-treatment issue.)

The Right to Treatment.   Although it is usually taken for granted that a person committed to a mental hospital will receive treatment, or a prisoner some form of rehabilitation, neither treatment nor rehabilitation is considered a constitutional right. Despite the fact that such "rights" are now contained in the statutes of several states as a result of circuit-court decisions, the Supreme Court has declined to issue an opinion on the constitutionality of these statutes.

Right to treatment first emerged as a specific legal issue when a man by the name of Rouse sued for release from St. Elizabeth's Hospital where he had been confined following a plea of insanity to the charge of carrying a weapon without a license (*Rouse v. Cameron,* 1966).

Rouse's confinement actually became a sentence of indefinite length inasmuch as his release from the hospital depended on his response to treatment, which, he claimed, he was not receiving. According to the plaintiff, the period of hospitalization was already four times greater than any sentence he would have received if the case had gone to trial.

Although the court reaffirmed Rouse's legal right to treatment, basing its decision on the already existing mental health statutes of the District of Columbia, he was not released from the hospital because, according to the decision, in fact, he had been receiving treatment but was not yet considered rehabilitated (Houts, 1979).

In 1972, a suit (*Wyatt v. Stickney*, 1972) on behalf of the patients at Portlow State Hospital in Tuscaloosa, Alabama, brought the right to treatment once more into the limelight. In addition to right to treatment, the court was also asked to rule on the question of patient privileges and employment while in the hospital —subjects of direct interest to practitioners of behavior modification.

On these matters the court ruled in the affirmative. Not only was the right to treatment upheld, but the patient also had rights to certain conditions while in the hospital: a residence unit with a screen, a comfortable bed, a locker, chair, and table, nutritional meals, social interaction with members of the opposite sex, visitors, clothes, laundry facilities, exercise, religious services, and a television set in the day room. The Wyatt decision also held that patients cannot be made to work for these privileges, and if employed in the hospital, they must be paid a minimum wage for their efforts. In two other cases (*Inmates of Boy's Training School v. Affleck*, 1972, and *Morales v. Turman*, 1973), the same decision was reached with respect to patient amenities (Brown et al., 1975; Houts, 1979). What effect have these decisions had on behavior modification?

Who defines treatment. While it may be simple enough to assert that all patients have a right to treatment, in making a legal decision on the subject the courts have placed themselves in the rather unenviable position of having to define just what treatment is. And, apparently, they are not unwilling to assume this responsibility. In the case of *Donaldson v. O'Connor* (1974), for example, the court explicitly ruled that if people are to be deprived of their liberty for the purposes of treatment, it is unacceptable to suggest that the courts are then powerless to determine whether or not treatment is, in fact, taking place. And, as if to emphasize their resolve in this matter of right to treatment, U.S. District Court Judge Frank Johnson went beyond the recommendations of the Mental Health Law Project attorneys for a court-appointed master to monitor compliance with the right to treatment decisions issuing from the Wyatt decision. He called for receivership status for the Alabama institutions if they did not meet court-ordered treatment and rehabilitation standards on their own (*APA Monitor*, 1979).

Clearly, as Houts (1979) points out, with this ruling the courts have placed themselves squarely in the position of defining treatment. As we see in the discussion on the right to refuse treatment, decisions have already been made based on the court's prerogative to define treatment.

Institutional privileges as "rights." The courts' rulings that most conditions of existence in an institution are rights rather than mere privileges places severe restraints on the use of contingency methods and token-economy procedures as forms of treatment. Many of the factors which were used to motivate and reinforce appropriate behavior are no longer available. The privilege of watching television, for example, can no longer be made contingent on personal appearance, socializing with others, or any of the behaviors that are regarded as goals in treatment. And the decision that patients must be paid at prevailing minimum wages for any work done in the hospital placed an even greater obstacle in the way of treatment. In effect, hospital budgets could no longer afford the one form of treatment—work —that has always been considered of paramount importance in the recovery from mental disorders.

Because privileges or work, both principal elements of treatment in behavior modification, can no longer be used as rewards and behavioral goals, patients will either have to agree to waive their rights to the privileges in order to motivate and reward themselves for more appropriate behavior (a highly unlikely prospect), or more unusual types of reinforcers will have to be found. It has also been suggested that the negative effects of such court decisions on treatment is likely to prompt a review of the *Wyatt v. Stickney* decision by the courts (Paul and Lentz, 1977).

The Right to Refuse Treatment.   By establishing a legal precedent for the right to obtain treatment, the courts were obviously attempting to ensure the welfare of institutionalized individuals. Were they accomplishing the same thing, however, in deciding that individuals also had the right to refuse treatment? If the individual's best interests are served through treatment and the institutions are legally responsible for providing it, then the right to refuse treatment appears to contradict the legal guarantee of treatment. Moreover, in allowing people the right to refuse treatment, it is conceivable that the law might be jeopardizing their welfare on the grounds that (1) patients do not have the technical knowledge to make judgments about treatment, and (2) they may be refusing something that may be ultimately beneficial to them (Houts, 1979).

According to some, however, what appears to be a contradiction in rights actually is not. The law can ensure people the right to treatment, they argue, and at the same time protect them from hazardous and intrusive procedures (Friedman, 1975; Houts, 1979).

In effect, this is precisely the way the courts have responded, and in the several cases concerned with the right to refuse treatment, the issues centered mainly around the use of aversive procedures in prisons (*MacKay v. Procunier*, 1973; *Knecht v. Gillman*, 1973). In each instance, however, the court's decision involved an assessment of what is proper treatment and what is not.

The case that appeared to set the legal precedent for the right to refuse treatment involved a patient, accused of murder and rape, who was diagnosed as a criminal psychopath. Although the patient had consented to psychosurgery (an experimental procedure) for the treatment of aggression, a suit was brought against the surgical procedure on behalf of the patient and others designated and confined as criminal sexual psychopaths (*Kaimowitz v. Michigan Department of Mental Health*, 1973). The court upheld the suit on the grounds that an involuntarily detained mental patient could not give legally adequate consent to experimental psychosurgery and that the treatment was deemed "unusually intrusive" into the right to privacy (Houts, 1979, p. 22).

While it is easy enough to agree with the courts in these instances where the treatment is questionable, there may be other occasions in which the judgment of the court may not be beneficial to the individual. For example, it is not difficult to imagine the ultimate result if pain and intrusiveness had been used as criteria to deny the use of surgical procedures in medicine.

The State of California has recently taken a much more enlightened attitude toward the use of aversive procedures in treatment. In a draft of a proposal entitled "Aversive Procedures in Education," the authors indicated that there are times when aversive procedures must be used to "fulfill the right to treatment of the individual." But these procedures should only be used after all appropriate alternatives have been tried and found wanting, and only then under the stringent conditions of the California Guidelines which spell out standards for planning and delivery, patient protection, review and evaluation, and responsibilities and qualifications of the personnel delivering the treatment (*APA Monitor,* 1979, p. 4).

CONCLUSIONS

Fifteen or twenty years ago, behavior modification was considered a new approach to treatment, and, like most new ideas, it rapidly became a persistent gadfly on the psychotherapy corpus (in fact, the acronym for the first journal in the area of behavior modification—Behaviour Research and Therapy—was BRAT). Today, behavior modification is an accepted form of treatment, and its advent has brought about a significant change in the role of psychotherapy. Its methods are readily communicable and, therefore, consistent with the needs of society for short-term mental health programs conducted by both professional and paraprofessionals in order to reach a larger and more diversified segment of the population than has hitherto been possible.

The following quote from a disinterested source (Walsh) is perhaps the most appropriate way to conclude. The statement confirms the purpose of this book—to demonstrate that psychological principles, learning and conditioning in particular, have indeed been applied in a most resourceful manner to establish new ways of bringing about beneficial behavior change.

Today, the content of clinical psychology has been significantly amplified by an explosion in the application of behavioral psychology. Psychologists can now do a number of things effectively in treating neurotic disorders, particularly in respect to phobias and compulsive behavior. And even before Masters and Johnson, behavior therapists were having substantial success in dealing with sexual dysfunction.

Psychologists working with children have made progress in the management of autistic children and the mentally retarded. Treatment of bed-wetting, hyperactivity, and disruptive classroom behavior in children has also shown good results. And with adults, stress-reduction methods have proved helpful in relieving anger, tension and anxiety.

Psychologists, in other words, have been applying knowledge in their field to an increasing number of problems. While they still have much to be modest about, there is a body of knowledge and technique much broader than that available to practitioners even a decade ago. (From J. Walsh. Professional psychologists seek to change roles and rules in the field. *Science,* 1979, *203,* 338–340. Copyright 1979 by the American Association for the Advancement of Science. Used by permission.)

References

Abramson, L. Y., Seligman, M. E. P., & Teasdale, J. D. Learned helplessness in humans: Critique and reformulation. *Journal of Abnormal Psychology,* 1978, *87,* 49–74.

Ackerman, S. H., Hofer, M. A., & Weiner, H. Early maternal separation increases gastric ulcer risk in rats by producing a latent thermoregulatory disturbance. *Science,* 1978, *201,* 373–375.

Adám, G. *Interoception and behaviour.* Budapest: Publishing House of the Hungarian Academy of Sciences, 1967.

Adams, H. E., Feuerstein, M., & Fowler, J. L. Migraine headache: Review of parameters, etiology, and intervention. *Psychological Bulletin,* 1980, *87,* 217–237.

Adelson, R., Liebert, R. M., Herskovitz, A., & Poulos, R. W. A modeling film to reduce children's fears of dental treatment. *International Association for Dental Research Abstracts,* March 1972, 114.

Addison, R. M., & Homme, L. E. The reinforcing event (RE) menu. *Journal of the National Society for Programmed Instruction,* 1966, *5,* 8–9.

Anthony, E. J. The developmental precursors of schizophrenia. In D. Rosenthal & S. S. Kety (Eds.), *The transmission of schizophrenia.* New York: Pergamon Press, 1968.

Anthony, E. J. The influence of maternal psychosis in children—Folie à deux. In E. J. Anthony & T. Benedeck (Eds.), *Parenthood.* Boston: Little, Brown and Company, 1970.

Anthony, E. J. From birth to breakdown: A perspective study of vulnerability. In E. J. Anthony, C. Kopernik, & C. Chiland (Eds.), *The child and his family: Vulnerable children.* Vol. 4. New York: John Wiley & Sons, 1978.

APA Monitor, December 1979, *10,* p. 1.

Arling, G. L., & Harlow, H. F. Effects of social deprivation on maternal behavior of rehesus monkeys. *Journal of Comparative and Physiological Psychology,* 1967, *64,* 371–377.

Association for Advancement of Behavior Therapy Newsletter. The domain of behavior therapy. July 1974, *1,* 7.

Association for Advancement of Behavior Therapy Newsletter. Oct., 1976, *3,* 2.

Association for Advancement of Behavior Therapy. Ethical issues for human services. *Professional Consultation and Peer Review Services.* New York: AABT, 1977.

Atthowe, J. M., Jr., & Krasner, L. A preliminary report on the application of contingency reinforcement procedures (token economy) on a "chronic" psychiatric ward. *Journal of Abnormal Psychology,* 1968, *73,* 37–43.

Atthowe, J. J., Jr., & McDonough, J. M. *Operations re-entry.* Washington, D. C.: U. S. Department of

Health, Education, and Welfare Social and Rehabilitation Services, 1969. (Film of Veterans' Administration Hospital, Palo Alto, Ca. Released by Indiana University.)

Atthowe, J. M., Jr. Token economies come of age. *Behavior Therapy,* 1973, *4,* 646–654.

Atthowe, J. M., Jr. Treating the hospitalized person. In W. E. Craighead, A. E. Kazdin, & M. J. Mahoney (Eds.), *Behavior modification: Principles, issues, and applications.* Boston: Houghton Mifflin Company, 1976, 243–259.

Averill, J. R., O'Brien, L., & DeWitt, G. W. The influence of response effectiveness on the preference for warning and on psychophysiological stress reactions. *Journal of Personality,* 1977, *45,* 396–418.

Ayllon, T., & Azrin, N. H. The measurement and reinforcement of behavior of psychotics. *Journal of the Experimental Analysis of Behavior,* 1965, *8,* 357–383.

Ayllon, T., & Azrin, N. H. *The token economy.* New York: Appleton Century Crofts, 1968.

Azrin, N. H., & Holz, W. C. Punishment. In W. K. Honig (Ed.), *Operant behavior: Areas of research and application.* Englewood Cliffs, N.J.: Prentice-Hall, Inc., 1966.

Azrin, N. H., Sneed, T. J., & Foxx, R. M. Dry-bed training: Rapid elimination of childhood enuresis. *Behaviour Research and Therapy,* 1974, *12,* 147–156.

Azrin, N. H., & Thienes, P. M. R. Rapid elimination of enuresis by intensive learning without a conditioning apparatus. *Behavior Therapy,* 1978, *9,* 342–354.

Bacon, M. K., Child, I. K., & Barry, H., III. A cross-cultural study of the correlates of crime. *Journal of Abnormal and Social Psychology,* 1963, *66,* 291–300.

Badia, P., & Culbertson, S. The relative aversiveness of signalled vs. unsignalled escapable and inescapable shock. *Journal of Experimental Analysis of Behavior,* 1972, *17,* 463–471.

Badia, P., Culbertson, S., & Harsh, J. Choice of longer or stronger signalled shock over shorter or weaker unsignalled shock. *Journal of The Experimental Analysis of Behavior,* 1973, *19,* 25–32.

Baer, D. M., Peterson, R., & Sherman, J. A. The development of imitation by reinforcing behavioral similarity to a model. *Journal of the Experimental Analysis of Behavior,* 1967, *10,* 405–416.

Bakal, D. Headache: A biopsychological perspective. *Psychological Bulletin,* 1975, *82,* 369–382.

Bakan, D. Behaviorism and American urbanization. *Journal of the History of the Behavioral Sciences,* 1966, *1,* 5–28.

Baker, B. L. Symptom treatment and symptom substitution in enuresis. *Journal of Abnormal Psychology,* 1969, *74,* 42–49.

Baker, B. L., Cohen, D. C., & Saunders, J. T. Self-directed desensitization for acrophobia. *Behaviour Research and Therapy,* 1973, *11,* 79–83.

Baker, T. B., & Cannon, D. S. Taste aversion therapy with alcoholics: Techniques and evidence of a conditioned response. *Behaviour Research and Therapy,* 1979, *17,* 229–242.

Bakwin, H. Emotional deprivation in infants. *Journal of Pediatrics,* 1949, *35,* 512–521.

Bandura, A. Influence of a model's reinforcement contingencies on the acquisition of imitative responses. *Journal of Personality and Social Psychology,* 1965, *1,* 589–595.

Bandura, A. A social learning interpretation of psychological dysfunctions. In P. London & D. Rosenhahn (Eds.), *Foundations of abnormal psychology.* New York: Holt, Rinehart and Winston, Inc., 1968(a), 293–345.

Bandura, A. Modelling approaches to the modification of phobic disorders. In R. Porter (Ed.), *Ciba foundation symposium on the role of learning in psychotherapy.* London: J. & A. Churchill Ltd., 1968(b), 201–217.

Bandura, A. *Principles of behavior modification.* New York: Holt, Rinehart and Winston, Inc., 1969.

Bandura, A. Social learning theory of aggression. In J. F. Knutson (Ed.), *Control of aggression: Implications from basic research.* Chicago: Aldine Publishing Company, 1971.

Bandura, A. The ethics and social purposes of behavior modification. In C. M. Franks & G. T. Wilson (Eds.), *Annual review of behavior therapy: Theory and practice,* Vol. III. New York: Brunner/Mazel, 1975, 13–20.

Bandura, A. Self-efficacy: Toward a unifying theory of behavioral change. *Psychological Review,* 1977(a), *84,* 191–215.

Bandura, A. *Social learning theory.* Englewood Cliffs, N.J.: Prentice-Hall, Inc., 1977(b).

Bandura, A., Blanchard, E. B., & Ritter, B. J. The relative efficacy of desensitization and modeling therapeutic approaches for inducing behavioral, affective and attitudinal changes. *Journal of Personality and Social Psychology,* 1969, *13,* 173–199.

Bandura, A., Grusec, J. E., & Menlove, F. L. Vicarious extinction of avoidance behavior. *Journal of Personality and Social Psychology,* 1967, *5,* 16–23.

Bandura, A., & Menlove, F. L. Factors determining vicarious extinction of avoidance behavior through symbolic modeling. *Journal of Personality and Social Psychology,* 1968, *8,* 99–108.

Bandura, A., Ross, D. A., & Ross, S. A. Transmission of aggression through imitation of aggressive models. *Journal of Abnormal and Social Psychology,* 1961, *63,* 575–582.

Bandura, A., Ross, D. A., & Ross, S. A. Imitation of film-mediated aggressive models. *Journal of Abnormal and Social Psychology,* 1963(a), *66,* 3–11.

Bandura, A., Ross, D., & Ross, S. Vicarious reinforcement and imitative learning. *Journal of Abnormal and Social Psychology,* 1963(b), *67,* 601–607.

Bandura, A., & Walters, R. H. *Adolescent aggression.* New York: The Ronald Press Company, 1959.

Bandura, A., & Walters, R. H. *Social learning and personality development.* New York: Holt, Rinehart and Winston, Inc., 1963.

Barling, J., & Wainstein, T. Attitudes, labeling bias, and behavior modification in work organizations. *Behavior Therapy,* 1979, *10,* 129–136.

Baron, A., Kaufman, A., & Stauber, K. A. Instructions and reinforcement-feedback in human operant behavior maintained by fixed-interval reinforcement. *Journal of the Experimental Analysis of Behavior,* 1969, *12,* 701–712.

Baum, M., & Poser, E. G. Comparison of flooding procedures in animals and man. *Behaviour Research and Therapy,* 1971, *9,* 249–254.

Bechterev, V. M. *General principles of human reflexology.* New York: International, 1932.

Beck, A. T. *Depressions: Causes and treatment.* Philadelphia: University of Pennsylvania Press, 1967.

Beck, A. T. *Cognitive theory and the emotional disorders.* New York: International Universities Press, Inc. 1976.

Beech, H. R., Watts, F., & Poole, A. D. Classical conditioning of sexual deviation: A preliminary note. *Behavior Therapy,* 1971, *2,* 400–402.

Bem, D. J. Self-perception theory. In L. Berkowitz (Ed.), *Advances in Experimental Social Psychology.* Vol. 6, New York: Academic Press, 1972.

Bennett, D. & Kennedy, J. F. Elimination of habitual vomiting using DRO procedures. *The Behavior Therapist,* 1980, *3,* 16–18.

Berger, S. M. Conditioning through vicarious instigation. *Psychological Review,* 1962, *69,* 450–466.

Bijou, S. W. Social variables and the beginning of self-control. Paper presented to the Society for Research in Child Development. Bowling Green, Ohio, 1965.

Bijou, S. W., & Baer, D. M. Some methodological contributions from a functional analysis of child development. In L. P. Lipsett & C. S. Spiker (Eds.), *Advances in child development and behavior* (Vol. 1). New York: Academic Press, Inc., 1963, 197–231.

Birk, L., Crider, A., Shapiro, D., & Tursky, B. Operant electrodermal conditioning under partial curarization. *Journal of Comparative and Physiological Psychology,* 1966, *62,* 165–166.

Birk, L., Huddleston, J. D., Miller, E., & Cohler, B. Avoidance conditioning for homosexuality. *Archives of General Psychiatry,* 1971, *25,* 314–325.

Black, A. H. The extinction of avoidance responses under curare. *Journal of Comparative and Physiological Psychology,* 1958, *51,* 519–524.

Black, A. H. Heart rate changes during avoidance learning in dogs. *Canadian Journal of Psychology,* 1959, *13,* 229–242.

Black, A. H., Carlson, N. T., & Solomon, R. L. Exploratory studies of the conditioning of autonomic responses in curarized dogs. *Psychological Monographs,* 1962, 76: 29 (whole #548).

Blanchard, E. B., & Young, L. Clinical applications of biofeedback training: A review of the evidence. *Archives of General Psychiatry,* 1974, *30,* 573–589.

Blanchard, E. B., Miller, S. T., Abel, G. G., Haynes, M. R., & Wicker, R. Evaluation of biofeedback in the treatment of borderline essential hypertension. *Journal of Applied Behavior Analysis,* 1979, *12,* 99–109.

Blaney, P. H. Contemporary theories of depression: Critique and comparison. *Journal of Abnormal Psychology,* 1977, *86,* 203–223.

Bolin, D. C., & Kivens, L. Evaluation in a community mental health center: Huntsville, Alabama.

Evaluation, 1974, *2,* 26–35. Quoted in M. T. Nietzel et al., *Behavioral approaches to community psychology.* New York: Pergamon Press, 1977.

Bootzin, R. R. Stimulus control treatment for insomnia. *Proceedings of the Annual Convention of the American Psychological Association,* 1972, *7,* 395–396.

Borkovec, T. D. The effect of instructional suggestions and physiological cues on analogue fear. *Behavior Therapy,* 1973, *4,* 185–192.

Borkovec, T. D. Heart rate process during systematic desensitization and implosive therapy for analogue anxiety. *Behavior Therapy,* 1974, *5,* 636–641.

Borkovec, T. D. Self-efficacy: Cause or reflection of behavior change? Unpublished manuscript, State University of Iowa, Iowa City, Iowa, 1978.

Boudewyns, P. A comparison of the effects of stress vs. relaxation on the finger temperature response. *Behavior Therapy,* 1976, *7,* 54–67.

Bousfield, W. A. Lope de Vega on early conditioning. *American Psychologist,* 1955, *10,* 828.

Bowlby, J. *Maternal care and mental health.* Geneva: World Health Organization, 1952.

Brady, J. V. Ulcers in "executive" monkeys. *Scientific American,* 1958, *199,* 95–100.

Bregman, E. An attempt to modify the emotional attitudes of infants by the conditioned response technique. *Journal of Genetic Psychology,* 1934, *45,* 169–196.

Broden, M., Bruce, C., Mitchell, M. A., Carter, V., & Hall, R. V. Effects of teacher attention and attending behavior of two boys at adjacent desks. *Journal of Applied Behavior Analysis,* 1970, *3,* 199–203.

Brody, G. H., Lahey, B. J., & Combs, M. L. Effects of intermittent modeling on observational learning. *Journal of Applied Behavior Analysis,* 1978, *11,* 87–90.

Brown, B. S., Wienckowski, L. A., & Stolz, S. B. *Behavior modification: Perspective on a current issue* (DHEW Publication #ADM 75-202). Washington, D. C.: U.S. Government Printing Office, 1975.

Brown, J. S. *The motivation of behavior.* New York: McGraw-Hill Book Company, 1961.

Brown, J. S., Martin, R. C., & Morrow, M. W. Self-punitive behavior in the rat: Facilitative effect of punishment on resistance to extinction. *Journal of Comparative and Physiological Psychology,* 1964, *57,* 127–133.

Brownell, K. D., Hayes, S. C., & Barlow, D. H. Patterns of appropriate and deviant sexual arousal: The behavioral treatment of multiple sexual deviations. *Journal of Consulting and Clinical Psychology,* 1977, *45,* 1144–1155.

Bruch, H. *Eating disorders—Obesity, anorexia, and the person within.* New York: Basic Books, Inc., 1973.

Buchwald, A. M., Coyne, J. C., & Cole, C. S. A critical evaluation of the learned helplessness model of depression. *Journal of Abnormal Psychology,* 1978, *87,* 180–193.

Budzynski, T. H., Stoyva, J. M., Adler, C. S., & Mullaney, D. J. EMG biofeedback and tension headaches #19. In N. E. Miller, T. X. Barber, L. V. DiCara, J. Kamiya, D. Shapiro, & J. Stoyva (Eds.), *Biofeedback and self-control.* Chicago: Aldine Publishing Company, 1973, 253–264.

Buehler, R. E., Patterson, G. R., & Furniss, J. M. The reinforcement of behaviour in institutional settings. *Behaviour Research and Therapy,* 1966, *4,* 157–167.

Bunck, T. J., & Iwata, B. A. Increasing senior citizen participation in a community-based nutritious meal program. *Journal of Applied Behavior Analysis,* 1978, *11,* 75–86.

Burgess, R., Clark, R., & Hendee, J. An experimental analysis of anti-litter procedures. *Journal of Applied Behavior Analysis,* 1971, *4,* 71–75.

Bykov, K. M., & Gantt, W. H. *The cerebral cortex and the internal organs.* New York: Chemical Publishing Company, Inc., 1957.

Caddy, G. R., Addington, H. J., Jr., & Perkins, D. Individualized behavior therapy for alcoholics: A third year independent double blind follow-up. *Behaviour Research and Therapy,* 1978, *16,* 345–362.

Caldwell, B. M. The effect of infant care. In M. Hoffman & L. Hoffman (Eds.), *Review of child development research* (Vol. 1). New York: Russell Sage Foundation, 1964.

Campbell, D., Sanderson, R. E., & Laverty, S. G. Characteristics of a conditioned response in human subjects during extinction trials following a single traumatic conditioning trial. *Journal of Abnormal and Social Psychology,* 1964, *68,* 627–639.

Carr, Edward G. The motivation of self-injurious behavior: A review of some hypotheses. *Psychological Bulletin,* 1977, *84,* 800–816.

Carr, E. G., Newsom, C. D., & Binkoff, J. A. Stimulus control of self-destructive behavior in a psychotic child. *Journal of Abnormal Child Psychology,* 1976, *4,* 139–153.

Carr, E. G., Newsom, C. D., & Binkoff, J. A. Escape as a factor in the aggressive behavior of two retarded children. *Journal of Applied Behavior Analysis,* 1980, *13,* 101–117.

Carver, C. S., & Blaney, P. H. Perceived arousal, focus of attention, and avoidance behavior. *Journal of Abnormal Psychology,* 1977, *86,* 154–162.

Castro, L., & Rachlin, H. Is self-reward like external reward? Unpublished manuscript, State University of New York at Stony Brook, Stony Brook, New York, 1978.

Chambless, D. L., Foa, E. B., Groves, G. A., & Goldstein, A. J. Flooding with Brevital in the treatment of agoraphobia: Countereffective? *Behaviour Research and Therapy,* 1979, *17,* 243–251.

Chapman, R. M., McCrary, J. W., & Chapman, J. A. Short-term memory: The "storage" component of human brain responses predicts recall. *Science,* 1978, *202,* 1211–1213.

Clark, H. B., & Risley, T. R. Experimentally specifying and effectively disseminating child-rearing procedures. Paper at sixth Banff International Conference on Behavior Modification, Canada, 1974. Quoted in M. T. Nietzel et al., *Behavioral approaches to community psychology.* New York: Pergamon Press, 1977, 256–258.

Clements, C. B., & McKee, J. M. Programmed instruction for institutional offenders: Contingency management and performance contracts. *Psychological Reports,* 1968, *22,* 957–964.

Clonce v. Richardson. No. 73 CV 373-S W.D. Mo. July 31, 1974.

Closs, R. G., & Globus, A. Spine stems on tectal interneurons in the Jewel fish are shortened by social stimulation. *Science,* 1978, *200,* 787–789.

Cohen, A. *Delinquent boys.* New York: The Free Press of Glencoe, Inc., 1955.

Cohen, H. L., & Filipsczak, J. A. *A new learning environment,* San Francisco: Jossey-Boss, 1971.

Cohen, H. L. *Responses to questions asked of a panel of experts.* U. S. District Court for the Western District of Missouri, Southern Division, 1974. Available from the National Prison Project, Washington, D. C.

Cohen, M., Liebson, I. A., Faillace, L.A., & Allen, R. P. Moderate drinking by chronic alcoholics. *Journal of Nervous and Mental Disorders.* 1971, *153,* 434–444.

Cook, J. W., Altman, K., Shaw, J., & Blaylock, M. Use of contingent lemon juice to eliminate public masturbation by a severely retarded boy. *Behaviour Research and Therapy,* 1978, *16,* 131–133.

Cooley, E. J. Cognitive versus emotional coping skills as alternative responses for the high test anxious college student. Unpublished doctoral dissertation, University of Texas at Austin, 1976.

Costello, C. G. A critical review of Seligman's laboratory experiments on learned helplessness and depression in humans. *Journal of Abnormal Psychology,* 1978, *87,* 21–31.

Coyne, J. C. Depression and the response of others. *Journal of Abnormal Psychology,* 1976, *85,* 186–193.

D'Amato, M. R. *Experimental psychology.* New York: McGraw-Hill Book Company, 1970, 371.

D'Zurilla, T. J. & Goldfried, M. R. Problem solving and behavior modification. *Journal of Abnormal Psychology,* 1971, *78,* 107–126.

D'Zurilla, T. J., Wilson, T. G., & Nelson, R. A preliminary study of the effectiveness of graduated prolonged exposure in the treatment of irrational fear. *Behavior Therapy,* 1973, *4,* 672–685.

Dalessio, D. J., Kunzel, M., Sternbach, R., & Sovak, M. Conditioned adaptation-relaxation reflex in migraine therapy. *Journal of American Medical Association,* 1979, *242,* 2102–2104.

Danaher, B. G. Rapid smoking and self-control in the modification of smoking behavior. *Journal of Consulting and Clinical Psychology,* 1977, *45,* 1068–1075.

Davison, G. Elimination of a sadistic fantasy by a client-controlled counterconditioning technique: A case study. *Journal of Abnormal Psychology,* 1968, *73,* 84–90.

Davison, G. C., & Neale, J. M. *Abnormal Psychology.* New York: John Wiley & Sons, Inc., 1974.

Davison, G. C. Homosexuality: The ethical challenge. *Journal of Consulting and Clinical Psychology,* 1976, *2,* 157–162.

Davison, G. C., & Stuart, R. B. Behavior therapy and civil liberties. Address delivered at bi-annual meetings of the American Civil Liberties Union, June 1974.

de Charms, R. *Personal causation: The internal affective determinants of behavior.* New York: Academic Press, Inc., 1968. Quoted in C. M. Franks, & G. T. Wilson, *Annual review of behavior therapy theory and practice* (Vol. 4). New York: Brunner/Mazel, 1976, 617.

Dekker, E., & Groen, J. Reproducible psychogenic attacks of asthma. *Journal of Psychosomatic Research,* 1956, *1,* 58–67.

Dekker, E., Pelser, H. E., & Groen, J. Conditioning as a cause of asthmatic attacks. *Journal of Psychosomatic Research,* 1957, *2,* 97–108.

Delude, L. A., & Carlson, N. J. A test of the conservation of anxiety and partial irreversibility hypotheses. *Canadian Journal of Psychology,* 1964, *18,* 15–22.

Deluty, M. A. Self-control and impulsiveness involving aversive events. *Journal of Experimental Psychology,* 1978, *4,* 250–266.

Depue, R. A., & Monroe, S. M. Learned helplessness in the perspective of the depressive disorders: Conceptual and definitional issues. *Journal of Abnormal Psychology,* 1978, *87,* 3–20.

DeRicco, D. A., & Garlington, W. K. An operant treatment procedure for alcoholics. *Behaviour Research and Therapy,* 1977, *15,* 497–499.

De Silva, P., Rachman, S., & Seligman, M. E. P. Prepared phobias and obsessions: Therapeutic outcome. *Behaviour Research and Therapy,* 1977, *15,* 65–77.

Diagnostic and Statistical Manual of Mental Disorders (DSM-II) (2nd. ed.). Washington, D.C.: American Psychiatric Association, 1968.

Diagnostic and Statistical Manual of Mental Disorders (DSM-III) (3rd. ed.). Draft. Washington, D.C.: American Psychiatric Association, 1979.

Dietz, S. M., & Repp, A. C. Decreasing classroom misbehavior through the use of DRL schedules of reinforcement. *Journal of Applied Behavior Analysis,* 1973, *6,* 457–463.

DiGiuseppe, R. A., & Miller, N. J. A review of outcome studies on rational-emotive therapy. In A. Ellis & R. Grieger (Eds.), *Handbook of rational-emotive therapy.* New York: Springer Publishing Co., Inc., 1977, 72–95.

Dohrmann, R.J., & Laskin, D.M. An evaluation of electromyographic biofeedback in the treatment of myofascial pain-dysfunction syndrome. *Journal of American Dental Association,* 1978, *96,* 656–662.

Doleys, D. M. Behavioral treatments for nocturnal enuresis in children: A review of the recent literature. *Psychological Bulletin,* 1977, *84,* 30–54.

Donaldson v. O'Conner. 493 F. 2d 507, 5th Cir., 1974.

Drabman, R. S. Behavior modification in the classroom. In W. E. Craighead, A. E. Kazdin, & M. J. Mahoney (Eds.), *Behavior modification principles, issues, and applications.* Boston: Houghton Mifflin Company, 1976.

Dubey, D. R. Organic factors in hyperkinesis: A critical evaluation. *American Journal of Orthopsychiatry,* 1976, *46,* 353–365.

Edwards, A. E., & Acker, L. E. A demonstration of the long-term retention of a conditioned GSR. *Psychosomatic Science,* 1972, *26,* 27–28.

Eisler, R. M., Hersen, M., & Miller, P.M. Effects of modeling on components of assertive behavior. *Journal of Behavioral Therapy and Experimental Psychiatry,* 1973, *4,* 1–6.

Ellis, A. Towards the improvement of psychoanalytic research. *Psychoanalytic Review,* 1949, *36,* 123–143.

Ellis, A. Outcome of employing three techniques of psychotherapy. *Journal of Clinical Psychology,* 1957, *13,* 344–350.

Ellis, A. The treatment of sex and love problems in women. In V. Franks and V. Burtle (Eds.), *Women in therapy.* New York: Brunner/Mazel, 1974.

Ellis, A. The basic clinical theory of rational-emotive therapy. In A. Ellis & R. Grieger (Eds.), *Handbook of rational-emotive therapy.* New York: Springer Publishing Co., Inc., 1977, 3–33.

Ellis, A. A note on the treatment of agoraphobics with cognitive modification versus prolonged exposure *in vivo. Behaviour Research and Therapy,* 1979, *17,* 162–164.

Emmelkamp, P. M. G. The behavioral study of clinical phobias. In M. Herson, R. M. Eisler & P. M. Miller, *Progress in Behavior Modification* (Vol. 8). New York: Academic Press, 1979.

Emmelkamp, P. M. G., & Wessels, H. Flooding in imagination vs. flooding in vivo: A comparison with agoraphobics. *Behaviour Research and Therapy,* 1975, *13,* 7–15.

Emmelkamp, P. M. G., & Kwee, K. G. Obsessional ruminations: A comparison between thought-stopping and prolonged exposure in imagination. *Behaviour Research and Therapy,* 1977, *15,* 441–444.

Emmelkamp, P. M. G., Kuipers, A. C. M., & Eggerat, J. B. Cognitive modification versus prolonged exposure *in vivo:* A comparison with agoraphobics as subjects. *Behaviour Research and Therapy,* 1978, *16,* 33–41.

Emmelkamp, P. M. G., Van Der Helm, M., Van Zanten, B. L., & Plochg, I. Treatment of obsessive-complusive patients: The contribution of self-instructional training to the effectiveness of exposure. *Behaviour Research and Therapy,* 1980, *18,* 61–66.

Engel, B. T., Nikoomanesh, P., & Schuster, M. M. Operant conditioning of rectosphincter responses in the treatment of fecal incontinence. *New England Journal of Medicine,* 1974, *290,* 646–649. Reprinted in L. V. DiCara, T. X. Barber, J. Kamiya, N. E. Miller, & J. Stoyva, *Biofeedback and self-control.* Chicago: Aldine Publishing Company, 1974, 407–410.

Engle, K. B., & Williams, T. K. Effect of an ounce of vodka on alcoholic's desire for alcohol. *Quarterly Journal of Studies on Alcohol,* 1972, *33,* 1099–1105.

English, H. B. Three cases of "conditioned fear response." *Journal of Abnormal and Social Psychology,* 1929, *34,* 221–225.

English, H. B. *The historical roots of learning theory.* New York: Random House, Inc., 1954.

Everett, P. B., Hayward, S. C., & Meyers, A. W. The effects of a token reinforcement procedure on bus ridership. *Journal of Applied Behavior Analysis,* 1974, *7,* 1–9.

Eysenck, H. J. The effects of psychotherapy: An evaluation. *Journal of Consulting Psychology,* 1952, *16,* 319–324.

Eysenck, H. J. *The dynamics of anxiety and hysteria.* New York: Frederick A. Praeger, Inc., 1957.

Eysenck, H. J. *Behavior therapy and the neuroses.* London: Pergamon Press, 1960.

Eysenck, H. J. *Fact and fiction in psychology.* Baltimore: Penguin Books, Inc., 1965(a).

Eysenck, H. J. The effects of psychotherapy. *Journal of Psychology,* 1965(b), *1,* 97–118.

Fairweather, G. W., Sanders, D. H., Cressler, D. L., & Maynard, H. *Community life for the mentally ill: An alternative to institutional care.* Chicago: Aldine Publishing Company, 1969.

Feather, B. W. A psychoanalytic contribution to behavior therapy. Unpublished manuscript, Department of Psychiatry, Duke University Medical School, Durham, N.C., 1971.

Feldman, M. P., & MacCulloch, M. J. The application of anticipatory avoidance learning to the treatment of homosexuality. I: Theory, technique and preliminary results. *Behaviour Research and Therapy,* 1965, *3,* 165–183.

Ferster, C. B. Animal behavior and mental illness. *The Psychological Record,* 1966, *16,* 345–356.

Ferster, C. B. A functional analysis of depression. *American Psychologist,* 1973, *28,* 857–870.

Ferster, C. B., Nurenberger, J. T., & Levitt, E. B. The control of eating. *Journal of Mathetics,* 1962, *1,* 87–109.

Fisher, E. B., Winkler, R. C., Krasner, L., Kagel, J., Batallio, R. C., & Basmann, R. L. Economic perspectives in behavior therapy: Complex interdependencies in token economies. *Behavior Therapy,* 1978, *9,* 391–403.

Fixsen, D. L., Phillips, E. L., Phillips, E. A., & Wolf, M. M. The teaching family model group home treatment. In W. E. Craighead, A. E. Kazdin, & M. J. Mahoney (Eds.), *Behavior modification, principles, issues, and applications.* Boston: Houghton Mifflin Company, 1976, 310–320.

Foa, E. B. Failure in treating obsessive-compulsives. *Behaviour Research and Therapy,* 1979, *17,* 169–176.

Foa, E. B., Steketee, G., & Milby, J. B. Differential effects of exposure and response prevention in obsessive-compulsive washers. *Journal of Consulting and Clinical Psychology,* 1980, *1,* 71–79.

Foxx, R. M., & Shapiro, S. T. The timeout ribbon: A non-exclusionary timeout procedure. *Journal of Applied Behavior Analysis,* 1978, *11,* 125–136.

Franchina, J. J., & Myers, L. W. Extinction effects following interpolation of instrumental trials among response prevention periods. *Behaviour Research and Therapy,* 1976, *14,* 471–477.

Frank, J. D. The present status of outcome studies. *Journal of Consulting and Clinical Psychology,* 1979, *2,* 319–334.

Franks, C. M. *Alcoholism.* In C. G. Costello (Ed.), *Symptoms of psychopathology.* New York: John Wiley & Sons, Inc., 1970.

Franks, C. M., & Wilson, G. T. (Eds.) *Annual review of behavior therapy theory and practice* (Vol. 4). New York: Brunner/Mazel, 1976, 685–695.

Freud, S. *Inhibitions, symptoms and anxiety.* London: Hogarth Press, 1936(a).

Freud, S. *The problem of anxiety.* New York: Quarterly Press and W. W. Norton & Company, Inc., 1936(b).

Freud, S. *The basic writings of Sigmund Freud.* New York: Modern Library, Random House, Inc., 1938.

Freud, S. Obsessive acts and religious practices (1907). In E. Jones (Ed.), *Collected papers* (Vol. 2). New York: Basic Books, Inc., Publishers, 1959(a).

Freud, S. Mourning and melancholia (1917). In E. Jones (Ed.), *Collected papers* (Vol. 4). New York; Basic Books, Inc., Publishers, 1959(b).

Frezza, D. A., & Holland, J. G. Operant conditioning of the human salivary response. *Psychophysiology,* 1971, *8,* 581–587.

Friedman, R., & Dahl, L. K. The effect of chronic conflict on the blood pressure of rats with a genetic susceptibility to experimental hypertension. *Psychosomatic Medicine,* 1975, *37,* 402–416.

Friedman, W. Legal theory: Law, justice, ethics and social morality. In S. Morgenbesser, P. Suppes, & M. White (Eds.), *Philosophy, science and method.* New York: St. Martin's Press, 1969, 333–361.

Frolov, Y. P. *Pavlov and his school.* London: Kegan Paul, Trench, Trubner & Co., Ltd., 1937.

Galef, G. G., Jr. The social transmission of acquired behavior. *Biological Psychiatry,* 1975, *10,* 155–160.

Garcia, J., Ervin, F., & Koelling, R. A. Learning with prolonged delay of reinforcement. *Psychonomic Science,* 1966, *5,* 121–122.

Gardner, J. Behavior therapy treatment approach to a psychogenic seizure case. *Journal of Consulting Psychology,* 1967, *31,* 209–212.

Gauthier, J., & Marshall, W. L. The determination of optimal exposure to phobic stimuli in flooding therapy. *Behaviour Research and Therapy,* 1977, *15,* 403–410.

Geller, E. S., Farris, J. C., & Post, D. S. Prompting a consumer behavior for pollution control. *Journal of Applied Behavior Analysis,* 1973, *6,* 367–376.

Gerst, M. S. Symbolic coding processes in observational learning. *Journal of Personality and Social Psychology,* 1971, *19,* 7–17.

Glaros, A. G., & Rao, S. M. Bruxism: A critical review. *Psychological Bulletin,* 1977, *84,* 767–781.

Glass, D. C. Stress, behavior patterns, and coronary disease. *American Scientist,* 1977, *65,* 177–187.

Gliner, J. A. Predictable vs. unpredictable shock: Preference behavior and stomach ulceration. *Physiology and Behavior,* 1972, *9,* 693–698.

Goetz, E. M., & Baer, D. M. Social control of form diversity and the emergency of new forms in children's blockbuilding. *Journal of Applied Behavior Analysis,* 1973, *6,* 105–113.

Goldfried, M. R., & Davison, G. C. *Clinical behavior therapy.* New York: Holt, Rinehart and Winston, Inc., 1976.

Goldiamond, I. Self-control procedures in personal behavior problems. *Psychological Reports,* 1965, *17,* 851–868.

Goldiamond, I. Fables, armadyllics, and self-reinforcement. *Journal of Applied Behavioral Analysis,* 1976, *9,* 521–525.

Goldstein, A. J., & Chambless, D. L. A reanalysis of agoraphobia. *Behavior Therapy,* 1978, *9,* 47–59.

Gralnick, A. Folie à deux: The psychosis of association. *Psychiatric Quarterly,* 1942, *16,* 230–263.

Graubard, P. S., Rosenberg, H., & Miller, M. B. Student applications of behavior modification to teachers and environments or ecological approaches to social deviancy. In E. A. Ramp & B. L. Hopkins (Eds.), *A new direction for education: Behavior analysis* (Vol. 1). Lawrence: University of Kansas, Support and Development Center for Follow Through, 1971.

Greist, J. H., Marks, I. M., Berlin, F., Gournay, K., & Noshirvani, H. Avoidance versus confrontation of fear. *Behavior Therapy,* 1980, *11,* 1–14.

Guthrie, E. R. *The psychology of learning.* New York: Harper & Row, Publishers, Incorporated, 1935.

Guthrie, E. R. *The psychology of human conflict.* New York: Harper & Row, Publishers, Incorporated, 1938.

Hall, C. S. & Lindzey, G. *Theories of personality.* New York: John Wiley & Sons, Inc., 1957.

Hall, R. Vance, *Behavior modification: Applications in school and home.* Lawrence, Kansas: H & H Enterprises, Inc., 1971.

Hall, R. V., Lund, D., & Jackson, D. Effects of teacher attention on study behavior. *Journal of Applied Behavior Analysis,* 1968, *1,* 1–12.

Hall, S. M., & Hall, R. G. Outcome and methodological considerations in behavioral treatment of obesity. *Behavior Therapy,* 1974, *5,* 357–365.

Hammen, C. L., & Glass, D. R. Depression, activity and evaluation of reinforcement. *Journal of Abnormal Psychology,* 1975, *84,* 718–721.

Hamner, W. C., & Foster, L. F. Are intrinsic and external rewards additive: A test of Deci's cognitive theory of task motivation. *Organizational Behavior and Human Performance,* 1975, *14,* 398–415. Quoted in C. M. Franks & G. T. Wilson, *Annual review of behavior therapy theory and practice* (Vol. 4). New York: Brunner/Mazel, 1976, 617.

Harless, J. H., and Lineberry, C. S. *Turning kids on and off.* Guild V Publications, 1971, p. 50.

Harlow, H. F., & Harlow, M. K. Social deprivation in monkeys. *Scientific American,* 1962, *207,* 473–482.

Harlow, H. F., Harlow, M. K., Dodsworth, R. O., & Arling, G. L. Maternal behavior of rhesus monkeys deprived of mothering and peer associations in infancy. *Proceedings of American Philosophical Society,* 1966, *110,* 58–66.

Harlow, H. F., & Zimmerman, R. R. The development of affectional responses in infant monkeys. *Proceedings of the American Philosophical Society,* 1958, *102,* 501–509.

Harlow, H. F., & Zimmerman, R. R. Affectional responses in the monkey. *Science,* 1959, *130,* 421–432.

Harris, C. W. Discrimination and facilitation of sexual responding in women: The application of biofeedback training. Doctoral dissertation, State University of New York at Stony Brook, 1978.

Haughton, E., and Ayllon, T. Production and elimination of symptomatic behavior. In L. P. Ullman and L. Krasner (Eds.), *Case studies in behavior modification.* New York: Holt Rinehart & Winston, Inc., 1965.

Hayes, S. C., Brownell, K. D., & Barlow, D. H. The use of self-administered covert sensitization in the treatment of exhibitionism and sadism. *Behavior Therapy,* 1978, *9,* 283–289.

Heckel, R. *Newsweek,* Feb. 21, 1977, p. 65.

Hefferline, R. F., Keenan, B., & Harford, A. Escape and avoidance in human subjects without their observation of the response. *Science,* 1959, *130,* 1338–1339.

Hefferline, R. F., & Perera, T. B. Proprioceptive discrimination of a covert operant without its observation by the subject. *Science,* 1963, *139,* 834–835.

Heider, F. *The psychology of interpersonal relations.* New York: John Wiley & Sons Inc., 1958.

Heiman, J. L. Response to erotica: An explanation of physiological and psychological correlates of human sexual arousal. Doctoral dissertation, State University of New York at Stony Brook, Stony Brook, New York, 1975.

Heller, M. S., & Polsky, S. *Studies in violence and television.* New York: American Broadcasting Company, 1975.

Herbert, E. W., Pinkston, E. M., Hayden, M. L., Sajwaj, T. L., Pinkston, S., Cordua, G., & Jackson, C. Adverse effects of differential parental attention. *Journal of Applied Analysis of Behavior,* 1973, *6,* 15–31.

Herman, H. H., Barlow, D. H., & Agras, S. W. An experimental analysis of classical conditioning as a method of increasing heterosexual arousal in homosexuals. *Behavior Therapy,* 1974, *5,* 33–47.

Herrnstein, J. R. Method and theory in the study of avoidance. *Psychological Review,* 1969, *76,* 46–69.

Hilgard, E. R., & Bower, G. H. *Theories of learning.* New York: Appleton Century Crofts, 1966.

Hillix, W. A. Theories of learning. In M. H. Marx & M. E. Bunch (Eds.), *Fundamentals and applications of learning.* New York: The MacMillan Company, 1977.

Hilts, P. J. *Behavior mod.* New York: Harper Magazine Press, 1974.

Hiroto, D. S. Locus of control and learned helplessness. *Journal of Experimental Psychology,* 1974, *102,* 187–193.

Hiroto, D. S., & Seligman, M. E. P. Generality of learned helplessness in man. *Journal of Personality and Social Psychology,* 1975, *31,* 311–327.

Hodgson, R., & Rachman, S. The effects of contamination and washing in obsessional patients. *Behaviour Research and Therapy,* 1972, *10,* 111–117.

Hodgson, R., & Rachman, S. The modification of compulsive behavior. In H. J. Eysenck (Ed.), *Case histories in behavior therapy.* London: Routledge & Kegan Paul, Ltd., 1976.

Hodgson, R., Rachman, S., & Marks, I. The treatment of obsessive-compulsive neurosis: Follow-up and further findings. *Behaviour Research and Therapy,* 1972, *10,* 181–189.

Hokanson, J. E., & Burgess, M. The effects of three types of aggression on vascular response. *Journal of Abnormal and Social Psychology,* 1962, *65,* 446–449.

Hokanson, J. E., Burgess, M., & Cohen, M. F. Effects of displaced aggression on systolic blood pressure. *Journal of Abnormal and Social Psychology,* 1963, *67,* 214–218.

Hokanson, J. E., DeGood, D. E., Forrest, M. S., & Brittain, T. M. Availability of avoidance behaviors for modulating vascular stress responses. *Journal of Personality and Social Psychology,* 1971, *19,* 60–68.

Holland, J. G. Behaviorism: Part of the problem or part of the solution? *Journal of Applied Behavior Analysis,* 1978, *11,* 163–174.

Holmes, T. H., & Rahe, R. H. The social readjustment rating scale. *Journal of Psychosomatic Research,* 1967, *11,* 213–218.

Holz, W. C., & Azrin, N. J. Discriminative properties of punishment. *Journal of the Experimental Analysis of Behavior,* 1966, *4,* 225–232.

Homme, L. E. Perspectives in psychology: XXIV control of coverants, the operants of the mind. *Psychological Record,* 1965, *15,* 501–511.

Homme, L. E. Human motivation and environment. *Kansas Studies in Education,* 1966, *16,* 30–39.

Homme, L. E., de Baca, P. C., Devine, J. V., Steinhorst, R., & Rickert, E. J. Use of the Premack principle in controlling the behavior of nursery school children. *Journal of the Experimental Analysis of Behavior,* 1963, *6,* 544.

Honigfeld, G., & Howard, A. *Psychiatric drugs.* New York: Academic Press, Inc., 1973.

Hornsveld, R. H. J., Kraaimaat, F. W., & van Dam-Baggen, R. M. J. Anxiety/discomfort and hand-washing in obsessive-compulsive control patients. *Behaviour Research and Therapy,* 1979, *17,* 223–228.

Houts, A. C. Ethical and legal issues in behavior modification. Unpublished paper, State University of New York, Stony Brook, New York, 1979.

Huesmann, L. R. Cognitive processes and models of depression. *Journal of Abnormal Psychology,* 1978, *87,* 194–198.

Hunt, G. M., & Azrin, N. H. A community-reinforcement approach to alcoholism. *Behaviour Research and Therapy,* 1973, *11,* 91–104.

Ince, L. P. Application of behavior modification techniques to the case of patients with spinal cord injuries. Unpublished manuscript, N.Y.U. Medical Center, Dept. of Rehabilitation Medicine, Goldwater Memorial Hospital, New York, New York 1975a.

Ince, L. P. Personal communication, 1975b.

Ince, L. P. *Behavior modification in rehabilitation medicine.* Springfield, Illinois: Charles C Thomas, Publisher, 1976.

Inmates of Boy's Training School v. Affleck. 346 F. Supp. 1354, D.R. I. 1972.

Jackson, B. Treatment of depression by self-reinforcement. *Behavior Therapy,* 1972, *3,* 298–307.

Jacobson, A. M., Hackett, T. P., Surman, O. S., & Silberberg, E. L. Raynaud's phenomenon. *Journal of the American Medical Association,* 1973, *7,* 739–740.

Jaffe, P. G., & Carlson, P. M. Relative efficacy of modeling and instructions in eliciting social behavior from chronic psychiatric patients. *Journal of Consulting and Clinical Psychology,* 1976, *44,* 200–207.

James, S. Treatment of homosexuality II. Superiority of desensitization/arousal as compared with anticipatory avoidance conditioning: Results of a controlled trial. *Behavior Therapy,* 1978, *9,* 28–36.

James, W. *Talks to teachers.* New York: W. W. Norton & Company, Inc., 1958, 133. (Originally published by Henry Holt and Company, 1899.)

Jaspers, K. *General psychopathology.* Manchester, England: Manchester University Press, 1963, p. 323.

Jehu, D., Morgan, R. T. T., Turner, R. K., & Jones, A. A controlled trial of the treatment of nocturnal enuresis in residential homes for children. *Behaviour Research and Therapy,* 1977, *15,* 1–16.

Jellinek. E. M. *The disease concept of alcoholism.* New Haven: Hillhouse Press, 1960.

Jeness, C. F. Comparative effectiveness of behavior modification and transactional analysis programs for delinquents. California Youth Authority, mimeo., 1974. Quoted in M. T. Nietzel et al., *Behavioral approaches to community psychology.* New York: Pergamon Press, 1977, 72.

Jenkins, W. O., Witherspoon, A. D., De Vine, M. D., de Valera, E. K., Muller, J. B., Barton, M. C., & McKee, J. M. The post-prison analysis of criminal behavior and longitudinal follow-up evaluation of institutional treatment. Elmore, Ala.: Rehabilitation Research Foundation, 1974.

Johnson, A. M. Factors in the etiology of fixations and symptom choice. *Psychoanalytic Quarterly,* 1953, *22,* 475–496.

Johnson, H. E., & Garton, W. H. Muscle re-education in hemiplegia by use of electromyographic device. *Archives of Physical Medicine Rehabilitation,* 1973, *54,* 320–325.

Johnson, W., & Turin, A. Biofeedback treatment of migraine headache: A systematic case study. *Behavior Therapy,* 1975, *6,* 394–397.

Jones, H. G. The application of conditioning and learning to the treatment of a psychiatric patient. *Journal of Abnormal and Social Psychology,* 1956, *52,* 414–419.

Jones, M. C. A laboratory study of fear: The case of Peter. *Pedagogical Seminar,* 1924(a), *31,* 308–315.

Jones, M. C. The elimination of children's fears. *Journal of Experimental Psychology,* 1924(b), *7,* 382–390.

Jones, R. T., & Kazdin, A. E. Programming response maintenance after withdrawing token reinforcement. *Behavior Therapy,* 1975, *6,* 153–164.

Kaimowitz v. Michigan Dept. of Mental Health. Filed July 10, 1973. Civil No. 73-19434-AW, Circuit Court of Wayne County, Mich.

Kanfer, F. H., & Phillips, J. S. *Learning foundations of behavior therapy.* New York: John Wiley & Sons, Inc., 1970.

Kantorowitz, D. A. An experimental investigation of preorgasmic reconditioning and postorgasmic deconditioning. *Journal of Applied Behavior Analysis,* 1978, *11,* 23–33.

Keefe, F. J., Surwit, R.S., & Pilon, R.N. Biofeedback, autogenic training, and progressive relaxation in the treatment of Raynaud's disease: A comparative study. *Journal of Applied Behavior Analysis,* 1980, *13,* 3–11.

Keller, D. J., & Goldstein, A. Orgasmic reconditioning reconsidered. *Behaviour Research and Therapy,* 1978, *16,* 299–300.

Keller, H. *The story of my life.* New York: Dell Publishing Co., Inc., 1968. (First printing, 1902.)

Keller, M. F., & Carlson, P. M. The use of symbolic modeling to promote social skills in preschool children with low levels of social responsiveness. *Child Development,* 1974, *45,* 912–919.

Kelly, G. A. *The psychology of personal constructs* (Vol. 2). *Clinical diagnosis and therapy.* New York: W. W. Norton & Company, Inc., 1955.

Kendler, H. H., & Kendler, T. S. Vertical and horizontal processes in problem solving. *Psychological Review,* 1962, *69,* 1–16.

Kennedy, R. E. Behavior modification in prisons. In E.E. Craighead, A.F. Kazdin, & M.J. Mahoney (Eds.). *Behavior modification, principles, issues, and applications.* Boston: Houghton Mifflin Company, 1976.

Kimble, G. A. *Hilgard and Marquis' Conditioning and learning.* New York: Appleton Century Crofts, 1961.

Kimmel, H. D. Instrumental conditioning of autonomically mediated behavior. *Psychological Bulletin,* 1967, *67,* 337–345.

Kimmel, H. D. Instrumental conditioning of autonomically mediated response in human beings. *American Psychologist,* 1974, *29,* 325–335.

Kimmel, H. D., & Hill, F. A. Operant conditioning of the GSR. *Psychological Reports,* 1960, 7, 555–562.

Kingsley, R. G., & Wilson, G. T. Behavior therapy for obesity: A comparative investigation of long-term efficacy. *Journal of Consulting and Clinical Psychology,* 1977, *45,* 288–298.

Kinsey, A. C., Pomeroy, W. B., & Martin, C. E. *Sexual behavior in the human female.* Philadelphia: W. B. Saunders Company, 1953.

Kleeman, S. T. Psychiatric contributions in the treatment of asthma. *Annals of Allergy,* 1967, *25,* 611–619.

Klein, D. C., & Seligman, M.E.P. Reversal of performance deficits in learned helplessness and depression. *Journal of Abnormal Psychology,* 1976, *85,* 11–26.

Kluger, J. M. Childhood asthma and the social milieu. *American Academy of Child Psychiatry,* 1969, *8,* 353–366.

Knecht v. Gillman. 488 F. 2d 1136, 8th Cir. 1973.

Kohlenberg, R. J. The punishment of persistent vomiting: A case study. *Journal of Applied Behavior Analysis,* 1970, *3,* 241–245.

Kohlenberg, R. J. Operant conditioning of human anal sphincter pressure. *Journal of Applied Behavior Analysis,* 1973, *6,* 201–208.

Köhler, W. *The mentality of apes.* New York: Harcourt, Brace & World, Inc., 1925.

Kolata, G. B. Obesity: A growing problem. *Science,* 1977, *198,* 905–906.

Konorski, J., & Miller, S. On two types of conditioned reflex. *Journal of Genetic Psychology,* 1937, *16,* 264–272. Quoted in H. D. Kimmel, Instrumental conditioning of automatically mediated responses in human beings. *American Psychologist,* 1974, *29,* 325–335.

Koslovskaya, I. B., Vertes, R. P., & Miller, N. Instrumental learning without proprioceptive feedback. *Physiology and Behavior,* 1973, *10,* 101–107.

Krapfl, J. E. Differential ordering of stimulus presentations and semi-automated versus live treatment in the systematic desensitization of snake phobia. Unpublished doctoral dissertation, University of Missouri, 1967.

Kuhn, T. S. *The structure of scientific revolutions.* Chicago: The University of Chicago Press, 1962.

Lacey, J. I. Somatic response patterning and stress: Some revisions of activation theory. In M. H. Appley & R. Trumbull (Eds.), *Psychological stress.* New York: Appleton Century Crofts, 1967.

Lacey, J. I., & Lacey, B. C. Some autonomic central nervous system inter-relationships. In P. Black (Ed.), *Physiological correlates of emotion.* New York: Academic Press, Inc., 1970.

Lamontagne, Y., & Marks, I. M. Psychogenic urinary retention: Treatment by prolonged exposure. *Behavior Therapy,* 1973, *4,* 581–585.

Landers, A. Advice II, *Newsday,* Jan. 13, 1978.

Landers, A. Advice II, *Newsday,* Nov. 4, 1978.

Lang, P. J. The mechanics of desensitization and the laboratory study of fear. In C. M. Franks (Ed.), *Behavior therapy: Appraisal and status.* New York: McGraw-Hill Book Company, 1969.

Lang, P. J., & Melamed, B. G. Avoidance conditioning therapy of an infant with chronic ruminative vomiting. *Journal of Abnormal Psychology,* 1969, *74,* 1–8.

Lang, P. J., Melamed, B. G., & Hart, J. H. A psychophysiological analysis of fear modification using an automated desensitization procedure. *Journal of Abnormal Psychology,* 1970, *76,* 220–234.

Langner, T. S., & Michael, S. T. *Life stress and mental health.* New York: The Free Press, 1963.

Lanyon, R. I., & Giddings, J.W. Psychological approaches to myopia: A review. *American Journal of Optometry and Physiological Optics,* 1974, *51,* 271–281.

Lazarus, A. A. Group therapy of phobic disorders by systematic desensitization. *Journal of Abnormal and Social Psychology,* 1961, *63,* 504–510.

Lazarus, A. A. Learning theory and the treatment of depression. *Behaviour Research and Therapy,* 1968, *6,* 83–89.

Lazarus, A. A. *Behavior therapy and beyond.* New York: McGraw-Hill Book Company, 1971.

Ledwidge, B. Cognitive behavior modification: A step in the wrong direction? *Psychological Bulletin,* 1978, *85,* 353–375.

Lefkowitz, M., Blake, R. R., & Mouton, J. S. Status factors in pedestrian violation of traffic signals. *Journal of Abnormal and Social Psychology,* 1955, *51,* 704–706.

Levis, D. J. Effects of serial CS presentations and other characteristics of the CS on the conditioned avoidance response. *Psychological Reports,* 1966, *18,* 755–766.

Levis, D. J. Implementing the technique of implosive therapy. Unpublished manuscript, State University of New York at Binghamton, Binghamton, New York, 1978.

Levis, D. J. & Boyd, T.L., Symptom maintenance: An infrahuman analysis and extension of the conservation of anxiety principle. *Journal of Abnormal Psychology,* 1979, *88,* 107–120.

Levis, D. J., & Hare, N. A review of the theoretical and empirical support for the extinction approach of implosive (flooding) therapy. In M. Hersen, R. M. Eisler, & P. M. Miller (Eds.), *Progress in behavior modification, IV.* New York: Academic Press, Inc., 1977.

Lewinsohn, P. M. The behavioral study and treatment of depression. In M. Hersen, R. M. Eisler, & P. M. Miller (Eds.), *Progress in behavior modification* (Vol. I). New York: Academic Press, Inc., 1974.

Lewinsohn, P. M., & Atwood, G. E. Depression: A clinical-research approach. *Psychotherapy: Theory, Research and Practice,* 1969, *6,* 166–171.

Lewinsohn, P. M., & Graf, M. Pleasant activities and depression. *Journal of Consulting and Clinical Psychology,* 1973, *41,* 261–268.

Lewinsohn, P. M., & Libet, J. Pleasant events, activity schedules, and depression. *Journal of Abnormal Psychology,* 1972, *79,* 291–295.

Liberman, R. P., Ferris, C., Salgado, P., & Salgado, J. Replication of the achievement place model in California. *Journal of Applied Behavior Analysis,* 1975, *8,* 287–299.

Libet, J., & Lewinsohn, P. M. The concept of social skill with special reference to the behavior of depressed persons. *Journal of Consulting and Clinical Psychology,* 1973, *40,* 304–312.

Lichtenstein, E., & Glasgow, R. E. Rapid smoking: Side effects and safeguards. *Journal of Consulting and Clinical Psychology,* 1977, *43,* 815–821.

Lichtenstein, E., & Rodrigues, M. P. Long-term effects of rapid smoking treatment for dependent cigarette smokers. *Addictive Behaviors* (Vol 2). Elmsford, N.Y.: Pergamon Press, 1977, 109–112.

Lick, J., & Bootzin, R. Expectancy factors in the treatment of fear: Methodological and theoretical issues. *Psychological Bulletin,* 1975, *82,* 917–931.

Liddell, H. S. The role of vigilance in the development of animal neurosis. In P. H. Hoch & J. Zubin (Eds.), *Anxiety.* New York: Grune & Stratton, Inc., 1951.

Liebert, R. M., & Allen, M. K. Effects of model's experience on children's imitation. *Psychonomic Science,* 1969, *14,* 198.

Liebert, R. M., & Fernandez, L. E. Vicarious reward and task complexity as determinants of imitative learning. *Psychological Reports,* 1969, *25,* 531–534.

Liebling, A. J. *The Press.* New York: Ballantine Books, Inc., 1961.

Linehan, M. M., Goldfried, M. R., & Goldfried, A. P. Assertion therapy: Skill training or cognitive restructuring. *Behavior Therapy,* 1979, *10,* 372–388.

Litin, E. M., Griffin, M., & Johnson, A. M. Parental influences in unusual sexual behavior in children. *Psychoanalytic Quarterly,* 1956, *25,* 37–55.

Lloyd, R. W., Jr., & Salzberg, H. C. Controlled social drinking: An alternative to abstinence as a treatment goal for some alcohol abusers. *Psychological Bulletin,* 1975, *82,* 815–842.

Logue, A. W., & Mazur, J. E. Determinants of self-control. Unpublished manuscript, State University of New York at Stony Brook, New York, 1979.

Lopez-Ibor, J. J. Problems presented by asthma as a psychosomatic illness. *Journal of Psychosomatic Research,* 1956, *1,* 115–119.

Lovaas, O. I. A behavior therapy approach to the treatment of childhood schizophrenia. In. J. P. Hall (Ed.), *Minnesota Symposium on Child Psychology* (Vol. 1). Minneapolis: The University of Minnesota Press, 1967.

Lovaas, O. I. *Reinforcement therapy.* Philadelphia: Smith, Kline and French Laboratories, 1966. (16-mm sound film)

Lovaas, O. I., Freitag, G., Gold, V. J., & Kassorla, I. C. Experimental studies in childhood schizophrenia. I. Analysis of self-destructive behavior. *Journal of Experimental Child Psychology,* 1965, *2,* 67–84.

Lovibond, S. H. *Conditioning and enuresis.* New York: The Macmillan Company, 1964.

Ludwig, A. O., & Ranson, S. W. A statistical follow-up of the effectiveness of treatment of combat-induced psychiatric casualties. I and II. *Military Surgeon,* 1947, *100,* 51–62, 169–175.

Luthans, F., & Kreitner, R. *Organizational behavior modification.* Glenview, Ill.: Scott, Foresman and Company, 1975.

McAdoo, H. P. Racial attitudes and self-concepts of black preschool children. Unpublished doctoral dissertation, University of Michigan, Ann Arbor, Michigan, 1970.

McClannahan, L. E., & Risley, T. R. Design of living environments for nursing-home residents:

Increasing participation in recreation activities. *Journal of Applied Behavior Analysis,* 1975, *8,* 261–268.

MacCorquodale, K., & Meehl, P. E. On a distinction between hypothetical constructs and intervening variables. *Psychological Review,* 1948, *55,* 95–107.

MacCulloch, M. J., Birtles, C. J., & Feldman, M. P. Anticipatory avoidance learning for the treatment of homosexuality: Recent developments and an automatic aversion therapy system. *Behavior Therapy,* 1971, *2,* 151–169.

McDavid, J., & Schroder, H. M. The interpretation of approval and disapproval of delinquent and non-delinquent adolescents. *Journal of Personality,* 1957, *25,* 539–549.

McFall, R. M., & Marston, A. R. An experimental investigation of behavioral rehearsal in assertive training. *Journal of Abnormal Psychology,* 1970, *76,* 295–303.

McFall, R. M., & Twentyman, C. T. Four experiments on the relative contribution of rehearsal, modeling, and coaching to assertive training. *Journal of Abnormal Psychology,* 1973, *81,* 199–218.

McGuire, R. J., Carlisle, J. M., & Young, B. G. Sexual deviations as conditioned behavior: A hypothesis. *Behaviour Research and Therapy,* 1965, *2,* 185–190.

MacKay v. Procunier. 477 F. 2d 877, 9th Cir., 1973.

McLaughlin, T. F., & Malaby, J. Instrinsic reinforcers in a classroom token economy. *Journal of Applied Behavior Analysis,* 1972, *5,* 45–51.

MacPhillamy, D. J., & Lewinsohn, P. M. Depression as a function of levels of desired and obtained pleasure. *Journal of Abnormal Psychology,* 1974, *83,* 651–657.

McSweeny, J. A. Effects of response-cost on the behavior of a million persons: Charging for directory assistance in Cincinnati. *Journal of Applied Behavior Analysis,* 1978, *11,* 47–51.

Madsen, C. H., Becker, W. C., Thomas, D. R., Koser, L., & Plager, E. An analysis of the reinforcing function of "sit down" commands. In R. K. Parker (Ed.), *Readings in educational psychology.* Boston: Allyn and Bacon, Inc., 1968.

Madsen, C. H., Madsen, C. D., Saudargas, R. A., Hammond, W. R., & Egar, D. E. Classroom RAID (Rules, Approval, Ignore, Disapproval): A cooperative approach for professionals and volunteers. Unpublished manuscript, University of Florida, Tallahassee, Florida, 1970.

Mahoney, M. J. Self-reward and self-monitoring techniques for weight control. *Behavior Therapy,* 1974a, *5,* 48–57.

Mahoney, M. *Cognition and behavior modification.* Cambridge, Mass.: Ballinger Press, 1974b.

Mahoney, M. J. Reflections on the cognitive-learning trend in psychotherapy. *American Psychologist,* 1977, *32,* 5–13.

Maletzky, B. M. "Assisted" covert sensitization in the treatment of exhibitionism. *Journal of Consulting and Clinical Psychology,* 1974, *42,* 34–40.

Marholin, D., II, & Gray, D. Effects of group response-cost procedures on cash shortages in a small business. *Journal of Applied Behavior Analysis,* 1976, *9,* 25–30.

Marks, I. M. *Fears and phobias.* New York: Academic Press, Inc., 1969.

Marks, I. Model 5: Phobias and obsessions. In J. D. Maser & M. E. P. Seligman (Eds.), *Psychopathology: Experimental Models.* San Francisco: W. H. Freeman and Company, 1977, 174–213.

Marks, I. Behavioral psychotherapy of adult neurosis. In S. Garfield & A. E. Bergin (Eds.), *Handbook of psychotherapy and behavior modification* (2nd ed.). New York: John Wiley & Sons, Inc., 1978.

Marlatt, G. A. A comparison of vicarious and direct reinforcement control of verbal behavior in an interview. *Journal of Consulting and Clinical Psychology,* 1971, *36,* 267–276.

Marlatt, G. A., Demming, B., & Reid, J. B. Loss of control drinking in alcoholics: An experimental analogue. *Journal of Abnormal Psychology,* 1973, *81,* 233–241.

Marquis, J. N. Orgasmic reconditioning: Changing sexual object choice through controlling masturbation fantasies. *Behavior Therapy and Experimental Psychiatry,* 1970, *1,* 263–271.

Marshall, H. C., & Gregory, R. T. Cold hypersensitivity: A simple method for its reduction. *Archives of Physical Medicine Rehabilitation,* 1974, *55,* 119–123.

Marshall, W. L. Satiation therapy: A procedure for reducing deviant sexual arousal. *Journal of Applied Behavior Analysis,* 1979, *12,* 377–389.

Marston, A. R., London, P., & Cooper, L. M. Observations of the eating behavior of children varying in weight. *Journal of Child Psychology and Psychiatry and Allied Disciplines,* 1976, *17,* 221–224.

Marston, A. R., London, P., Cooper, L. M., & Cohen, N. In vivo observation of the eating behavior of obese and nonobese subjects. *Journal of Consulting and Clinical Psychology*, 1977, *45*, 335–336.

Masserman, J. H. *Behavior and neurosis: An experimental psychoanalytic approach to psychobiologic principles.* Chicago: The University of Chicago Press, 1943.

Masserman, J. H., & Yum, K. S. An analysis of the influence of alcohol on experimental neurosis in cats. *Psychosomatic Medicine*, 1946, *8*, 36–52.

Masters, W. H., & Johnson, V. E. *Human sexual inadequacy.* Boston: Little, Brown and Company, 1970.

Mathew, R. J., Largen J. W., Dobbins, K., Meyer, J.S., Sakai, F., & Claghorn, J.L. Biofeedback control of skin temperature and cerebral blood flow in migraine. *Headache*, 1980, *20*, 19–28.

Meichenbaum, D. Toward a cognitive theory of self-control. In G. E. Schwartz & D. Shapiro (Eds.), *Consciousness and self-regulation* (Vol. 1). New York: Plenum Press, 1967, 223–259.

Meichenbaum, D. *Cognitive behavior modification.* New York: Plenum Press, 1977.

Meichenbaum, D., Bowers, K. S., & Ross, R.R. Modification of classroom behavior of institutionalized female adolescent offenders. *Behaviour Research and Therapy*, 1968, *6*, 343–353.

Meichenbaum, D. H., & Cameron, R. The clinical potential of modifying what clients say to themselves. In A. Ellis & R. Grieger (Eds.), *Handbook of rational-emotive therapy.* New York: Springer Publishing Company, Inc., 1977, 327–351.

Meichenbaum, D., & Goodman, J. Reflection-impulsivity and verbal control of motor behavior. *Child Development*, 1969, *40*, 785–797.

Meichenbaum, D., & Goodman, J. Training impulsive children to talk to themselves: A means of developing self-control. *Journal of Abnormal Psychology*, 1971, *77*, 115–126.

Melamed, B. G., & Siegal, L. J. Reduction of anxiety in children facing hospitalization and surgery by use of filmed modeling. *Journal of Consulting and Clinical Psychology*, 1975, *43*, 511–521.

Melnick, J., & Stocker, R. B. An experimental analysis of the behavioral rehearsal with feedback technique in assertiveness training. *Behavior Therapy*, 1977, *8*, 222–228.

Melzack, R., & Thompson, W. R. Effects of early experience on social behavior. *Canadian Journal of Psychology*, 1956, *10*, 82–90.

Menninger, W. C. *Psychiatry in a troubled world.* New York: The Macmillan Company, 1948.

Merry, J. The "loss of control" myth. *Lancet*, 1966, *1*, 1257–1268.

Milan, M. A. When behavior modification fails. Paper presented at the 10th Annual Convention of the Association for the Advancement of Behavior Therapy, New York, 1976.

Milan, M. A., & McKee, J. M. Behavior modification: Principles and applications. In D. Glaser (Ed.), *Handbook of Criminology.* Chicago, Ill.: Rand McNally & Company, 1974, 745–776.

Milan, M. A., & McKee, J. M. The cellblock token economy: Token reinforcement in a maximum security correctional institution for adult felons. *Journal of Applied Behavior Analysis*, 1976, *9*, 253–275.

Miller, G. A. *Psychology: the science of mental life.* New York: Harper & Row, Publishers, Incorporated, 1962.

Miller, N. E. Studies of fear as an acquirable drive: I. Fear as motivation and fear reduction as reinforcement in the learning of new response. *Journal of Experimental Psychology*, 1948, *38*, 89–101.

Miller, N. E. Introduction, current issues and key problems. In N. Miller, T. X. Barber, L. V. Dicara, J. Kamiya, D. Shapiro, & J. Stoyva (Eds.), *Biofeedback and self-control.* Chicago: Aldine Publishing Company, 1973, xi–xx.

Miller, N. E., & Dollard, J. *Social learning and imitation.* New Haven: Yale University Press, 1941.

Miller, P. M. *Behavioral treatment of alcoholism.* New York: Pergamon Press, 1976.

Miller, S. M. Controllability and human stress: Method, evidence and theory. *Behaviour Research and Therapy*, 1979, *17*, 287–304.

Miller, W. R., & Seligman, M. E. P. Depression and perception of reinforcement. *Journal of Abnormal Psychology*, 1973, *82*, 62–73.

Miller, W. R. Behavioral treatment of problem drinkers: A comparative outcome study of three controlled drinking therapies. *Journal of Consulting and Clinical Psychology*, 1978, *46*, 74–86.

Mills, H. L., Agras, W.S., Barlow, D.H., & Mills, J.R. Compulsive rituals treated by response prevention. *Archives of General Psychiatry*, 1975, *32*, 933–936.

Milne, A.A. *When we were very young.* E.P. Dutton & Co.: New York, 1924.

Mischel, W., & Baker, N. Cognitive appraisals and transformations in delay behavior. *Journal of Personality and Social Psychology,* 1975, *31,* 254–261.

Mischel, W., & Gilligan, C. Delay of gratification, motivation for prohibited gratification, and responses to temptation. *Journal of Abnormal and Social Psychology,* 1964, *69,* 411–417.

Mischel, W., & Staub, E. The effects of expectancy on working and waiting for larger rewards. *Journal of Personality and Social Psychology,* 1965, *2,* 625–633.

Monti, P., & Smith, N. F. Residual fear of the conditioned stimulus as a function of response prevention after avoidance or classical defensive conditioning in rats. *Journal of Experimental Psychology,* 1976, *105,* 148–162.

Moot, S. A., Cebulla, R. P., & Crabtree, J. M. Instrumental control and ulceration in rats. *Journal of Comparative and Physiological Psychology,* 1970, *71,* 405–410.

Morales v. Turman. 364 F. Supp. 166, E.D. Tex, 1973.

Moreno, J. L., & Kipper, D. A. Group psychodrama and community-centered counseling. In G. M. Gazda (Ed.), *Basic approaches to psychotherapy and group counseling.* Springfield, Ill.: Charles C Thomas, Publisher, 1968.

Morgan, C.L. *Introduction to comparative psychology,* London: Scott, 1894.

Morgan, R. T. T. Relapse and therapeutic response in the conditioning treatment of enuresis: A review of recent findings on intermittent reinforcement, overlearning, and stimulus intensity. *Behaviour Research and Therapy,* 1978, *16,* 273–279.

Mosher, L. R., & Feinsilver, D. *Special report: Schizophrenia.* Rockville, Md.: National Institute of Mental Health Studies of Schizophrenia, 1971.

Moss, F. E. *Nursing home care in the U.S.: Failure in public policy.* Introductory report prepared by the Subcommittee on Long-Term Care of the Special Committee on Aging. U. S. Senate, Washington, D. C.: Government Printing Office, 1974. Quoted in M. T. Nietzel et al., *Behavioral approaches to community psychology.* New York: Pergamon Press, 1977.

Mowrer, O. H., & Mowrer, W. M. Enuresis: A method for its study and treatment. *American Journal of Orthopsychiatry,* 1938, *8,* 436–459.

Mowrer, O. H. A stimulus-response analysis of anxiety and its role as a reinforcing agent. *Psychological Review,* 1939, *46,* 553–565.

Mowrer, O. H. On the dual nature of learning: A reinterpretation of "conditioning" and "problem-solving." *Harvard Educational Review,* 1947, *17,* 102–148.

Mowrer, O. H. *Learning theory and behavior.* New York: John Wiley & Sons, Inc., 1960.

Munford, P. R., Reardon, D., Liberman, R. P., & Allen L. Behavioral treatment of hysterical coughing and mutism: A case study. *Journal of Consulting and Clinical Psychology,* 1976, *44,* 1008–1014.

Munjac, D. J. Overcoming obstacles to desensitization using *in vivo* stimuli and Brevital. *Behavior Therapy,* 1975, *6,* 543–546.

Munroe, R. L., Munroe, R. H., & Whiting, J. W. M. Structure and sentiment: Evidence from recent studies of the couvade. American Anthropological Association Meetings, 1965.

National Advisory Commission on Criminal Justice, Standards, and Goals. Report on corrections. Washington, D.C.: 1973. Quoted in M. A. Milan & J. M. McKee, The cellblock token economy: Token reinforcement in a maximum security correctional institution for adult male felons. *Journal of Applied Behavior Analysis,* 1976, *9,* 253–275.

Nettelbeck, T., & Langeluddecke, P. Dry-bed training without an enuresis machine. *Behaviour Research and Therapy,* 1979, *17,* 403–404.

Newsday, Sept. 27, 1977.

N.Y. Times, March 11, 1978.

N.Y. Times, July 28, 1978.

Nietzel, M. T., Winett, R. A., MacDonald, M. L., & Davidson, W. S. *Behavioral approaches to community psychology.* New York: Pergamon Press, 1977.

Nigl, A. J. Electromyographic training to increase oral cavity functioning in a postoperative cancer patient. *Behavior Therapy,* 1979, *10,* 423–427.

Nisbett, R. E., & Wilson, T. E. Telling more than we can know. Verbal reports on mental processes. *Psychological Review,* 1977, *84,* 231–257.

Noelp, B., & Noelp-Eschenhagen, I. Bedingte reflexe beim Asthma bronchiale: Ein experimentelle beitrag zur pathogenses des Asthma bronchiale. *First International Congress for Allergy.* Zurich, 1951(a), 783.

Noelp, B., & Noelp-Eschenhagen, I. Die rolle bedingte reflexe beim Asthma bronchiale. Ein experimenteller beitrag zur pathogenese des Asthma bronchiole. *Helv. med. Acta.,* 1951(b), *18,* 142.

Noelp, B., & Noelp-Eschenhagen, I. Das experimentelle Asthma bronchiale des Meerschweinchens. *International Archives for Allergy,* 1951(c), 1952, *2,* 308, 321; ibid. 3, 108, 127.

Norman, R. J., Buchwald, J. S., & Villablanca, J. R. Classical conditioning with auditory discrimination of the eye blink in decerebrate cats. *Science,* 1977, *196,* 551–553.

Novaco, R. *Anger control: The development and evaluation of an experimental treatment.* Lexington, Mass.: D.C. Heath and Company, 1975.

O'Brien, J. S., & Raynes, A. E. Treatment of compulsive verbal behavior with response contingent punishment and relaxation. *Journal of Behavior Therapy and Experimental Psychiatry,* 1973, *4,* 347–352.

O'Connor, R. D. Modification of social withdrawal through symbolic modeling. *Journal of Applied Behavior Analysis,* 1969, *2,* 15–22.

O'Connor, R. D. Relative efficacy of modeling, shaping and the combined procedures for modification of social withdrawal. *Journal of Abnormal Psychology,* 1972, *79,* 327–334.

Öhman, A., Fredrickson, M., Hugdahl, K., & Rimmo, P. The premise of equipotentiality in human classical conditioning: Conditioned electrodermal responses to potentially phobic stimuli. *Journal of Experimental Psychology,* 1976, *105,* 313–337.

O'Leary, K. D. *The etiology of hyperactivity.* Paper presented at the Second Annual Italian Behavior Therapy Association Meeting, Venice, Italy, June 1978.

O'Leary, K. D. Pills or skills for hyperactive children. *Journal of Applied Behavior Analysis,* 1980, *13,* 191–204.

O'Leary, K. D., & Drabman, R. S. Token reinforcement programs in the classroom: A review. *Psychological Bulletin,* 1971, *75,* 379–398.

O'Leary, K. D., O'Leary, S., & Becker, W. C. Modification of a deviant sibling interaction pattern in the home. *Behaviour Research and Therapy,* 1967, *5,* 113–120.

O'Leary, K. D., Pelham, W. E., Rosenbaum, A., & Price, G. H. Behavioral treatment of hyperkinetic children. *Clinical Pediatrics,* 1976, *15,* 510–515.

O'Leary, K. D., & Wilson, G. T. *Behavior Therapy.* Englewood Cliffs, N.J.: Prentice-Hall, Inc., 1975.

O'Leary, S., & Pelham, W. E. Behavior therapy and withdrawal of stimulant medication with hyperactive children. Unpublished manuscript, State University of New York, Stony Brook, New York, 1978.

O'Leary, S. G., & O'Leary, K. D. Behavior modification in the school. In H. Leitenberg (Ed.), *Handbook of behavior modification.* Englewood Cliffs, N.J.: Prentice-Hall, Inc., 1976.

Ottenberg, P., Stein, M., Lewis, J., & Hamilton, C. Learned asthma in the guinea pig. *Psychosomatic Medicine,* 1958, *20,* 395–400.

Overmier, J. B., & Bull, J. A. On the independence of stimulus control of avoidance. *Journal of Experimental Psychology,* 1969, *79,* 364–367.

Overmier, J. B., & Brackbill, R. M. On the independence of stimulus evocation of fear and fear evocation of responses. *Behaviour Research and Therapy,* 1977, *15,* 51–56.

Padfield, M. The comparative effects of two counseling approaches on the intensity of depression among rural women of low socioeconomic class. *Journal of Counseling Psychology,* 1976, *23,* 209–214.

Page, H. A. The facilitation of experimental extinction by response prevention as a function of the acquisition of a new response. *Journal of Comparative and Physiological Psychology,* 1955, *48,* 14–16.

Page, H. A., & Hall, J. F. Experimental extinction as a function of the prevention of a response. *Journal of Comparative and Physiological Psychology,* 1953, *46,* 33–40.

Page, S., Caron, P., & Yates, E. Behavior modification methods and institutional psychology, *Professional Psychology,* 1975, *9,* 694–695.

Patterson, G. R., Shaw, D.A., & Ebner, M.J. Teachers, peers, and parents as agents of change in the classroom. In F.A. Benson (Ed.) Modifying deviant social behaviors in various classroom settings. Eugene, Oregon, *Department of Education Special Monographs, 1969, 13.*

Paul, G. L. Behavior modification research: Design and Tactics. In C. M. Franks (Ed.), *Behavior therapy: Appraisal and status.* New York: McGraw-Hill Book Company, 1969(a), 29–62.

Paul, G. L. Chronic mental patient: Current status—future directions. *Psychological Bulletin, 1969(b), 71,* 81–94.

Paul, G. L. Personal communication. 1979.

Paul, G. L., & Lentz, R. J. *Psychosocial treatment of chronic mental patients.* Cambridge, Mass.: Harvard University Press, 1977.

Paulsen, K., Rimm, D. C., Woodburn, L. T., & Rimm, S. A. A self-control approach to inefficient spending. *Journal of Consulting and Clinical Psychology, 1977, 45,* 433–435.

Pavlov, I. P. *Lectures on conditioned reflexes.* New York: International Universities Press, Inc., 1941.

Pavlov, I. P. *Conditioned reflexes: An investigation of the physiological activity of the cerebral cortex.* London: Oxford University Press, 1927. (Republished, New York: Dover Publications, Inc., 1960.)

Paykel, E. S., Meyers, J. K., Dienelt, M. N., Klerman, G. L., Lindenthal, J. J., & Pepper, M. P. Life events and depression: A controlled study. *Archives of General Psychiatry, 1969, 21,* 753–760.

Perkins, C. C. The relation of secondary reward to gradients of reinforcement. *Journal of Experimental Psychology, 1947, 37,* 377–392.

Perri, M. G., Richards, C. S., & Schultheis, K. R. Behavioral self-control and smoking reduction: A study of self-initiated attempts to reduce smoking. *Behavior Therapy, 1977, 8,* 360–365.

Peterson, D. R. *The clinical study of social behavior.* New York: Appleton Century Crofts, 1968.

Peterson, R. F., & Peterson, L. R. The use of positive reinforcement in the control of self-destructive behavior in a retarded boy. *Journal of Experimental Child Psychology, 1968, 6,* 352–359.

Phillips, C. Tension headache: Theoretical problems. *Behaviour Research and Therapy, 1978, 16,* 249–261.

Phillips, D. P. Airplane accident fatalities increase after newspaper stories about murder and suicide. *Science, 1978, 201,* 748.

Phillips. E. L. Achievement place: Token reinforcement procedures in a home-style rehabilitation setting for "pre-delinquent boys." *Journal of Applied Behavior Analysis, 1968, 1,* 213–223.

Polich, J., Armor, D. J., & Braiker, H. B. *The course of alcoholism: four years after treatment.* Rand/R-2433-NIAAA, Santa Monica, Calif., January, 1980.

Powers, R. B., & Osborne, J. G. *Fundamentals of behavior.* St. Paul, Minn.: West Publishing Company, 1976.

Premack, D. Reinforcement theory. In D. Levine (Ed.), *Nebraska symposium on motivation.* Lincoln: University of Nebraska Press, 1965, 123–180.

Premack, D., & Woodruff, G. Chimpanzee problem-solving: A test for comprehension. *Science, 1978, 202,* 532–535.

Prindaville, P., & Stein, N. Predictability, controllability and innoculation against learned helplessness. *Behaviour Research and Therapy, 1978, 16,* 263–271.

Purcell, K., Brady, K., Chai, H., Muser, J., Molk, L., Gordon, N., & Means, J. The effect on asthma in children of experimental separation from the family. *Psychosomatic Medicine, 1969, 31,* 144–164.

Quarti, C., & Renaud, J. A new treatment of constipation by conditioning: A preliminary report. In C. Franks (Ed.), *Conditioning techniques in clinical practice and research.* New York: Springer Publishing Company, Inc., 1964, 219–227.

Quay, H. C. Personality dimensions in delinquent males as inferred from factor analysis of behavior ratings. *Journal of Research on Crime and Delinquency, 1964, 1,* 33–37.

Rabavilas, A. D., Boulougouris, J.C., & Stefanis, C. Duration of flooding sessions in the treatment of obsessive-compulsive patients. *Behaviour Research and Therapy, 1976, 14,* 349–355.

Rachlin, H. Self-control. *Behaviorism, 1974, 2,* 94–107.

Rachlin, H. *Behavior and learning.* San Francisco: W. H. Freeman and Company, 1976.

Rachlin, H., & Green, L. S. Commitment, choice and self-control. *Journal of the Experimental Analysis of Behavior, 1972, 17,* 15–22.

Rachman, S. Spontaneous remission and latent learning. *Behaviour Research and Therapy, 1963, 1,* 133–137.

Rachman, S. Sexual fetishism: An experimental analogue. *Psychological Record,* 1966, *16,* 293–296.

Rachman, S. The modification of obsessions: A new formulation. *Behavior Research and Therapy,* 1976, *14,* 437–443.

Rachman, S. The conditioning theory of fear acquisition: A critical examination. *Behaviour Research and Therapy,* 1977, *15,* 375–387.

Rachman, S. *Fear and courage.* San Francisco: W. H. Freeman and Company, 1978.

Rachman, S., & Hodgson, R. J. Experimentally induced "sexual fetishism": Replication and development. *Psychological Record,* 1968, *18,* 25–27.

Rachman, S., De Silva, P., & Roper, G. The spontaneous decay of compulsive urges. *Behaviour Research and Therapy,* 1976, *14,* 445–453.

Rachman, S., Hodgson, R., & Marks, I. Treatment of chronic obsessive-compulsive neurosis. *Behaviour Therapy and Research,* 1971, *9,* 237–247.

Rapaport, D. The structure of psychoanalytic theory: A systematizing attempt. In S. Koch (Ed.), *Psychology: A study of a science* (Vol. 3). New York: McGraw-Hill Book Company, 1959, 58–183.

Rappaport, J., & Chinsky, J. M. Models for delivery of service: An historical and conceptual perspective. *Professional Psychology,* 1974, 42–50.

Razran, G. H. S. The observable unconscious and the inferable conscious in current Soviet psychophysiology: Interoceptive conditioning, semantic conditioning, and the orienting reflex. *Psychological Review,* 1961, *68,* 81–147.

Redfield, J., & Stone, A. Individual viewpoints of stressful life events. *Journal of Consulting and Clinical Psychology,* 1979, *47,* 147–154.

Rees, L. The significance of parental attitudes in childhood asthma. *Journal of Psychosomatic Research,* 1964, *7,* 253–262.

Rehm, L. P., & Marston, A. R. Reduction of social anxiety through modification of self-reinforcement. *Journal of Consulting and Clinical Psychology,* 1968, *32,* 564–574.

Reid, J. B. (Ed.). *A social learning approach to family intervention* (Vol. 2). Observation in home settings. Eugene, Ore.: Castalia Publishing Co., 1975.

Reppucci, N. D., & Saunders, J. T. Social psychology of behavior modification. Problems of implementation in natural settings. *American Psychologist,* 1974, *29,* 649–660.

Rescorla, R. A. Pavlovian conditioning and its proper control procedures. *Psychological Review,* 1967, *74,* 71–80.

Rescorla, R. A. Effect of inflation of the unconditioned stimulus value following conditioning. *Journal of Comparative and Physiological Psychology,* 1974, *86,* 101–106.

Rescorla, R. A., & Solomon, R. L. Two-process learning theory: Relationships between Pavlovian conditioning and instrumental learning. *Psychological Review,* 1964, *74,* 151–182.

Restle, F. *Learning: Animal behavior and human cognition.* New York: McGraw-Hill Book Company, 1975.

Ribble, M. A. *The rights of infants.* New York: Columbia University Press, 1965.

Richards, C. S. The politics of token economy. *Psychological Reports,* 1975, *36,* 615–621.

Rinn, R. C., Vernon, J. C., & Wise, M. J. Training parents of behaviorally disordered children in groups: A three years' program evaluation. *Behavior Therapy,* 1975, *6,* 378–387.

Roethlisberger, F. J., & Dickson, W. J. *Management and the worker.* Cambridge, Mass.: Harvard University Press, 1939.

Rohrer, J. H., & Edmonson, M. S. *The eighth generation.* New York: Harper & Row, Publishers, Incorporated, 1960.

Rotter, J. B. Generalized expectancies for internal versus external control of reinforcement. *Psychological Monographs,* 1966, *80* (1, Whole No. 609).

Rouse v. Cameron, 373 F. 2d 451, D.C. Cir., 1966.

Rowland, N. E., & Antelman, S. M. Stress-induced hyperaphagia and obesity in rats: A possible model for understanding human obesity. *Science,* 1976, *191,* 310–311.

Ruch, F. L., & Zimbardo, P. G. *Psychology and life.* Glenview, Ill: Scott, Foresman and Company, 1971.

Ruppenthal, G. C., Arling, G. L., Harlow, H. F., Sackett, G. P., & Suomi, S. J. A 10-year perspective of motherless-mother monkey behavior. *Journal of Abnormal Behavior,* 1976, *85,* 341–349.

Rush, A. J., Beck, A. T., Kovacs, M., & Hollon, S. Comparative efficacy of cognitive therapy and pharmacotherapy in the treatment of depressed outpatients. *Cognitive Therapy and Research,* 1977, *1,* 17–37.

Sajwaj, T., Libet, J., & Agras, S. Lemon-juice therapy: The control of life-threatening rumination in a six-month infant. *Journal of Applied Behavioral Analysis,* 1974, *7,* 557–563.

Santayana, G. Living without thinking. *Forum,* 1922, 731–735.

Sargent, J., Green, E., & Walters, E. The use of autogenic training in a pilot study of migraine and tension headaches. *Headache,* 1972, *12,* 120–124.

Sargent, J., Green, E., & Walters, E. Preliminary report of the use of autogenic-feedback techniques in the treatment of migraine and tension headaches. *Psychosomatic Medicine,* 1973, *35,* 129–135.

Sargent, J., Walters, E., & Green, E. Psychosomatic self-regulation of migraine headaches. *Semin Psychiatry,* 1973, *5,* 415–428.

Satterfield, J. H. EEG issues in children with minimum brain dysfunction. In S. Walzer & P. H. Wolff (Eds.), *Minimal cerebral dysfunction in children.* New York: Grune & Stratton, Inc., 1973.

Saunders, A., Jr. Behavior therapy in prisons: Walden II or Clockwork Orange? Paper presented at the Eighth Annual Convention of the Association for the Advancement of Behavior Therapy, Chicago, Nov. 1974.

Schachter, S. Some extraordinary facts about obese humans and rats. *American Psychologist,* 1971, *26,* 129–144.

Schachter, S., & Singer, J. E. Cognitive, social and physiological determinants of emotional state. *Psychological Review,* 1962, *69,* 279–299.

Schaefer, H. H., & Colgan, A. H. The effect of pornography on penile tumescence as a function of reinforcement and novelty. *Behavior Therapy,* 1977, *8,* 938–946.

Schiff, R., Smith, N., & Prochaska, J. Extinction of avoidance in rats as a function of duration and number of blocked trials. *Journal of Comparative and Physiological Psychology,* 1972, *81,* 356–359.

Schnelle, J. F., Kirchner, R. E., Macrae, J. W., McNees, M. P., Eck, R. H., Snodgrass, S., Casey, J. D., & Uselton, P. H., Jr. Police evaluation research: An experimental and cost-benefit analysis of a helicopter patrol in a high crime area. *Journal of Applied Behavior Analysis,* 1978, *11,* 11–21.

Schroeder, H. E., & Rich, A. R. The process of fear reduction through systematic desensitization. *Journal of Consulting and Clinical Psychology,* 1976, *44,* 191–199.

Schwartz, G. E. Biofeedback as therapy: Some theoretical and practical issues. *American Psychologist,* 1973, *28,* 666–673.

Schwitzgebel, R., & Kolb, D. A. Inducing behavior change in adolescent delinquents. *Behaviour Research and Therapy,* 1964, *1,* 293–304.

Schwitzgebel, R., & Kolb, D. A. *Changing human behavior.* New York: McGraw-Hill Book Company, 1974.

Seeley, John R. *Americanization of the unconscious.* New York: International Science Press, 1967.

Seer, P. Psychological control of essential hypertension: Review of the literature and methodological critique. *Psychological Bulletin,* 1979, *86,* 1015–1043.

Seligman, M. E. P. Phobias and preparedness. *Behavior Therapy,* 1971, *2,* 307–321.

Seligman, M. E. P. *Helplessness: On depression, development and death.* San Francisco: W. H. Freeman and Company, 1975.

Seligman, M. E. P. Comment and integration. *Journal of Abnormal Psychology,* 1978, *87,* 165–179.

Seligman, M. E. P., Abramson, L. Y., Semmel, A., & von Bayer, C. Depressive attributional style. *Journal of Abnormal Psychology,* 1979, *88,* 242–247.

Seligman, M. E. P., & Hager, J. L. *Biological boundaries of learning.* New York: Appleton Century Crofts, 1972.

Seligman, M. E. P., & Johnston, J.C.A. A cognitive theory of avoidance learning. In F.S. McGuigan and D.B. Lumsden (Eds.). *Contemporary approaches to conditioning and learning.* New York: Wiley, 1973.

Seligman, M. E. P., & Maier, S. F. Failure to escape traumatic shock. *Journal of Experimental Psychology,* 1967, *74,* 1–9.

Serbin, L. A., & O'Leary, K. D. Sexual bondage begins in the nursery school. Unpublished manuscript, State University of New York at Stony Brook, Stony Brook, New York, 1977.

Shapiro, D. & Surwit, R. S. Learned control of physiological function and disease. In H. Leitenberg

(Ed.) *Handbook of behavior modification and behavior therapy,* Englewood Cliffs, N.J.: Prentice-Hall, 1976.

Shapiro, A. K. Contributions to a history of the placebo effect. *Behavior Science,* 1960, *5,* 109–135. Reprinted in Miller et al. (Eds.), *Biofeedback and self-control.* Chicago: Aldine Publishing Company, 1973, 224.

Shaw, B. F., & Beck, A. T. The treatment of depression with cognitive therapy. In A. Ellis & R. Grieger (Eds.), *Handbook of rational-emotive therapy.* New York: Springer Publishing Co., Inc., 1977, 309–326.

Shaw, D. W., & Thoresen, C. E. Effects of modeling and desensitization in reducing dentist phobia. *Journal of Counseling Psychology,* 1974, *21,* 415–420.

Singer, I. B. *The Spinoza of Market Street.* New York: Avon Books, 1963, 129.

Skinner, B. F. Two types of conditioned reflex and a pseudo type. *Journal of General Psychology,* 1935, *12,* 66–77.

Skinner, B. F. *Walden II.* New York: The Macmillan Company, 1948.

Skinner, B. F. Are theories of learning necessary? *Psychological Review,* 1950, *57,* 193–216.

Skinner, B. F. *Science and human behavior.* New York: The Macmillan Company, 1953.

Skinner, B. F. Teaching machines. *Scientific American,* 1961, *205,* 90–102.

Skinner, B. F. Behaviorism at fifty. *Science,* 1963, *140,* 951–958.

Skinner, B. F. *Contingencies of reinforcement.* New York: Appleton Century Crofts, 1969.

Skinner, B. F. *Beyond freedom and dignity.* New York: Alfred A. Knopf, Inc., 1971.

Skinner, B. F. *Science and human behavior.* Quoted in H. D. Kimmel, Instrumental conditioning of autonomically mediated responses in human beings. *American Psychologist,* 1974, *29,* 326.

Sloane, R. B., Staples, F. R., Cristol, A. H., Yorkston, N. J., & Whipple, K. *Psychotherapy vs. behavior therapy.* Cambridge, Mass: Harvard University Press, 1975.

Slutskaya, M. M. Converting defensive reactions into food reflexes in oligophrenics and in normal children. *Zhurnal Nevropatolgii,* 1928, *21,* 195–110. Quoted in G. H. S. Razran, Conditioned responses in children. *Archives of Psychology,* 1933, *148,* 86.

Smith, M., & Glass, G. Meta-analysis of psychotherapy outcome studies. *American Psychologist,* 1977, *32,* 752–760.

Smith, R. E. The use of humor in the counterconditioning of anger responses: A case study. *Behavior Therapy,* 1973, *4,* 576–580.

Smith, S., & Guthrie, E. R. *General psychology in terms of behavior.* New York: Appleton Century Crofts, 1921.

Sobell, M. B., Schaeffer, H. H., & Mills, K. C. Differences in baseline behavior between alcoholics and normals. *Behaviour Research and Therapy,* 1972, *10,* 257–269.

Sobell, M. B., & Sobell, L. C. Individualized behavior therapy for alcoholics. *Behavior Therapy,* 1973, *4,* 49–72.

Solnick, J. V., Kannenberg, C. H., Eckerman, D. A., & Waller, M. B. An experimental analysis of impulsivity and impulse control in humans. Unpublished manuscript, University of Kansas, Lawrence, Kansas, 1979.

Solomon, R. L. Punishment. *American Psychologist,* 1964, *19,* 239–253.

Solomon, R. L., & Turner, L. H. Discriminative classical conditioning in dogs paralyzed by curare can later control discriminative avoidance responses in the normal state. *Psychological Review,* 1962, *69,* 202–219.

Solomon, R. L., & Wynne, L. C. Traumatic avoidance learning: The principles of anxiety conservation and partial irreversibility. *Psychological Review,* 1958, *61,* 353–385.

Solomon, R. W., & Wahler, R. G. Peer reinforcement control of classroom problem behavior. *Journal of Applied Behavior Analysis,* 1973, *6,* 49–56.

Spates, C. R., & Kanfer, F. H. Self-monitoring, self-evaluation, and self-reinforcement in children's learning: A test of a multistage self-regulation model. *Behavior Therapy,* 1977, *8,* 9–16.

Spence, K. W. The nature of theory construction in contemporary psychology. *Psychological Review,* 1944, *51,* 47–68.

Spiess, W. Toward a psycho-physiological theory of premature ejaculation. Doctoral disseration, State University of New York at Stony Brook, Stony Brook, New York, 1977.

Spitz, R. A. *The first year of life.* New York: International Universities Press, Inc., 1965.

Stampfl, T. G., & Levis, D. J. Essentials of implosive therapy: A learning-theory-based psychodynamic behavioral therapy. *Journal of Abnormal Psychology,* 1967, *72,* 496–503.

Steele, B. F. Parental abuse of infants and small children. In E. J. Anthony & T. Benedek (Eds.), *Parenthood.* Boston: Little, Brown and Company, 1970.

Stern, R., Lipsedge, M., & Marks, I. Obsessive ruminations: A controlled trial of thought-stopping technique. *Behaviour Therapy and Research,* 1973, *11,* 659–662.

Steuer, F. B., Applefield, M. M., & Smith, R. Televised aggression and interpersonal aggression of preschool children. *Journal of Experimental Child Psychology,* 1971, *11,* 442–447.

Stokes, T. F., & Baer, D. M. Preschool peers as mutual generalization-facilitating agents. *Behavior Therapy,* 1976, *7,* 549–556.

Stokes, T. F., & Baer, D. M. An implicit technology of generalization. *Journal of Applied Behavior Analysis,* 1977, *10,* 349–367.

Stokes, T. F., Baer, D. M., & Jackson, R. F. Programming the generalization of a greeting response in four retarded children. *Journal of Applied Behavior Analysis,* 1974, *7,* 599–610.

Stokes, T. F., Fowler, S. A., & Baer, D. M. Training preschool children to recruit natural communities of reinforcement. *Journal of Applied Behavior Analysis,* 1978, *11,* 285–303.

Stone, L. J., & Hokanson, J. E. Arousal reduction via self-punitive behavior. *Journal of Personality and Social Psychology,* 1969, *12,* 72–79.

Stone, N. M., & Borkovec, T. D. The paradoxical effect of brief CS exposure on analogue phobic subjects. *Behaviour Research and Therapy,* 1975, *13,* 51–54.

Stout, M. Stress and the vascular response in migraine headache: Biofeedback treatment implications, Doctoral dissertation, State University of New York at Stony Brook, Stony Brook, New York 1979.

Stroebel, C.F., & Glueck, B.C. Psychophysiological rationale for the application of biofeedback in the alleviation of pain. In M. Weisenberg and B. Tursky (Eds.), *Pain: New perspectives in therapy and research.* Plenum Publishing Corporation, New York, 1976.

Stuart, R. B. Behavioral control of overeating. *Behaviour Research and Therapy,* 1967, *5,* 357–365.

Stuart, R. B. Situational versus self-control. In R. B. Burin, J. D. Fensterheim, J. D. Henderson, & L. P. Ullman (Eds.), *Advances in Behavior Therapy.* New York: Academic Press, Inc., 1972.

Stuart, R. B. *How to manage the blues, tension, anger or boredom.* Manhasset, New York: Weight Watchers, 1975.

Stunkard, A. J. Eating patterns and obesity. *Psychiatric Quarterly,* 1959, *33,* 284–295.

Stunkard, A.J., & Mahoney, M.J. Behavioral treatment of the eating disorders. In H. Leitenberg (Ed.), *Handbook of behavior modification.* New York: Appleton Century Crofts, 1976.

Surwit, R. S. Biofeedback: A possible treatment for Raynaud's disease. *Seminars in Psychiatry,* 1973, *5,* 483–489.

Surwit, R. S., Pilon, R. N., & Fenton, C. H. Behavioral treatment of Raynaud's disease. *Journal of Behavioral Medicine,* 1978, *1,* 323.

Surwit, R. S., Shapiro, D., & Good, M.I. Comparison of cardiovascular biofeedback, neuromuscular biofeedback, and meditation in the treatment of borderline essential hypertension. *Journal of Consulting and Clinical Psychology,* 1978, *46,* 252–262.

Tanner, J., Weissman, M., & Prusoff, B. Social adjustment and clinical relapse on depressed outpatients. *Comprehensive Psychiatry,* 1975, *16,* 547–556.

Tarler-Benlolo, L. The role of relaxation in biofeedback training: A critical review of the literature. *Psychological Bulletin,* 1978, *85,* 727–755.

Thelen, M. H., Fry, R. A., Ehrenbach, P. A., & Frautschi, N. M. Therapeutic videotape and film modeling: A review. *Psychological Bulletin,* 1979, *86,* 701–720.

Thomas, J. D., Presland, I. E., Grant, M. D., & Glynn, T. L. Natural rates of teacher approval and disapproval in grade-7 classrooms. *Journal of Applied Behavior Analysis,* 1978, *11,* 91–94.

Thoresen, C. E., & Mahoney, M. J. *Behavioral self-control.* New York: Holt, Rinehart and Winston, Inc., 1974.

Thorndike, E. L. *Animal intelligence.* New York: The Macmillan Company, 1911.

Tighe, L. S., & Tighe, T. J. Discrimination learning: Two views in historical perspective. *Psychological Bulletin,* 1966, *66,* 353–370.

Timberlake, W., & Allison, J. Response deprivation: An empirical approach to instrumental performance. *Psychological Review,* 1974, *81,* 146–164.

Todd, F. J. Coverant control of self-evaluative responses in the treatment of depression: A new use for an old principle. *Behavior Therapy,* 1972, *3,* 91–94.

Tolman, E. C., & Honzik, C. H. "Insight" in rats. *University of California Publications in Psychology,* 1930, *4,* 215–232.

Trollope, A. An autobiography. London: Williams & Norgate, 1946.

Trotter, S. Experimental prison opened in Butner, N.C. *APA Monitor,* June 1976, p. 5.

Turin, A., & Johnson, W. Biofeedback therapy for migraine headaches. *Archives of General Psychiatry,* 1976, *33,* 517–519.

Turner, S. M., & Adams, H. F. Effects of assertive training on three dimensions of assertiveness. *Behaviour Research and Therapy,* 1977, *15,* 475–483.

Ullmann, L. P., & Krasner, L. *A pscyhological approach to abnormal behavior* (2nd ed.). Englewood Cliffs, N.J.: Prentice Hall, Inc., 1975.

Valarianai, R. Pet journal: That Kissinger dog! *Ladies Home Journal,* 1976, *93,* 126–129.

Valins, S., & Ray, A. A. Effects of cognitive desensitization on avoidance behavior. *Journal of Personality and Social Psychology,* 1967, *1,* 345–350.

Van Buren, A. Dear Abby. *Newsday,* Nov. 4, 1978.

Verden, P., & Shatterly, D. Alcoholism research and resistance to understanding the compulsive drinker. *Mental Hygiene,* 1971, *55,* 331–336.

Voegtlin, W. L., & Lemere, F. Treatment of alcohol addiction: A review of the literature. *Quarterly Journal of Studies in Alcoholism,* 1942, *11,* 717–803.

Voegtlin, W. L., & Lemere, F. An evaluation of aversion treatment of alcoholism. *Quarterly Journal of Studies in Alcoholism,* 1950, *11,* 199–204.

Vogler, R. E., Weissbach, T. A., Compton, J. V., & Martin, G. T. Integrated behavior change techniques for problem drinkers in the community. *Journal of Consulting and Clinical Psychology,* 1977, *45,* 267–279.

Wagner, A. R., & Rescorla, R. A. Inhibition of Pavlovian conditioning: Application of a theory. In R. A. Boakes & M. S. Holliday (Eds.), *Inhibition and Learning.* New York: Academic Press, Inc., 1972, 301–336.

Wallace, I. W., & Pear, J. J. Self-control techniques of famous novelists. *Journal of Applied Behavior Analysis,* 1977, *10,* 515–525.

Wallerstein, R. S. (Ed.) *Hospital treatment of alcoholism.* New York: Basic Books, Inc., Publishers, 1957.

Walsh, J. Professional psychologists seek to change roles and rules in the field. *Science,* 1979, *203,* 338–340.

Walton, D. The application of learning theory to the treatment of a case of neurodermatitis. In H. J. Eysenck (Ed.) *Behaviour therapy and the neuroses.* New York: Pergamon Press, 1960.

Walton, D., & Mather, M.D. The application of learning principles to the treatment of obsessive-compulsive states in the acute and chronic phases of illness. *Behaviour Research and Therapy,* 1963, *1,* 163–174.

Watson, J. *The double helix.* New York: Atheneum Publishers, 1968.

Watson, J. B. Psychology as the behaviorist views it. *Psychological Review,* 1913, *20,* 158–177.

Watson, J. B. The place of the conditioned reflex in psychology. *Psychological Review,* 1916, *23,* 89–116.

Watson, J. B. *Behaviorism.* New York: The Peoples' Institute Publishing Co., Inc., 1924.

Watson, J. B. The heart or the intellect? *Harper's Monthly Magazine,* 1928, *156,* 345–353.

Watson, J. B., & Rayner, R. Conditioned emotional reaction. *Journal of Experimental Psychology,* 1920, *3,* 1–14.

Weiher, R. G., & Harmann, R. E. The use of omission training to reduce self-injurious behavior in a retarded child. *Behavior Therapy,* 1975, *6,* 261–268.

Weinberg, N. M. Effects of detainment on extinction of avoidance CR. Unpublished doctoral dissertation, Western Reserve University, Cleveland, Ohio, 1961.

Weiner, H. M. *Psychobiology and human disease.* New York: Elsevier, 1977.

Weisberg, P., & Waldrop, P. B. Fixed-interval work habits of Congress. *Journal of Applied Analysis of Behavior,* 1972, *5,* 93–97.

Weiss, J. M. Effects of coping behavior with and without a feedback signal on stress pathology in rats. *Journal of Comparative and Physiological Psychology,* 1971, *77,* 22–30.

Weiss, J. M. Model 7: Psychological and behavioral influences on gastrointestinal lesions in animal models. In J. D. Maser & M. E. P. Seligman (Eds.), *Psychopathology: Experimental methods.* San Francisco: W. H. Freeman and Company, 1977, 253–269.

Wenar, A. E., & Rehm, L. P. Depressed effect: A test of behavioral hypotheses. *Journal of Abnormal Psychology,* 1975, *84,* 221–227.

Whiting, Beatrice B. (Ed.). *Six cultures: Studies of child rearing.* New York: John Wiley & Sons, Inc., 1963.

Whiting, B. Sex identity conflict and physical violence: A comparative study. In L. Nader (Ed.), The ethnology of law. *American Anthropologist,* 1965, *67* (Special Issue, Part 2), 126.

Whiting, J. W. M., & Whiting, Beatrice B. Contributions of anthropology to the method of studying child rearing. In P. H. Mussen (Ed.), *Handbook of research methods in childhood development.* New York: John Wiley & Sons, Inc., 1960.

Williams, R. J. Alcoholics and metabolism. *Scientific American,* 1948, *179,* 50–53.

Willis, J., & Giles, D. Behaviorism in the twentieth century: What we have here is a failure to communicate. *Behavior Therapy,* 1978, *9,* 15–27.

Wilson, G. T., & Davison, G. C. Processes of fear reduction in systematic desensitization. *Psychological Bulletin,* 1971, *76,* 1–14.

Wilson, G. T., & Davison, G. C. Behavior therapy and homosexuality: A critical perspective. *Behavior Therapy,* 1974, *5,* 16–28.

Wincze, J., Hoon, P., & Hoon, E. A. A comparison of the physiological responsivity of normal and sexually dysfunctional women during erotic stimulus exposure. *Psychosomatic Research,* 1976, *20,* 44–50.

Wine, J. Investigations of an attentional interpretation of test anxiety. Unpublished doctoral dissertation, University of Waterloo, Waterloo, Ontario, 1970.

Wine, J. Test anxiety and direction of attention. *Psychological Bulletin,* 1971, *76,* 92–104.

Wolpe, J. Experimental neuroses as learned behavior. *British Journal of Psychology,* 1952, *43,* 243–268.

Wolpe, J. *Psychotherapy by reciprocal inhibition.* Stanford: Stanford University Press, 1958.

Wolpe, J. The experimental foundations of some new psychotherapeutic methods. In A. J. Bachrach (Ed.), *Experimental foundations of clinical psychology.* New York: Basic Books, Inc., Publishers, 1962, p. 554.

Wolpe, J. Cognition and causation in human behavior and its therapy. *American Psychologist,* 1978, *33,* 437–446.

Wolpe, J., & Lazarus, A. A. *Behavior therapy techniques.* New York: Pergamon Press, 1966, 48.

Wood, R., & Flynn, J. M. A self-evaluation token system versus an external evaluation token system alone in a residential setting with predelinquent youth. *Journal of Applied Behavior Analysis,* 1978, *11,* 503–512.

Woodruff, G., Premack, D., & Kennel, K. Conservation of liquid and solid quantity by the Chimpanzee. *Science,* 1978, *202,* 991–994.

Woodworth, R. S. *Contemporary schools of psychology.* New York: The Ronald Press Company, 1931.

Wooley, S. C., Wooley, O. W., & Dyrenforth, S. R. Theoretical, practical, and social issues in behavioral treatments of obesity. *Journal of Applied Behavior Analysis,* 1979, *12,* 3–25.

Woolfolk, A. E., Woolfolk, R. L., & Wilson, G. T. A rose by any other name . . . : Labeling bias and attitudes toward behavior modification. *Journal of Consulting and Clinical Psychology,* 1977, *45,* 184–191.

Wright, D. F., Brown, R. A., & Andrews, M. E. Remission of chronic ruminative vomiting through the reversal of social contingencies. *Behaviour Research and Therapy,* 1978, *16,* 134–136.

Wright, L., Nunnery, A., Eichel, B., & Scott, R. Behavioral tactics for reinstating natural breathing in infants with tracheotomy. *Pediatric Research,* 1969, *3,* 275–278.

Wyatt v. Stickney, 344 F. Supp, 373 and 374 F. Supp. 387 (M.D. Ala 1972).

Yahraes, H., & Gunders, S. M. An anthropological investigation of child-rearing and adult personality. In E. A. Rubinstein & G. V. Coelho (Eds.), *Behavioral sciences and mental health: An anthology of program reports.* Washington, D.C.: National Institute of Mental Health, Public Health Service Publication, No. 2064, 1973.

Yarrow, L. J. Maternal deprivation: Toward an empirical and conceptual reevaluation. *Psychological Bulletin,* 1961, *58,* 459–490.

Yates, A.J. *Behavior Therapy.* New York: John Wiley & Sons. Inc. 1970..

Young, G. C. The treatment of childhood encopresis by conditioned gastro-ileal reflex training. *Behaviour Research and Therapy,* 1973, *2,* 499–503.

Young, G. C., & Morgan, R. T. T. Overlearning in the conditioning treatment of enuresis: A long-term follow-up study. *Behaviour Research and Therapy,* 1972, *10,* 419–420.

Yukl, G. A., Latham, G. P., & Pursell, E. D. The effectiveness of performance incentives under continuous and variable schedules of reinforcement. *Personnel Psychology,* 1976. Quoted in C. M. Franks & G. T. Wilson (Eds.), *Annual review of behavior therapy theory and practice* (Vol. 4). New York: Brunner/Mazel, 1976, 619.

Zeiss, A. M., Rosen, G. M., & Zeiss, R. A. Orgasm during intercourse: A treatment strategy for women. *Journal of Consulting and Clinical Psychology,* 1977, *45,* 891–895.

Zlutnick, S., Mayville, W. J., & Moffat, S. Behavioral control of seizure disorders: The interruption of chained behavior. In R. Katz & S. Zlutnick (Eds.), *Behavior therapy and health care: Principles and applications.* New York: Pergamon Press, 1975.

Zwart, C. A., & Lisman, S. A. Analysis of stimulus control treatment of sleep-onset insomnia. *Journal of Counseling and Clinical Psychology,* 1979, *47,* 113–118.

Name Index

Subject Index